THE REIGN OF CHRIST ON EARTH

OR

THE VOICE OF THE CHURCH IN ALL AGES

CONCERNING

The Coming and Kingdom of the Redeemer

BY

DANIEL T. TAYLOR

REVISED AND EDITED, WITH A PREFACE, BY

H. L. HASTINGS

EDITOR OF "THE CHRISTIAN," BOSTON

"**Thy** kingdom come, thy will be done on earth as it is in heaven."

Wipf & Stock
PUBLISHERS
Eugene, Oregon

Wipf and Stock Publishers
199 W 8th Ave, Suite 3
Eugene, OR 97401

The Reign of Christ on Earth
The Voice of the Church in All Ages Concerning
The Coming and Kingdom of the Redeemer
By Taylor, Daniel T.
ISBN 13: 978-1-55635-564-6
ISBN 10: 1-55635-564-5
Publication date 8/1/2007
Previously published by Repository Press, 1893

CONTENTS.

INTRODUCTORY SYNOPSIS.

Extracts exhibiting the character of the volume. Antiquity. New Heavens and Earth. Kingdom of God. The Judgment Day. The Age's Crisis. Present Evil Times. It hasteth greatly. Signs of the times. Author's Excuse. Loving Christ's Appearing. Author's method. Pre-millennialists are missionaries. . . . . page 1

CHAPTER I

Definition of Terms. Millennium. Chiliasts. The great question of the age Principles of interpretation. Critics. Taylor. Ernesti. Vitringa. Luther. Rosenmuller. Smith. 13

CHAPTER II.

TRADITIONARY TESTIMONY. Criticism on Dan. 12: 2. Hebrew Church Rabbins. Targums. Gamaliel. Talmuds. Zohar. Jonathan. Kimchi Maimonides. FIRST RESURRECTION. Book of Wisdom. Antiquity. SIX THOUSAND YEARS. Rabbi Elias. Other Jewish Doctors. The Gemarah Heathen nations. Zoroaster. The general belief of all nations. Sibylline Oracles Book of Enoch. Testament of the twelve patriarchs. Fourth Book of Ezra. Ascension of Isaiah. Second Book of Esdras. GENERAL CONFLAGRATION. Jews and Heathen. Greeks. Romans. Persians Egyptians. Geologists. ADVENT AND RESTITUTION. Classic writers. Mohammedans. Ancient belief. Modern heathen nations. Karens. Aztecs. Jews. Arabs. Hindoos. Jewish view of the kingdom. Chalmers. Charnock. Watts. 19

CHAPTER III.

The early church from Hermas to Origen. All Pre-millennialists. Hermas Clement. Barnabas. Ignatius. Polycarp. Papias. Justin Martyr. Irenæus. Epistle of the Churches of Vienna and Lyons. Three Millions of Premillenialists. Hippolytus. Melito. Tertullian. Montanists. The Alogi. Clement of Alexandria. Cyprian. Methodius. Nepos. Coracian. Other witnesses. Character of the opponents of the doctrine of the Lord's reign on earth. 47

CHAPTER IV.

Voice of the Church from Origen to Augustine. Origen. His erroneous principles of intepretation. His admissions. The first anti-millennarian of any note. Victorinus. Lactantius. Dionysius. Relatives of our Lord. Commodian. Gregory. Sulpicius. Paulinus. Apollinaris. Other witnesses. Some begin to reject the Apocalypse. The Nicene Fathers. The doctrine still prevalent. Eusebius. Cyril. Epiphanius. Apostacy. Ambrose. Chrysostome. Hilary. Jerome—an opposer. His character and admissions. Who crushed the truth? Augustine. A new millennial theory. Testimony of Dr. Lardner. Chillingworth. Russell. Bush. Moshiem. Burton. Neander Gibbon. Encyclopedias. Newton. Mede Maitland Kitto. Milner. Taylor. Whitby. Stuart. Giesler. The Septuagint Chronology. 76

CHAPTER V.

From Augustine to Luther. Truth dying. An onward creeping Apostacy. Character of the times. Origenism. The Apocalypse rejected as not being canonical. Why? Chiliasm once orthodoxy—now heresy. Rome's opposition. The infant harlot extirpates an apostolic truth! Still it lives. The new view. Papal Divines. Andreas. Anti-millennarianism. Dark Ages. Romish Doctors—Joachim Abbas. Anselm. Almeric. Jean Pierre d'Olive. Jewish Rabbis of the middle ages. The Paulikians. Thomas Aquinas. Waldenses. The Noble Lesson. A line of witnesses. Wickliff. Day Breaking 110

CHAPTER VI.

Views of the great reformers. Era and century of the reformation. Miscellaneous testimony—Tyndale. Bradford. Piscator. Latimer. Ridley. Sandys. Chytræus. Augsburg Confession. Catechism of the time of Edward Sixth. Becon. Leo Juda. Bullinger. Knox. Perkins. Calvin. Osiander. Flacius. Luther's Expectation of the judgment near—yearnings for its coming. Melancthon. Bale. Foxe. Brightman. Pareus. . 136

CHAPTER VII.

The seventeenth century. The illustrious Mede. Millennarianism rises to eminence. No creed opposed to it. Twisse. Usher. Maton. Adams. Goodwin. Reformers view the end approaching. Milton, the Christian Homer. Janeway. Baxter. Ambrose. Durant. Alleine. Taylor. Watson. Westminster Assembly Divines. Most of them believed in Christ's personal reign. Rutherford. Heart yearnings. Farmer. Sterry. Burroughs. Vincent. Hall. Anti-millennarian testimony. Bunyan. Baptists of 1660. Boughton. Hall. Beverly. Tillinghast. Prideaux. Jurieu. Charnock. Henry's Golden Thoughts. Burnet Cressener. Ames. Howe. Mennonites. Coccoius. Davenant. Alstead. Napier. Many voices. Post-millennialism had no where an existence. 166

CONTENTS.   v

CHAPTER VIII.

The eighteenth century. History continued. A new millennial view, but not a divine one. Fleming. Whitby. A "New Hypothesis," with comments upon it by Henshaw, Woodhouse, Russell, and Duffield. Hurd. Whiston. Reader. Sir Isaac Newton. Wells. Daubuz. Gill. Bengel. Doddridge. John Wesley. Newcome. Bishop Newton. Lancaster. Dr. Watts. Pirie. Hort. Horsely. Browne. King. Whitefield. Benson. C. Wesley. Hall. Fletcher. Perry. Toplady. Early Methodism. Romaine. Cooper. Coke. Glas. Homes. Butler. T. Taylor. Lambert. Rudd. Hussey. Pope. Priestley. Dr. A. Clarke's admissions. Character of the times.   224

CHAPTER IX.

Christians in America. Christopher Columbus. The seventeenth century. New England pastors. Eliot. R. Mather. J. Higginson. J. Dury. J. Baily. J. Moody. J. Mitchel. Williams. Norton. Bulkley. Shepherd. Cotton. Huet. Parker. Holyoke. Stoughton. Oaks. Lee. Sewall. Willard. Davenport. Cheever, the N. E. school-master. Aspenwell. Jooke. S. Mather. Clarke. Holmes. The whip and the hope. Whiting. Hutchinson. I. Mather. Noyes. No openly avowed post-millennial views cherished among these New England fathers. Whitbyism unknown. Sharp words from Spalding.   293

CHAPTER X.

Christians in America, continued. The eighteenth century. The "New Hypothesis" obtains with Edwards, Bellamy, and Hopkins. The early church view still cherished. C. Mather. Bowers. Flint. Webb. Burnet. Gookin. Chauncy. Byles. Prince. Siegvolck. Imbrie. Torrey. Edwards. Marsh. Murray. Gale. Winchester. Fish. Watkins. Cummings. Farnham. Dow. A fair representation. The old faith never died out. New England Christians have loved His appearing.   .   324

CHAPTER XI.

Prophetic conferences. First conference at Albury, in England, in 1826. The twenty students. A great cry goes forth. An English opinion. First conference in America, 1840. Fifteen hundred preachers of His coming. Time setting. The London conference of 1873. The opinion of a British earl. The Mildmay Park conference of 1878. The great prophetic conference at New York in 1878. One hundred and twenty-two responses to its call. Fifty thousand *Tribune* reports. The addresses. A mighty theme. A deep interest. Christendom agitated with the question of our Lord's coming.   346

CHAPTER XII.

Doom of Antichrist. The grand argument. Principles of interpretation. What Paul meant. Barnabas' view. Justin. Irenæus. Antichrist to come. Cyprian. Hippolytus. Origen. Tertullian. Lactantius. Cyril. Gregory. Ambrose. Chrysostom. Evagrius. Jerome. Hilarion. Theodoret. Augustine. Cassidorus. Andreas. Antichrist come. Pope

CONTENTS.

Gregory. Time of the Papal rise. Serenus. Alcuin. Paulinus. Agobard. Claude. Arnulph. Gonthier. Tergand. Berenger. Bernard. Arnold. Peter De Bruys. Joachim. Peter Olive and others. Waldenses. Walter Brute and others. Huss. Jerome. Wickliff. Protestantism and what the Pope knows. "*Epiphania*" and "*Parousia*." Lexicographers. Fifty testimonies concerning Antichrist's doom. The Advent pre-millennial. 365

CHAPTER XIII.

Our Warrant. Criticisms on Dan. 12:4. The nineteenth century. Millenarian authors. Millenarian preachers. Millenarian expositors. Millenarian missionaries. Millenarian revivalists. The Adventists. The doctrine preached everywhere. The day near. Voice of church creeds. Thirty creeds. No church inculcates a post-millennial advent. The first resurrection. Many churches endorse the doctrine. The Lord at hand. A solemn charge. 408

CHAPTER XIV.

Extracts. The Startling Cry—"He Cometh," by Krummacher. Signs of the Times, by Charlotte Elizabeth. First Resurrection, by Stuart. Advent Experience, by Charlotte Elizabeth. The New Earth, by Chalmers. The Vindication and Great Incentive, by Bonar. The Blessed Hope, by Andrews. The Solemn Warning, from the Journal of Prophecy. Looking for His Coming, by Barnes. Coming of the Bridegroom, by Alford. The Church's Last Testimony, by Melville. Count on Christ's coming, by Radstock. The Spirit and the Bride Say, Come, by Martyn. The Faith that Sustains, by Connor. The End of the World, by Tait. The New Creation, by Van Oosterzee. Where Are We? by Spurgeon. Distinguish the Times, by M'Neile. The Coming of the Lord Jesus, by Müller. The Gospel a Witness, by Gilfillan. Our Great Want is Christ, by Stockton. The Ancient Hope, by Patterson. Loving His Appearing, by Seiss. The Triumphant Kingdom of God, by Van Oosterzee. The Final Consummation, by Hodge. The Universal Song, by Spurgeon. Pre-millennial Creed, by Ryle. Essay on the first Resurrection, by Gordon. Two Resurrections, by Alford. The Coming of the Lord in its Relation to Christian Doctrine, by Brookes. History of the Pre-millennial doctrine, by West. Defense of Pre-millenarianism, by Duffield. Return of Christ and Foreign Missions, by Mackay. The Second Coming of Christ, by Varley. Christ's Second Coming, by Moody. Relative Period of the Second Advent, by Guinness. The Final Farewell, by Cumming. Author's Adieu. Dying Words, — "Tell the Church to hold on till Christ comes!" 442

APPENDIX.

Comparative Chronological Table. 538

EDITOR'S PREFACE.

It is not necessary to apologize for calling the attention of Christian men to the testimony of a multitude of the most eminent servants of God in all ages, regarding the greatest event in human history, the Coming of the Judge of quick and dead, and the establishment of his kingdom in the world which he has made. The assurance that this globe is yet to be the theatre of the grandest displays of divine goodness, mercy, grace, and glory, is confined to Christians of no sect or age; it is the universal faith of the universal Church. Since the time when man went out from his lost paradise, separated by sin from the presence of his God, the hope of the triumph of good over evil, and of the bruising of the serpent's head by the woman's conquering Seed, has been the joy of every faithful heart. The promise of universal blessing through Abraham and his Seed can never fail of its accomplishment; and He who said, "As truly as I live, all the earth shall be filled with the glory of the Lord;" and who has declared that "The earth shall be filled with the knowledge of the glory of the Lord, as the waters cover the sea," will not fail to make good all that he has promised. For eighteen hundred years the prayer,"Thy kingdom come, thy will be done IN EARTH as it is done in heaven," has ascended to the throne. And that this prayer will eventually be answered, and that God's will shall yet be done in earth as it is now done in heaven, admits of no doubt in the mind of the believing child of God.

Just how and when this state of glory shall be introduced, is with some a matter of question; but the ultimate conclusion is beyond all dispute or cavil. To give light upon this subject is the purpose of the present volume, the aim of which is, not to present new theories, nor to advocate the opinions or advance the interests of any sect, but to direct attention to the old paths, and invite those who search the Living Oracles to listen to the consenting testimony of the most eminent servants of God in all the ages, upon this important theme.

The present treatise is by no means exhaustive, for to exhaust this subject would be to explore all sacred literature, and reproduce elaborate treatises and massive volumes which have come down from ages past; but the plan of the work has been, not only to present a summary of the views of different individuals, but to allow each writer to state for himself his own conclusions in his own language, and thus give the reader the benefit of the personal testimony of each witness, upon the point in question. Hence the author of this volume instead of writing a mere history, has largely suppressed his own reflections, and held in check his graphic pen, allowing THE CHURCH to speak upon the point at issue, through its most eminent and eloquent teachers.

It has been often stated that the opinion that the world is to be converted to God through the existing instrumentalities of gospel preaching and publication, is an opinion peculiar to modern days, and in entire opposition to the faith of the earlier ages of the church. In this volume that statement is proved true, and proved beyond the possibility of successful contradiction. The Voice which speaks from these pages is not the voice of the author or the editor; nor is it the voice of despised and obscure students of prophecy, nor unwise and over-excited fanatics; but it is the Voice of THE CHURCH;—the Church of many ages and of many lands. It is not the voice of a single generation, but it is the voice of those who, catching the words of inspiration from apostolic lips, and following in apostolic footsteps, have run with patience the race that was set before them, and have been able to say, as their course was finished, "I have kept the faith."

Upon this important question The Church is entitled to a hearing: and this book is prepared that she may have it. And if this voice seems strange to some who are sunk in the easy slumbers of luxury and worldliness, it is nevertheless the Voice of the Church; if it seems stern and rugged to those who wear soft raiment and dwell in the palaces of kings, it is yet the Voice of the Church. If its utterances seem like the words of those that mock, it is nevertheless the Voice of the Church; and The Church must be heard; and in this volume The Church of the living God, the light of the world for seventeen hundred years, through some FOUR HUNDRED of its most ancient, eminent, learned, eloquent, and steadfast men,—martyrs, confessors, preachers, teachers, expounders, reformers, orators and poets, representing the church during the whole pc iod of its existence, and including all its branches and departments, —utters its solemn protest against the prevailing doctrine of the world's conversion,—the syren song of those who say "peace and safety," while sudden destruction draweth nigh.

In view of the array of evidence presented in this volume, the question will arise, What is truth? Shall we accept the prevailing opinion, that this world is calmly gliding on to days of millennial blessedness and peace?—an opinion of which no traces can be found in the early history of the Church of Christ,— or shall we embrace that ancient faith which, undazzled by the glare of worldly prosperity, and the fancies of a false philosophy, views the world as in rebellion against God, as living in the grasp of the Wicked One, as ripening for the harvest of judgment, as waxing old like a garment, and destined to be changed, convulsed, dissolved and renewed by the mighty power of Him who created and redeemed it, and who shall yet renew it and rule it forever?

The illustrious line of witnesses here testifying, goes back through "the noble army of the martyrs" to the "goodly fellowship of the Apostles." The records of the church do not furnish *four hundred other names* so famed as these; there is no chance to accumulate a mass of rebutting testimony; and these men have uttered in no uncertain tones the Voice of the Church upon this important theme. Were they all mistaken in their understanding of Scripture statements for many hundreds of years? Was it reserved for modern divines to correct the faith of those who listened to apostolic teachings, and who followed in their teachers' paths? Has that which was an unknown doctrine or a condemned error in the church for seventeen hundred years, come at last to be the true faith of the gospel? And shall we, the successors of those who have steeled themselves against earth's flatteries and earth's frowns for many generations, with the solemn watchword, "The coming of the Lord draweth nigh!" now fold our arms in lazy lock, and say in our hearts, or with our lips, the Lord "delayeth his coming"? How are we certain that the judgment is hundreds of years distant from us, when for ages past the church has considered it near to *them?* Have we a new revelation? Has God sent forth men to declare that all things do and will "continue as they were" for ages yet to come? Has he not rather proclaimed that the hour of his judgment is at hand? Has he not said, "Behold, I come as a thief"?—and that too, in connection with events that are now occurring before our eyes? And has he not said, "Blessed is he that watcheth"? Shall we then cease to watch? If the early disciples were bidden to watch because they knew "neither the day nor the hour" of the coming of the Son of Man, have we learned that that day and hour are so far distant that we may be excused from the watchers' wakeful care?

And what are the present prospects of a church that has set out in all confidence to convert the world? How may those now putting on the harness, boast of greater expected success than is warranted by the experience of those who have put it off after having fought the good fight? The prophets could not convert the world; are we mightier than they? The Apostles could not convert the world; are we stronger than *they?* The martyrs could not convert the world; can we do more than *they?* The Church for eighteen hundred years could not convert the world; can *we* do it? They have preached the gospel of Christ, so can we. They have gone to earth's remotest bounds, so can we. They have saved "some," so can we. They have wept as so few believed their report, so can we. They have finished their course with joy, and the ministry which they have received to testify of the gospel of the grace of God; we can do the same. Can we reasonably hope to do more? "It would take to all eternity to bring the Millennium, at the rate that modern revivals progress," said the venerable Dr. Lyman Beecher, before a ministerial convention, held close by old Plymouth Rock. And what hope is there that they will progress more rapidly? Is it in the word of God? Glad would we be to find it there. Sadly we read that "Evil men and seducers shall wax worse and worse, deceiving and being deceived."

Has God a mightier Saviour—a more powerful Spirit? Has he another Gospel which will save the world? Where is it? Is there any way to the kingdom other than that which leads through much tribulation? Is there another way to the crown besides the way of the cross? Can we reign with Him unless we first suffer for his sake?

No doubt the world might be converted if men desired to know the Lord. And so had all who heard, received with gladness the word of God, the world might have been converted within twenty years from the day of Pentecost. If each

Christian had brought a single soul to God with each successive year, the calm splendors of the Millennial era might have shone upon the declining years of the apostles of Jesus Christ. But instead of this, ages of darkness came on. The world did not repent, but the church apostatized. The darkness did not become light, but much of the light became darkness; and to this hour, as in the apostles' time, the whole world lieth in the wicked One.

If the gospel were to convert the world, we should have seen tokens of it ere this. But where are such omens to be found? Shall we look to missionaries, who sometimes labor for years before one sinner yields to the claims of the gospel? Shall we look to the dense darkness of the heathen world? Shall we look at the formalism of the professed church? Shall we look at the wide extension of infidelity? Shall we look at the abounding of iniquity and the waxing cold of love? Shall we look at a world where eighteen hundred years of toil and tears has not brought one-twentieth part of mankind even to a profession of true Christianity; and where not more than one-fifth claim for themselves the dubious title of Christian nations? Shall we look over a world in which we cannot find one nation of Christians, nor one tribe of Christians, nor one city of Christians, nor one town of Christians, nor one village of Christians, nor one hamlet of Christians, save here and there, where a questionable faith has led a few, with hypocrites even then among them, to withdraw themselves from the world, and cherish the untried virtues of a secluded life? Surely, after eighteen hundred years of experiment with a system designed to convert the world, men might point to some country, to some province, to some nation, and say, "Behold the commencement of a converted world."

Where shall we look to find the tokens of the speedy dawning of the hoped-for day of peace? Shall we look at Christendom, where for every missionary sent forth to convert the heathen, a thousand soldiers are trained and supported that they may cut each others' throats? Shall we look at the dense masses of godless, hopeless toilers, who journey on in darkness to perdition, in the chief cities of boasted Christian lands? Shall we look at those nations which claim to be mentally and morally in advance of all the inhabitants of the globe, but who spend more money for strong drink than they do for bread, and whose yearly expenditure for all religious and secular instruction; and for all purposes of Christian charity, would not pay for the cost of the intoxicating drinks consumed by them in a single month?*

Shall we look to the centres of Christian civilization, where squalor crowds on splendor, and where Lazarus still lies, licked by dogs, hard by the rich man's gate; where in the midst of lavished wealth and wasted treasure, thousands of helpless women make their dire election between hunger and shame, starvation and damnation? Shall we explore the great cities of Christendom, where, surrounded by sky-piercing steeples and sweetly chiming bells, poor motherless, friendless outcasts wander wet and weary through the midnight hours, scorned by Simon the Pharisee and his proud wife and silk-robed daughters; finding no way to draw near to Him who calls the heavy laden to come and rest; no place in the rich man's house to bathe His feet with penitential tears; no path open but the downward way; no gate ajar but the broad gate that leadeth to destruction? Shall we visit the gorgeous temples erected to Him who, more homeless than the foxes and the birds, was cradled in a wayside manger, and was buried in a stranger's tomb,—but the price of whose blood bought a potter's field where *strangers* might be buried?—we shall find by the smell of mint, and anise, and cummin, that the tithes are promptly paid by the proud Pharisee whose "God-I-thank-thee," echoes through the sounding aisles; but shall we not also find Fraud and Greed sitting side by side in the chief seats of the Synagogue, and unclean reptiles swarming like frogs of Egypt, while the tables of the money changers still stand right side up, and no scourge of small cords drives the buyers and the sellers from the sacred place?

Shall we look to China, along whose borders a few mission

*"The income of all our missionary societies does not equal a hundredth part of the sum raised in Great Britain by taxation, nor does it amount to a ten thousandth part of the sum annually spent on tobacco, or a *hundred thousandth* part of the cost to the kingdom of intoxicating drinks."—*Foreign Missions*, by Dr. JOSEPH ANGUS. *Religious Condition of Christendom*, p.172.

"Was there ever a time when charity was more eagerly solicited, when pauperism was more appallingly rampant? and yet, amidst all this want and suffering, this nation is annually pouring out a perfect pyramid of gold upon a mere indulgence—an enormous sum of money, which outstrips all the other national expenses. 150,000,000 pounds sterling are wasted—aye, ten thousand times worse than wasted—in intoxicating drinks; a sum which is 60,000,000 pounds sterling in excess of our whole national revenue, and one-sixth of our national debt—a sum which means more than 20 pounds sterling spent in intoxicating drinks upon an average by every family in the United Kingdom; and thus, mark you, all the legitimate trades of this country, *except one*, are depressed, and toil-worn men and women groan under the burden of their local taxation."—*Discourse on the Use and Sale of Intoxicating Drink*, delivered by CANON WILBERFORCE, in ST. PAUL'S CATHEDRAL, London, 1877.

stations twinkle like tapers in the midst of a darkness wide reaching and almost impenetrable? While we rejoice at the salvation of some in the far-off land of Sinim, let us not forget that every passing day witnesses the horrible death of not less than one thousand Chinamen, diseased, debauched, degraded, murdered, damned, by the use of that opium which is raised and sold by the British Government, and forced on the unwilling heathen by Christian England at the cannon's mouth and at the bayonet's point; and that while the British and Foreign Bible Society reports an income of *one million of dollars* per year for the diffusion of the Word of God, the Christian Government of Great Britain derives an annual income of *forty-five millions of dollars from the opium trade.**

Shall we turn to India with its myriad populations, where the rulers of this same Christian nation long barred the way against the Gospel of Christ, which has at last effected an entrance, but where intemperance and dissipation have made such havoc, that, to use the words of Archdeacon Jefferies, a missionary there, "For one really converted Christian as a fruit of missionary labor, the drinking practices of the English have made fully a thousand drunkards in India"? †

---

* For facts and statistics regarding the opium trade, and other horrible infamies of these days, see "*Crimes of Christendom,*" in THE SIGNS OF THE TIMES, by H. L. HASTINGS, pp. 47-92.

† "This blighting curse is not only robbing men of money, but is robbing Jesus of the souls He loves. It is desolating our churches, it is swelling infidelity and sin, it is originating, strengthening, and fostering prostitution and Sabbath-breaking. Let me tell you that at a census which was taken not long since in a teeming London parish upon a Sunday night, 18,000 persons were found in various places of worship, but not less than 20,000 were found in the drink-shops and gin-palaces of the same parish on that single night—a clear gain of something like 2,000 for the devil—and it is simply notorious that wherever the English name and the English flag are borne by British enterprise and British commerce, there rises up the wail which follows in the track of British intemperance. A native prince of high rank in India, in a published speech delivered in this metropolis, has openly said, "The helpless widows of India are uttering their curses against the British Government for having introduced this thing into their midst;" and the cry of India is echoed back to us from the far, far West. "What do you preach?" asked a North American Indian not long since of a missionary. "Christ," was the answer. "Then away with you," he said; "we don't want Christ. We were once a powerful nation, and our enemies feared us, and our wigwams were wealthy, and our young men were brave; but the white man came, and he preached Christ to us, and he brought the accursed fire-water with him, and now our wigwams are poor, our glory is gone--we do not want Christ." Vide. WILBERFORCE'S SERMON.

"The Queen of Madagascar forbids the drinking and sale of intoxicating spirits, but these are *forced into the land to a fearful extent by the nations of England, France, and America.* The present state of the coast of Madagascar, in consequence of the quantity of spirits brought into the country is most deplorable— *much worse than when the people were in heathen darkness. If Christian nations* would do what is right in the matter, we should have no need of a temperance movement on the island of Madagascar."—Letter of HELEN GILPIN, *Missionary to Madagascar, in Nat. Temp. Advocate, July,* 1877.

Shall we look at the far off islands of the Southern Seas, where heathenism has been banished by the light of gospel truth, and barbarism has given place to an enlightened civilization? We shall find that those races which lived in health and strength in spite of barbarism and cannibalism, are now slowly dying out, from unreportable diseases and vices, unknown in their barbarous condition, but which have been brought to their shores by sailors from Christian lands, and which, spreading like the gangrene of hell, are eating out the sources of the national life.*

Where shall we go to find the evidence of this glad era of universal peace and blessing which is proclaimed as so sure to come and so near at hand? It is easy on platforms and at anniversaries to speak of the spread of the gospel and the diffusion of the Word of God, and in this we do rejoice and will rejoice with joy unspeakable; but while many are exhibiting to delighted assemblies these gracious tokens of divine favor and blessing, who keeps an account of the statistics of the work of the Prince of Darkness, the god of this world? A company of Christian people assemble and congratulate themselves upon the rescue of a dozen or a hundred men from ruin, in some great city: suppose on the other hand all the dealers in strong drink, and the panderers to vice and crime, should gather themselves together and count up the victims ensnared, the hearts broken, the homes desolated, the lives blighted and the souls ruined by their infernal craft: suppose *their* annual reports were issued, in which they gave the number of drunkards made during the year, the number induced to take the first glass, the number of murders and suicides due to their terrible traffic, the souls enticed from paths of innocence and peace, and led in ways of darkness and of death: suppose that such a report could be laid upon our tables fresh from the press, or suppose it should meet us as we read our morning papers: suppose along with it were placed the statistics of wealth lavished by Christians on vanities, and follies, set over against the amount doled out for purposes of Christian endeavor;—would not such an exhibition as this speedily cause us to hide our faces in the very dust, and instead of boasting of the work accomplished, cry out to God for mercy and for help?

We have no doubts nor misgivings regarding the importance nor the success of Christian efforts, nor would we for one

*See *The Morals of Christendom*, in SIGNS OF THE TIMES. p. 169.

moment discourage those ardent souls who, with their sickles in their hands, are entering this wide spread harvest field. But facts are facts; and it is well for the Christian soldier to know that he is summoned to service more stern than sham fights and dress parades; that the warfare of the church is a mighty struggle, with overwhelming odds against her; and that only the Captain of Salvation can give victory to his saints. It is useless to shut our eyes to sins and dangers which exist on every hand. It is easy to talk about converting the world, but do those who talk about it, know much about converting men? Do not some of them need converting themselves? Let them enter into this work with all their souls, and it will not be strange if with others who have tried the experiment, they conclude that the world is a wrecked vessel, doomed to go down, and it is their business to launch the gospel life-boat and rescue all they can.

But if the world is not converted, will not the gospel then prove a failure? That depends upon what is to be expected of it. If the life-boat was intended to keep the ship from sinking, then it proves a failure if it only saves the crew. If the gospel was to effect the eternal salvation of all mankind, then failing to accomplish that work is a failure of the gospel. If the gospel was to convert the world, it will prove a failure if that is not done. But if the gospel was preached "*to take* OUT OF *the Gentiles a people for His name*," then it is not a failure. If it was given that God might in infinite mercy and love "*save* SOME," then it is not a failure. If it was given that every repentant sinner might have eternal life, and that every good soldier might receive a crown of glory, then it is not a failure. If it was given that an innumerable company might be redeemed "OUT OF *every kindred, and tongue, and nation, and people*," then it is not a failure. If it was given that the vales and hills of paradise restored, might teem with a holy throng who shall be "equal unto the angels, the children of God, being the children of the resurrection," then it is not a failure. If it was given that the elect might be brought into one great family of holy ones, then it is not a failure.

And was not this its object, rather than the exaltation of a worldly church to the splendors of earthly prosperity, while beneath the theatre of their easy triumph there slumber the ashes of prophets and the dust of apostles? Are we to hold jubilee a thousand years, while the martyrs' unceasing cry, "How long, oh Lord?" goes up to God? Are we to have our songs of triumph, while "the whole creation groaneth for deliverance," and while that longed-for day of the redemption of our body is postponed? Nay, verily, the hope of the Body is one hope;—the hope of the completeness and perfection of the church which Christ has redeemed. It reaches beyond the splendors of temporal prosperity; it looks beyond death's shadowy vale; and the church only finds its home and rest, with Abraham, and Isaac, and Jacob, in the Kingdom of our God, and in the presence of our King.

Thus teaches the word of the Lord. Thus responds the universal church. There are, I know, with regard to the details, differences of opinion. But this only strengthens the argument. It shows that the church were not led by blind reverence for the traditions of their fathers. But on the leading features they all agree. Wide apart as the poles in their estimate of various other matters, they all agree in one point, that the coming of Jesus and the scenes of judgment must precede the rest of the church of God. They all agree that the church shall never reign till she reign complete in the presence of her Lord. They all agree that earth is not her rest until renewed by the power of God. They agree that the world will not be converted, but that the Judge of quick and dead must come upon a race not ready for the harvest of glory, but ripe for the sickle of wrath. And is not this the voice of the prophets and apostles? Is not this the teaching of the Sacred Word?

If the Lord has said to his Son, "Ask of me, and I shall give thee the heathen for thine inheritance, and the uttermost parts of the earth for thy possession," has he not also said, "Thou shalt break them with a rod of iron, thou shalt dash them in pieces like a potter's vessel"?—Psa. ii: 8, 9. If it is written, "The earth shall be full of the knowledge of the Lord, as the waters cover the sea," is it not also written that "He shall smite the earth with the rod of his mouth, and with the breath of his lips shall he slay the wicked"?—Isa. xi: 4, 9. If we read that "The wilderness and the solitary place shall be glad, and the desert shall rejoice and blossom as the rose," do we not also read, "Behold, your God shall come with vengeance, even God with a recompense, he will come and save you."— Isa. xxxv: 1, 4. If the glory of the Lord shall be revealed, and all flesh shall see it together, so also, "The Lord God will come with a strong hand, and his arm shall rule for him;

behold his reward is with him, and his work before him."—Isa. xl: 5, 10. If we are called to rejoice with Jerusalem when God shall extend peace to her like a river, we are also told that "The hand of the Lord shall be known toward his servants and his indignation toward his enemies; for, behold, the Lord will come with fire, and with his chariots like a whirlwind, to render his anger with fury, and his rebuke with flames of fire." —Isa. lxvi: 10-15. If we read that The God of heaven shall set up a kingdom that never shall be destroyed, we also read that earth's kingdoms are first to be broken in pieces together, and to become "like the chaff of the summer threshing floor." —Dan. ii: 35, 44.. If it is declared that "The kingdom and dominion and the greatness of the kingdom under the whole heaven shall be given to the people of the saints of the Most High," we must not forget that before all this, the Ancient of Days appears upon his fiery throne, surrounded by ten thousand holy ones, while ten thousand times ten thousand stand before him; the judgment is set, and the books are opened.— Daniel vii: 10, 27. If the righteous are to "shine forth as the sun in the kingdom of their father," it is not until the angel reapers have gathered out of that kingdom "all things that offend, and them which do iniquity," and have "cast them into a furnace of fire."—Matt. xiii: 41,43. If we read that the kingdoms of this world are to become our Lord's and his Christ's, and that He shall reign for ever and ever, we also read of angry nations and divine wrath, and of the time of the dead that they should be judged, and that God should give reward to his prophets and his saints, and all that fear his name, and destroy those that destroy the earth. Rev. xi. 15, 18. If the Arch-deciever is to be cast into the abyss and shut up that he may no more seduce the nations, it is not until after the King of kings and Lord of lords appears with his celestial hosts, and smites the apostate and rebellious powers of earth, and hurls them into the lake of fire burning with brimstone. Rev. xix. xx. And so the glorious pages of Revelation which describe the new creation and the scenes of glory there, tell first of the solemn judgment, of the great white throne, the resurrection of the dead, and the casting of death and hell into the burning lake. Rev. xx., xxi.

The predicted glory that awaits this earth is connected, not with temporal, but with eternal scenes. It is not the sunset glow which gilds the eventide of a disordered world as it hastens on to the blackness of darkness forever and ever, but it is the rising of the Sun of Righteousness with healing in its wings, when the darkness of night has vanished, and the sun shall never more go down. The kingdom which God shall set up is "a kingdom which shall never be destroyed; which shall not be left to other people, but which shall stand forever. Dan. ii. 44. To the babe of Bethlehem shall be given "the throne of his father David," and he shall reign over the house of Jacob forever, and of his kingdom there shall be no end. Luke i. 32. The kingdoms of this world shall become our Lord's and his Christ's, and HE shall reign forever and ever. Rev. xi. 15. Thus the stamp of eternity is set upon all the prophetic pictures of "the glory that shall be revealed." The whole Scripture agrees in these representations. This present world is dark and evil, and grows darker and more evil to the end; and when the darkness passes, then comes the light of life forevermore. There is first the gloom and then the glory; first the storm and then the calm; first the darkness and then the light; first the great struggle with the powers of sin and evil, and then the eternal triumph of the ransomed host. The old world must be dissolved before the new one can appear; Satan must be dethroned ere Christ shall reign; and death itself must be swallowed up in victory, before the ransomed saints can sing the conquerors, joyful song.

It is sometimes asserted that these predictions of the future glory of the Messiah, are to be figuratively interpreted; but it is well for us to be cautious how we invoke the aid of fancy and allegory to evade the conclusions enforced by the plain statements of Scripture. Quite probably the Jewish Rabbis held that the prediction that Christ was to be born of a virgin was allegorical. Unquestionably they regarded the prophecies of his sorrows, his rejection, and his suffering, as couched in "highly figurative language." They could believe the predictions of his glory, but they could not accept those which foretold his sorrows and his shame. Doubtless they may have had plausible theories and reasonable conjectures, which may have commanded the assent and respect of their followers; but when in the fulness of time, God sent forth his Son to accomplish all that he had spoken, it speedily became evident that he had no need of their figures, fancies, or theories to accomplish the fulfillment of his own word. And if in opening to his disciples the Scriptures, and expounding unto them all things in the Law and in the Prophets and in the Psalms, concerning himself, he demonstrated his Messiahship by the accuracy with which every prediction was fulfilled: if his birth of the virgin, his nativity in Bethlehem, his ministry and work, were all foretold; if prophecy was fulfilled by the beast that carried him, by the nation that rejected him, by the disciple that betrayed him, by the price of his betrayal, by the nails that pierced his hands; by his death, and burial, and resurrection, and ascension;—if in all these instances God fulfilled his word with the utmost literality and precision, by what rule shall we, when we read the words of those same prophets concerning his future glory, refuse to accept them as precise and unquestionable statements of things which must shortly come to pass? If the prophecies of his shame were literally fulfilled, shall the predictions of his glory be cast aside as vague and shadowy? If the cross on which he hung was a reality, shall the throne which he shall inherit be a figure of speech? If the sufferings which he endured were real, shall the glory which is to follow, be an empty vision or an idle dream? Surely if any portion of the prophecy were to be figuratively expounded, it should be that portion which told of the shame, and sorrow, and suffering of the Son of God. If we can believe that God "spared not his own Son, but delivered him up for us all," we can believe *anything* which God has promised to do for Him or for us.

It is sometimes asserted that this earth is a very insignificant planet in the vast array of orbs that stud the heavens, and that it is unreasonable to suppose that the Son of God will ever come and make his abode in a world like this. There are other grander orbs; there are starry hosts wheeling in limitless space; there are far off radiant centres around which suns and systems roll and shine; why should we imagine that the Christ of God would select this poor world as the theatre of the revelation of his glory, and the place of the establishment of his throne?

These considerations have force, and if it were left to our imagination to decide the matter, we certainly might reach a different conclusion. But we deal with facts; and dark and insignificant as this world is, the Son of God *has* already trod its desert wastes. Strange as it may seem, he *has been here*, and for more than thirty years has been a pilgrim on this world's highway. We could not have anticipated such condescension, but it is his nature to do exceeding abundantly above all that we ask or think. Granted that his coming to our world is unreasonable, nevertheless *it is true;* he has been here once;—why may he not come here again? His glorious body had its origin here, and he has borne with him to the right hand of the Majesty on high, a physical form which partakes of the elements of this world in which we dwell. And if he has already entered into such an alliance with this shadowed, blighted, sin-cursed earth, can we deny that he may yet more gloriously manifest his love for the world which he has created, and which at the beginning God pronounced very good?

We may not judge of this world's importance by its visible magnitude. Doubtless there may be in the universe of God other and grander orbs than this, but there are associations connected with this planet, for which we might elsewhere search in vain. Where in all the wide creation can we find an orb which has been the theatre of events so strange and wonderful as this? Where can we find another Bethlehem, another Gethsemane, another Calvary? What other soil has been moistened by the tears and crimsoned by the blood of the Son of God? What other planet has been the theatre of such sorrow, such suffering, such conflict, and such victory as has been witnessed in this world? Do we ask why *this* earth should become the theatre of the grandest displays of divine grace and mercy? Is there not a sufficient answer found in the fact that this world has been the seat of the darkest and most terrible rebellion against a God of grace and truth? And is there not a glorious fitness in the thought that in this poor, dark, dishonored world, where God's law has been broken, his love despised, his Gospel rejected, his servants persecuted and his Son slain,—that here at last his Tabernacle should descend, and his glory be revealed as in no other portion of the universe which he has made? Thus where sin abounded grace shall so much the more abound, and in the very realm where Satan long has ruled and reigned, shall God magnify his love and power, by making it the abode of his people, and the habitation of his own glory.

And if this be the divine purpose, shall not every loyal heart rejoice to hear the news? Our exiled King shall return, and earth and heaven shall rejoice to hail his approach. He who was crowned with thorns, shall then be crowned with glory and honor. He who was crucified on Calvary, shall then reign on Zion. He who was despised and rejected, shall then be honored and esteemed. He who was mocked, and scourged, and spurned, and buffeted, shall be hailed and honored, and adored by a world which he has redeemed. And here, beneath skies once darkened above his cross, but then illumined with the splendors of his throne, they shall,

> "Bring forth the royal diadem,
> And crown him Lord of all."

To-day Christ sits enthroned, but it is not upon the throne of his own eternal kingdom. An exile from his rightful, blood-bought realm, he sits at the right hand of the throne of God, from henceforth expecting until his enemies be made his footstool. He, like the nobleman, has gone "into a far country, to receive for himself a kingdom, and to return," and by and by he shall come again and reckon with his servants, and destroy his foes who hated him, and said," We will not have this man to reign over us." Luke xix. 11-15. But he is not without honor or authority. As Pharaoh said to Joseph in Egypt: "Thou shalt be over my house, and according unto thy word shall all my people be ruled: only in the throne will I be greater than thou," so God hath "highly exalted Him, and given him a name which is above every name." And as of old they cried before Joseph, "Bow the knee," and made him ruler over all the land, so the great antitype of Joseph, having passed through his years of suffering and of shame, is set on high, and before him every knee shall bow and every tongue confess, to the glory of God the Father. Presiding over the destinies of the world, and carrying forward the work of human redemption, the resources of the universe are at his command. All power in heaven and earth is given into his hands, and, no matter whose decree opposes, he bids his servants go into all the world, and preach the Gospel to every creature, and win the rebels back to their allegiance to him.

But when "This Gospel of the kingdom shall be preached in all the world, for a witness unto all nations: then shall the end come." Matt. xxiv. 14. He, who to-day, as the great High Priest and Mediator, holds in his hands the reins of power and government, shall, when his work of grace is accomplished, deliver up the kingdom to God, even the Father; and the dispensation of grace having ended, the work of judgment shall begin. 1 Cor. xv. 24. His enemies shall then be made his footstool, and he, having authority to execute judgment, shall tread down all his foes. The kingdoms of this world shall first become "our Lord's," and then, subjected by Almighty power, they shall become "his Christ's, and he shall reign forever and ever." Rev. xi. 15. "The Lord God shall give unto him the throne of his father David: and He shall reign over the house of Jacob forever: and of his kingdom there shall be no end." Luke i. 32. One like the Son of Man shall come in the clouds of heaven to the Ancient of Days, and shall be brought near before him, and there shall be given him a kingdom and dominion and glory, that all people, nations and languages may serve him. Dan. vii: 14. "And when all things shall be subdued unto him, then shall the Son also himself be subject unto him that put all things under him, that God may be all in all." 1 Cor. xv. 28.

"But of the times and the seasons, brethren, ye have no need that I write unto you. For yourselves know perfectly that the Day of the Lord so cometh as a thief in the night. For when they shall say, Peace and safety; then sudden destruction cometh upon them, . . . and they shall not escape." And as it is not for us to "know the times or the seasons, which the Father hath put in his own power," it will appear evident that the Church should live in constant watchfulness, neither uttering rash alarms on the one hand, nor saying "Peace and safety" on the other, but standing in constant vigilance, with girded loins and burning lamps, waiting for the coming of the King. And if at times we grow weary of this long delay, we are yet to remember that "the Lord is not slack concerning his promise, as some men count slackness; but is long-suffering to us-ward, not willing that any should perish, but that all should come to repentance."

Our estimates of times and seasons partake of our own frailty and imperfection. That which God pronounces near at hand might yet seem far off to finite mortals. An eagle's estimate of distance is very different from a snail's; and periods which to us seem vast and almost illimitable, are but the dust of rolling ages in the sight of Him of whom it is written. "A thousand years in thy sight are but as yesterday when it is past, and as a watch in the night." "One day is with the Lord as a thousand years, and a thousand years as one day." Gazing through the pure ether which surrounds the heights of prophetic inspiration, the annointed eye of faith beholds at hand, events that, to the dim-eyed dwellers among the fogs and mists of worldliness and doubt, seem very far away. And the eagle glance that leaps from height to height along the distant landscape, may sometimes take no note of intervening vales, which must be entered by slow descents, and trodden with worn and weary feet. In a single sentence the prophet Isaiah connected "The acceptable year of the Lord, and the day of vengeance of our God." Only the slightest pause divides between those grand events; yet at the very point when our Saviour had read of "the acceptable year of the Lord," he "closed the book... and sat down." Isa. lxi. 2. Luke iv. 19. He knew *when to close the Book;*—he knew that between that acceptable year of the Lord and the day of vengeance of our God, a whole dispensation intervened: unfortunately we do not always know just where to close the Book, and sit down.

It seems, notwithstanding these considerations, clearly demonstrable that we are living in the closing period of this world's history. Long ago was it written, "The night is far spent, the day is at hand;" and again, "Knowing the time, that now it is high time to awake out of sleep: for now is our salvation nearer than when we believed." The apostles spoke of the times in which they lived as "*these last days*" wherein God had spoken unto men by his Son, "who verily was foreordained before the foundation of the world, but was manifest in *these last times* for you." The time when the Spirit of God was poured out as upon the day of Pentecost is definitely described as "in the *last days*," and the Scriptures, as a whole, coincide with these representations. But we may be sure that we could not reach " the last days " in the world's history, until we had passed the *middle period of its course.* On a journey of six thousand miles we do not reach the last miles until we have passed the middle milestone. Standing in the earlier portion of such a journey, we might call the whole of the latter half of the pilgrimage the *last* portion of it, but on arriving at the middle of the course we should still look forward and speak of the *last* part of it as that which immediately preceded the journey's end. The last miles of the journey, cannot include any portion of the *first half* of a journey, but they may include *all*, they *must* include a part of the *latter half*, and they *must* include the *last mile* of the course. So when the apostles spoke of living themselves "in the last days," they clearly indicated that the middle portion of the journey had been passed; and when, standing at that point, they looked still farther on and warned us of the dangers to come "in the last days," they certainly gave us no reason to conclude that they were then in the *opening period of this world's history*. Hence all these vague ideas that the world is in its infancy, that we have but just entered upon the flow of ages which are to roll on without limit or interruption, is contrary to the plain revelation of the inspired Word.

What do men know of the world's infancy? As much as a cricket knows of the infancy of the oak under which it chirps. Who can tell what uncounted ages may have swept over this globe between the time when it was " without form and void," and the time when God said, " Let there be light," and prepared it for the abode of mankind. The world may be in its infancy, in respect to the divine purpose, but it will never reach its maturity until He who made it " very good " at first, shall come back to remove its curse and enshroud it with his blessing, and make it the abode of righteousness and peace and truth.

A terrible infancy this world has passed! For six thousand years it has been in rebellion against its Maker and its God. Here his name has been blasphemed, his law broken, his love despised, his grace spurned, his servants hated, his prophets stoned, and his Son slain. Here plains have shook with the tread of rushing armies, mountains have trembled with the thunder of battle, heaven has been pierced with cries of anguish, and earth has been slippery with human gore. From the time that the first man born of woman quenched his wrath in his brother's blood, this world has been the theatre of violence, oppression, injustice, iniquity, carnage, strife, jealousy, lust, pollution, idolatry, blasphemy, covetousness, and devilishness, so vast, so black, so terrible, that no eye but the eye of God could bear to contemplate the scene. From those in this world who view a little of this seething hell of vice and woe and sin, the cry, " How long, O Lord?" goes up before the throne. And from Him who sitteth in the heavens and declares the end from the beginning, the answer comes, "Yet a little while, and He that shall come, will come, and will not tarry." The long-suffering of God is salvation; he bears with all that he may save some; " But the Day of the Lord will come," even "the day of judgment and perdition of ungodly men;" and then, when the reign of sin is past, we may look for the days of joy and sunshine for the world, under the dominion of her rightful King.

There is another consideration which is not without weight. The statements of Scripture are in agreement with the facts of science and the nature of things; and until we enter that world where they neither marry nor are given in marriage, but are equal with the angels, we may assume that like causes produce like effects, and that the laws which govern the human race in its present condition, would govern them in the millennial state. At present we have a general knowledge of the extent of our globe. There are no new continents to be discovered or explored, and geographical science informs us as to the extent of man's earthly habitation. We are also aware that the practice of religion, virtue, temperance and moderation, tend naturally to increase any population where these principles prevail. Now it is estimated that under such favorable circumstances, the population of any country will double itself in the space of about thirty-three years. Suppose then, for example, that at some period, say in the year A. D. 2,000, the fourteen hundred millions comprising the present population of this globe, will have increased to two thousand millions, and that then, the millennium will have dawned, with every condition favorable to the increase and longevity of the race; with no wars, famines, or pestilences to hurt or destroy the human family; with knowledge universally diffused, and the principles of piety, temperance, and pure religion everywhere regarded; with an utter absence of all these nameless vices and abominations which at present so largely deteriorate the physical vigor of the race;—certainly a virtuous, healthful, peaceful, pious, happy population, surrounded by all material blessings and comforts, could not fail to double itself once in *thirty-three years*, or three times in the course of a century.

But if we start with these undeniable premises, the simplest possible calculation will show us that long ere the close of the millennium, the population of this world will have entirely outgrown its habitation; and that long before a thousand years would have elapsed, to say nothing of the much vaster periods to which some men extend their millennial expectations, this globe would be covered by a solid mass of human beings, *far more numerous than could obtain standing room upon its surface.* Hence a theory which involves such consequences must be regarded as not only unscriptural but impossible.

It has been objected to the doctrine of the personal coming and reign of Christ on earth, that its adherents and advocates are like the apostles of old, "unlearned and ignorant men," of humble station and of small repute; and that their conclusions are hence unworthy of confidence and respect.

But the Gospel takes mankind as they are. Not many mighty or noble are called; "the poor in this world, rich in faith," are chosen to be heirs of the kingdom; and any doctrine which is beyond the reach of the common mind, gives little evidence that it pertains to that Gospel which of old was preached to the poor, and which is especially adapted, not to the exceptional few who have learning, wealth, and fame, but to the common people who heard the Saviour gladly, and who still make up the vast majority of the Church of Jesus Christ, and the world of mankind.

But we have no more need to be ashamed of the men who now hold this "faith once delivered to the saints," than we have to blush for that noble army of elect souls who have believed and published it in years gone by. Can we find more eminent preachers than Chalmers, and Krummacher, and Cumming, and Charles H. Spurgeon, and Newman Hall, and S. H. Tyng? Can we find evangelists more laborious than D. L. Moody, and D. W. Whittle, and E. P. Hammond, and Henry Varley, and their associates and helpers? Can we point to philanthropists more devoted than Lord Shaftesbury and George Müller of Bristol? Can we find commentators more learned than Lange, and Alford, and Fausett? Can we find sacred poets more fervid than Bonar, and Bliss, and Denny? Can we find critics who have studied to better purpose than Tregelles, and Kelly, and Craik, and Hudson? Can we find singers that have sung the songs of Zion in sweeter strains than Sankey, and Bliss, and their fellow-singers? Can we, in their several departments, find men more honored of God, or less tainted with folly and fanaticism than these? And yet, we believe every one of them has been taught by the grace of God to live "looking for that blessed hope," and waiting "for the Son of God from heaven;" and that every one of them holds the personal coming of the Lord Jesus Christ to reign over the earth, as a personal and a precious faith.

Is it not time to drop such objections as these? "Have any of the rulers . . . believed on him?" is an old question, but it savors of the old man, rather than the new. The fact that the foremost men of the Church in *all* ages, the present included, unite their testimonies in favor of this faith, while it is not urged as a *proof* of the truth of that which the Word of God alone can establish, may perhaps serve as an answer to those who would reject the teaching of inspiration because ignorant or erratic people have unhappily mingled their own errors with the teachings of divine revelation. And the fact that these representative men, with many others that might be found, hold and declare these truths unchallenged, simply indicates that the heart of the church of God gravitates towards this ancient faith. The multitudes throng to listen to the utterances of men like these, because they believe their testimony, and because the "gospel of the kingdom" is no less glad tidings to the saints, than "the gospel of the grace of God" which saves them from their sins is to sinners. In their faith they link together the cross and the crown, "the sufferings of Christ, and the glory that should follow;" and while they proclaim "the acceptable year of the Lord," they also proclaim "the day of vengeance of our God."

In a conversation with the late P. P. Bliss, at his residence in Chicago, in the autumn of 1875, the writer, who had recently returned from attending the special religious services in London, conducted by the American Evangelists, referred to the stirring Gospel Hymns which he had heard sung with such effect by the vast assemblies congregated in the London Tabernacles; and expressed his gratification at the prominence with which the ancient hope of the church, the coming of the Lord, was set forth in those sacred lyrics. The sweet singer replied substantially as follows:

"God has seemed to set *special honor* upon those hymns which speak of Christ's second coming. The hymns that have gone around the world, are those that refer to that event, such as:

>'Hold the fort, for *I am coming*,
>Jesus signals still.'

>'Down life's dark vale we wander,
>*Till Jesus comes.*'

>'When he cometh, when he cometh
>To make up his jewels.'"

How near this subject lay to his heart, was well known to all his acquaintances, and his latest hymns show that his love for Christ's appearing glowed with a still intenser ardor, as he drew near his journey's end. His friend and co-worker, D. W. Whittle, in a large assembly in Boston, declared that, during the last year of his life every hymn he wrote, had in it something on this great subject. Thus he sang:

> "*When he comes*, our glorious King,
> All his ransomed home to bring,
> Then anew this song we'll sing:
> Hallelujah, what a Saviour!"

And again:

> "Children of the living God, take courage;
> Your great deliverance sweetly sing;
> Set your faces toward the hill of Zion,
> Thence to hail our coming King!"

> "Are your windows open toward Jerusalem,
> Though as captives here a 'little while' we stay?
> For the *coming of the King in his glory*,
> Are you watching day by day?"

And finally, the last production he sent to the press, before he went down in the fiery wreck of Ashtabula, had these words as its burden:

> "Thy Saviour is *coming* in tenderest love,
> To make up his jewels and bear them above:
> Oh, child, in thy anguish, despairing or dumb,
> Remember the message, 'Hold fast till I come.'
> Hold fast till I come, Hold fast till I come;
> A bright crown awaits thee; *Hold fast till I come.*"

In giving to the world these hymns of grace and glory, this evangelist of song not only poured forth his own personal aspirations and desires, as did Watts, and Wesley, and Dodridge, and many others, but he also voiced the emotions of ten thousand glowing hearts in every quarter of the globe. It is by no mere accident that those hymns that speak of Christ's glorious appearing "have gone round the world," stirring the souls of multitudes, and winning their way to every land; but it is because they strike those deep, grand chords the church so longs and loves to hear, and give expression to the glad anticipations of those who, having the first fruits of the Spirit, wait for the adoption, to wit, the redemption of our body; and to whom the grace of God that bringeth salvation has appeared, teaching them that, denying ungodliness, and worldly lusts, they should live "soberly, righteously and godly in this present world; looking for that blessed hope, and the glorious appearing of the great God and our Saviour Jesus Christ." Titus ii. 12, 13.

Not only now, but through all past ages, has this tremendous theme been the burden of some of the grandest songs of the universal church. It has been one of the mightiest inspirations of those who prepare praises for the Most High, and give voice to the deepest emotions of the human heart. From the solemn judgment hymn of unknown antiquity, quoted by the Venerable Bede more than twelve hundred years ago,

> "At last the great day of the Lord shall arise
> As a thief in the night to dismay and surprise,"

down through the strain of St. Bernard, beginning with,

> "The world is very evil, the times are waxing late,
> Be sober and keep vigil, the Judge is at the gate,"

and rolling on until, having run its tossing current through the rugged scenes of sin and judgment, it sweeps out at last in the glad sunshine of

> "Jerusalem the golden, with milk and honey blessed;"

and also in the awful majesty of "Dies Iræ," that noblest hymn of the ages,

> "Day of wrath, that day of burning,
> All shall melt, to ashes turning;"

and in that midnight hymn of the Greek church:

> "Behold, the Bridegroom cometh in the middle of the night,
> And blest is he whose loins are girt, whose lamp is burning bright;"

as also that ancient Greek hymn of Theodore of the Studium,

> "The day is near, the judgment is at hand:
> Awake, my soul! awake and ready stand!"

likewise in the rich treasury of German hymnology, where so many precious hymns proclaim that day, such as the judgment hymn of Ringwalt:

> "Surely at the appointed time,
> The Son of God in glory
> Shall come to judge the human kind,
> The sinful and the holy"—

and Philip Nicolai's solemn *Wachet Auf:*

> "Wake! the startling watch-cry pealeth,
> While slumber deep each eyelid sealeth;
> Awake! Jerusalem, awake!"

and Laurentius Laurenti's beautiful hymn, commencing,

> "Rejoice, all ye believers,
> And let your lights appear;"

and in others, far too numerous to mention, in the Greek, Latin, Syrian, German, French, and other churches, this thought of the coming judgment, sudden, awful, and impending, rings its solemn cadence through all the ages and generations.

The grandest songs of Christendom are upon this theme; and the sweetest singers swell these solemn hymns. Watts exclaims,

> "When shall thy lovely face be seen,
> When shall our eyes behold our God?"

Wesley sings,

> "Lo, he comes, with clouds descending!"

Heber lifts up the song,

> "The Lord shall come, the earth shall quake."

Milman chants,

> "The chariot, the chariot, its wheels roll in fire,
> As the Lord cometh down in the pomp of his ire;"

and thus through all the years, rings this deep and solemn strain of those who, like the Psalmist, say, "I will sing of mercy and judgment; unto thee, O Lord, will I sing."

We offer no array of names as evidence of the correctness of a position, nor do we seek to sustain by reference to authority a cause which cannot be maintained by argument. But when men heap opprobrium upon a truth because it is accepted and advocated by men who are, like Christ's first disciples, ignorant and unlearned, it becomes necessary to show that there stand among the advocates of this ancient faith, men the latchet of whose shoes some of its despisers might count themselves honored to stoop down and unloose.

There is probably no living author whose hymns are more widely and justly prized than those of Dr. Horatius Bonar. In glancing over the latest and choicest Hymnals prepared for various churches, we find no other living writer so fully represented as he; several recent collections containing more than a score of Bonar's hymns, many of which have taken their place among the permanent hymnology of the English tongue.

And what has been the inspiration of these holy hymns? It is well known that their author is, and has been for many years, a firm and fervent believer in this gospel of the kingdom of God at hand; and that the "blessed hope" has been the joy of his life and the inspiration of his writings and his songs. The evidences of this fact would fill volumes. As editor for many years of the *Quarterly Journal of Prophecy*, and author of numerous sermons, tracts, and Scripture expositions, he has ever, with sobriety of judgment and soundness of speech, made prominent this grand and glorious theme. And on almost every page of the various collections of his published poetry, shines the light of this bright and morning star; and this truth, pervading his entire faith, and linking the cross which the Saviour bore, to the crown that he is yet to wear, lends to his hymns a charm which touches the hearts of many who do not yet clearly see the fountain whence these songs have sprung. A few lines will serve to indicate the tenor of many of these sacred hymns:

"Come, Lord, and tarry not;
Bring the long looked for day.
Oh, why these years of waiting, why
These ages of delay?

"Come, for thy saints still wait;
Daily ascends their sigh;
The Spirit and the Bride say, Come;
Dost thou not hear the cry?"

Again,

"The church has waited long,
Her absent Lord to see,
And still in loneliness she waits,
A friendless stranger, she.
Age after age has gone,
Sun after sun has set;
And still in weeds of widowhood,
She weeps, a mourner yet.
Come, then, Lord Jesus, come."

Again he thus tells of the hope of the Church of God:

"Oh, long expected, absent long,
Star of creation's troubled gloom,
Let heaven and earth break forth in song,
Messiah! Saviour! art thou come?
For thou hast bought us with thy blood,
And thou wast slain to set us free;
Thou madest us kings and priests to God,
And we shall reign on earth with thee!"

Once more he pours forth the warning cry of coming doom:

> "Time's sun is fast setting, its twilight is nigh.
> Its evening is falling in cloud o'er the sky:
> Its shadows are stretching in ominous gloom,
> Its midnight approaches, the midnight of doom.
> Then haste, sinner, haste, there is mercy for thee;
> And wrath is preparing, flee, lingerer, flee."

The songs of Watts and Wesley, breathing this longing for the coming of the King, and heralding and celebrating his visible and personal reign on earth, may be expurgated from the hymn books of those who hold their names in honor; but they cannot be erased from the memories of those who "love His appearing," and find in them the words that express their sorrows and their joys. A living and loving church will sing these hymns of faith and hope; and we rejoice that in the later and better collections of sacred song, this grand theme is resuming its appropriate place and prominence. As Mr. Spurgeon says in his preface to "*Our Own Hymn Book*," "Subjects frequently passed over or pushed into a corner, are here made conspicuously the themes of song, such, for instance, as the great doctrine of sovereign grace, the *personal advent of our Lord*, and especially the sweetness of present communion with him."

These hymns have made their way through the length and breadth of the church of Christ, because they expressed, not only the ancient faith embodied in the creeds of Christendom, but also the universal, scriptural hope and true Christian sentiment of the church which is redeemed by the blood of Christ.

However Christians may contend about creeds, differ about doctrines, and divide into denominations, they agree in sacred song; and the new song which God has put into the mouth of his redeemed children who sing with the spirit and the understanding also, more truly expounds the living faith of a living church than all the creeds which men frame, or the systems of divinity about which they divide and dispute.

In the early spring of 1863 two armies of brothers estranged, confronted each other on the opposite hills of Stafford and Spottsylvania, Va. The shadows of evening were falling, and two military bands chanced at the same hour to be discoursing sweet music on the opposite banks of the river. The soldiers of both armies gathered to listen to the pleasing strains, and soon the bands began to answer each other. First the band on the northern bank would play the various national airs,—the listening soldiers cheering the strain. The band on the southern bank would respond with some southern melody, and receive the applause of their comrades. Presently one of the bands struck up a sweet and plaintive strain which was wafted across the Rappahannock, caught up by the band upon the other shore, and like a grand anthem the strain, "Home, Home, Sweet Home," swelled forth upon the evening air, thrilling every heart, and causing the tear of sympathy to roll down many a weather-beaten cheek, while a simultaneous shout went up from either side the rolling stream, and the hills which had so recently resounded with the thunder of hostile artillery, echoed and reëchoed the glad acclaim. They sung their national and their sectional tunes by themselves, but here was a strain which struck a responsive chord in every heart, and awoke an answering shout from every voice.

It is by no mere accident that those hymns which speak of Christ's glorious appearing have gone around the earth, stirring the heart of the universal church, and winning their way to every land; but it is because they go beneath the sectional and sectarian solos and quartets which speak of narrow ideas and personal interests, and strike those deeper, grander chords the church so longs and loves to hear, giving expression to the glad anticipations of those who, having the first fruits of the Spirit, wait for the adoption, to wit, the redemption of our body, in the immortal glory of the resurrection of the just.

The great question at issue is not so much concerning "the times or the seasons, which the Father hath put in his own power;" it is not a question of dates and periods, and visions and symbols; but it has respect to the habitual attitude of the church of Christ toward her absent Lord.

The Christians of Thessalonica, under the teaching of Paul the apostle, turned "from idols to serve the living and true God, and to *wait* for his Son from heaven." The early Christians were to "come behind in no gift, waiting for the coming of our Lord Jesus Christ." They were taught by divine grace to live, "looking for that blessed hope, and the glorious appearing of the great God and our Saviour Jesus Christ;" and they were also taught that a crown of righteousness was laid up for "all them also that love his appearing." Hence this grand event was their inspiring motive, their watchword, their guiding star.

Now is it not impossible for any church to be looking for and waiting for an event which they are taught may never come at all, or which they are certain never can come during the period of their natural lives? Yet it has come to pass that teachers have recently arisen who, forgetting that no man knoweth the day nor the hour when the Son of man cometh, have substituted for that wisely ordained uncertainty which enforces the exhortation, "Watch, therefore, for ye *know neither the day nor the hour* wherein the Son of man cometh," definite statements that that day *can not come* for hundreds, or thousands, or millions of years, and perhaps will never come at all. Of course persons accepting such teaching *do not* and *cannot* live, "looking for that blessed hope," nor can they live, waiting for the Son of God from heaven; and if they do not become evil servants, smiting their fellows and eating and drinking with the drunken, they can hardly avoid saying *in their hearts*, "My Lord delayeth his coming." But such a position is as unscriptural as it is unsafe. If it was right to wait for the Son of God from heaven, in the days of the apostles, it is much more needful now; for now is our salvation nearer than when we believed; and if our Lord has left the time of his return unrevealed, that Christians may be ever ready and watching, surely he has sent no man to tell them that that day *cannot come* for ages, and hence that watching for it is utterly in vain. It is true that the apostle declared that that day could not come until an apostasy should occur, but it is also true that he had no assurance, and gave no assurance, that the events to which he referred would occupy a long period of time. This was one of those times and seasons which the Father had put in his own power.

Nor must we lose sight of the fact that the great truths concerning the coming and kingdom of the Lord, are no matters of idle and indifferent speculation. The "resurrection of the dead" and "eternal judgment," are among the very "principles of the doctrine of Christ," ranking with "repentance from dead works" and "faith toward God." Heb. vi. 1, 2. They are the things which were to be taught first, and which even babes in Christ were expected to receive. And further, the expectant attitude of the church of Christ is an indication and proof of her love for the person and presence of her Master.

They do greatly err who suppose that the children of God derive this hope only from dim prophetic symbols or mysterious apocalyptic visions. These, no doubt, have their meaning, their place, and their use; but if these are all that men have on which to build their faith, they come very far short of the apostolic church. A universal faith must have a broader foundation; a universal hope must have a surer anchorage. And so this question is not more a question of prophecy than of piety, for the church's expectation does not so much depend upon wisdom in the head, as upon grace in the heart. "The *grace* of *God* that bringeth salvation, hath appeared to all men, *teaching* us" to "live . . . *looking* for that *blessed hope.*" It is not, then, the book of Daniel, nor the symbols of Revelation, but it is "*the grace of God* that bringeth salvation," which teaches us to live, looking for that blessed hope of our Lord's return. It is that grace by which we are saved, through faith; that grace without which we cannot *be* saved: that grace which "bringeth salvation" to a lost world, that teaches us how to live, and for what to look; and the same grace that teaches us to live soberly, righteously, and godly, teaches us to look for "that blessed hope."

This matter is too plain for argument. The man who knows the grace of God in truth, does not need long arguments to teach him to deny ungodliness and worldly lusts, and live a sober, righteous, and godly life. These principles are taught him by the grace that saves him, and are inwrought in his heart by the Holy Spirit. But the same grace which teaches men to live the Christian life, also teaches them to look for "that blessed hope." No one admits that a difference of opinion among Christians is a sufficient ground for ceasing to live soberly, righteously, and godly; and the man who claimed that his "views" led him in a different direction, would be regarded as one ignorant of the gospel, and unacquainted with Christ and his grace. But the same grace of God also teaches men to look for that blessed hope, and if they fail to do this, they must be either deficient in the experience of the grace that bringeth salvation or slow to learn the lesson which it conveys.

These considerations lift this theme entirely above the realms of theological strife, and the niceties of speculative criticism, and assign it its true position as a normal element in the life of the redeemed church. And hence, while this waiting attitude is independent of special theories, opinions, or interpretations, any theory or interpretation, the direction and effect of which is to turn men's eyes from "looking for that blessed hope," and hinder them from waiting for the Son of God from heaven, is necessarily and palpably faulty, contrary to, and subversive of, the teaching of that "grace of God which bringeth salvation."

Nor are we to fall into a mistaken notion that this subject is one of slight importance, upon which the sacred penmen touch lightly or incidentally. There are many writings from which this theme is omitted, but they were not written "by inspiration of God." There are many sermons that ignore this subject, but they were not preached by prophets or apostles. There are systems where the doctrine of Christ's glorious appearing has no place, but they are neither apostolic nor primitive; they are the product of an age wise in its own conceit, and indifferent to that word "which liveth and abideth forever."

The Scriptures say far more about Christ's coming in glory, than they ever said about his coming in poverty and humiliation. The Scriptures say a hundred times as much about the coming of the Lord in judgment as they do about preparing to die; and yet ministers ring perpetual changes about death and a preparation for death, when they cannot even find *one* passage of scripture for a text to sanction such ideas, and are obliged, when talking of accidents, calamities, collisions, and explosions, causing unexpected death, to quote and *misapply* the words, "Be ye also ready, for in such an hour as ye think not, the *Son* of *man cometh.*"

A more glaring perversion of scripture it would be difficult to produce. Death is in no sense whatever the coming of the Lord. Not one passage of scripture inculcates or sanctions such an idea. Death is an enemy, Christ is a friend. Death destroys our living friends, Christ restores our dead friends. Death sinks man into the sepulchre, Christ brings him out again. Death came by sin, Christ was manifested to take away sin. Death comes as a curse, Christ comes as a blessing, to redeem us from the curse. Death conquered Christ on Calvary, Christ has conquered death, and will destroy death and him that had the power of death, that is, the devil, when he comes. Death will be cast into the lake of fire, while Christ will reign in the new Jerusalem. Death shall then be no more; Christ shall endure forever. Can death be the coming of Christ? Mary and Martha knew better than this, and each of them said, as they met him in the day of their sorrow, "Lord, if *thou* hadst been here, my brother HAD NOT DIED." John xi. 21, 32.

So far as we know, no person ever died in Christ's presence. Though he was appointed to "comfort all that mourn," yet he preached no funeral sermons, and was present at no death-bed scenes. Death knew its conqueror, and vanished at his approach; and whether he walked among the sick and dying, or came where the ruler's daughter lay dead among the mourning throng, or met the funeral procession bearing out the widow's son to his burial, or stood by the sepulchre of the departed Lazarus,—wherever he confronted death, the monster quailed, and the lawful captives were delivered from his power. Even as he hung upon the cross, it was not until after He expired, that the malefactors beside him died; and his dying groan not only smote the heart of nature with earthquake shocks, but also burst the graves and startled the slumberers there.

He lives who was dead, and he is now alive forevermore. He has the keys of hell and of death, and he shall redeem his people and destroy death, the last enemy, in the lake of fire. And to intimate that death is, *in any sense whatever*, *the coming of Christ*, is to betray a carelessness of study unworthy a well-instructed scribe, or an inexactness of statement not justifiable in dealing with that word whose jots and tittles shall abide when heaven and earth shall pass away.

Nor will the indefinite allegation that the scriptures which predict Christ's coming and reign on earth are merely figurative language, serve to settle this question, for those who assert this have no exclusive knowledge upon this point. They are disciples, not masters, and others can find figures as well as they, and can interpret them quite as authoritatively. If the Scriptures do not mean what they *say*, then surely these teachers have no special authority to tell us what they *do* mean; and to say that the plain sense of Scripture is to be set aside to give place to fanciful, allegorical meanings, is to subvert all faith, and make the word of God subject to the caprices of men. To claim that these words of Scripture are to be understood in an unusual and special sense, is to beg the whole question. If the plain teaching of the Scripture sustains a position, there is no necessity for resorting to such expedients; and if it does not sustain it, it is better to admit an error of opinion than to tamper with the sacred record.

Figures of speech are common to every tongue, but these figures represent and express facts. There were plenty of figures of speech in the predictions of our Saviour's coming, eighteen hundred years ago. The lamb, the passover, the turtle-doves, the young pigeons offered in sacrifice, foreshadowed the one great offering for the sins of men. He was the root, the branch, the light, the rock, and the corner-stone: but beneath all these figures there was a *fact*, and under all these shadows there was *a person* who came to do the will of God, and who, from Bethlehem's manger to Calvary's cross, fulfilled in all their minuteness, not only the types and shadows which prefigured him, but also those plainer, more specific statements in all the scriptures concerning himself. And it was by reference to these express statements of Scripture, minutely fulfilled, that his claim to the Messiahship was made good. The same arguments which prove that Jesus of Nazareth, the despised and rejected sufferer, was the true Messiah, prove from the same scriptures, that the same despised and rejected Jesus shall come again in the clouds of heaven, and reign over the house of Jacob forever, and of his kingdom there shall be no end. The arguments by which men disprove that he will come, disprove that he has come, and warrant the Jews in denying his Messiahship. If the foundations be destroyed, what can the righteous do?

It is asserted by some, that the acceptance of the doctrine of the personal coming and reign of Christ on earth, as the one grand hope of the church, tends to diminish zeal, paralyze missionary effort, and cause people to sit down in listless indifference, while the world is rushing onward to perdition. This is a very broad and sweeping charge which should not be lightly made, but if made, should be abundantly sustained. It would not be sufficient to show that persons cherishing this hope were indifferent to the cause of missions, because there are thousands who do *not* cherish it who are equally indifferent; nor would it be sufficient to prove that some persons who are expecting days of millennial peace are interested in missionary labor, for it would be easy to find other persons cherishing similar opinions who have no deep, vital, active interest in such matters. The current theory of the past generation has been, that the world is to be converted by the preaching of the gospel; and yet the churches who have held this theory, have probably expended more money for tobacco and strong drink, than they have to publish the gospel in all the world. Would it be a logical deduction from these facts, that a belief in the doctrine of the conversion of the world operated as a powerful incentive to the use of rum and tobacco?

There are many people who feel no special interest in the work of missions; but it is fair to remember that the interest of modern Christendom in missionary work only dates back to the beginning of the present century, and that previous to that time, the interest in missions was paralyzed throughout Christendom. Shall we conclude that the doctrine of the world's conversion was answerable for the general indifference which pervaded Christendom a hundred years ago? Or shall we conclude that the doctrine of the world's conversion is so new that up to the beginning of this century, the missionary zeal of the church was paralyzed because the doctrine of the world's conversion had not yet been invented? In order to give this argument logical force and coherence, it would need to be shown that all men who believe in the conversion of the world, know what conversion *is*, and are trying to convert the world; and that persons who have been zealous in the work of saving men, uniformly lose their zeal when they become convinced that the world is not to be converted by the preaching of the gospel. It would be necessary to show that these results uniformly followed and flowed from the causes specified, and that zeal uniformly dies out of the hearts of those who hold this ancient hope.

Solitary instances and occasional examples settle nothing. Of course certain men are liable to abuse any scriptural truth, for no one can tell how ill-ordered minds may be affected by any doctrine. In apostolic days men even turned the grace of God into lasciviousness, continuing in sin that grace might abound. The founder of Christianity chose twelve apostles, and one of them was a devil who abused his position, stole the funds entrusted to him, and finally betrayed his Lord; but we have not been accustomed to regard this fact as a proof that Christ was an impostor or Christianity a delusion. Nor should we reject any doctrine because unworthy or unstable men have perverted it or made it an instrument of wrong-doing for personal gratification or advantage.

There may be men holding the most precious truths, whose theoretical beliefs have no influence upon their hearts and lives,—ungodly men who have crept into the church, and who in all sects and all quarters, prove themselves to be in the direct line of succession from the Apostle Judas, who carried the bag, and stole the money, and betrayed his Lord. Whatever their opinions may be, such ungodly men, ordained of old to this condemnation, pervert every truth, and prove by inconsistent and unholy lives that they do not really know the grace of God. But these men, found everywhere, are no more to be accepted as representatives of any doctrine, than Judas the traitor was to be accepted as a fair representative of Christ and his religion. Truth is harmonious; and while a partial knowledge of its principles may lead to mistaken views and injudicious action, thorough acquaintance with the same truth is the best possible corrective for such errors. No Christian man has a right to abandon important truths to the custody of fanatics or hypocrites. If set for the defense of the gospel he must defend it, holding forth the faithful word against the oppositions of foes or the perversions of pretended friends.

Those persons who suppose that to abandon the hope of the world's conversion is to cease from Christian labor, confound two essentially different things. They assume that those scriptures that teach us that the gospel shall be *preached* in all the world, warrant us in believing that by it all the world shall be *converted*. Such a conclusion seems entirely unwarranted, and tends to obscure the subject under discussion.

There is no question but that the gospel is to be preached in all the world and to all nations. Our Saviour plainly said, "This gospel of the kingdom shall be preached in all the world for a witness unto all nations; and *then* shall the *end* come." Matt. xxiv. 14. He does not say that this gospel shall be received by all nations, nor that through its proclamation all nations shall be converted: he does not say that when this gospel of the kingdom is preached in all the world, then days of millennial peace shall dawn, and all the nations yield obedience to Christ: but he plainly predicts, first, the preaching of the gospel in all the world as a witness unto all nations, and then the coming of "*the end*," as if that consummation were to follow without interval or delay. There is not the slightest hint that after this gospel is preached in all the world, long years of peace and blessing and prosperity shall follow before the completion of this dispensation. On the contrary, the language conveys an entirely opposite idea.

We read again in the book of Revelation, of an angel flying through the "midst of heaven, having the everlasting gospel to preach unto them that dwell on the earth, and to every nation and kindred and tongue and people." But this message thus sent from one end of the world to another, is not a proclamation of the world's conversion, nor of the incoming of a golden age, but rather a command to "fear God and give glory to him, for the hour of his judgment is come."

On the other hand, those predictions which describe the state of glory yet to occur on earth, carry us beyond the era of gospel preaching and prophetic labor. When that day shall come, we are taught that "the earth shall be filled with the knowledge of the Lord, as the waters cover the sea." To preach the gospel under such circumstances would be like sprinkling drops of water into the ocean; and we are expressly told, that "They shall *teach no more* every man his neighbor, and every man his brother, saying, Know the Lord; for they shall all know me, from the least of them unto the greatest of them, saith the Lord." Jer. xxxi. 34. The era here contemplated is certainly beyond the period of preaching, praying, inviting, or instructing. When from the least of them to the greatest, all shall "know the Lord," we shall have entered upon a state of things entirely different from that which now exists; we shall have passed beyond all gospel labor and missionary enterprise.

Hence it is not easy to see how a faith in the personal coming and reign of Christ can retard the efforts and paralyze the zeal of those unto whom the word of reconciliation is committed in order that they may prepare a people for his coming. In fact the proximity of that event is one urgent motive to earnest endeavor for the salvation of men. It was when all things were *ready* that the invitation was given with increasing urgency to come to the marriage feast. The thought that the hope of the world's conversion is the mainspring to Christian effort, would require a new version to the sacred Scriptures, and then we might expect to read, "The hope of *success* constraineth us." But this was not the power which constrained the Apostle Paul, nor is it the power which constrains the people of God to-day. It is "the love of Christ" which constraineth men to seek and save the lost; and if that love has not vanished from our hearts, and if we still acknowledge our subjection to our risen and ascended Lord, we have no choice in this matter, but are to go into all the world and preach the gospel to every creature.

If it be said that Christians will not labor to save the lost unless they have the assurance that all the world will be converted, we reply, such a Christianity as that is not described or illustrated in the New Testament. Prophets and apostles have been obliged to exclaim, "Lord, *who* hath believed our report? and to whom hath the arm of the Lord been revealed?" But they have not despaired, but have struggled on through years of reproach and sorrow, becoming all things to all men, that thereby they might save *some;* and rejoicing in the hope of a resurrection to immortal life, and the assurance that their labor was not in vain in the Lord.

The assertion that the ancient faith of the church of Christ paralyzes missionary effort, is best met by an appeal to facts. Was not the Thessalonian church, which turned from idols "to serve the living and true God, and to wait for his Son from heaven," the very church from which "sounded out the word of the Lord" in Macedonia and Achaia, and in every place? Was not the church of the first three centuries, which held this faith, in the most emphatic sense a missionary church? And are not those who look for that blessed hope, to-day among the leaders in the van of modern missionary labor? Does this faith paralyze their zeal?

Did this faith paralyze the zeal of the godly Henry Martyn,

who, embarking for India in 1805, toiled through seven long, lonely years in the mission field; who, when worn with labors and broken by disease, started homeward, journeying overland on horseback in weariness and anguish, from Persia towards Constantinople, and while resting and suffering in an orchard by the way-side, October 6, 1812—just ten days before he died among strangers, at Tokat, Asia Minor, penned in his journal these, his last recorded words: "Oh! when shall time give place to eternity? When shall appear that new heaven and new earth, wherein dwelleth righteousness? There, there shall in no wise enter anything that defileth. None of that wickedness which has made man worse than wild beasts, none of these corruptions which add still more to the miseries of mortality, shall be seen or heard of any more"?

Did this faith paralyze the zeal of Heber, the Bishop of Calcutta, who sung in his missionary hymn of the time,

"When o'er our ransomed nature, The Lamb, for sinners slain,
Redeemer, King, Creator, In bliss RETURNS TO REIGN;"

and who also spent his strength in missionary toils and journeyings, and at last rested from his labors on "India's coral strand"? Has this hope paralyzed the zeal of the Moravian church, which for more than a century has maintained its existence mainly to preach the gospel to the heathen? Did this hope paralyze the zeal of Krapf, the explorer of Africa, or Gutzlaff, the opener of China, or Bettleheim, the pioneer missionary of Japan, or of a multitude of others who have borne the glad tidings of salvation to a lost and dying world?

Did this faith paralyze the zeal of that mighty Scottish evangelist, William C. Burns, the early co-worker of McCheyne and Somerville and Bonar, who wrote soon after his conversion: "This is not our home, for we are dead, and our life is hid with Christ in God; when he who is our life shall appear, then shall we also appear with him in glory. What a hope is this, that our eyes shall see him, and that we shall dwell with him forever!" who, standing at the head of the quay at Leith, and preaching to the throng of sailors, cried: "The breakers are ahead, the storm is rising, you are running upon a lee shore! In a few moments the ship (the world) will strike and go down! The life-boat is Christ; it is ready to move off. Come away, sailors, come away, or it will be too late;" who, in 1842, preached in the open air to a tearful congregation for nearly four hours on Heb. ix. 27, 28; who, in September, 1844, stood in a dense crowd in 'Spital Square, Newcastle, prayerfully inquiring what he should say, until he opened the Bible and his eye fell on Rev. xx. 15, "And I saw a great white throne and him that sat on it," and preached with solemn power on the rising of the dead, and the appearing of each indivdual at the judgment bar; who, when Great Britain had become too narrow a field, and he had crossed the ocean and plowed the Canadian snows, went finally to far off China, and toiled for nearly a quarter of a century; so winning the love of the people that when all other Europeans were surrounded by tumults and encompassed by foes, he, "the man of the book," "the Chinaman's friend," could go and come in peace; who, after proclaiming the gospel of God's grace to the swarming myriads of the land of Sinim, while lying upon his dying bed at Nieu-chwang, said to the Chinese, "Come to my bedside, I will still preach to you;" and there preached his last sermon, December 29, 1867, from Rev. xx. 11-15; witnessing in his last testimony to that solemn judgment message which he proclaimed so powerfully in the streets of Newcastle twenty-seven years before, with that overwhelming conviction which imparted an almost preternatural terribleness and grandeur to his words; whose dying meditations were upon the words, "If I go and prepare a place for you, I will come again;" and who, after nearly thirty years of arduous toil, left behind him, as befitted a servant of Him who was rich, but for our sakes became poor; a trunk which contained nearly all his earthly possessions,—a few sheets of Chinese printed matter, a Chinese and an English Bible, and an old writing-case, one or two small books, a Chinese lantern, a single Chinese dress, and the blue flag of his gospel boat,—the earthly wealth of one whose treasures were in the heavens?

Such are the moral heroes whose lives illustrate the power of this ancient faith as an incentive to missionary enterprise and exertion. A returned missionary who had labored many years in the foreign field writes: "In my own class, in the theological seminary, between forty and fifty were graduated. Seven of these held Pre-millennial views; they *all* offered themselves for the foreign work. The four who were accepted, went to the heathen; the three whom the doctor's verdict forbade to go, went as domestic missionaries to the far West. *No other person in the class offered to go.**

Passing from this topic, we come to consider an objection to the doctrine of the literal first resurrection. It is sometimes asserted that the doctrine of a special resurrection of the people of God, is only mentioned once in Scripture, and that in the Apocalypse, - an obscure and mysterious book. It is true that the Apocalypse has much that is obscure and mysterious, nevertheless it is a *Revelation*, and if so, it reveals something previously unknown. And if nothing which it contains is to be accepted unless it were previously revealed, then its value as a "revelation" is not apparent.

The acts of rulers and the changes of empires are no doubt veiled under symbols, that the foreknowledge of them might not affect the freedom of human agents during the period of their probation; but those prophecies which refer to the material universe, or which affect the destinies of men beyond the period of mortal probation, seem to furnish no occasion for such mysterious symbolism; and may consequently be accepted in their simplest and most obvious sense.

But the assumption that the doctrine of "the first resurrection" is only found in the twentieth chapter of Revelation, while the doctrine of the "general resurrection" is continually taught in the Scriptures, seems to indicate a singular forgetfulness of the actual facts in the case. Indeed the "general resurrection" is a phrase entirely unknown to the Scripture; and though the universality of the resurrection is clearly taught, yet it will not be easy to find proof that all the dead are to rise simultaneously. In fact the *universality* of the resurrection may be regarded as one of the later developments of divine revelation; while the idea of a *special resurrection* of the *people of God* runs through the entire Scripture.

The faith of Abraham, that God was able to raise his son even from the dead, "from whence also he received him in a figure" (Heb. xi. 19), was certainly a faith in a special resurrection. The resurrection hope of Job, who said, "I know that my Redeemer liveth," and "in my flesh shall I see God" (Job xix. 25, 26), was a personal and special hope, which

---

* The Presbyterian, January 25, 1879.

decided nothing definitely concerning the human race at large. The Psalmist's anticipation of being quickened again and brought up from the depths of the earth, and thus being satisfied when awaking in the divine likeness (Psalms lxxi. 20; xvii. 15), was an expression of his personal hope; and so far as it bears upon the subject, it intimates his faith in a special resurrection. The resurrection which Ezekiel foresaw and foretold, when God should open the graves of his people and cause them to come up out of their graves (Ezek. xxxvii. 12), was a special resurrection, in which only the people of God are brought to view. The resurrection which Hosea foretold, when God's people were to be ransomed from the power of the grave and redeemed from death (Hos. xiii. 14), was clearly a special resurrection. The "better resurrection" to which the martyred Hebrews looked forward when they were tortured, not accepting deliverance (Heb. xi. 35), could not have been a "general resurrection." The "resurrection of the just," at which those who care for the poor, the maimed, the lame, and the blind, shall be recompensed (Luke xiv. 14), is manifestly a special resurrection. "The resurrection from the dead" which they that "are accounted worthy" shall obtain, when they shall be equal with the angels, being the children of God and of the resurrection (Luke xx. 25, 26), was not a general resurrection of the dead, but a special "resurrection *from* the dead," leaving others behind. The argument of our Lord which silenced the cavils of the Sadducees, who denied the resurrection of any of the dead (Matt. xxxii. 31, 32), though amply sufficient for that purpose, had reference only to a special resurrection of those of whom, as of Abraham, Isaac and Jacob, the Lord proclaimed himself the God; and it had no bearing upon the question of a universal resurrection. The *outrising* (*exanastasin*) from the dead, for which Paul labored, "if by any means" he might attain unto it (Phil. iii. 11), was certainly no general resurrection. The resurrection of those "that are *Christ's* at his coming" (1 Cor. xv. 23), is certainly a special resurrection. The resurrection of the dead in Christ who "shall rise first" (1 Thess. iv. 16), can not be made to include the whole human family; and the prophecy of the first resurrection which is of the "blessed and holy" (Rev. xx. 6), clearly stands in the same line of truth which has pervaded the pages of divine revelation from the earliest ages down.

In addition to these passages where the resurrection of individuals, or of a *class*, and *that class* the *people of God*, is foretold, there are other passages where *two classes* are mentioned as destined to be raised; but these classes are always mentioned in a certain order; and in every instance the people of God are *named first* in that order. Thus, the prophet Isaiah declared: " *Thy* dead men shall live, together with *my* dead body shall they arise. Awake and *sing* ye that dwell in dust: for thy dew is as the dew of herbs, AND the earth shall cast out the dead"(*r'phah-eem*). Isaiah xxvi. 19. Here we have, first, the resurrection of the Lord's dead, who, together with the dead body of the prophet, are to awake and sing, arising from their dwelling in the dust. But after this it is declared that the earth shall cast out THE DEAD, *r'phah-eem;* — an entirely different Hebrew word being used to describe the latter class, which the earth is to cast out; a word which, though rendered in English "the dead," is never applied to a righteous man, whether dead or alive, but was a Hebrew term which designated the ancient giants, the enemies of God and his people. *

Again in the prophecy of Daniel we are told, that "many of them that sleep in the dust of the earth shall awake, some to everlasting life, and some to shame and everlasting contempt." Daniel xii. 2. Here, as in other passages, the class awaking to life are mentioned *first*, the others afterwards. So also our Saviour informs us, that "the hour is coming in the which all that are in the graves shall hear his voice, and shall come forth; they that have *done good* unto the resurrection of life, and they that have *done evil* unto the resurrection of damnation." John v. 28, 29. Here those who come to the resur-

---

* The Hebrew word *r'phah-eem* occurs eight times in the Hebrew Scriptures. It is rendered *deceased* in Isa. xxvi. 14; *dead* in Job xxvi. 5; Ps. lxxxviii. 10; Prov. ii. 18; ix. 18; xxi. 16; Isa. xiv. 9, and Isa. xxvi. 19, where Bp. Lowth renders it: "The earth shall cast forth, as an abortion, the *dead tyrants.*" The term is defined by Gesenius: "The quiet, the silent, *i. e.*, the *shades, manes* dwelling in Hades. . . . As a proper name, the founder of a race of tall men. See Gen. xiv. 5; xv. 20; Deut. ii. 11, 20; iii. 11, 13; Joshua xii. 4, etc. In later writings, after their extermination, they were accounted as *dead*, as tenants of the dark abodes of Sheol; and the man who wandered out of the way of understanding, went down to join this congregation of the *r'phah-eem.*"

rection of life are mentioned first. The same order of expression occurs in the Acts of the Apostles, where Paul declares: "After the way which they call heresy, so worship I the God of my fathers, believing all things which are written in the law and in the prophets; and have hope toward God, which they themselves also look for, that there shall be a resurrection of the dead, both of the just and unjust." Acts xxiv. 14, 15.

In all these instances where the resurrection of both classes is named, we have *first* the resurrection to life and glory, and afterwards the resurrection to shame and contempt; so that the entire course and current of Scripture statement seems to imply a *special* and *prior* resurrection of the people of God, followed by a resurrection of "the unjust," — of "all that are in the graves," "the dead, small and great."

In strict harmony with these representations of the prophets and apostles, we find in the book of Revelation the doctrine of a twofold resurrection clearly brought to view. First the resurrection of the "blessed and holy," and subsequently the resurrection of "the dead, small and great," who shall stand before God. Throughout the Scriptures there is no previous intimation of the precise time which may elapse between the first and the subsequent resurrection; but here this closing revelation informs us that "the rest of the dead lived not again until the thousand years were finished,"—or that, as in the prophecy of Isaiah, between "the acceptable year of the Lord, and the day of vengeance of our God," many centuries must be interposed; so here, between the "resurrection of the dead, both of the just and unjust," a period of a thousand years must elapse.

There are interpreters who regard the thousand years of Revelations xx. as past, and the binding of the dragon as a figurative representation of the subjugation of some civil power. But it may be questioned whether a personage so accurately described, under so many different *aliases*,—as the dragon, the old serpent which is the devil and Satan, who deceiveth the nations,—can be thus disposed of. And the difficulties in the way of thus locating the fulfillment of this prophecy, are neither few nor small.

To grasp the true sense of the prediction, we must omit the unauthorized division into chapters, and commence as far back as the sixteenth chapter, and read to the close of the book. We note first that it is said: "And I saw coming out of the mouth of the dragon, and out of the mouth of the beast, and out of the mouth of the false prophet, three unclean spirits, as it were frogs: for they are spirits of demons, working signs; which go forth unto the kings of the whole world, to gather them together unto the war of the great day of God, the Almighty. (Behold, I come as a thief. Blessed is he that watcheth, and keepeth his garments, lest he walk naked, and they see his shame.)" In the seventeenth and eighteenth chapters we read of the judgment upon great Babylon, and in the nineteenth chapter, of the triumphal song in heaven over her downfall, and over the marriage of the Lamb. Next, the prophet sees heaven opened, and beholds him who is called Faithful and True, coming forth, in righteousness to judge and make war. The armies of heaven follow him, as he smites the nations, and treads the wine-press of the fierceness of the wrath of Almighty God. Against him are now arrayed those hosts which have been marshaled by the three unclean spirits sent forth by the dragon, the beast and the false prophet. Their fate is thus described: "I saw the beast, and the kings of the earth, and their armies, gathered together to make war upon him that sat upon the horse, and against his army. And the *beast* was taken, and with him the *false prophet* that wrought the signs in his sight, wherewith he deceived them that had received the mark of the beast, and them that worshiped his image: they twain were cast alive into the lake of fire that burneth with brimstone: and the rest were killed with the sword of him that sat upon the horse, even the sword which came forth out of his mouth: and all the birds were filled with their flesh. And I saw an angel coming down out of heaven, having the key of the abyss and a great chain in his hand. And he laid hold on the *dragon*, the old serpent, which is the devil and Satan, and bound him for a thousand years, and cast him into the abyss, and shut it, and sealed it over him, that he should deceive the nations no more, until the thousand years should be finished: after this he must be loosed for a little time."

The three grand agents who instigate and prosecute this war against the King of kings and Lord of lords, are described as the dragon, the wild beast and the false prophet. In the struggle here described, the dragon is not visible; but the wild beast appears with the kings of the earth and their armies. These are overthrown, and the wild beast, and the false prophet who wrought signs before him, are taken, and cast alive into the lake of sulphurous fire. The nineteenth chapter of the Apocalypse thus records the overthrow of *two* of the instigators of this rebellion. The twentieth chapter, without the slightest break in the narrative, disposes of the *third* member of this unholy alliance, the dragon, who is arrested by an angel from heaven, and cast into the abyss and shut up, that he may deceive the nations no more "until the thousand years are finished," after which he is to emerge from his prison for a little season, practice his last deception, and meet his final doom in the lake of fire and brimstone.

We do not here undertake to explain this prophecy in its minutiæ, or to apply all these names or terms. The prophecies were not intended to make prophets of us, and their fulfillment often puts their interpreters to shame. And while the Lord never fails to accomplish his own word, he does not undertake to fulfill the expositions and comments of those who rashly misinterpret and apply it. We may perhaps be able to trace, even at the present time, indications of the workings of unclean spirits, like frogs, deceiving and deluding the nations; and if we watch and pray we shall in due time learn all that we need to know concerning these mysterious things. The church of God is not in darkness, that the day of God should overtake it as a thief. They are the children of the light and of the day. But light not only enables us to see whatever *is* to be seen, but also prevents our seeing things which do *not* exist. Gloom and obscurity are often peopled with distorted and hideous forms; a clearer light assists us to look more carefully, to see less, to restrain the exuberance of imagination, to perceive that which God reveals, and to wait for further information concerning things which he has not disclosed.

But, whatever obscurity may linger about the details of this prophecy, there seems no good ground for dividing asunder things which God has here joined together, and thus applying a part of one connected prophecy to some indefinite period in the past, while the rest is unquestionably in the future. When the King of kings shall come, these events here predicted will transpire. The Wild Beast and the False

Prophet will be overthrown and consigned to the flames, and the Dragon also will be bound and hurled into the abyss. At that time, the dead in Christ shall arise, and they shall live and reign with him a thousand years.

We are not from this to infer that their reign is then to terminate. They *live* and *reign* a thousand years. The passage no more asserts that they cease to *reign* at the end of the thousand years, than that they cease to *live*. They *live* and *reign* a thousand years. But they live forever; the life given is an everlasting life; and as for their reign, "they shall reign forever and ever." The end of the thousand years is *not* marked by the termination of the *reign* of Christ or of his saints, but it *is* marked by the loosing of Satan from his prison, the consequent overthrow of the last rebellion that he shall ever instigate, and the introduction of those happy ages of immortal joy and perfection, when sin and pain and death shall be no more, and God shall be all and in all.

There are numerous questions which may be raised in connection with these grand events, but into these matters of detail we do not enter. It is not our purpose to dogmatize or speculate concerning questionable things, but simply to call the attention of the devout student to the consideration of those facts which seem to be unquestionable, and which have commanded the general assent of the great majority of careful students of the holy scriptures. Hence we confine ourselves to the leading outlines of those coming events which are foreshadowed in the word of God, and confessed in the testimony of his Church. And though we now see as in a glass darkly, and may not be able to understand the precise order of those wonderful scenes that are before us, yet the general outlines are broadly drawn, and are matters of distinct promise and prediction in the scriptures of truth.

And while we may not know the times and the seasons which the Father hath put in his own power, we may yet be well assured that "the coming of the Lord draweth nigh." More than eighteen hundred years ago, John, the forerunner of our divine Master, said, "The kingdom of heaven is at *hand!*" Christ, the great teacher, made the same announcement, saying, "Repent: for the kingdom of heaven is at *hand!*" Twelve apostles were sent forth by him to proclaim the same fact; and though the Jews rejected that kingdom, which was taken from them to be given "to a nation bringing forth the fruits thereof;" and though the disciples were in darkness when they inquired, "Lord, wilt thou at *this time* restore again the kingdom to Israel?" as they were also in error when they thought "the kingdom of God should immediately appear" instead of at some future time, when the absent and rejected nobleman should return from " a far country;" yet throughout the teaching of the apostles there ran the thought of the nearness and possible imminence of this great event. "Let your moderation be known unto all men; the Lord is at *hand*." Phil. iv. 5. "The night is far spent, the day is *at hand:* let us therefore cast off the works of darkness, and let us put on the armor of light." Rom. xiii. 12. "The end of all things is *at hand:* be ye therefore sober, and watch unto prayer." 1 Pet. iv. 7. "Seal not the sayings of the prophecy of this book: for the time is *at hand.*" Rev. xxii. 10.

This expression, "at hand," is not without significance. By tracing the prophetic Image, described in the second chapter of Daniel, we find there five great universal kingdoms delineated, four of which are earthly and temporary, and the fifth heavenly, divine and eternal. The first of these great kingdoms was Babylon; and when this was in its glory, Medo-Persia was "at hand," as this was the next in succession. When Medo-Persia had conquered and supplanted Babylon, the next kingdom "at hand" was the kingdom of Græcia. When Græcia had conquered Persia, and bore sway, the next kingdom "at hand" was Rome; and when Rome stretched the scepter of universal dominion over the earth, then came the message, "The kingdom of heaven is *at hand.*" This kingdom follows next after Rome, which, though divided, declining and tottering to its fall, still, as embodied in European civilization, maintains its hold on the world; and will, until it is overthrown, destroyed and succeeded by the everlasting kingdom of God. That kingdom, then, is "*at hand.*" And when the disciples heard our Saviour predict the desolation of Jerusalem and its temple, they said, "When shall these things be, and what shall be the sign of thy coming and the consummation of the age?" The Saviour, after answering this important question by giving a connected chain of events running through this dispensation, said, "When ye see these things coming to pass, know ye that the kingdom of God is *nigh.*" The kingdom was "at hand" when our Saviour was upon earth; it seems now to be emphatically "*nigh.*"

Again, we read in the New Testament such expressions as these: "God who at sundry times and in divers manners spake in time past unto the fathers by the prophets, hath in *these last days* spoken unto us by his Son." Heb. i. 1, 2. "Who verily was foreordained before the foundation of the world, but was manifest in *these last times* for you." 1 Peter i. 20. "It shall come to pass in the *last days,* saith God, I will pour out of my Spirit upon all flesh." Acts ii. 17. "Little children it is the *last time*: and as ye have heard that Antichrist shall come, even now are there many Antichrists; whereby we know that it is the *last time.*" 1 John ii. 18.

Now if the days when our Lord Jesus Christ appeared were denominated "the *last days,*" then the world at that time had certainly run more than one half its destined course. The first days are not the last days. If we are to-day in the world's infancy, then these Scriptures would seem to be misleading, for they evidently imply that, even at our Saviour's first coming, the world had run more than half its appointed course.

On a journey of six thousand miles, we cannot reach the last miles until we have passed the three thousandth mile stone. From that point, we shall be on the last miles of our journey, but still we may look forward again and speak of the last miles, as yet in the distance before us. And so, while the apostles already declared that they were then "in the last days," they yet looked forward to still later times which they also described by similar expressions. "In the *latter times* some shall depart from the faith, giving heed to seducing spirits and doctrines of demons." 1 Tim. iv. 1. "In the *last days* perilous times shall come; for men shall be lovers of their own selves, covetous, boasters, proud, blasphemers, disobedient to parents, unthankful, unholy." 2 Tim. iii. 1, 2. "There shall come *in the last days* scoffers, walking after their own lusts, and saying, Where is the promise of his coming? for since the fathers fell asleep, all things continue as they were from the beginning." 2 Pet. iii. 3, 4. And the apostle James says in his warning to the rich, "Ye have heaped treasure together for the *last days.*" James v. 3.

It is obvious that if we extend the period of this world's history on through many ages, then our Saviour was *not* manifested in "these *last* times;" nor was the outpouring of the spirit on the day of Pentecost "in the *last* days." But if these statements are to have weight, and the dispensation in which we live, is fitly called "the last days," then we are apparently, near its close. And we may well adopt the language of the apostle, "Knowing the time, that now it is high time to awake out of sleep: for now is our salvation nearer than when we believed. The night is far spent, the day is at hand: let us therefore cast off the works of darkness, and let us put on the armor of light." Rom. xiii. 11, 12.

The times in which we live are ominous. We stand amid the rush and thunder of earth's most restless age. The gospel of Christ is speeding on its way to every land and tribe; many run to and fro, and knowledge is increased; art, science, invention and discovery wing their way over the globe; but meanwhile, iniquity abounds, the love of many waxes cold, dark shapes of evil stand in the pathway before us, infidelity, atheism, anarchy, confusion and turmoil swarm around us, and the church, divided into petty sects and weakened by intestine strifes, is confronted by the legions of darkness, who march in solid column to the final fray. Against such hosts, the doctrines of men and the inventions of worldly wisdom are vain. Nothing will avail in such a battle, but the word of truth, the power of God, and the armor of righteousness on the right hand and on the left. The coming conflict may be fierce and terrible, but it will be brief and decisive. It will end, not by human might or human power, but by the power of Him who "giveth us the victory, through our Lord Jesus Christ." He shall break in upon the world's disorder and misrule, and shall crush the usurpers, and "destroy them that destroy the earth." He in his time shall show, who is the blessed and only Potentate, the King of kings and Lord of lords; and they who have borne his cross and endured his reproach, shall hear with gladness the trump that heralds his approach, and shall answer back, "Lo, this is our God; we have waited for him, and he will save us; this is the Lord; we have waited for him, we will be glad and rejoice in his salvation." Isa. xxv. 9.

Toward these scenes we hasten; for we are of that number

"upon whom the ends of the world are come." "The coming of the Lord draweth nigh." Eternal rest is before us, and the toil is very brief. But alas for a world that lieth in the wicked one! woe to a race that will not repent! The deluge and the Dead Sea tell us what God has done; the Scriptures tell us what he will do. The sword of wrath shall not always sleep in its scabbard. Ere we are aware it shall be unsheathed and stretched forth to smite a rebellious race. Watchman, upon the walls of Zion, set the trumpet to thy lips. Sound in the ears of a slumbering world the dread alarm. "But if the watchman see the sword come, and blow not the trumpet, and the people be not warned; if the sword come, and take away any person from among them, he is taken away in his iniquity; but HIS BLOOD WILL I REQUIRE AT THE WATCHMAN'S HAND."

H. L. H.

SCRIPTURAL TRACT REPOSITORY,
November, 1881.

INTRODUCTORY SYNOPSIS.

ANTIQUITY OF THE DOCTRINE OF THE PERSONAL ADVENT AND REIGN OF CHRIST ON EARTH.

" *Behold a king shall reign in righteousness and princes shall rule in judgment.*"—ISAIAH.

Says *Rev. H. H. Milman*, " The future dominion of some great king to descend from the line of David, to triumph over all his enemies, and to establish a universal kingdom of peace and happiness, was probably an authorized opinion long before the advent." And on the part of the heathen world, *Plato* exclaims, " It is necessary that a lawgiver be sent from heaven to instruct us. O how greatly do I desire to see that man, and who he is. He must be more than man."

Rev. Edward Bickersteth has well remarked, " There have been from age to age those who have held the personal coming of Christ before the millennium, but where is the voice of the Church as to a spiritual millennium, uncommenced, and to last 1000 years before His real coming ? The idea of a spiritual millennium, which is not yet begun, before our Lord's return, is sometimes called the old way, the old paths; but is it not an entire novelty of modern times ? Has it any plea of general antiquity whatever to urge in its behalf? I believe not. Bishop Hall in his list of varied opinions on this subject gives no intimation of it. I have not been able to trace it higher than *Dr. Whitby*, who speaks of it as a ' new hypothesis' at the beginning of the eighteenth century."

INTRODUCTORY SYNOPSIS.

"In later ages," says *Dr. Burnet*, "they seemed to have dropped one-half, namely, the renovation of nature, which Irenæus, Justin Martyr, and the ancients, join inseparably with the millennium: and by this omission, the doctrine hath been made less intelligible, and one part of it inconsistent with another." "We are well aware," says *Professor Bush*, "of the imposing array of venerable names by which it is surrounded, as if it were the bed of Solomon guarded by three score valiant men of Israel, all holding swords, and expert in war."

In the language of *Rev. J. W. Brooks*, "It is still further encouraging to find the number daily increasing of able and pious ministers who are becoming sensible of the duty of investigating this important branch of Scripture, and are beginning to be persuaded of the premillennial advent of our Lord."

The *Rev. W. Burgh* in one of his sermons relates the following conversation between a Christian minister and a Jew. "Taking a New Testament and opening it at Luke i: 32, the Jew asked, 'Do you believe that what is here written shall be literally accomplished—the Lord God shall give unto him the throne of his father David; and he shall reign over the house of Jacob forever?' 'I do not,' answered the clergyman, 'but rather take it to be figurative language, descriptive of Christ's spiritual reign over the church.' 'Then,' replied the Jew, 'neither do I believe literally the words preceding, which say that this Son of David should be born of a virgin; but take them to be merely a figurative manner of describing the remarkable character for purity of him who is the subject of the prophecy.' 'But why,' continued the Jew, 'do you refuse to believe literally verses 32 and 33, while you believe implicitly the far more incredible statement of verse 31?' 'I believe it,' replied the clergyman, 'because it is a fact.' 'Ah!' exclaimed the Jew, with an inexpressible air of scorn and triumph, '*you* believe

Scripture because it is a *fact;* *I* believe it because it is the Word of God.'"

THE NEW HEAVENS AND THE NEW EARTH.

Calvin in his notes on Isa. xi : 6–8, remarks, " He asserts here the change of the nature of wild beasts, and the restitution of the creation as at first." On Isa. xxiv : 23, " Christ shall hereafter establish his Church on earth in a most glorious estate. At length God shall enjoy his own right among us, and have his due honor, when all his creatures being gathered into order, he alone is resplendent in our eyes."

Says *Matthew Henry,* " Christ's second coming will be a *regeneration* (Matt. 19 : 28,) when there shall be new heavens and a new earth, and a restitution of all things."

In his Commentary on 2 Peter 3, *Dr. A. Clarke* writes as follows: " All these things will be dissolved, separated, be decomposed; but none of them will be destroyed. And as they are the original matter out of which God formed the terra queous globe; consequently they may enter again into the composition of a new system; and therefore the apostle says, ' We look for a new heaven and a new earth ;' the others being decomposed, a new system is to be formed out of their materials."

" I do not believe," says *William Anderson,* " that the earth shall be annihilated, but that rectified, and beautified, it shall last forever as the happy abode of the saints."

THE KINGDOM OF GOD.

Says *Dr. J. Pye Smith,* " The prophecies respecting the kingdom of Messiah, its extent and duration, and the happiness of his innumerable subjects are in a much greater proportion than those which describe his humiliation to sufferings and his dreadful death."

In the language of *Dr. Stephen Tyng,* " The covenant made by God to Abraham remains to this day utterly unful filled. The fifth universal monarchy remains to be established upon the earth. The king that is to rule is the Son of Man, who will make a personal manifestation of himself."

In view of these facts, well may we exclaim, in the words of *Dr. William Channing*, " O come, thou kingdom of heaven for which we daily pray. Come, ye predicted ages of righteousness and love for which the faithful have so long yearned !"

THE JUDGMENT DAY.

Milton's faith.—" He believes," says *Dr. Channing*, " that Christ is to appear visibly for the judgment of the world, and that he will reign a thousand years on earth, at the end of which period Satan will assail the Church with an innumerable confederacy, and be overwhelmed with everlasting ruin. He speaks of the judgment as beginning with Christ's second advent, and as comprehending his whole government through the millennium as well as the closing scene, when sentence will be pronounced on evil angels and on the whole human race." That Christ will come to earth again is certain, and in the language of *Charles Beecher*, " Earth needs but one such man to dwell therein to produce a day of judgment."

In view of that solemn day, how appropriate the language of *Jerome*, " Whether I eat or drink, or in whatever other action or employment I am engaged, that solemn voice always seems to sound in my ears, ' Arise ye dead and come to judgment !' As often as I think of the day of judgment, my heart quakes, and my whole frame trembles. If I am to indulge in any of the pleasures of this present life, I am resolved to do it in such a way that the solemn realities of the future judgment may never be banished from my recollection."

THE AGE'S CRISIS.

Says *Sir Robert Peel*, " Every aspect of the present times

viewed in the light of the past warrants the belief that we are on the eve of a universal change."

In the language of *Mrs. H. B. Stowe*, "This is an age of the world when nations are trembling and convulsed. A mighty influence is abroad, surging and heaving the world as with an earthquake."

Says *Dr. Wm. Channing*, "History and philosophy plainly show to me in human nature the foundation and promise of a better era, and Christianity concurs with these."— And as *Dr. Tyng* remarks, "While all human appearances indicate the approach of changes more important than any man has ever seen before, God's Word lays before us just what that change is to be."

PRESENT EVIL TIMES.

Says *Dr. Arnold*, "My sense of the evils of the times that are coming, and of the prospects to which I am bringing up my poor children is overwhelming; times are coming in which the devil will fight his best and that in good earnest."

Says the learned *Dr. Cotton Mather*, "They who expect the rest promised for the Church of God, to be found anywhere but in the new earth, and they who expect any happy times for the church in a world that hath death and sin in it, —these do err, not knowing the Scriptures nor the kingdom of God."

Says the gifted *Charlotte Elizabeth :*—"We shall soon need to exercise judgment in the discerning of spirits. The sixth vial, under which there can be no doubt that we now live, is marked by the going forth of the three unclean devils, of whose miracle-working powers we are forewarned, and He who has deigned to show us things to come, has not set forth cunningly devised fables to amuse our fancy, but revealed solemn truths to guide our steps aright, when our path becomes perplexed beyond all that we have known hitherto, or that the experience of the church has recorded."

And the great *Luther* declares:—" The older the world the worse. A something strikingly awful shall forewarn that the world will come to an end, and that the ast day is even at the door."

In the language of President *Nathan Lord*, " Evangelical Protestantism has gained nothing for a hundred years. It has been merely struggling for its life."

IT HASTETH GREATLY.

Says *Dr. Thomas Goodwin*:—" It hasteth greatly. And although we may think this dismal and black hour of temptation not likely to come so soon (seeing the clouds rise not fast enough so suddenly to overcast the face of the sky with darkness); yet we are to consider that we live now in the extremity of times, when motions and alterations being so near the centre, become quickest and speediest; and we are at the verge, and, as it were, within the whirl of that great mystery of Christ's kingdom, which will, as a gulf, swallow up all time; and so, the nearer we are unto it, the greater and more sudden changes will Christ make, now hasting to make a full end of all."

Says " *The Edinburg Presbyterian Review:*"—" Never was there a time when events developed themselves with such rapidity. As the world moves on, it seems to accelerate its speed, and precipitate itself with headlong haste. Events seem to ripen before their time. The crisis comes ere we were aware of the commencement. Speed,—whirlwind speed—is the order of the day."

" It seems to me," remarks *William Cuninghame*, " we have entered into that last period of awful expectation during which the church is likened unto virgins."

Says the sainted *Rutherford:*—" Tell her (the church) that the day is near the dawning, the sky is cleaving: our Beloved will be on us ere ever we are aware."

SIGNS OF THE TIMES.

Says *Dr. Hales:*—" Our blessed Lord graciously proposed these signs, destined to precede his second appearance at the regeneration for the comfort and support of his faithful disciples in these latter times." How significant the inquiry of *Bishop Chase:* " Are not these signs of our prognostics of the speedy coming of our Lord to judgment? When the Son of Man cometh shall he find faith upon the earth? He will not find much faith upon the earth. How awful to reflect that this sign seems so exactly the fact."

Says *William Cuninghame:*—" If we, who have marked every sign in the spiritual horizon for a long series of years, **were now** asked, 'Is there any sign of His coming yet unaccomplished?' we should be constrained to answer: 'To our view not one sign remains unaccomplished.' If we were further asked, 'Shall He come this year?' our answer would be, 'We know not; but this much we know and believe, that Christ is near at hand, even at the door.' * * * Amidst this commixture of dread and alarm, and these groanings of distressed nations, and fond whisperings of 'peace, peace,' suddenly as the blaze of forked lightning, unexpectedly as the fall of the trap upon the ensnared animal, and as the dark and concealed approach of the midnight thief, a voice like that of ten thousand thunders shall burst on the ears of the astonished inhabitants of the earth. IT IS THE VOICE OF THE ARCH-ANGEL. IT IS THE TRUMP OF GOD. HE COMETH—HE COMETH TO JUDGE THE EARTH! His **dead** saints spring from the dust,—his living saints in a moment, in the twinkling of an eye are changed, and both together are rapt up far above the clouds to meet Him."

THE AUTHOR'S EXCUSE FOR WRITING THIS VOLUME

Is well expressed in the words of the venerated *Joshua Spaulding,* " I have written these things with great trembling, not so much because I know they must be unpopular, and must be considered by this earthly minded generation, as the height of fanaticism, and the most consummate folly; and that to all careless unbelieving lazy worldlings, I must seem like Lot to his sons-in-law, as one that mocketh; but fearing most of all lest I should add unto, or take from the word of prophecy: yet I dared not be silent, and see the world slumbering until the day of God break. I have also experienced great discouragement in thinking to attempt something of this kind, from the consideration that if I am right I shall not be believed; on the contrary the songs of peace—peace—happy times yet in this world, will still prevail, and prevail until the end; but the farther considerations have engaged me to proceed, that possibly some few may be benefited, and also what I owed myself to some attempts of this kind by others, which were the means of opening my eyes, that had been held in errors, as I now think them, for a number of years of adult age."

"It is right," says *Silvo Pelico*, "to profess an important truth at all times; because, if we may not hope that it will be immediately acknowledged, still it may so prepare the minds of others, as one day to produce greater impartiality of judgment, and the consequent triumph of light."

And the ministry may well give heed to the solemn charge of *Dr. Hugh McNeile:* "My Reverend Brethren, watch, *preach the coming of Jesus*—I charge you, in the name of our common Master, *preach the coming of Jesus*—solemnly and affectionately in the name of God, I charge you, *preach the coming of Jesus*, "Watch ye, therefore, (for ye know not when the master of the house cometh, at even or at midnight, or at cock-crowing, or in the morning,) lest, coming suddenly, he find the porter sleeping." Take care—"what I say unto you, I say unto you all—watch."

LOVING CHRIST'S APPEARING.

Says **Tertullian,** "For since the times of our whole hope

are fixed in the sacred writings, and it cannot be placed before the coming of Christ, our desires pant after the end of this age, the passing away of the world at the great day of God."

How sweet the words of the eloquent *Edward Irving*, " Blessed consummation of this weary and sorrowful world! I give it welcome, I hail its approach, I wait its coming more than they that watch for the morning. Over the wrecks of a world I weep; over broken hearts of parents; over suffering infancy, over the unconscious clay of sweet innocents, over the untimely births that have never seen the light, or have just looked upon it and shut their eyes for a season until the glorious light of the resurrection morn. O, my Lord, come away. Hasten with all thy congregated ones. My soul desireth to see the King in his beauty, and the beautiful ones whom He shall bring along with him."

Says *Milton*, England's greatest sacred poet : " Come forth out of thy royal chambers, O Prince of all the kings of the earth. Put on the visible robes of thy imperial majesty. Take up that unlimited sceptre which thy Almighty Father hath bequeathed thee. For now the voice of thy bride calls thee, and all creatures sigh to be renewed."

> " Like as the flaming comet—doubles wide
> Heaven's mighty cape; and then revisits earth,
> From the long travel of a thousand years;
> Thus at the destined period shall return
> He, once on earth, who bids the comet blaze;
> And with Him all our triumph o'er the tomb."
> YOUNG'S NIGHT THOUGHTS.

Such are the views in general advanced in the volume now before the reader, and sustained by the concurrent testimony of a literal interpretation of the Holy Scriptures, and by the voice of the Church. In compiling a work of this character, it has been deemed proper to condense as much as possible, avoiding unnecessary repetition, and prolixity, so that if in many testimonies there is an appearance of too much brevity, or more at least than some might wish, the reader will at once perceive the reasonableness of the same on this ground. The method of presentation is somewhat peculiar, and is chosen for the sake of presenting a wider range of mind. The compiler has spoken himself as seldom as practicable, but has chosen rather to make use of the language of others, and instead of permitting one to relate the whole as is usually done, he has preferred that all should testify, and thus each and every mind be mirrored on the page in harmonious support of the same grand truths. He has endeavored in most cases to let the witnesses speak for themselves, and though but briefly in numerous instances, yet enough is given to exhibit the constant hope of the faithful in all ages.

And the names herein presented are no mean and insignificant ones. They are the names of the men who under God have controlled His church on earth, and led her in the hour of conflict and in the fight of faith. They are many of them not only enrolled high on the lists of human fame, but which is far better, are doubtless also "written in the Lamb's book of Life." And though but frail and feeble men, they are not to be despised. The doctrine of the personal reign of Christ in the new earth, is of the Bible, and in presenting the combined testimony of a "cloud of witnesses" in its favor, to bear upon the church in this century, it is not with the view of promulgating novelty. We are no innovators. Pre-millennialism has had its advocates among the orthodox in all ages. We seek the old paths, feeling assured they are the safest and most desirable. We have taken our position. To oppose POST-millennialism and its kindred errors we feel bound, and here we throw down the gauntlet. Being strongly impressed with the nearness of that day when the everlasting kingdom of God shall be established in the renewed earth, and the whole human race broken up and strangely and forever separated; under this solemn conviction strengthened by every passing event, we send forth the present volume of testimonies, fraught with many a gem of truth, and many a thrilling cry, to awaken, if possible, in all our readers, a deeper interest on the momentous subject of the speedy and visible coming of the Son of Man.

Time is short. The season of toil is well nigh spent. Let us be active. Every Christian in this day should be a missionary in earnest. We are not against missions. Rather do we wish there were an army of five hundred thousand missionaries like Brainard, and Wolffe, and Judson. Let this gospel of the kingdom be "preached in all the world for a witness unto all nations," and then let the end—the kingdom, come. There are thousands of Pre-millennialists in the Protestant churches of Great Britain and America, and Mr. Lord affirms that among missionaries of all denominations that go abroad, there is as great a proportion of them Pre-millenialists as among the ministry who stay at home.

And surely the extensive travels and writings of Ben Ezra, in South America; the unremitted toils of Joseph Wolffe and Rev. Dr. Poor in Asia, for a long series of years, who preached the speedy coming of Jesus; the happy results of the labors of James McGregor Bertram, the "man of peace," on St. Helena, in South Africa, and elsewhere, who not only preached the gospel of faith and repentance, but also urged upon all the consideration of Christ's soon coming; the preaching of L. D. Mansfield, in the West Indies; of many others in Newfoundland; the extraordinary efforts of Gonsalves, Dr. Kalley, and Hewitson, on the Madeira Islands, resulting in the conversion of hundreds; the Christian labors of H. W. Fox, missionary to the Teloogoo people, with many other instances we could name, now unnoticed and unknown, are sufficient proofs that Pre-millennialists are not opposed to missionary efforts, and lack none of the missionary spirit. They labor as did the great apostle to "save some" from wrath to come,—yea, almost come. "I have a strong anticipation," wrote the pious Fox, "that the time is not far distant." So Pre-millennialists labor. And their faith and hope is acknowledged to impart to their preaching greater earnestness and power. And why should it not? May God speed every effort to win souls from remediless woe, for oh! how solemn, how terrible to be found among the eternally lost.

Commending our volume, with all its imperfections, to the candid and careful perusal of every Christian, we send it forth with many a prayer and tear that it may be blessed to the everlasting good of all who read its pages. It is the congregated cry of a great multitude, saying, with a loud voice, The King cometh. The kingdom is at hand! Are we ready? Oh, that reader and writer may so live and act that the stern disclosures of the day of Eternity shall not give the lie to all the fond anticipations of Time. Blessed is he that watcheth!

DANIEL T. TAYLOR

Rouse's Point, N. Y., 1855.

CHAPTER I.

DEFINITION OF TERMS—THE GREAT QUESTION WHEN IS THE MILLENNIUM TO OCCUR?—PRINCIPLES OF INTERPRETATION.

MILLENNIUM (*Latin*) *Mille*, a thousand, and *annus*, year. A thousand years; a word used to denote the thousand years mentioned in Rev. 20; during which period Satan will be bound, and holiness become triumphant throughout the world. During this period, as some believe, Christ will reign on earth in person with his saints.[*] "MILLENNIUM. Thousand years; generally taken for the thousand years in which some Christian sects expected, and some still expect the Messiah to found a kingdom on earth full of splendor and happiness."[†]

"MILLENNIUM, thousand years: generally employed to denote the thousand years during which, according to an ancient tradition in the church, our blessed Saviour will reign upon earth, after the first resurrection, before the final completion of beatitude. The time when the millennium will commence cannot be fully ascertained, but the common idea is that it will be in the seven-thousandth year of the world."[‡] "The seventh chiliad (or 1000 years) from the creation. All sober commentators take this literally."[§]

"MILLENNIARIANS or CHILIASTS. A name given to those who believe that the saints will reign on earth with Christ a thousand years."[‖]

---

[*] Webster's Dictionary.   [†] Encyclopedia Americana.
[‡] Encyclopedia of Religious Knowledge.   [§] Cottage Bible.
[‖] Buck's Theological Dictionary.

DEFINITION OF TERMS.

It is generally conceded by the Christian world at the present time, that the Apocalyptic millennium is yet to occur in the future, and to commence immediately upon the expiration of six thousand years from the creation of the world, it seeming to be more decidedly proper and Scriptural thus to chronologically locate it: but as there have been and still are some who deny this, and as those who maintain its futurity are divided both in regard to the manner of the events and the events themselves, which are to introduce and occupy the millennial era, manifestly composing at least *three classes* of millennial believers; to avoid a multiplicity of terms and introduce simplicity, it has been thought proper in the following pages to classify under *three heads*, all who have at any time written concerning the millennium of the Apocalypse; denominating them severally as follows:

ANTI-MILLENNARIANS, or *Anti-M.*, all those who deny that the Apocalyptic millennium is in the future, or those who locate it in the *past*, though not denying the future personal reign of Christ on earth.

POST-MILLENNIALISTS, or *Post-M.*, all those who hold that the Apocalyptic millennium is in the future, and who postpone the personal advent of the Redeemer, and literal resurrection of the holy dead till its close, thus *denying* the *personal* millennial *reign*.

PRE-MILLENNIALISTS, or *Pre-M.*, all those who hold that the Apocalyptic millennium is future,—the seventh thousand years,—and that it is to commence with, and be introduced by, the *personal advent* of Christ, and literal resurrection of the just: thus *affirming* the *personal* reign of Christ on earth.

These terms are frequently varied throughout these pages and others in common use are substituted, as *Temporal Millennialists, Post-millennialists, Whitbyans*, etc., to denote the *second class;* and *Literalists, Pre-millennialists, Chiliasts*, etc., to signify the *third class*, whose view or doctrine, of the *personal reign of Christ on earth*, is advocated in the present volume.

Says *Professor Bush:* "The etymological import of the word millennium is, as is well known, the space of a thousand years. The term considered by itself does not point to any particular period of that extent, but may be applied indifferently to any one of the five millenniums which have elapsed since the creation, to the sixth, now verging to its close, or to the seventh, which is yet to come. But long established usage has given the word a restricted application, and where it occurs without specification, it is universally understood to refer to the period mentioned by the prophet of Patmos, Rev. 20: 1–.7"*

THE GREAT QUESTION.

Says *Bishop Henshaw:* "In our day much is said of the millennium. It is a common theme in the pulpit and on the platform. It animates the conceptions of the poet, and the glowing periods of the orator. It is held forth as the great incentive to missionary effort; the glorious reward of self-denial, liberality and prayer in the good work of propagating the Gospel."†

"And here," remarks *Dr. Elliott,* "the famous question opens: In what way are we to understand this vision and prophecy of the millennium? What the first resurrection spoken of, literal or figurative? Who the persons who partake of it? What the nature of the devil's synchronous binding and incarceration? What the state of things on earth corresponding? What the chronological position and duration of the millennium? What the sequel of events on the devil's being loosed again at its termination? Finally what the relation of the millennary period and its blessedness to the New Jerusalem afterwards exhibited in the

* Bush on the Millennium, p. 1.
† "The Second Advent."

Apocalypse, and what also to the paradisiacal state predicted in the Old Testament prophecies?"*

Says *Dr. Duffield:* "Whether that long predicted and expected coming of Jesus Christ and of the kingdom of heaven are matters of literal verity according to the grammatical import of the expressions, or anagogically to be understood, and therefore to be interpreted altogether figuratively or spiritually, is a question of deep and wonderful bearing: nor is it to be slighted and sneered at by any one professing to love and reverence the sacred oracles of God. It is vital to all our hopes, and forms the very warp and woof of all the Scriptural revelations on the subject. It must be met; and will be candidly examined by every man who loves the truth, and is unwilling to be swayed by the dogmas of others. The decision, we contend, must be had from the word of God itself."†

Charles Beecher thus earnestly inquires: "Is the second coming of the Son of Man now nigh at hand? Is it in other words the commencement and the cause, or the climax and the product of the millennium? This is the simple question now in the providence of God first claiming the solemn attention of the churches. That he shall return in majesty to judge the earth, we all believe. The simple question where we differ is,

WHEN?

To the answer of this question, I believe, the church is solemnly called."

PRINCIPLES OF INTERPRETATION.

Says *Bishop Jeremy Taylor:* "In all the interpretations of Scripture, the *literal sense* is to be presumed and chosen unless there be evident cause to the contrary.

* Horæ Apocalypticæ, Vol. iv. p. 177.
† Duffield on the Prophecies, p. 7.

PRINCIPLES OF INTERPRETATION.

Says *Prof. J. A. Ernesti:* "There is in fact but one and the same method of interpretation common to all books whatever be their subject. And the same grammatical principles and precepts, ought to be the common guide in the interpretation of all. * * Theologians are right, therefore, when they affirm the *literal sense*, or that which is derived from the knowledge of words, to be the *only true one;* for that mystical sense, which indeed is incorrectly called a sense, belongs altogether to the thing and not to the words."*

Says the learned *Vitringa:* "We must never depart from the *literal meaning* of the subject mentioned in its own appropriate name, if all or its principal attributes square with the subject of the prophecy—an unerring canon, he adds, and of great use."†

Says *Martin Luther:* "That which I have so often insisted on elsewhere, I here once more repeat, viz.: that the Christian should direct his first efforts toward understanding the *literal sense* (as it is called) of Scripture, which alone is the substance of faith and of Christian theology. * * The allegorical sense is commonly uncertain and by no means safe to build our faith upon: for it usually depends on human opinion and conjecture only, on which if a man lean, he will find it no better than the Egyptian reed. Therefore Origen, Jerome, and similar of the fathers are to be avoided with the whole of that Alexandrian school which, according to Eusebius and Jerome, formerly abounded in this species of interpretation. For later writers unhappily following their too much praised and prevailing example, it has come to pass that men make just what they please of the Scriptures, until some accommodate the word of God to the most extravagant absurdities; and, as Jerome complains of his own times, they extract a sense from Scripture repugnant

---

* Biblical Repertory, Vol. iii., pp. 125, 131.
† Doctrine of Prophetic Types. 1716.

to its meaning : of which offence, however, Jerome himself was also guilty."*

Says *Rosenmuller :* " All ingenuous and unprejudiced persons will grant me this position, that there is no method of removing difficulties more secure than that of an accurate interpretation derived from the words of the texts themselves, and from their true and legitimate meaning, and depending upon no hypothesis !"†

Says *Hooker :* " I hold it for a most infallible rule in expositions of sacred Scripture, that when a literal construction will stand, the farthest from the letter is commonly the worst. There is nothing more dangerous and delusive than that art, which changes the meaning of words, as alchemy doth or would the substance of metals; making of anything what it listeth, and bringing in the end all truth to nothing."

Dr. John Pye Smith defines the literal sense as " The common rule of all rational interpretation, viz. : the *sense* afforded by a cautious and critical examination of the terms of the passage, and an impartial construction of the whole sentence, according to the known usage of the language and the writer."‡

Such is the system adopted in this volume, it being regarded as the only safe principle of interpreting the Bible.

* Annotations on Deut. Cap. i., Fol. 55.
† Cox's Immanuel Enthroned, p. 70.
‡ Scripture Testimony to the Messiah. Vol. 1, p. 214.

CHAPTER II.

UNIVERSAL TRADITIONARY TESTIMONY.

JEWISH FAITH IN THE FIRST RESURRECTION.

"*Then multitudes that sleep in the dust of the ground shall awake, some to everlasting life and others to reproaches and to confusion everlasting.*"—DAN. 12:2. *Thomas Wintle's Translation.*

The doctrine of a two-fold resurrection did not originate with the Apocalypse. The period between the two resurrections was not defined, but the distinction between them was apparent from early days.

The ancient resurrection hope was, in some sense, personal. "In my flesh shall *I* see God." "Thou shalt call and *I* will answer thee." Job 19:26; 14:15. "*I* shall be satisfied when I awake in thy likeness." Ps. 17:15. "Thou shalt quicken *me* again, and shalt bring me up again from the depths of the earth." Ps. 71:20. Such anticipations as these would naturally be shared by all the faithful; as "the hope of the promise made of God unto the fathers" depended for its fulfillment upon the resurrection of the dead. Acts 26:6-8.

A universal resurrection was implied in the fact of future retribution, but the resurrection, as looked upon as an object of hope, was the resurrection of the people of the Lord. *They* were to be ransomed from the power of the grave (Hosea 13:14); they were to be brought up out of their graves into the land of Israel (Ezekiel 37: 13, 14); they were to "awake and sing" (Isa. 26:19).

Hence the passages which express this ancient hope usually have reference to the resurrection of the just; and so well known was this, that some of the Pharisees held that the resurrection was the exclusive privilege of the children of Israel.

But much as the scriptures say concerning the resurrection of the just, they are not silent concerning the resurrection of others. Not only is this fact implied, in the predictions of future retribution, but it is definitely stated in various scriptures. Thus, for example, after the saints who "dwell in the dust" are summoned to awake and sing, the prophet still continues: "*And* the earth shall cast out the dead tyrants." * "The earth shall disclose her blood and shall no more cover her *slain*." Isa. 26:21. And the prophet Daniel, when predicting the resurrection of the multitudes that sleep in the dust of the ground, declares that they "shall awake, some to life everlasting, and others to reproaches and confusion everlasting." While other passages express only the hope of Israel in the resurrection of the blessed, in these passages two classes are specified; and though the prophet does not define the interval that shall elapse between the resurrection of the just and of the unjust, yet the righteous are ever mentioned *first*, for their's is "the first resurrection." †

Professor Stuart remarks, "That the great mass of Jewish Rabbins have believed and taught the doctrine of the resurrection of the just in the days of the Messiah's development, there can be no doubt on the part of him who has made any considerable investigation of this matter. The specific limitation of this to the commencement of the millennium, seems to be peculiar to John." ‡

With *Dr. Duffield* we would say, "These traditions we do not quote as authority, but as historical evidence of what the views and expectations of the church were during the

---

* Isaiah 26: 19, Bishop Lowth's translation.
† For additional remarks on this subject, see Preface, p. xlv.-xlviii.
‡ Commentary on Apocalypse, vol. i. p. 177.

period that elapsed from the captivity to the coming of Christ.

The millennium John predicts, is exactly coincident in its leading features, with the expectations of the pious Jews before the coming of Christ."*

We gather the following Rabbinic testimonies from the Commentaries of Dr. Clarke, Scott, Prof. Stuart, the works of Mede, Bishop Newton, and others, as they were by them extracted from the Jewish Targums and Talmuds, together with the book of Zohar, a production of the early ages of Christianity, Maimonides and other Jewish authors.

The Jerusalem Targum, or Paraphrase of the Law, written A. D. 300, on Gen. 49 : 10, says: "The King Christ shall come whose is the kingdom, and all nations shall be subject to him."

The Babylonian Targum, written A. D. 500, on the same passage reads : "Messiah shall come whose is the kingdom, and him shall the nations serve."

Rabbi Eliezar the Great, applies Hosea 14 : 8, to the pious Jews who would die without seeing the glory of the Lord, paraphrasing it thus: "As I live, saith Jehovah, I will raise you up in the time to come, in the resurrection of the dead, and I will gather you with all Israel." Capitula, c. 34.

Rabbi Gamaliel, the preceptor of St. Paul, was asked by the Sadducees whence he could prove that God would raise the dead, and he finally silenced them on the authority of Deut. 11 : 21. "Which land the Lord moreover sware he would give to your fathers." The Rabbi argued, as Abraham, Isaac, and Jacob had it not, and God cannot lie, therefore they must be raised from the dead to inherit it.† Christ's argument in Luke 21, is substantially the same.

* Duffield on the Prophecies, pp. 186, 190.
† Brooks on Prophecy, p. 33.

Rabbi Simai of later date argues the resurrection from Exodus 6: 4, insisting that the law in asserting, "And I have also established my covenant with them to give them the land of Canaan, &c.," teaches the resurrection from the dead; "for," he adds, "it is not said to *you* but to *them.*"

Jonathan, the Paraphrast, who lived about B. C. 30, on Hos. 14: 8, says, "They shall be gathered from their captivity; they shall live under the shadow of Messiah; the dead shall rise and good shall increase in the earth."*

Rabbi Kimchi of the thirteenth century on Obadiah, says, "When Rome shall be laid waste, there shall be redemption for Israel." On Isaiah 26: 19, he observes that "The holy blessed God will raise the dead at the time of deliverance." And on Jer. 23: 20, he argues, "In that he saith, *ye* shall consider it, and not *they*, he intimateth, the resurrection."

On the second Psalm, *Kimchi* thus quotes an ancient apothegm. "The benefit of the rain is common to the just and the unjust, but the resurrection from the dead is the peculiar privilege of those who have lived righteously."

Rabbi Chabbo says, "The dead in the land of Israel shall live or be quickened first in the days of the Messiah, and shall enjoy the years of the Messiah."

In the *Jerusalem Talmud* on Gen. 13: 15-17, *Rabbi Eliezer* and *Rabbi Chanina* both affirm that "these words respect some other text." *Resh Lekish* refers them to Psalm 116: 9, and on the authority of *Bar Kaplud*, explains it as "the land whose dead shall live or be raised first in the days of the Messiah."†

R. Saadias Gaon,‡ of the tenth century, on Dan. 12: 2, thus writes: "This is the resurrection of the dead of Israel whose lot is to eternal life; but those who do not awake,

* Vide Mede's Works. † Yaacob. fol. 4, 2.

‡ "The excellent ruler of the Academy of the Jews at Sora, near Babylon." Dr. A. Clarke's "Succession of Sacred Literature," p. 56.

they are the destroyed of the Lord, who go down to the habitation beneath; that is, Gehenna, and they shall be an abhorrence to all flesh." This agrees with Bush's translation of this text, evincing its prior resurrection sentiment.

Rabbi Jochannan agrees with Gaon, and says, "There are some who study in the law as they ought, and those are they who shall rise first to everlasting life, as it is said, "And many of them that sleep in the dust of the earth shall awake *some* to everlasting life," &c.*

Again, we read: "Our Rabbins have taught us that in the times of the Messiah he will restore to life the just," &c.†

In another place, commenting on Isaiah 25 : 8, it says:—"The world cannot be free from its guilt until King Messiah shall come, and the blessed God shall raise up those who sleep in the dust." Maimonides testifies this is the opinion of many Rabbis.

In *Yalcut Rubeni*, fol. 182—1, we read, "Know that we have a tradition that when the Messiah with the collected captivity, shall come to the land of Israel, in that day the dead in Christ shall rise again; and in that day the fiery walls of the city of Jerusalem shall descend from heaven; and in that day the temple shall be builded of jewels and pearls."

Rabbi Jeremias affirms the same, saying : "The Holy blessed God shall renew the world, and build Jerusalem, and shall cause it to descend from heaven."‡

Rabbi Eliezer, son of Rabbi Jose, of Gallilee, observes "The days of the Messiah are a thousand years," and, in *Sanhedrin*§ it is written thus: "There is a tradition in the house of Elias, that the righteous whom the holy blessed God shall raise from the dead, shall not return again to the dust, but for the space of a thousand years, in which the holy blessed God shall renew the world, they shall have wings like the wings of eagles, and shall fly above the waters."

* Zohar in Gen. fol. 100–3, 61, 73. † Genes. fol. 61.
‡ Midrash Hanalem, Zohar Genes, fol. 69 § Fol. 92–1.

In the *Book of Wisdom*, the writer of which was a Jew of the highest antiquity, we find the following concerning the holy dead: "In the time of their visitation they shall shine, and run to and fro like sparks among the stubble; they shall judge the nations, and have dominion over the people, and their Lord shall rule forever."*

Prof. Stuart declares that "the doctrine of a *first* resurrection as taught by John was not novel to the men of his time, and in his notes on Romans says it was a common opinion among the ancient commentators that the Jews were cast off until the end of the world, and hence understood the expression in Rom. 11: 15, 'life from the dead,' literally."†

Bickersteth says that the Jewish writers generally mention together the coming of the Messiah, and the resurrection of the dead, and frequently consider them as branches of the same proposition; asserting from the first Psalm, verse 4, that the resurrection was peculiar to the just.‡ Mr. Humphrey of England, also affirms the same.

Calmet in his Dictionary, says that "the doctrine of a two-fold resurrection—which he allows that the early fathers taught—is found clear enough in the second book of Esdras, in the Testament of the Twelve Patriarchs, and in several of the Rabbis."

Joseph Mede on this subject wisely remarks: "I can hardly believe that all this smoke of tradition could arise but from some fire of truth, anciently made known unto them. Besides, why should the Holy Ghost on this point speak so like them unless he would induce us to mean with them? In fine, the second and universal resurrection with the state of the saints after it, seems to have been less known to the ancient church of the Jews, than the first and the state to accompany it.§

* Wisdom, ii, 7–8. † Comment on the Apocalypse, vol. 1, p. 178
‡ Bickersteth on Prophecy.
§ Mede's Works.

THE SIX THOUSAND YEARS.

In six days the Lord made Heaven and Earth—
On the seventh day he rested and was refreshed. Exodus 31: 17.
One day is with the Lord as a thousand years. 2 Pet. 3: 8.
There remaineth therefore a rest—[keeping of a Sabbath]—to the people of God. Heb. 4: 9.

Bishop Russell, of Scotland, an Anti-Millennarian, says: "With respect to the millennium it must be acknowledged that the doctrine concerning it stretches back into antiquity so remote and obscure, that it is impossible to fix its origin. * * The tradition that the earth, as well as the moral and religious state of its inhabitants, were to undergo a great change at the end of 6,000 years, has been detected in the writings of Pagans, Jews and Christians. It is found in the most ancient of those commentaries of the Old Testament, which we owe to the learning of the Rabbinical school; and although the arguments by which it is recommended to our belief will not make a deep impression upon any intelligent reader, this will nevertheless leave no room for doubt that the notion of the millennium preceded by several centuries the introduction of the Christian faith."*

Rabbi Elias, a Jewish Doctor of high antiquity—lived, says Bishop Russell, about two hundred years before Christ. His opinion is called by the Jews "A tradition of the house of Elias." He taught that the world would be "2000 years void of the law; 2000 years under the law, and 2000 years under the Messiah." He limited the duration of the world to 6000 years, and held that in the seventh millennary "the earth would be renewed and the righteous dead raised; that

* Discourse on the Millennium, p. 39.

these should not again be turned to dust, and that the just then alive should mount up with wings as the eagle: so that in that day they would not fear though the mountains be cast into the midst of the sea. Psa. 46: 3"* on which Russell observes, "That by this resurrection he meant a resurrection prior to the millennium is manifest from what follows."

David Gregory, a learned mathematician and astronomer of Oxford, Eng., who died in 1710, says: "In the first verse of the first chapter of Genesis, the Hebrew letter Aleph, which in the Jewish arithmetic stands for 1000, is six times found. From hence the ancient Cabalists concluded that the world would last 6000 years. Because also God was six days about the creation, and a thousand years with him are but as one day; Psa. 90: 4. 2 Pet. 3: 8, therefore after six days, that is 6000 years duration of the world, there shall be a seventh day, or millennary sabbath of rest. This early tradition of the Jews was found also in the Sibylline Oracles, and in Hesiod, as we have seen; in the writings of Darius Hystaspes, the old king of the Medes, derived probably from the Magi; and in Hermes Trismegistus, among the Egyptians; and was adopted by the early Christian fathers, Clemens, Timotheus and Theophilus, Bishop of Antioch."†

Baal Katturim, a Rabbi, observes "There are six millenniums in the first verse of the first of Genesis, answering to the 6000 years which the world is to continue."‡

Rabbi Gedaliah says: "At the end of 6000 years the world shall return to its old state, without form and void, and after that it shall wholly become a Sabbath."

The author of *Cespar Mishna*, in his notes on Maimonides, writes: "At the end of 6000 years will be the day of judgment, and it will also be the Sabbath, the beginning of the

---

* Mede's Works, pp. 776, 893.
† Hale's Analysis of Chronology, vol. i. p. 79.
‡ Dr. Rudd's Essay, p. 369.

world to come. The Sabbath year, and year of jubilee, intend the same thing."*

In the *Gemarah*, or comment on the Mishna, we read:—
"Rabbi Ketina has said in the last of the thousands of years of the world's continuance, the world shall be destroyed; of which period it is said, 'the Lord alone shall be exalted in that day.' Isa. 2. And tradition agrees with Rabbi Ketina; for even as every seventh year is a year of release, so of the seventh thousand years of the world, it shall be the thousand years of release."

Henry D. Ward says: "This view of the course of time in six days of a thousand years, appears not to have been confined to Jews. The Chaldeans, according to Plutarch, believed in a struggle between good and evil for the space of 6000 years; 'and then Hades is to cease, and men are to be happy, neither wanting food nor making shade.' Zoroaster taught the same. Plutarch assigns no reason for these opinions; but Daubuz from whom I extract them, supposes they are of patriarchal origin. He adds: The Tuscans had an opinion which the Persians still hold, that 'God has appointed twelve thousand years to his works, the first 6,000 were employed in creation, the other six are appointed for the duration of mankind.' "†

Theopompus, who flourished 340 B. C., relates that the Persian Magi taught the present state of things would continue 6000 years, after which Hades or death, would be destroyed, and men would live happy. Bishop Russell, from whom we extract, adds, that the opinion of the ancient Jews on this point may be gathered from the statement of a Rabbi who said, "The world endures 6000 years, and in the 1000, or millennium that follows, the enemies of God will be destroyed."

Mr. Faber also affirms it to have been the doctrine of the

* Rudd's Essay, p. 369. † History of the Millennium. p. 2.

ancient *Persians* and *Etruscans*, particularly the latter, who taught that "The world was formed in the course of six periods; each period comprehending a millennary; while 6000 years are allotted for a seventh period, viz., that of its duration."

Zoroaster, an ancient Persian philosopher, and founder of the Magians: whom Dr. Prideaux* supposes to have been a student of the Hebrew prophets, taught that in the last times after much evil of every kind had afflicted the earth, two beings of supernatural powers appear and extensively reform mankind. In the end another superior personage, viz., Sosioch—a name resembling in sound the Hebrew Messiah—makes his appearance, under whose reign the dead are raised, the judgment takes place, and the earth is renovated and glorified. And finally, a still superior righteous judge, Ormuzd, from an elevated place commands Sosioch to render to all men their deserts, and takes the pure to his own presence. He also taught the sex-millennial duration of the world. Dr. Hengstenberg thinks he stole and adulterated the truths of revelation.†

Dr. Gill, commenting on 2d Pet. 3: 8, observes, "The Jews interpret days, millenniums; the seventh is the Sabbath and the beginning of the world to come."

Joseph Mede remarks, "The divine institution of a sabbatical or seventh years solemnity among the Jews, has a plain typical reference to the seventh chiliad, or millennary of the world, according to the well known tradition among the Jewish Doctors, adopted by many in every age of the Christian Church, that this world will attain to its limit at the end of 6000 years. Mede informs us that the whole school of Cabbalists call the seventh millennium 'the great day of judgment' because then they think God will judge the souls of all men; and he quotes many of their Rabbis to prove it."‡

* Connection, vol. 1, p 205. † Christology, vol. 1, p. 16
‡ Works, p. 535.

Prof. Bush, though denying the authoritative nature of this ancient tradition says :—" At the same time it is but fair to admit that as there is nothing in the Scriptures which directly contradicts it, the tradition may be well founded. It has perhaps more of an air of internal probability than most of the Rabbinical fancies which have laid a tax upon human credulity."

Dr. Cumming writes :—" I state the very remarkable fact, that dating time from the commencement of the globe, and on the supposition that the Jewish idea is a right one, that as there are six days in the week and the seventh is the sabbath, so there will be six millennaries or periods of a thousand years in the lapse of time, and the seventh will be the millennium ! It will follow from that interpretation that we are now at the close of the thousand years that constitutes the world's Saturday, and on the very dawn of the seventh thousand years that shall constitute the world's Sabbath."*

In " *The Investigator and Expositor of Prophecy*," a writer says :—" There is another event apparently at hand, viz., the conclusion of the sixth millennary of the world. The expectation indeed that at the end of the six thousand years the millennium should commence, is not supported by any direct testimony of Scripture with which we are acquainted; but it is so very ancient and general a tradition in the church, having been maintained by the Jews anterior to Christ's advent, by the Christians of the first centuries, and by the most judicious of our reformers; that we cannot help regarding it ourselves with feelings of great interest. We look at no particular year, but are persuaded that the true position of the Christian church should be that of expecting the coming of the Bridegroom in any and every year, and to stand with the loins girt and the lights burning ready to receive **Him.**"†

---

* Apocalyptic Sketches. First Series.
† Investigator, vol. v. pp. 6, 7.

"Thus," in the language of Dr. Cumming, "all fingers point to this rapidly approaching crisis. All things indicate that the moment that we occupy is charged with intense and inexhaustible issues. Never was man so responsible! Never, in the prospect of what is coming on the earth, was man's position so solemn! But evil shall not gain the day. Truth and love will emerge from every conflict, beautiful, and clothed with victory. The days of Infidelity and Popery are numbered. The waters of evil will soon ebb from the earth they have soiled. The approaching genesis will surpass in beauty and in glory the old. The church of Christ will lay aside her soiled garments, her ashen raiments, and put on her bridal dress, her coronation robes; and the nations will look up to her in admiration, earnest as the waves of the ocean rise up to the bright full moon enthroned above them. The sunrise of approaching day will soon strike the earth, and awaken its long silent hymns, and clothe creation's barest branches with amaranthine blossoms. Poor Nature, that has so long moaned like a stricken creature to its God from its solitary lair, shall cease her groans, and travail, and expectancy; for God will wipe away her tears, and on her fair, and beautiful and holy brow, crowned and kingdomed, other orbs in the sky, her handmaidens, will gaze in ecstacy, and thankfulness, and praise. 'And God shall wipe away all tears from their eyes; and there shall be no more death, neither sorrow, nor crying; neither shall there be any more pain. And there shall be no more night there. For these sayings are faithful and true.' "*

---

* "The Signs of the Times"—a Lecture before the Young Men's Christian Association, p. 42.

THE SIBYLLINE ORACLES.

As certain also of your own poets have said. Acts 17: 28.
One of themselves even a prophet of their own said, &c. Titus 1: 12.

These are rare and ancient writings, and come to us in the form of Greek verses, comprising fourteen books in all. They seem to be written by various authors, embracing Heathen, Jewish, and Christian, and are of different ages; some being written before Christ and some after. "The Sibyls," says Dr. Burnet, "were the Prophetesses of the Gentiles, and the Romans thought they had the fates of their empire in their books, which were kept by their magistrates as a sacred treasure." Some of the early Fathers frequently quoted them. We abridge them on the points in question from Stuart's Commentary on the Apocalypse.

THE FIRST BOOK commences with a description of the creation of the world by the Supreme Being, mostly modeled after Gen. 1. The Sibyl then describes the fall of man, the antediluvian age, the flood, the building of Babel, &c. She then predicts a future Messiah, his miracles, death, resurrection, and ascension, and finally, the dispersion of the Jews by the Romans.

THE SECOND BOOK, which appears to be a continuation of the first, commences with fearful woes on the "seven hilled city," followed by great slaughter and distress. A crown is held out for all who enter the lists against sin, especially will the crown be given to martyrs. The Sibyl then predicts the disastrous times which will precede the final judgment, in which war, famine, pestilence, &c., will rage. Elijah will come from heaven and fiery flames will consume all things. The resurrection of the body will take place and the judgment by the Eternal on his throne, and

Christ at his right hand. The Sibyl concludes by a prayer that she may obtain mercy in that tremendous day.

Book Third begins with a description of Belias, (or Belial) who with pretended miracles will deceive many and lead them astray; after which comes the judgment. The Sibyl proceeds with threatenings against all countries—then predicts the Messianic age, which is always preceded by wars, tumults, and distresses. When these end, the "Prince of Peace" shall come and wars shall cease. "He will fill the earth with blessings, and set up a perpetual kingdom among all men. The holy king of all the earth shall come, who shall wield the sceptre during all the ages of swiftly moving time."

In Book Fourth the Sibyl begins by declaring herself to be the "Prophetess of the great God, the creator of all things." She then describes his empire, and recommends obedience to him. Wars, pestilences, famines, earthquakes are as usual threatened to many countries. The Romans destroy the Jews. An Antichrist appears, and great persecution arises, then the destruction of the earth, the resurrection and judgment follow. After this comes the millennial state upon the earth. "Again the friends of piety shall live on the earth, God giving life and breath and support to all the pious—most blessed the man who shall live at such a time."

Book Fifth represents the Antichrist as "whetting his sharp teeth" and destroying many men, princes, and laying waste all the world. Great horror is excited, and all the elements join in the battle which finally ends for want of victims. Then comes the reign of peace, when the "divine Jewish race inhabit a great city in mid earth." Jesus, the crucified, shall return and speak words of consolation and peace to its inhabitants. He is "the man from the heavenly heights" who restores all things, subdues all enemies, rebuilds the city beloved of God, and makes it more splendid than stars, or sun, or moon; builds its tower so that it reaches to the clouds; the east and west celebrate the honor of God, and no more evils shall come.

Book Sixth contains but twenty-eight verses, which are in the form of a hymn to the Son of God " to whom the most High has given a throne." It describes his universal dominion and the peaceful state of the earth under his reign.

In Book Seventh the Sibyl introduces the Messiah as creator of the stars: He will be King of all and King of peace: all shall be completed by the Davidic house; for God has given him—the Messiah—the throne, and angels sleep at his feet. To a time of general destruction shall succeed the renovation of the earth, which shall then spontaneously produce all that is needed, and God shall dwell with men and teach them.

The Eighth Book. The Sibyl announces her intention of disclosing the wrath of God against the whole world. Every thing shall be consumed. Rome shall first fall. The Antichrist — whom she supposes was Nero — comes, and nothing shall stand before him. Then comes the end of all things and the judgment of God. Rome shall be plunged into a lake of fire and brimstone, and her wailings be heard by all; Antichrist loses his sceptre, and goes down to Hades. " Then shall a pure King reign over all the earth forever, raising the dead." A millennial season, says Stuart, is described as following after the resurrection.

Books IX and X are wanting. They remain as yet undiscovered, or at least unpublished. Books XI, XII, XIII, XIV, resemble the others in tone and manner. The Sibyls all limit the world's duration to 6,000 years.*

Such are their predictions with regard to the advent and millennial Kingdom, many of them being in perfect harmony with the Sacred Scriptures.

---

* Stuart on the Apocalypse, vol. i pp. 87. *et seq.*

THE BOOK OF ENOCH.

This work is apocryphal. It was first found in Ethiopia by James Bruce. The author is unknown, but is supposed to have been a Hebrew. It was written previous to the Christian era, and is often alluded to and quoted by the early Fathers. It is supposed to be the work from which Jude quotes, though many doubt it. It is certainly antique. Its dedication is, "The blessing of Enoch upon the elect and the righteous who are to exist in the time of trouble." Enoch says that what he sees has reference to a distant period—i. e. the days of the Messiah—and that God will hereafter reveal himself on earth: the earth be burned and all things in it perish: but to the righteous peace and mercy will be given; they shall all be blessed and glorified, and the martyrs obtain a rich reward: the time of judgment and separation is coming; that the elect One, clothed with power to subdue the rebellious kings, shall dwell among his people, changing the face of heaven and earth, rejecting the wicked, and a new heaven and earth will appear. Enoch describes a millennial period as coming for the righteous subsequent to the destruction of the wicked.

Jude's quotation in Enoch, chap. 2d, reads thus:—"Behold, He the Lord cometh with ten thousands of his saints, to execute judgment upon them and destroy the wicked, and reprove all the carnal for every thing which the sinful and ungodly have done, and committed against Him." The quotation, if from this work, is doubtless paraphrastic. Enoch ends with a benediction on the good.

THE TESTAMENT OF THE XII PATRIARCHS.

This, too, is an apocryphal work, and probably written during the first century. Prof. Stuart thinks the author was a Christian Jew. It teaches that a King of the race of Judah is coming who will restore all things and reign for ever: that God will appear dwelling among men on earth and save the race of Israel, and gather the just from all nations. "The Most High will visit the earth, and coming as a man eating and drinking with men in quiet, he shall crush the head of the dragon: the saints shall rise from the dead and each worship on his sceptre the King of the heavens. His kingdom is an eternal Kingdom which shall not pass away."

THE FOURTH BOOK OF EZRA.

This is an apocryphal work; author and date unknown. It is quoted by Clement and others of the early writers. It teaches the coming of more corrupt times; that man's evil heart still blinds and perverts him, and will do so till the time of harvest come, i. e. when the number of the wicked is completed; that great changes will take place and strange things happen; that the earth will have its old age, which will bring many evils with it. The consummation will be preceded by great commotions of the natural elements and nations—the end will follow; a new age shall come; the earth shall give up the dead; sinners shall be plunged into the bottomless abyss; and Paradise shall appear in all its glory. In chapter 6, a millennial period of bliss is described, when evils shall cease.

THE ASCENSION OF ISAIAH.

This work is also apocryphal. It was probably written during the first century by a Christian Jew. It was found in London, and brought before the world in 1819, by D. Laurence, Professor of Hebrew at Oxford. In it we are taught that the Messiah will come take the form of a man, suffer, be crucified, rise again, and commission his disciples to preach; and that afterwards some will forsake the doctrine of the apostles respecting the second advent of Christ, and contend much about the proximity of his approach; that there will be great defections in doctrine and practice in the church; but few faithful teachers will be left, and a lying, worldly, ambitious and avaricious spirit will prevail. Then the Berial (Satan) in the form of an impious monarch, will much oppress the saints; claim divine honors; overturn all the usual and established course of things; be worshiped as a God, and erect his image every where—only a few believers will be left waiting for the coming of their Lord. Soon the Lord and his saints will descend from heaven and dwell in this world; Berial and his powers shall be dragged into Gehenna, and the saints enjoy the promised rest on earth in great splendor. The wreck of the material world will ultimately follow, and this will be the forerunner of the general resurrection and judgment, in which the ungodly will be devoured by fire from the Beloved. "The writer," says Prof. Stuart, "appears to have been a decided millennarian." We gather these testimonies from Stuart's Commentary on the Apocalypse.

THE SECOND BOOK OF ESDRAS.

This apocryphal writer says: "How much the world shall be weaker through age, so much the more shall evils increase upon them that dwell therein."* In the thirteenth chapter, through a dream, Esdras teaches that after a time, the days will come when the Most High will begin to deliver them that are upon the earth, he coming to the astonishment of all. The latter time comes, signs shall happen—the Son of God shall be declared, and a great battle will ensue, in which all the wicked will be rebuked and destroyed, and when this is accomplished, He will defend his people that remain who are a peaceable multitude, and will show them great wonders. Chapter 11, verse 46, describes a millennial season as occurring at the destruction of the fourth monarchy.

* 2 Esdras, xv. 17

THE CONFLAGRATION OF THE EARTH.

"Looking for and hasting unto the coming of the day of God, wherein the heavens being on fire shall be dissolved, and the elements shall melt with fervent heat. Nevertheless we, according to his promise, look for new heavens, and a new earth, wherein dwelleth righteousness." 2 Peter 3: 12-13.

Josephus gives a singular tradition concerning Seth, who he says having found out the knowledge of the celestial bodies, and having received from Adam a prophecy that the world should have a double destruction, one by fire and the other by water, raised two pillars with inscriptions upon them to survive the fire, and so transmit their astronomical knowledge to posterity*—" which," says Burnet, " seems to imply a foreknowledge of this fiery destruction even from the beginning."

Dr. Burnet, in his Theory of the Earth† on the conflagration, says, " We find little in antiquity contrary to this doctrine." He then quotes *Plato* as admitting a general conflagration and ultimate succession of worlds. The *Stoics* also made this doctrine a part of their philosophy. The school of *Democritus* and *Epicurus* made all their worlds subject to destruction, and by a new concourse of atoms restored them again; and the *Ionic* philosophers who had *Thales* for their master, and were the first naturalists among the Greeks, taught the same doctrine. *Origen* in his answer to Celsus, tells him that his own (the heathen) authors did believe and teach the renovation of the world after certain ages or periods. Among the Greeks not only the *Stoics* but *Heraclitus* and *Empedocles* also, more ancient than *Zeno* the master of the *Stoics*, taught the final conflagration. Among the Romans

---

* Antiquities, Book i. chap. 2. † Vol. i.

Tully, *Lucretius*, *Lucan*, and *Ovid* have spoken openly of the conflagration. Says *Ovid*:—

> "A time, decreed by fate at length will come,
> When heavens, and earth and sea shall have their doom;
> A fiery doom; and nature's mighty frame,
> Shall break, and be dissolved into a flame."

As for *Seneca*, he being a Stoic, we need not doubt of his opinion on this subject. The eastern nations, the *Egyptians*, the *Persians* and *Phœnicians* all taught the final catastrophe of the world by fire. Fire was the God of the *Persians*, and they made it at length to consume all things. The eastern fable of a species of bird, the Phœnix, which appeared at the end of a great year making herself a nest, which being set on fire by the sun consumed her in the flames, and then out of her ashes there arose a second Phœnix—Burnet regards as an emblem of the world which after a long age will be consumed in the last fire, and from its ashes will arise another world or a new heavens and earth. The *Scythians*, the *Celts*, the *Chaldeans*, the *Indian Philosophers*, all say that the world will be renewed after a general conflagration. The *Druids* as *Strabo* tells us, gave the world a kind of immortality by repeated renovations, the destroying principle being always fire or water. *Hesiod* and *Orpheus*, authors of the highest antiquity, sung of this last fire in their philosophic poetry. The heathen all speak of an *Annus Magnus*, or great year, at the expiration of which the world would be renovated, particularly after the conflagration, and use the same words in describing it that the Scriptures do. *Chryssippus* calls this golden age αποκαταστασις *apokatastasis* or "restitution," as Peter does Acts 3: 21. *Marcus Antoninus*, in his "Meditations," several times calls it παλιγγενεσία *palingenesia* or "regeneration," as our Saviour does Matt. 19: 28. And *Numenius* has two Scripture words "resurrection" and "restitution" to express this renovation of the world.*

* Theory of the Earth, vol. 1.

Dr. Adam Clarke in his commentary, testifies that :—"It was an ancient opinion among heathens, that the earth should be burned up with fire; so Ovid, Met. l. 5, 256. *Minucius Felix* tells us 34 : 2, that it was a common opinion of the Stoics, that the moisture of the earth being consumed, the whole world would catch fire. The Epicureans held the same sentiment. And indeed it appears in various authors, which proves that a tradition of this kind has pretty generally prevailed in the world. But it is remarkable that none have fancied that it will be destroyed by water. The tradition founded on the declaration of God was against it ; therefore it was not received."

Gibbon in his " Decline and Fall of the Roman Empire," testifies as follows: " In the opinion of a general conflagration, the faith of the Christian very happily coincided with the tradition of the East, the philosophy of the Stoics, and the analogy of nature; and even the country, which, from religious motives, had been chosen for the origin and principal scene of the conflagration, was the best adapted for that purpose by natural and physical causes: by its deep caverns, beds of sulphur, and numerous volcanoes, of which those of Ætna, of Vesuvius, and of Lipari, exhibit a very imperfect representation. The calmest and most intrepid skeptic could not refuse to acknowledge that the destruction of the present system of the world by fire, was in itself extremely probable. The Christian, who founded his belief much less on the fallacious arguments of reason than on the authority of tradition and the interpretation of Scripture, expected it with terror and confidence as a certain and approaching event.*"

Dr. Hitchcock, of Amherst College, remarks : " Some author has remarked that, from the earliest times, there has been a loud cry of fire. We have seen that it began with the ancient Egyptians, and was continued by the Greeks

---

* Gibbon, chap. xv.

But in recent times it has waxed louder and far more distinct. The ancient notions about the existence of fire within the earth were almost entirely conjectural, but within the present century the matter has been put to the test of experiment. Wherever, in Europe and America, the temperature of the air, the waters, and the rocks in deep excavations has been ascertained, it has been found higher than the mean temperature of the climate at the surface; and the experiment has been made in hundreds of places. It is found, too, that the heat increases rapidly as we descend below that point in the earth's crust to which the sun's heat extends. The mean rate of increase has been stated by the British Association to be one degree of Fahrenheit for every forty-five feet. At this rate, all known rocks would be melted at the depth of about sixty miles. Shall we hence conclude that all the matter of the globe below this thickness (or, rather, for the sake of round numbers, below one hundred miles) is actually in a melted state? Most geologists have not seen how such a conclusion is to be avoided. And yet this would leave only about one-eight hundredth part of the earth's diameter, and about one-fourteenth of its contents, or bulk, in a solid state. How easy, then, should God give permission, for this vast internal fiery ocean to break through its envelope, and so to bury the solid crust that it should all be burnt up and melted! It is conceivable that such a result might take place even by natural operations. And certainly it would be easy for a special divine agency to accomplish it."*

Pliny the Elder, the celebrated Roman Naturalist, born A. D. 23, in contemplating the abundant existence of fire, sc devouring an element, in the earth, air, and all the terrestrial universe, both in a latent and active state, made the following startling remark: "It exceeds all miracles, in my opinion,

---

* Lecture on the New Earth.

that one day should pass without setting the world all on fire !!"

THE ADVENT AND RESTITUTION.

' *The Lord Jesus Christ who shall judge the quick and the dead at his appearing, and his kingdom.*"—2 Tim. 4 : 1.

The London Quarterly Journal of Prophecy testifies that : " All classic myths relative to the expected era of bliss announce a Mighty One to come. Sibylline verses, deriving their name from a Chaldee word, which signifies 'to prophecy,' are traditional predictions, and as we have them presented by Virgil, they point us to an 'age to come,' and ' a new birth of nature,' and at the same time link the glorious kingdom they depict with an exalted Personage, who would, they say, ' reduce all mankind into a single empire.' "

The Encyclopædia of Religious Knowledge informs us that the Mohammedans all believe in a general resurrection and future judgment, adding : " The time of the resurrection they allow to be a perfect secret to all but God alone—however, they say the approach of that day may be known from certain signs which are to precede it."

Sir Paul Ricaut, in his work on the " Ottoman Empire," published in the seventeenth century, says : " There is a sect of Mohammedans called Haictites, who believe that the Messiah took a true natural body ; and that being eternal, he became incarnate, as the Christians believe." " Wherefore,' says Ricaut, " they have inserted this article into their confession of faith, that Christ shall come to judge the world at the last day. For the proof whereof, they cite a text out of the Koran, in these words, ' O Mahomet! thou shalt see thy Lord, who shall come again in the clouds !' They affirm that this is foretold of the Messiah, and confess that this Messiah can be no other than Jesus, who is to return into the world with the same flesh which he assumed."

Robert Hort, A. M., in the seventeenth century, in a sermon on the millennium, wrote as follows: "In Plato's dialogue, the philosopher having spoken of the first happy condition of the world and its fall, adds: 'But in the end, lest the world should be plunged into an eternal abyss of confusion, God, the author of the primitive order, will appear again, and resume the reins of empire; then he will change, embellish, and restore the whole frame of nature; and put an end to decay of age, sickness and death." Hort again continues: "*Plutarch* having related the doctrine of the ancient *Persians* concerning the evil introduced into the world by Arimanius, concludes it thus: 'But there will come a time, appointed by fate, when *Arimanius* shall be entirely destroyed and extirpated; the earth shall change its form, and become plain and even; and happy men shall have one and the same life, language, and government.' According to the authority of Strabo, the ancient *Gymnosophists* had a similar tradition, and believed in a time when 'the ancient plenty shall be restored.' All the heathen nations believed that the renovation would be brought about by some divine hero. Virgil in his fourth eclogue describes the renovation both of the physical and moral world, in a manner very little differing from the sacred writings; and the Chinese philosophers entertain the same notions concerning the corruption, and the future renovation of the world."*

THE KARENS.—This nation exists in Tavoy, a province near Siam, in Asia, and number about five thousand. From the "Memoir of Mrs. Mason," we gather the following beautiful tradition among them concerning a coming deliverer. Fifty years ago one of their number, to whom a white man presented a copy of the Psalms, was thrown into jail on the charge of "praying, and teaching others to pray for the arrival of the white foreigners." He was a religious teacher

* Sermons, p. 10.

and had much influence over the natives of Tavoy and Mergui, and went every where, making his followers assemble for the worship of God, exhorting them to remember their ancient tradition, "that God once dwelt among them, and that he had departed to the west, that they had the promise of his return, and though long delayed, he would assuredly reappear, and would come with the white foreigners, with whom he had departed, and whose ships were from time to time then seen on their coasts." "When God comes," said he, "the dead trees will bloom again; the tigers and serpents will become tame; there will be no distinction between rich and poor; and universal peace will bless the world."

THE AZTECS. From the same "Memoirs" we learn that this ancient people of South America maintain a similar view. Among them a tradition existed concerning a demi-god or superior intelligence of some kind, who had formerly reigned among them, but at length had departed westward with the promise of a return and a more brilliant reign, to which the natives looked forward as to a certain Millennium, and when the Spanish ships first reached their coast many of them believed it was their returning deity.

Dr. Joseph Wolffe. From his travels in the east we gather the following traditions, current among the Asiatic nations.

In ARABIA the Jews of *Yemen*, the *Rechabites*, and the children of Israel, of the tribe of *Dan*, expect the speedy arrival of the Messiah in the clouds of heaven. The children of Rechab say: "We shall one day fight the battles of the Messiah and march towards Jerusalem." *Rabbi Alkaree*, one of the Jews of Yemen, said: "We do expect the coming of the Messiah. * * There is war in the wilderness unprecedented in our memory."

In THIBET, one of their chiefs said: "When you shall see corn growing upon my grave, then the day of resurrection is nigh at hand." The people of *Cashmere* assured me that corn had begun to grow upon his grave, and therefore they considered my words to be true, that Jesus will come.

THE JEWS IN PERSIA say the world is to exist six thousand years, and that the Messiah will appear, and the sabbatical year shall have its commencement. One of their Rabbis read to Mr. Wolffe, from Maimonides, that "The King Messiah shall rise to make the kingdom of David return to its former condition and power," that "whosoever does not hope in his coming denies the words of the prophets and the law of Moses," that "in his days the Messiah shall rule alone, and only he," that "on his arrival the battle of Gog and Magog shall be fought," that "we must wait for his coming," and that, "at that time there shall be hunger and war no more, and envy and anger shall cease among us."

THE GUEBERS of India and Persia who worship fire are acquainted with the history of the fallen angels, and believe in the deluge, and that a time is coming when this world will pass away and another will be created. The Musselmans, the worshippers of Ali and Mahammedan Jews and Mullahs, many of them believe in the coming of a deliverer called "Mohde," (translated from Shiloh) who shall restore all things before the day of judgment, and be proclaimed sovereign: a messenger going on before him. They told Wolffe that they were glad to find he expected the speedy arrival of the Messiah Jesus; for the signs of the times prove that Mohde must soon come, one stating to him that she had discovered by the book called "Khorooj Namah," that Christ will come again in the year 1861. "They derive," says Wolffe, "most of this from their *Hadees* or traditional prophecies."

THE HINDOOS have a tradition that VISHNOO is to come to destroy the world for a season, a belief analogous to the advent of Christ to judgment. They have also a record of the submersion of the world by a deluge.

The following dialogue occurred between **Mr. Wolffe** and a Persian Dervish.

Wolffe.—What will become of this world?

Dervish.—The world will become so good that the lamb and the wolf shall feed together, and there shall be general peace and fear of God upon the earth; there shall be no more controversy about religion, all shall know God truly; there shall be no more hatred, &c.

Wolffe.—Who then shall govern the earth?

Dervish.—JESUS.

Dr. *Wolffe* says they got this from their *Hadees;* and he adds, that in his opinion more light is to be found among them than among the most learned neologists and infidels in Europe.

In Yemen (Teman of Scripture) a Rabbi told Mr. Wolffe that his tribe did not return to Jerusalem after the Babylonish captivity. When Ezra by letters invited their princes in Tanaan to return, they replied, "Daniel predicts the murder of the Messiah, and another destruction of Jerusalem and the temple; therefore we will not go up until He shall have scattered the power of the holy people—till the 1290 days (meaning years) are over. * * * But we do expect the coming of the Messiah," &c.

Seiler a German spiritualist opposing the faith of the ancient Jews in relation to a personal reign of the expected Messiah, makes the following admission:—" Concerning many things they formed erroneous conceptions, some of the prophets themselves not excepted. * * * They expected it—the kingdom of God—to arrive earlier than it did. They fancied that God would subdue the heathen by miraculous punishments. They believed that they should continue to live forever on earth in this kingdom. They expected a new state of paradise on earth and an abundance of the pleasures of sense. They had no conception of supersensuous or heavenly happiness, and therefore as being persons whose notions were entirely sensuous, they could not conceive of a kingdom of God otherwise than as possessing a visible king, ruling on earth in splendid majesty."*

Nevertheless this kingdom will come. It will be a literal kingdom. Immanuel will reign on David's throne "in splendid majesty" forever. He will be a "visible King,' making " all things new." O those will be happy times! We are confidently expecting them, and they are at hand:

> " These eyes shall see them fall,
>   Mountains and skies and stars;
> These eyes shall see them all
>   Out of their ashes rise;
> These lips his praises shall rehearse
> Whose nod restores the universe."

So read we the Scriptures. So we believe. So taught the eminent Stephen Charnock,† and so the lamented Thomas Chalmers, who writes, " The object of the administration we are under is to extirpate sin, but it is not to sweep away materialism. There will be a firm earth as we have at present, and a heaven stretched out over it as we have at present. It is not by the absence of these, but by the absence of sin that the abodes of immortality will be characterized. It will be a paradise of sense, but not of sensuality. It is then that heaven will be established upon earth, and the petition of our Lord's prayer be fulfilled, THY KINGDOM COME."‡

> " The world to come, redeemed from all
>   The miseries which attend the fall,
>   New made and glorious shall submit
>   At our exalted Saviour's feet."—DR. WATTS.

* Seiler's Bible Hermeneutics, p. 270.
† Works, vol. 1. pp. 204–207.   ‡ Sermon on the New Earth.

CHAPTER III.

THE EARLY CHURCH, FROM HERMAS TO ORIGEN.

"Blessed and holy is he that hath part in the first resurrection; on such the second death hath no power, but they shall be priests of God and of Christ, and shall reign with him a thousand years."—REV. 20: 6.

THE early church was eminently pre-millennial in her cherished expectations of the Lord's advent. His coming and kingdom was her constant hope, and she deemed it, says Massillon, "one step in apostacy not to sigh after his return." And this faith and hope, with her, was practical: even Gibbon admitting it to be "an opinion which may deserve respect, from its usefulness and antiquity." With her, too, Millennarianism was connected with all that is orthodox. On this point Mosheim is somewhat unfair. He places Chiliasm among the heresies of Cerinthus, in the first century, and yet affirms it had "met with no opposition till the third." The infidel saw and rebuked this unfairness. Says Gibbon, this "learned divine is not altogether candid on this occasion."

We have introduced Hermas into this catalogue, who, while he may be apocryphal, is still antique. Like Paul, he writes of a "world to come." Clement, too, advocates a future kingdom at the Redeemer's advent. Of Barnabas, we observe in the language of Professor Bush: "the genuineness of this epistle is disputed, but as far as the present argument is concerned, it is immaterial who the real author was. There is sufficient testimony that it is the production of a very early period of the Christian church."* Ignatius says nothing of the millennium. His hope lay in the better resurrection. So also Polycarp, who was a strenuous advocate of the personal advent of Christ. Papias' testimony is both interesting and credible. Of Justin Martyr, the following testimony is borne by Semisch: "Justin dwells with deep emotion on this hope. It was in his esteem a sacred fire, at which he kindled afresh his Christian faith and practice. That this hope in its pure millennarian character and extent might possibly be vain, never entered his thoughts. He believed that it was supported by scripture. He expressly appealed to the New Testament Apocalypse, and such passages in the Old Testament as Isaiah 65 : 17, in evidence of the personal reign of Christ in Jerusalem. From the Apocalypse, and Isaiah 65 : 22, in connection with Genesis 2 : 17; 5 : 5, and Psalm 90 : 4, he deduced the millennial period. How could he doubt it?"

And Irenæus—how explicit and weighty his testimony. In the language of Edward Winthrop, we ask, "Is it credible that that excellent and pious father, with the advantage of being instructed by Polycarp, who was himself instructed by St. John, did not know what the beloved disciple held, as to the fact, whether the second coming of Christ would usher in the millennium, or be delayed to its close. We think not."† Still, it is said by Post-millennialists, that the Hebrew church believed the same, and that the early Christians drew their Chiliasm from this source. "It is, therefore," writes Bishop Russell, "a Rabbinic fable." "No mistake," says David N Lord, "could be greater. Justin Martyr, Irenæus, Tertullian, and Lactantius, expressly found their doctrines of the millennium on the twentieth chapter of the Apocalypse, and the prophecies of Isaiah 65th, Zech. 14th, and other pas-

* Bush on the Millennium, p. 10. † Letters on Prophecy p 43.

sages of the Old Testament, that are alleged by millennarians as foreshowing the reign of Christ and the saints on the earth. Not a hint is uttered by them that they were led to their belief in that reign by Jewish interpretations, or traditions; or that they drew their notions of it in any manner from the opinions that were entertained by the Jews of the reign of the Messiah."* Such are the men to whose authority and writings we are about to refer. The opponents of pre-millennialism, cannot quote them without being condemned. "Jerome never mentions Justin Martyr," says Mede, "being afraid of the antiquity and authority of the man." In the midst of these early Christians we love to linger, while as yet the dark cloud of apostasy had not come over the path of the church.

But we give place to permit the early Christian Fathers to speak for themselves. Let us listen with patience and candor to the voice of the Church.

HERMAS, ABOUT A. D. 100.

Says Dr. A. Clarke: "This writer is generally allowed to be the same that Paul salutes, Rom. 16: 14."† Dr. Hagenbach remarks that his work, "The Shepherd or Pastor," "enjoyed a high reputation in the second half of the second century, and was even quoted as a part of Scripture."‡ According to Eusebius, this book was regarded as a part of the sacred canon by some in the days of Irenæus.‖

Dr. Burton and Prof. Stuart date its production about A.D. 150. Dr. Elliott allows the same and pronounces it a spurious publication, but as Irenæus calls it a useful book, and both Jerome and Eusebius say it was read in the churches, we give a few extracts for what they are worth, remarking,

---
* Theological and Literary Journal, vol. p. 426.
† Succession of Sac. Lit. p. 90.   ‡ Hist. of Doctrines, Vol. 1. p. 56.
‖ Eccl. Hist., B. v. ch. viii.

that the real Hermas mentioned by Paul, is supposed to have died about A.D. 81.

Hermas predicts great tribulation for the church, and says: "Happy ye as many as shall endure the great trial that is at hand." He says: "This world is as the winter to the righteous men, because they are not known but dwell among sinners; but the world to come is as summer to them."

Again he says: "The Great God will remove the heavens and the mountains, the hills and the seas: and the end will be accomplished that all things may be filled with his elect, who will possess the world to come." "This age," he says, "must be destroyed by fire, but in the age to come the elect of God shall dwell." Hermas no where describes a millennial era or rest for the church till the end of time.*

CLEMENT, A. D. 96.

The third Bishop of Rome, and "fellow laborer" of Paul, whose name is "in the book of Life." Phil. 4 : 3. Says Eusebius, "Of this Clement there is one epistle extant, acknowledged as genuine, of considerable length, and of great merit. This we know to have been read for common benefit, in most of the churches, both in former times, and in our own."†

Nor does he deny the genuineness and authenticity of the second Epistle, though he does not speak of it so approvingly. Clement wrote about A. D. 95. In his first Epistle, he says, "Let us be followers of those who went about in goat skins and sheep skins, preaching the coming of Christ. Such were the Prophets." Again, alluding to some who scoff at the apparent delay of the advent, he says,—"You see how in a little while the fruit of the trees comes to maturity. Of a

---

* Hermas, pp. 270, 288. Library of the Apostolical Fathers—Oxford Translation. † Eusebius, B. iii. ch. xvi.

truth, yet a little while and His will shall be accomplished suddenly, the Holy Scripture itself bearing witness that He shall quickly come and not tarry; and the Lord shall suddenly come to his temple, even the Holy One whom ye look for." In his second Epistle he says, "If therefore we shall do what is just in the sight of God, we shall enter into his kingdom, and shall receive the promises, which neither eye hath seen, nor ear heard, nor have entered into the heart of man. Wherefore let us every hour expect the kingdom of God in love and righteousness, because we know not the day of God's appearing." He uses the phœnix to demonstrate the possibility of the resurrection.*

Dr. Duffield, says "there is not in Clement's writings the most remote hint of a millennium of religious prosperity before the coming of Christ." Roman Catholics count him a saint. Clement of Alexandria calls him "an Apostle," which Jerome qualifies by styling him "an Apostolic man." If a companion of Paul, how valuable his testimony—he plainly putting the kingdom at the coming of Christ. Clement was martyred A. D. 100, by being drowned in the sea, under the reign of the Emperor Trajan.

BARNABAS, A. D. 71.

He was the companion of St. Paul. He was a Levite, and was born on the Island of Cyprus. He was brought up with Paul at the feet of Gamaliel, and is declared by Clement to have been one of the seventy sent out by the Saviour.† He first introduced Paul to the other Apostles (Acts 9: 27.) "He was a good man, and full of the Holy Ghost and faith." An Epistle is extant bearing his name, in which the writer speaks as though he were Barnabas the Apostle. It was read in the churches at an early period, and was cited by Clement of Alexandria, Origen, and others, the latter styling

* See His. Epistles, pp. 21, 30, 357.
† Quoted by Euseb. Eccl. Hist., B. ii. Ch. 1.

it, "The Catholic Epistle of Barnabas." Jerome and Eusebius pronounce it Apocryphal. Vossius, Dapuis, Dr. Mill, Dr. Cave, Dr. Burnet, Dr. S. Clarke, Archbp. Wake, Bishop Fell, Whiston, and many others esteemed it genuine.

Barnabas recognizes the Abrahamic covenant as surviving and superseding the Mosaic, and as yet to be perfected by Christ, who is the covenant pledge of its fulfillment. He uses the style of Peter in speaking of the Advent, and says, "The day of the Lord is at hand, in which all things shall be destroyed, together with the wicked one. The Lord is near and his reward is with him." On the creation-week he says, "Consider, my children, what this signifies, he finished them in six days. The meaning of it is this; that in six thousand years the Lord God will bring all things to an end. For with him one day is as a thousand years; as himself testifieth, saying, Behold, this day shall be as a thousand years. Therefore, children, in six days (i. e. 6000 years) shall all things be accomplished. And what is that he saith, 'and he rested the seventh day;' he meaneth this, that when his Son shall come and abolish the wicked one, and judge the ungodly; and shall change the sun, and moon and stars; then He shall gloriously rest on that seventh day," i. e. millennium. He taught the "restitution," or "renewing of all things," and said that we should "call to our remembrance day and night the future judgment."*

Mr. Brooks and Dr. Duffield esteem this extract as of good authority, and the Fathers who call his Epistle apocryphal, do not deny that Barnabas wrote it. If this be so, and if he was the associate of the apostle Paul, was not the latter very likely to have been a pre-millennialist? and is not this testimony overwhelming? Barnabas is supposed to have been martyred about A.D. 75 by being stoned to death by the Jews.

* Apostolic Fathers, p. 186.

IGNATIUS, A. D. 100,

He was Bishop of Antioch. Of his parentage and birth, nothing is known. Greek and Syriac writers affirm that he was the little child the Saviour took in his arms and sat in the midst of his disciples, as a model of innocency and humiliation. Chrysostom, Mosheim, Chalmers, Fox, and others affirm, that he was the disciple and familiar friend of the apostles, and was educated and nursed up by them. He wrote about A. D. 100. Dr. Elliot highly commends him, and says, his seven Epistles are almost universally acknowledged to be genuine.

To the Ephesians, Ignatius expresses his faith thus: " The last times are come upon us ; let us therefore be very reverent and fear the long suffering of God, that it be not to us condemnation." He also bids them " stop their ears" when one shall speak contrary to the evangelical record of Jesus Christ. To Polycarp he wrote: " Be every day better than another ; consider the times, and expect Him who is above all time, eternal, invisible, though for our sakes made visible." To the Smyrnians he says, that Peter and the other disciples did actually prove by the sense of touch, the real presence and resurrection of Christ, " being convinced both by his flesh and spirit." And being thus assured of his personal resurrection, and consequently their own at his coming, for this cause they despised death and were found to be above it." To the Romans, he expressed his hope that all the churches would " suffer him to be food for wild beasts ; to encourage them that they might become his sepulchre and leave nothing of his body ; may I enjoy the wild beasts ; I wish they may exercise all their fierceness on me ; to this end I will encourage them that they may be sure to devour me ; I would rather die for Christ's sake than to rule to the utmost ends of the earth ; for I am the wheat of God, and being ground by the teeth of the wild beasts, I shall be found the pure bread of Christ." His reason for this thirst for **martyrdom** was this, "If I suffer, I shall then become the free man of Jesus Christ, *and shall rise free,*" evidently in the first resurrection. He was devoured by lions in the amphitheatre at Rome, courting death, and dying in great triumph,[*] A. D. 107.

Not one word of a temporal millennium or spiritual reign, but instead the advent of the Redeemer and resurrection of the body, appears to have been his blessed hope. And if, as Eusebius says, he succeeded Peter at Antioch, they were doubtless of the same faith.

POLYCARP, A. D. 108.

This eminent man was born, it is supposed, in Smyrna. Spanheim says, he was ordained Bishop over the church in that city by John; and Usher and others affirm that John in the Apocalypse addresses him as the "angel of the church of Smyrna." He was the disciple and familiar friend of John the revelator, and contemporary with Ignatius, Papias, and Irenæus. Eusebius bears the highest testimony concerning him, and makes him a pattern of orthodoxy. His epistle is both authentic and genuine.

Polycarp taught in this epistle that God had raised up our Lord Jesus from the dead, and that he will come to judge the world and raise the saints, and that if we walk worthy of him we shall reign together with Him. He alludes to the other life, or world to come, and asks, Who of you are ignorant of the judgment of God? "Every one," he adds, "that confesses not that Jesus Christ is come in the flesh, is Anti-Christ; and he who doth not acknowledge his martyrdom on the cross, is of the devil; and whosoever shall pervert the oracles of the Lord to his own lusts, and shall say that there is neither resurrection nor judgment to come, that man is the first born of Satan."[†]

Polycarp taught no spiritual reign, but otherwise. **Dr.** Burnet pronounces him a decided millennarian, and Irenæus

[*] Apos. Fath., p. 60—137.　　　[†] Apostolic Fathers, p. 56.

hints the same. He must have received the doctrine from St. John. Duffield, Brooks, and Ward, quote him as confirming millennarian views. Who has not read of the sainted Polycarp? He was burned at the stake about A. D. 167. His tormentors urging him to blaspheme Christ, he thus nobly answered, " Four score and six years have I served Him, and he never did me any harm ; how then can I blaspheme my King, and my Saviour ?" When further urged, his answer was, "I am a Christian." Being threatened with wild beasts, he cried, " Bring them forth !"*

PAPIAS, A. D. 116.

He was Bishop of Hierapolis, where he was probably born. Eusebius and Jerome, both anti-millenarians, pronounce him to have been the disciple and friend of John the Revelator. Irenæus testifies he was one of John's auditors, and being a staunch millennarian, he doubtless obtained his views from John. He was also the intimate friend and companion of Polycarp, who was as we have seen, another of John's disciples. He taught the millennium in all the churches. His writings, consisting of five books, entitled "A narrative of the sayings of our Lord," are not extant, but they come to us through Eusebius. He seems to have been a personal acquaintance of the apostles. He drew his Chiliasm from the Apocalypse, and Irenæus intimates that he claimed the sanction of John for it. Eusebius denies him talent for interpreting the prophecies, because he interpreted them literally, but on other points speaks of him as being "eloquent and learned in the Scriptures."

Papias in his preface, says that " He did not follow various opinions, but had the apostles for his authors; and that he considered what Andrew, what Peter said, what Phillip, what Thomas, and other disciples of the Lord ; as also what

* Eusebius Eccl. Hist., B. iv. chap. 15.

Aristion, and John the senior, disciples of the Lord, what they spoke; and that he did not profit so much by reading books, as by the living voice of those persons which resounded from them." Jerome who did not believe in the millennium, gives this account of Papias. Eusebius thus records the words of Papias. " Nor will you be sorry, that, together with our interpretations, I commit to writing those things which I have formerly learned from the elders, and committed to memory. For I never (as many do), have followed those who abound in words, but rather those who taught the truth; not those who taught certain new and unaccustomed precepts, but those who remembered the commands of our Lord, handed down in parables, and proceeding from truth itself, i. e. the Lord. If I met with any one who had been conversant with the elders, from him I diligently enquired what were the sayings of the elders. * * The elders who had seen St. John, the disciple of our Lord, taught concerning those times, (the millennium), and said, ' The days shall come when the vine shall bring forth abundantly, * * and all other fruits, * * and all animals shall become peaceful and harmonious, one to the other, being perfectly obedient to man. But these things are credible only to those who have faith.' Then Judas, the betrayer, not believing, and asking how such fertility should be brought about, our Lord said, ' They shall see who come to those times.' And of these very times Isaiah prophesying said, ' The wolf and the lamb shall dwell together.' "* This is recorded by Papias as a discourse of our Lord, handed down by John the Evangelist. Eusebius himself thus speaks of Papias: " Other things also, the same writer has set forth, as having come down to him by unwritten tradition, some new parables and discourses of the Saviour. Among these, he says, that there will be a certain thousand years after the resurrection of the

* Eusebius Hist., B. iii., chap. 39.

dead, when the kingdom of Christ will be established visibly on this earth." Daniel Whitby admits that Papias taught "It shall be a reign of Christ bodily on earth;" and Eusebius affirms that "most of the ecclesiastical writers" believed with Papias. Such are the admissions made by the opponents of pre-millennialism. Such their testimony concerning the faith of the Apostolic Fathers.

Dr. Elliot says that "Papias' millennary doctrine was founded in part on the Apocalyptic Book, as well as on the many other Scriptures well agreeing therewith, both in the Old and New Testaments." Dr. Burton admits that Papias' "proximity to the apostolical times, if not his personal acquaintance with some of the apostles, would put him in possession of many facts;" and the learned Greswell oberves, that "Papias' honesty has never been impeached, and his antiquity makes his testimony to the millennium so much the more valuable."

JUSTIN MARTYR, A. D. 150.

He was a learned writer of Greek origin, born at Neapolis or Sichem, in the province of Samaria, in Palestine, A. D. 89; some say later. He was converted to Christianity, A. D. 132-3, and flourished as a writer A. D. 140-160. He was in part contemporary with Polycarp, Papias and Irenæas. Eusebius says his works stood in high credit among the early Christians. His "Dialogue with Trypho," the Jew, is considered authentic and genuine. Justin was a real convert to Chiliasm, of a pure character, and looked for no millennium in this world. He speaks of those as "destitute of just reason who did not understand that which is clear from all the Scriptures, that two comings of Christ are announced." He argued that the millennium would be beyond the resurrection, and in the restitution of all things, quoting Isaiah 65, and others of the Prophets as proof especially these verses, "Behold I create new heavens and a new earth, &c." When questioned by Trypho in regard to this faith, he answered, "I am not such a wretch, Trypho, as to say one thing and mean another. I have before confessed to thee that I, and many others, are of their opinion (the millennial reign) so that we hold it to be thoroughly proved that it will come to pass. But I have also signified unto thee on the other hand that many, even those of that race of Christians who follow not godly and pure doctrine—do not acknowledge it. For I have demonstrated to thee that these are indeed called Christians, but are atheists and impious heretics, because that in all things they teach what is blasphemous, ungodly, and unsound." Then after saying that he will commit his dialogue to writing that others may know his faith, because it is of God, he continues, "If therefore you fall in with certain who are called Christians, who confess not this truth, but dare to blaspheme the God of Abraham and Isaac and Jacob, in that they say there is no resurrection of the dead, but that immediately when they die, their souls are received up into heaven—avoid them and esteem them not Christians, &c. But I and whatsoever Christians are orthodox in all things, do know that there will be a resurrection of the flesh, and a thousand years in the city of Jerusalem, built, adorned, and enlarged according to the Prophets." The foregoing is according to the original of Justin's printed copies. The reader is referred to Brooks and Duffield for the argument in relation to Justin's writings having been interpolated by Romish writers. Justin thus continues: "For thus hath Isaiah spoken of this thousand years; 'For there will be a new heaven,' &c. He then quotes Isaiah 65, making the "tree" of verse 22, the tree of life, and adds: "We believe a thousand years to be figuratively expressed. For as it was said to Adam, 'In the day that he should eat of the tree he should surely die.' Gen. 2: 17. So we know that he did not live a thousand years. We believe, also, that this expression, 'The day of the Lord is a thousand years.' Ps. 90 : 4, and 2 Peter 3 : 8, relates to this. Moreover a certain man among us whose name is John, being one of the twelve Apostles of Christ, in that revelation which was shown to him, prophesied that those who believe in Christ, should live a thousand years in Jerusalem; and after that there would be a general, and in a word, an universal resurrection of every individual person, when all should arise together with an everlasting state and a future judgment." And in proof that he looked for no carnal millennium, but a pure state, he immediately quotes the Saviour's prediction in Luke 20 : 35-36. Justin taught that the Abrahamic promise of land would be fulfilled at the resurrection, in the renovated or new earth. He also says: "We may conjecture from many places in Scripture that those are in the right who say six thousand years is the time fixed for the duration of the present frame of the world."*

Milner highly lauds the character of Justin, and Semisch, a German writer, remarks, that "Chiliasm constituted in the second century so decidedly an article of faith, that Justin held it up as a criterion of perfect orthodoxy," and Dr. Burnet calls Justin "a witness beyond all exception." Dr. Cave, though seemingly opposed to his faith, admits that "Justin expressly asserts, that after the resurrection of the dead is over, our Saviour, with all the holy patriarchs and prophets, the saints and martyrs should visibly reign a thousand years," and also adds, that Justin and Irenæus held the millennium in "an innocent and harmless sense." Dr. Elliott calls him a man to whose learning and piety testimony has been borne by nearly all the succeeding Fathers." Dr. Adam Clark declares that "he abounds in sound, solid sense, the produce of an acute and well cultivated mind." Let the reader weigh well the testimony of Justin in favor of the pre-millennial advent. Farther comment is unnecs

* See his Dialogue with Trypho.

sary. He was crowned with martyrdom at Rome, A. D. 163 or 165, by being beheaded.*

IRENÆUS, A. D. 178.

Irenæus was Bishop of Lyons. He was born, it is supposed, at Smyrna, not far from the beginning of the second century, and flourished as a writer about A. D. 178. Basil styles him " one near the apostles." He was pupil to and trained up under the tutorage of Papias and Polycarp, both of whom were disciples of John the Revelator. The words and memory of Polycarp were deeply graven upon his mind, and by him preserved fresh and lively to his dying day. We give his language on this point both for its interest and to confirm his testimony. Writing to Florinus he says: "When I was very young, I saw you in the lower Asia with Polycarp. I can remember circumstances of that time better than those which have happened more recently; for the things which we learn in childhood grow up with the soul and unite themselves to it; insomuch that I can tell the place in which the blessed Polycarp sat and taught, and his going out and coming in, the manner of his life, the form of his person, and the discourses he made to the people; and how he related his conversation with John, and others who had seen the Lord; and how he related their sayings, and the things which he heard of them concerning the Lord, both concerning his miracles and doctrine, as he had received them from the eye witnesses of the Lord of Life; all of which Polycarp related agreeable to the Scriptures." For learning, steadfastness and zeal, he was among the most renowned of the early Fathers. Milner highly commends him, and calls him a man of exquisite judgment. His works now extant, and which Mosheim calls " a splendid monument of antiquity," are five books on the Heresies of his times. He says that certain heretical opinions had arisen, proceeding

* Eusebius' Ecclesiastical History.

THE COVENANT—RESURRECTION NECESSARY. 61

from ignorance of the arrangements of God, and the mystery of the resurrection and kingdom of the just; and it therefore became needful to speak of them. Then he proceeds: " For it is fitting that the just, rising at the appearing of God, should in the renewed state receive the promise of the inheritance which God covenanted to the fathers, and should reign in it. * * It is but just that in it they should receive the fruits of their suffering, so that where for the love of God they suffered death, there they should be brought to life again, and where they endured bondage, there also they should reign. For God is rich in all things, and all things are of him; and therefore, I say, it is becoming, that the creature being restored to its original beauty, should without any impediment or drawback be subject to the righteous." Quoting Rom. 8: 19, 22, in proof, he continues—" The promise likewise of God, which he made to Abraham, decidedly confirms this, for he says,—' Lift up now thine eyes.' " Quoting farther, Gen. 13: 14–17, he adds,—" For Abraham received no inheritance in it,—not even a foot-breadth, but always was a stranger and a sojourner in it. And when Sarah, his wife, died, and the children of Heth offered to *give* him a piece of land for a burial place, he would not accept it, but *purchased* it for four hundred pieces of silver, from Ephron, the son of Zohar, the Hittite; staying himself on the promise of God, and being unwilling to seem to accept from man what God had promised to give him, saying to him, ' To thy seed will I give this land, &c.' Thus therefore as God promised to him the inheritance of the earth, and he received it not during the whole time he lived in it, it is necessary that he should receive it, together with his seed, that is, with such of them as fear God, and believe in him, in the resurrection of the just." He then shows that Christ and the church are the true seed, and partakers of the promises, and concludes the chapter by saying,—" Thus, therefore those who **are of** faith are blessed with faithful Abraham and the same are the children of Abraham. For God repeatedly promised the inheritance of the land to Abraham and his seed; and as neither Abraham nor his seed—that is, not those who are justified—have enjoyed any inheritance in it, they will undoubtedly receive it at the resurrection of the just. For true and unchangeable is God; wherefore also he said, 'Blessed are the meek, for they shall inherit the earth.'" He supports his statements by numerous quotations from the old Testament, reference to which we give that the student of prophecy may know what was the method of ap plying and expounding the prophetical Scriptures in times so near to the apostles. We give his texts in his own order. Isa. 26 : 19. Ez. 37 : 12–14; and 38 : 25, 26. Jer. 23 : 7, 8. Isa. 30 : 25, 26; and 58 : 14. Luke 12 : 37–40. Rev. 20 : 6. Isa. 6 : 11. Dan. 7 : 27. Jer. 31 : 10–15. Isa. 31 : 9; and 32 : 1; and 54 : 11–14, also Isa. 65 : 18–28.

Irenæus gives a famous hyperbolic tradition concerning the marvellous fertility of the earth in its renewed state, referring it to the kingdom or millennial era, and says it was related by those clergy—Papias and Polycarp—who saw St. John, the disciple of Christ, and heard from him what our Lord had taught concerning those times "which," observes Burnet, "goes to the fountain head. He relates it as from John, and John from our Lord. Irenæus, like Justin, calls those "heretics" who expected the saints glorification to follow immediately after death, and before their resurrection. He also made the Roman kingdom to be the fourth described in Dan. 7th chap., and on the duration of the world, he says, "In as many days as this world was made, in so many thousand years it is perfected; for if the day of the Lord be as it were a thousand years, and in six days those things that are made were finished, it is manifest that the perfecting of those things in the six thousandth year, when Anti-Christ having reigned 1260 years * * then the Lord shall come from heaven in the clouds, with the glory of his Father, casting him and them that obey him, into a lake of fire; but bringing to the just the times of the kingdom, that is, the rest, or Sabbath, the seventh day sanctified, and fulfilling to Abraham the promise of the inheritance." He thus identifies the millennium with the Kingdom of God, placing both at the end of the sixth chiliad.*

Thus have we quoted this great man at length, but we trust not without profit. Chillingworth says that Irenæus made the doctrine of Chiliasm apostolic tradition. Eusebius and Jerome both affirm that he believed in the thousand years reign of Christ on earth according to the *letter* of the Revelations of John; and Whitby allows that he taught " Christ will be every where seen," his proof being Math. 26: 29, and adding, " this cannot be done by him while he remains in the celestial regions." Irenæus sealed his testimony with his blood by being *beheaded* under the reign of Severus, about A.D. 203–5.

How copious and scriptural is the testimony and voice of Irenæus! And will not the *beheaded* ones live pre-millennially? The Seer of Patmos answers "I saw them live and reign a thousand years!"

THE CHURCHES OF VIENNE AND LYONS, A.D. 177.

Their Epistle, which Eusebius has inserted at length in his Ecclesiastical History, was written about A.D. 177, to the churches in Asia and Phrygia. Dr. Elliott says it was penned by one of the Lyonese Christians, and Prof. Stuart thinks that not improbably Irenæus wrote it himself. We give an extract exhibiting the hope of the early church.

After describing the tortures and modes of martyrdom of the Christians during their persecution under Marcus Aurelius, the epistle proceeds to narrate the death of Ponticus

* Irenæus Adversus Hæreses, Lib. v. cap. 35. pp. 452–464.

a youth of fifteen, and Blandina, a Christian lady, and says: "The bodies of the martyrs having been contumeliously treated and exposed for six days, were burned and reduced to ashes, and scattered by the wicked into the Rhone, that not the least particle of them might appear on the earth any more. And they did these things as if they could prevail against God, and prevent their resurrection, and that they might deter others, as they said, 'from the hope of a future life, relying on which they introduced a strange and new religion, and despise the most excruciating tortures, and die with joy. Now let us see if they will rise again, and if their God can help them and deliver them out of our hands.'"*

Here from the lips of their enemies we have evidence of the practical bearing of the doctrine of the resurrection of the body as held by the primitive martyrs. Mr. Faber on this point observes, that "The doctrine of the literal resurrection of the martyrs prior to that epoch certainly prevailed to a considerable extent throughout the early church, and often animated the primitive believers to seal the truth with their blood,"—and on the same subject, the learned Dodwell writes:—"The primitive Christians believed that the first resurrection of their bodies would take place in the kingdom of the millennium; and as they considered that resurrection to be peculiar to the just, so they conceived the martyrs would enjoy the principal share of its glory. Since these opinions were entertained, it is impossible to say how many were inflamed with the desire of martyrdom."† From this it is demonstrably evident that the martyrs' hope lay in the first resurrection of Rev. 20: 6. Ignatius craving death that he might "rise free," Ponticus and Blandina hoping for "a future life," Cyprian attesting that those who suffered

* Eusebius Eccl. Hist., Book v. chap. i.
† Dodwell's Dissertations, Sect. 20.

expected a prior resurrection and "a more prominent place in God's kingdom," and to crown all, Tertullian affirming that the martyr's express prayer was that he "might have a part in the first resurrection."

Let the honest reader compare this Epistle with the testimony of Ignatius, Cyprian, Tertullian, Gibbon, and Bush, and then decide whether it be not highly probable that the three millions of martyrs put to death by Pagan Rome were mostly pre-millennialists.

HIPPOLYTUS, A. D. 220.

He was Bishop of Porto. He flourished, according to Dr. Cave and Lardner, about A. D. 220. Photius says he was in early life a disciple of Irenæus, and eulogizes his style as being clear, grave, and concise. Jerome and Andreas say he wrote a treatise on the Revelation, but if so, it has perished. His treatise now extant, on Antichrist, bears every mark of genuineness. So remarks Elliott, from whom we give an abstract. Hippolytus was evidently a pre-millennialist. He declared, none of the mysteries of the future, foreshown by the prophets, will be concealed from God's servants. He gives a full exposition of Daniel's prophecies of the four kingdoms, which, with all the other fathers, he pronounces to be Babylon, Persia, Macedon, and Rome, then existing, "and what then," he adds, "remains for accomplishment but the division of the iron image into its ten toes—the growing out of the fourth Beast's head of its ten horns?" And though Rome should fall, and Antichrist arise out out of the ten horns or kingdoms, he being the two horned lamb-like beast, and "being a man of resource would heal and restore it, so that it shall revive again through 'he laws established by him," and would on this account be called "The Latin man," a name containing the fatal number, 666; Antichrist, he says, would reign his predicted time, greatly persecuting the saints, whose only hope will be in Christ crucified, and that then and thereupon would take place Christ's coming, personal, in glory, for, as Elliott observes, "no other coming ever entered the minds of the early Christians"—Antichrist be destroyed by its brightness; the first resurrection of the saints follow; the just take the kingdom prepared for them (Math. 25) and shine forth as the sun; the judgment of the conflagration being meanwhile executed on the wicked. Following the Septuagint, he fixed the termination of the six thousand years and end of the world about A.D. 500.*

He suffered martyrdom under Alexander Severus. No millennium, until Christ comes, is the voice of Hippolytus.

MELITO, A.D. 177.

He was Bishop of Sardis. He was born in Asia, and was contemporary with Justin Martyn. He was bishop of one of the apocalyptic churches, and was so eloquent and deeply pious, that Tertullian affirms, " he was by most Christians considered a prophet," and Polycrates says of him, "he was in all things governed by the Holy Ghost."† He made extracts from the scriptures respecting the Messianic prophecies, and wrote a treatise on the Apocalypse, and also made out a complete list of the canonical books of the Old Testament, but his works are not now extant. He was a Chiliast. In regard to his views of that period, he probably followed Papias : Jerome and Gennadius both affirming that he was a declared millennarian. And even Neander admits that Polycarp, Papias, Irenæus, and Melito, "endeavored to maintain the pure and simple apostolic doctrine, and defend it against corruption." The time and manner of his death is unknown, but he lies buried at Sardis, waiting with hi "name in the book of life," for the first resurrection, at the coming of our Lord.‡

---

* Elliott's Horæ Apoc., vol. iv. p.   † Euseb., B. v., ch. 24.

‡ Cave's Lives of the Fathers, p. 337. Burnet's Theory of the Earth, vol. ii. p. 166.

TERTULLIAN, A. D. 200.

He was born at Carthage, in Africa, about A. D. 160, and flourished as a writer, A. D. 199—220. Jerome reckons him among the first Latin millennarians, and Vincentius as the "Prince of those writers." Prof. Stuart calls him "a truly eloquent writer of extensive information." Mosheim says of him, "which were the greater, his excellencies or defects, it were difficult to say." Neander says of him, "This great Father united great gifts with great faults." Milner speaks harshly of him, but allows him to have been "an orator and a scholar." Spanheim calls him "one of the first of the Fathers," and Cyprian thought much of Tertullian, and never passed a day without reading some portion of his works, thus showing his high estimation of them. Dr. Elliott commends him, and on Tertullian's view of the Apocalypse, says, that with one or two exceptions, "there is but little in it on which we might not join hands in concord with the venerable and sagacious expositor." He also says that Tertullian's view of the New Jerusalem was, that it was of heavenly fabric, and would descend from heaven to be the abode of resurrection saints during the millennium, &c., which he said would come from heaven on the destruction of Antichrist. He was a rough writer, but was a Christian, and his testimony in regard to the faith of the church in his day is plain and interesting. He says, "We confess that a kingdom is promised us on earth, before that in heaven, but in another state— namely—after the resurrection; for it will be one thousand years in a city of divine workmanship, viz., Jerusalem brought down from heaven; and this city Ezekiel knew, and the Apostle John saw, &c. This is the city provided of God to receive the saints in the resurrection, wherein to refresh them with an abundance of all spiritual good things, in recompense for those which in the world we have either despised or lost. For it is both just and worthy of God, that his servants should there triumph and rejoice, where they have been afflicted for His name's sake. This is the manner of the heavenly kingdom." He was a decided pre-millennialist, and affirms it was customary for Christians in his times, "to pray that they might have part in the first resurrection." In regard to the triumph of truth in this world, he refers to their persecutions, and thus eloquently writes: "Truth wonders not at her own condition. She knows that she is a sojourner upon earth; that she must find enemies among strangers: that her origin, her home, her hopes, her dignities, are placed in heaven."* Tertullian died about A. D. 245, where or how it is not known.

MONTANISTS, A. D. 150.

These were the followers of MONTANUS: a sect which flourished in the second century. As we have said, Tertullian leaned towards the faith of this sect. They are reputed by some to have been "heretics," and by others as "real Scriptural Christians." Being all of them decided millennarians and somewhat rigorous and ultra in other views cherished by them, they have doubtless been misrepresented by their opponents, through whose hands most of their writings have reached us. Says Mr. Brooks, "What is Montanism? According to some, it is an error comprehending every species of indefinable theological evil that the imagination of man can apprehend; but according to others it was more immediately the heresy of "commanding to abstain from meats," as being unlawful to be eaten." Bishop Jeremy Taylor says, that "Epiphanius put Montanus and his followers into the catalogue of heretics for commanding abstinence from meats, as if they were unclean and of themselves unlawful. Now the truth was, Montanus said no such thing; but commanded frequent abstinence, enjoined dry diet, and an ascetic table not for conscience sake, but for discipline; and thus Epi-

* Tertullian against Marcion, Lib. iii., p. 680.

phaneous affixes that to Montanus which Epiphanius believed a heresy, and yet which Montanus did *not* teach."* Tertullian affirms that it was because Montanus urged such abstinence by the way of discipline, and no more, that the primitive church disliked him, thinking his views came too near Judaism. Mr. Brooks farther remarks, that "the apologies of the Montanists (excepting what is contained favorable to them in Tertullian,) have not been permitted to come down to us; and we may well pause before we brand them with the name of heretics."† The eminent John Wesley observes, "by reflecting on an old book which I have read in this journey, (The general delusion of Christians, &c.,) I was fully convinced of what I had long suspected, that the Montanists in the second and third centuries were real Scriptural Christians."‡ In regard to other errors imputed to Montanus, Mr. Lee, in his History of Montanism, shows that he was grossly aspersed and misrepresented. Munscher, a German neologian, and no friend to the Millennarians, makes the following statement: "How widely the doctrine of millennarianism prevailed in the first centuries of Christianity, appears from this, that it was universally received by almost all teachers; and even some heretics agreed with them§ referring we presume to the Montanists. This is partly true, but we deny that, in general, Chiliasm has been the associate of heresy. Prof. Stuart says of the Montanists, they were all Chiliasts, and, at the same time, justly admits that Chiliasm existed apart from Montanism. It is yet to be proved by unprejudiced witnesses, that the Montanists were real heretics. And if they were Montanism but hung itself upon Chiliasm, as more subsequently Munzerism hung itself upon Protestantism. Anti-millennarianism, on the other hand, has been all along the associate and ally of heresy. The here-

* Liberty of Prophesying, Sect. 11. † Brooks on Prophecy, p. 71
‡ Journal, Aug. 1750.
§ Munscher's Dogmengeschichte, vol. ii. p. 415.

tics were the opponents of Millennarianism. The Gnostics could not tolerate it. The unsound and mystical Origenists opposed it. The whole Alexandrian School with the Arian Dionysius took weapons against it. The Alogi hated it. Platonism and heathen philosophy set itself with zeal to overthrow it. Socinus, of later date, attacked it, and Rome has ever been its enemy. "The Millennarian Fathers," says the London Journal of Prophecy, "were the great upholders of orthodoxy. They fought the battle with the Gnostics, and most vigorously condemned and confuted Cerinthianism; that very Cerinthianism which they have been not seldom identified with, but which they ably opposed. Millennarianism and orthodoxy went hand in hand; Millennarianism and heresy were resolute and irreconcilable foes."

But we must leave the Montanists. We admit in doing so, it is possible they had errors which connected with the Millennial truth, tended at last to bring it into disrepute.

THE ALOGIANS. CAIUS, A. D. 212.

The name or word Alogi signifies without Logos, or Word. This sect, with *Caius*, flourished about the end of the second century. Both opposed the Montanists and the Millennium. Dr. Lardner says the Alogi are not mentioned by contemporary writers, and intimates that they were not numerous. They complained that the Apocalyse was dark, enigmatical, unintelligible, and unreasonable, and rejected it together with John's gospel. "These," says Prof. Stuart, "are subjective reasons, and belong to their understanding and judgment, rather than to the book itself." Lucke also affirms that "The Alogi rejected the Apocalyse not on historical ground, &c., but only and simply because of their exegetical ignorance of it."[*] They evidently denied the canonical author

---

[*] Stuart's Apoc., Vol. 1, pp. 337-344.

ity of John's gospel, because it taught that Christ was the Logos, or Word, and did the same with the Revelations because of its Chiliasm. Mede says that Caius "did his best to undermine the authority of the Apocalyse." "Nor," he adds, "did any one know of such Caius, but from his relation; and if there were any such, he should seem to be one of the heretics called Alogi." Mosheim admits that "the first open opposer of Chiliasm that he met with was Caius, a teacher of Rome, toward the end of the second century. On this ground he denied that the Apocalypse was written by John, and ascribed it rather to Cerinthus. But he effected very little." Dr. Burnet says that Caius called the visions of John, "monstrous stories." He ascribed a gross sensualism to the Millennium of the Revelations, which John never taught. Prof. Stuart says "the ground of his opposition is merely, and only his antipathy to Chiliasm," and also remarks that "his judgment has very little claim to our respect or consideration. The fact that he palmed a carnal Millennium upon the Apocalyse is enough to show how little he understood the book, and indeed how little he had studied it."

Here we have the character of that opposition which, still in embryo, began to develop itself against the Millennium. What was its character? Readers, "Judge ye!"

CLEMENT, A. D. 192.

Clement, Bishop of Alexandria, was born at Athens, and flourished, A. D. 192, and he himself affirms that he had heard those preach whose doctrines had been immediately received from the Apostles. Eusebius calls him an "incomparable master of the Christian philosophy." Clement was contemporary with Tertullian. Neander attributes to him "great knowledge about divine matters;" but Dr. Murdoch, while allowing the same, declares that "he construed the Bible allegorically, and fancifully." H. D. Ward affirms

that Clement "takes no notice of the Millennium:" he does not directly, but still he hints at it. Dr. Burnet says, "He has not said any thing that I know of, either for or against the Millennium: but he takes notice 'that the seventh day has been accounted sacred both by the Hebrews and Greeks, because of the revolution of the world, and the renovation of all things.'" Giving this as a reason for keeping that day, Burnet remarks, that "it can be in no other sense than that the seventh day represents the seventh Millennium, in which the kingdom and renovation are to be." G. H. Wood, of England, seems to put Clement among the Millennarians, but it may be for the same reason that Jeremy Taylor reckons Origen as one, because he believed in the consummation at the end of six chiliads. Clement addresses the heathen thus: "Therefore Jesus cries aloud, personally urging us, because the kingdom of heaven is at hand: he converts men by fear," &c. "This," says Dr. Duffield, "is Peter's argument, (1 Peter 4: 7) and it proves that he regarded the kingdom of heaven, as the prophets testify, to be introduced by judgment: his ideas of that kingdom must have been radically different from those of the spiritualists."*
The place, time, and manner of Clement's death is unknown.

CYPRIAN, A. D. 220.

He was Bishop of Carthage, which was his birth-place. In early life he was a heathen teacher of rhetoric, but afterward became a zealous Christian, and flourished as a writer, A. D. 220–250. Lactantius says of him, "Cyprian alone was the chief and famous writer;" and Erasmus declares that he spoke the purest Latin of any of the Latin Fathers. Mosheim calls him "a prelate of eminent merit;" and both Milner and Neander highly laud his character. He was a sincere admirer of Tertullian and professed to be his disciple,

* Cave, p. 355. Burnet's Theo. Earth, Vol. 2, p. 188. Duff. on Proph., p. 29. Ward's Hist. of Mill., p. 17.

calling him "master." Mede regarded him as a decided believer in the Millennium. Cyprian said to his Christian brethren, " Christ is coming to avenge our sufferings ;" and Mr. Ward remarks of him that " he appeared to have been waiting for the coming of the Lord to overthrow Antichrist and to give his saints the kingdom."

Cyprian writes as follows: "It were a self-contradictory and incompatible thing for us, who pray that the kingdom of God may quickly come, to be looking for long life here below.   *   *   Let us ever in anxiety and cautiousness be awaiting the sudden advent of the Lord, for as those things which were foretold are come to pass, so those things will follow which are yet promised ; the Lord himself giving assurance and saying, ' When you see all these things come to pass, know that the kingdom of God is nigh at hand.' Dearest brethren, the kingdom of God has begun to be nigh at hand ; reward of life, joy, eternal salvation, perpetual happiness, and possession of Paradise, lately lost, are already coming nigh while the world passes away."* He certainly looked for no Millennial kingdom prior to the advent of Christ. Dr. Burnet says that with the other Fathers he fixed the period of 6000 years, and made the seventh Millennium "the consummation of all," and Dr. Elliott confirms the same. Cyprian informs us that the thirst for martyrdom which existed among Christians, arose from their supposing that those who suffered for Christ would obtain a more distinguished lot in his kingdom, and which expectation is in perfect keeping with Hebrews 11 : 35-40. He coveted martyrdom, and when his sentence of death was read to him, he said, "I heartily thank Almighty God." He was led to the block, A. D. 258, amid the weeping and lamentations of the people who loved him, and who cried, "Let us also be beheaded with him." Reader, are you with the pious Cyprian, awaiting "the sudden advent of the Lord ?"

* Oxford Translation of Cyprian, pp. 149, 217. See Cave, p. 443

METHODIUS, A. D. 260.

He was first Bishop of Olympus, and afterwards of Tyre. This Christian writer flourished about A. D. 260-290, and is allowed by Neander to have been a Chiliast.[*] He was the firm opponent of Origen, and charged that fanciful interpreter with heresy. His work is not known to be extant, but the following passage from it is quoted by Proclus in Epiphanius. He says: "It is to be expected that, at the conflagration, the creation shall suffer a vehement commotion, as if it were about to die: whereby it shall be renovated, and not perish: to the end that we, then also renovated, may dwell in the renewed world free from sorrow. Thus it is said in Psalm 104: 'Thou wilt send forth thy Spirit, and they shall be created, and thou wilt *renew* the face of the earth.' For seeing that after this world there shall be an earth, of necessity there must be inhabitants; and these shall die no more, but be as angels, irreversibly in an incorruptible state, doing all most excellent things."[†] He was evidently a Pre-millennialist, and Whitby at antipodes with his sentiments, allows that " Methodius held to a *pure* Millennium—free from every thing sensual." He was crowned with martyrdom under the reign of Decius, A. D. 312.

NEPOS AND CORACION, A. D. 250.

These both flourished about A. D. 250, the former being a learned Egyptian Bishop. We have none of their writings. Prof. Stuart says that Nepos was a strong Millennarian, and Coracion joined him. Nepos wrote a book against the Allegorists, and in defence of his Millennarian views; in which he everywhere appeals to the Apocalypse in support of them." Says Mr. Brooks, " he wrote a book entitled ' The Reprehensions of Allegorizers,' which was specially directed against

---

[*] Neander's Ch. Hist. vol. i. p. 451-452. [†] Epiphanius Her. 74.

APOCALYPTIC CHILIASM—LITERALISM.

who now began to explain the Millennium figuratively." Mosheim says, " Nepos attempted to revive its (the Millennium's) authority in a work written against the Allegorists, as he contemptuously styled the opposers of the Millennium." Dr. Cave says " he was a man skilled in the Holy Scriptures, and also a poet, and that he had fallen into the *error* of the Millennarians, and had published books to show that the promises made in the Scriptures to good men were according to the sense and opinions of the Jews to be literally understood."* Nepos's views have been denominated sensual, but like many others of the Millennary Fathers, he has probably been misrepresented and misunderstood. That he was a Pre-millennialist is most certain, even Whitby allowing that Nepos taught "after this (first) resurrection the Kingdom of Christ was to be upon earth a thousand years, and the saints were to reign with him."

Such was the Scriptural faith of Nepos; but the reader can perceive by this testimony the sad departure from the faith of the earlier Christians, and the exhibition of that blighting spiritualism which had begun imperceptibly to creep into the church of God through the influence of Origen.

* Cave's Lives, p. 510.

CHAPTER IV.

FROM ORIGEN TO AUGUSTINE.

*"For the time will come when they will not endure sound doctrine;
* * and they shall turn away their ears from the truth, and shall be turned unto fables."*—2 Tim. 4: 3-4.

UP to this period, we meet with no writer of reputed soundness in the faith, or of distinction in the church, who opposed the doctrine of Christ's millennial reign. The most that can be said of some of them, is, that they do not mention the doctrine in their writings, but at the same time, all that do refer to it adopt the Pre-millennial view, and do not even appear to dream of any other. We have traced the doctrine back through the Hebrew church for many centuries prior to the Lord's first advent. We have traced it through the early Church back to the inspired apostles, and forward to times of apostacy. And for the first time in the whole history of Chiliasm, it now began to be strenuously opposed. Would that we could speak well of the soundness of its opposers. But we cannot. Truth forbids it. We are obliged in some instances at least, to rank them among the most unreliable and spiritualizing interpreters of God's sacred Word. And we begin with

ORIGEN, A. D. 250.

Origen had his birth at Alexandria, A. D. 185. He was unquestionably a man of great talents, an indefatigable student, and the well known champion of Anti-millennarianism. But what shall we say of him? He was certainly a strange professor of Christianity. He circulated two books on magic attributed to Jannes and Jambres, representing those two prime magicians of the court of Pharaoh as inspired prophets. He taught that magic was a true and lawful science. From his master Ammonius, he learned the art of communicating with the demons. "He went so far," says Hagenbach, "that contrary to general opinion, he did not even take from Satan all hope of future pardon."* Dr. Clarke says, that according to his plan of interpretation, "The sacred writings may be obliged to say *anything*, everything, or *nothing*, according to the *fancy*, peculiar *creed*, or *caprice* of the interpreter."†

Glassius says that "it was from the allegorical system of Origen that Porphyry, his pupil, drew the strength of his arguments, as well as the point of his ridicule against Christianity." Origen taught that "the Scriptures were of little use, if we understand them as they are written;" that "words in many parts of the Bible convey no meaning at all;" that "the Scriptures are full of mysteries, and have a three-fold sense, viz., a literal, a moral, and a mystical, and that the literal sense was worthless." He also taught the pre-existence of human souls previous to the creation, and perhaps from eternity; their condemnation to animate mortal bodies in order to expiate faults committed in their pre-existent state; a spiritual or etherial resurrection of the body; the universal restoration of the damned, after a limited punishment, to a state of probation, &c., &c. The Universalists have usually claimed Origen as one of their faith. He brought in a torrent of allegory on the church which, according to Mosheim, Duffield, and other good authority

* Hagenbach's History of Doctrines, vol i. p. 147.
† Sacred Literature, p. 153.

evidently laid the foundation for the rise of the Papal hierarchy; the monks being his enthusiastic admirers. Church historians speak of Origen as follows: Spanheim says, "The genius of Origen was too luxuriant, and inclined to allegory; and he fell into several doctrinal errors, which afterward supplied fuel for the flames of discord, and produced deplorable effects in the church."* Mosheim observes: "After all the encomiums we have given to Origen, * * it is not without deep concern, we are obliged to add that he also, by an unhappy method of interpretation, opened a secure retreat for all sorts of errors, which a wild and irregular imagination could bring forth." He then alludes to Origen's system of interpretation, and calls it "wild, fanciful, chimerical, mystical, licentious." He says again on the doctrine of the Millennium: "Now its credit began to decline, principally through the influence and authority of Origen, who opposed it with the greatest warmth, because it was incompatible with some of his favorite sentiments."† Milner declares that, "No man, not altogether unsound and hypocritical, ever injured the church of Christ more than Origen did. From the fanciful mode of allegory introduced by him, uncontrolled by Scriptural rule and order, arose a vitiated method of commenting on the Scriptures, which has been succeeded by a contempt of types and figures altogether, just as his fanciful ideas of letter and spirit tended to remove from men's minds all right conception of genuine Christianity. A thick mist for ages pervaded the Christian world, supported by his absurd allegorical mode. The learned alone were looked at as guides implicitly to be followed, and the vulgar, when the literal sense was hissed off the stage, had nothing to do but to follow the authority of the learned. It was not till the days of Luther and Melancthon that this evil was fairly and

* Spanheim's Hist., p. 219.   † Eccl. Hist., vol. i, pp. 181, 186.

successfully opposed."* "He was famous," says Saurin, "for the extent of his genius, and at the same time for the extravagance of it; admired on the one hand for attacking and refuting the errors of the enemies of religion, and blamed on the other for injuring the very religion that he defended, by mixing with it errors monstrous in their kind, and almost infinite in their number." . . . . " In spite of all his Greek and Hebrew, he was a sorry philosopher, and a very bad divine. The Church has condemned his doctrine in the gross. All his philosophy was taken from the ideas of Plato."†

Dr. A. Clarke justly observes, that "every friend of rational piety and genuine Christianity, must lament that a man of so much learning and unaffected godliness, should have been led to countenance, much less to recommend a plan of interpreting the Divine Oracles, in many respects the most futile, absurd, and dangerous that can possibly be conceived."‡ No orthodox Bible student will for a moment admit the soundness of his system of Biblical interpretation. The great Martin Luther wrote, " Origen is to be avoided."

But, the Emperor patronized him, and finally Origen and his fellows prepared the way of Mystery, Babylon. Well may the London Quarterly Journal of Prophecy, ask, " Are we to call Origen a Christian ?" At least his opposition to Chiliasm should by the church be accounted as nothing, and those who mention his name in such connection, get to themselves no honor.

We are aware that Origen died a martyr, but his principles of Scripture interpretation we deplore and condemn. " Origen, Augustine, and Jerome," observes the critical author of the Theological and Literary Journal, "do not deny that the prediction of the restoration of the Israelites, the rebuilding of Jerusalem, the first resurrection, and the reign

* Milner's Ch. Hist., vol. i, p. 435.
† Sermon xl., vol. i, pp. 335, 337. ‡ Sacred Literature, p. 150.

of the Messiah, teach, if taken in their literal sense, what the Chiliasts ascribe to them. They admit it; but they maintain that that is not their true sense." How could they do otherwise, we ask, when Origen had "laid down the broad principle," writes President Porter, " that the scriptures are of little use to those who understand them as they are written!"

Still the Anti-millennarian Fathers held to the earth's renovation. "God will make new heavens and a new earth," wrote Jerome, " not other heavens and another earth, but the former ones changed into better;" and even as late as Gregory the Great, we find him saying, " others are not to be created, but these same renewed." Again, on Eccl. 3 : 14, he thus comments—" They will pass as to their present figure or appearance, but as to their substance, they will remain for ever."* This doctrine, like that of the world's sex-millennial duration, seems never to have been utterly abandoned, even during the middle ages, when the millennial reign was laid aside or deemed in the past.

ORIGEN'S ADMISSIONS.

Origen was an Anti-millennarian, but still we do not give him to the modern Post-millennialists. He allows a first and second resurrection, and we have yet to learn that he postpones the advent of Christ till the end of the seventh thousand years; "on the contrary," says Mr. Brooks, " he states his expectation of the renovation of all things in the seventh millennary of the world," and for this declaration of faith, Bishop Jeremy Taylor ranks Origen among the decided Millennarians, as also some others have done. Origen also denied, says Bishop Taylor, the reception of pious souls into heaven, immediately at death, but places their reward at the resurrection. Origen himself says, in the thirteenth book of

* Lib. xvii., ch. 2 and 5.

his work, against Celsus, "We do not deny the purging fire of the destruction of wickedness, and the renovation of all things," and the "Encyclopedia of Religious Knowledge" states that he taught "that the earth, after its conflagration, shall become habitable again, and be the mansion of men," and as this "renovation by fire" was to take place in the seventh millennium, he gives no support to the modern Whitbian system, but was virtually a Pre-millennialist. In his thirteenth Homily on Jeremiah, he says: "If any man shall preserve the washing of the Holy Spirit, he shall have his part in the first resurrection; but if any man be saved in the second resurrection only, it is the sinner that needeth the baptism of fire. Let us lay the Scriptures to heart, that we may be raised up with the saints, and have our lot with Jesus Christ." To admit two resurrections, is to admit a cardinal point in Millennarian doctrine. It is but just to say of Origen, that unlike Caius, he received the Apocalypse as genuine and canonical. In being an Anti-millennarian, he seems simply to have laid aside the Millennium as being the seventh thousand years, and expected an eternal age to commence at the coming of the Lord. Had he been a literalist he would not have done so, for he admits that "they who deny the millennium, are they who interpret the sayings of the prophets by a trope; but they who assert it are styled disciples of the letter of scripture only."

Says Mr. Brooks, "The majority of Christians did nevertheless continue some time after Origen, to maintain the Millennarian view."

VICTORINUS, A. D. 280—290.

He was the Bishop of Pettaw and the author of an Apocalyptic Commentary, which is mentioned by Jerome, who speaks of it as one of Millennarian views. From Dr. Elliott who has published an abstract of the same, we give the following items on the points under consideration. Victorinus made the twenty-four elders mean the twelve patriarchs and twelve apostles seated on thrones of judgment; the voices and thunderings from the throne he made notices of Christ's threats and of his coming to judgment. He speaks of the last times, and mingled with the continuous persecution of the saints, alludes to wars, pestilences, and famines which would precede Christ's coming. The earthquake of the sixth seal meant the last one, and the silence of the seventh seal he made to be the eternal rest. He contended that chronological order was not followed in the Apocalypse, but the Holy Spirit when He came to the end, returns, often, and repeats. He, with all the Fathers, who had not as yet adopted the year-day theory, made Antichrist's time three years and a half; and taught that he was at hand. The first beast meant Rome; the ten horns ten kings that would rise, three of whom would be plucked up by Antichrist; the woman was the city of Rome. The rider on the white horse was Christ, who will come and take the kingdom, a kingdom extending from the river to the world's end—the greater part of the earth being cleansed introductorily to it; and, finally, the last judgment and the eternity of the kingdom; the millennium itself not ending it."* Mede asserts that the writings of Victorinus and Sulpicius, who maintained Millennarian opinions, were authoritatively suppressed by Pope Damasus.† Victorinus was martyred during the persecution by Dioclesian, being faithful unto death, and evidently expecting a part in the first resurrection.

LACTANTIUS, A. D. 300.

Lactantius was born about A. D. 250, and flourished as a writer A. D. 310. He was tutor to Constantine's heir, and the purity of his Latinity gained for him the title of "the Christian Cicero." Mosheim styles him "the most eloquent

---

* Horæ Apoc., vol. iv. † Mede's Works p. 664.

of the Latin Fathers." He often quotes the Sibylline verses and probably for the same reason that Paul quotes the Pagan poets. (Acts 17: 28.) Says Stuart, "that he makes such appeals for the sake of the heathen seems very evident." Stuart allows him to have been "a zealous Chiliast." Jerome, the Anti-millennarian, charges him with the error of the Manichees, but Dr. Lardner, in his "Credibility of the gospel history," has satisfactorily vindicated him from this charge. Says Dr. Lardner: "It is well known that Lactantius expected a terrestrial reign of Christ for a thousand years before the general judgment. Jerome has ridiculed his millennary notions, and took the same freedom with Irenæus, Tertullian, and other Christians who held the same sentiment."* Lactantius taught a mixed Millennium, as do many now, but Dr. Duffield and Mr. Brooks have vindicated him from the charge of sensualism preferred against him by Jerome. He asserted two resurrections according to the Revelation, and speaks at large upon the Millennial period, which he denominates "the thousand years of the heavenly empire, when righteousness shall reign on earth." In his Book of Divine Institutions, he says: "Let philosophers know, who number thousands of years since the beginning of the world, that the six thousandth year is not yet concluded or ended. But that number being fulfilled, of necessity there must be an end, and the state of human things be transformed into that which is better. Because all the works of God were finished in six days, it is necessary that the world should remain in this state six ages; that is, six thousand years. Because having finished the works he rested on the seventh day and blessed it, it is necessary that at the end of the six thousandth year all wickedness should be abolished out of the earth, and justice should reign for a thousand years. When the Son of God shall have destroyed

---

* Lardner's Credibility, vol. iii. pp. 316, 319, 520.

injustice, and shall have restored the just to life, he shall be conversant among men a thousand years, and shall rule with a most righteous government. At the same time the Prince of Devils shall be bound with chains, and shall be in custody for a thousand years of the heavenly kingdom, lest he should attempt anything evil against the people of God. When the thousand years of the kingdom, that is, seven thousand years, shall draw toward a conclusion, Satan shall be loosed again; and then shall be that second and public resurrection of us all, wherein the unjust shall be raised."* Having enlarged on this topic, he thus concludes: "This is the doctrine of the holy prophets which we Christians follow, this is our wisdom." Whitby allows that Lactantius taught "this Millennium belongs to all the just which ever were from the beginning of the world." Following the erroneous chronology of the Septuagint, as did other of the early Christians, Lactantius supposed the Millennium or consummation would commence about 200 years from his time. Dr. Elliott gives an abstract of the Apocalyptic scheme of Lactantius.† It is interesting, and we refer the reader to it for a better understanding of the views of this eloquent Chiliast, who, in his time, nobly endeavored to sustain the Millennial truth. Lactantius died at Treves about A. D. 325.

DIONYSIUS, A. D. 250.

Dionysius was Bishop of Alexandria. He was a disciple of Origen, and of course an Anti-millennarian. He opposed Nepos, his contemporary, and won over Coracion to his faith, but in his opposition questioned the cannonical authority of the Apocalyse, and denied it was written by John the apostle: "From which," says Brooks, "a fair inference may be drawn that he found himself hard pressed by passages in that book," and Dr. Duffield has shown that he only received

---

* Lactantius Div. Inst., Book vii ch. 24.   † Hor. Apoc., vol. iv. p. 824.

the book at all from mere motives of policy. Prof. Stuart intimates that his object in denying that John wrote it was to take away from the Montanists their apostolic authority for the Millennial doctrine; and says, "It may well be doubted, I think, whether he would have thought of assailing the Apocalypse if he had never heard of Nepos' book," and Dr. Elliott declares that "It was in the act of writing against Millennarians that he pronounced judgment against it." Here again we have the character of the opposition, and it amounts to this: that if the Revelation is to be received as canonical, the primitive doctrine of the Millennium is of God. The Chiliastic party were still strong after this; and therefore as Burnet remarks, "We do not find that Dionysius' opposition had any great effect," though doubtless the doctrine had begun to be corrupted by its advocates. Dionysius charged his opponents with persuading men "to hope for only small and mortal things in the kingdom of God (i. e. the Millennium), even such as are visible now," on which Henry D. Ward justly remarks: "From this it appears how little he regarded the Millennium of time." As yet we observe the Augustinian Millennial theory had not been broached, and both Origen and Dionysius, instead of locating the Millennium in the past, simply laid it aside, commencing an eternal unbroken age at Christ's coming.*

THE RELATIVES OF OUR LORD. A. D. 95

Hegesippus, a converted Jew, who flourished A. D. 150, relates that in the fifteenth year of Domitian, while he was engaged in persecuting the church of God, there were yet living the grandchildren of Judas, called the brother of our Lord according to the flesh. Upon the Emperor's issuing an edict that all the descendants of David should be slain, on

---

* See Eusebius, B. vi. ch. xxxv. Ward's Hist. Mill., p. 19 Stuart vol. i. p. 844.

account of his fear that Christ would appear, these persons were brought before Domitian. In his presence they witnessed the following "good confession."

"He put the question whether they were of David's race, and they confessed that they were. He then asked them what property they had, or how much money they owned. And both of them answered that they had between them only nine thousand denarii,* and this they had not in silver, but in the value of a piece of land, containing only thirty-nine acres; from which they raised their taxes and supported themselves by their own labor. Then they also began to show their hands, exhibiting the hardness of their bodies, and the callousity formed by incessant labor on their hands, as evidence of their own labor. When asked also, respecting Christ and his kingdom, what was its nature, and when and where it was to appear; they replied that it was not a temporal nor an earthly kingdom, but celestial and angelic: that it would appear at the end of the world, when, coming in glory, he would judge the quick and the dead, and give to every one according to his works. Upon which Domitian, despising them, made no reply, but treating them with contempt, as simpletons, commanded them to be dismissed, and by a decree ordered the persecution to cease. Thus delivered, they ruled the churches both as witnesses and relatives of the Lord. When peace was established, they continued living even to the times of Trajan."†

MANY NAMES, A. D. 125–430.

Proceeding, we notice *Commodian*, a Latin author, who flourished A. D. 270, of whom Dr. Lardner writes: "He heartily embraced the doctrine of the expected Millennium;" *Gregory*, of *Nyssa*, who died A. D. 389; *Sulpicius*, of the 4th century; *Paulinus*, Bishop of Antioch, who died 431

---

* About $1.450. † Eusebius' Eccl. Hist., B. iii., Chap. xix, xx.

and also *Apollinaris* had not entirely renounced Chiliasm; *Quadratus*, Bishop of Athens, A. D. 125, also, *Aristides*, his contemporary; *Pantænus*, who flourished A. D. 150; *Theophilus*, who died 182; *Hermias* and *Athenagoras*, of the 2d century; also, the names of *Seraphion*, *Agrippa Castor*, *Claudius Apollinarius*, *Philip*, of *Gortyra*, *Miltiades Modestus*, and *Apollonius*, the most of whose writings are lost; others of whom do not mention the subject, but when they do revert to it, says Brooks, they support Chiliastic views.

COUNCIL OF NICE. A D. 325

This first general Church Council was called by Constantine the Great, (who was present,) and was, according to Eusebius, composed of 250 Bishops; Socratés says 318. Moshcim affirms we know very little about their acts and doings. It assumed authority over the conscience, expelled Arius, and framed what is called the Nicene Creed, which Gelasius Cyzicenus has given in his history of this Council. "We quote from these acts," says Dr. Duffield, "because it furnishes incidentally, some valuable testimony as to what continued to be at that period the method of interpretation most prevalent." On the resurrection state, the Council says: "We expect new heavens and a new earth, according to the Holy Scriptures, at the appearing of the great God, and our Saviour, Jesus Christ. And then, as Daniel says, ' the saints of the Most High shall take the kingdom,' and there shall be a pure earth, holy, a ' land of the living and not of the dead,' which David foreseeing by the eye of faith, ' I believe to see the goodness of the Lord in the land of the living'—the land of the meek and humble. Christ says, ' Blessed are the meek, for they shall inherit the earth,' and the prophet says, ' the feet of the meek and humble shall tread upon it.'"[*] Says Mr. Brooks: "The majority of the

[*] History Act. Council of Nice, by Gelasius.

churches must, at the period of this Council, have still held to the primitive method of interpretation." Mede remarks: "Judge by this (notwithstanding fifty years' opposition,) how powerful the Chiliastic party yet was at the time of this Council. By some of whom, if this formula were not framed and composed, yet was it thus moderated as you see, that both parties might accept it as being delivered in the terms and language of Scripture."* The London Quarterly Journal of Prophecy says: "It is obvious that nearly a century after the days of Origen and Dionysius, Chiliastic doctrine was still truly the creed of the church, or at least of the greater part of it. In this Council it stands before us, not only dissociated from heresy, but opposed to it; nay, not only opposed to heresy, but united to what was sound and holy." And Dr. Burnet writes as follows: "The Millennial kingdom of Christ was the general doctrine of the primitive church from the times of the Apostles to the Council of Nice, *inclusively*. According to the opinion of these Fathers, there will be a kingdom of Christ upon earth, and moreover in the new heavens and new earth."† Such is the testimony of the Nicene Fathers. Still the Millennial truth which received their sanction was crushed to death at last under the iron heel of Antichrist. But it died hard!

EUSEBIUS, BISHOP OF CÆSAREA. A. D. 325.

He was born A. D. 267, and died A. D. 340. He was the first writer of ecclesiastical history, and we are indebted to him for many things concerning the early church, but as Burnet observes, "he was a back friend to the Millennary doctrine, and represented every thing to its disadvantage;" and Brooks affirms that "his statements on this head are contradictory and absurd." He represents Irenæus as hav-

---

* Mede's Works p. 813   † Burnet, Vol. ii. p. 184. Mosheim, chap. 5.

ing obtained his Millennary views from Pa*' .s,* whereas we know from the writings of Irenæus that his faith n this doctrine was founded on the Scriptures. He also sets forth Papias as having received the doctrine solely by the way of "oral tradition," as though Papias knew nothing of the Apocalypse, nor received his Millennial views from it, which, says Elliott, is not true, farther remarking, that " his untrustworthiness and tendencies to inaccuracies on any Millennary subject, are sufficiently apparent." Jerome pronounces him a learned man, but not a catholic, (i.e. as then understood, not orthodox,) and also calls him the " Prince of the Arians." Dr. Elliott, (who gives his language,) Mr. Brooks, and Prof. Stuart, affirm that he disparaged the authority of the Apocalypse, and insinuated that perhaps it was the work of Cerinthus. Jeremy Taylor suspects him of having endeavored to corrupt and falsify the Nicene creed,† and Dr. Duffield accuses him of time serving, having boasted of his conversations with the Emperor Constantine. Eusebius was moreover a miserable expounder of the Bible, for he quotes Ps. 46: 9, 10, Isa. 35, also Rev. 21, and other Millennial prophecies as being fulfilled in the Constantinian glory of the church, which he affirmed at that time "looked like the very image of the kingdom of Christ." The city built by the Emperor, at Jerusalem, with the church of the Holy Sepulchre, he suggested, was the New Jerusalem of Revelation; which was indeed, as Burnet exclaims, "A wonderful invention!" And to sum up all, at the very time when, as Elliott declares, intimations were every where given, that the great apostacy had begun, the splendor-blinded Eusebius, in the language of Dr. Cumming, " dreamed the Apocalyptic Millennium had commenced!"

* Eccl. Hist., iii.29.   † Liberty of Proph., p. 954.

CYRIL, A. D. 350.

Cyril was Bishop of Jerusalem. He was born A. D. 315. Though an Anti-millennarian, as Mosheim observes, he "is justly celebrated for his Catechetical Discourses," in which he is often truly eloquent. Cyril was of the age of Julian, the apostate, who reviled the Christians of his day for expecting the kingdom of God. This kingdom Cyril looked for, insisting much upon its eternity, and teaching no temporal Millennium. He, says Elliott, like the Fathers before him, explained the four wild beasts of Daniel 7th to be the Babylonian, Persian, Macedonian, and Roman empires, and thought that when Rome fell it would be dissolved into ten cotemporaneous kingdoms, and then Antichrist,—whom he called "some great man raised up by the Devil"—at first mild, &c., —would come and eradicate three of the ten kings, and subjugate the other seven, and reign three years and a half, persecuting the church; then Christ would destroy him. Dropping the Millennium or seventh chiliad, he looked for Christ to come, and renovating the earth, introduce an eternal state.[*]
Cyril says, "Do thou look for the true Christ, the Son of God, the only Begotten, who is henceforth to come not from the earth, but from heaven, appearing to all more bright than any lightning, or other brilliance, with angels for his guards, that he may judge quick and dead, and reign with a kingdom heavenly, eternal, and without end. Be sure to settle your belief in this point also, since there are many who say that Christ's kingdom has an end." Again he says, "Adam received the doom, 'cursed be the ground—thorns and thistles, &c.' For this cause Jesus wears the thorns that he might cancel the doom; for this cause also was he buried in the earth, that the cursed earth might receive, instead of the curse, the blessing. Our Lord Jesus Christ then comes from heaven with glory at the end of this world, in the last

[*] Hor. Apoc. vol. 4.

day. For this world shall have an end, and this created world shall be made anew; for since corruption and theft and adultery, and every sort of sins have been poured forth over the earth, and blood has been mingled with blood in the world, therefore that this wondrous dwelling place may not remain filled with iniquity, this world shall pass away that that fairer world may be made manifest." He then quotes Isa. 34 : 4, also Matt. 24 : 29, and adds that the Lord will roll up the heavens, not that he may destroy them, but that he may raise them up again more beautiful. He also bids us " venture not to declare when these things shall be, nor on the other hand abandon thyself to slumber, for he saith, 'Watch, &c.' But it behoveth us to know the signs of the end, and we are looking for Christ."* He says nothing about a spiritual reign, but as Mr. Ward observes, reproves those sentiments advocated by Post-millennialists. He died A. D. 386.

EPIPHANIUS, A. D. 375.

Epiphanius was Bishop of Salamasis. He was born A. D. 322, and died in 403. Epiphanius was a Millennarian, and testifies that the doctrine was held by many of his time. Quoting the words of Paulinus, Bishop of Antioch, concerning one Vitalius, whom he highly commends for his piety, orthodoxy, and learning, he says: " Moreover, others have affirmed that the venerable man would say, that in the first resurrection we shall accomplish a certain Millennary of years :" on which Epiphanius observes: " And that indeed this Millennary term is written of in the Apocalypse of John, and is received of very many of them that are godly is manifest."*

Here are one or two more voices on the Millennium in the fourth century, but it had evidently become corrupted and

* Cyril, Ox. Ed. pp. 152, 184, 186, 190, 199. † Epiph. Lib., 3, 2.

unpopular, and was dying away. Still the Fathers of this century, though Anti-millennarian, looked for no blissful era for the church this side the resurrection of the just. And they believed a pure and unmixed age would then commence. So *we* believe.*

AMBROSE, A. D. 400.

Ambrose, Bishop of Milan, was born in A. D. 333, and died 420. We do not know as this Father says any thing about the Millennium. Dr. Elliott says that "he explained the apostacy of St. Paul, to mean an apostacy from true religion, and that Antichrist would come and seize on the kingdom, claiming for himself divine authority, and that he referred to the strife between the Goths and Romans, as well as other rumors of war, pestilence, &c., as evidences that the world was near its end."† He looked for no restoration of the Jews prior to the resurrection of the dead, and with Cyril made the Sabbath a type of an endless age. He cannot be regarded as at all favoring the Whitbian system of postponing the advent till the end of the seventh chiliad, and the completion of the world's conversion, for he says, "The gospel is preached that the world may be destroyed; for the preaching of the gospel has gone out into the whole world, and therefore we see the end of the world approaching, &c." Thus his voice is virtually Pre-millennial.

CHRYSOSTOM, A. D. 400.

Chrysostom was Bishop of Constantinople. He was born A. D. 354. He was learned and eloquent, and is styled the Homer of orators; and though an ecclesiastical writer, as Dr. Duffield observes, he is silent with regard to the Millennium. Elliott says that he explains the four kingdoms of Daniel as did Cyril, and made the fourth, or Roman empire, to be the let or hindrance to Antichrist's manifestation

* Brooks on Proph., p. 55.   † Hor. Apoc., vols. ii, iv.

alluded to by St. Paul. He also regards the "mystery of iniquity" as being the persecuting spirit working in Nero, in Paul's time, and the abomination of desolation spoken of by Daniel, he made the Roman armies under Titus. With his cotemporaries, he looked for no glad era for the church before the advent, but concerning the approaching future, out of which loomed up the dark form of Antichrist, he says: "We are now at the twelfth hour: the purity of justice is leaving the world; the sun is gathering in his rays, and darkness is covering the whole earth;" and again he truly sketches the dispensation, when he observes that, "As Rome succeeded Greece, so Antichrist is to succeed Rome, and Christ our Saviour Antichrist." Though he was a monk, and, perhaps, an Anti-millennarian, still this testimony affords no support to the spiritual view. And he confirms it still more by quoting Math. 24: 14; making its fulfillment a sign of the "last day," saying, "Attend with care to what is said. He said not when it hath been believed by all men, but when it hath been preached to all. For this cause, he also said for a witness to the nations to show that he doth not wait for all men to believe, and then for him to come: since the phrase, 'for a witness,' hath this meaning,—for accusation, for reproof, for condemnation of them that have not believed."*
So speaks Chrysostom, who died A. D. 404.

HILARY, A. D. 350.

Hilary, Bishop of Poictiers, flourished in the 4th century, and wrote on the Apocalypse. He understood the reign of Christ, and the final judgment to be introduced at his second coming, when, as he thought, the 6th and 7th seals were to be broken. He also attached a Christian sense to the Jewish symbols of the Old Testament, such as Zion, Jerusalem, Israel, the Temple, &c., and looked for the Antichrist to be

* Vide Homilies, part i. p. 141, Oxford Trans.

developed within the professing Christian church. While commenting on the transfiguration, (" after six days, &c.,") Hilary refers to the old idea of a seventh sabbatical Millennary; saying that as Christ was transfigured in glory after the six days, so after the world's 6000 years there would be manifested the glory of Christ's eternal kingdom. He constantly insisted that the day and hour of the consummation was a secret with God, but knowing the doubtfulness of our world's chronology, he still maintained the idea of the world's sex-millennial duration.* He died A. D. 367.

JEROME, A. D. 380.

Jerome was born in Dalmatia, A. D. 330. Died A. D. 420. He was a learned and voluminous writer, but was a bitter Anti-millennarian, and decidedly a monk and a Roman Catholic. The Encyclopedia of Religious Knowledge informs us that he founded a convent at Bethlehem, and through his exhortations many fashionable ladies there and at Rome became nuns. Mosheim affirms that he with many other Fathers of the fourth century were tinctured with the corrupt principle of the two monstrous errors of the age, namely, " It is an act of virtue to deceive and lie, when by that means the interests of the church may be promoted; second, Errors in religion when maintained and adhered to after proper admonition are punishable with civil penalties and corporeal torture," and in everything, while he applauds his labor and genius, he gives Jerome a miserable character. The London Quarterly Journal of Prophecy, says of this century: " Jerome, in whose works the seeds of most every Popish error may be found, led the opposition against the Millennium." And the learned Elliott has shown that Jerome virtually advocated saint and martyr worship, veneration of relics, the well nigh infallibility of the Bishop of Rome, prac

---

* Hilary. Benedictine Ed. See abstract in Elliott's Hor. Apoc.

ticed penance, &c., &c. Such were the principles of Jerome, and with regard to the form of his opposition, as Dr. Duffield justly observes, "He teems with abuse and ridicule in relation to the Millennium, and by his general character for fierceness, acrimony, and ribaldry, toward all who differ from him, has forfeited all claims upon our respect." All Millennial historians represent him as harsh and unfair. Brooks calls him "a vehement adversary of the doctrine." H. D. Ward, "an unmerciful scoffer, not always regarding fairness." Mede, "a most unequal relator of the opinions of his adversaries," and the Journal of Prophecy calls him one of the most resolute enemies of the doctrine that ever wrote." Dr. Burnet styles him, "a rough and rugged saint, and an unfair adversary, that usually ran down with heat and violence what stood in his way," and that "he always represents the Millennary doctrine after a Judaical rather than a Christian manner." He held the Origenistic system, and says Elliott, he taught that "the Apocalypse was all to be spiritually understood, because otherwise Judaic fables would have to be acquiesced in ; such as the rebuilding of Jerusalem, and the renewal in its temple of carnal ceremonies ;" a false conclusion obvious to every Bible student. But perhaps the Millennium was made carnal by its advocates, thus giving some occasion for Jerome's laughter, and the more we presume did he wish to oppose it, it being now unpopular, and he being secretary to Pope Damasus, (who used every means to suppress it,) and desiring like many now to keep in with public opinion. Said Luther, "Jerome is to be avoided!"

But Jerome made some capital admissions, and held much truth, and we cannot give him to Post-millennialists. He taught the doctrine of the redemption of the earth and its renovation by fire, with which he believed its interior filled and held, says Elliott, to only the conversion, not the national restoration of the Jews. On the prayer "Thy kingdom come," he says: "They ask for the kingdom of the whole world, that Satan may cease to reign in the world." His views of the metalic image; the four wild beasts; the man of sin, his origin, &c., were similar to those of Cyril, Hippolytus and other Fathers, and he makes a twofold destruction of the Roman Empire: the one its desolation and dissolution by a breaking up into ten kingdoms, introductory to Antichrist's manifestation; the other its total and final destruction, to take place on account of Antichrist's blasphemies at "the triumphant advent of the Great God," and "we are perfectly sure," he says, "that after the second advent of our Lord nothing will be base, nothing terrestrial; but then will be the celestial kingdom which was first promised in the gospel," which, observes Henry Ward, is "sound doctrine." He also taught that the world would endure but 6,000 years, and at their termination (which he placed A. D. 500,) the consummation would occur, and Christ come: thus giving no support to Post-millennialism, but was virtually a Pre-millennialist, while like many others an Anti-millennarian. Jerome used to say, that it seemed to him as if the trumpet of the last day was always sounding in his ear, saying, "Arise, ye dead, and come to judgment!" And now we call the reader's attention to Jerome's admission, where he is constrained to allow the truth, and by which we may learn that if the Chiliasts of A. D. 400 were really in the minority, they were still a great multitude in spite of opposition. On Jer. 19:10, he says, that "he durst not condemn the (Millennial) doctrine, because many ecclesiastical persons and martyrs affirm the same." And again, speaking of the Millennarian Apollinarius, he remarks: "An author whom not only the men of his own sect, but most of our people likewise, follow on this point (Chiliasm) so that it is not difficult to prove what a multitude of persons will be offended with me." So much for Jerome. We have been particular that the reader may know through whose opposition the Millennium fell. Rev. Henry Morris, a Post-millennialist, in his work entitled "Modern Chiliasm Refuted," truly says, "Jerome and other writers of this period were *great scoffers* at the doctrine, and the consequence was, that it fell into disrepute, and entirely dwindled away, so that we hear scarcely no more of it, until the tenth and a portion of the eleventh century, the Reformation and the present time."*

But this admission of Mr. Morris every close thinker will at once see is prejudicial, nay, even fatal to Post-millennialism! It allows that Rome banished the true Millennium, and more even than this!

AUGUSTINE. A. D. 390.

Augustine was Bishop of Hippo. Born A. D. 358, and died in 434. He was contemporary with Jerome, and is acknowledged to have been a great and justly celebrated divine. Though not thoroughly free from the superstitions of his times, yet with regard to the doctrines of free grace in Christ, as Dr. Cumming says, "Augustine was a brilliant exception, and continued evangelical," and Milner also states that "the light from his writings glimmered through many ages, down even to the Reformation," Gibbon hinting that Rome had a secret repugnance to them on this account. He was once a Chiliast, but abandoned that view through the influence and misrepresentations of his enemies, particularly Eusebius, as Mr. Brooks argues. He then developed what is usually called the Augustinian view of the Millennium, which afterwards became very prevalent, and which constitutes a new era in its history. On the first view he expresses himself: "Those who have supposed from these words, Rev. 20 : 6, that there shall be a first corporeal resurrection, have been moved among other things chiefly

* See Jerome's Comment on Jeremiah, 19 : 10. De Instit. Cap. xv. Horæ. Apoc., vol. 4. Lond. Quar. Jour. Proph., No. 7. Mede's Works, p. 602. Ward's Hist. Mill., p. 21. Mosheim, vol. 1, p. 116.

by the number of the thousand years; as if there ought to be among the saints a sabbatism, as it were in a holy vacation after their six thousand years of trouble; which opinion would indeed be tolerable if it should be believed that spiritual delights should redound to the saints in that Sabbath, by the presence of the Lord, for we also were ourselves formerly of that opinion." Augustine's objection does not militate against *us*, for we hold to a pure Millennium of spiritual delights by the personal presence of the Lord, and his admission is that such an one can be tolerated. The abuse of Millennial truth evidently caused him to reject it as of carnal tendency; so Elliott supposes.

On the four kingdoms of Daniel's prophecy, Augustine made the first three to be Babylon, Chaldea, and Macedon, and the fourth to be Rome, as did, according to Jerome, all the previous Fathers. He identifies the little horn of the fourth beast with St. Paul's man of sin, and St. John's Antichrist; the Roman empire he thought hindering the revelation of the latter, who would bring in a great religious apostacy, pretended miracles, etc. On the question of the Jews, "Augustine," says Elliott, "only speaks of their conversion, never, I believe, of their national restoration in Palestine." In this he agreed with Jerome, who held that the local Jerusalem would never be rebuilt, but remain in ruins to the end of the world. He thus describes the character of the virgins of Math. 25th: "But men continually say to themselves, 'Lo the day of judgment is coming now, so many evils are happening; so many tribulations thicken; behold all things which the prophets have spoken have well nigh fulfilled, the day of judgment is already at hand.' They who speak thus and speak in faith, go out as it were, with such thoughts, to meet the bridegroom." He represented the world as "old and full of troubles; distressed by the heavy breathing of old age," and taught the earth's renovation at Christ's coming: saying on the Lord's prayer, Math. 6:10, "His kingdom will come when the resurrection of the dead shall have taken place; for then He will come himself. And when the dead are raised, he will divide them, as he himself says, and he shall set some on the right hand and some on the left. To those who shall be on the right hand he will say, 'Come ye blessed.' This is what we wish and pray for when we say, 'Thy kingdom come,' that it may come to us. For if we shall be reprobate, that kingdom will come to others but not to us. But if we shall be of that number who belong to the members of his only begotten Son, his kingdom will come to us and will not tarry. For are there as many ages yet remaining as have already passed away? The apostle John hath said, 'My little children, it is the last time.' Let us watch now, &c." On the earth's renovation, he writes: "By the change of things the world will not entirely perish or be annihilated. Its form, or external appearance, will be changed, but not its substance. The figure of this world will pass away by the general conflagration. The qualities of the corruptible elements of which our world is composed, which were proportioned to our corruptible bodies, will be entirely destroyed by the fire; and the substance of those elements will acquire new qualities which will be suitable to our immortal bodies, and thus the world by becoming more perfect, will be proportioned to the then improved state of the human body." So taught Augustine. The world's duration he made sex-millennial, and says Dr. Elliott, "with the other Anti-millennarian Fathers of the fourth and fifth centuries, explained the Sabbatical seventh day, not of a seventh Sabbatical Millennium of rest, but an eternal Sabbath—a view generally adopted afterwards."[*] In viewing the advent and end of the world, as occurring on the termination of 6000 years, Augustine negatives a Post-millennial advent.

---

[*] Augustin De Civit, Lib. 20, c. 5, 14, 16. Homil., vol. i. pp. 48, 358, 252, 83, 70. Ox. ed.

CONFIRMATORY TESTIMONY TO THE PRE-MILLENNIAL FAITH OF THE EARLY CHURCH.

NATHANIEL LARDNER, D. D. Born in Kent, England, 1684. Died 1768. An erudite, voluminous author, and a name—says Dr. Clarke—never to be mentioned but with respect. An Anti-m. he is, but of the early church, and Chiliasm he thus testifies: "The Millennium has been a favorite doctrine of some ages, and has had the patronage of the learned as well as the vulgar among Christians."* "It must be owned that the orthodox Millennarians do speak of one thousand years reign of Christ before the general resurrection; which good men, having been raised from the dead should spend on this earth, when there shall be extraordinary plenty of the fruits of the earth." "They certainly grounded their sentiments upon the Revelation and upon other books of the Old and New Testament universally received."† Such is the testimony of one who, like Bishop Russell, denies the theory we advocate.

WILLIAM CHILLINGWORTH. Born at Oxford, England, 1602. Died a captive, 1644. He was Chancellor of Salisbury, and a powerful theologian. On the early catholicity of Chiliasm, he writes as follows, while controverting Romanism: "That this doctrine is by the present Romish Church held false and heretical, I think no man will deny. That the same doctrine was by the church of the next age after the Apostles (mark this!) held true and catholic, I prove by these two reasons: First, whatever doctrine is believed and taught by the most eminent Fathers of any age of the church, and by none of their contemporaries opposed or condemned

---

* Credibility of the Gospel History, Vol. iv. p. 513. † Ibid, Vol. iv., pp. 640, 641.

that is to be esteemed the catholic doctrine of the church of those times; but the doctrine of the Millennaries was believed and taught by the most eminent Fathers of the age next after the Apostles, and by none of that age opposed or condemned; therefore, it was the catholic doctrine of those times." Quoting the Fathers in proof, he continues: "And Second, whatever doctrine is taught by the Fathers of any age, not as doctors, but as witnesses of the tradition of the church, that is, not as their own opinion, but as the doctrine of the church of their time, neither did any contradict them in it: *ergo*, it is undoubtedly to be so esteemed."* Again, he says: "It appears manifest out of this book of Irenæus, that the doctrine of the Chiliasts was in his judgment Apostolic tradition, as also it was esteemed (for aught appears to the contrary) by all the doctors, and saints, and martyrs of, or about his time, for all that speak of it, or whose judgments in the point are any way recorded, are for it; and Justin Martyr professeth that all good and orthodox Christians of his time believed it, and those that did not, he reckons among heretics."†

JOHN LAURENCE MOSHEIM, D. D. Born 1695. Died 1755. He was a celebrated German Protestant theologian, and writer of a well known and valuable Ecclesiastical History. He was a Post-m. Under the "Third Century," he says: "Long before this period, an opinion had prevailed that Christ was to come and reign a thousand years among men, before the entire and final dissolution of this world. This opinion, which had hitherto met with no opposition, was variously interpreted by different persons, &c. But in this century its credit began to decline, principally through the influence and authority of Origen, who opposed it with the greatest warmth, because it was incompatible with some of his favorite sentiments."‡

* Works, fol. ed., p. 174. † Ibid, p. 347. ‡ Ecclesiastical History, Vol. i., p. 89, Chap. 3, Sec. 2.

Bishop Russell, Professor of Eccl. History of the Scottish Episcopal Church, writing on the Millennium, says:— "The Jews and their followers in primitive times, understood the Millennium literally: the word had no double sense in their creed; it was not in their estimation the emblem or shadow of better things to come; on the contrary, it denoted the actual visible appearance of the Messiah, and the establishment of his kingdom upon earth as the Sovereign of the elect people of God." * * "The hope of such a consummation was not superseded by his (Christ's) residence on earth. The first Christians, on the contrary, looked with a more earnest desire for the new heavens and new earth promised to their fathers, and connected their expectations, too, with the ancient opinion that this globe was to undergo a material change at the end of 6000 years, throwing off all the imperfections which had arisen from the guilt of its inhabitants, and being fitted for the habitation of justice, benevolence, and purity, during a blessed Millennium—the Sabbath of this terrestrial globe. * * So far as we view the question in reference to the sure and certain hope entertained by the Christian world, that the Redeemer would appear on earth, and exercise authority during a thousand years, there is good ground for the assertion of Mede, Dodwell, Burnet and other writers on the same side, that down to the beginning of the fourth century, the belief was universal and undisputed."*

Such is the testimony of an extreme Anti-millennarian, and one who styles the doctrine a "Rabbinical fable which had no connection with the Gospel."

Professor George Bush, of New York city, the justly celebrated Hebrew scholar. An Anti-m. He admits that "There is ample evidence that the doctrine of the Chiliasts

* Discourse on the Millennium, pp. 47, 84, 89, 236.

was actually the catholic faith of more than one century," that even "during the first three centuries it was very extensively embraced. Again, "During the first ages of the church, when the style of Christianity was 'to believe, to love, and to suffer,' this sentiment seems to have obtained a prevalence so general, as to be properly entitled to all but absolute catholic," and that "the belief of it was calculated to produce, and did produce results of a most auspicious character, which, under the circumstances, a different and even a more correct construction of the Sacred Oracles would have failed to effect."* Such is the language of one who commences the Apocalyptic Millennium with the Constantinian epoch.

Dr. BURTON, Regius Professor of Theology at Christ's church, Oxford, England, whom the late Dr. Welsh styles "the learned and excellent." Though a decided Post-m. he says: "Papias, who heard the apostle John, and was a companion of Polycarp, held that there would be a period of a thousand years after the resurrection of the dead, when the kingdom of Christ would be established on the earth." Again, "It cannot be denied that Papias, Irenæus, Justin Martyr, and all the other ecclesiastical writers, believed, literally, that the saints would rise in the first resurrection, and reign with Christ upon earth previous to the general resurrection," but he observes, "Upon the whole, we may safely conclude that after the middle of the third century, the doctrine was not received as that of the catholic church, though it continued to be held by a few who were called Milliarri, Millenarri, Chiliastæ," &c.†

JOHN WM. AUGUSTUS NEANDER, D.D. born 1789. A late distinguished German Protestant Theologian, of Jewish origin, Professor of the University at Berlin, a mem-

* Bush Mill., chap. i., ii. † Burton's Bampton Lecture for 1829.

ber of the Lutheran church, and author of an Ecclesiastical History. He is doubtless of the school of Post-m's. Though he affirms that "the minds of some took a fanciful turn, and they propagated a gross and sensual Chiliasm," yet he bears the following noble testimony to the Pre-millennial faith of the early church:

"They were accustomed to consider the church only in its opposition to the heathen state, and it was far from entering their thoughts, that by the natural development of circumstances, under the guidance of Providence, this opposition should hereafter cease. They believed that the struggle of the Christian church with the heathen state would continue on, until the victory should be conceded to it, through the immediate interposition of God, and through the return of Christ. It was natural enough that the Christians should willingly employ their thoughts in the prospect of this victory, during the seasons of persecution. It was thus that many formed a picture to themselves which had come to them from the Jews, and which suited with their condition. This was the idea of a Millennial reign, which the Messiah should establish on earth at the close of the whole career of the world, during which all the saints of all ages, were to live together in holy communion with each other. As the world was created in six days, and according to Psa. 90: 4, a thousand years in the sight of God is but as one day, so the world was supposed to endure six thousand years in its present condition; and as the Sabbath day was the day of rest, so this Millennial reign was to form the seventh thousand year period of the world's existence, at the close of the whole temporal dispensation connected with the world. In the midst of persecution it was an attractive thought for the Christians to look to a period when their church, purified and perfected, should be triumphant even on earth, the theatre of their present sufferings. In the manner in which this notion was conceived by many, there was nothing unchristian in it. They imagined the happiness of this period, in a spiritual manner, and one that corresponded well with the real nature of Christianity; for they conceived under that notion only the general dominion of God's will, the undisturbed and blessed union and intercourse of the whole communion of saints, and the restoration of harmony between man as sanctified, and all nature as refined and ennobled."*

EDWARD GIBBON.—Born at Putney, England, 1737. Died 1794. He was very learned, and is accounted as one of the greatest of the English historians. Was at first a Papist, but afterwards settled into a confirmed Infidel. He sneers at the doctrine of the Millennium, and also misrepresents it, as he does the entire Christian system, but contributes his testimony relating to the Pre-millennialism of the early church in the following language: "The ancient and popular doctrine of the Millennium was intimately connected with the second coming of Christ." Then stating the early views with his own gloss, etc., he continues: "The assurance of such a Millennium was carefully inculcated by a succession of Fathers from Justin Martyr and Irenæus, who conversed with the immediate disciples of the apostles down to Lactantius, who was preceptor to the son of Constantine. Though it might not be universally received, it appears to have been the reigning sentiment of the orthodox believers; and it seemed so well adapted to the desires and apprehensions of mankind, that it must have contributed in a very considerable degree to the progress of the Christian faith. But when the edifice of the church was almost completed, the temporary support was laid aside. The doctrine of Christ's reign on the earth was first treated as a profound allegory, was considered by degrees as a doubtful and useless opinion, and was at length rejected as the absurd invention

* Neander's Church History, vol. i. pp. 403, 404.

of heresy and fanaticism. A mysterious prophecy, which still forms a part of the sacred canon, but which was thought to favor the exploded sentiment, has very narrowly escaped the proscription of the church."* We suppose he means the Apocalypse.

From THE AMERICAN ENCYCLOPÆDIA we give the following extracts. "Chiliasm, or the expectation of a blessed Millennium, became a universal belief among the Christians of the first centuries, which was strengthened by the prophecies contained in Revelations of the times which were to precede and indicate the happy times of the Millennium."

"Before it began, human misery, according to their opinion, was to rise to the highest degree; then the overthrow of the Roman empire would follow, and from its ruins would proceed a new state of things; in which the faithful who had risen from the dead, with those still living would enjoy ineffable happiness * * * and the blessed reside in the heavenly Jerusalem, which would descend from heaven in extraordinary splendor and grandeur to receive them in its magnificent habitations."

"This faith the Christian teachers of the first centuries were unanimous in adopting and promulgating. * * * When Christianity became the predominant religion of the Roman Empire, it lost its interest for the multitude; victory, liberty, and security, which the Millennium was expected to bring, being now actually enjoyed." The Encyclopædist is careful to notice the fact, as do the others, that they regarded the Apocalyptic Millennium as being the seventh Chiliad of the world's existence.†

Quotations to any amount like the foregoing, might be made. We will abridge a few others thus:—Gieseler says of the first centuries, "Millennarianism became the general

* Decline and Fall, vol. i. pp. 411, 413,
† Encyclopædia Amer., Art. Millennium.

belief of the time." Dr. Kitto remarks that "The Millennial doctrine may be regarded as generally prevalent in the second century." Bp. Newton says, "The doctrine of the Millennium was generally believed in the three first and purest ages." Mede, "This was the opinion of the whole orthodox Christian church in the age immediately following St. John." Maitland, of the first two centures, says:—"As far as I know no one, except such as were notoriously out of the pale of the church, had impugned the doctrine of the Millennium, as held by Justin, or taught any doctrine contrary to it." Bishop Russell admits that "The Apostles clung to the expectation of the Millennium during their whole lives." Of the days of Nepos, a German historian of Chiliasm, says "At that time the number and respectability of its supporters was not small." Whitby, on the Pre-millennial views of the early church, says: "They held that this (first) resurrection was not confined to the martyrs only, but that all the just were then to rise and reign with Christ." Jeremy Taylor admits that "The doctrine of the Millennium was in the best ages esteemed no heresy, but true Catholic doctrine." Stuart affirms that Justin Martyr, Irenæus, Tertullian, &c., regarded the descriptions of the thousand years reign on earth, of the first resurrection of the dead, and of the New Jerusalem, as designed to be literally interpreted in order to elicit the true meaning of the Apocalypse." Milner on the Pre-millennarian faith of the early church, says: "This fact is not disputed," and we would add in conclusion that he who doubts it after perusing these pages thus far, would not believe though one rose from the dead. Says the London Quarterly Journal of Prophecy: "Thus, by the testimonies of men, many of whom are wholly unfriendly to our doctrine, we have established this point, that, during the first two centuries and a half, Pre-millennialism, or Chiliasm, as it was then called, was the faith of the church. We can distinctly trace it back to the days of the Apostles, nay, to the very lips of the Apostles."

THE SEPTUAGINT CHRONOLOGY.

The chronological calculus of the early church, leading them to expect the termination of the 6000 years in their day or later, the reader will perceive is incorrect. Says Gibbon, "The primitive church of Antioch, computed almost 6000 years from the creation of the world to the birth of Christ." Their calculations were founded on the Septuagint, i. e., the ancient Greek version of the Old Testament, which was universally received during the first six centuries, on which Dr. Burnet says: "The reason why so many of the Fathers were mistaken in supposing the end at hand was because they reckoned the 6000 years according to the chronology of the Septuagint; which, setting back the beginning of the world many ages beyond the Hebrew, the six thousand years were nearly expired in the times of those Fathers; and this made them conclude the world was very near an end."* Prof. George Bush thus observes of the primitive Christians:— " Owing to a radical error in their chronological calculus, they conceived themselves as actually having arrived at the eve of the world's seventh Millennary, or in other words, as having their lot cast on the Saturday of the great anti-typical week of the creation."† Dr. Elliott also affirms the same, and exhibiting a vast discrepancy of hundreds of years between the chronology of the Hebrew and Septuagint text, there being then extant different copies of the latter, he instances, Clement of Alexandria, as terminating from then the 6000 years about A. D. 374; (others earlier), Eustathius, Lactantius, Hillarion, Jerome, and perhaps Hippolytus, in A. D. 500; Sulpitius Severus, in A. D. 581; Augustine, in A. D. 650; and Cyprian, about A. D. 243; this being, he says, the earliest application of the world's supposed nearness to its

---

* Theory of the Earth, vol. ii.   † On the Mill., p. 23

seventh Millennary in proof of the nearness of the consummation, save the Sibylline Oracles, Book seventh which fix on A. D. 196. As proof of the incorrectness of the chronology of the Septuagint, he observes that it makes Methuselah to have lived till fourteen years after the flood !*

And now taking our leave of the early church, after noticing more at length the decline of the primitive doctrine of the Millennium, and the introduction of a new Millennial theory we plunge into the ages of darkness.

* Hor. Apoc., vol. ii. pp 206-7, &c.

CHAPTER V.

FROM AUGUSTINE TO LUTHER.

"In the latter times some shall depart from the faith." 1 Tim. 4: 1.
"Others were tortured not, accepting deliverance, that they might obtain a better resurrection."—Heb. 11: 35.

PRE-MILLENNIALISM, we hold, is Apostolic; but in reviewing the testimony of the early church on the question of Chiliasm, it is of course admitted that they mixed errors with the doctrine. We remember that "the mystery of iniquity" worked in Paul's day, and we have read his solemn prediction in his farewell charge given to the church at Ephesus. An English writer has well observed, "I do not appeal to the writings of the early Christians as authority; so far from it, I regard their writings as the history of truth perverted; so that while on the one hand I should be surprised to find any truth taught by the apostles, unnoticed in the Fathers, I should be almost equally surprised to find it taught Scripturally and unincumbered by human additions, so early did the apostacy begin to work." Above antiquity, tradition or human opinion, in the words of Burnet, "we should always require a higher witness, viz: the Bible." This is the first. But we highly esteem the faith of that church whose characteristics, says Milner, were "to believe, to love, and to suffer." "Whatever is first," says Tertullian, "is true, whatever is later is adulterate," and Mr. Faber has truly said: "If a doctrine totally unknown to the primitive church, which received her theology immediately from the hands of the apostles, and which continued long to receive it from the hands of the disciples of the apostles, springs up in a subsequent age, let that age be the fifth century, or let it be the tenth century, or let it be the sixteenth century, such doctrine stands on its very front, impressed with the brand of mere human invention."* Such, we argue, is Post-millennialism, and such also Anti-millennialism, of which we are now to speak, after first giving the character of the times.

Having now arrived in our history of Millennarianism at the commencement of the fifth century, when the great apostacy had begun, and this Apocalyptic truth was deemed a heresy and accounted unpopular, we here purpose giving, through the combined testimony of many voices, a brief but fuller account of its decline. Paganism was fallen, but the Papacy was hastening to its birth, and even in its embryo was hung all over with idolatry. From Gibbon, Neander and Mosheim, we learn that in the fourth century monks, monasteries, convents, penance, church councils, with church control of conscience, excommunication, the perfume of flowers, the smoke of incense, wax tapers in the churches at noon day, prostrate crowds at the altar drunk with fanaticism or wine, imprinting devout kisses on the walls and supplicating the concealed blood, bones, or ashes of the saints, idolatrous frequenting martyrs' tombs, pictures and images of tutelar saints, veneration of bones and relics, gorgeous robes, tiaras, croises, pomp, splendor and mysticism, were seen everywhere, and were the order of the day; and says Mosheim: "The new species of philosophy imprudently adopted by Origen and many other Christians, was extremely prejudicial to the cause of the gospel, and to the beautiful simplicity of its celestial doctrines," and Gibbon writes that

* Primitive Doctrine of Election, p. 158

"If in the beginning of the fifth century Tertullian or Lactantius had been suddenly raised from the dead to assist at the festival of some popular saint or martyr, they would have gazed with astonishment and indignation at the profane spectacle which had succeeded to the pure and spiritual worship of a Christian congregation." Martyr worship was very common, and Eunapius the Pagan, A. D. 396, exclaimed, "These are the gods that the earth now-a-days brings forth, these the intercessors with the gods—men called martyrs: before whose bones and skulls, pickled and salted, the monks kneel and lay prostrate, covered with filth and dust." The mystery of iniquity worked like leaven, and to use the words of Coleridge, "The Pastors of the Church had gradually changed the life and light of the gospel into the very superstitions they were commissioned to disperse; and thus paganized Christianity in order to christen Paganism." Dr. Cumming remarks that "The great multitude consisted of embryo papists, and what we call Pusyism in the nineteenth century, was the predominating religion of the fourth." Milner says that "while there was much outward religion the true doctrines of justification were scarcely seen." All of this Dr. Duffield does not hesitate to affirm was the genuine offspring of the allegorical system and Platonic philosophy of Origen, who made the church on earth the mystic kingdom of heaven. "Vigilantius," says Elliott, "remained true, and was the Protestant of his times," but Jerome, remarks Dr. Cumming, "became utterly corrupted," and Augustine, as Elliott has shown, scarcely escaped the universal contagion. Eusebius said "the church of the fourth century looked like the very image of the kingdom of Christ," but it was not the Millennium, as he dreamed, says Cumming, but the mystery of iniquity, ripening and maturing. It rapidly approached its predicted maturity, and Antichrist loomed into view. Such was the character of the times, and need we wonder that the true Millennium was laid aside, and with it the Apocalypse that taught it? "Rome," says Burnet, "always had an evil eye on the Millennium!" Truly spoken! Says Newman, the Roman Catholic writer: "Whereas at first certain texts were inconsistently confined to the letter, and a Millennium was in consequence expected; the very course of events, as time went on, interpreted the prophecies about the church more truly," &c., i. e. in a mystical or anagogical manner.

Continuing our quotations on this point, we give the testimony of Bishop Russell, of Scotland, a strong Anti-millennarian, who writes as follows: "It is worthy of remark, that so long as the prophecies regarding the Millennium were interpreted literally, the Apocalypse was received as an inspired production, and as the work of the apostle John; but no sooner did theologians find themselves compelled to view its annunciations through the medium of allegory and metaphorical description, than they ventured to call in question its heavenly origin, its genuineness, and its authority Dionysius, the great supporter of the allegorical school, gives a decided opinion against the authenticity of the Revelation." Joseph Mede truly says of the Anti-millennarians of the fourth century, "They denied the Apocalypse to be Scripture, nor was it re-admitted till they thought they had found some commodious interpretation of the thousand years." Dr. Cumming observes, "Some divines of the fourth century rejected the Apocalypse, on the ground that it contained, as they alleged, prophecies of what they erroneously believed to be a carnal Millennium; just in the same way as some persons still argue that the Bible cannot be God's word, because it contains truths that cross their prejudices." Dr. Elliott testifies, that from the Constantinian revolution in the eastern empire, with but few exceptions, we find the Apocalypse "passed over in silence by the great Greek Fathers of the remainder of the fourth century;" and he also shows that nearly all who rejected it, were evidently under prejudices against, and misconceptions of the Apocalyptic doctrine of a Millennium. The pointed testimony of Prof. Stuart is as follows: " In the end of the fourth century to guard against Chiliasm, quite a number doubted the genuineness of the Apocalypse,—did not receive it as canonical, and carefully abstained from appealing to it, but after this period we find only here and there a solitary voice raised against it, until at length the reception became all but universal. When the question of Chiliasm had ceased to excite any special interest in the churches * * * all opposition to the Apocalypse either ceased or became quite inactive and indifferent." Gibbon, too, adds his testimony to this remarkable fact, and says: " In the Council of Laodicea, A. D. 360, the Apocalypse was tacitly excluded from the sacred canon, by the same churches of Asia to which it was addressed; and we may learn from the complaint of Sulpicius Severus, that their sentence had been ratified by the greater number of Christians of his time." And to sum up this array of evidence with regard to the Millennium, as held by the church up to this period, together with its rejection, as also that of the Apocalypse, we give the following striking and truthful language of Horatius Bonar. On Rev. 20th chapter, he writes:—

"In the first centuries great stress was laid upon this passage. It was considered the stronghold of Chiliasm—so strong and decided was its testimony deemed, that the Antichiliasts deemed their only escape from it, was the total denial of the Apocalypse. Chiliasm, and the Apocalypse, were deemed inseparable. They could only get rid of the former, by rejecting the latter. They never thought it possible to deny that the Apocalypse taught Chiliasm. This was not disputed; and hence those who disliked Chiliasm could not tolerate the Apocalypse. It was not till the church had learned to Platonize, or had taken lessons in the school of Origen, that they could condemn Chiliasm without disputing the inspiration of the Revelation."

A SALUTARY FAITH.—THE HERESY.

Such is the voice of History, with regard to the doctrine of the Millennium, and its subsequent depression. We have been sufficiently copious, so that the intelligent and candid reader might know both the character of its advocates and opponents—its firm adherents, and its ultimate destroyers. Orthodoxy had sided with it, but heterodoxy waged war against it. The true church believed in it, but the apostate church crushed it. If this be true, ought not the church of Christ in the nineteenth century to unanimously maintain Chiliasm ? We think so. Rome, with those in her employ, rose up against it. Brooks affirms that the works of Papias and Nepos, and Mede adds those of Victorinus and Sulpicius, containing Millennarian views, were authoritatively suppressed by Pope Damasus. The extraordinary admission of Gibbon is that, " as long as for wise purposes this *error* was permitted to subsist in the church, it was productive of the most salutary effects on the faith and practice of Christians, who lived in the awful expectation of that moment when the globe itself, and all the various races of mankind, should tremble at the appearance of their divine Judge," but now the great Antichrist was at hand, and the way must be prepared for him to reign, and be worshipped. That which Chillingworth, Lardner, Taylor, Russell and others affirm to have been orthodox in the first centuries, began to be deemed heretical. The Council of Rome under Pope Damasus, in A. D. 373, formally denounced Chiliasm, and so effectual was the condemnation that Baronius, a Roman Catholic historian of the sixteenth century observes that, " the heresy, however loquacious before, was silenced then, and since that time has hardly been heard of." And of the fifth century he writes, " Moreover the figments of the Millennaries being now rejected everywhere, and derided by the learned with hisses and laughter, and being also put under the ban, were entirely extirpated !"

Says Bush—" through the dreary tract of the ages of

darkness, scarcely a vestige of Millennarian sentiment is to be traced!"

Thus have we seen that through the rejection of the Apocalypse by Caius, Dionysius, and finally the church in general; through the Platonism and allegorizing of Origen and his numerous followers; through the misrepresentations of Eusebius; through the scoffing of the monk Jerome; through the hatred and opposition of a great church of embryotic Papists; through the denunciations of church councils; through the comminations and bitterness of Popes; through the laughter and hisses of Popish doctors; through the influence of an onward creeping and awful apostacy; through perhaps, the abuse of Millennarian truths by their advocates; and, finally, through the presentation and final reception of a new and erroneous Millennial theory more suited to the times, the true Apocalyptic doctrine of the Millennium, as held by the primitive church, wasted away, and ultimately well nigh died—died, not at the hands of orthodox Christians, but at the hand of men noted for their unsoundness in the faith—died at the hands of the infant harlot, Rome! And, alas! how much truth died with it—how much error lived when it died! But it did not die utterly, for

"Truth crushed to earth shall rise again,
The eternal years of God are hers!"

Resuming our history of the doctrine under consideration, we now give from Elliott's Horæ Apocalypticæ, the Augustinian view of the Millennium, a belief which, when the primitive views were silenced, generally prevailed for nearly a thousand years afterwards. That Millennial scheme was:— That the Millennium of Satan's binding, and the saints' reigning, dated from Christ's ministry, when he beheld Satan fall like lightning from heaven; it being meant to signify the triumph over Satan in the hearts of true believers; and that the subsequent figuration of Gog and Magog indicated the coming of Antichrist at the end of the world—the 1000 years being a figurative numeral, expressive of the whole period intervening. It supposed the resurrection taught, to be that of dead souls from the death of sin to the life of righteousness; the beast conquered by the saints, meant the wicked world; its image, a hypocritical profession; the resurrection being continuous, till the end of time, when the universal resurrection and final judgment would take place. This view, says Dr. Elliott, prevailed from Augustine's time, among certain writers throughout the middle ages, down to the Reformation. He then instances Primasius, Andreas, Bede, Ambrose, Ansbert, and other Catholic divines as holding it, and even after the Reformation, with some modifications, various Protestant doctors, Luther, Bullinger, Bale, Pareus, &c., it being held by them more ecclesiastical than by Augustine, and the Constantinian era being made a commencing epoch; and, finally, in the language of Professor Stuart—and as Elliott also affirms—(Stuart erroneously attributing its origin to Andreas)—This view ultimately originated the crusades, and the monstrous deception and consternation, into which the whole Roman world was betrayed in regard to the coming of Christ in the year 1000.* Comment or refutation is unnecessary.

For the purpose of exhibiting to the minds of our readers in a fuller and clearer manner, the character of the tide of Millennial views now setting in upon the Romish church, in the advancing establishment of the Papacy, to be received by her, never to be abandoned, we give one more testimony, that of her own expounder,

ANDREAS, A.D 550 OR 600.

Andreas was Bishop of Cesarea. Drs. Cave and Lardner say he flourished about A.D. 550. Dr. Elliott argues for

* Elliott's Horæ Apoc. Also, Stuart on the Apoc.

A. D. 550 or 612–615. "In his Apocalyptic Commentary, says Stuart, "he took a mystical view, and commenced the 1000 years from the first institution of the Christian church." Dr. Clarke speaks of Andreas' Commentary, as one of "mystical interpretations." Elliott says, "the Millennium he explains anagogically, as Augustine." But we will let Andreas speak for himself. On Rev. 20—"Some confine this thousand years to the short period of our Lord's ministry, from his baptism to his ascension to heaven, being no more than three years or three years and a half. Others think that after the completion of six thousand years shall be the first resurrection from the dead, which is to be peculiar to the saints alone; who are to be raised up that they may dwell again on this earth, where they had given proofs of patience and fortitude; and that they may live here a thousand years in honor and plenty, after which will be the general resurrection of good and bad. But the CHURCH receives neither of these interpretations. * * By the thousand years we understand the time of the preaching of the gospel, or the time of the gospel dispensation."* Antichrist, says Stuart, was to appear, and the end of the world immediately follow their termination. This was the Millennial scheme now adopted by the church, though it is manifestly evident from the words of Andreas, that some, even as late as his day, held to the primitive view. Albert Bengel writes: "When Christianity, in the age of Constantine, was made the religion of the empire, a notion began to be entertained that the Millennium must have already commenced; men dated its commencement from Christ's nativity or crucifixion; and dismissing the opinion that Antichrist had come, they regarded this event as still future, and expected the appearance of Antichrist to take place at the termination of their own imaginary Millennium."†

* Lardner's Credibility, vol. v. p. 79. † Memoirs, p. 334.

"Mistaking," says Dr. Cumming, "the spiritual character of the church of Christ, and identifying its earthly grandeur with its real success, they believed that the Millennium had at last dawned upon the world—and even in more modern times, such writers as Grotius and Hammond, and the venerable martyrologist, Fox, have expressed their conviction that the reign of Constantine was the realization of the Millennium of the Apocalypse!"*

Dr. Burnet, who possessed a thorough knowledge of the Millennial history, says—"I never yet met with a Popish doctor that held the Millennium; Baronius would have it pass for an heresy, with Papias for its author; whereas, if Irenæus may be credited, it was received from St. John, and by him from the mouth of our Saviour. It never pleased, but always gave offence to the church of Rome; because it did not suit that scheme of Christianity which they have drawn. The Apocalypse of John supposed the true church under hardships and persecutions, but the church of Rome supposing Christ reigns already, by his vicar, the Pope, hath been in prosperity and greatness, and the commanding church in Christendom for a long time. And the Millennium being properly a reward and a triumph for those that come out of persecution, (i. e the martyrs,) such as have lived always in pomp and prosperity, can pretend to no share in it, or be benefitted by it. This has made the church of Rome always have an ill eye upon this doctrine, because it seemed to have an ill eye upon her; and as she grew in splendor and greatness, she eclipsed and obscured it more and more; so that it would have been lost out of the world, as an obsolete error, if it had not been revived by some at the Reformation."†

Bishop Newton thus wisely and truely speaks: " In short, the doctrine of the Millennium was generally believed in the

* Apocalyptic Sketches, First Series.
† Theory of the Earth, vol. ii, p. 193.

three first and purest ages; and this belief, as the learned Dodwell has justly observed, was one principal cause of the fortitude of the primitive Christians; they even coveted martyrdom, in hopes of being partakers of the privileges and glories of the martyrs in the first resurrection. Afterwards this doctrine grew into disrepute for various reasons. Some, both Jewish and Christian writers, have debased it with a mixture of fables; they have described the kingdom more like a sensual than a spiritual kingdom, and thereby they have not only exposed themselves; but what is infinitely worse, the doctrine itself to contempt and ridicule. It hath suffered by the misrepresentations of its enemies, as well as by the indiscretions of its friends; many, like Jerome, have charged the Millennarians with absurd and impious opinions, which they never held; and rather than they would admit the truth of the doctrine, they have not scrupled to call in question the genuineness of the book of the Revelation. It hath been abused even to worse purposes; it hath been made an engine of faction, and turbulent fanatics, under the pretext of saints, have aspired to dominion, and disturbed the peace of civil society. Besides, wherever the influence and authority of the church of Rome have extended, she hath endeavored by all means to discredit this doctrine, and indeed, not without sufficient reason, this kingdom of Christ, being founded on the ruins of the kingdom of Antichrist. No wonder, therefore, that this doctrine lay depressed for many ages; but it sprang up again at the Reformation, and will flourish together with the study of the Revelation. All the danger is on one side, of pruning and lopping it too short; and on the other, of suffering it to grow too wild and luxuriant. Great caution, soberness, and judgment are required to keep the middle course. We should neither with some interpret it into an allegory, nor depart from the literal sense of Scripture without absolute necessity for so doing. Neither should we with others indulge an extravagant fancy nor explain too curiously the manner and circumstances of this future state. It is safest and best faithfully to adhere to the words of Scripture, or to fair deductions from Scripture; and to rest content with the general account till time shall accomplish and eclaircise all the particulars."* With all of these facts before us, how true and impressive is the language of Mr. Cox, of England, when he observes that,— "The great chasm in the history of Chiliasm, seems to be those awful centuries of Rome's supremacy when almost every truth was hidden!"†

ANTI-MILLENNARIANISM.

It is obviously seen that the singular theory of the Apocalyptic Millennium, being in the past, is Romish in its origin and nature. With regard to this view, we present but one argument, and that from Dr. Gill. He says: "The continuance and duration of the reign of Christ and the saints together, will be a thousand years. It is expressly said, 'The rest of the dead lived not again till the thousand years were finished.'—Rev. 20: 5. It may be inquired,

"Whether these thousand years are past or to come? To the solution of which, this observation is necessary, that the binding of Satan, and the reign of Christ, are contemporary. These thousand years have been dated from the birth of Christ, who came to destroy the works of the devil, and before whom Satan fell as lightning from heaven; yet this falls short of the binding and casting him into the bottomless pit. Others date these thousand years of Satan's binding from the resurrection of Christ; but Satan was not then bound. Others begin these thousand years of Satan's binding at the destruction of Jerusalem; but in these times, the devil

---

* Dissertations on Proph. ch. 55, p. 592.
† A Millennarians Answer, p. 43.

could never be said to be bound, when he had a synagogue of corrupt men.—Rev. 2: 9.

"Others begin the date of Satan's binding, and Christ's reigning, from the times of Constantine; and reckoning the thousand years from hence, they will reach to the beginning of the fourteenth century. But that the devil was not then bound, appears by the flood he cast out of his mouth to destroy the woman, the Church, who was obliged to disappear and flee into the wilderness, the remnant of whose seed he persecuted.—Rev. 12: 13–17. Some begin the thousand years reign, and the binding of Satan, at the reformation from Popery; but whether the date is from Wickliff, John Huss, and Jerome of Prague, or of Luther, they all of them either suffered death or met with great inhumanity and ill treatment, from the instruments of Satan, and therefore he could not be bound. Satan will not be bound till Christ, the mighty Angel, descends from heaven to earth, which will not be till the end of the world."*

We pass over this period almost in silence. The Man of Sin had come, and stretching his magic wand over the whole church, the "heresy of the Chiliasts" was silenced, and Popish error and Millennial darkness reigned supreme. The Romish Church silenced it; but when in the burning light of history we consider her character, we regard Post and Antimillennarians as getting to themselves no honor by referring to the fact. Will our Protestant brethren of the other view look at this? Tichonius, of the 4th century; Primasius, of the 6th; Andreas, of the 6th or 7th; Ambrose, Ansbert and probably Bede, of the 8th; and Berengaud in the 9th century; all either Romish or Greek Apocalyptic writers, expound the Millennium on the Augustinian system, but in doing so they predict trouble for the church till the end of the world; frequently limiting its duration to 6,000 years.†

---

* Gill's Body of Divinity.   † Vide Horæ. Apoc., vol. iv. pp. 329–468.

Andreas, one of the most distinguished of these, makes six ages or Millenniums for the world's duration, and argues that at their conclusion, and in the days of the Seventh Trumpet, all would end, and the saints' rest begin. Indeed this idea seems never to have been abandoned even during the dark ages. Then, as before and since the world's duration, has generally been made to be sex-millennial.

JOACHIM ABBAS, A. D. 1190.

Joachim Abbas. He was born at Calabria, and was an Apocalyptic writer of much celebrity, Dr. Elliott affirming that, as a prophetic expounder, he had " a greater influence than any other man in the middle ages." Joachim lived in the times of Richard Cœur d'Lion, before whom he lectured on the Apocalypse at Messina, while the latter was on his way in a crusade to the Holy Land. His prophetic scheme in regard to the Millennium, etc., Elliott calls bold, original and new for his times, and regards it as an innovation of the Augustine and Romish view. We condense from Elliott his thoughts on the subject in question.

Great troubles were to come on Rome—" the proud city"—he thought, on the pouring out of the sixth vial, his own church (the Romish) would be scourged for its sins. Much tribulation would occur under the reign of the Antichrist, but at the end of his rule, and the treading down of the witnesses, Christ would appear and take to himself the earth's dominion, as in Psalms 2nd. The angel's oath, Rev. 10, he supposed indicated " a proclamation of the last time, and day of judgment as near at hand;" which warning cry however, the wicked world would not hear: the cessation of time predicted meaning the final Sabbath. The seventh trumpet he makes to correspond with the " sabbath state" of Rev. 20: the voices in heaven meaning preachers on earth announcing that coming good; and the judgments of that trump as accomplishing the extermination of the Beast, the false Prophet, and Antichrist. The blessing of Rev. 14: 13, meant, he thought, the glorious Sabbath awaiting the church at last. The song of exultation on the fall of Babylon given in Rev. 19, Joachim expounds as the rejoicing of the Church on her liberation and triumph; and so, he says, "will begin that kingdom for which we continually pray 'Thy Kingdom come.'—O, how good will it be for us to be there! Christ being our shepherd, king, meat, drink, light, life!" On the advent of Rev. 19: 11, &c., remarking that it was a point in dispute among doctors, as to whether it would be personal or providential, he decided on the former, and gives his own opinion that it would be personal: the sword from the rider's mouth, he says, corresponding with St. Paul's prediction in 2 Thess. 2: 8. He made six periods, or ages, for the duration of the world, and regarded Rev. 20, as treating of that great Sabbath which is to be at the end of time: i. e. the Millennium, (which he says would be longer or shorter, as God pleased.) He commences this Millennium with the personal advent of the Redeemer. The binding of Satan, he says, which began incipiently to have its fulfillment at Christ's resurrection, would now have its perfect fulfillment in this Sabbath time, after the Beast's destruction. The first resurrection, which he makes identical with Daniel's prophecy of the saints possessing the kingdom, Daniel 7,—and also Ezekiel's, of the resuscitation of Israel—Ezk. 37—Joachim intimates may be literal. "Perhaps," he says, "the saints are then to rise and enter at once on life eternal." The battle of Gog, or Antichrist, would follow the Millennium. The new heavens and earth is "the final blissful state when the tares shall have been gathered from the wheat, and the just shine as the sun in the kingdom of their Father.*

* Horæ Apoc., vol. iv., pp. 372, 403.

The voice of Joachim is decidedly Pre-millennial; harmonizing measurably in its sentiments with that of the Church in earlier and purer times.

Anselm, Bishop of Havilburg, A. D. 1145, in a Treatise on Revelation, advocated a similar view, making six ages for the world, and these followed by a seventh, which would be the "Saint's Rest."* Almeric, Professor of Logic and Theology at Paris, and Jean Pierre d'Olive,† a leader in the church, were disciples, and followed in the footsteps of Joachim, whose views—says Elliott—exercised an influence on subsequent interpreters.

JEWISH RABBIS

Saadias Gaon. A Jewish Rabbi, who died in A. D. 943. He was eminent as an expositor, and wrote a book on the Belief of the Jews. On Daniel 7: 18, he thus comments: "Because Israel have rebelled against the Lord, their kingdom shall be taken from them, and shall be given to these four monarchies, which shall possess the kingdom in this age, and shall lead captive, and subdue Israel to themselves, in this age, until the age to come, until Messiah shall reign."‡

The celebrated Spanish Rabbi, Abraham Aben Ezra, who died in 1174, and whose commentaries are so highly valued as to win for him the title of "wise, great, and admirable," is said to have looked for the end, resurrection, and restitution, at the expiration of the 6000 years. Ben-Israel Menasse, a Portuguese Rabbi of the sect of the Pharisees, who died in 1660, thus expresses his own faith, and also speaks of Aben Ezra. He says: "As for my opinion, I think that after six thousand years the world shall be destroyed, upon one certain day, or in an hour; that the arches of heaven shall make a stand, as immovable; that there will be no more generation or corruption; and all things by the resurrection shall be

---

* Ibid., p. 370.   † Mosheim, Cent. xiii.   ‡ Mede's Works, Book 3.

renovated, and return to a better condition." He then adds that "this, out of doubt, is the opinion of the most learned ABEN EZRA," who looked for it in the new earth of Isa. 65 : 17. And MOSES MAIMONIDES, a Spanish Rabbi, called "The eagle of the Doctors," held and taught similar views. He died about A. D. 1201. Cunninghame says that ISAAC ABARBANEL, SAADIAS GAON, SOLOMON JARCHI, HANNANEEL, BECHAY, LABAN, BEN NACHMAN, RASHI, and BEN ABRAHAM, all Jewish Rabbis, adopt the year-day theory thus according with the majority of Protestant expositors.

THE PAULIKIANS, A. D. 600, AND LATER.

These were an ancient sect of Christians declaring themselves to be followers of the doctrines of Paul, and suffering with the Waldenses persecution by the church of Rome. They were quite numerous in the middle ages, and though charged with heresy and Manicheism by their persecutors, Dr. Elliott vindicates them entirely from every charge, and styles them "A line of true witnesses for the Lord Jesus." Among other things, for which they were anathematized, was the charge of holding that "God has no authority in this world, but in that which is to come; and that the Maker of this world is another, and has authority over this present," or as their Abjuration reads, "God, the Heavenly Father, has merely authority over the world to come; inasmuch as that the present state ($\alpha\iota\omega\nu$, i. e. age) and the world were not made by Him but by his adversary, the Evil One, the ruler of the world." Dr. Elliott says that their peculiar doctrine, on this head, appears to have related not to the original creation, but to the present constitution and the present ruling authority in the world: the wording of the charge especially in the Formula of Anathema in Photius and in Cedrenus, the use of the word age, and the contrast of this age, or world, not with another cotemporaneous, but with that of the "age to come." With Elliott, we accord the Scripturalness of this view, it agreeing well with Rom. 8: 20-23; John 14:30; 2 Cor. 4:4; 1 John 5:19; Job 9: 24, and Luke 4:6. The Paulikians called themselves *Christians* and their enemies *Romans*, and there was in this view of the present subordinate rule of the Evil One, so plainly taught in the above Scriptures, something so decidedly alien from the then—and alas! too much now—prevalent belief of an ecclesiastical reign and Millennial era—a faith so antagonistical to Rome as to be apparent to all, and call down the maledictions of the great Antichrist. We would that all Christians would draw a lesson from these humble, yet faithful witnessing Protestants of the middle ages, as also from the folly of the Corinthian church, so ironically rebuked by Paul, in 1 Cor. 4:7, 8, &c. The Paulikians spoke of Christ, says our informant, as Him whose footsteps they wished to follow in this world, Him who was their forerunner to the heavenly Jerusalem, and as their king, marked them from his meditorial throne in heaven. And as the great object of their hopes, they looked, as we have before seen, to His introduction of the age to come; in which age the usurper should have no more authority, but all the power and all the authority be with the Lord Christ. They saluted each other when they met as "fellow-pilgrims, or fellow-exiles," and their home was in "THE WORLD TO COME."*

We would here observe, that the evidence in confirmation of Pre-millennialism, derived from the voice of the church during the dark ages, and even at the opening of the Reformation, as seen in the testimonies of the Paulikians, the Waldenses, Wickliff, etc., is of a negative character, and comes to us in the form of a constant expectation of the end of the world and the coming of Christ; precluding the faith of an

* Horæ Apoc., vol. ii, p. 292-315.

intervening Millennium of blessedness, a doctrine totally unknown to the martyrs and reformers. Thus, while there be nothing in their testimonies clearly affirming Millennarianism, the grand fact therein presented, of the true church waiting for the Lord, and him only, and even of fixing dates making his advent proximate, is, we affirm, decidedly at variance with the faith of every Post-millennialist of the modern school of Whitby.

THOMAS AQUINAS, A. D. 1250.

Thomas Aquinas was born A. D. 1224. Died A. D. 1274. He was a learned doctor of the Romish Church, and was canonized A. D. 1323. Expounding the Millennium, Elliott says of him: "Of the Millennial binding of Satan he in one place gives the old Augustinian explanation, as having eference to time past, and commencing from Christ's ministry; yet seems elsewhere to apply it to a judgment on the Devil after Antichrist's destruction. It was another step in the track of Joachim Abbas to the abandonment of the so long received Millennial theory of Augustine."*

Almeric, before mentioned, declared that Rome was Babylon, and the Roman Pope Antichrist, for which he was pronounced a heretic, and his bones dug up and publicly burnt, in the year 1209.† Both Almeric and his disciples pro claimed the approach of an era of light and reformation, or as Joachim had called it, "a third Age, the Age of the Holy Spirit." The passing away of the Millennial year 1000 without the expected awful mundane catastrophe, tended to make men earnestly reason and question, both on the long received Millennial theory, and also on that of the prophetic Antichrist, Tissington, a writer of the 14th century, calling the developed Augustinian scheme, as cherished by Berenger, a "day dream!"‡ Dr. Elliott says, even of the 11th century.

---

* Horæ Apoc., vol. iv., p. 407.   † Mosheim, Century xiii.
‡ Faber on the Waldenses, p. 394.

that as it wore away everything prepared for, and symptoms very significantly betokened that a new era of prophetic interpretation was approaching. Thank God, the morning of this long night dawned at last! The Reformation came and light came with it. "After ages of superstition, and the reign of ignorance," says Milner, the historian, "we see the Sun of Righteousness rising over Europe, with healing under his wings."

THE WALDENSES, A.D. 314, TILL NOW.

The Waldenses, Valdenses, Vaudois or "People of the Valleys." "Who has not heard," says Elliott, "of the Waldenses?" "this most ancient stock of religion," to use the words of the great Milton. In the language of Dr. Cheever, "They are an unconquered community of Protestant Christians, who have always existed directly at the doors of the Romish court, and beneath the reverberating thunders of the Vatican." Romish and Protestant writers of the best authority have demonstrated their existence since the time of Pope Sylvester, and perhaps even from the days of the Apostles, and it is well known that they acknowledge no founder. But we need not stop to eulogize them, for their praise is in every mouth. We come to notice their faith, and on this we remark that, "They have always regarded the Papal Church as the Antichrist: the Babylon of the Apocalypse."

'They condemned the mystical or allegorical interpretations of Scripture."* If the latter be true, could they have been anything else than Literalists? Their "Treatise on Antichrist," and "Noble Lesson," written in the 12th century, are both pronounced by the best judges to be genuine and authentic.† The latter (translated by Faber and quoted

* Vide Encyc. Relig. Knowl. Art. Waldenses.
† Elliott, vol. ii. p. 328.

by Brooks, Elliott, etc.) is originally in the form of a Poem Elliott pronounces it to have been written among the Cottian Alps, about A. D. 1150 or 1160, and thinks Peter Waldo was its author. The Poem is very beautiful, and in its style and sentiment resembles the Epistles of the early Chiliastic Fathers. We give extracts.

THE NOBLE LESSON.

"O Brethren, hear a Noble Lesson.

"We ought always to watch and pray; for we see that the world is near to its end. We ought to strive to do good works; since we see that the world approaches to its termination.

"Well have a thousand and a hundred years been entirely completed, since it was written that we are in the last times.

"We ought to covet little; for we are at what remains. Daily, we see the signs coming to their accomplishment, in the increase of evil, and in the decrease of good. These are the perils which the Scripture speaks of; which the gospels have recounted, and which St. Paul mentions; that no man who lives can know the end. Therefore ought we the more to fear; since we are not certain whether death will overtake us to-day or to-morrow. But when the day of Judgment shall come, every one shall receive his entire payment; both those who have done ill and those who have done well. For the Scripture saith, and we ought to believe it, that all men shall pass two ways; the good to glory, the wicked to torment. But if any one shall not believe this dipartition, let him attend to Scripture from the commencement. Since Adam was formed, down even to the present time, there may he find, if he will give his attention to it, that few are the saved in comparison with those that remain.

"We ought to love our neighbor, for God hath commanded it: not only those who do good to us, but likewise thos who do evil. We ought, moreover, to have a firm hope in the Celestial King, that at the end he will lodge us in his glorious hostelry."

Referring at length to their persecutions, the writer says

"But he who is thus persecuted strengthens himself greatly through the fear of the Lord; for the kingdom of heaven shall be given to him at the end of the world."

After writing about many things and repeating sound doctrine and good instruction, the lesson ends thus:—

"Many signs and great wonders shall be from this time forward to the day of judgment. The heaven and the earth shall burn; and all the living shall die. Then all shall rise again to life everlasting. Every building shall be laid prostrate; and then shall be the last judgment; when God shall separate his people according as it is written. Then shall he say to the wicked, depart from me ye accursed, into the infernal fire, which shall have no end. There shall they be straightened by three grievous conditions; namely, by multitude of pains, and by sharp torment, and by an irreversible damnation."

"From this may God deliver us, if it be his pleasure, and may he give us to hear that which He will say to his people without delay: when He shall say, come unto me ye blessed of my Father, and possess the kingdom which is prepared for you from the beginning of the world. In that place you shall have delight, and riches, and honor."

"May it please the Lord who formed the world, that we may be of the number of his elect to stand in his courts! Thanks unto God! Amen!"[*]

Such is the tone of "the noble lesson," emphatically a Protestant voice from the ages of darkness, coming from the cherished and martyred Waldenses, of whom the Congregational Journal[†] says "they preserved alive the teachings of the primitive church," and in which, in the language of Elli-

[*] Horæ Apoc. vol. ii., pp. 315-350, 363   [†] Nov. 1851.

ott, is simply and beautifully drawn out, "the world's near ending and the hope of coming glory at the revelation of Jesus Christ." We pronounce it as decidedly favoring Pre-millennialism, and giving no sanction to an opposite theory. The shortness of time, the advent of the "Celestial King,' the signs of the times, perils and wonders till the judgment, the fires of the last day, a heavenly kingdom when the world ends, and not before, are the themes of the Noble Lesson. There is not one hint even of a temporal Millennium, such as many have looked for, since the time of Whitby, but instead, it harmonizes beautifully in its Pre-millennial tone with the faith of the Fathers and Reformers. Even Rome admits the Waldenses' warm attachment to the Scriptures, and if in interpreting them they condemn the mystical and anagogical system, they strike a blow and lift a voice against the wide spread Origenistic, and more modern *Whitbian* method of Biblical interpretation that should be felt and heard throughout Christendom.

Rev. Mr. Morris, in his work against Pre-millennarianism, says, that "The seed of Chiliasm has always remained in the church."* We believe it. We have found it among the Paulikians, the Waldenses and others of the dark ages, and are happy to trace our *credo* geneology back through this "noble army of martyrs" to the church of the purest age—nay, to the Seer of Patmos himself, and we are neither ashamed of the antiquity and apostolicity of our doctrine, or of our theological lineage, or of our company.

WICKLIFF, A. D. 1350.

John Wickliff, D. D., was born in Yorkshire, England, in 1324. He was the zealous antagonist of Rome, the "Morning star of the Reformation," and, says Mosheim, "a man of an enterprising genius and extraordinary learning."† In 1356 he put forth to the world a small tract, entitled "The

* Modern Chiliasm Refuted, p. 97   † Mosheim, Vol. 1, p. 399.

Last Age of the Church." The occasion of its production was the frequent occurrence of terrible earthquakes and the ravages of a fearful pestilence, which is supposed to have swept away full one-third of the population of Europe. Did Wickliff hail this fearful sign as a harbinger of an approaching temporal Millennium? Nay, the idea seemed farthest from his mind. Adopting the sentiments afterward echoed by Wesley,

> "Whatever ills the world befall,
> A pledge of endless good we call—
> A sign of Jesus near;"

he thought that the plagues with which the nations had recently been scourged, were indications that the great designs of God were hastening to a close; and that with the fourteenth century, the world would come to an end. He supposed, on the authority of Bede and St. Bernard, that four periods of heavy tribulation were to intervene between the first and second advent of Christ, and that two of these visitations were being passed, and that the last two would take place during that century, which was accordingly styled by him as "The Last Age of the World."

The above tract has never been printed, but exists only in MS. in the Library of Trinity College, Dublin. Albert Bengel in his writings, intimates that Wickliff put the thousand years in the past.* From the foregoing we gather the following conclusions: That this celebrated Reformer, whose intimate acquaintance with the Holy Scriptures gained for him the title of the "Gospel Doctor," looked for no intervening period of Millennial blessedness to occur prior to the second advent of Christ, but instead regarded the Redeemer's appearing as the object of the hope and constant expectation of the church of God.† So shone this "Morning Star," who

* Brooks on Proph., p. 353. † Le Bas Life of Wickliff, p. 105. Hor. Apoc. Vol. ii., 380.

faded from time's sky in 1384. The Waldenses, the Lollards, Walter Brute, the martyrs, Huss and Jerome of Prague, and the lamented Lord Cobham, were all either followers of, or intimately associated with, Wickliff.

Here, for the present, we pass from the ages of darkness. When the great Reformation came, and the Man of Sin was discovered, with it came the solemn impression on the mind of the true church, that she was nearing the end of the world. "The first Christians," says President Lord, "expected the return of Christ, and the setting up of his kingdom almost in their own time. Paul corrected them. He testified prophetically to the longer probation of the Gentile church; to its falling away, and the revelation of the Man of Sin. That prophetic apostacy is now a matter of history, or of present observation. . . . Rome attained its climacteric, and God sent Luther to announce that the day of redemption would not be long delayed. Another testimony, another shorter experiment, said the confessors of Germany, the Calvinists and the Puritans generally of Europe, and the last revolution cometh!" And Luther thus speaks, "The great day is drawing near, in which the kingdom of abominations shall be overthrown." "This aged world is not far from its end," said Melancthon, as he counted the numbers in the great creation-week of time. If the elder Reformers said the day was near in their time, what should we say who have entered the stream three centuries after them? And if the only Apostolic argument against the proximity of the last advent, be now obsolete and invalid, what look we for? If "that prophetic apostacy be now history," where are we? A master spirit anticipates the coming crisis. Surveying the Reformation he says: "The first day was the battle of God, the second the battle of the priest, the third the battle of reason. What will be the fourth? In our opinion, the

* Sermon on Heb. 7, 1.

confused, the deadly contest of all these powers together, to end in the victory of Him to whom triumph belongs."* We are past the ages of darkness. A mighty voice began three centuries ago to " proclaim the hour of God's judgment at hand." It waxeth louder and louder. **The Lord cometh!**

* D'Aubigne's Hist. Ref., p. 418.

CHAPTER VI.

THE ERA AND CENTURY OF THE REFORMATION.

" I beheld, and the same horn made war with the saints and prevailed against them; until the Ancient of days came, and judgment was given to the saints of the Most High: and the time came that the saints possessed the kingdom." DAN. 7: 21, 22.

THE period when Luther entered upon the labors of a reformer, and which is generally adopted as the era and century of the Reformation, is A. D. 1517.

Rev. Henry Morris admits that the doctrine of Millennarianism, as held by the early church, though it fell into disrepute, and was lost during the dark ages, was revived again "at the Reformation." "At the Reformation," observes Spaulding, "this doctrine was revived, and we may judge from the unreserved manner in which the Millennarian sentiments are expressed by many Protestant writers, that they were not thought new or doubtful."* The London Quarterly Journal of Prophecy† testifies that, " Millennarianism during the first century after the Reformation rose again into notice, and was held by several learned and godly men, and in the second it rose into still greater eminence, being taught by great numbers among all denominations who had no participation in the fanaticism of the ' Fifth Monarchy Men.' " "Whilst," says Mr. Brooks, " the single tenet of the thousand years was by the generality of the early reformers avoided; still they often avow what in the present day would

* Lectures, p. 252. † No viii., 1850.

generally be considered decided Millennarian doctrine. They came back decidedly to that important point, the looking for the speedy revelation in glory, of the Lord Jesus Christ,—a point of doctrine which we constantly find pressed upon the church in the writings of the Apostles."* A writer in the Protestant Churchman has shown that the great Reformers, unlike modern spiritualists, did not expect the Golden Age to be brought about by human agency, or that it would occur in this world. Dr. Duffield writes, that the faith of the Reformers as set forth in the Augsburg Confession, " strikes directly against the modern notions of the Millennium, one essential item of which is, that the governments of the earth will be administered by pious rulers in the flesh."† Modern Protestantism, we affirm, is at variance with the Protestantism of the early Reformers. The former holds to the world's entire conversion, whereas the Reformation under Luther was commenced with no such view, and while the latter has accomplished its work, the former is daily proving to be a fallacy—Macaulay, a prince among Protestants, affirming that " during the past two hundred and fifty years, Protestantism has made no conquests worth speaking of. Nay, we believe that as far as there has been a change, that change has been in favor of the Church of Rome." The great Luther, the gentle Melancthon, as also Calvin and Knox, also the Augsburg Confession, all deny the modern doctrine of the world's entire evangelization before the Lord's advent. And when it was proposed to Zuingle to found a church in which there should be no sin, he replied, " We cannot make a heaven upon earth,—and Christ has taught us that we must let the tares grow up along with the wheat." " The wise and extraordinary men," says Mr. Ward, " whom the Lord raised up for the great work of the Reformation, saw and rebuked the carnal doctrine of a kingdom of the church in the flesh and

* Elements of Prophetic Inter., pp. 78, 86.   † Duffield, p. 248.

blood, and explicitly condemned the doctrine of a Millennium in this world, a faith that was never received into the church in any of its acknowledged branches until the eighteenth century." Dr. Elliott justly writes, "Our Anglican reformers, and those too of the continental churches, had no notion of any such spiritual Millennium intervening before Christ's coming, as Whitby afterwards advocated and which has since his time been so much received."* Dr. Watkins, of England, on the general opinion of the world's duration for six thousand years only, says, "At the time of the Reformation this notion was very prevalent." Junckner informs us that in 1546 a medal was in use, representing Christ as come down to judgment, and the dead rising, with the legend, 'Watch, for ye know not at what hour the Lord cometh.' It was struck just after Luther's death, and shows, says Junckner, the then general apprehension among Protestants of the judgment day being at hand."† But let us remember the words of Bickersteth, "because men hundreds of years back said the coming of Christ was near to them, let us not say it cannot be near to us."

THE TESTIFYING ANGEL.—THE REFORMERS.

Dr. Elliott, the learned commentator, translates Rev. 10: 5, 6, as follows, "And the angel * * * sware * * * that the time should not yet be; but in the days of the voice of the seventh angel, (whensoever he may be about to sound,) then the mystery of God shall be finished; according to the glad tidings that He hath declared to his servants, the prophets," and regarding this Apocalyptic chronological notice, as " the prefiguration of some proportionably strong and definite expectation of the consummation impressed in its due order of time on the minds of the Reforming Fathers, impressed too, not as an evanescent, though momentarily

---

* Hor. Apoc., vol. ii, p. 141.   † Ibid, p. 137.

strong idea, but abidingly," he commenting, thus exclaims, "It declared the end to be approaching, and comparatively nigh at hand. It would not indeed, the angel swore, be just as yet. But He swore also that there should intervene but one more trumpet-sounding before it. "How joyous," he exclaims, "this striking as it were, of the hour on the chronometer of heaven; to tell that the mystery was indeed near its ending, the grand, the long-desired consummation at length drawing nigh!"*

On the general expectation of the great Reformers, Elliott states that "Commencing immediately from the time of Luther and Zuingle's first heaven-made discovery of the Antichrist, of prophecy being none other than the Roman Popes, there was also impressed on them with all the force and vividness of a heavenly communication, the conviction of the fated time being near at hand, though not indeed yet come, of Antichrist's final fore-doomed destruction, and therewith also of Christ's kingdom coming, and God's great prophetic mystery ending, that the Reformers considered the Papal Antichrist's time of empire as being then not at its commencement, nor at its middle epoch, but already far advanced toward its ending," and that "this idea fixed itself upon the whole reforming body, alike in Germany, Switzerland, and in England," the Reformers in Germany grounding their strong and hopeful impressions chiefly, (though not wholly,) on the prophecies of Daniel and John, while those in Switzerland and England, seized on, and applied "the angel's oath and prophecy," and regarded their chronological place, "as being under the sixth trumpet in the evolution of the Apocalyptic drama, and the seventh only having to blow in order to the consummation," the whole of them regarded the brilliant unfoldings of Scripture light then evolving as a "sign of the promised brighter day soon coming." Elliott also notices

* Hor. Apoc., vol. ii., pp. 128, 129.

the striking fact "that the view thus communicated (save partially in the case of the church under Pagan Rome's persecution) considered as a prophetic chronological discovery, was all but unprecedented, it being then, for the first time, distinctly revealed to Christians whereabouts they were in God's grand prophetic calendar of the world's history, and that the impression and discovery was no barren piece of prophetic chronological information, but one most influential and practical, in fact, precisely that which was best suited to animate them for the great work before them."

He then instances Foxe, Bale, Bullinger, Osiander, Leo Juda, Latimer, Ridley, Ecolampadius, Melancthon, and Luther, as regarding the great day of judgment "not very far distant:" Melancthon as "strongly insisting on the predicted fact of there rising up no fifth earthly universal empire, after the Roman in its last form under the Little Horn, but only the kingdom of Christ and his saints," and Luther as "at one time fancying it might be less than twenty years; at another deprecating the extension of the interval to fifty years, and at another mentioning 300 as the very furthest limit that entered his imagination," to the consummation,—the judgment,—the end of time!!*

TYNDALE, A.D. 1530.

William Tyndale, the celebrated English reformer, was born in the fifteenth century, educated at Oxford and Cambridge, and is claimed as a Baptist in sentiment. He was connected with the Wickliffites, and imbibed the doctrines of Luther, and in 1532, translated into English, and printed the first English edition of the Bible. The following is his principle of interpreting the sacred Scriptures:

"No man dare abide by the literal sense of the text, but under a protestation, if it shall please the Pope. Thou shalt

* Hor. Apoc., vol. ii. pp. 121–145.

understand, therefore, that the Scripture hath but one sense, and that is the literal sense; and that literal sense is the root and ground of all, and the anchor that never faileth, whereunto if thou cleave, thou canst never err nor go out of the way. * * * The greatest cause of which captivity and decay of faith and this blindness wherein we are now, sprang first from allegories; for Origen, and the doctors of his time, drew all the Scripture into allegory, insomuch as that twenty doctors expounded one text twenty different ways, as children make descant upon plain song. Yea, they are come into such blindness that they not only say the literal sense profiteth not, but also that it is hurtful and killeth the soul." *

Carrying out these principles, Tyndale could, we are of opinion, arrive at no other conclusion respecting the "first resurrection," than that it would be literal. That he postponed the rewarding and glorification of the church until the advent, is obvious from his language to the Papists, arguing with whom he says: "If the souls be in heaven, tell me why they be not in as good a case as the angels be? and then what cause is there of the resurrection?"† Again he says: "Christ and his apostles taught no other, but warned to look for Christ's coming again every hour; which coming again, because ye believe it will never be, therefore have ye feigned that other merchandize?" ‡ On Math. 6:10, he says: "'Thy kingdom come'—that is, the time when thy Son shall surrender his kingdom unto thee, as it is in 1 Cor. 15:24. This kingdom is also mentioned, Romans 8:21-22, where it is declared that all creatures descry that day as the time of their rest and perpetual Sabbath."§ Tyndale was burnt at the stake at Flanders, 1536, praying, "Lord, open the eyes of the king of England." He evidently, like Joseph of Arimathea, "waited for the kingdom of God."

* Works, vol. i., p. 307. † Answer to More, B. iv., chap. ii.
‡ Answer to More, B. iv., ch. 8. § Literalist, vol. ii., p. 44.

BRADFORD, A. D. 1550.

John Bradford, A. M., was prebendary of St. Paul's, in London. The following extracts from his writings beautifully illustrate his faith.

On Rom. 8, he thus comments: "This renovation of all things, the prophets do seem to promise, when they promise new heavens and a new earth. For a new earth seemeth to require no less renovation of earthly things, than new heavens do of heavenly things. But these things the apostle doth plainly affirm, that Christ will restore, even whatsoever be in heaven and in earth. Therefore, methinks, it is the duty of a godly mind simply to acknowledge, and thereof to boast in the Lord, that in our resurrection all things shall be repaired to eternity, as for our sin they were made subject to corruption. The ancient writers out of 2 Peter iii, have as it were agreed to this sentence, that the shape of this world shall pass away, through the burning of earthly fire, as it was drowned with the flowing of earthly waters." He then quotes St. Augustine as saying, that "the world changing into the better, may openly be made fit for man when returned in the flesh into the better state."

"But this my Saviour and my Head, Jesus Christ, died for my sins, and therewith, as he took away death, so hath he taken away all the corruption and labor of all things, and will restore them in his time. Now every creature travaileth and groaneth with us; but we being restored, they also shall be restored: there shall be new heavens, new earth, and all things new.*

"Covet not the things that are in this world, but long for the coming of the Lord Jesus. God will one day restore our bodies to us, like to the body of our Lord and Saviour Jesus Christ, whose coming is now at hand. Let us look for it, and lift up our heads for our redemption draweth nigh.* * *

* Richmond's Fathers of the Eng. Ch., vol. vi., p. 608.

He—our Lord—now is not seen elsewhere than in heaven, or otherwise than by faith; until he shall be seen as he is, to the salvation of those that look for his coming, which I trust is not far off; for if the day of the Lord drew near in the Apostles' time, which is now above 1500 years past, it cannot be, I trust, long hence now. I trust our Redeemer's coming is at hand."*

How sweet indeed, is this voice from the prisons of earth; the yearnings of the bride for His coming and the day of redemption! In company with John Leafe, this pious reformer was burnt at the stake in 1555, exclaiming, "O England, England, repent thee of thy sins! Beware of Antichrist! Beware of idolatry; take heed they do not deceive you!"† and may England in her present peril heed the warning voice of the martyr Bradford.

PISCATOR, A. D. 1530.

John Piscator, Professor of Theology at Strasburgh, who died 1546, seems to have had his hopes fixed upon the Redeemer's advent. In his valuable Commentary, he says, "The advent of the Lord to judgment is to be looked for with perpetual vigilance; especially by the ministers of the word." Com. on 1 Thess. 4: 14. A solemn injunction! Mr. Brooks says, Piscator "professed Millennarian sentiments."‡

LATIMER, A. D. 1535.

Hugh Latimer was born in Leicestershire, Eng., 1470. In early life he was a Papist, but embracing Protestantism at the age of fifty-three, he became a zealous champion of the Reformation. In 1535, Henry VIII. made him Bishop of Worcester, but this office he soon after resigned, refusing the mitre. He had the courage to write a letter to King Henry

---

* "Letters from Prison," 1554.   † Chris. Index, p. 118.
‡ El. Prop. Int. p. 70.

against a proclamation just published, forbidding the use of the Bible in English, in which he told that monarch, "the day is at hand when you shall give account of your office, and the blood which hath been shed by your sword."*

Having spoken in his third Sermon on the Lord's Prayer, of a future Parliament, different from the parliaments of this world: "A parliament in which Christ shall bear the rule and not men; and which the righteous pray for when they say, 'Thy kingdom come,' because they know that therein reformation of all things shall be had:" he says: "Let us therefore have a desire that this day may come quickly; let us hasten God forward; let us cry unto him day and night, 'Most merciful Father, thy kingdom come.' St. Paul saith, 'The Lord will not come till the swerving from faith cometh,' 2 Thess. 2: 3, which thing is already done and past: Antichrist is already known throughout all the world. Wherefore the day is not far off. Let us beware, for it will one day fall on our heads. St. Peter, 'The end of all things draweth very near.' St. Peter said so at his time; how much more shall we say so? for it is a long time since St. Peter spake these words. The world was ordained to endure, (as all learned men affirm, and prove it with Scripture,) six thousand years. Now, of that number there be past 5552 years; so there is no more left but 448 years. And furthermore, those days shall be shortened: it shall not be full six thousand years; the days shall be shortened for the elects' sake. Therefore all those excellent and learned men, which, without doubt, God hath sent into the world in these latter days to give the world warning, all those men do gather out of the Scriptures that the last day cannot be far off.† Peradventure, it may come in my days, old as I am, or in our children's days. * * * There will be great alterations in that day; there will be hurly burly, like as you see when a man dieth, &c. There will be such alter-

* Chris. Index, p. 137. † Third Sermon on the Lord's Prayer.

ations of the earth and elements, they will loose their former nature, and be endued with another nature. And then shall they see the Son of Man come in a cloud, with power and great glory. Certain it is that he shall come to judge; but we cannot tell the time when he shall come."

After saying that the saints in that day " shall be taken up to meet Christ in the air, and so shall come down with him again," he adds, " That man or that woman that saith these words, ' Thy kingdom come,' with a faithful heart, no doubt desireth in very deed, that God will come to judgment, and amend all things in this world, and put down Satan, that old Serpent, under our feet."*

Bishop Latimer became a victim of Queen Mary's persecution, and in company with Ridley, was burned at an advanced age, 1555; and this is his eulogy; no other is wanting, and the first resurrection awaiteth him.

RIDLEY, A. D. 1530.

Nicholas Ridley, D. D., and Bishop of London. He was erudite and deeply pious, and the result of his zeal in the great work of reformation is well known to all readers of martyrology. In 1554 he wrote as follows: ." The world, without doubt—this I do believe and therefore I say it—draws towards an end. Let us, with John, the servant of God, cry in our hearts unto our Saviour Christ, Come, Lord Jesus, come."† He was burned with Latimer, suffering death with great fortitude, and evidently expecting no Millennial glory for the church of God in time.

SANDYS, A. D. 1550.

Edmund Sandys, D. D., and Archbishop of York, was born in England, 1519, and educated at Cambridge. He was

* Sermon for the Second Sunday in Advent.
† Ridley's Lamentation for the Change of Religion.

a man of learning and influence, Middleton affirming that "he was consulted on every occasion." He was one of nine Protestant divines who were appointed by Elizabeth to hold a disputation with an equal number of Romanists, in the presence of both houses of Parliament. He looked for the end—his language being thus: "As his (Christ's) coming is most certain, so the hour, day, month, and year is most uncertain. Now, as we know not the day and the time, so let us be assured this coming of the Lord is near. * * That it is at hand, may be probably gathered out of the Scriptures. The signs mentioned by Christ in the gospel, which should be the foreshadows of this terrible day, are almost already all fulfilled."* His view of the nearness of that "terrible day," excludes the faith of an intervening Millennium. Sandys died 1588.

CHYTRÆUS, A. D. 1590.

David Chytræus, D. D., born at Bostock, 1571. He was the author of an Apocalyptic Commentary. He interpreted the sixth trumpet as having reference to the Turks; the angel-vision of Rev. 10, as prefiguring the light of the reformation; and the seventh trumpet as bringing "the end of the world." He expounded the 1260 prophetic days as meaning so many years, and thus writes: "If they are numbered from the time of Phocas, A. D. 606, when the Pope's supremacy began, then the end may be expected A. D. 1866."† He began the 1000 years with the first advent, and consequently looked for no future Millennium in time. This author died 1600.

THE AUGSBURG CONFESSION, A. D. 1530.

Charles V., in 1530, convened a Diet at Augsburg, for the purpose of composing the then existing religious troubles, at

---

* Sermon on "The End of all Things at hand."
† Hor. Apoc., Vol. iv., p. 433.

THE AUGSBURG CONFESSION. 147

which there were present the Emperor himself, the princes of the empire, the Pope's legates, and the nobles and prelates of the Latin kingdom. On this occasion the great Melancthon drew up this famous confession of faith, "which," says Newton Brown, "may be considered as the creed of the German Reformers." It consists of twenty-one articles, and among the rest who signed it was the Elector of Saxony, and three or four other German princes.

We give translations from both the German and the Latin translation of Article 17th. *Ger.*—"In like manner they (our churches) condemn those who circulate the Judaizing notion, that prior to the resurrection of the dead, the pious will establish a separate temporal government, and all the wicked be exterminated."

Lat.—"In like manner they (our churches) condemn those who circulate the Judaizing notion that prior to the resurrection of the dead, the pious will engross the government of the world, and the wicked be every where oppressed." In the language of H. D. Ward: 'This is a miniature portrait of the doctrine now current in the church, worthy of the master-hand of Melancthon; and if it should make some ears tingle, to hear their loved doctrine of the Millennium, 'prior to the resurrection of the dead,' publicly stigmatized as 'a Judaizing notion,' they may know with whom, in this world, they must reckon for it, and count the cost before they begin the war with the bold Martin Luther, the gentle Melancthon, and their brave coadjutors; who not only brand this child of modern adoption 'a Judaizing notion,' but they solemnly 'condemn all those who circulate' the carnal doctrine."*

Says Dr. Duffield: "The Augsburg Confession disowns altogether a spiritual Millennium before the coming of

---

* Hist. Mill., p. 26.

Christ;"* and the Protestant Churchman remarks that "Rome and Augsburg agree to condemn the doctrine of a Golden Age in this world."

There are in the various Lutheran churches scattered throughout the world, a population of nearly thirty millions of members, and "The Encyclopædia of Religious Knowledge" informs us, that "The Augsburg Confession is the acknowledged standard of faith for the Lutherans wherever they are found!" Do they hold to the doctrine of their fathers on this great and important question?

CATECHISM OF EDWARD VI., A. D. 1550.

This monarch ruled on the English throne from 1547 until 1553, in which year he died. The Catechism was authorized by him. Bishop Burnet declares that Cranmer owned himself to be its author.† If so, we have presented in it the views of this celebrated and martyred arch-bishop, on the doctrines in question.

"Q. How is that petition, Thy kingdom come, to be understood?

"ANS. We ask that his kingdom may come, because that as yet we see not all things subject to Christ: we see not yet how the stone is cut out of the mountain without human help, which breaks into pieces and reduces to nothing the image described by Daniel: or how the only rock, which is Christ, doth possess and obtain the empire of the whole world, given him of the Father. As yet Antichrist is not slain; whence it is that we desire and pray that at length it may come to pass and be fulfilled; and that Christ alone may reign with his saints, according to the divine promises; and that he may live and have dominion in the world, according to the decrees of the holy Gospel, and not according to the tradition and laws of men, and the wills of the tyrants of this world."

* Duffield, p. 250.   † Burnet's Hist., vol. iii., p. 4.

"Q. The sacred Scriptures call the end of the world the consummation and perfection of the mystery of Christ, and the renovation of all things, for thus the Apostle (Peter) speaks in his second epistle, chapter 3, ' We expect,' &c. Now, by what means or circumstances those things shall be brought to pass, I desire to know of thee ?

"Ans. I will declare, as well as I can, the same Apostle attesting. The heavens, in the manner of a stormy tempest, shall pass away, and the elements estuating, shall be dissolved, and the earth, and the works therein shall be burnt. As if the Apostle should say, the world, like as we see in the refining of gold, shall be wholly purged with fire, and shall be brought to its utmost perfection ; man, imitating, shall likewise be freed from corruption and change. And so for man's sake for whose use the great world was created, being at length renovated, it shall put on a face that shall be far more pleasant and beautiful."*

Brooks affirms that this Catechism " was sanctioned by certain chief ecclesiastics of that day ;" and Dr. Duffield remarks that " this was the faith of the Episcopal Church of England in the days of Edward VI."

BECON, A. D. 1567.

Thomas Becon, of Queen Elizabeth's time, 1567, in a sermon on the judgment, expressed his belief that the great day was near. JOHN CARELES who was martyred 1556, died looking for Christ's coming, " unto which," says he, " now I hope it is not very long." They "loved His appearing."

LEO JUDA, A. D. 1500.

Leo Juda was born in Alsace, Germany, 1482. Encyclopedias refer to him as " a great and good divine, and one of the burning lights of the reformation. ' He was skilled

---

* Catechism, p—: Investigator, vol. i. p. 171.

in the Oriental languages, and had studied the writings of the Fathers. He was pastor at Zurich, and is numbered among the Swiss reformers. On the angel's oath of Rev. 10 he thus writes, applying the prophecy to the Reformation:

"Christ takes an oath, and swears by God, his heavenly Father, even with great fervency and holiness, that the time of his glorious last coming to judge all the world, both quick and dead, is now already nigh and at hand; and that when the victory that was prophesied to be fulfilled of Antichrist, which victory the seventh angel must blow forth according to his office, were once past, then should altogether be fulfilled what all prophets did ever prophecy of the kingdom of Messiah the Saviour; which is the highest mystery."* The reader will not fail to observe that he puts the kingdom and judgment at the seventh trumpet. He applied Rev. 9: 20–21 to Rome, and the tenth chapter to the Reformation. He died 1542.

BULLINGER, A. D. 1530.

Henry Bullinger was born in Zurich, 1504. He succeeded Zuingle as pastor at Zurich, and was one of the authors of the Helvetic Confession. He was the author of a Commentary on the Revelation, in which, according to Dr. Elliott, he explained the sixth trumpet (nearly as Luther's comment does) of the desolation of the Mahommedan Saracens and Turks, and on the seventh trumpet says, "It must come soon, therefore our redemption draweth nigh." He, like Leo Juda, applies the angel's descent and oath of Rev. 10 to the work of the Reformation, and on the passage says: "Christ swears that there is but one trumpet remaining: therefore let us lift up our heads because our redemption draweth nigh." The bridal in Apocalypse, 19th Bullinger makes to coincide with the saint's resurrection: the

* Vide His. Com. on the Apoc.

vision of Christ and his army on white horses, to symbolize the last judgment. The Millennium he commences nearly with the ascension of Christ, or as he says, he "objects not if any prefer to follow the Chiliasm of Papias," and finally in the new heavens and new earth he recognizes the renovation of this, our world.* Here again, as in the writings of all the other reformers, we can discern gleams of Pre-millennialism. He died in 1575.

KNOX, A. D. 1550,

John Knox, the great champion of the Scottish Reformation and founder of the Presbyterian Church, was born at East Lothian, 1505. He was eloquent, influential and intrepid, and so mighty with God that Queen Mary said she feared his prayers more than an army of twenty thousand men. On the doctrine of the earth's renovation Knox writes, "to reform the face of the whole earth, which never was, nor yet shall be till that righteous King and Judge appear for the restoration of all things." Acts 3. In his letter to the faithful in London, dated 1554, he, on the Redeemer's advent, asks, "Has not the Lord Jesus, in despite of Satan's malice, carried up our flesh into heaven? And shall he not return? We know that He shall return, and that with expedition." He died 1572, evidently looking for the Lord, and when laid in the grave the Regent of Scotland said, "There lies he who never feared the face of clay!" What do Presbyterians think of John Knox?

WILLIAM PERKINS, A. D. 1580.

William Perkins. Born at Maton Eng., 1538. He was ducated at Cambridge, and became rector of St. Andrews parish. He was of a philosophic mind, and was a powerful preacher. He wrote many valuable works, and on the signs

---

*Hor. Apoc., vol. ii. p. 140.

of Christ's coming, says, "The first is, this gospel of the kingdom shall be preached, &c., Math. 24: 14, which must be understood, not that the gospel must be preached to the whole world at any one time, for that I take it, was never yet seen, neither shall be, but it shall be published distinctly and successively at several times." The other signs are the revealing of Antichrist, 2 Thess. 2: 3, a general departing from the faith, 2 Thess. 2: a universal corruption of manners, 2 Tim. 2: 3; terrible and grievous calamities, Math. 24: 6, 16; exceeding deadness of heart, Luke 17: 26. "These, he says, are the signs that go before the coming of Christ; all of which are almost past, and therefore the end cannot be far off. The second coming of Christ is sudden as the coming of a thief in the night. He will come when the world thinketh not of him, as a snare doth on the bird.'* This eminent divine who died in 1602, in much triumph, could not have believed in the world's entire evangelization as do Post-millennialists.

CALVIN, A. D. 1535.

John Calvin, the justly renowned French Reformer, was born at Noyon, in France, A. D. 1509. Scaliger pronounced him at the age of 22, "the most learned man in Europe;" but we pause, not for commendations, for the world knows him. Calvin quotes Dan. 7: 10, as referring to "the last day."† Dan. 12: 3, he argues, proves a literal resurrection of the body, and on Joel, says that Peter's quotation, Acts 2: 17–20, extends to "the last resurrection." He also in his Com. on Acts maintains the "refreshing" of Acts 3: 19, is at the day of judgment. He repudiates the Millennium, rebuking those who would limit the kingdom to a thousand years, but with Luther looked for a renewed earth, saying, "I expect with Paul a reparation of all the evils caused by sin, for which he represents the creatures as groan-

* Exposition of the Creed. † Institutes, B. 3, chap. 11.

NO WORLD'S CONVERSION.—THE ADVENT. 153

ing and travailing;" and also allows that " the Scriptures more commonly exhibit the resurrection to the children of God alone, in connection with the glory of heaven, because, strictly speaking, Christ will come, not for the destruction of the world, but for purposes of salvation."* He places the kingdom at the advent, contending that " Christ is our Head whose kingdom and glory have not yet appeared. If the members were to go before their Head, the order of things would be inverted and preposterous : but we shall follow our Prince then, when he shall come in the glory of his Father, and sit upon the throne of his majesty."† And on the time of full reward, he remarks, that " The Scripture uniformly commands us to look forward with eager expectation to the coming of Christ, and defers the crown of glory that awaits till that period."‡ Commenting on Math. 24 : 30, he rejects the world's conversion, as taught by Post-millennialists, pointedly saying, " There is no reason why any person should expect the conversion of the world : for at length (when it will be too late, and will yield them no advantage), they shall look on him whom they have pierced." By his comments on Math. 24, 1 Cor. 15 : 51; 1 Thess. 4 : 15; 2nd Thess. 2 : 2, &c., he evidently understood the Bible as teaching that the day of the Lord's advent is to be expected at all times, precluding the faith of an intervening Millennium. He bids them " not to hesitate, ardently desiring the day of Christ's coming as of all events most auspicious;" and maintained that " the whole family of the faithful will keep in view that day."§ And finally, " We must hunger after Christ, we must seek, contemplate, &c., till the dawning of that great day when our Lord will fully manifest the glory of his kingdom."‖ Such are the words of this eminent divine on the second advent and its kindred doctrines. Are Calvinists in the succession

---

* Institutes, B. 3, chap. 25. † Psychopannychia, p. 55.
‡ Institutes, B. 3, chap. 25. § Inst. B. 3, chap. 9. ‖ Ibid. ch. 18.

hero as in other tenets of their great leader ? Calvin died in 1564.

OSIANDER, A. D. 1530.

Andrew Osiander was a German Reformer, born in Bavaria, and one of Luther's first disciples. He was celebrated as a divine, and was a voluminous writer. This Reformer—says Elliott—measurably endorses the year-day system of interpreting the prophetic days, and like Luther, somewhat curiously notes Phocas' decree, A. D 606, as constituting a notable Papal commencing epoch. He also argues like Melancthon, from the tradition of Elias; observing that as not all the sixth day was employed in creation, but its evening partly taken into the Sabbath, so it might be expected that all the sixth Millennium would not pass before the sabbatism; but the sabbath begin ere it had all run out.* He seems, unlike those of the school of Whitby, to have looked for the end at, or near, the expiration of the sixth chiliad. Osiander died 1552.

FLACIUS, A D. 1560.

Matthias Flacius, a Professor of Greek and Latin languages at Wittemburg, in the sixteenth century, in his "Catalogue of Witnesses," represented the twelve hundred and sixty days of the wild Beast, as having commenced in A. D. 606, with the decree of Phocas, and consequently referred its destruction, and the advent of Christ to the year 1866. Flacius was a Protestant divine, and a pupil of Luther and Melancthon. He died in 1575.†

LUTHER, A. D. 1520.

Martin Luther, the master-spirit of the reformation, was born at Saxony, in Germany, 1483. 'Luther! a name that shines in greater lustre than Milton or Shakspeare; a name

---

* Hor. Apoc., vol. ii., p. 139. † Lord on the Apoc., p. 240

ploughed into the hearts of millions; and on the brightest place in the roll of the illustrious dead." Such is the beautiful eulogium of the eloquent Cumming, and to all who would learn the worth and greatness of this extraordinary man, we recommend a perusal of D'Aubigne's History of the Reformation. We give extracts from his writings on various subjects, showing his views on the doctrines we advocate.

"About the time of Easter, Pharaoh was destroyed in the Red sea, and Israel led out of Egypt; about the same time the world was created; Christ rose again; and the world is renewed. Even so, I am of opinion, the last day shall come about Easter, when the year is at its finest and fairest."*

"How does Satan rage everywhere against the Word! This I reckon by no means the slightest mark of the approaching end, viz., that Satan perceives that the day is at hand, and pours forth his final fury."†

"It is now time to watch; for we are the mark they shoot at. Our adversaries intend to make a confederacy with the Turk; for Antichrist will war and get victory against the saints of God, as Daniel says."‡

"I am not so much afraid of the Pope and tyrants, as of our own unthankfulness and contemning of God's word:—the same, I fear, will help the Pope again into the saddle. When that comes to pass I hope the day of judgment will soon follow."§

"The world has grown very stubborn and headstrong since the revelation of the word of the gospel. It begins to crack sorely; and I hope will soon break and fall on a heap through the coming of the day of judgment, for which we wait with yearning and sighs of heart."‖

In 1545, he said of the passing events: "I do most earnestly hope that these are the blessed signs of the immediate

* Table Talk, chap. 57. † Milner, p. 896.
‡ Table Talk, chap. 15. § Ib. chap. 4. ‖ Ib. chap. 4.

end of all things."* Again, "I ardently hope that amidst these internal dissensions on the earth, Jesus Christ will hasten the day of his coming, and that he will crumble the whole universe into dust."† Maître Phillipe having said that the Emperor Charles would live to be eighty-four, Luther replied, " the world itself will not live so long. Ezekiel tells us to the contrary. And again, if we drive forth the Turks, the prophecy of Daniel will be accomplished, and then, you may rely upon it, the day of judgment is at hand."‡

Of printing, Luther said: " Printing is the latest and greatest gift, by which God enables us to advance the things of the Gospel. It is the last bright flame, manifesting itself just previous to the extinction of the world. Thanks be to God, it came before the last day came."§

Writing to Melancthon, 1541, he said, "I have no time to write to thee at any length, for though I am overwhelmed with age and weariness; old, cold, and half blind as the saying is, yet I am not permitted as yet to take my repose, besieged as I am by circumstances which compel me to write on, on, on. I know more than thou dost about the destiny of our world; that destiny is destruction; it is inevitably so —seeing how triumphantly the devil walks about, and how mankind grow daily worse and worse. There is one consolation, that the day of judgment is quite close at hand. The Word of God has become a wearisome thing to man, a thing viewed with disgust. . . . . Nothing remains but to pray : '*thy will be done.*'|| All around me I observe an unconquerable cupidity prevalent; this is another of the signs which convince me that the last day is at hand; it seems as though the world in its old age, its last paroxysm, was growing delirious, as sometimes happens to dying people."¶

"I pray the Lord to come forthwith and carry me hence

---

* Michelet's Life of Luther, p. 255. †Ibid. p. 257 ‡ Ibid. p. 290
§ Ibid. p. 291. || Ib. p. 344. ¶ Ib. p. 344.

LUTHER'S HOPES.

Let him come above all with his last judgment: I will stretch out my neck, the thunder will burst forth, and I shall be at rest." One of his guests observing that if the world were to subsist another fifty years, a great many things would happen which they could not then foresee, Luther said:

"Pray God it may not exist so long; matters would be even worse than they have been. There would rise up infinite sects and schisms, which are at present hidden within men's hearts, not yet mature. No; may the Lord come at once! Let Him cut the whole matter short with the day of judgment, for there is no amendment to be expected."*
"The judgment must needs be at hand, for what help is there for the world? The Papal church will not reform itself; that is out of the question; and the Turks and the Jews are as little inclined to amendment. Our empire makes no progress towards improvement: here have we been for the last thirty years assembling diets from time to time, yet nothing is done. When I am meditating, I often ask myself, what prayer I ought to offer up for the diet. I see no other prayer that is fitting but only this, *Thy kingdom come!*"†

Again, Luther said: "You will see that before long such wickedness will prevail, life will become so terrible to bear, that in every quarter the cry will be raised, God, come with thy last judgment." And having a necklace of white agates in his hand at the time, he added, "O God, grant that it may come without delay. I would readily eat up this necklace to-day for the judgment to come to-morrow."‡

The computation of those who confidently fixed the year and the day of the final judgment being once referred to, he said: "No, verily, the text is too plain in Matthew 24th, concerning the day and the hour, knoweth no man; no, not the angels in heaven, but alone my Father; therefore, neither I nor any man, nor angel, can fix the day or the hour."§

* Michelet's Life of Luther, p. 342. † Ibid. p. 343. ‡ Ib. p. 342.
§ Meurer's Life of Luther.

Again, "The world is, as it ever has been—the world—and desires to know nothing of Christ. Let it go its own way. They continue to rage and grow worse from day to day, which indeed is a solace to the weary soul, as it shows that the glorious day of the Lord is at hand. The world is given up to its own ways, that the day of its destruction and of our salvation should be hastened. Amen. So be it!"*

Near the time of his death, he said, "I persuade myself verily, that the day of judgment will not be absent full 300 years more. God will not, cannot suffer this wicked world much longer."†

"And the prevalent idea," says Elliott, "of its being near at hand, remained with him even to his dying hour, and was a perpetual topic of consolation, encouragement, and hope; nor did the circumstance of the fanatics of his day—Munzer and others—adopting, and making unsound and unscriptural use of this expectation of the near advent of Christ, affect his belief in, or declaration of it; for it seemed but Satan's well known artifice, by abuse or by a counterfeit to bring contempt on what was important and true."‡

Commenting on the passage, "Other sheep I have," &c., he says: "Some in explaining this passage say, that before the latter days, the whole world shall become Christians. This is a falsehood, forged by Satan, that he might darken sound doctrine, that we might not rightly understand it. Beware, therefore, of this delusion." (Com. on John 10: 11–16.) Luther's views of the Apocalypse were somewhat meagre and obscure. On the Millennium, Dr. Elliott says,§ he endorsed the Augustinian system, somewhat modified, and made it the "1000 years between St. John and the issuing forth of the Turks," and in the language of Bengal: "He believed also with many others, that the duration of the world, from its commencement, would be only 6000 years; and

---

* Horæ Apoc., vol. 2, p. 136. † Table Talk, ch. 1 and 9
‡ Horæ Apoc., vol. ii., p. 134. § Ib. vol. iv.

hence considered its end so near, that he could see no space for any future Millennium."* Luther puts the saints rewarding and the establishment of the kingdom of Christ, at the period of the second advent. We recommend to the reader a perusal of his " Sermon of consolation on the coming of Christ, and the signs that shall precede the last day." Luther died 1546.

We might multiply extracts, but have already given sufficient to show that the great Luther had no faith in the modern notion of a spiritual Millennium, but on the contrary, was a firm believer in the speedy coming of Christ and the renovation of all things. Has the voice of Luther no weight with the church of God in the nineteenth century?

MELANCTHON, A.D. 1530.

Philip Melancthon was born 1497, at Bretten, in Germany. He was one of the greatest men of his age. He was Luther's fellow-laborer in the Reformation, and is distinguished for his intellectual endowments, piety, and extraordinary erudition. Regarding his views on the prophecies and Pre-millennial advent, Elliott says that " he expounds 'the abomination of desolation' of Dan. 11, primarily of Antiochus Epiphanes, but secondarily and chiefly of Antichrist ;" that " he conceived Daniel's numbers 1260 and 1335 days might be understood on the year-day system ; that he regarded the reformation as the consumption of the Antichrist predicted to occur just before his final destruction at Christ's coming;" that he made but five universal kingdoms for the earth, the fourth being Rome, and the fifth the " kingdom of Christ and his saints," and these to come in numerical order; that like Luther he intently fixed his mind on Daniel and St. Paul's prophecies of Antichrist, and like Luther, conceived the " fated end to be near and iminent."

* Memoir of Bengel, p. 335.

In the British Museum is a copy of the first edition of Luther's German Bible, in two volumes. Upon the third page of the fly leaf of the second volume, are the following words, in the writing of Melancthon:

"THE WORDS OF THE PROPHET ELIAS.

'Six thousand years this world shall stand, and after that be burned.

'Two thousand years void (or without the law).

'Two thousand years, the law of Moses.

'Two thousand years, the day of the Messiah, but on account of our sins, which are many and great, these years which are not fulfilled shall be shortened.'

"Written in the year 1557, after the birth of our Lord Jesus Christ of the Virgin Mary. Year from the creation of the world, 5519. From this number we may be assured that this aged world is not far from its end. May Jesus Christ, the Son of Almighty God, graciously preserve, govern, keep, protect it by the power of his arm.

Written by the hand of Philip, 1557. W."

Again, he says: "It is known that Christ was born about the end of the fourth Millennary, and one thousand five hundred and forty-two years have since revolved. We are not, therefore, far from the end. Daniel asked in respect to the time of the end, and the number was given, which, although it seems to respect the time of the Macabees, yet undoubtedly has a reference to the end of the world, and the application is easy, if days be taken for years. They will be two thousand six hundred and twenty-five. We do not endeavor to ascertain the moment when the last day is to dawn. That is not to be sought. But inasmuch as this number happily agrees with the words of Elias, I regard it as denoting the years through which the world was to subsist from the time of Daniel. There were six hundred, or near that, from

Daniel to the birth of Christ. There remained, therefore two thousand years as the last age of the world.

"God showed to Daniel a series of monarchies and kingdoms, which it is certain has already run to the end. Four monarchies have passed away. The cruel kingdom of the Turks, which arose out of the fourth, still remains, and as it is not to equal the Roman in power, and has certainly, therefore, already nearly reached its height, must soon decline, and then will dawn the day in which the dead shall be recalled to life."*

Melancthon regarded the term Antichrist as denoting both the Mohammedan empire and the Papacy, and held that they were not to be overthrown till the time of the resurrection of the dead, and personal advent of the Messiah, who would then destroy Antichrist, and set up his kingdom. He opposed the Annabaptists, and said they "were infatuated by the devil," "hypocritical," &c. The standing up of Michael, Dan. 12: 1, Melancthon expounded as meaning Christ coming to judgment; and on the prospect of his coming—says Elliott—it became Christians, he thought, much and earnestly to dwell.†

Such is the testimony of this celebrated man, to whom the great Erasmus gave the praise of "uncommon research, correct knowledge of classical antiquity and eloquence of style;" and on whose character all biographical writers pronounce splendid eulogiums. His words beautifully harmonize with the concurrent testimony of the primitive church. Melancthon died in 1560.

BALE, A. D. 1530.

John Bale, Bishop of Ossory, was born in England 1496, and was educated at Cambridge. He was a converted Romanist, and became a zealous reformer and author while

---

* Lord's Expos, of Apoc., pp. 238-240.   † Comment. 1555.

called to the see of Ossory in Ireland. He published an Apocalyptic Commentary, in which he identifies the seven seals, seven trumpets, and seven vials, and made them to prefigure seven different stages of Christ's church; the angel of Rev. 10, the same as Bullinger; and the seventh trumpet sounding as at hand. On the world's six ages he follows Joachim Abbas. On the Lamb's bridal, Rev. 19, he says: "Since the beginning of the world, the faithful have been preparing for this heavenly marriage, and in the resurrection of the righteous it shall be perfectly solemnized; such time as they appear in full glory with Christ."* And again elsewhere, he says: "This (the Beast's) will be the rule of this present age. No doubt of it. Unto kings has not God given to subdue these beasts. This is reserved to the victory of his living Word. Only shall the breath of His mouth destroy them. Let the faithful believer, considering the mischief of this time, appoint himself to persecution, loss of goods, exile, prison, sorrow, and death for the truth's sake; thinking that his portion is in the land of the living. For now are the perilous days under the voice of the sixth trump; whereas, under the seventh the carnal church shall be rejected, Antichrist overthrown, and the right Israel, tokened with faith, peaceably restored into the possession of God." Further, respecting this oath that all shall be finished in the seventh age of the church, he adds: "Necessary it is that both good and bad know it: the faithful to be ascertened that their final redemption is at hand, to their consolation; the unfaithful to have knowledge that their judgment is not far off, that they may repent and be saved."† Bale understood the Millennium on the Augustinian system, and on the new heavens and new earth—says Elliott—looked for an earth purified and renovated by the fires of the judgment. He died 1563.

* Horæ Apoc., vol. ii. p. 142.   † Horæ Apoc., vol. ii., p. 142.

FOXE, A. D. 1580.

John Foxe, the celebrated author of "The Book of Martyrs," was born at Boston, England, 1517; was educated at Oxford, and became a zealous reformer. Foxe, as his biographers have shown, was no ordinary man. He was the author of a comment on the Revelations, which appeared after his death. Says Dr. Elliott: "He explains the woe of the sixth trumpet to be that of the Turks; adding that, after the Protestant restoration of Gospel-preaching, figured in Rev. 10, the seventh trumpet's sounding could not be far off, (Christ's coming and the resurrection occurring under it). Then he dwells on this passage—Rev. 10: 5-7—thus: 'Oh, what an adjuration! Of the truth and certainty of which we can no more doubt, than we can of the existence of God himself.' And, after arguing against the skepticism of ungodly men on the subject of the world's ending, he urges from the angel's oath the certainty of that end coming, and certainty, too, as appears from the angel's prophetic caution, (though the exact time was not to be known,) that it could not be very far off from the time then present."* "Which being so," says Foxe, "let both all pious Christians, and all the multitude of the ungodly, diligently listen to, and observe what the angel says and swears. For in the whole of Scripture, I think there is no passage more clear, none more suited to our times, none more calculated to strengthen the faith and minister consolation to the pious; and, on the other hand, to alarm the minds and break off the attacks of the ungodly." He regarded the judgment as certainly occurring under, or at the seventh trumpet. The Millennium, or 1000 years of Satan's binding, Foxe very singularly made to commence at the Constantinian era, and was, says Elliott, "I believe, the first so to compute it."† Post-millennarians affirm that the world will be converted at the seventh trumpet, but not so the venerable Foxe. He died 1587.

* Horæ Apoc., vol. ii., p. 142. † Horæ Apoc., vol. 4, p. 438.

BRIGHTMAN, A. D. 1600

Thomas Brightman was Rector of Hawnes, England. His Apocalyptic Commentary was first published in 1600. Dr. Elliott says it is one of great vigor both in thought and language, and was popular with the Protestant Churches of the times. Brightman interpreted the prophetic periods of the Apocalypse on the year-day theory; the 9th chapter as referring to the ravages of the Saracenic and Turkish armies; the five months of the locusts meant 150 years; the "hour, day, month and year," he regarded as a period of 396 years, and measuring the duration of the Turkish power. The two witnesses he makes to be the Scriptures and the assemblies of the faithful. The Beast, the dragon's accomplice, meant the Pope of Rome; and finally, the 1000 years began with Constantine. Under the seventh vial we add, the enemies of the church are destroyed, and her period of rest and triumph appears.* Brightman died 1607.

PAREUS, A D. 1590.

David Pareus, D. D., was born 1548, in Silesia. He was celebrated as a divine and reformer, and his fame as a professor of Theology was quite extensive. He was a Calvinist. In his Apocalyptic Commentary, Pareus seems to regard the six seals as covering the duration of the gospel dispensation; the white horse under the first seal as symbolizing the primitive purity of the church during the first three centuries; the sixth seal as denoting the Lamb's wrath and judgment against the world; then the vision returns and a new series commence. The trumpets he makes to correspond with the seals: the fifth and sixth referring to the conquest of Mahomedanism; the seventh "the consummation." The 1260 days are so many years, commencing A. D. 605, and ending

---

* Horæ Apoc., vol. 4.

he says, 1866. The first Beast out of the sea is the Papal Antichrist, whom he says, the ten kings will not destroy, "he being destined to survive Rome's destruction, and to be destroyed only by the brightness of Christ's coming." Pareus explains the Apocalyptic Millennium nearly on the Augustinian principle, controverting Chiliasm, and yet the reader will not fail to perceive his antagonism with the modern spiritual view. The following is his comment on Matt. 24 · 14. " Now, this universal preaching is not to be understood strictly—in which sense it never will happen that the gospel shall be preached absolutely to all nations at once; (for there will be a perpetual separation of the church and the world,) but by synecdoche or distribution; it shall be preached, not to the Jews alone, but to other nations also, without distinc tion of people. * * *. However it may be with the new world or other regions still hidden from us, it is a false interpretation of our Lord's words, as if there were not to be a spot on the earth's surface where the gospel shall not be preached. For it is a thing never to be looked for, that the whole world shall become Christian; since the enemies of the church, together with Antichrist, shall not cease but at the last coming of Christ."* He died 1622.

* Horæ Apoc. vol. 4, p. 445.

CHAPTER VII.

THE SEVENTEENTH CENTURY.

"The saints of the Most High shall take the kingdom and possess the kingdom forever, even for ever and ever."—Dan. 7th chap.

PRE-MILLENNIALISM rose to much eminence in this century. First and highest on the list stands the illustrious Mede, whom Rev. David Brown, of Scotland, styles "The Prince of Millennarians." Twiss and Usher sit as pupils at his feet, and Baxter modestly says, "I cannot confute him." Bunyan, "the Prince of dreamers," also sides with him in the personal reign, and Taylor makes good concessions. Henry's golden thoughts sustain Pre-millennialism, and Burnet is eloquent upon the theme. Burroughs testifies to the general faith in the year-day theory, which Stuart calls "a general and almost universal custom, so understood by the great mass of interpreters in the English and American world for many years." Some in this century had set times for the advent, but says John Cox, of England, "because some have made mistakes in fixing dates, let us beware of saying 'my Lord delayeth his coming.' Very solemn are the words of God by Ezekiel 12: 22–28." The "current axiom" of literal interpretation is set forth by Maton, the approaching end by Goodwin, and Alleine and Durant teach us to love our Lord's appearing. Bunyan, in the words of Pilgrim to Apollyon, expressed the hope of the saints:

"For present deliverance they do not much expect it, for they stay for their glory; and then shall they have it, when their Prince comes in His and the glory of the angels." But we pass on. May the mantle of our fathers fall upon us as we go.

MEDE, A. D. 1720.

Joseph Mede, B. D., styled " the illustrious Mede," was born in Essex, England, 1586. His " Clavis Apocalypticæ" is well known to prophetic students, and all his biographers concur in pronouncing him "a pious and profoundly learned man," and add that " in every part of his works the talents of a sound and learned divine are eminently conspicuous."

Dr. Elliott gives his Apocalyptic scheme, and says that " his works have generally been thought to constitute an era in the solution of the Apocalyptic mysteries, for which work he was looked on and written of, as a man almost inspired."[*] We extract copiously from his writings. Like the Reformers he interpreted the fifth trumpet of the Saracens; the sixth of the Turks explaining the prophetic periods of both on the year-day theory, referring the smoke and brimstone of verse 17, to the Turkish cannon. Rendering Rev. 11 : 7, "when they shall be about finishing their testimony," he makes the two witnesses to be trodden down 1260 years; the drying up of the Euphratean flood, Rev. 16th, meant the exhaustion of the Turkish empire; the seventh trumpet covers the Millennium.

1 Thess. 4 : 14–18. Paraphrasing verse 17th thus, "After this, our gathering together unto Christ at his coming, we shall from henceforth never lose his presence, but always enjoy it," &c. He argues that the redeemed will reign neither in heaven, nor in the air, but " on the earth,"—Rev. 5 : 10, he then gives the cause of this " rapture of the saints on high." " The saints being translated into the air, is to do honor to their Lord and King at his return, and * * * that they may be preserved during the conflagration of the earth,

[*] Horæ Apoc., vol. iv. p. 450

and the works thereof; that as Noah and his family were preserved from the deluge by being lifted up above the waters in the ark, so should the saints at the conflagration be lifted up in the clouds, unto their ark, Christ, to be preserved there from the deluge of fire, wherein the wicked shall be consumed."* 2 Peter 3: 8, he paraphrases thus,—" But whereas, I mentioned the day of judgment, lest ye might mistake it for a short day, or a day of few hours, I would not, beloved, have you ignorant that one day is with the Lord as a thousand years, and a thousand years as one day;" then remarking that the style and sentiment is that of the Jewish doctors, he adds:—

"The words are commonly taken as an argument why God should not be thought slack in his promise, (which follows in the next verse,) but the first Fathers took it otherwise, and besides it proves it not. For the question is not whether the time be long or short in respect of God, but whether it be long or short in respect of us, otherwise not only a thousand years, but an hundred thousand years, are in the eyes of God no more than one day is to us, and so it would not seem long to God if the day of judgment should be deferred till then."†
On the Millennium of Rev. 20, he in his letter to Wm. Twiss, thus argues:—

"The rising of the martyrs is that which is called 'the first resurrection,' being as it seems a prerogative to their sufferings above the rest of the dead, who as they suffered with Christ in the time of his patience, so should they be glorified with Him in the reign of his victory before the universal resurrection of all. 'Blessed and holy is he that hath part in the first resurrection, for on such the second death hath no power;' namely, because they are not in *via* but in *patria*, being a prerogative, as I understand it, of the first sort of reigners only, and not of the second. Thus I yet admit the

* Mede's Works, B. iv. p. 776. † Ibid. B. iii. p. 611.

first resurrection to be corporeal, as well as the second, though I confess, I have much striven against it, and if the text would admit another sense less free of paradox, I had yet rather listen unto it, but I find it not. However, to grant a particular resurrection before the general is against no article of faith, for the gospel tells us, Math. 27 : 52–53, that at our Saviour's resurrection, ' The graves were opened, and many bodies of the saints which slept, arose and came out of their graves, and went into the holy city, and appeared unto many.' Neither was the number of them a small number, if we may credit the Fathers, or the most ancient records of Christian tradition. For of this was that famous saying, ' That Christ descended alone, but ascended with a multitude,' which is found in the heads of the sermons of Thaddeus, as they are reported by Eusebius, out of the Syriac records of the city of Edessa, in Ignatius' Epistle to the Trallians, and in the disputation of Macarius, Bishop of Jerusalem, in the first general Council of Nice, also in Cyril's Catechism. Nay, this Cyril of Jerusalem, Chrysostom, and others, suppose this resurrection to have been common to all the saints that died before our Saviour. However it may be, it holds no unfit-proportion with this supposed of the martyrs. And how it doth more impeach any article of our faith to think that may be of the martyrs, which we believe of the patriarchs, I yet see not."*

He says again, "When at first I perceived that Millennium to be a state of the church consequent to the times of the beast, I was averse from the proper acceptation of that resurrection, taking it for a rising of the church from a dead estate ; yet afterward, more seriously considering and weighing all things, I found no ground or footing for any sense but the literal. (His biographer says : ' He tried all ways imaginable to place the Millennium elsewhere than after the

* Works, B. iii. p. 304.

literal first resurrection, and, if it were possible, to begin it at the reign of Constantine. But after all his striving, he was forced to yield,' &c.) For first, I cannot be persuaded to forsake the proper and usual importment of Scripture language, where neither the insinuation of the text itself, nor manifest tokens of allegory, nor the necessity and nature of the things spoken of (which will bear no other sense) do warrant it. For to do so, were to lose all footing of divine testimony, and instead of Scripture, to believe mine own imagination. Now the 20th of the Apocalypse, of all the narrations of that book, seems to be the most plain and simple, most free from allegory and the involution of prophetic figures; only here and there sprinkled with such metaphors as the use of speech makes equivalent to vulgar expressions, or the former narrations in that book had made to be as words personal or proper names are in the plainest histories; as old serpent, beast, &c. How can a man, then, in so plain and simple a narration, take a passage of so plain and ordinarily expressed words (as those about the first resurrection are) in any other sense than the usual and literal?

"*Secondly.*—Howsoever the word resurrection by itself might seem ambiguous, yet in a sentence composed in this manner,—viz., 'of the dead, those which were beheaded for the witness of Jesus,' &c., 'lived again when the thousand years began; but the rest of the dead lived not again till the thousand years were ended,'—it would be a most harsh and violent interpretation to say that dead, and consequently living again from the dead, should not in both cases be taken in the same meaning. For such a speech, in ordinary construction, implies, that some of the dead lived again in the beginning of the thousand years, in that sense the rest should live again at the end of the thousand years; and *e contra*, in what manner the rest of the dead should live again at the end of the thousand years, in that manner those who were beheaded for Jesus lived again in the beginning of the

MASTERLY ARGUMENTS.—THE NEW STATE. 171

thousand years; which living again of those some, is called the first resurrection."*

Then after referring to the fact that the ancient Jews and the early church believed, and taught a prior resurrection of the righteous, he continues: "Thus I have discovered my opinion of the thing which I suppose the Scripture hath revealed shall be; but *de modo* how it shall be, I would willingly abstain from determining. We must be content to be ignorant of the *manner of things*, which for the matter we are bound to believe. Too much adventuring here, without a sure guide, may be dangerous, and breed intolerable fancies, as it did among some in those ancient times, which occasioned as may seem, the death and burial of the main opinion itself so generally at first believed.

"Yet thus much I conceive the text seems to imply, that these *saints of the first resurrection should reign here on earth in the new Jerusalem* in a state of beatitude and glory partaking of divine presence and vision of Christ their king; as it were in an heaven upon earth, or new paradise immutable, unchangeable, &c." (Mr. Mede would often say that to make Jerusalem *descending out of heaven* to signify *ascending up thither*, was more absurd than that of the Canonist, who expounded *constuimus* we constitute by *abrogamus* we abrogate.)

Secondly. That, for the better understanding of this mystery we must distinguish between the state of the *New Jerusalem* and state of the *nations which shall walk in the light thereof;* they shall not both be one, but much differing. Therefore what is spoken particularly of the *New Jerusalem*, must not be applied to the whole church which then shall be; New Jerusalem is not the whole church, but the metropolis thereof, and of the new world. * * I make this state of the church to belong to the second advent of Christ, or day of the great judgment, when Christ shall appear in the clouds

* Works, B. iv., p. 770.

of heaven to destroy all the professed enemies of his church and kingdom, and deliver the creature from that bondage of corruption brought upon it for the sin of man. * * But the truth is, this state is neither before nor after [the day of judgment], but *the day of judgment itself*, the *time itself of the second appearing of Christ*. And it is to be remembered here, that the Jews, who gave this time the name of *the day of judgment*, and from whom our Saviour and his apostles took it, never understood thereby [anything] but a time of many years continuance, yea some (*mirabile dictu*) of a thousand years."*

Mede taught the sex-millennial duration of the world, the renovation of the earth, and looked for the kingdom not far in the future.

Such is the voice of Joseph Mede, whom Prof. Bush styles, " One of the profoundest Biblical scholars of the English Church, of whom it was said that in the explication of the mysterious passages of Scripture, ' he discerned the day before others had opened their eyes,'"* and whose works, to use the language of Dr. Duffield, have done more to revive the study of the prophecies, and to promote Millennarian doctrine than those perhaps of any other man. May we, like him, not only be Christians, but also Bible students! Mede died in 1638.

TWISS, A. D. 1625.

William Twiss was a pupil of Mede's, and in all his Letters to him—numbering fifteen, and preserved in Mede's Works—expressed the highest admiration for his views, saying at one time, " O, Mr. Mede, I would willingly spend my days in hanging upon your lips,"&c., " to hear you discourse upon the glorious kingdom of Christ here on earth, to begin with the ruin of Antichrist." Again he says: " I heartily

* Works, B. iv., p. 770.   *Bush on the Mill p. 28.

thank you for all, and particularly for that speculation of the untimely advancing of the martyrs;"* referring, we suppose, to their prior resurrection, as taught in Revelation, 20th chapter. So, too, writes Usher, who observed of Mede's Comment on the Apocalypse, " I cannot sufficiently commend it.' These two great men seemed to sit at Mede's feet and learn prophetic truth. Twiss was President of the Westminster Assembly.

USHER.

James Usher, D. D., Archbishop of Armagh, Ireland, was born 1581, at Dublin. He was distinguished for his native talent and great learning, and is well known to have been the author of the common chronology of the Bible. Instead of looking for a joyous time in the future, this celebrated prelate anticipated severe tribulation to come on the church, observing, " The greatest stroke upon the Reformed Church is yet to come; and the time of the utter ruin of the see of Rome shall be when she thinks herself most secure." "Again he says, "A very great persecution will fall upon all the Protestant Churches of Europe. I tell you, all you have yet seen hath been but the beginning of sorrows to what is yet to come upon the Protestant Churches of Christ, which will, ere long, fall under sharper persecution than ever. Therefore look ye, be not found in the outer court, but a worshipper in the temple, before the altar. * * And this shall be one great difference between the last and all other preceding persecutions. For in the former the most eminent and spiritual ministers and Christians did generally suffer most. But in this last persecution these shall be preserved by God as a seed to partake of that glory which shall immediately follow and come upon the church, as soon as this storm shall be over. For as it shall be the sharpest so shall it be the shortest persecution of them all,"† &c. Brooks

*Mede's Works, B. iv. p. 845.   † Elm. Proph. Int., p. 232.

says that he uttered these sentiments in the immediate prospect of death, and also refers them to expected Pre-millennial judgments; Usher saying they would take away "only the gross hypocrites and formal professors." On the Millennium, Usher followed the Augustinian theory, but Mr. Brook affirms that "From the manner, however, in which he afterwards concurred in much which was submitted to him by Mede and others (as may be seen from his communications published in Mede's Works,) we must conclude that he latterly renounced this opinion and became a Millennarian."*

Mede, writing to Twiss of Usher, says: "He did not discover any aversion or opposition to the notion I represented thereabout. The like, Mr. Wood told me of him after he read his papers; nay, that he uses this compliment to him at their parting: 'I hope we shall meet together in *resurrection prima.*'" Then remarking that Usher was shy of committing himself on the question, he adds: "Yet the speeches I observed to fall from him were no wise discouraging. He told me once he had a brother who would say, he could never believe but the 1000 years were still to come."†

MATON, A. D. 1642.

Robert Maton, A. M., Minister and Commoner at Oxford in 1642, was a Pre-millennialist. After remarking that "We may justly doubt whether our Saviour hath as yet executed the office of king," he refers to Coll. 2: 15; Eph. 4. 8; Coll. 2: 10; Heb. 1: 3, &c., allowing their fulfillment, and then proceeds to argue as follows: "Yet that he doth not now reign in that kingdom which he shall govern as man, and consequently in that of which the prophets spake, his own words in Rev. 3: 21, do clearly prove, 'To him that overcometh I will grant to set with me in my throne,' &c., from whence it follows that the throne which here he calls his

---

* Elm. Proph. Int., p. 89.   † Mede's Works, B. iv., p. 851.

own; and which he hath not yet received, Heb. 2 : 8 and 10. 12, 13, must needs belong unto him as a man: because the place where now he sits is the Father's throne, a throne in which he hath no proper interest but as God. Again, it follows, that seeing he is now in his Father's throne, therefore neither is this the time nor the place in which his own throne is to be erected; not the place, for in one kingdom there can be but one throne, and not the time, for then he should sit in his own throne, which now he doth not do, and the reason of it (as it is intimated in the first words) is because the time in which all that shall ever come are to be called, is not yet at an end. And this also the answer to the souls under the altar doth fully confirm."

Quoting Rev. 6: 11, also 2: 26, in connection with Luke 22: 28, Maton further adds: " I know these words are taken by interpreters for a metaphorical expression of those joys which we shall receive in heaven, but it is a current axiom in our schools that we must not forsake the literal and proper sense of the Scriptures, unless an evident necessity doth require it, or the truth thereof would be endangered by it. And I am sure here is no cause for which we should leave the natural interpretation of the place," &c. He then urges from these passages the certainty of the personal reign. On Rev. 20th, he says: " When our Saviour comes to reign over all the earth he comes not alone, but brings all the saints with him : which words establish the literal sense of the first resurrection in Revelation, 20th chapter."* Maton's whole argument is clear, Scriptural and convincing.

ADAMS, A. D. 1650.

Thomas Adams, a learned tutor of Cromwell's time, at London, in his exposition of 2nd Peter, chapter 3rd, though he controverts the sex-millennial duration of the world, admits

* Israel's Redemption. Pub. 1642.

that it was taught by the Jewish Rabbins and Talmuds, also in the early church and later by others, and on verse second says: "The end in the Apostle's times was not far off; now it must be very near. If that were the last day, this must be the last hour; or if that were the last hour, this is the last minute. From all this we may gather, that so deep are we fallen into the latter end of these last times, that for aught we know, before we depart from this place, we may look for the last fire to flash in our faces."* This is the right method of preaching.

GOODWIN, A. D. 1650.

Thomas Goodwin, D.D., was born in Norfolk, Eng., in 1600. He was celebrated as a dissenter: Anthony Wood calling him and Dr. Owen "the two atlasses and patriarchs of independency." He advocated the year-day theory of the prophetic numbers, and of the 1335 days of Daniel, says, it would reach to the time "of the full and final end which shall be the great resurrection and thousand years reign of Christ." He observes, "There is a special world, called the world to come, appointed for Jesus Christ eminently to reign in; and therefore, though all the other senses to which I have referred, are true and good, yet let me add this to it, that God did not content himself to bestow this world upon Christ, for him to rule and reign in, and to order and dispose the affairs of it as he doth, and, after the day of judgment to reign in that sense you heard spoken of afore forever, more gloriously than he did before; but he hath appointed a special world on purpose for him, between this world and the end of the day of judgment (and the day of judgment itself is part of it, if not the whole of it,) wherein our Lord and Saviour Jesus Christ shall reign; which world the Scriptures eminently calleth "the world to come," Christ's world as I may call it, that as this present world was ordained for the first

* Adam's Expositions.

Adam, and God hath given it unto the sons of men; so there is a world to come appointed for the second Adam, as the time after the day of judgment is God the Father's in a more eminent manner, who then shall be " all in all." Quoting Heb. 2 : 5, also 2nd Pet. 3rd chapter as proof, he afterwards continues, " Yea, my brethren, let me add this to it also that God doth take the same world that was Adam's, and make it new and glorious. The same creation groaneth for this new world, this new clothing—as we groan to be clothed upon so doth this whole creation. And as God takes the same substance of man's nature and engrafteth the new creature upon it, the same man still; so he takes the same world that was Adam's, and makes it new and glorious, a new world for the second Adam. For the substance of the same world shall be restored to a glory which Adam could never have raised it unto—the same world that was lost in Adam. And this God will do before he hath done with it, and this restitution is ' the world to come.' Read the prophets and you shall find promises of strange and wonderful things, of glorious times, and that here upon earth."

" Now it is said that the first resurrection is a spiritual resurrection of men's souls from the death of sin. But consider with yourselves a little: first, it is the souls of men dead; that is plain, for he saith they were slain with the sword, they were beheaded for the witness of Jesus; and as their death is, so must their resurrection be; their death was certainly a bodily death, for they were beheaded, therefore their resurrection must be answerable to it. And, to mention no other arguments, ' they reigned with Christ a thousand years.' This is not the glory of heaven, for that is for ever; and so they had reigned from the first time they were slain, if that glory were meant; but they reign upon their rising, for he says, ' the rest of the dead lived not again till the thousand years are expired.' Therefore the opposition implies, that it is a living again, and a proper resurrection

Now where do these reign? It should seem on earth by this argument; because why else is the devil bound up? He need not be bound up for their reigning in heaven."

Dr. Goodwin, on his chronological position, says, in 1676, "Let an indefinite warning that these things are approaching, and we within the reach of them, suffice, for to move us to prepare for them; which is the only use of knowing them. It may be said of the time of these things, as it is said of the day of death, *Latet hic dies, ut observetur omnis dies*; the day and year of the accomplishment of these great matters are hid from us, that so each day and year we may be found ready, whenever they shall come upon us (as in this age wherein we live they are likely to do.)*

Such is the voice of the pious Goodwin, who was a member of the Westminster Assembly, and who died in 1679.

MILTON, A. D. 1660.

John Milton, "The Christian Homer," the renowned author of Paradise Lost, was born in London, 1608. His genius, creative imagination, mental sublimity, and power exhibited in the production of this great work is the admiration of all. An Arian Baptist in sentiment, he entered fully into the doctrine of the second advent; taught the final re-creation of the earth and the near coming and personal reign of the Lord Jesus. In a prayer for England, he thus addresses the Deity: "When thou, the eternal, and shortly expected King, shall open the clouds, to judge the several kingdoms of the world, and shalt put an end to all earthly tyrannies, proclaiming thy universal and mild monarchy through heaven and earth, &c." On the personal reign, he justly remarks—"That this reign will be on earth is evident from many passages." Quoting Psa. 2: 8, 9; Rev. 2: 25-27; Psa. 110: 5, 6; Isa. 9: 6, 7; Dan. 7: 22-27; Luke 1: 32, 33; Math. 19: 28, and Luke 22: 29, 30, in order,

* Goodwin's Expositions.

as proof-texts, on the last one he adds, that, "The judgment here spoken of will not be confined to a single day, but will extend through a great space of time; the word being used to denote not so much a judicial enquiry, properly so called, as an exercise of dominion; in which sense Gideon, Jepthah and others judged Israel," referring the reader then to Rev. 5 : 10, 11, 15, and 20 : 1–7.*

He also teaches that—

"The world shall burn and from her ashes spring
New heaven and earth wherein the just shall dwell;
And after all their tribulations long
See golden days." *Par. Lost*, iii. 3 : 334.
"For the earth
Shall all be Paradise, far happier place
Than this of Eden, and far happier days." *Ibid.* xii : 461.

And on the world's course and destiny, again he says—

"Truth shall retire
Bestuck with slanderous darts, and works of faith
Rarely be found; so shall the world go on,
To good malignant, to bad men benign,
Under her own weight groaning till the day
Appear, of reparation to the just,
And vengeance to the wicked at return
Ot him—thy Saviour and thy Lord;
Last in the clouds from heaven to be revealed,
In glory of the Father, to dissolve
Satan, with his perverted world; then raise
From the conflagrant mass, purged and refined,
New heavens, new earth, ages of endless date,
Founded in righteousness and peace and love,
To bring forth fruits, joy and eternal bliss."
Par. Lost, xii : 535.

Such is the clear and "precious" Pre-millennial "faith" of Milton—whose doctrines in the seventeenth century made Europe tremble, and who quoted the Scriptures as though he

* Treatise on Christian Doctrine vol. ii. ch. 33

believed they literally meant as they spoke. What do his million of admirers, of the spiritual and Post-millennial school, think of him? He died 1674.

JANEWAY, A. D. 1660.

James Janeway, a pious dissenting divine, at Oxford, and who also died in 1674, thus sweetly writes: "Of this I am confident, through infinite mercy, that the very meditation of that day (of judgment) hath ever ravished my soul; and the thought of the certainty and nearness of it is more refreshing to me than the comforts of the whole world." Blessed Janeway! may thy spirit be mine. He loved the "appearing" of Jesus, 2 Tim. 4: 8.

JEREMY TAYLOR, A. D. 1665.

Jeremy Taylor, D. D., Bishop of Down and Connor, was born 1613, at Cambridge, England. He was a pious and eloquent writer, and his works stand high among those of British theologians. While he condemns the early Chiliastic belief, he at the same time admits the primitive catholicity of the doctrine, and evidently argues a prior resurrection for the just, saying: "The resurrection shall be universal; good and bad shall rise; yet not all together; but first Christ—then we that are Christ's—and then there is another resurrection, though it is not spoken of here. My text speaks only of the resurrection of the just—of them that belong to Christ. * * * But there is one thing more in it yet: every man in his own order. First, Christ, and then they that are Christ's; but what shall become of them that are not Christ's? Why, there is an order for them too; first, they that are Christ's, and then they that are *not* his: 'Blessed and holy is he that hath his part in the first resurrection.' There is a *first* and a *second* resurrection even after this life; 'the dead in Christ will rise first;' now blessed are they that have their portion here; for upon these the second death shall have no power. * * * Paul *implies* the more universal resurrection unto judgment, wherein the wicked also shall rise to condemnation."* The reader will not fail to see that he makes the first resurrection of Rev. 20, a literal one: the admission of a cardinal point in Pre-millennialism. So the English prophetical writers regard it.† Showing how doctrines of antiquity were contradicted by modern ecclesiastics and councils, he gives the views of primitive Christians on the delay of rewards and glorification until the Advent, as follows:

"That is a plain recession from antiquity, which was determined by the council of Florence, 'that the souls of the pious, being purified, are immediately at death received into heaven, and behold clearly the triune God just as he is:' for those who please to try, may see it dogmatically resolved to the contrary, by Justin Martyr, Irenæus, Origen, Chrysostom, Theodoret, Arethas, Cæariensis, Euthymius, who may answer for the Greek Church. And it is plain that it was the opinion of the Greek Church, by that great difficulty the Romans had of bringing the Greeks to subscribe to the Florentine Council, where the Latins acted their master-piece of wit and stratagem,—the greatest that hath been till the famous and super-politic Council of Trent. And for the Latin Church, Tertullian, Ambrose, Austin, Hilary, Prudentius, Lactantius, Victorinus, and Bernard, are known to be of opinion, that the souls of the saints are in '*abditis receptaculis et exterioribus atriis*,' where they expect the resurrection of their bodies and the glorification of their souls; and though they all believe them to be happy, yet that they enjoy not the beatific vision before the resurrection."‡ Mr. Brooks remarks on this that "the testimony of the church is

---

* Sermon on 1st Cor. 15: 23. † Vide Elem. Proph. Int., p. 78.
‡ Liberty of Prophesying, Sec. viii. p. 216.

uniform on this point down to Popish times: the early Reformers maintaining the same primitive faith."*

Jeremy Taylor maintained the literal system of Biblical interpretation, and as exhibited in his writings, evidently cherished an ardent love for the appearing of the blessed Saviour. He was chaplain to king Charles the First, and died in 1677.

WATSON, A. D. 1670.

Thomas Watson, a pious divine, who died in 1673, thus writes: "For the time of the general judgment is a secret kept from the angels, but this is sure, it can not be far off. When the elect are all converted, then Christ will come to judgment."†

BAXTER, A. D. 1670.

Richard Baxter was born in Shropshire, England, 1615. He was minister at Kidderminster, and also chaplain in th: army, refusing the see of Hereford. His works are univer sally admired, and no eulogy upon him is here required. Expecting the personal return of Jesus, he thus sweetly and calmly writes: "Would it not rejoice your hearts if you were sure to live to see the coming of the Lord, and to see his glorious appearing, and retinue? If you were not to die, but to be caught up thus to meet the Lord, would you be averse to this? Would it not be the greatest joy that you could desire? For my own part, I must confess to you, that death as death, appeareth to me as an enemy, and my nature doth abhor and fear it. But the thoughts of the coming of the Lord are most sweet and joyful to me, so that if I were but sure that I should live to see it, and that the trumpet should sound, and the dead should rise, and the Lord appear

* Elem. Proph. Int., p. 64. † Body of Divin., p. 208

before the period of my age, it would be the joyfullest tidings to me in the world. Oh, that I might see his kingdom come!"*

"Whether He will come before the general resurrection and reign on earth a thousand years, I shall not presume to pass my determination; but sure I am, it is the work of faith and character of his saints to love his appearing and to look for that blessed hope; 'The Spirit and the Bride say come; even so come, Lord Jesus, come quickly,' is the voice of faith, and hope, and love. But I find not that his servants are thus characterized by their desire to die. It is the presence of their Lord that they desire, but it is death that they abhor, and therefore, though they cannot submit to death, it is the coming of Christ that they love and long for. If death be the last enemy to be destroyed at the resurrection, we may learn how earnestly believers should long and pray for the second coming of Christ, when this full and final conquest shall be made. There is something in death that is penal even to believers: but in the coming of Christ and their resurrection there is nothing but glorifying grace."†

"Though I have not skill enough in the exposition of hard prophecies, to make a particular determination about the thousand years reign of Christ on earth before the final judgment, yet, I may say, that I cannot confute what such learned men as Mr. Mede, Dr. Twiss, and others (after the old Fathers) have hereof asserted. * * * But I believe there will be a new heaven and earth on which will dwell righteousness."‡

"This is the day that all believers should long, and hope, and wait for, as being the accomplishment of all the work of their redemption, and all the desires and endeavors of their souls. * * * Hasten, O Lord, this blessed day! Stay

---

* Works, vol xvii., p. 555.   † Works, vol. xvii., p. 500.
‡ Ibid, vol. ii. p. 513.

not till faith have left the earth; and infidelity, and impiety, and tyranny have conquered the rest of thine inheritance! Stay not till selfish, uncharitable pride hath vanquished love and self-denial, and planted its colonies of heresy, cruelty, and confusion in thy dominions; and earth and hell be turned into one! Stay not till the eyes of thy servants fail, and their hearts and hopes do faint and languish with looking and waiting for their salvation! But if the day be not at hand, O keep up faith, and hope, and love till the sun of perfect love arise, and time hath prepared us for eternity and grace for glory."*

On Christ's most glorious coming and appearance, he says: "We daily behold the forerunners of his coming foretold by himself. We see the fig tree putteth forth leaves, and therefore know that summer is nigh. Though the riotous would say my Lord delayeth his coming, yet the saints lift up their heads, for their redemption draweth nigh. Alas! fellow Christians, what should we do if our Lord should not return?"†

In his "Farewell Sermon"‡ he obviously negatives the doctrine of the world's conversion, as taught by many divines. So speaks the "Sainted Baxter." He was a dissenter, and died 1691.

AMBROSE, A. D. 1650.

Isaac Ambrose, a divine of England, of some celebrity, and who during the civil wars became a Presbyterian. In his sermon on Doomsday, he connected the second advent with the seventh trumpet, and also looked for the restoring of all things at the expiration of the 6000 years, exclaiming, "This time is at hand, and is it not time to petition to the judge of heaven? What a dangerous course it is never to call to

* Baxter's Works, vol. iv., p. 164.   † Saint's Rest, ch. 2.
‡ Works, vol. iv., p. 931.

mind that time of times until we see the earth flaming, the heavens melting, the judgment hastening, the Judge with all his angels coming in the clouds, &c. See you now not many signs, as the heralds and forerunners of his glorious coming?"*
His hope was evidently in the coming of the Lord, and no false view of intermediate Millennial blessedness dimmed its glories. We know not the dates of his birth or death.

DURANT, A. D. 1653.

John Durant, a pious Pre-millennialist of the Commonwealth time. "Sweet old Durant," as Rev. D. Brown calls him, advocated the personal reign, and in his work, "Christ's appearance the second time for the salvation of believers," published in 1653, thus enrapturingly writes. " O how glorious will that salvation be, when all the heirs of salvation shall meet together! Now, all are not saved; the whole body now is in trouble for a part. Then all the children of the Father shall meet together in their Father's presence; they shall come from the east and west, from north and south, and sit down in that kingdom; yea, and then all saints shall be sweetly conjoined. Jewels scattered are not so resplendent; but joined in some rich pendant, O how glorious are they! In that day Christ will gather up all his jewels—he will bring in every saint into one—gather them into one great jewel, one precious pendant, which shall jointly lie in his bosom. Now a saved soul sighs and cries, Where is Israel? where is Judah? When will the Lord save them? Why, poor hearts, you shall all meet at that day— be saved with an universal salvation. All, always, altogether in the presence of your Saviour!—surely, then, you will say, that salvation is very sweet. Not one saint shall be missing in that day; but all shall altogether meet and enjoy the salvation of Christ. * * I have heard of a poor man, who it seems loved and longed for Christ's appearance,

* Ambrose's Works, p. 408.

that when there was a great earthquake, and when many cried out, the day of judgment was come, and one cried, Alas! alas! what shall I do? and a third, How shall I hide myself? That poor man only said, 'Ah! is it so? Is the day come? Where shall I go? Upon what mountain shall I stand to see my Saviour?'"*

How does this love for 'His appearing' rebuke the cold and unloving spirit of very many modern Christians!

ALLEINE, A. D. 1660.

Joseph Alleine, A. B. Born in Wiltshire, Eng., 1623, was educated at Oxford, and became a classic scholar and eminent preacher, and lived and died universally beloved. Brooks calls him a Millennarian. In a letter written to his flock while in Ilchester goal for preaching the gospel, he says:—

"But now, my brethren, I shall not so much call upon you to remember the resurrection of Christ as the return of Christ. Behold he cometh in the clouds, and every eye shall see him—your eyes and mine eyes—and all the tribes of the earth shall mourn because of him. But we shall lift up our heads because the day of our redemption draweth nigh. This is the day I look for and wait for, and have laid up all my hopes in. If the Lord return not, I profess myself undone—my preaching is vain, and my suffering is vain, and the bottom in which I have entrusted all my hopes is for ever miscarried. But I know whom I have trusted; we are built upon the foundation of his sure word, and how fully doth that word assure us that this same Jesus who is gone up into heaven, shall so return. O, how sure is the thing! How near is the time! How glorious will his appearing be! What generous cordials hath he left us in his parting sermons and his last prayer; and yet of all the rest, these words are the sweetest; I will come again and receive you to myself, that where

* D. Brown on the Second Advent, second edition, pp 74–7.

I am there ye may be also. And will He come? Tremble then, ye sinners; but triumph, ye saints! Clap your hands all ye that look for the consolation of Israel. O children of the Most High, how will you forget your travail and be melted into joy! This is he in whom you have believed; whom not having seen ye have loved. O my soul, look out and long! O my brethren, be you as the mother of Sisera, looking out at the windows, and watching at the lattice, saying, Why are his chariot wheels so long in coming? Though the time till ye shall see him be very short, yet love and longing make it seem tedious. My beloved, comfort your hearts with these words: look upon these things as the greatest realities, and let your affections be answerable to your expectations. I would not have told you these things unless I had believed them; it is for this hope that I am bound with this chain.* Mr. Brooks justly observes that " these passages " afford an evidence of the practical tendency of the Saviour's advent, and of the proper mode of handling the subject." Alleine was a non-conformist, was the author of the " Alarm," and died 1668.

WESTMINSTER ASSEMBLY, A. D. 1643.

The Westminster Assembly was convened by Parliament during the reign of Charles I., 1643, and composed of 10 Lords, 20 Commoners, and 121 Divines, Episcopalians, Dissenters, Independents, &c. Buck says: " They were called for the purpose of settling the government, liturgy, and doctrines of the Church of England, and the divines were men of eminent learning and godliness." They framed " The Directory for Public Worship," " The Confession of Faith," " The Larger and Shorter Catechisms," and signed the " Solemn League and Covenant," and several of them published the "Assemblie's Annotations," " sentences in which," says Mr. Brooks, " it cannot be reasonably questioned, were

* Elem. Proph. Int., p. 98

intended to be understood in a Millennarian sense."* Dr Duffield also affirms that "they express Millennarian doctrines."† Robert Bailee, Principal of the University of Glasgow, died 1662, one of the members of this Assembly, and a strong Anti-millennarian, thus records the Pre-millennial faith of this august body. Writing to Wm. Spang at the time, he says, "Rev. and dear Bro. * * *, Send me the rest of Forbes: I like the book very well, and the man much better for the book's sake. I marvel I can find nothing in it against the Millennarians. I cannot think the author a Millennary. I cannot dream why he should have omitted an error so famous in antiquity, and so troublesome among us; for the most of the chief divines here, not only Independents, but others, such as Twiss, Marshall, Palmer, and many more are express Chiliasts."‡ The celebrated John Selden, the erudite Henry Ainsworth, D. D., the learned Thomas Gataker, the admired Daniel Featly, D. D., together with Wm. Twiss, who was Moderator of this body, Thomas Goodwin, D. D., Stephen Marshall, Jeremiah Burroughs, Herbert Palmer, Joseph Caryll, Simeon Ash, Wm. Bridge, A. M., Wm. Gouge, D. D., J. Langley, and Peter Sterry, of London, some of whose writings are lost, but most of whom speak for themselves, were among the "chief divines" of the Westminster Assembly, the majority of whose members, as Duffield, Brooks, Anderson and others argue, were evidently Pre-millennialists.

What do Congregationalists and Presbyterians every where think of the doings and doctrines of the Westminster Assembly?

RUTHERFORD, 1643.

Samuel Rutherford was Professor of Divinity at St. Andrews, in Scotland, 1643, and he and Bailee were styled "the

* Elem. Proph. Int., p. 92. † Duffield on Proph., p. 255.
‡ Letter 117, vol. ii., p. 156.

greatest lights of their day." In his "Letters" he constantly refers to the nearness of Christ's day in language like the following: "Indeed our fair morning is at hand, the day-star is near the riseing, and we are not many miles from home."* "That fallen Star, the Prince of the bottomless pit, knoweth it is near the time when he shall be tormented."† "This day is fast coming; yet a little while and the vision will speak, it will not tarry."‡ "The day is near the dawning, the sky is riving, our Beloved will be on us ere ever we be aware."§ "It is time enough for us to laugh when our Lord Christ laugheth, and that will be shortly. For when we hear of wars and rumors of wars, the Judge's feet are then before the door, and he must be in heaven, giving order to the angels to make themselves ready, and prepare their sickles for that great harvest. Christ will be on us in haste. Watch but a little, and, ere long, the skies shall rend, and that fair, lovely person, Jesus, will come in the clouds, fraught and loaded with glory."‖ "We are in the last days." "The day of the Lord is now near at hand." "The blast of the last trumpet is now hard at hand. This world's span-length of time, is drawn now to less than half an inch, and to the point of the evening of the day of this old gray-haired world."¶

That Rutherford did not hold to the conversion of the whole world before the Lord's advent, seems evident from his saying that "The Lord's Bride will be up and down, above the water swimming, and under the water sinking, until her lovely and mighty Redeemer and Husband set his head through these skies, and come with his fair court to settle all their disputes and give them the hoped for inheritance."** Again he says, on the doctrine of Christ's personal reign, that the church ought to "Avouch the royal crown and

* Letters, p. 62.   † Ibid, p. 77.   ‡ Ibid, p. 84.   § Ibid, p. 89
‖ Ibid, p. 94.   ¶ Ibid, p. 367.   ** Letters, p. 111.

absolute supremacy of our Lord Jesus Christ, the Prince of the kings of the earth, as becometh, for certain it is that Christ will reign the Father's king in Mount Zion; and his sworn covenant will not be buried."* Again, "Put on thy glittering crown, O thou Maker of kings, and make but one stride, or one step of the whole earth, and travel in the greatness of thy strength; Isa. 63: 1, and let thy apparel be red, and all dyed with the blood of thy enemies thou art fallen righteous heir by line to the kingdoms of the world."† And on the bringing in of Israel he says, "O for a sight in this flesh of mine of the prophesied marriage between Christ and them. The kings of Tarshish, and of the isles, must bring presents to our Lord Jesus. Psa. 72: 10. And Britain is one of the chiefest isles; why then but we may believe, that our kings of this island shall come in, and bring their glory to the New Jerusalem, wherein Christ shall dwell in the latter days? It is our part to pray, 'that the kingdoms of the earth may become Christ's."‡

Whether "the seraphic Rutherford," as D. Brown, of Scotland, calls him, was Pre-millennial, or Post-millennial in his views of Christ's advent, we know not certainly, but we judge from his letters that the latter was the case; this we do know, that he loved his Lord's appearing, and seemed to be like one of whom Wesley sings, that "waited in an agony" for his advent. He says:

"The Lord hath told you what ye should be doing till He come; wait and hasten, saith Peter, for the coming of your Lord. All is night that is here, in respect of ignorance and daily ensuing troubles, one always making way to another as the ninth wave of the sea to the tenth; therefore, sigh and long for the dawning of that morning, and the breaking of that day of the coming of the Son of Man, when the shadows shall flee away. Persuade yourself that the King is coming

* Letters, p. 549. † Ibid, p. 470. ‡ Ibid, p. 460

Read his letter sent before Him, Rev. 22 : 20, Behold I come quickly. Wait with the wearied night-watch, for the breaking of the eastern sky, and think that ye have not a morrow; as the wise father said, who, being invited against to-morrow to dine with his friends, answered, 'These many days I have had no morrow at all.'"*

I half call his absence cruel; and the mask and vail on Christ's face, a cruel covering that hideth such a fair face from a sin sick soul. I dare not challenge himself, but his absence is a mountain of iron upon my heavy heart. O, when shall we meet ? Oh, how long is it to the dawning of the marriage day ! O, sweet Lord Jesus, take wide steps ! O, my Lord, come over mountains at one stride ! O, my beloved, flee like a roe, or a young hart, on the mountains of separation. Oh, that He would fold the heavens together like an old cloak, and shovel time and days out of the way, and make ready in haste the Lamb's wife for her husband. Since He looked upon me my heart is not mine own, he hath run away to heaven with it."†

"O day, dawn ! O time, run fast ! O bridegroom, post, post fast, that we may meet ! O, Heavens, cleave in two, that that bright face and head may set itself through the clouds ! Oh, that the corn were ripe, and this world prepared for his sickle."‡

"The wife of youth, that wants her husband some years, and expects he shall return to her from over sea lands, is often on the shore; every ship coming near shore is her new joy; her heart loves the wind that shall bring him home. She asks at every passenger news, O, saw ye my husband ? What is he doing ? When shall he come ? Is he shipped for a return ? Every ship that carrieth not her husband is the breaking of her heart."

"The bush hath been burning above five thousand years,

* Letters, p. 37. † Letters, p. 276. ‡ Ib. p. 349.

and we never yet saw the ashes of this fire. He cannot fail to bring judgment to victory. O, that we could wait for our hidden life! O, that Christ would remove the covering, draw aside the curtain of time, and rend the heavens, and come down! O, that he who feedeth among the lilies would cry to his heavenly trumpeters, 'make ready, let us go down and fold together the four corners of the world, and marry the bride!' "*

Rutherford was born about 1600, and died in 1661 a saint of blessed memories.

FARMER, A. D. 1660.

Joseph Farmer, of England, in 1660, wrote and published a little volume, bearing the title of "A sober Enquiry, or Christ's reign with his saints, modestly asserted from the Scriptures." This work was republished in 1843, by Rev. J. Lillie, of New York, who endorses its sentiments. The Edinburgh Presbyterian Review says, "The spirit of this little piece of antiquity, is admirable calm, candid and christian."†

Farmer says, "I argue as followeth:—The kingdom of the Son of Man, and of the saints of the most high in Daniel, begins when the great judgment sits. The kingdom in the Apocalypse, chap. 20: 4; wherein the saints reign with Christ a thousand years, is the same with the kingdom of the Son of Man, and the saints of the Most High in the prophet Daniel; therefore it also begins at the great judgment. The one thousand years begin with the day of judgment, which is not consummated till Gog and Magog's destruction at their end; therefore the whole thousand years is included in that great day of judgment. The resurrection of the just will take place in the morning of the day of judgment, or beginning of the thousand years, and is called 'the

---

* Letters, p. 507, Carter's edition. † Jan. No. 1843.

first resurrection,' literally in the Greek, 'this resurrection that first,' a singular emphasis to denote some first resurrection known and spoken of in the writings of the prophets and apostles."*

"Yea, Paul himself declares this first resurrection in 1 Thess. 4: 16, 'The dead in Christ shall rise first.' The Vulgate hath the word *primi*, but the Greek is the adverb; still it comes to all one. And hence Chrysostom upon the place saith, 'The just shall rise before the wicked, that they may be first in the resurrection, not only in dignity, but in time.' Now if the dead *in Christ* shall rise first, when shall the wicked arise but in a second resurrection? And if the resurrection St. Paul speaks of be the resurrection of the body, why is not the resurrection of St. John, Rev. 20: the resurrection of the body too?"†

Again he says, "It will be a Millennium *aureum* or *aureum siculum*. It will be a golden day and age indeed, for the holy city, the New Jerusalem, that city of gold and pearl doth contemporate and synchronize with the thousand years, as might be abundantly proved, if Mede had not done it to my hand." Farmer regarded that day as near, and writes: "Pray we therefore for the ruin of Antichrist. Arise, O Lord, and hasten thy coming!"

STERRY, A. D. 1653.

Peter Sterry, a minister and author at London, in 1653, was a decided Pre-millennarian. In his recommendation of Dr. Holmes, "Resurrection Revealed," he writes in the following beautiful strain:—"The subject, (which is the reign of our Saviour, with his saints on the earth) is of a transcendant glory in itself, of universal consequence to all persons and states, and of very great reasonableness for present times. Like a piece of rich coin, it hath long been buried in

* Sober Enquiry, &c., p. 115. † Ibid, p. 115.

the earth; but of late days digged up again, it begins to grow bright with handling; and to pass current with great numbers of saints, and learned men of great authority. As the same star at several seasons is the evening star, setting immediately after the sun, and the morning star shining immediately before it; so was this truth the evening star to the first coming of Christ, and giving of the Spirit, setting together with the glory of that day in a night of Antichristianism: now it appears again in our times as a morning star to that blessed day of the second effusion of the Spirit, and the second appearance of our Saviour in the glory of the Father."* Sterry was a member of the Westminster Assembly. His illustration is a good one, and we would add that the "Morning Star" is shining yet and will until its light is lost in the Rising Sun.

BURROUGHS, A. D. 1643.

Jeremiah Burroughs, was a preacher at Stepney and Cripplegate, England, and a member of the Westminster Assembly. Dr. Wilkins reckons him among the most eminent of the English divines, for practical divinity. He looked for the advent, and says: "But now if you ask me when shall these things be; when shall Jerusalem be made the praise of the whole earth? It is very hard to determine the particular time, but surely at the end of Antichrist's reign it must be. And how long Antichrist shall reign, that we know certainly; the only difficulty is to reckon the very time of the beginning of his reign. He shall reign for 1260 years, and we have such parallel Scriptures for this, that there is nothing more evident, and generally divines agree upon it."†

Citing several texts in proof, he adds: "Now all the difficulty is about the beginning of the 1260 years;" then saying

* Extracts from English Writings.
† Jerusalem's Glory, p. 89.

some expected them to terminate in his day, he continues: "But there is another computation of those who think the reign of Antichrist did not begin so soon, and they conceive it will be a matter of some 200 years or more, before the beginning of these times. But I think God hath not left it very clear to determine about the time. Only this: God by his strange kind of work among us doth seem as if he were hastening the time, as if it were near at hand; * * * there will be troubles and wars continually till this time. There will be no certainty nor settledness of things till Jerusalem come to be made as the praise of the earth. There will attend affliction to the people of God, yea, and to others too; yea, and there is a curse upon men's spirits which will not be taken off till this time come." Mr. Brooks pronounces him Millennarian in his sentiments.* He died in 1646.

VINCENT, A. D. 1656.

Thomas Vincent, a Dissenting minister at London, who died in 1761, and of whose Millennial views we know nothing, in a sermon on "Christ's sudden appearance to judgment," preached on the occasion of the great plague, 1666, says: "Citizens of London! Give me leave to sound another trumpet in your ears, and to forewarn you of a ten thousand times more dreadful judgment; I mean the last and general judgment of the whole world, at the second appearance of our Lord Jesus Christ, who will most certainly and very quickly be revealed from heaven in flaming fire."† Such preaching is in the style of the angel of Rev. 14 : 6. This he says in his Preface, and quoting still further, Vincent says in his work:—

"'Surely I come quickly. Amen. Even so come, Lord Jesus.'—Rev. 23 : 20. The last words of a dear friend are usually most remarked and best remembered, especially when

* Elem. Proph. Int., p. 93.   † From the English Writings.

they speak great affection. These are the last words of Jesus Christ, the best friend that the children of man ever had, which he sends his angels from heaven, after he had been some years in glory with the Father, to speak in his name unto his churches upon the earth, ver. 16, 'I, Jesus, have sent mine angel to testify these things in the churches; and of all the things which he testifieth by his angel, this is the last and the sweetest in the text, ' Surely I come quickly. Which words of promise coming down from heaven, and expressing so much love to the church, are followed with an echo, and resound of the church's earnest desire, ' Amen. Even so come, Lord Jesus,' &c. Hence observe—

"Doct. 1. That the Lord Jesus Christ will certainly and quickly appear.

"Doct. 2. That there is an earnest desire and longing in the church after Christ's appearance."

Oh, that this were true of the church generally in these days! After speaking at length of the manner and object of Christ's coming, and the attending resurrection and judgment, applying the subject, with great power, to the hearts of all, he proceeds:

"The third thing promised, is to show that the Lord Jesus will quickly appear; that is, he will come within a short time.

"'He that shall come, will come,' there is the certainty of his coming, and 'yet a little while, he will come, and will not tarry,' there is the speediness of his coming. 'The Lord is at hand,' Phil. 4:5. 'The coming of the Lord draweth nigh,' James 5:8. 'The Judge standeth at the door,' ver. 9. 'The end of all things is at hand,' 1 Peter 4:7. Therefore our days are called the 'last days,' 2 Tim. 3:1. 'And upon us the ends of the world are come,' 1 Cor. 10:11. We live in the end of the world, in the last days, in the old age thereof The world hath as it were three ages: the youth, the middle age, and the old age; the youth of the world was from the creation to the flood; the middle age from the flood to the first coming of Christ; the old age from the first coming of Christ to the second coming. The old age and last days of the world began in the apostles' time; now many of them are spent, and we are come not only to the declining years, but also to the decrepid age of the world. And if the Lord Jesus Christ were to come shortly in the days of the apostles, *much more shortly* will he come now, when so many years are past since the Scriptures were writ, and these things foretold."*

HALL, A. D. 1657

Thomas Hall, B. D., pastor of Kingsnorton, England, was the author of a work against Pre-millennialism, published in London, 1657. We extract from it to exhibit the faith of our elder divines, while as yet the Whitbyan theory of the Millennium was unknown. Writing in opposition to Dr. Homes, after saying "that ever the church should come to that height of happiness on earth, as to be free from troubles, internal and external, and to reign with Christ here for a thousand years in a sinless, sorrowless, temptationless condition, is a mere dream, and hath no ground in Scripture,"—in a final summary of his arguments he thus writes:—

"Against the Doctor's thesis I shall set down this antithesis:

"That Christ shall not reign personally with the saints or martyrs here on earth for a thousand years, neither before the day of Judgment, in the day of judgment, nor after it. If ever there be such a reign it must be in one of those times. But it is in neither.

"1. It cannot be before the day of judgment for these reasons. 1. Because the last days will be perilous, not pleasant

* English Writings.

days, 2 Tim. 3 : 1, 2, 3. *They will be full of security, sensuality and iniquity*, insomuch that when Christ comes he shall scarce find any faith on earth, Luke 18: 8, Math. 24: 37, 38, WICKEDNESS WILL MOST ABOUND TOWARDS THE END OF THE WORLD.

"2. If the church of Christ on earth be a mixt society, consisting of good and bad to the end of the world, then it cannot subsist for a thousand years only of good men. But the church of Christ on earth to the end of he world, is a mixt society, consisting of tares and wheat, good and bad, a Gog and Magog to molest the saints to the end of the world. Matthew 13: 40; Rev. 20: 7, 8.

"3. If Christ remain in heaven till the day of judgment, then he cannot reign corporally a thousand years on earth before that day. But the antecedent is true, and therefore the consequent. Acts 3: 21 ; John 14: 3. Whom the heaven must contain till the time that all things be restored, i. e., until the time of his coming to judgment, when he shall appear again for the full consummation of the glory of his elect, and perfect accomplishment of his kingdom ; then all shall be repaired which sin hath disordered, and the creature be delivered from the bondage of corruption, into the glorious liberty of the sons of God, Rom. 8: 21; it is from heaven, and not from earth, (saith our creed,) that Christ shall come to judge the quick and the dead.

"4. If God's church (whilst in this world) must look for afflictions, temptations, persecutions; then this imaginary reign without sin or sorrow cannot be expected here. But God's church (whilst on earth) must look for afflictions, temptations, and persecutions here. 2 Tim. 3: 12. All Christ's disciples must take up their cross daily, though they be righteous, yet must they look for many troubles, Ps. 34: 19 ; Acts 14: 22.

"5. Christ's kingdom is not of this world, John 18: 36. And therefore, when the Jews would have made him a king, he conveyed himself from amongst them, John 6 : 15. His kingdom in this world is spiritual, not carnal; it is not without any worldly pomp, neither doth it consist in meat, drink or marriage, Matt. 22 : 30. 1 Cor. 6 : 13. Rom. 14 : 27 A woe is denounced against those that have their carnal delights, and their portion of pleasures here. Luke 6: 25. James 5 : 5.

"6. That tenet which is *contrary to the judgment of all the church of Christ*, ought to be suspected by us.

"9. It makes the ruin of Antichrist to be a thousand years or more before the day of judgment, WHEN THE SCRIPTURE JOINS THEM TOGETHER, 2 Thess. 2 : 8.

"10. It makes the church triumphant when Christ comes, contrary to the tenor of the Scripture, Math. 37 : 38. 2 Tim. 3 : 1.

"11. It is a means to breed security in men when they shall hear that it is yet above a thousand years to the day of judgment; whereas the learned conceive the end of the world to be *much nearer*. And the apostles thought *it was not far off* in their time."

This is a powerful, because an impartial, testimony to the great truths we hold. These propositions prove a temporal Millennium impossible.*

BUNYAN, A. D. 1660.

John Bunyan was born 1628, in Bedfordshire, England. He is the widely known and ingenious author of "Pilgrim's Progress," "The Holy War," and other noted works, and is universally acknowledged to have been one of the most original and interesting writers of the seventeenth century. He was a Baptist in faith and practice. Though his name was not attached to the Baptist Confession of Faith, presented to King Charles in 1660, yet he doubtless approved of it, and evidently believed, with the Baptists of his day, in the personal reign of Christ on the Throne of David, forever.

* From the English Writings.

On Zech. 14: 4, "His feet shall stand in that day upon the Mount of Olives," arguing against the spiritualizers of God's Word, he says, "This is the day of His second coming," and then asks, "Where is the Mount of Olives? Not within thee! But that which is without Jerusalem, before it, on the east side."* A pointed and summary argument truly.

On the Millennium, Bunyan writes as follows: "God's blessing the Sabbath day, and resting on it from all his works, was a type of that glorious rest that saints shall have when the six days of this world are fully ended. This the Apostle asserts in the fourth chapter to the Hebrews, 'there remaineth a rest (or the keeping of a Sabbath) to the people of God;' which Sabbath, as I conceive, will be the seventh thousand of years which are to follow immediately after the earth has stood six thousand years first. For as God was six days in the works of creation, and rested on the seventh, so in six thousand years he will perfect his works and providences that concern this world. As also he will finish the travail and toil of his saints, with the burden of the beasts, and the curse of the ground, and bring all into rest for a thousand years. A day with the Lord is a thousand years; wherefore this blessed and desirable time is also called a day, a great day, that great and notable day of the Lord, Isa. 2; Joel 2: 31; Rev. 16: 14, which shall end in the eternal judgment of the world. God hath held this forth by several other shadows, such as the Sabbath of weeks, the Sabbath of years, and the great Jubilee."†

"None ever saw this world as it was in its first creation but Adam and his wife, neither will any see it until the manifestation of the children of God; that is, until the redemption or resurrection of the saints. But then it shall be delivered from the bondage of corruption into the glorious lib-

---

* Works, vol. v., p. 486. † Ibid, vol. vi., p. 301.

erty of the children of God. Adam, as a type of Christ reigned in the church almost a thousand years. The world, therefore, beginning thus, doth show us how it will end,— viz., by the reign of the second Adam, as it began with the reign of the first. * * * In the seventh thousand years of the world will be that Sabbath when Christ shall set up his Kingdom on earth: according to that which is written, 'They lived and reigned with Christ a thousand years.'"*

Of the New Jerusalem, Bunyan thus beautifully writes: "Now I saw in my dream, that the two pilgrims went in at the gate: and lo! as they entered they were transfigured; and they had raiment put on that shone like gold. Just as the gate was opened to let in the men, I looked in after them, and behold! the city shone like the sun! The streets also were paved with gold, and in them walked many men with crowns on their heads, and golden harps to sing praises withal.

"There were also of them that had wings, and they answered one another without intermission, saying, '*Holy, holy, holy is the Lord!*' And after that, they shut up the gates; which, when I had seen, I wished myself among them."

The "Prince of Dreamers" speaks the language of the early Church, and with every Baptist of the time of King Charles II., lifts his voice against the great error of the day —Post-millennialism. Bunyan died 1688.

BAPTIST CHURCHES, A. D. 1660.

Baptist Confession of Faith, 1660. This confession was presented to Charles II. in the above year, in the city of London, and was signed by forty-one elders, deacons, and brethren, and approved by more than 20,000 others; "for which," say they, "we are not only resolved to suffer persecution to the loss of our goods, but also life itself, rather than decline from the same."

* Works, vol. vi., p. 329.

We give one or two extracts exhibiting its decided Millennarian character:

I. "WE believe, and are very confident, That, &c. * * * *

XX. "THAT there shall be (through Christ, who was dead, but is alive again from the dead) a resurrection of all men from the graves of the earth, *Isa.* xxvi. 19, both the just and the unjust, *Acts* xxiv. 15, that is, the fleshly bodies of men, sown into the graves of the earth; corruptible, dishonorable, weak, natural, (which, so considered, cannot inherit the kingdom of God) shall be raised again, incorruptible, in glory, in power, spiritual; and so considered, the bodies of the saints (united again to their spirits) which here suffer for Christ, shall inherit the kingdom, *reigning* together with Christ. 1 Cor. xv. 21, 22, 42, 43, 44, 49.

XXI. "THAT there shall be, after the resurrection from the graves of the earth, *an eternal judgment*, at the appearing of Christ and his kingdom, 2 *Tim.* iv. 1; *Heb.* ix. 27, at which time of judgment, which is unalterable, and irrevocable, every man shall receive according to the things done in his body. 2 Cor. v. 10.

XXII. "THAT the same Lord Jesus who showed himself alive after his Passion, by many infallible proofs, *Acts* i. 3, which was taken up from the disciples, and carried up into heaven, *Luke* xxiv. 51, *shall so come in like manner as He was seen to go into heaven*, Acts i. 9, 10, 11. *And when Christ, who is our life, shall appear, we shall also appear with him in glory.* Col. iii. 4. *For then shall He be King of kings, and Lord of lords.* Rev. xix. 16. *For the kingdom is His, and He is the Governor among the nations*, Psa. xxii. 28, *and king over all the earth*, Zech. xiv. 9, *and we shall reign with Him on the earth.* Rev. v. 10. The kingdoms of this world (which men so mightily strive after here, to enjoy) shall become the kingdoms of our Lord, and his Christ. *Rev.* xi. 15. *For all is yours* (O, ye that overcome this world) *for ye are Christ's, and Christ* as

God's. 1 Cor. iii. 22, 23. *For unto the saints shall be given the kingdom, and the greatness of the kingdom under* (mark that) *the whole heaven. Dan.* vii. 27. Though (alas!) now many men be scarce content that the saints should have so much as a being among them; but when Christ shall appear then shall be their day; then shall be given unto them power over the nations, to rule them with a rod of iron. *Rev.* ii. 26, 27. Then shall they receive a crown of life, which no man shall take from them, nor they by any means [be?] turned, or overturned from it; for the oppressor shall be broken in pieces, *Psa.* lxxii. 4, and their now vain rejoicings turned into mourning and bitter lamentations; as it is written. *Job* xx. 5, 6, 7. *The triumphing of the wicked is short and the joy of the hypocrite but for a moment: though his excellency mount up to the heavens, and his head reach unto the clouds, yet shall he perish forever, like his own dung; they which have seen him, shall say, Where is he?*"

XXIV., on liberty of conscience, closes thus: "And that the tares and the wheat should grow together in the field (which is the world) until the harvest (which is the end of the world)." *Matt.* xiii. 29, 30, 38, 39.*

BOUGHTON AND OTHERS A. D. 1600.

John Boughton, of London, in 1603, in his catechism, treated of the signs of the second advent, and bade to watch for Christ. Bishop JOSEPH HALL, of Norwich, an Anti-m., who died in 1656, bearing the title of the English Seneca, said, "For my part, I am persuaded in my soul, that the coming of our Saviour is near at hand." THOMAS BEVERLY, in 1687, maintained the doctrine of a literal first resurrection, and expected the Millennium. MATTHEW MEAD, a Dis-

---

* Crosby's History of the Baptists, vol. ii., Appendix, p. 85, 86, 87. See also Irving's Dialogues on Prophecy, vol. ii., p. 269, for other matter on this subject.

senter, who died in 1699, wrote these words: "Christ will visibly appear at the beginning of the seventh trumpet." TILLINGHAST, in 1665, taught that the second coming of Christ was "but a little way from the door, and finally DR. PRIDEAUX, a very learned Episcopalian of England, born in 1648, admits that the Dissenters of his day, took the word "souls," Rev. 20, as meaning "souls and bodies united," interpreting them synechdochically, thus allowing their Pre-millennialism.

JURIEU, A. D. 1700.

Peter Jurieu, a French Protestant Calvinist minister, was born 1637. He was a preacher at Rotterdam, and in England, and an Apocalyptic writer, in which he avowedly takes Mede as his master, except in those portions of prophecy of later application. He advocates the year-day theory, makes the tenth part of the city in Rev. 11: 13, also the city in which the witnesses were slain, to be France; explains the beast as Mede, making its seventh head to be the Papal Antichrist, whose ruin he expected in 1710–15, saying, " Many things, without reckoning the modern prophecies, made me hope that we were near the end of that period, of 1260 years, at the close whereof Babylon must fall. It is much nearer than is commonly thought. In a few years you will see the light of that fire which is shut up, without being extinguished. We are now in those last days when Christ should come and not find true piety, or true faith upon earth." And once more: "That which is to follow his (Antichrist's) fall is the famous reign of Christ upon earth."* The foregoing are detached extracts. We now give an argument from him on the Pre-millennial advent. On Dan. 12: 3, he writes:—
" What, I pray, should the resurrection do here in the middle of the chapter, in which the adventures only of Antiochus

* Jurieu's Apocalypse.

Epiphanes are spoken of? 'Tis plain that this is perfectly the same prophecy as that of St. John in the 20th chap. of the Revelations, where the apostle predicts the deliverance of the church, and the coming of the kingdom of Christ by a resurrection. They that were beheaded for the name of Jesus must be raised up, and reign with him a thousand years. This is what Daniel saith here, that they that have turned many to righteousness, by their doctrine, and by their martyrdom, shall be as shining and ruling stars in the kingdom of Jesus Christ. It is not the last resurrection nor the last coming of Christ that St. John speaks of, no more than Daniel. 'Tis of that coming that St. Paul speaks of when he saith that Jesus Christ shall destroy Antichrist by the brightness of his coming; when he shall come to establish his kingdom of a 1000 years on the earth. 'Tis that resurrection which the Revelation calls '*the first resurrection*.' And therefore Daniel doth not say, and *all* those that sleep in the dust shall awake, but he only saith *many* of those that sleep in the dust; even as St. John saith expressly that then all the dead shall not arise. 'Tis true, that Daniel also joins the resurrection of the wicked; but we must not conclude that this resurrection of the wicked must be at the same time; one prophecy must be explained by the other. The resurrection of the wicked, which Daniel joins here with the first resurrection, is distant from it at least a 1000 years. But he speaks of it as of two things joined together, because he who speaks of it is God, before whom a thousand years are but as one day."*

Jurieu used language that Pre-millennialists are obliged to make use of now, for Dr. Whitby now lived, and so unpopular had this truth become, that though a firm believer in the personal reign, he says "many divines in this country (England) have greatly murmured at it, even so far as to

---

* Jurieu on the Apocalypse, p. 254.

threaten to complain of me. I am sorry it is so, for I should be glad not to displease my brethren." We must hold fast to the truth, cost what it will. Jurieu, " the Goliah of Protestantism," as he was styled, died in 1713.

CHARNOCK, A. D. 1660.

Stephen Charnock, D. D., was born at London in 1628. He was eminent as a dissenter, and was a powerful theologian. His views of the Millennium we know not, but on the doctrine of the world's restitution he says:

"How could 'the creature'—the world, or any part of it—be said to be delivered from the bondage of corruption, into the glorious liberty of the sons of God, if the whole frame of heaven and earth were to be annihilated (Rom. 8: 21)? The apostle saith also, that the creature ' waits, with earnest expectation, for this manifestation of the sons of God,' (verse 19,) which would have no foundation if the whole frame should be reduced to nothing. What joyful expectation can there be in any, of a total ruin? How should the creature be capable of partaking in this glorious liberty of the sons of God? As the world, for the sin of man, lost its first dignity, and was cursed after the fall, and the beauty bestowed on it by creation defaced, so shall it recover that ancient glory, when he shall be fully restored, by the resurrection, to that dignity he lost by his first sin. As man shall be freed from his corruptibility, to receive that glory which is prepared for him, so shall the creatures be freed from that imperfection or corruptibility, those stains and spots upon the face of them, to receive a new glory suited to their nature, and answerable to the design of God, when the 'glorious liberty' of the saints shall be accomplished. As when (see Mestrazat on Heb. 1,) a prince's nuptials are solemnized, the whole country echoes with joy, so the *inanimate creatures*, when the time of the marriage of the Lamb is come, shall have a delight and pleasure from that renovation. The apostle sets forth the *whole world* as a person *groaning*, and the Scriptures are frequent in such metaphors, as when the creatures are said to 'wait upon God and to be troubled;' the hills are said to 'leap, and the mountains rejoice.' (Psalm 104, 27: 29.) The creature is said to '*groan*,' as the heavens are said 'to declare the glory of God,' passively, naturally, not rationally. . . . . If the creatures be subject to vanity by the sin of man, they shall also partake of a happiness by the restoration of man. The earth hath borne thorns and thistles, and venomous beasts; the air hath had its tempest and infectious qualities; the water hath caused its floods and deluges; the creature hath been abased to luxury and intemperance, and been tyrannized over in man, contrary to the end of its creation. 'Tis convenient that some time should be allotted for the creature's attaining its true end, and that it may partake of the peace of man as it hath done of the fruits of his sin which prevailed more than grace, and would have had more power to deface, than grace to restore things into their due order. Again, upon that account should the Psalmist exhort the heavens to rejoice, and earth to be glad, when *God comes to judge the world* with righteousness, if they should be annihilated, and sink for ever into nothing? It would seem, saith Daille— (on Psalm 96: 12, 13)—to be an impertinent figure, if the Judge of the world brought them to a total destruction. An entire ruin could not be matter of triumph to creatures who naturally have that instinct or inclination put into them by their Creator, to preserve themselves, and to effect their own preservation. . . . . Again, '*The Lord is to rejoice in his works*, (Psalm 104, 31.) Since God can rejoice only in goodness, the creatures must have that goodness restored to them which God pronounced them to have at their first creation, and which he ordained them for, before he can again rejoice in his works."* This divine died in 1680, much beloved.

HENRY, A. D. 1700.

Matthew Henry, born in Flintshire, England, 1663. He was a pious Dissenter, and deservedly eminent as a commentator of the Scriptures, Wm. Romaine declaring, "There is no comment upon the Bible, either ancient or modern, in all respects equal to Mr. Henry's." We give copious extracts. On the Millennium he is somewhat vague, affirming of the "angel" of Rev. 20: 1, "It is very probable that this angel is no other than the Lord Jesus Christ; the description of him will hardly agree with any other," yet on the resurrection of verse 4, he says: "This may be taken either literally or figuratively." Still, throughout his Commentary he advances sentiments utterly at war with modern Post-millennialism.

On Luke 12: 45, 46: "Our looking at Christ's second coming as a thing at a distance, is the cause of all those irregularities which render the thought of it terrible to us."

On watching: "To watch implies not only to believe that our Lord will come, but to desire that he would come, to be often thinking of his coming, and always looking for it as sure and near, and the time of it uncertain. To watch for Christ's coming is to maintain that gracious temper and disposition of mind which we would be willing that our Lord, when he comes, should find us in. To watch is to be aware of the first notices of his approach, that we may immediately attend his motions and address ourselves to the duty of meeting him. On 2d Pet. 3d chap., of the final fire he says: "It is yet to come, and will surely come, though we know not when nor upon what particular age or generation of men; and therefore we are not, we cannot be sure that it may not happen in our own times."

* Charnock on the Attributes of God.

On John 18: 19: "It is meet that disciples should be warned of the haste and end of time, and apprised as much as may be of the prophetic periods of time."*

On Rom. 8 ch., Henry makes "the creature" to mean "the whole frame of nature, especially that of this lower world, the whole creation, the compages of inanimate and sensible creatures;" the vanity and bondage and corruption is the curse to which the whole creation is subject, now "hastening to a total dissolution by fire."

He says, "the creature, that is now thus burdened, shall, at the time of the restitution of all things, be delivered from this bondage into the glorious liberty of the children of God. They shall no more be subject to vanity and corruption, and the other fruits of the curse; but, on the contrary, this lower world shall be renewed, when there will be new heavens and a new earth, 2nd Pet. 3, 13; Rev. 21, 1; and there shall be a glory conferred upon all the creatures which shall be (in the proportion of their natures,) as suitable and as great an advancement as the glory of the children of God shall be to them. The fire at the last day shall be a refining, not a destroying, annihilating fire. Compare with this Psa. 96, 10—13; Ps. 98: 7—9, "Let the heavens rejoice, &c."

On verse 19, "At the second coming of Christ there will be a manifestation of the children of God. Now, the saints are God's hidden ones, the wheat seems lost in a heap of chaff; but then they shall be manifested * * And this redemption of the creature is reserved till then; for as it was with man and for man that they fell under the curse, so with man and for man shall they be delivered. All the curse and filth that now adheres to the creature shall be done away then, when those that have suffered with Christ upon earth shall reign with him upon earth. This the whole creation looks and longs for."

* Vide Henry's Commentary.

"Verse 23. We groan within or among ourselves. It is the unanimous vote, the joint desire of the whole church; all agree in this. Come, Lord Jesus, come quickly. The groaning notes a very earnest and importunate desire, the soul pained with the delay, * * groans not as the pangs of our dying, but as the throes of a woman in travail, groans that are symptoms of life, not of death."*

2 Pet. 3. "That time which men think to be the most improper and unlikely, and therefore are most secure, will be the time of the Lord's coming. Let us then beware how we in our thoughts and imaginings put that day far away from us; let us rather suppose it to be so much nearer in reality, by how much further off it is in the opinion of the ungodly world."

"The first coming of our Lord Jesus Christ was what the people of God earnestly waited and looked for; that coming was for the consolation of Israel. How much more should they wait with expectation and earnestness for his second coming, which will be the day of their complete redemption, and of his most glorious manifestation?"

"They (the wicked,) will still attack us till the end of time; till our Lord is come, they will not themselves believe that he will come; nay, they will laugh at the very mention of his second coming, and do what in them lies to put all out of countenance who seriously believe and wait for it."

On Luke 18 : 8, "Now when he comes, will he find faith in the earth? The question implies a strong negative; no, he shall not, he himself foresees it. * * In general he will find but few good people, few that are really and truly good; many that have the form and fashion of godliness, but few that have faith. Even to the end of time there will be occasion for the same complaint; the world will grow no better, no, not when it is drawing towards it period. Bad it is, and

---

* Vide Henry's Com.

bad it will be, and worst of all just before Christ's coming, the last times will be the most perilous. In particular he will find few that have faith concerning his coming. It intimates that he will delay his coming so long that wicked people will begin to defy it, and to say, "Where is the promise of his coming?" They will challenge him to come.—Isa. 5: 18, 19, and Amos 5: 18, 19, and his delay will harden them in their wickedness. Even his own people will begin to despair of it, and to conclude he will never come, because he has passed their reckoning.

On Matt. 25, "As Christians, we profess not only to believe and look for, but love and long for, the appearing of Christ, and to act in our whole conversation with regard to it. The second coming of Christ is the centre in which all the lines of our religion meet, and to which the whole of the divine life hath a constant reference and tendency."

"The Bridegroom tarried, that is, he did not come as soon as they expected. But though Christ tarry past our time, he will not tarry past the due time."

On Dan. 12: 10, Henry, though looking for an extensive proclamation of the gospel, looked not for its universal reception, but says: "As long as the world stands there will still be in it such a mixture as now we see there is of good and bad. We long to see all wheat and no tares in God's field; all corn and no chaff in God's floor; but it will not be till the time of ingathering, till the winnowing-day comes; both must grow together until the harvest. There is no remedy but that wicked people will do wickedly; and such people there are and will be in the world till the end of time."

On Rev. 22: 20, "This is Christ's farewell to his church, and the church's hearty echo to Christ's promise. Come, Lord Jesus! thus beats the pulse of the church, thus breathes that gracious spirit which actuates and informs the mystical body of Christ, and we should never be satisfied till we find such a spirit breathing in us, and causing us to look for that blessed hope, and the glorious appearing of the great God, and our Saviour Jesus Christ. What comes from heaven in a promise should be sent back to heaven in a prayer. Come, Lord Jesus, put an end to this state of sin, and sorrow, and temptation, and gather thy people out of this present evil world!" So writes the pious Henry in a commentary, the superior excellencies of which, says Dr. A. Alexander, are admitted by "thousands of judicious theologians," and of which Dr. Adam Clarke affirms, "It is always orthodox!" Henry died in 1714.

BURNET, 1700.

Thomas Burnet, D. D., was born in Yorkshire, Eng., 1635, and being educated at Cambridge, became Chaplain to King William, and master of the Charter House. Burnet was eloquent and of unquestioned ability and learning. He is very copious, and we glean and extract as follows: He says that "the sex-millennial duration of the world is much insisted upon by the christian fathers, not so much on the bare authority of tradition, as because they thought it was founded in the six days creation and the Sabbath succeeding." He then instances Barnabas, Irenæus, Hippolytus, Cyprian, Lactantius, Jerome, Augustine, John Damascenus, Justin Martyr, Hilary, Anastasius, Sinaita, Sanctus Gaudentius, Julius Hillarion, Isidorus Hispalensis, Cassidorus, Gregory the Great, and others who all taught it, adding, "we may be bold to say that nothing yet appears, either in nature or Scripture, or human affairs, repugnant to this belief of the 6000 years."*

On the conflagration and renovation of the earth, its restoration to Edenic beauty, as the eternal residence of Christ

---

* Theory of the Earth.

and the redeemed, Burnet is voluminous and clear. He thus writes · "When we speak of the end or destruction of the world, whether by fire or otherwise, it is not to be imagined that we understand this of the *great universe:* sun, moon and stars, and the highest heavens; as if these were to perish or be destroyed some few years hence, whether by fire or any other way. This question is only to be understood of the *sublunary world,* of this earth and its furniture; which had its original about six thousand years ago, according to the history of Moses; and hath once already been destroyed, when the exterior region of it broke, and the abyss, issuing forth, as out of a womb, overflowed all the habitable earth. --Gen. 7 : 17; Job 38 : 8. The next deluge is that of fire, which will have the same bounds, and overflow the surface of the earth, much-what in the same manner. But the celestial regions, where the stars and angels inhabit, are not concerned in this fate; those are not made of combustible matter; nor, if they were, could our flames reach them. Possibly those bodies may have changes and revolutions peculiar to themselves, but in ways unknown to us, and after long and unknown periods of time. Therefore when we speak of the conflagration of the world, these have no concern in the question; nor any other part of the universe, than the earth and its dependences. As will evidently appear when we come to explain the manner and causes of the conflagration.

And as this conflagration can extend no farther than to the earth and its elements, so neither can it destroy the matter of the earth, but only the form and fashion of it, as it is an habitable world. Neither fire, nor any other natural agent, can destroy matter, that is, reduce it to nothing: it may alter the modes and qualities of it, but the substance will always remain. And accordingly the apostle, when he speaks of the mutability of this world, says only, *The figure* or fashion of *this world passes away.*—1 Cor. 7: 31. This structure of the earth and disposition of the elements, and all the *works* of the earth, as St. Peter says, 2 Epist. 3, all its natural productions, and all the works of art or human industry, these will perish, be melted or torn in pieces by the fire, but without an annihilation of the matter, any more than in the former deluge."

Of the Millennium, Burnet writes that "it doth begin and end the Apocalypse, as the soul of that body of prophecies," and that we can "as well open a lock without a key as interpret the Apocalypse without the Millennium;" that, "after the conflagration this earth will be renewed," that " in this new heavens and earth the Millennium will be enjoyed;" that "this was the doctrine of all the ancient Millennaries," "and we ought to be careful and locate it thus :" that " the new Jerusalem state is the same as the Millennial state," which he contends is ushered in by the seventh trumpet, and the judgment; in the Millennium, there being a lustral appearance of Christ and the Shechinah. He also affirms that placing the Millennium in this earth before the renovation, was what brought the doctrine anciently into discredit and decay, the earlier Millennarians identifying the Millennial era with the kingdom and renovation or restitution of all things ; those are "happy days ! when the temple of Janus shall be shut up for a thousand years."*

We here give an argument from him on Rev. 20 : 6th, &c.

" This resurrection, you see, is called the *first resurrection*, by way of distinction from the second and general resurrection ; which is to be placed a thousand years after the first. And both this first resurrection, and the reign of Christ, seem to be appropriated to the martyrs in this place : for the prophet says, ' the souls of those that were beheaded for the witness of Jesus,' etc., ' they lived and reigned with Christ a thousand years.' From which words, if you please, we

---

* Theory of the Earth.

will raise this doctrine: that those who have suffered for the sake of Christ, and a good conscience, shall be raised from the dead a thousand years before the general resurrection, and reign with Christ in an happy state. This proposition seems to be plainly included in the words of St. John, and to be the intended sense of this vision; but you must have patience a little, as to your inquiry into particulars, till in the progress of our discourse we have brought all the parts of this conclusion into fuller light.

"In the meantime, there is but one way, that I know of, to evade the force of these words, and of the conclusion drawn from them; and that is, by supposing that the *first resurrection*, here mentioned, is not to be understood in a literal sense, but is allegorical and mystical, signifying only a resurrection from sin to a spiritual life; as we are said to be *dead in sin* and to be *risen with Christ*, by faith and regeneration. This is a manner of speech which St. Paul does sometimes use, as Eph. 2: 6, 14, and Col. 3: 1. But how can this be applied to the present case? were the martyrs dead in sin? it is they that are here raised from the dead; or, after they were beheaded for the witness of Jesus, naturally dead and laid in their graves, were they then regenerate by faith? There is no congruity in allegories so applied. Beside, why should they be said to be regenerate a thousand years before the day of judgment? or to reign with Christ after this spiritual resurrection, such a limited time, a thousand years? why not to eternity? for in this allegorical sense of *rising* and *reigning*, they will reign with him for everlasting. Then, after a thousand years, must all the wicked be regenerate, and rise into a spiritual life? It is said here, 'the rest of the dead lived not again, until the thousand years were finished.'—v. 5. That implies, that at the end of these thousand years, the rest of the dead did live again; which, according to the allegory, must be, that, after a thousand years, all the wicked will be regenerate, and raised into a spiritual life. These absurdities arise upon an allegorical exposition of this resurrection, if applied to single persons:

"The Scripture speaks only of the resurrection of the martyrs, (Apoc. 20 : 4, 5,) but not a word concerning their ascension into heaven: will that be visible? We read of our Saviour's resurrection and ascension, and therefore we have reason to affirm them both. We read also of the resurrection and ascension of the witnesses, (Apoc. 11) in a figurative sense; and in that sense we may assert them upon good grounds. But as to the martyrs, we read of their resurrection only, without any thing expressed or implied about their ascension. By what authority then shall we add this new notion to the history or scheme of the Millennium? The Scripture, on the contrary, makes mention of the descent of the new Jerusalem, (Apoc. 21 : 2,) making the earth the theatre of all that affair: and the camp of the saints is upon the earth (v. 9,) and these saints are the same persons, so far as can be collected from the text, that rose from the dead, and reigned with Christ, and were priests to God.—vs. 4–6. Neither is there any distinction made, that I find, by St. John, of two sorts of saints in the Millennium, the one in heaven, and the other upon earth."*

Dr. Burnet on the celestial signs of the advent, thus remarks : "We may conclude that when the last great storm is coming, and all the volcanoes of the earth ready to burst, and the frame of the world to be dissolved, there will be previous signs in the heavens and on the earth, to introduce this tragical fate; nature cannot come to that extremity without some symptoms of her illness, nor die silently without pangs or complaint. The Scripture plainly tells us of signs that will precede the coming of our Saviour, and the end of the world. The sun, moon, and stars will be disturbed in their

* Theory of the Earth.

motions or aspect; earth and the sea will roar and tremble, and the mountains fall at his presence. In determining these signs let us take the known and approved rule for interpreting Scripture, not to recede from the literal sense without necessity, or when the nature of the subject will admit of a literal interpretation."

"As to earthquakes, these will necessarily be multiplied toward the end of the world, when by an excess of drought and heat, exhalations will more abound within the earth. Inflammations will be more frequent. They will reach to a vast compass of ground, and whole islands or continents be shaken at once. These concussions will not only affect mankind, but all the elements.'

"The sun and the moon will be darkened, or of a bloody or pale countenance. This will be produced by an infectious and corrupted air, filled with thick vapors and fumes or turbid exhalations: atmospheric obscurities, to a great extent, intercepting the sun's rays, causing it thus to appear and proportionably diminishing the light of the moon. Before this mighty storm the disposition of the air will be quite altered, or, the sun may contract at that time some spots greater than usual, thus making it dark."*

"Of the falling stars, we are sure from the nature of the thing, that this cannot be understood either of fixed stars or planets; for if either of these should tumble from the skies, and reach the earth, they would break it all in pieces, or swallow it up as the sea does a sinking ship; and at the same time would put all the inferior universe in confusion. It is necessary, therefore, by these stars, to understand either fiery meteors falling from the middle region of the air, or comets and blazing stars. No doubt there will be all sorts of fiery meteors at that time, and among others those called falling stars, which, though they are not considerable singly

* Theory of the Earth.

yet if they were multiplied in great numbers, falling, as the prophet says, as leaves from the vine, or figs from the fig tree, they would make an astonishing sight. The last sign before the coming of Christ is the falling stars, and all these things will literally come to pass as they are predicted."

Burnet makes the quaking and reeling to and fro of the earth, and its being thrown out of posture, fulfill the appearance of " the shaking of the powers of heaven"—" like as in a ship at sea by night, in a tempest, tossed with uncertain motions, giving the heavens a fluctuating, tremulous action, and making the stars to dance; so the motions of the atmosphere, and also the earth will make all the starry canopy shake and tremble."

Dr. Burnet regarded the time as being short, and says " He that does not err above a century, in calculating the last period of time, from what evidence we have at present, (1697), hath in my opinion, cast up his accounts very well. But the scenes will fast change toward the evening of this long day, and when the sun is near setting they will more readily compute how far he hath to run."*

So much for Burnet, who has written much truth, and who being dead, yet speaketh. We invite our readers to a perusal of his work, " The Theory of the Earth."

He fell asleep 1715

CRESSENER, A. D. 1690.

Dr. Cressener was a learned divine, and prophetical writer of the seventeenth century. His work on the " Protestant applications of the Apocalypse," dedicated to Queen Mary, and written in 1690, advocates Pre-millennialism. He writes: " The kingdom of the Son of Man in the 7th of Daniel, is the second coming of Christ in glory.

" One would easily be persuaded of this, at the first sight

---

* Theory of the Earth, vol. ii. chap. 2.

of the glorious properties of it, and especially upon the account of its universal command, and the eternal duration of it. For what else is his coming in glory for, but to take possession of the whole world, and to reign with the Father and his saints to all eternity, and though he delivers up his kingdom to his Father at the last end, yet he has so much share in it as to have it here called his 'everlasting kingdom.'

But it may be said this was verified of Christ at his first coming, for at his ascension into heaven, he is said to have all power given unto him, both in heaven and in earth. It must, therefore, be shown that, by the characters of the kingdom of the Son of man in this place, it cannot be that universal power which was given to Christ at his ascension into heaven, and his sitting at the right hand of power."*

" For this purpose, it is to be considered that the kingdom of the Son of man, and that of the saints in the 7th chapter of Daniel, is the same kingdom, for they both are described as beginning at the same time, at the destruction of the 'little horn,' and have the same characters of an universal and eternal dominion, which it is impossible for two different kingdoms to have at the same time. And the kingdom of the saints hath these properties in it: 1st. To begin at the destruction of a kingdom that did devour the whole earth, and of a great tyrannizing power in it, that did wear out the saints of the Most High. 2ndly. To be in the actual possession of the obedience of all people, nations, and languages, and all dominions under heaven. 3dly. To be eternal from that first beginning of such an universal dominion. And this can be nothing but Christ's second coming in glory; for though all power, both in heaven and earth, was given to him at his ascension into heaven, yet St. Paul tells us that all things were not yet put under him Heb. 2: 8."*

* Cressener's Work, p. 75.   † Ibid, p. 76.

Dr. Cressener, unlike some more modern writers, also shows that the coming of the Son of man in Math. 24 : 30 is his coming in glory, to judge the world. Giving his argument—which is too lengthy to be quoted here—he finally adds, " we do find an almost unanimous consent among all sorts of interpreters that this coming of the Son of man in Math. 24 : 30, must be his second coming in glory. Grotius himself in this is forced to be of the same mind as the rest."*

In this view Cressener is sustained by Justin Martyr, Tertullian, Chrysostom, Cyril, and nearly, if not quite all of the early Fathers, to whom, in the language of Cunninghame, " the modern fancy of a figurative coming of the Son of man in the clouds of heaven was altogether unknown."

AMES, A. D. 1640.

William Ames, D. D., of Norfolk, England, 1641, in his Exposition of the Epistles of Peter, says, that " The reason why iniquity doth now abound in the last days is, 1st, because knowledge doth more abound, which being held in unrighteousness, makes it the more sinful; and 2nd, the last days, by reason of that depravedness and corruption which hath ever prevailed among men, are as it were the *sink* of all ages that went before to receive the dregs!"† Such testimony certainly accords with the inspired Apostles in 2nd Timothy and 3d chapter.

HOWE, A. D. 1660.

John Howe, an eminent and pious English Dissenter, born in 1630, wrote as follows: " Nor will the time of expectation be long when I shall awake—when He shall appear; put it to the longest term. It was said sixteen hundred years ago, to be but a little while; three times over in the shutting up of the Bible, He tells us, I come quickly."‡

* Cressener's Work, p. 81.   † Ame's Expositions.
‡ Works, vol. 1., p. 263.

MENNO, A. D. 1550.

Simon Menno, the founder of a sect called Mennonites, taught at the Reformation, the true principles of primitive Millennarianism. Menno's followers are said by Mosheim to have maintained " the ancient hypothesis of a visible and glorious church of Christ upon earth."*

COCCEIUS, A. D. 1650.

John Cocceius, who died in 1669, and who was Professor of Theology at Bremen, and who became the founder of a sect bearing his name, strenuously maintained the principles of a literal interpretation of the prophecies, and taught Millennarianism to his followers, maintaining, says the English Encyclopedia, " among other singular opinions, that of a visible reign of Christ in this world."† The same opinion prevailed generally among the *Pietists* in Germany, and the *Mystics* of England and the Continent. Vitringa, Grotius, Horne, and others, highly commend the piety and learning of Cocceius.

DAVENANT, A. D. 1630.

John Davenant, Bishop of Salisbury, England, who died in 1641, writes, that " the glory of Christians is to be expected at the second coming of Christ, whose day will arrive both quickly and suddenly." Very many works on Millennarianism were written and published in this century. In 1641 a tract of thirty-nine pages was circulated through Europe, advocating the doctrine, observing, " Let every saint search into this doctrine; it is our harvest of joy and gladness, and may Christ pardon our hitherto so much neglect of it."‡

---

* Mosheim's Hist., vol. v., p. 497.   † Brooks on Proph., p. 97.
‡ In the Antiquarian Library, Worcester, Mass.

ALSTEAD, A. D. 1627.

John H. Alstead, a divine of great erudition and a Professor of divinity and philosophy, at Nassau, and afterward at Julia Alba, in Transylvania. His " Prophetical Work," published 1640, affirmed that a majority of the divines of his day held that " the last judgment was even at the doors," such being the general belief. " In defending the doctrine of the Millennium, he fixed the beginning of Christ's reign on earth in 1694. He died in 1638."*

NAPIER, A. D. 1600.

John Napier, Lord Baron of Marchestoun, a Scottish nobleman, born 1550, and celebrated as the inventor of logarithms, was, in the opening of this century, the author of a work on the Revelations of St. John, in which he made the seven trumpets and seven vials synchronal in their fulfillment and symbolical of so many equal ages, supposing the last age would end in 1786, adding, in explanation, " Not that I mean that that age or yet the world shall continue so long, because it is said that for the elect's sake the time shall be shortened ;" and the result of his calculations was, that he confidently expected, from the fulfilment of the numbers and woe trumpets, that the awful day of judgment would take place at some time between 1688 and 1700. Dr. Adam Clarke commends his piety and erudition, and says, " So very plausible were the reasonings and calculations of Lord Napier, that there was scarcely a Protestant in Europe who read his works who was not of the same opinion."†

We, of course admit, with Dr. Clarke, the error of these calculations concerning the time of the Lord's advent, but on the strength of these statements would candidly ask,

---

* Becket's Biog. Dictionary.
† Clarke's Commentary, vol i., p. 22. Preface,

SOLEMN QUESTIONS. 223

Where, in all the seventeenth century, among the entire Christian church, was cherished the faith of an intervening temporal Millennium, such as many Protestants at the present time vainly expect? Assuredly the thought is worthy of our solemn and candid consideration, that from the days of the apostles up to this period, Post-millennialism had nowhere an existence! And can it then be the truth? Is it possible that that is the doctrine of Christ and his apostles, which was never heard of in the church till sixteen hundred years from the time of their preaching? Can it be that that which was condemned and accounted as a heresy for the first sixteen centuries of the Christian era, is really the truth? Can it be that that of which the immediate successors of the apostles were ignorant, and upon which they were silent, has now come to be the doctrine of the prophets and apostles?

Church of Christ in the nineteenth century, ponder these questions! Watchman on Zion's walls, ponder these questions! and take heed lest while dreaming of a golden age of mercy, you see the gleaming of the sword of justice. Watch! lest in the midst of Peace and Safety sudden destruction overtake a sinful world, and their blood be required at the hand of the slumbering watchman.

CHAPTER VIII.

THE EIGHTEENTH CENTURY.

"To him that overcometh, will I grant to sit with me in my throne, even as I also overcame, and am set down with my Father in his throne."
—*Rev.* 3: 21.

THIS century is distinguished for the rise of a new Millennial theory—viz., the Whitbyan; a theory that we are of opinion, were there no other argument, finds its own successful refutation in the admitted fact that Pre-millennialism, its opposite, was believed and taught by the early Church and all "the best of Christians for 250 years as a tradition apostolical." The admission is Whitby's, and is fatal to his scheme. By the rule of Faber, given in another place, Post-millennialism is a "mere human invention," and, to use the language of this venerable divine, "with whatever plausibility it may be fetched out of a particular interpretation of Scripture, and with whatever practical piety on the part of its advocates, it may be attended, we cannot evidentially admit it to be part and parcel of the divine revelation of Christianity."* But the doctrine of a personal reign still had its advocates, and the great names of the age were on its side. We invite special attention to the evidence given in this, as also in preceding centuries, that the early founders and creed-makers of the present existing evangelical denominations were mostly Pre-millennialists. Such were the Baptists of King Charles' time—the noble assembly of West-

---

* Doctrine of Election, p. 159.

minster divines, and later among the Methodists, Toplady, Fletcher, Charles Wesley, &c.; and the concessions of John Wesley, Dr. A. Clarke, and also Whitefield, are not a few; Dr. Clarke affirming that "probably no such time shall ever appear in which evil shall be wholly banished from the earth, till after the day of judgment, when the earth having been burned up, a new heavens and a new earth shall be produced out of the ruins of the old by the mighty power of God"*—Whitefield declaring that the Church will suffer persecution—in Henry's language—"till the end of time," and the others admitting a cardinal doctrine of our faith— namely, the earth's renovation, and eternal possession by the meek.

Not only did Pre-millennialism find advocates among the great lights of the Church," but it also enlisted astronomers, philosophers, nobles, and poets in its defense. The names of Sir Isaac Newton, Tycho Brahe, Lord Napier, Cowper, Heber, and Watts, as well as those of Bishops Horsely, Newton, Clayton, Newcome, &c., are not to be despised by the divines of the nineteenth century. "But time would fail to speak" of all—even Rome contributing her single testimony to the truth.

And who can resist the arguments of a Fletcher, a Gill, and a Spaulding, or the pious longings of a Doddridge, a Mather, or the holy impatience of the "seraphic Rutherford," who would fain "shovel time and days out of the way," and bring "that day, for which all other days were made?" O Christian! love your Lord's appearing! With Gill, we urge you to "be hastening in your warm affections and earnest desires after those glorious times, and in the darkest season look for the morning," and harmonious with the prayer, "Thy kingdom come," let your cry be with Milton, "Come forth out of thy royal chambers, O Prince of all the Kings of the earth!"

* Comments on Rev. 20th and 21st.

FLEMING, A. D. 1700.

Robert Fleming, Jr., was born in Scotland, in the seventeenth century. He was minister at Leyden and Rotterdam, and afterwards of the Presbyterian Church at Lothbury, Scotland; was distinguished for his piety and learning, and as the author of a work on the rise and fall of the Papacy, in which, among other things, he calculated the humiliation of the French monarchy in the close of the eighteenth century, about 1794, remarking that " we may justly suppose that that monarchy, after it has scorched others, will itself consume, by doing so, wasting insensibly till it be exhausted as one of the chief supporters of Antichrist"—a prediction which, when Louis XVI. was about to perish on the scaffold, was remembered, and produced a thrilling sensation in Great Britain. He looked also for the commencement of the downfall of the Papal power in 1848, the judgment of the fifth vial which was to be poured upon the seat of the Beast, or the dominions that belong to it, and depend on the Roman See, beginning in the year of France's humiliation, and expiring at this time. "But yet," he says, " we are not to imagine that this vial will totally destroy the Papacy, (though it will exceedingly weaken it, for we find this still in being and alive when the next vial is poured out."* From 1848 to 2000 he looked for the decay of the Papacy, and finally for its entire destruction at the date last mentioned, when he says the 6000 years will end, and the Millennium commence. He dates the rise of Antichrist at the decree of Phocas, A. D. 606, and says, " If we may suppose that Antichrist began his reign in the year 606, the additional 1260 years of his duration, were they Julian or ordinary years, would lead us down to the year 1866, as the last period of the seven-headed monster; but seeing they are prophetical years only, we must cast away eighteen years in order to

---

* " Rise and Fall of the Papacy," p. 70.

bring them to the exact measure of time that the Spirit of God designs in this book; and thus the final period of Papal usurpations, (supposing that he did indeed rise in 606,) must conclude with the year 1848."*

We give these calculations of Fleming as being of some interest and for what they are worth. After stating that the "militant state of the Christian church will run out in the year 2000, and the glorious sabbatical Millennary then begin," he says, "Christ himself will appear in his glory and destroy his enemies with fire from heaven, which denotes the great conflagration in 2 Pet. 3 : 10, &c., which is followed with the resurrection and Christ's calling men before him into judgment. And perhaps the time of this judgment will take up the greatest part of the whole of another Millennary of years; that as there were four thousand years from the creation to his first coming, there may be four from thence to his triumphal entry into heaven with all his saints; for though the Scriptures call this time a day, yet we know what Peter says—that a thousand years and a day are the same thing in a divine reckoning. That all men that ever lived should be publicly judged in a day, or year, or century, so as to have all their life and actions tried and searched into, is to me, I confess, inconceivable; not indeed in relation to God, but in relation to men and angels, who must be convinced of the equity of the procedure and sentence of the Judge."† On Rev. 20th, he hints that "the first resurrection" might be a revival of the Jewish Church, but in his Christology he corrects himself, and maintains that this is "a real and corporeal resurrection of the apostles and other most eminent saints of the New Testament, who died before the Millennium began,"‡ thus interpreting it, as he also does Dan. 12 : 2, in a literal sense. Fleming departed this life at London in 1716.

* Rise and Fall, p. 35.   † Ibid, p. 41.   ‡ Christology, pp. 36, 40

WHITBY, A. D. 1680.

Daniel Whitby, D. D., was born in Northamptonshire England, 1638. His ability and erudition is unquestioned yet we are at antipodes with the Millennial scheme of which he is the acknowledged originator. But he bears a noble testimony for Pre-millennialism. Hear him: "The doctrine of the Millennium, or the reign of saints on earth a thousand years, is now rejected by all Roman Catholics, and by the greatest part of Protestants, and yet it passed among the best of Christians for two hundred and fifty years for a tradition apostolical; and as such is delivered by many Fathers of the second and third century, who spake of it as the tradition of our Lord and his apostles, and of all the ancients that lived before them; who tell us the very words in which it was delivered, the Scriptures, which were then so interpreted, and say that it was held by all Christians who were exactly orthodox." Then quoting the Fathers in proof, he sums up with the following statements: "It was received not only in the eastern parts of the church by Papius (in Phrygia,) Justin (in Palestine,) Irenæus (in Gaul,) Nepos (in Egypt,) Apollinarius, Methodius, but also in the west and south, by Tertullian (in Africa,) Cyprian, Victorinus (in Germany,) Lactantius (in Italy,) and Severus, and by the first Nicene Council. These men taught this doctrine, not as doctors only, but as witnesses of the tradition which they had received from Christ and his apostles, and which was taught them by the elders, the disciples of Christ. * * * They pretend to ground it upon numerous and manifest testimonies, both of the Old and New Testaments, and speak of them as texts which would admit no other meaning."*

"The above," says the London Quarterly Journal of Prophecy, "comes to us with the weight of an irresistible testimony."†

---

* Whitby's Treatise on Tradition.   † April No., 1850.

"The fact is," says the late pious Bishop Henshaw, "that the commonly received opinion of a spiritual Millennium consisting in a universal triumph of the gospel and conversion of all nations for a thousand years before the coming of Christ, is a novel doctrine, unknown to the church for the space of sixteen hundred years. So far as we have been able to investigate its history, it was first advanced by the Rev. Dr. Whitby, the commentator, and afterwards advocated by Hammond,* Hopkins, Scott, Dwight, Bougue, and others, and has been received without careful examination by the majority of evangelical divines in the present day. But we may safely challenge its advocates to produce one distinguished writer in its favor, who lived before the commencement of the eighteenth century. If antiquity is to be considered as any test of truth, the advocates of the Pre-millennial advent and personal reign of Christ with his saints upon earth, need have no fears of the result of a comparison of authorities with the supporters of the opposite theory."† The foregoing argument in favor of Pre-millennialism our opponents never have seen proper to answer. The statement of Bishop Henshaw in relation to Dr. Whitby, being the first open propounder of Post-millennialism and its kindred doctrines, is affirmed by all Millennial historians, and no person will risk their reputation for learning by denying it.

Archdeacon Woodhouse, a decided Post-millennialist, justly observes: "It is remarkable that Dr. Whitby, who had declined to comment on the Apocalypse, assigning as his motive, that he felt himself unqualified for such a work, has ventured to explain this particular prediction of the Millennium; which, being, as all agree, a prophecy yet unfulfilled is, of all others, the most difficult."‡

---

* Dr. H. Hammond held the Augustinian view.
† Henshaw on 2nd Advent. p. 115.   ‡ Woodhouse on Apoc. p. 470.

The following is the opinion of one unbiased by any Millennial theory, yet a thorough student of its history:

"Modern Divines have concurred in the use of certain professional terms, which undoubtedly owe their reception to a feeling of convenience rather than to the authority of sound criticism. For example, the phrase 'coming of Christ,' which in former times conveyed the most exalted ideas in regard to the destiny of the world, is conventionally employed in our days to mean the hour of every individuals death. The first resurrection, again, according to Whitby and his followers, implies nothing more solemn than the conversion of the Jews; the reign of the saints with the Redeemer, a thousand years on earth, denotes simply the revival of evangelical doctrine; and by the rest of the dead we are to understand a generation of bad men, who are to be born about the end of the Millennium, and to annoy the congregations of the faithful. Those very persons who were not to have fathers or mothers for 900 years afterwards, are, agreeable to this hypothesis, described as the rest of the dead, at the moment the martyrs were raised to live and reign with Christ. * * * In short, the main object of the allegorical school is to explain away the proper Millennium by endeavoring to prove that the language of the New Testament has no reference to any personal advent prior to the general judgment, nor to any kingdom except that which is in heaven. That their aim is good and justifiable, I should be very slow to call in question, inasmuch as it is high time to relinquish the hopes of such a Millennium, as was expected by the Jews and early Christians; but that the means which they have adopted to accomplish their end will prove effectual, is a position which no one will maintain who compares the language of primitive times with the glosses which they have been pleased to put upon it. Every person who reads the book of Revelation without any bias on his mind, and then turns to the far-fetched commentaries of Dr. Whitby and his pupils, will perceive either that undue liberties have been used by them in expounding the original, or that John the Divine did not know the meaning of his own words." * "Such," says Bonar, "are the sentiments of one who had brought himself to deny any Millennium, either spiritual or literal." † Whitby's Millennial theory, now so prevalent, is confessed to be, and is called by him, "A NEW HYPOTHESIS." His treatise was written to support it, or, as he says, "framed according to it." Now, a *thesis* is defined to be a proposition, a position, a statement; while a *hypothesis* means a supposition, a conjecture, an opinion, or a system formed upon some principle not proved. Says Duffield: "His arguments and explanations of Scripture in favor of his hypothesis, are based on assumptions which have not been proved; and his attempts to show the falsity of Millenarian expositions are founded on the assumption of his own hypothesis." ‡ It is an occurrence without a parallel in the history of theology, that a theory without antiquity, without support from the plain, literal sense of Scripture, a theory named by its originator at its birth, "new," and hypothetical, and which impugns the faith of the Church for more than sixteen centuries, has come to be at this time almost universally received and taught, among all classes of men, as a part of the Christian faith. Reader, is it not passing strange? Did you ever soberly think of this?

HURD, A. D. 1772.

Richard Hurd, D. D., lord bishop of Gloucester, Eng., in 1772 published lectures on the sacred prophecies. We extract a few of his thoughts. He says: "The contempt of the prophecies has a natural tendency

---

* Bishop Russell's Discourse on the Mill., pp. 113, 115.
† London Quarterly, etc., April, 1850.   ‡ Duffield on Proph., p. 263.

to corrupt the temper and harden the heart." * He asserted that the Papacy "is now on the decline, whensoever that declension began, or how long soever it may be before it will be finished." † Also, "The prophecies concerning Antichrist deserve, at least, to be considered with care, since in so many striking particulars they appear, on the face of them, to have been completed." ‡ And he declares that righteousness shall at last "obtain a firm and permanent establishment, till the *saints reign* (not in a fanatical, but in a sober and evangelical, sense of that word), *reign* in the earth; till the Lord God omnipotent reigneth." § The bishop, in this volume, fails to commit himself to any Millennial view.

WHISTON, A. D. 1706.

William Whiston, M. A., born in 1667, was at first an Episcopalian, and chaplain to the bishop of Norwich; then a Baptist clergyman at London. He succeeded Sir Isaac Newton as professor, in 1703. He wrote a dozen works, several of which were on the sacred prophecies. He was accused of heresy, but his learning was undisputed. Whiston sustained the year-day theory, often cites Mede, and thought the end would come in 1766. Of the fourth kingdom in Daniel he wrote: "As it was to be in being before the first setting up of our Saviour's kingdom, so was it also to continue in being until his second coming to set up his own kingdom, which can no way agree to the kingdom of the Seleucidæ, nor indeed to any but the Roman empire." ‖ He cites Mede, Dr. More, Cressener, Dr. P. Allix, and Mr. Stephens, as sustaining this view.

Of the Apocalypse he says: "The prophetic part of it contains the most remarkable revolutions and muta-

---

* Hurd on Prophecy, p. 435. † Ibid., p. 277. ‡ Ibid., p. 402. § Ibid., p. 415.
‖ Essay on the Revelation, 1706, pp. 25, 26.

tions relating to the Roman empire and the Christian church, from the days of St. John till the setting up of Christ's kingdom, and the day of judgment." Hence he says: "We may observe the great error of those who would apply all the Revelation to the earliest ages of the church." * Of the personal reign of Christ he wrote: "That happy and glorious state of the church which concludes the Revelation, and is sometimes described as the marriage of the Lamb, or the New Jerusalem, sometimes as the thousand years wherein Satan is bound, and wherein the saints live and reign with Christ upon earth, belongs to one and the same period, which is still future, and immediately succeeds the events contained in the sealed book, and in the open codicil, taking up the entire space from thence to the second resurrection, or till the general judgment and consummation." † Whiston died in 1752. Brooks regards his works as containing much useful information.

READER, A. D. 1778.

Thomas Reader, of England, a dissenting minister of some ability, in 1778 put forth a volume on Revelation. The world will stand 6000 years, he taught; then comes the Millennium, which he supposed would occur between A. D. 2016 and A. D. 3016. Of the new earth he says: "It is not probable that Infinite power and wisdom should ever remand any part of the material creation into its primitive nothing. . . . . For there is to be a grand restitution or restoration of all things (Acts 3: 21), called the regeneration in Matt. 19: 28, by which God will reconcile all things in heaven and earth to his own delightful enjoyment. But polluted matter cannot be reconciled without dissolving its substance by fire, taking it all to pieces, and gloriously changing every

---

* Essay on the Rev., pp. 43, 44. † Ibid., p. 97.

thing which has been defiled by sin. Purged by fire, the earth resembles some resplendent diadem, reflecting from every part the glories of its maker." *

"It is not for us to know in what part of illimitable space the new heavens and new earth will be situated, but as they are to remain before God (Isa. 66:22), no doubt they will be inhabited; for he makes them not in vain. Isa. 45:18. And they will be inhabited by rational but not by miserable beings, viz., the human race." "This" new world, says Reader, "is the kingdom prepared for the church from the foundation of the world."†

On Rev. 22:20 he writes: "As though our apostle had said, 'Whatever you forget, do not forget this one word, Quickly;' and that you may not, as his minister I thankfully take it up from the lips of my Master and his angel; and Oh! that God would sound it out so loud as to drown the noise of every intruding vanity. At the final judgment he comes quickly to all. Reader, are you ready? Can you welcome him? Where is the heart that says Amen to this declaration? Can the creatures whom he came to save, wish his continued absence or delay?" ‡

ISAAC NEWTON, A. D. 1700.

Sir Isaac Newton, "the greatest of philosophers," was born, 1642, in Lincolnshire, Eng. He was the first to discover the laws of gravitation, and his name, connected with all sciences, is renowned throughout the world. "He gave," says Dr. Duffield, "his powerful mind two whole years to the study of the prophecies, and has avowed his belief in the Pre-millennial coming of Christ." §

On the seals and trumpets, also, in explaining Rev. 12th and 13th chapters, Sir Isaac Newton generally agrees with Mede. The hour, day, month, and year of Rev.

---

*Rem. on Rev., p. 316. †Ib., p. 318. ‡Ib., p. 349. §Duffield on Proph., p. 258.

9th, he calculates as 391 years; not 396, as Mede. The vials he makes synchronal with the trumpets; the little book of Rev. 10, he explains as a new prophecy, and he adopts the year-day theory. He alludes to Peter, in his third chapter of Epistle second, as predicting the destruction of all false systems, and then the " future kingdom," he says, is described. On Heb. 12, he speaks of " the shaking of the heavens and earth, and removing of them, that the new heavens and earth, and kingdom, may remain." On the design of prophecy, Sir Isaac observes: " For as the few and obscure prophecies, concerning Christ's first coming, were for setting up the Christian religion, which all nations have since corrupted, so the many and clear prophecies concerning the things to be done at his second coming, are not only for predicting, but also for effecting a recovery and establishment of the long lost truth, and setting up a kingdom wherein dwelleth righteousness." On Daniel 12 : 4, 10, he writes: " It is a part of this prophecy that it should not be understood before the last age of the world; and therefore it makes for the credit of the prophecy, that it is not yet understood, but if the last age, the age of opening these things, be now approaching, (as by the great success of late interpreters it seems to be,) we have more encouragement than ever to look into these things. If the general preaching of the gospel be approaching, it is to us and our posterity that these words mainly belong. But in the very end the prophecy shall be so far interpreted as to convince many, for then, says Daniel, " many shall run to and fro, and knowledge shall be increased."

" The time is not yet come for the understanding the old prophets, (which he that would understand must begin with the Apocalypse,) because the main revolution predicted in them is not yet come to pass. In the days of the voice of the seventh angel the mystery of God shall be finished. * *

Among the interpreters of the last age, there is scarce one of note who hath not made some discovery worth knowing; whence I seem to gather that God is about opening these mysteries."*

Sir Isaac used to say that "about the time of the end, in all probability, a body of men will be raised up, who will turn their attention to the prophecies, and insist upon their literal interpretation in the midst of much clamor and opposition." "How exactly," says Wm. Thorp, "has this observation of that sagacious man been verified."

Of the Beast whose number was 666, Sir Isaac agrees with Irenæus in his application, saying, "His mark is $\chi\xi\varsigma$, and his name *Lateinos*, and the number of his name 666." In this he is not alone, as Foxe, the martyrologist, Dr. Henry More, Lord Napier, Mede, Bishop Newton, and more recently, Faber, Elliott, and a host of others adopt Irenæus' solution, referring the prophecy to the Latin or Roman kingdom. Sir Isaac died in 1727.

WELLS, A. D. 1720

Edmund Wells, D. D., who was Professor of Greek at Oxford, and died in 1730, thus paraphrases Rev. 20 : 4, "The martyrs and other righteous persons, being every one in his proper order arisen from the dead, lived and reigned with Christ a thousand years. Now this resurrection of the righteous is therefore fitly styled 'the first resurrection.'"

DAUBUZ, A. D. 1720.

Charles Daubuz, born in France in the seventeenth century. He was a scholar of the first rank, and published an Apocalyptic Commentary in 1720. Prof Bush calls him "the ablest of all commentators on the visions of John"

---

* Observations on the Prophecies.

Daubuz explained the trumpets, mainly, as did Mede and Jurieu, the first four of the desolations and fall of the Roman Empire, the fifth and sixth of the Saracenic and Turkish Mahomedans, and the seventh evidently of the Millennium. The angel of Rev. 10, as did the Reformers, of the great Lutheran Reformation; advocated strongly the year-day theory, and also the literality of the first resurrection and Millennial reign, and synchronizing it with the New Jerusalem state, teaching that the church being in the saints' mortal state betrothed to Christ, but after the resurrection his wife.*

We give from him two extracts, the first on the reasonableness of the year-day theory. He says: "It would be monstrous and indecorous to describe a beast raging during the space of 1260 years; or a witness which is a man, prophesying so long; or a woman dwelling in the wilderness so many years. Therefore, that the duration of the events may be represented in terms suitable to the symbols of the visions, it is reasonable to expect that the symbols of duration be also drawn in miniature, or in a proportionable arithmetic to the symbols of the events, which are also drawn in miniature. So that as a lion, a leopard, a bear, may represent vast empires, and a woman the whole church, and the like, it is more proportionable to the nature of those things that are thus used for symbols to express their acts by such short measures of time, as bear the same proportion to the duration of that great event which is represented by such small matters. * * If, therefore, it is proper in the symbolic language to represent the *extent* of things in miniature, why shall we think it improper to represent their *duration* in a proportionable manner, by revolutions of time shorter in proportion than the event represented?"† He then makes

---

* Horæ Apoc., vol. iv. p. 468. † Perpetual Commentary, p. 56

the five months of Rev. 9: 5, 10, to mean 150 days, *i. e.* 150 years. On the Millennium he writes:

"It may be observed that as the Jewish Church had no absolute rest or sabbatism, as the Millennium is, so the Holy Ghost could not derive the symbol from that ceremony, but was, as it were, obliged to draw it from an higher fountain or original of ideal types and events. But, however, even this original idea was known to the Jews. They had a tradition of it, and the notion was current even before St. John wrote. He has not then treated of the Millennium as a new thing, but has described it in some measure by the old notions, with improvements: and beside that, showed us how it is accomplished by Christ, by giving us a full account of the antecedents and consequents. Now that tradition was grounded upon the allegorical exposition of the creation of the world in six days, and the rest of God in the seventh, and that a thousand years are with God as one day. Whence it is argued that as God created the world in six days and rested on the seventh, so he will redeem mankind and work out their redemption in six thousand years, and procure his and their sabbatism in the seventh thousand: this *rest* to be proportionable to the duration of the *work*. By consequence, that term of one thousand years is to be taken in a literal sense, and must consist of a thousand years in the common acceptation of the word, and needs no farther evolution, as some of late have pretended, because it is fixed by that traditional allegory. Now, that the Jews had it, must be plain from this, that we find it in St. Barnabas, who wrote before St. John, many years. And indeed we give very good reasons in our Commentary, to think that the notion is as old as the deluge, because we find it pretty plainly to be also the tradition of the Chaldean Magi, and perhaps, too, of the Egyptians."*

* Perpetual Com., p. 64.

On Rev. 19 : 11, he says : "This is Christ himself, who rides upon his white horse; as appears by what is said hereafter. He is to act therein himself visibly, without deputies, at least such as he has already employed. * * * Christ comes now to settle himself in his kingdom, with his saints, who are now to be gathered to him."

On chapter 20 : 4, giving his reasons why the dead bodies of the martyrs are denominated souls : "The first is, that Ψυχὴ is said of a dead man, upon the account of the shedding of his blood, which is as his soul; the second is that ψυχὴ signifies a dead body. Num. 5 : 2; Lev. 19 : 28; 22 : 4; 21 : 11; Num. 6 : 6; Hag. 2 : 13; and in this sense one may also understand that place of Rev. 6 : 9. Now these souls thus shed or dead are to live and reign. It being therefore certain that these very souls are they which must be understood thus dead and living, and that it is not possible to understand it of any other sort of men, but of the primitive martyrs, it is now as certain that in this Millennial state they revive and reign with Christ."*

GILL, A. D. 1750

Dr. John Gill was born in England, 1697. He was eminent as a divine, theologian, and orientalist, and as all are aware who are conversant with his Prophetical Sermons, Body of Divinity and Commentary, was a thorough Pre-Millennialist. He argues thus :

"THE MILLENNIUM, OR PERSONAL REIGN OF CHRIST

"I observe, I. That Christ will have a special, peculiar, glorious, and visible kingdom, in which he will reign personally on earth. 1. I call it a special, peculiar kingdom, different from the kingdom of nature, and from his spiritual kingdom 2. It will be very glorious and visible; hence his

* Perpetual Com., p. 64.

appearing and kingdom are put together.—2 Tim. 4: 1
3. This kingdom will be, after all the enemies of Christ and of his people are removed out of the way. 4. Antichrist will be destroyed; an angel, who is no other than Christ, will then personally descend to bind Satan and all his angels. 5. This kingdom of Christ will be bounded by two resurrections; by the first resurrection, or the resurrection of the just, at which it will begin; and by the second resurrection, or the resurrection of the wicked, at which it will end, or nearly. 6. This kingdom will be before the general judgment, especially of the wicked. John, after he had given an account of the former, (Rev. 20,) relates a vision of the latter. 7. This glorious, visible kingdom of Christ will be on earth, and not in heaven; and so is distinct from the kingdom of heaven, or ultimate glory.

" II. Having explained the nature of Christ's kingdom, I shall proceed to give the proof that there will be such a glorious, visible kingdom of Christ on earth. Now the proof of this point may be taken," &c.

He then quotes Psalms 45, 96; Isa. 24 : 23; Rev. 21: 23; Isa. 30: 26, 27, 30; Jer. 23: 5, 6; Ezk. 21: 27; Dan. 2: 44; Zech. 14: 9; Matt. 6: 10; also 20: 21–23; Luke 1: 32–33; also 23: 42, 43; Acts 1: 7; 2 Tim. 4: 1, in proof.

Then proceeding to show, *Third*, that all the saints will have a share in this reign. *Fourth*, it will be those who rise in the first resurrection. *Fifth*, the 1000 years are literal and future. He concludes thus:

" VI. I close all with an answer to a few of the principal objections. 1. It may be objected, to what purpose will Satan be bound a thousand years to prevent his deception of the nations, when there will be no nations to be deceived by him during that time, since the wicked will be all destroyed in the general conflagration, and the saints will be with Christ, out of the reach of temptation and seduction. I answer this will not be the case at the binding of Satan; the same nations (Satan by being bound, is prevented from deceiving,) are those that will be deceived by him after his being loosed, as appears by comparing Rev. 20: 3, with verse 8. 2. That though the saints are said to reign with Christ a thousand years, (Rev. 20: 4-6,) yet they are not there said to reign on earth. But it is elsewhere said, the meek shall inherit the earth. They are manifestly the camp of the saints, who will be upon the breadth of the earth, and therefore must be on the earth. 3. It is objected to the personal reign of Christ with the saints on earth, that they, by reason of the frailty of nature, will be unfit to converse with Christ. This objection proceeds upon a supposition, that the saints will then be in a sinful, mortal state; which will not be the case. 4. It is suggested, that for the saints to come down from heaven, and leave their happy state there, and dwell on earth, must be a diminishing of their happiness, and greatly detract from it. No such thing; for Christ will come with them. 3. The bodies of the wicked lying in the earth till the thousand years are ended, may be objected to the purity of the new earth, and to the glory of the state of the saints upon it. The purification of it by fire will, indeed, only affect the surrounding air, and the surface of the earth, or little more. As for the bodies of the wicked, that will have been interred in it from the beginning of the world to the end of it, those will be long reduced to their original earth, and will be neither morally impure, nor naturally offensive; and if any thing of the latter could be conceived of, the purifying fire may reach so far as entirely to remove that; and as for the bodies of the wicked, which will be burnt to ashes at the conflagration, how those ashes, and the ruins of the old world, after the burning, will be disposed of, by the Almighty power, and all wise providence of God, it is not easy to say; it is very probable they will be disposed of under ground: all the wicked that ever were in the world, will be under the feet of the saints in the most literal sense; they will tread upon the very ashes of the wicked.—Mal. 4: 3. II. As to the questions.—1. What will become of the new earth, after the thousand years of the reign of Christ and his saints on it are ended? whether it will be annihilated or not? My mind has been at an uncertainty about this matter; sometimes inclined one way, and sometimes another; because of the seeming different accounts of it in Isa. 66: 22, where it is said to remain before the Lord, and in Rev. 20: 11, where it is said to flee away from the face of the Judge. My last and present thoughts are, that it will continue forever.—Rev. 20: 11. 2. Who the Gog and Magog army are, that shall encompass the camp of the saints when the thousand years are ended? They are the rest of the dead, the wicked, who live not till the thousand years are ended. 3. What the fire will be, which shall come down from heaven, and destroy the Gog and Magog army? The wrath and indignation of God.

He thus writes on Rev. 3: 20: "Behold, I stand at the door and knock," &c. The phrase "standing at the door" may be expressive of the near approach of Christ to judgment; and his knocking may signify the notice that will be given of it by some of the immediate forerunners and signs of his coming; which yet will be observed by a few, such a general sleepiness will have seized all professors of religion; and particularly may intend the midnight cry; which will, in its issue, rouse [awaken the attention] of them all. 'If any man hear my voice,' in the appearances of things, and providences in the world, 'and open the door,' or show a readiness for the coming of Christ, look and wait for it and be like such that will receive him with a welcome, 'I will come in and sup with him, and he with me.' To and among these will Christ appear when he comes in person, and these being likewise virgins, ready, having his grace in their hearts, and his righteousness upon them, he will take them at once into the

marriage chamber, and shut the door upon the rest, when they shall enjoy a thousand years' communion with him in person here on earth, when the Lamb on the throne shall feed them with the fruit of the tree of life, and lead them to fountains of living waters, and his tabernacle shall be among them."*
Dr. Gill died in 1771.

BENGEL, A. D. 1720.

John Albert Bengel, was born in Wurtemberg, Germany, in 1687. He is celebrated as a prophetical writer, Dr. Clarke affirming that "in him were united two rare qualifications— the deepest piety and the most extensive learning." His Millennial views were singular, he arguing from Rev. 20th a double Millennium, viz., a thousand years reign on earth, followed by a thousand years reign in heaven; the first the seventh, the second the eighth thousand years from the creation. The first thousand years beginning, as he thought, in 1836, would be preceded by rapid changes and great judgments. Wesley took Bengel for his master in interpreting the Apocalypse. We extract but briefly.

"Apart from all the details of chronological computation, we cannot but think ourselves approaching very near to the termination of a great period; neither can we get rid of the idea, that troublous times will soon supersede the repose we have so long enjoyed. At the approaching termination of any great and remarkable period, many striking events have been found to take place simultaneously, and many others in quick succession; and this after a course of intermediate ages in which nothing unusual has occurred."†

"As long as nothing extraordinary befals Rome or Jerusalem, things in general will proceed pretty smoothly; but while they continue much as they are, the news in the journals will be alternating and fluctuating every quarter of a year. One novel scene of things and then another, will be

* Vide Commentary.   † Memoirs and Writings, p. 311

perpetually engaging public notice, till the children of men become ripe at length for a visitation from Him who is higher than the high ones. When events have arrived just at the finishing of the mystery of God, we shall hear the striking of that clock which has so long been silent. I mean that partly before, and partly at this period, many events of a terrible, yes, also of a joyful kind will rapidly succeed one another. * * The aspect of the present season in the church indicates the approach of winter; for ours is a poor, frigid, slumbering age, which needs an Awakener; and surely an Awakener is coming."

"Men are now but novices to those who will appear in the last age of general profligacy, when fleshly security and scoffing at religion shall have gained completely the upper hand; when it will not be so much as dreamed that the end is so near, when the dream will be that all things shall continue as they were from the beginning of the creation. But even that season will have a few who shall continue in the faith, and in patient waiting for Christ; though their numbers will be small indeed, compared with the multitudes then wholly given to infidelity."

"Surely we cannot feel at home in such a world as we now find it; at best it is but an inn upon the road; and the summons 'Arise, and depart, for this is not your rest, because it is polluted,' surely cannot be unwelcomed when it comes. For folly is practised exceedingly in our own days, because it is taken for granted that we can know nothing about futurity."

"A period is coming when the pure Millennial doctrine will be duly regarded as an article of the true faith, and then teachers will be so well acquainted with the whole detail of the Apocalypse, as to make it the subject of common juvenile instruction."*

* Memoirs and Writings, pp. 311, 312.

DODDRIDGE, A. D. 1740.

Philip Doddridge, D. D. He had his birth at London, in 1702, and became pastor at Northampton, and director of an academy. He was the author of valuable writings. In his "Rise and Progress of Religion in the Soul," we see exhibited an abiding love for the Lord's advent, worthy of emulation. He says:—

"Nor is it long before the Judge who standeth at the door, will appear also for universal judgment; and though, perhaps, not only scores but hundreds of years will lie between that period and the present moment, yet it is but a very small point of time to Him who views at once all the immeasurable ages of a past and future eternity. A thousand years are with him but as one day, and one day as a thousand years. He comes quickly; and I trust you can answer with a glad Amen that the warning is not troublesome or unpleasant to your ears, but rather that his coming, his certain, his speedy coming, is the object of your delightful hope, and of your longing expectation.

"For with regard to his final appearance to judgment, our Lord says—'Surely I come quickly:' and will you not here also sing your part in the joyful anthem—Amen, even so come, Lord Jesus?

"Let this illustrious day come, even with all its horrors. We shall go from the ruins of a dissolving world, to the new heavens and new earth, wherein righteousness forever dwells."[*]
Doddridge was a dissenter, and died 1751.

JOHN WESLEY, A. D. 1750.

John Wesley, A. M., was born at Epworth, England, in 1703. He was the distinguished founder of Methodism, and our readers are doubtless familiar with his name and superior excellencies. In 1754 he published his "Notes on the New Testament," from which we make extracts bearing on

---

[*] Rise and Progress, p. 419.

the advent and kingdom. On Math. 24 : 36, he says : "But of that day—the day of judgment—knoweth no man; not while our Lord was on earth. Yet it might afterwards be revealed to St. John, consistently with this." On 2 Pet. 3 : 12, he thus comments : " Hastening on, as it were, by your earnest desires and fervent prayers, the coming of the day of God." In interpreting Revelation, his views nearly coincide with those of Bengel. " Yet," he observes, " I by no means pretend to understand or explain all that is contained in this mysterious book. I only offer what help I can to the serious inquirer, and shall rejoice if any be moved thereby more carefully to read, and more deeply to consider the words of this prophecy. Blessed is he that does this with a single eye : his labor shall not be in vain." He remarks that this revelation " reaches from the old Jerusalem to the New," and also that the seven trumpets extend " nearly from the time of St. John to the end of the world." Applying as others the sixth trumpet to Mohammedanism, he observes that the dominion of Christ " appears in an entirely new manner, as soon as the seventh angel sounds," and that " this trumpet contains the most important and joyful events, and perhaps shall once be heard on earth"—Christ now having " actually come." On the importance of the study of the Apocalypse, he says : " Some have miserably handled this book : hence, others are afraid to touch it; and while they desire to know all things else, reject only the knowledge of those which God hath shown. They inquire after anything rather than this, as if it were written, Happy is he who doth not read this prophecy. Nay, but happy is he that readeth, and they that hear and keep the words thereof, especially at this time when so considerable a part of them is on the point of being fulfilled. * * * It behoves every Christian at all opportunities to read what is written in the oracles of God, and to read this precious book in particular, frequently, reverently and attentively; for the time of its beginning to be accomplished is near—even when St. John wrote. How much nearer to us is even the full accomplishment of this weighty prophecy!" On chapter 5th, verse 4, he comments: "And I wept much: the Revelation was not written without tears, neither without tears will it be understood. How far are they from the temper of St. John, who inquire after anything rather than the contents of this book; yea, who applaud their own clemency if they excuse those that do inquire into them!" The message of the first angel of chap. 14, he says, is not the gospel proper, but a specific joyful message to all, that the hour of God's judgment is come. He says: "We are very shortly to expect, one after another, the calamities occasioned by the second beast, the harvest and the vintage; the pouring out of the vials, the judgment of Babylon, the last raging of the beast and his destruction, the imprisonment of Satan. How great things these! And how short the time!" Like Bengel, he singularly gathers two Millenniums from Revelation 20th—the one ending when the other begins: the first "a flourishing state of the Church on earth," the second "a reign of the saints with Christ in heaven," allowing verse 6th to teach a literal resurrection of the martyrs and saints. Wesley looked for the Millennium in 1836, remarking that, "In a short time those who assert that they (the thousand years) are now at hand, will appear to have spoken the truth." Of Satan's binding, he says: "This fulfillment approaches nearer and nearer, and contains things of the utmost importance, the knowledge of which becomes every day more distinct and easy." On chap. 22: 17,—" The Spirit of adoption in the Bride, in the heart of every true believer says with earnest desire and expectation, Come and accomplish all the words of this prophecy, &c. He that adds (to this book) all the plagues shall be added to him; he that takes from it, all the blessings shall be taken from him. And doubtless this guilt is incurred by all those who lay hindrances in the way of the faithful, which prevent them from hearing their Lord's *I come!* and answering, Come, Lord Jesus!"* John Wesley taught the doctrine of Hades being the receptacle of the soul during the intermediate state, observing of the idea entertained by many, that the soul at death departed immediately to glory and the presence of Christ, that "This opinion has no foundation in the Scriptures." He evidently follows the early Fathers and reformers, postponing the full reward until Christ's appearing.

In his "Sermon on the New Earth," he declares his faith, as does Charles Wesley, in his hymns,

> "By faith we find the place above;"
> "Righteous God, whose vengeful vials;"
> "How happy are the little flock,"

and numerous others, found in the complete collection of his poems. John Wesley died in 1788.

NEWCOME, A. D. 1780.

William Newcome, the learned Archbishop of Armagh, who died in 1799, on Rev. 20 : 4, thus speaks : "I understand this not figuratively of a peaceable and flourishing state of the church on earth, but literally of a real resurrection, and of a real reign with Christ, who will display his royal glory in the New Jerusalem. This is the great Sabbatism or rest of the Church."†

THOMAS NEWTON, A. D. 1775.

Thomas Newton, D. D., Bishop of Bristol, England, was born in 1703, and is distinguished for his piety, and extensive research, as exhibited in his valuable writings on the prophecies. On the Millennium he speaks as follows : " Nothing is more evident than that this prophecy of the Millennium, and of the first resurrection hath not been yet fulfilled, even though the resurrection be taken in a figurative sense. For reckon the thousand years with Usher, from the time of

* Vide Wesley's Notes. † Bickersteth on Prophecy p. 106.

Christ, or reckon them with Grotius from the time of Constantine, yet neither of these periods, nor indeed any other, will answer the description and character of the Millennium, the purity and peace, the holiness and happiness of that blessed state."* Then referring to the persecutions of Christians by the church of Rome, he asks, " If Satan was then *bound,* when can he be said to be *loosed?* Or could the *saints* and the *Beast,* Christ and Antichrist reign at the same period ? This prophecy therefore remains yet to be fulfilled, even though the resurrection be taken for an allegory, which yet the text cannot admit, without the greatest torture and violence. For with what propriety can it be said that some of the dead who were beheaded, lived and reigned with Christ a thousand years, but the rest of the dead lived not again until the thousand years are finished, unless the *dying* and *living again* be the same in both places, a proper death and resurrection ? Indeed the *death* and *resurrection* of the ' witnesses,' before mentioned, chapter 11, appears from the concurrent circumstances of the vision, to be figurative; but the death and resurrection here mentioned must for the very same reasons, be concluded to be real. If the martyrs rise only in a spiritual sense, then *the rest of the dead* rise only in a spiritual sense, but if *the rest of the dead* really rise, the martyrs rise in the same manner. There is no difference between them, and we should be cautious and tender of making the first resurrection an allegory, lest others should reduce the second into an allegory too, like Hymeneus and Philetus. In the general, that there shall be such a happy period as the Millennium ; that the kingdom and dominion, and the greatness of the kingdom under the whole heaven, shall be given to the people of the saints of the Most High, Dan. 7 : 27 ; that Christ shall have the heathen for his inheritance, and the uttermost parts of the earth for his pos-

---

* Dissertations on Prophecy, vol. iii. p. 331.

session, Ps. 2 : 8 ; that the earth shall be full of the knowledge of the Lord, as the waters cover the sea, Isa. 11 : 9 ; that the fullness of the Gentiles shall come in, and all Israel be saved, Rom. 11 : 25 ;—in a word, that the kingdom of heaven shall be established upon earth,—is the plain and express doctrine of Daniel, and all the prophets, as well as of John ; and we daily pray for the accomplishment of it in praying, 'Thy kingdom come.' But of all the prophets John is the only one who hath declared particularly, and in express terms, that the martyrs shall rise to partake of the felicities of this kingdom, and that it shall continue upon earth a thousand years; and the Jewish Church before him, and the Christian church after him have farther believed and taught that these thousand years will be the seventh Millennary of the world."* Bishop Newton referred the prophetic periods of Daniel 12th, to the downfall of Antichrist, and the ushering in of the Millennial period, and also the trumpet of Rev. 11: 15 This excellent man died in 1784

LANCASTER, 1730.

PETER LANCASTER, A. M., in 1730 translated and published Daubuz's Commentary, fully endorsing the millennarian views. On Rev., 20th ch., he says, " This resurrection of the martyrs is called the first resurrection, as being the first in the order of time, and the most excellent."†

ISAAC WATTS, A. D. 1720.

Isaac Watts, a dissenter, born at Southampton, Eng., in 1674. His mental gifts and poetic genius are too well known to require comment or farther praise, he being esteemed as one of the standard British poets. His prose writings we have not at hand, nor do we know his views in regard to the Millennium, but in his hymns the doctrines of the personal advent, the literal resurrection of the saints,

*Dissertations on Prophecy, vol. iii. p. 331. †Perpetual Com. p. 568

the terrestrial reign, and the recreation of the earth, and descent of the New Jerusalem stand forth conspicuous. We transpose and quote a few of them.

On Isa. 9: 6, styling it "The kingdom of Christ," he sings that the government of the earth and seas shall be laid upon the shoulders of "The Wonderful, the Counsellor," who shall have honor and wide dominion. The holy child Jesus shall sit high on the throne of his father David, and crushing all his foes beneath his feet, he shall reign to unknown ages. On Rev. 11 : 15, "The kingdoms of the world become the kingdoms of the Lord, or, as he calls it, "*The day of judgment;*" he prays, "Let the seventh angel sound on high" when the kings of the earth shall give up their kingdoms to God, who assumes his power, and Jesus the Lamb once slain shall live and reign forever. The angry nations fret and roar, God flies on wings of vengeance to pay the long arrears of blood, the rising dead appear and hear the decisive sentence, and the martyrs receive an infinite reward. Of Sol. Songs 3: 11, "The coronation of Christ," he sings

"O, that the months would roll away,
And bring the coronation day."

In Hymns 102 and 110, Book 2d, he sings of the literal resurrection of the body, "at the revival of the just;" chides the Redeemer's long delay, and prays that he would let the sacred morning break through the sky and cut short the hours by appearing again. In Hymn 13, B. 2, on "The creation, preservation, desolation and restoration of the world," he sings of the creation era, the hasty years, the passage of time; this orb rolls on till the saints are all gathered in, and the trumpet's dreadful blast shakes all nature to dust again:

"Yet, when the sounds shall tear the skies,
And lightnings burn the globe below,
° Saints, you may lift your joyful eyes,
There's a new heaven and earth for you."

Psa. 50, he treats of "the last judgment," when "God comes amid clouds, bright flames, thunder, darkness, fire and storm." Psa. 110, concerning "The kingdom and Priesthood of Christ." He teaches that Christ's reign shall spread through the whole earth, the rebelling powers will be crushed, the rising dead judged, and the guilty world sent to hell. Watts' beautiful "Lyric Poem," entitled, "Come, Lord Jesus," and commencing with

"When shall thy lovely face be seen,"

together with another, beginning, "How long shall death the tyrant reign, &c," express an intensity of love for Christ's appearing, only equalled by Wesley's hymn, beginning, "The church in her militant state," or by the closing words of John, in the Apocalypse. Will the reader carefully peruse the following hymn, composed by our sacred poet, and sung in all the churches? We refer to Hymn 21, Book 3d, entitled, "A vision of the kingdom of Christ among men:"

"Lo, what a glorious sight appears
To our believing eyes, &c."

It contains pure advent sentiment, and all will be ready to admit with Dr. Duffield, that "Watts has sung in noblest strains of the bright hope of a fallen, ruined world."[*] Watts died in 1748.

PIRIE, A. D. 1700.

Alexander Pirie, of Newburg, Scotland, in the eighteenth century, was a staunch Millennarian. He wrote on the subject, and we give the following argument from him. He says:—"It has been argued by Dr. Whitby and his numerous followers, that a proper and literal resurrection is never in the whole New Testament expressed or represented by the living of the *soul*, but by the living, raising, and resuscitation

---

[*] Duffield on Proph., p. 258

of the dead—the raising of the *bodies* of the saints—of them that slept in the dust or in their graves. A very confident assertion this! Let us see whether it be just or not. In Peter's sermon on the day of Pentecost—Acts 2 : 27–31— we find the resurrection of Christ expressed in the very words employed by David for that purpose : ' Thou wilt not leave my *soul* in hell, neither wilt thou suffer thine Holy One to see corruption.' This, says Peter, David as a prophet ' spake of the resurrection of Christ that his *soul* was not left in hell, neither did his flesh see corruption.' Now it will be allowed that the clauses of this verse, or distich of David, are parallel and synonymous, expressing the same thing in different words. Consequently the hell in the first line is the same as the place of corruption in the second, and the soul in the one corresponds with the flesh in the other. Here then it is evident that the soul of our Lord is said to live again, or to be raised from the dead, and also that the resurrection of the soul includes the resurrection of the body; so that it is a matter of indifference whether you say the soul or the body rose, since the one can neither die nor rise again without the other—only to die and to live again are more immediately and properly applied to the soul or life, than to the body, for reasons formerly given.

"Two consequences necessarily follow :—1st. The above remark of Dr. Whitby is unfounded in truth. Here is a proper and literal resurrection expressed in the N. T., by the living again of the soul, and as the resurrection of the first-born from the dead is so expressed, was it not proper to express the resurrection of his younger brethren in the same terms ? Yea, might we not have expected that John as a prophet would use the language common to all the ancient prophets? 2d. When we hear John saying, ' I saw the souls of them that were beheaded, &c., and they lived and reigned with Christ,' we must necessarily understand this as spoken of their reänimated and risen bodies, because Peter has taught us so to explain the resurrection of the soul of Christ, the Lord and Head of the resurrection. Beside this, how could John see a soul separated from the body?"*

HORT, A. D. 1747.

Robert Hort, A. M., Chaplain to his Grace Josiah, Lord Archbishop of Tuam, in a sermon preached at Dublin, in 1747, says: "The opinion of those who are called Millennaries, is far from being new, since it is confirmed in substance by the united testimony of the ancient Heathen nations, of the Jews, and of the whole Christian Church, in its earliest and purest ages. And if we consider the great probability there is that the heathen nations derived it from some revelation earlier than the dispersion of mankind; that the Jews were a people governed and instructed by prophets divinely inspired; that our Lord himself allows their expectations in this matter to be just; that the primitive Christians, unexceptionable witnesses in this case, declare that they receive this doctrine from the immediate disciples of St. John; that it is itself reasonable, and even necessary, in order to render the redemption from the curse complete; that it is taught by many plain and express texts of Scripture, which cannot, without violence and constraint, such as no man would be allowed to use in the explanation of any human writings, be interpreted to any other purpose; if these things are duly considered, it will appear, I think, that the truth as well as the antiquity of this opinion is sufficiently established, nor can I see how it possibly could have been established with more certainty. For if a multitude of Scripture texts, understood in their plain and natural sense, according also to the general tenor of the Scriptures, and supported by so great an authority, be not a sufficient proof I am utterly at a loss to know what is."†

---

* Posthumous Works, published 1805. † Tracts on Prophecy, p. 14

HORSLEY, A. D. 1788.

Samuel Horsley, D. D., born, 1733, educated at Cambridge, and made a bishop of the Church of England in 1788, possessed an original and giant mind, was eloquent as a preacher, and powerful as a theological and scientific writer. Mr. Brooks classes him among the Millenarians of the century, and a volume of his sermons before us confirms this classification. In three masterly discourses on James 5: 8, and Matt. 24: 3, the bishop strongly inveighs against the Whitbyan school of interpreters, who saw in our Lord's splendid prophecies of his own advent, only the destruction of Jerusalem, eighteen centuries ago. He says the phrase, Coming of the Son of man, it is now "the fashion to understand of the ruin of Jerusalem by the Roman arms within half a century after our Lord's ascension; and that to those who take the sense of Scripture from some of the best modern expositors, it must seem doubtful whether any clear prediction is to be found in the New Testament of an event in which, of all others, the Christian world is most interested." *

Clearing up the sense of our Lord's predictions in Matt. 24 and 25, he says in all places the phrase, Our Lord's coming, "is to be taken literally for our Lord's personal coming at the last day;" that those texts that seem to announce his arrival in the apostle's days were intended to be understood in a comparative sense: "Thus, although the day of judgment removed undoubtedly by an interval of many ages from the age of the apostles, yet it might in their days be said to be near at hand, if its distance from them was but a small part of the whole period of the world's existence, which is the standard in reference to which, so long as the

* Horsley's Sermons, London, 1839, p. 18.

world shall last, all other portions of time may be by us most properly denominated long or short." * Very sensibly he regards "the great tribulation" predicted by our Lord, Matt. 24: 21, 29, as not limited to the destruction of the Jews' city and nation in the first century, but as extending over a long period and nearly covering this age; then would come the signs, Israel's release, and the Lord's advent. "Our Lord will come," he exclaims; "he will come unlooked for, and may come sooner than we think." †

In a sermon on Ps. 45: 1, "touching the King," he says the words of this Psalm are "the marriage song" of the holy Bridegroom and elect bride, and "for eighteen hundred years have been the means of perpetuating in Christian congregations the grateful remembrance of what has been done, anxious attention to what is doing, and of the cheering hope of the second coming of our Lord; who surely cometh to turn away ungodliness from Jacob, and to set up a standard to the nations which yet sit in darkness and in the shadow of death. He that witnesseth these things saith, Behold, I come quickly. And the Spirit saith, Come; and the bride saith, Come; and let every one that hears, say, Amen. Even so, come, Lord Jesus." ‡

BROWNE, A. D. 1642.

Sir Thomas Browne, a physician and writer of eminence, born at London, 1605, a man of learning and benevolence, gave to the world the following thoughts, which suggest that he was no believer in a millennium of peace and safety, this side the end of time. He wrote: "We cannot hope to live so long in our names as some have done in their persons; one face of Janus holds no proportion to the other. It is too late to be

* Sermons, p. 23.   † Sermons, p. 43.   ‡ Sermons, p. 89.

ambitious. The great mutations of the world are acted, or time may be too short for our designs. To extend our memories by monuments whose death we daily pray for, and for whose duration we cannot hope, without injury to our expectations in the advent of the last day, were a contradiction to our beliefs. We, whose generations are ordained in this setting part of time, are providentially taken off from such imaginations; and being necessitated to eye the remaining particle of futurity, are naturally constituted unto thoughts of the next world, and cannot excusably decline the consideration of that duration which maketh pyramids pillars of snow, and all that is past, a moment." *

KING, A. D. 1788.

Edward King, Esq., was a Fellow of the Royal Society and the critical and sagacious author of a work entitled, "Morsels of Criticism," first published in 1788. Mr. Brooks places him among the Millenarians.† King was a layman of the Church of England, and was deeply pious. He believed that the world would stand 6000 years; and of the last 2000 years of this period he wrote, "We cannot but apprehend the end and closing of this third great day to be near at hand." ‡ Commenting on Luke 18: 8, he thought that "before the second coming of the Lord, there shall indeed be a most dreadful and too general apostacy of those once called Christian nations, from the true faith in Christ their Saviour, and from the truth of his Holy Word." §

Our author touched on many of the prophecies that relate to the last great day. In a section of his work devoted to "The Second Coming of our Lord," and the famous three-fold question of the disciples recorded in

---

* Hydriotaphia, or Urn Burial; by Sir Thomas Browne, M. D., of Norwich, Eng.; p. 258.   † Elements Proph. Int., p. 79.
‡ Morsels, 2d edition, vol. iii. p. 375.   § Morsels, vol. iii. p. 367.

Matt. 24:3, he flings aside the old scholastic notion that the judgment period will be an instantaneous and hurried scene of adjudication, and, with Mede, supposes it will be "a long day, an era, a prophetical day, even of many years, and perhaps of ages;" and "a season of wise and deliberate arrangement, and a final perfecting and rectifying of all things." * With Horsley, he says the questions did not all relate to Jews and Jerusalem, but covered the last glorious advent of Jesus. Long after the destruction of Jerusalem, and at the end of the unexampled season of tribulation on Israel and the church, the signs would literally occur, the sun and moon be obscured, and the stars fall in showers. "The second coming," he wrote, "shall not be (as some have imagined) merely a gradual, progressive improvement of human nature, and a regular, slow, melioration of the state of things on earth produced by that means, but it shall be almost instantaneous, or as the lightning." Matt. 24:27. † The grand era of our Lord's reign, King argues, is to be a "very long one; so long a one, that the end is as yet unrevealed." And again he says, "And, although it be impossible to form any conjecture concerning the end of this, yet this much, perhaps, we may gather from several intimations of Scripture, without presumption: that as the original duration of man upon earth in the first paradisiacal state seems to have been intended to have been about one thousand years, and as each one is to be raised in his own order,— some early in the morning of the day of judgment and resurrection (Ps. 49:14), and some late in the day, even towards the very evening of that great and long day (Ps. 59:6, and Rev. 20:8; 22:15),— so, probably, the duration of each one of the servants of God upon earth, in this paradisiacal state, after his resurrection, may be

* Morsels, vol. i., pp. 371-373.   † Ibid., vol. 1, p. 406.

about a thousand years. . . . But concerning this matter, I speak with great awe and fear." * King sets forth precious thoughts on this interesting subject.

WHITEFIELD, A. D. 1760.

George Whitefield was born at Gloucester, 1714. He was educated at Oxford, and was associated with Wesley; from his youth exhibiting extraordinary talents. His system was Calvinistic Methodist. What his views were in regard to the personal Millennial reign, we know not, but if we are left to judge by the tenor of his published sermons, we should regard him as not at all favoring Post-millennialism, or the doctrine of the complete evangelizing of the world. He makes constant and pointed references to the "coming of Christ and the judgment day," alluding mournfully to the fact, that by some, "Our Lord's coming in the flesh at the day of judgment is denied;" affirming that "Christ ascended to heaven with the body which he had here on earth," and though we have him in spirit "in our hearts," yet will he "come hereafter the second time, and summon every soul of every nation and language to appear before his dread tribunal," when "earth, air, fire, and water shall give up the scattered atoms," and the saints be literally resurrected; in several places alluding to that day as the accomplishment of the Lord's prayer, saying earnestly: "Hasten, O Lord, that blessed time! Oh, let thy kingdom come!" † On the parable of the Virgins, Matt. 25:1, he makes the "Bridegroom, Jesus Christ;" his tarrying, all "the space of time which passeth between our Lord's ascension, and his coming again to judgment;" the slumbering and sleeping, means, "the wise as well as the foolish died, for dust we are and unto dust we must return;" the cry, "Behold, he cometh,"

* Morsels, vol. 1, pp. 415–417. † Memoirs and Sermons by Gillie.

is "the voice of the archangel, and the trump of God; the solemnizing of the sacred nuptials being reserved till the day of judgment." He says, "Because he tarried for awhile to exercise the faith of saints, and give sinners space to repent, scoffers were apt to cry out, 'Where is the promise of his coming?' but perhaps to-day, perhaps this midnight, the cry may be made. * * Let that cry, Behold, the bridegroom cometh! be continually sounding in your ears, and begin now to live as though you were assured this night you were to go forth to meet him." He often used the expressions, "in these last times," "in these last days," "scoffers of these last days," and, like Usher, anticipated " persecution for the church," justly remarking that "without a spirit of prophecy, we may easily discern the signs of the times," and warning his hearers that "in a little while," or " ere long," and perhaps " very shortly," Christ would come. In his sermon on Mark 16: 15, 19, where he would naturally have spoken on the triumphs of the Gospel, he does not even intimate that every person will receive it, or be saved by it, but otherwise. The following are extracts from his discourse on "The Burning Bush," and "Persecution every Christian's lot."*

"The bush burned—what is that for? It shows that Christ's church, while in this world, will be a bush burning with fiery trials and afflictions of various kinds." "This bush is typical of the church of God in all ages. Pray, is not that the case of the church in all ages? Yes, it has been; read your Bibles, and you may instantly see that it is little else than an historical account of a burning bush; and though there might be some periods wherein the church had rest, yet these periods have been of a short date; and if God's people have walked in the comforts of the Holy Ghost, it is only like a calm that precedes an earthquake." On texts of a

---

* Memoirs and Sermons.

character with this, he says that they are "Passages which though confined by false prophets to the first, I am persuaded will be verified by the experience of all true Christians in this and every age of the church." * * "Hence it is that as it was formerly, so it is now, and so will it be to the end of time; he that is born after the flesh, the natural man, does and will persecute him that is born after the Spirit, the regenerate man. Notwithstanding some may live in more peaceful times of the church than others, yet all Christians in all ages will suffer persecution." "The enmity of the serpent * * * will continue to rage and show itself in a greater or less degree to the end of time."* Such was the faith and teaching of the eloquent Whitefield; a faith we regard as differing from that of Dr. Hopkins, the Post-m., who taught that in the Millennium "every individual person who shall then live will be a real Christian;"† and one that gives no countenance to the views of modern spiritualists. This "Apostle of the British empire, and Prince of preachers," as he is styled by Toplady, died at Newburyport, Mass., in 1770, where his body, committed to the tomb, lies buried "in sure and certain hope of a resurrection."

BENSON, A. D. 1750.

Dr. George Benson, a very distinguished Dissenter, born in England, in 1699, seems to advocate the personal reign in the following notes on Psalms 96: 10-13, and 98: 4-9. He says, "Here we have the subjects of the general joy—the coming of the Messiah to reform the world, to execute judgment upon the wicked, and to establish a kingdom of righteousness upon the earth. We expect his second advent to restore all things, to judge the world, to condemn his enemies, and to begin his glorious reign. Then shall heaven and earth rejoice, and the joy of the redeemed shall be full."‡ He died in 1763.

* Memoirs and Sermons.   ‡ Treatise on the Mill., p. 48.
† Benson's Notes.

CHARLES WESLEY, A. D. 1770

Charles Wesley, A. M., was born at Epworth, 1708, and was educated at Westminster and Christ Church, England. One of the early Methodists, he was decidedly talented and pious, and is the author of hymns, poems, and sermons. His prose writings we have not; but concerning his hymns, whatever our readers may judge, we argue there is taught in them pure Pre-millennialism. As with Watts, we give them, transposing some for the sake of brevity. On Job 19 : 25. he says that—

> "Jesus shall reappear below,
>   Stand in that dreadful day unknown,
>   And fix on earth his dreadful throne."

On Isa. 2 : 17, he sings of Jesus coming, and of his being seated in full glorious power on his Millennial throne. On Isa. 49 : 23, he represents Christ as saying that his people are expecting him to come and reign on the earth. On Isa. 59 : 19, he sings of the time when Christ shall be the universal King on his Millennial throne. Isa. 60 : 13. Christ will descend to his footstool, and fill the world with peace unknown, and with endless joy. The new earth of Isa. 65, like his brother John, he seems to interpret literally, and joyfully exclaims: "We long to see thy throne appear: bid the new creation rise: bring us back our Paradise, and create the universe fair beyond its first estate." On Ezek. 37 : 24, he prays that "God would place Christ our heavenly David on his (Christ's) terrestrial throne;" and on verse 25 sings—

> "Trusting in the literal Word,
>   We look for Christ on earth again;
>   Come, our everlasting Lord,
>   With all thy saints to reign."

On Dan., 2 chapter—

> "Lord, as taught by thee, we pray
>   That sin and death may end;
>   In the great Millennial day
>   With all thy saints descend."

On Dan., 12 chapter, he sings of "the Redeemer's descending from the skies, and beginning on earth his glorious reign with his ancients." On Zech. 14, he prays that Christ "would hasten to erect his throne below, in that last great divine monarchy." On Mal. 4, he sings of Elijah's coming first to prepare the way of the Lord, and then, to Christ—

> "When the seventh trumpet's sound
> Proclaims the grand Sabbatic year,
> Come thyself with glory crown'd,
> And reign triumphant here."

On Math. 24 chapter, he represents "Christ as coming to reign *before* the general doom;" and on Rev. 1 : 5, he prays that "Christ's kingdom may come, and he reign *previous* to the everlasting day." On Heb. 9 : 28, and Rev. 1 : 5, he petitions that Christ would appear a second time, and ascend his bright Millennial throne, and give pure Millennial joy to his people, he reigning the King of glory here; and finally —though much more of the same kind might be added—on Rev. 5 : 10. "We shall reign on the earth," our sweet Millennial poet thus sings—

> "Mightier joys ordained to know
> When thou comest to reign below;
> We shall at thy side sit down,
> Partners of thy great white throne;
> Kings a thousand years with thee—
> Kings to all eternity!"*

HALL, A. D. 1800.

Robert Hall was born 1766. He was a Baptist preacher and author of great talent, and one of the most eloquent and extraordinary men of his time. In his "Sermon on the Advance of Knowledge," he said : "Everything in the condition of mankind announces the approach of some great crisis." Like Lowth and Faber, Mr. Hall looked for a supernatural interposition of the Messiah at the commencement

* C. Wesley's Hymns, published 1762.

of the Millennium.* Mr. Thorp, of England, says that Millennarianism "formed part of the subject of the last evening's conversation enjoyed by him with that extraordinary man, only a few days before his decease, and upon each point the most perfect unanimity of opinion prevailed,"†— Mr. Hall to use the language of Dr. Duffield, " regretting on his dying bed he had not preached the Millennarian views he entertained."‡

FLETCHER, A. D. 1775.

Rev. John Fletcher was born in Switzerland, 1729; became vicar at Madely, and was associated with Wesley; was not only one of the most pious men that ever lived, but also was a close student of prophecy, and, like Toplady, was a Premillenialist. In his "Letter on the Prophecies," dated 1775, he refers to a certain "great and learned divine," who, with Sir Isaac Newton, held that "we are come to the last times," and that Christ was coming to destroy the wicked, and raise the righteous dead a thousand years before the final judgment, whose opinions he endorses, quoting him as saying, on Daniel 8th, that "the end," in verse 19, was the "end of God's universal scheme" at the "revelation of our Lord Jesus Christ," and that though "Chronologists may mistake in a few years, but cannot err upon the whole; and as God is true and faithful, so it is manifest that the prophecy of 2300 years must be fully accomplished in our days, or those of the next generation." Having fully stated his friend's views, Fletcher adopts him as his master, and says:

"Give me leave to conclude with some reflections, that naturally flow from what has been said on that system. '1. Many people, I know, look on meditations on the prophecies, so expressly enjoined by St. Peter, as one of the greatest

---

* Hall's Works, vol. iv., p. 404. † Thorp's Destinies of the British Empire, p. 16. ‡ Duffield on Proph., p. 259.

.nstances of presumption and enthusiasm; because they believe there is no sure ground to build upon, and that it is a land of darkness, in which the most enlightened Christians will never fail to stumble and fall shamefully. But is it probable that God, who foretold to a year, and very clearly, the deliverance of the Jews from their captivity in Babylon, and the building of the second temple, and the birth and death of the Messiah;—is it probable, I say, that He should have been silent, or not have spoken as clearly concerning his coming to destroy the destroyers, and to set up that kingdom which we pray for, when we daily say, according to our Lord's appointment, *Thy kingdom come?* If God has exactly foretold, for the comfort of believers, the various revolutions that have happened to his Church in past ages, is it possible that he should have left himself without a witness concerning the most important of all—I mean the last? If he showed the prophets the first acts of his drama, is it not highly probable he has not forgot the last, without which his wisdom, justice, and mercy would always remain hid under a thick cloud?"

Discarding all knowledge of the hour, day, or even the year of the second advent, yet he says, "the day is fixed, it is foretold; and though the vision was to be after many days, as an angel said to Daniel, yet it may be fulfilled in a few days for us, who live in the last times." He then adds, that, "it is lawful to meditate on the prophecies," observing, "let but those objectors ponder the word *Apocalypse*, and they will be ashamed to say that we must not look into those things, because they were never revealed to us," and that "if Jesus told his disciples that it was not theirs to know the times when those things shall be accomplished, it does not follow that it must be hid from *us* who are far nearer concerned in them than they were;" presenting as authority that Daniel's vision was to be closed up and sealed, till the time of the end, and consequently could not be perfectly known till near its fulfillment. "It is remarkable," he continues "that more books have been written upon the prophecies these last hundred years, than were ever known before, and all—those, at least, which I have read—agree that these things will, in all probability, soon come upon the earth. I know many have been grossly mistaken as to the years; but because they were rash, shall we be stupid? Because they said '*to-day*,' shall we say 'never?' and cry 'peace, peace,' when we should look about us with eyes full of expectation? Let us not judge rashly, nor utter vain predictions in the name of the Lord; but yet let us look about us with watchful eyes, lest the enemy take advantage of us, and we lose the opportunity of rousing people out of their sleep, of confirming the weak, and building up in our most holy faith, those who know him in whom they have believed. If we are mistaken in forming conjectures, if the phenomena we hear of everywhere are but common providences, if these things happen not to us, but to our children, (as they most certainly will, before the third generation is swept away,) is it not our business to prepare ourselves for them, to meditate on them, and to warn as many people as we can prudently, lest their blood should be required at our hands, were they to fall, because of a surprise? Let us pray to God more frequently, that for the elect's sake he would still more shorten the days of the tribulation, and add daily to the true church such as will be saved. But let us not forget to rejoice with Abraham, in seeing by faith the glorious day of our Lord; and to hasten by our fervent prayers that glorious kingdom, those happy days, when narrow shall be the way to destruction, when saints raised from the dead, shall converse with living saints, and the world of spirits be manifested in a great measure to the material world,—in a word, when Jesus shall be all in all. What a glorious prospect is this! Let us then often think of these words of our Lord, 'Behold, I come quickly.' 'Blessed is he that mindeth the sayings of this prophecy.' Let us join 'the Spirit and the bride' who say, 'come.' O, 'let him that heareth, say, come; and let him that is athirst, come; for he that testifieth these things saith, surely I come quickly. Amen: even so, come, Lord Jesus!"* This pious man departed this life in 1785.

PERRY, A. D. 1721.

Joseph Perry, of Northampton, England, was a Pre-millennialist, and like Dr. Burnet, before him, held to a pure and unmixed Millennial age. In a work called "The Glory of Christ's Visible Kingdom in this World," published in 1721, he says:

"The last restitution, or the restitution of all things, will not be, as I conceive, until Christ's personal coming. As the heaven received him, so it will retain him until this time, in which all things shall be restored .... What though this restitution of all things takes in the restitution of the creation unto its paradisiacal state; yet it is certain that the bringing in of the elect by regenerating grace, and completing the whole mystical body of Christ, is the principal part of that restitution, they being principally concerned in it, and for whose sake all other creatures are to be restored; all which shows that there will be no more conversion when Christ is come."†

TOPLADY, A. D. 1770.

Augustus M. Toplady was born in Surrey, England, in 1740. He was distinguished as a Calvinistic divine and author, and was eminently a Pre-millennialist. He says: "I am one of those old fashioned people who believe the doctrine of the Millennium, and that there will be two distinct resurrections of the dead: 1st, of the just, and second of the unjust; which last resurrection of the reprobate will not com-

---

* Vide Fletcher's Works, vol. x.   † Glory, &c., p. 224.

mence till a thousand years after the resurrection of the elect. In this glorious interval of a thousand years, Christ I apprehend, will reign in person over the kingdom of the just; and that during this dispensation, different degrees of glory will obtain, and every man shall receive his own reward according to his own labor, 1 Cor. 3: 8."

"In the course of the present argument, I have been forced to take the doctrine of the Millennium for granted; time not allowing me to even intimate an hundredth part of the proof by which it is supported. I would only observe to those who have not considered that subject that it would be prudent in them to suspend their judgment about it, and not be too quick in determining against it, merely because it seems to lie out of the common road. As doctrines of this kind should not be admitted hastily, so they should not be rejected prematurely.*

"It is enough for us to know that a day will dawn when a period shall be put to every disorder under which nature at present labors, and the earth will become just what it was, perhaps considerably better than it was, ere sin destroyed the harmony and broke the balance of the well-according system. The stupendous accomplishment of this predestined restoration is largely and explicitly foretold, Rev. 20, where we read that the apostate angels shall be restrained by the coercive power of God, &c. The next chapter opens with acquainting us, that prior to the commencement of the Millennium, a new heaven, that is, a new body of surrounding air, and a new earth shall be prepared for the residence of Christ and his elect: 'I saw new heaven and a new earth; for the first heaven and the first earth were passed away;' intimating that this terraqueous globe and its circumambient atmosphere will be so purified by the preceding general conflagration, as to be totally

---

* Works, vol. iii., p. 470.

changed in their qualities, and divested of everything noxious or that can cause disgust and pain."

Oh, pray to Him for faith, and he who prepares your heart to call upon him will hearken to your cry. Throw yourself for eternal life on the merits of Jesus; and then, whether you believe the doctrine of the Millennium or not, you will certainly have a part in the blessedness of the state itself, and the second death shall have no power over you."* In his sermon on " Jesus Seen of Angels," he says: "They perhaps will, when Christ gives the signal, set fire to the world, and regulate that conflagration which shall issue in the new heavens, i.e., new body of air, and new earth." He died in much peace, 1778.

ROMAINE, A. D. 1790.

William Romaine, an eminent and learned theologian and divine, who was born in 1714 and died 1795, thus writes: " The marks and signs of Christ's second advent are fulfilling daily. His coming cannot be far off. If you compare the uncommon events which the Lord said were to be the forerunners of his coming to judgment, with what hath lately happened in the world, you must conclude that the time is at hand." He could not have embraced the Whitbyan theory.

COWPER, A. D. 1789.

William Cowper, England's " Christian Poet," of imperishable fame, was born in 1731. He was obviously a Premillennialist, and in his " Task," has sung in glorious numbers of the signs of the times, the world's age, the advent, the restitution, the New Jerusalem, and of all those " scenes surpassing fable," but just before us. He says:

* Toplady's Works and Sermons.

"The world appears
To toll the death-bell of its own decease.
And by the voice of all its elements
To preach the general doom. When were winds
Let slip with such a warrant to destroy?
When did the waves so haughtily o'erleap
Their ancient barrier, deluging the dry?
Fires from beneath, and meteors from above,
Portentous, unexampled, unexplained,
Have kindled beacons in the skies. The old
And crazy earth has had her shaking fits
More frequent, and foregone her usual rest;
And nature seems with dim and sickly eye
To wait the close of all. * *

" The groans of nature in this nether world,
Which heaven has heard for ages, have an end,
Foretold by prophets, and by poets sung,
Whose fire was kindled at the prophet's lamp,
The time of rest, the promised Sabbath comes.
Six thousand years of sorrow have well nigh
Fulfilled their tardy and disastrous course
Over a sinful world; and what remains
Of this tempestuous state of human things,
Is merely as the working of a sea
Before a calm that rocks itself to rest;
For He whose car the winds are, and the clouds
The dust that waits upon his sultry march,
When sin hath moved him and his wrath is hot,
Shall visit earth in mercy; shall descend,
Propitious, in his chariot paved with love;
And what his storms have blasted and defaced
For man's revolt, *shall with a smile repair.*

* * * * * *

Behold the measure of the promise filled;
See, Salem built, the labor of a God!
Bright as a sun the sacred city shines;
All kingdoms and all princes of the earth
Flock to that light; the glory of all lands
Flows into her; unbounded is her joy,
And endless her increase. * * *

* * * From every clime they come
To see thy beauty and to share thy joy,
O Sion! an assembly, such as earth
Saw never, such as heaven stoops down to see.
* * * * * *
Come, then, and added to thy many crowns,
Receive yet one, the crown of all the earth,
Thou who alone art worthy! It was thine
By ancient covenant 'ere nature's birth;
* * * * * *
Thy saints proclaim thee King; and thy delay
Gives courage to their foes, who, could they see
The dawn of thy *last advent*, long desired,
Would flee for safety to the falling rocks."*

The reader is referred to the whole extract, found in Book sixth. Cowper, after a life of suffering, died in 1800.

COKE, A. D. 1800.

Thomas Coke, LL. D., was born in South Wales, in 1747, and educated at Oxford, England. Coke was associated with Wesley, and was very active, accomplishing nine missionary voyages to America. In his Commentary, like all other modern writers, he locates the four predicted earthly monarchies, and also Antichrist's principal time, in the past. He regards the third woe-trumpet as ushering in the Millennium—the end of the world, which will begin with great judgments on all nations. On 2 Pet. 3d ch., he writes: "Peter told them that in the last days scoffers would arise, avowed infidels, who, because Christ's coming was so long delayed, would ridicule the promise of it as a mere fable, and from the permanency of the mundane system, without any alteration since the beginning, would argue that there is no probability of its ever being destroyed." On the Millennium of Rev. 20th, he is not original, but follows and quotes Daubuz, Mede, Newton and Faber, as indeed he does on all

* Cowper's Task, B. ii. and vi.

Revelation, advocating firmly Pre-millennialism. Satan being bound, he says: "Wickedness being restrained, the reign of righteousness succeeds; and the martyrs and confessors of Jesus, not only those who were beheaded or suffered any kind of death under the Roman emperors, but also those who refused to comply with the idolatrous worship of the beast and his image, are raised from the dead and have the principal share in Christ's kingdom upon earth. 'But the rest of the dead,' &c., so that this was a peculiar prerogative of the martyrs and confessors above the rest of mankind. This is the first resurrection, a particular resurrection preceding the general one at least a thousand years. * * The sons of the resurrection, therefore, shall not die again, but shall live in eternal bliss, as well as enjoy all the glories of the Millennium."* By the following sentences, gleaned from his Commentary, the reader will not fail to see Dr. Coke's cherished expectation of the approach of the last day: "Near, even at the door, is the great day of judgment. The period of time which yet remains we know is short; how short, who can tell! We ought to be in constant and hourly expectation of it At the coming of Christ to avenge and deliver his faithful people, the faith of his coming will in a great measure be lost. Chronological calculation, and the general appearance of the world, all conspire to tell us that the events of the latter days are even come upon us, and that the time of God's controversy with the earth is near at hand. It is already on the wing. If these things are insufficient to alarm the guilty, neither will they be persuaded though one rose from the dead."*

SCOTT, A D. 1800.

Thomas Scott, DD., the noted commentator, was born in 1747, in Lincolnshire, Eng. and became rector of Aston

* Vide Coke's Commentary.

Sanford. Dr. Scott, as all are aware, was a determined Post-millennialist, showing the opposite view but little favor, and too often lamentably spiritualizing the Sacred Word, as do many others; still we make a few extracts from him, exhibiting his admissions.

On Acts 3: 19, &c., "Diverse opinions still prevail in respect of the reign of Christ during the Millennium, whether it be personal or spiritual; and his coming to set up his kingdom all over the earth has been very generally, even by diligent expositors and other learned writers, confounded with his coming to judge the world," &c.

"Luke 18: 8. Some think that a great prevalence of infidelity will take place just before Christ shall come to judge the world, as it is probable there will be immediately before the introduction of the Millennium."

Rev. 1. He remarks at some length on the blessing pronounced upon those who read and understand the Apocalypse, exhorts to its study, and says: "An acquaintance with this revelation concerning the purposes of God with respect to his church to the end of time, when connected with humility, sobriety, and the obedience of faith, must greatly conduce to the Christian stability, constancy, hope, peace and patience."*

"God's vast design (in the creation) is already in a considerable measure accomplished, and is evidently hastening to an entire completion," &c.

Rev. 11: 15, 18. "Thus we arrive at the consummation of all things through a series of prophecies, extending from the Apostle's days to the end of the world."

Rev. 20th ch. Of the Millennium, he says: "We have as just grounds to expect such a happy event as the Jews had to look for a Messiah; but those who suppose it will be a carnal Millennium are as much mistaken as the Jews were

* Scott's Commentary.

in waiting for a temporal Deliverer. It is our duty to pray for the promised glorious days. * * * Whether the general opinion that this thousand years will be the seventh thousand from the creation—or the Sabbatical Millennary—the event must determine; it is evident, however, that the dawn of this glorious day cannot be very distant, &c. Nor can I doubt that in proportion as the Scriptures are diligently and impartially searched and understood, the more generally and unreservedly will the persuasion prevail that there shall be a Millennium; that it is at hand, even at the door; and that we ought to advert to it, and to those things which may prepare the way for it, in all our studies and writings."*

Dr. Scott, like all other modern writers, locates the four universal kingdoms of Daniel's prophecy, together with the persecuting reign of Antichrist, in the past. On Dan. 8: 13, 14, he speaks approvingly of the views of Newton and Lowth, adding, that "No doubt the end of the two thousand three hundred days or years is not very distant." He fully sustains the year-day theory, and terminates the 1260 years of Papal tyranny in 1866. Scott died in 1821.

GLAS, A. D. 1761.

John Glas, of Scotland, in this century was a Millennarian. From his works in four volumes published at Edinburgh, in 1761, we extract the following argument.

"By the seventh vial comes all the wrath of God, and the destruction of them that destroyed the earth, when God comes to set up that kingdom which was foretold by Daniel. The beast is destroyed, and given to the burning flame, or cast into the lake of fire, at the coming of Christ; and this is the time of the resurrection of all the saints to reign over the world a thousand years, while Satan is restrained from tempting and deceiving the nations. Then it is that the stone cut out of the mountain fills the whole earth, having

* Scott's Commentary.

become a great mountain; and then dominion and glory is given to the Son of man, that all peoples, nations, and languages, should serve him, Dan. 7: 13, 14, 26, 27. And this is the time when the kingdoms of this world become our Lord's and his Christ's. Rev. 11: 15.*

"Further we may observe, that as this kingdom will come with the utter destruction of the enemies of Christ and his saints, so it will be the reward of all the saints, even that same recompense of which our Lord speaks, Luke 14: 13, 14,—'thou shalt be recompensed at the resurrection of the just.' This is that resurrection which is described, Rev. 20, and called the first resurrection, at the beginning of the saints' reign; for by 'it we cannot understand, as some do, the resurrection from trespasses and sins, which is spoken of Eph. 2, because it is expressly declared to be the resurrection of them who had been slain for the witness of Jesus, and for the word of God, and who had not worshipped the beast, nor his image, nor received his mark. These are their characters before they arise and live to reign; but before men rise from trespasses and sins, they are dead in trespasses and sins, wherein in time past they walked after the course of this world, and the prince of the power of the air.†

"Neither can this resurrection be understood, as others incline to understand it, to be a remarkable revival of the testimony and cause of the martyrs of Christ—for this would turn only to the temporal advantage of some saints living this mortal sinful life on the earth, while the departed sufferers in former ages, are crying 'How long, O Lord.' Neither is this opinion consistent with the answer given to that cry of the souls of the slain, wherein their hope is deferred only till the sufferings of their brethren should be fulfilled; for they must all in some shape or other suffer with Christ, who are to be glorified together with him at his appearing.‡

---

* Glas' Works, vol. ii. p. 425. † Ib. vol. ii. p. 425. ‡ Ib. vol. ii. p. 429.

"Further, this reign with Christ, unto which they rise, is the same which is set forth as the hope of the whole redeemed body, when the Lamb takes the book to open it. Compare Rev. 5 : 9, 10, with chap. 20 : 6. It is the reward of God's servants, the prophets, and them that fear his name small and great, Rev. 11 : 18, and chap. 20 : 4. John saw thrones and them who sat on them—compare Math. 19 : 28, and the souls of them who were beheaded for the witness of Jesus, and for the word of God (which is the designation the Apocalypse gives to them who suffered from the Jews, and from Rome heathen, before Antichrist was revealed, chap. 6 : 9, and 12 : 11,) and which had not worshipped the beast nor his image, (which comprehends all the saints that live under Antichrist, to the time of his final destruction;) he saw that all these lived and reigned with Christ a thousand years before the resurrection of the rest of the dead. Now, these descriptions comprehend all the saints in all ages, and cannot be confined to them who live in any one period only. And for this reason, this first resurrection and reign of the saints cannot be understood to be a resurrection only of some eminent sufferers unto death, while the rest of the elect remain in their graves, and those who are living in this mortal life, are enjoying a prosperous outward state. As this opinion cannot be reconciled with the aforesaid texts; so it is not agreeable to the faith of the primitive Christians on this head, from which there was a remarkable departure when Antichrist's kingdom came; for they believed that at the destruction of the empire, there would be a resurrection of all the just, and that all the elect should reign with Christ a thousand years before the judgment of the rest of the dead."*

"Thus the saints will have the dominion over the whole world, and 'the kingdom shall not be left to another people but it shall stand forever.'"

* Glas Works, vol. ii. p. 430.

BUTLER, A. D. 1736.

Bishop Joseph Butler, born in England in 1692, distinguished for his genius and learning, author of the celebrated "Analogy," a work of very superior merit, appears to have endorsed the personal, millennial reign of the Messiah. In his Analogy he makes use of the following language, viz.: "Things of this kind naturally turn the thoughts of serious men towards the full completion of the prophetic history concerning the final restoration of that people (Israel), concerning the establishment of the everlasting kingdom among them, the kingdom of the Messiah, and the future state of the world under this sacred government." * In his life we find him arguing for the future kingdom thus: "Since they (Christians) are not already invested with that degree of glory that will be communicated to them, they could not, under the notion of members of that kingdom, claim any earthly dominion before the glorious reign of Christ shall commence, when they shall indeed reign with him upon the earth." † It is evident that Butler's profound mind grasped the faith and views of Mede on this question. He died in 1752.

HOMES, A. D. 1653.

Nathaniel Homes, D. D., a Puritan writer of learning and ability, was author of "Sermons on 2 Pet. 3:13," published in 1641, and other works, in which clear millenarian doctrines appear. His staunchest and most famous defense of the early church view, is presented in his great work, "Resurrection Revealed," published at London, 1653, and which, along with a further defense of the work, was reprinted in 1833. Mr. Brooks pronounces the volume "an admirable exposi-

---

* Analogy, part 2, chapter 7.   † Memoirs, p. 298.

tion."* Homes amply quotes the early Christian writers, rabbins, and later authors; and was an admirer of Mede, Twiss, Maton, Burroughs, and other Chiliasts of his time. He vigorously refutes Mr. Bailee and Dr. Prideaux, who wrote against the personal millennial reign.

Homes taught that "the time of the saints' reigning with Christ upon earth is so punctually and positively put down to be a thousand years, that I know not how, without perverting the Scripture, to make it more or less. It would seem to me a presumptuous thing to hear the Holy Spirit tell John six times over *in six verses together*, namely, Rev. 20, verses 2, 3, 4, 5, 6, 7, of a thousand years precisely, touching the same business, never varying the phrase to a weakening, but four times (of the six) to a strengthening, of it, with mighty emphasis in the Greek, so as to say, *the* or *that same* thousand years, if I, the mean while, should imagine another number. I know no such phrase in all the Bible, of a thousand years put for another number, to encourage me to such a boldness of imagination." †

Dr. Homes makes the "refreshing from the presence of the Lord" (Acts 3:19–21) to mean "from the *face* of the Lord;" this, he says, is literally from the Greek original, and it "evidently signifies a *sight of Christ*." ‡

His argument that Jesus has never yet reigned on the throne of David according to the promise in Isa. 9:6, 7, is very strong, but too long to quote here. Arguing for a personal and future reign, he cites John Calvin, on Isa. 24:23, as "favoring a visible, glorious kingdom of Christ on earth;" Calvin's words being, "So he reigns, that we may perceive him present with us." §

On Isa. 65:20, a difficult text, Dr. Homes thus criticises: "Now, as far as I can see into languages and

* J. W. Brooks, Dictionary of Writers on Prophecy.
† Resurrection Revealed, c. 3, pp. 74, 75. ‡ Ibid., p. 97. § Ibid., p. 202.

the context, these words, 'For the child shall die an hundred years old,' may be more fitly translated, '*That* the child should die an hundred years old.' For the word in the Hebrew is exceedingly often used, yea, and so rendered by the translators, to signify *that*, as we have here rendered it. As for turning shall into should, it is not worth the mentioning before a grammarian, who knows that the Hebrew so rendered will infer that the verb speaks subjunctively. Now read the words so easily altered in the English, and without the least violence to the native acceptation of the Hebrew, and the meaning will be quite contrary to any intimation of the mortality of the saints in this glorious time of the thousand years, but of their immortality; the sense being, There shall be no more thence (or from that time, viz., the beginning of the thousand years of the new creation) an infant of days, or an old man that hath not filled his days, that the child, or young man, should die at an hundred years old." *

Homes is generally powerful and convincing.

LOWTH, A. D. 1730.

William Lowth was born in London in 1661. He was distinguished as a theologian and commentator, and writes as follows: "The glory of the Lord, that is, the Shekianh, or symbol of God's presence, when it departed from the city and temple, settled itself upon the Mount of Olives. Ezek. 11 : 23. So when God shall return to Jerusalem and make it the seat of his presence again, it shall return by the same way it departed. Ezek. 43 : 2. We may add, that when the Lord ascended from the Mount of Olives, the angels told his disciples he should come again in like manner, that is, in a visible and glorious appearance at the same place." †

---

* Resurrection Revealed, p. 518. † Vide Lowth's Commentary.

Commenting on Daniel 7: 9, he says: "The fourth monarchy being to continue till the consummation of all things, the general judgment is described in this and the following verses, wherein sentence was to pass upon the Fourth Beast, and an end be put to his dominion." Again, on verse 26, he says: "This being the last of the four earthly kingdoms or monarchies, when that is destroyed, there will be an end to the present state of things, when all human power, rule, and authority shall cease, and the kingdoms of this world shall become the kingdoms of our Lord and of his Christ." And on verse 27th he writes: "This denotes the reign of Christ on earth, where his saints are described as reigning with him."* He evidently held the personal reign. Died 1732.

RUDD, A. D. 1730.

Sayer Rudd, M. D., an eminent physician in this century. His "Essay on the Resurrection, Millennium, and Judgment," was published in London 1734. He takes strong ground on the Pre-millennial advent, reasoning admirably and powerfully. After confuting, in a masterly manner, the theory of Whitby, in answer to the question, "Where Christ and the raised saints are to reside during the 1000 years,"† he says: "My opinion on this head can be no secret to those who are the least read in this argument. Every one who hath heard of the Millennary doctrine, and has taken a cursory view of this treatise, must know that I agree both with the ancient Chiliasts (Papias said the reign of Christ shall be upon the new earth, after the bodily resurrection of the dead,) and the most considerable of the moderns on this point; and that I suppose Christ will live and reign with his saints a thousand years on the earth, that is, in this world, not in the form or condition in which it now is, but as renewed

---

* Lowth's Com.   † Rudd's Essay, p. 407.

and refined after the general conflagration. For this is at present to be allowed me, and I imagine it will be readily done, that though the present world is to be burned up, yet that it is not to be annihilated; that the fire of the last day will only alter the figure of the matter composing this ball, and not entirely consume or reduce it to nothing; and that after this deluge of fire a new earth, attended with a new heaven, will arise out of the ashes of this present world. Now, this new earth, together with the new heaven attending, I suppose, will be the seat of Christ's personal kingdom; that he will here transact the great matters of judgment, both with respect to the saints and the wicked, the former during the 1000 years, and the latter at the end of them."*
He then, quoting the usual Scriptures, gives ten reasons for thus believing.

HUSSEY, A. D. 1730.

Joseph Hussey, of Cambridge, who lived in this century, was an author of some distinction, and says John Cox, "he is the most decided Millennarian I ever met with."

Hussey writes: "The glory of this text, viz., Rev. 22: 16, 17, is a thing evidently to be fulfilled in the glorious kingdom of Christ on earth, immediately after the first resurrection of the Lamb's wife, at her making ready in her glorified body, even as the 21st and 22nd chapters of Revelation speak." On Acts 3: 19, he says, "This doctrine of Christ's reign on earth, stands with the witness of all the holy prophets, and it is lodged upon record that the times of refreshing shall come from the presence of the Lord." Hussey taught that this reign would precede the time of eternity, and called it "the reign of Christ through the happy Millennium," "the rest, or Sabbatism, or keeping of the glory-sabbath which remaineth for the people of God, of

---

* Essay, p. 406.

which the first day of the week now under the gospel **is the** earnest penny."*

POPE, A D. 1740.

Alexander Pope, the celebrated English poet, was born in London, 1688. He was, we believe, a Roman Catholic, and is the author of the "Essay on Man," also, "The Messiah." In the latter, after describing the wonderful birth of Jesus, he speaks of his being "the promised Father of the future age," describing his reign as follows:

> " No more shall nation against nation rise,
> Nor ardent warriors meet with hateful eyes,
> Nor fields with gleaming steel be cover'd o'er,
> The brazen trumpets kindle rage no more;
> But useless lances into scythes shall bend,
> And the broad falchion in a plowshare end.
> Then palaces shall rise; the joyful son
> Shall finish what his short-liv'd sire begun;
> Their vines a shadow to their race shall yield,
> And the same hand that sow'd, shall reap the field.
> The swain in barren deserts with surprise
> Sees lilies spring, and sudden verdure rise;
> And starts, amidst the thirsty wilds, to hear
> New falls of water murmuring in his ear.
> On rifted rocks, the dragon's late abodes,
> The green reed trembles, and the bulrush nods.
> Waste sandy valleys, once perplex'd with thorn,
> The spiry fir and shapely box adorn:
> To leafless shrubs the flowery palms succeed,
> And odorous myrtle to the noisome weed.
> The lambs with wolves shall graze the verdant mead,
> And boys in flowery bands the tiger lead;
> The steer and lion at one crib shall meet,
> And harmless serpents lick the pilgrim's feet.
> The smiling infant in his hand shall take
> The crested basilisk and speckled snake,
> Pleas'd, the green lustre of the scales survey,
> And with their forky tongue shall innocently play.

---

* Hussey's Glories of Christ, p. 664.

> Rise, crown'd with light, imperial Salem, rise;
> Exalt thy towery head, and lift thy eyes!
> See a long race thy spacious courts adorn;
> See future sons, and daughters yet unborn,
> In crowding ranks on every side arise,
> Demanding life, impatient for the skies!
> See barbarous nations at thy gates attend,
> Walk in thy light, and in thy temple bend!
> See thy bright altars throng'd with prostrate kings
> And heap'd with products of Sabean springs!
> For thee Idume's spicy forests blow,
> And seeds of gold in Ophir's mountains glow.
> See Heaven his sparkling portals wide display,
> And break upon thee in a flood of day!
> No more the rising Sun shall gild the morn,
> Nor evening Cynthia fill her silver horn;
> But lost, dissolv'd in thy superior rays,
> One tide of glory, one unclouded blaze
> O'erflow thy courts: the Light himself shall shine
> Reveal'd, and God's eternal day be thine!
> The seas shall waste, the skies in smoke decay,
> Rocks fall to dust, and mountains melt away!
> But fix'd his word, his saving power remains:
> Thy realm for ever lasts, thy own Messiah reigns!" *

Pope died in 1744.

T. TAYLOR, A. D. 1789.

Thomas Taylor, of Hull, England, was one of the first Methodists, and an associate with the Wesleys. In a work entitled, "Ten Sermons on the Millennium, and Five Sermons on what appears to follow that happy Era," 1789, he sets forth opinions that seem a cross between those of Mede and Whitby. The Millennium will open with "a partial resurrection, namely, of the martyrs and eminent confessors of Jesus," who, he says, will rise and reign a thousand years in the invisible world. This will constitute the first resurrection, and

---

* Vide Pope's Messiah.

to this Paul may refer where he says the dead in Christ shall rise first." 1 Thess. 4 : 16.* Rome will perish by an earthquake, Jerusalem be the metropolis of the millennial kingdom, the 1000 years be a period of extraordinary gladness and glory. At the end will occur the conflagration, from which the earth will emerge fair and eternally new. "The topography or place of this glorious bliss, will, very probably, be this earth after the grand conflagration; for it does not appear to me that the fire will annihilate but refine, agreeable with Isa. 65 : 17 ; 2 Pet. 3 : 13; and Rev. 21 : 1. The purging fire having done its office, a beautiful frame will arise, a meet habitation for the spirits of just men made perfect, and to which they will repair after the resurrection, each to their own place. And that the place will be within our solar system, and probably where the earth now is, appears to me from what follows in Rev. 21 : 2, 3."

"Here is the ever-blessed God restoring all things! Here is full redemption, so that the wreck and ruin occasioned by the defection of the angels, remains no longer a dreary waste; but a habitation is restored for the true God, and a residence for blessed souls. The Repairer of the breach (Isa. 58 : 12) restores all things; and harmony, order, and sweet concord shall forever dwell." †

LAMBERT, A. D. 1750.

Francis Lambert, a Roman Catholic ecclesiastic of some eminence, born in France about the beginning of the eighteenth century. He is the author of a work on the prophecies, which was first published in Paris, 1806, and which, contrary to the doctrines of his Church, contains a striking testimony in favor of millennial views. On the phrase, "end of the world," he writes:

---

* Sermons, p. 253. † Sermons, pp. 341-343.

"In order that we may rightly understand what the Holy Scriptures announce concerning the destruction of the ungodly, and the punishments which are to fall upon apostate Gentiles—among whom he includes Roman Catholic nations as well as Protestant—we must distinguish three great judgments of God, which are the consummation of three periods which the Scriptures call worlds. The first of these worlds commenced at the creation, and was ended by the deluge, which is the first universal judgment pronounced by the Creator against all flesh. Peter calls this first world the world that then was, or the old world. The second world commenced when Noah left the ark with his family to re-people the earth. It comprehends the time from Noah to Moses, before the law—from Moses and the giving of the law to the advent of the Lord Jesus Christ, and that which shall elapse from thence till the reprobation of the Gentiles, and the return of the Jewish people—that is, the time which shall intervene between the first and second advent of our Lord. This second period, or rather the last portion of it, is often called by the sacred writers the last times—the last days. It was in reference to this corrupted world (or age) our Lord said to Pilate: 'My kingdom is not of this world.' In fact, it will not be until the third world, or 'the world to come,' as Paul calls it, that the kingdom of the Messiah, so often spoken of in the Scriptures, will be established. This second world, which still continues, will be ended by a judgment, which is called by Malachi 'the great and terrible day of the Lord.' Then the Lord will 'shake the heavens and the earth,'—or, as it is immediately explained, 'will overthrow the throne of kingdoms.' Hag. 2: 21. In fine, the third world, which is yet future, is that which the Apostle calls 'the world to come;' or (Gr.) 'the habitable earth to come.' Heb. 2: 5. Elsewhere as in Isa. 65: 17; 2 Pet. 3: 13, the Scriptures call this third world the new heavens and the new earth. This last or third world will be ended by the general resurrection and the last judgment, and the eternal separation of the righteous and the wicked. The first of these great judgments—viz., the deluge—is to us now nothing more than a lesson for instruction; the last of these judgments is still very remote, and its remoteness is still made a pretext or an occasion for impenitence and carnal security. But every thing indicates that the second of these judgments is advancing rapidly, and that it may burst at any moment, when least expected, upon the apostate Gentiles, and enclose them as in the net of a fowler!" He then quotes Joel 2: 10, 30, 31; 2 Thess. 1: 1–7; Psalms, 10-50–97; Isa. 30: 27–30; Isa. 66: 12–16; chap. 13: 5–18; chap. 24: 1-6-16-22; and chap. 34: 1–18; Math. 24: 29, &c.; Mark 13: 24; Jer. 25: 30, and explains them in order as applying and having their fulfillment at the period of the second judgment, which he ushers in with the personal advent of the Saviour.* Lambert's Pre-millennial argument is very lucid, and not without force. He died in A. D. 1763.

HEBER, A. D. 1800.

Reginald Heber, Bishop of Calcutta, was born in England in 1783. He was a poet and divine of much piety and eminence, and evidently a Millennarian. From his spirited poem, "Palestine," which gained the prize for him at Oxford, we extract as follows:

> "And who is He! the vast, the awful form, (Rev. 10: 1-2.)
> Girt with the whirlwind, sandal'd with the storm?
> A western cloud around his limbs is spread,
> His crown a rainbow, and a sun his head.
> To highest heaven he lifts his kingly hand,
> And treads at once the ocean and the land;
> And hark! his voice amidst the thunder's roar,
> His dreadful voice, that time shall be no more!
> Lo! cherub hands the golden courts prepare,
> Lo! thrones are set, and every saint is there; (Rev. 20: 5-6,)

---

* Lambert's Expositions, vol. i., pp. 97, 98.

Earth's utmost bounds confess their awful sway,
The mountains worship, and the isles obey:
Nor sun, nor moon they need—nor day—nor night;—
God is their temple and the Lamb their light; (Rev. 21: 22.)
And shall not Israel's sons exulting come,
Hail the glad beam and claim their ancient home?
On David's throne shall David's offspring reign,
And the dry bones be warm with life again. (Ezk. 37.)
Hark! white rob'd crowds their deep hosannahs raise,
And the hoarse flood repeats the sound of praise;
Ten thousand harps attune the mystic song,
Ten thousand thousand saints the strain prolong!
"Worthy the Lamb! omnipotent to save,
"Who died, who lives triumphant o'er the grave."

Dr. Duffield observes that "Heber sung in noblest strains of the bright hope of a fallen world," or to use the language of Mr. Cox, of England, he "sung sweetly of Millennial glories." The beautiful hymn found in most of our hymn books, commencing,—

"In the sun and moon and stars
Signs and wonders there shall be, &c,"

is the production of Bishop Heber, as also the following,—

"The world is grown old, and her pleasures are past;
The world is grown old, and her form may not last;
The world is grown old, and trembles for fear!
For sorrows abound, and judgment is near!

The sun in the heaven is languid and pale;
And feeble and few are the fruits of the vale;
And the hearts of the nations fail them for fear,
For the world is grown old, and judgment is near.

The king on his throne, the bride in her bower,
The children of pleasure, all feel the sad hour;
The roses are faded, and tasteless the cheer;
For the world is grown old, and judgment is near.

> The world is grown old, but should we complain
> Who have tried her, and know that her promise is vain?
> Our heart is in heaven, our home is not here,
> And we look for our crown when judgment is near."

Bishop Heber died suddenly of apoplexy, at Trichinopoly in India, 1826.

PRIESTLEY, A. D. 1775.

Joseph Priestley, LL. D., F. R. S., born in 1733, and eminent as an author, philosophical writer, and dissenting divine, was led in his later years to regard Christ's personal second coming as to take place at the beginning of the apocalyptical thousand years. In his notes on Revelation he writes: "It is evident from Rev. 20, that the proper reign of Christ, whatever it be, commences with these thousand years, and continues through the whole of them; and that his disciples, at least those who suffered in his cause, will reign with him." Adverting to the opinion that this was only a reign of Christianity, and no proper resurrection of any who are dead, Priestley says, "I was formerly of this opinion, as appears in my 'Institutes,' but I am not so at present." He then proceeds to give scriptural reasons for the change in his belief. "Christ," he says, "will come in the clouds, so as to be seen by all;" but he may not be ever present during the Millennium. The thousand years will be a mixed age of mortals and immortals, and the Jews have special honor therein. At the end comes the general judgment.

While Dr. Priestley's views in some theological questions have been sharply contested by the orthodox writers, it is still pleasant to find him classed with those who hold the early faith.[*]

---

[*] Notes on all the Books of Scripture, 1804, vol. iv. pp. 646-656.

T. GALE, A. D. 1673.

Theophilus Gale was a learned non-conformist divine, who was born in 1628, and whose remarkable work, entitled, "The Court of the Gentiles," gave him celebrity. In 1673 he published a work on the second coming of our Lord, and, by Brooks, Mr. Gale is classed as a Millenarian. We have not seen the volume, but quote the following testimony from it, as given by Mr. Bonar. Gale wrote: "We see the true reason why so many professors, and some truly godly, are so far behind in their Christian race, and have so much of their work before them. . . . Whence comes all this, but from want of serious, lively expectations of their Lord's approach? Believe it, there is a deep mystery, a spiritual art and skill in godliness, which none arrive unto so soon as they who wait for the coming of their Lord. What made the Thessalonians in a short time, to arrive unto such a high state of Christianity, but that they imbibed at their first conversion this principle of waiting for his coming? 1 Thess. 1:10. Oh that professors would try this experiment! Verily, we should not have such complaints among professors as we now everywhere find. It is a sure and fixed rule, that no one has made a further proficiency in the school of Christ, than he can with hope and joy expect the second coming of Christ." *

Gale died in 1678.

CLARKE, A. D. 1800.

Dr. Adam Clarke was born in England, 1762. His name, labors, and learning, are too widely known to require comment. With regard to the prevalence of Pre-millennialism in his day, he writes in his Commentary: "It is

---

* Discourse on Christ's Coming, London, 1673; copied from the London Quar. Jour. of Prophecy, vol. vii., p. 289.

generally supposed from these passages, *i. e.* Rev. 20, that all who have been martyred for the truth of God, shall be raised a thousand years before the other dead, and reign on earth with Christ during that time; after which, the dead in general shall be raised"—" but," he adds, "this also is very doubtful." Though a decided Post-millennialist, yet, like Dr. Burnet, of an opposite faith, he looked for the earth's renovation, observing on 2 Peter, 3d chapter, that " The present earth, though destined to be burned up, will not be destroyed but be renewed, and refined, purged from all moral and natural imperfections, and made the endless abode of blessed spirits. But this state is certainly to be expected after the day of judgment," &c.*

On Daniel 12, he writes: " The world has now lasted nearly six thousand years, and a very ancient tradition has predicted its termination at the close of that period." Referring to the oft repeated words of Elias, he proceeds to terminate the 6000 years at the expiration of 2000 years from the Christian era, and then commenting, thus solemnly observes: " Are we indeed so near that time when the elements of all things shall be dissolved by fervent heat; when the heavens shall be shrivelled up like a scroll, and the earth and all it contains burned up? Are all vision and prophecy about to be sealed up, and the whole earth to be illuminated with the bright beams of the Sun of Righteousness? Are the finally incorrigible and impenitent about to be swept off the face of the earth by the besom of destruction, while the righteous shall be able to lift up their heads with ineffable joy, knowing their final redemption is at hand? Are we so near the eve of that period when they who turn many to righteousness shall shine as the stars forever and ever? What sort of person should we be then in all holy conversation and godliness? Where is the sounding of our

---

* Comments on Peter.

bowels over the perishing nations who have not yet come under the yoke of the gospel? Let us beware lest the stone that struck the motley image, and dashed it to pieces, fall on us, and grind us to powder."

Dr. Clarke, as some others already quoted, seems at times, from the obviously natural construction of the text, to advocate Pre-millennial sentiments *nolens volens*, for, on Math. 13 : 25, in presenting his third sense, he explains the end of the world, verse 36, to be the consummation of all things, observing, that Christ " seems to refer also to the state in which the world will be found when He comes to judge it: The righteous and the wicked shall be permitted to grow together till God comes to make a full and final separation."*

We present such extracts from Clarke and Scott as we might also from Hopkins, Edwards, Bellamy, and others of the Whitbyan school, to show how difficult it is to explain certain Scriptures consistent with the theory of a Post-millennial advent and previous entire conversion of the world.

JOHN B. MASSILLON, a talented French divine and consummate master of eloquence, who died in 1742, admits, that " In the first ages it would have been deemed a kind of apostacy not to have sighed after the day of the Lord,"† but says it was very difficult in his day, on account of the worldly minded and luke warm state of the church, " to call up the minds of the people to attend to the subject of the Lord's advent."

Dr. GILL, too, testifies that the churches, in this century, had a name to live and were dead : " a sleepy frame of spirit,' he says, " having seized upon us, both ministers and churches are asleep." Bengel also called it "a poor, frigid, slumbering age, that needed an Awakener." Such was the complaint, both in England and on the Continent. And there

* Vide Clarke's Com. † Sermons, p. 1.

was a cause for this coldness. Whitby had lived and wrote, and his "New Hypothesis," by which the advent is necessarily postponed a thousand years, had stifled the warning note of, "Behold, I come quickly." That "belief in the speedy advent of the Saviour, and habitual contemplation of the last things, which adds weight and impressiveness to the ordinary preaching of the gospel, giving it earnestness, fervor, and solemnity not often attained," * was now getting unpopular, and, as in the fourth century, truth measurably dimmed before wide-spread error, and spiritual life died away.

As men contemplated an intervening Millennium of peace and safety before the day of judgment, they ceased to be on the alert for the sudden coming of the Son of man. Mark 13:37. Then the principle of accommodation was seized upon, and mistaken believers came more and more to substitute death for Christ's coming, until, in the creed of many, there was little or no difference between them. A laudable and growing desire to see the gospel diffused, caused the faith of the world's conversion to take the place of the scriptural doctrine that the gospel is to be proclaimed as a *witness* or testimony only, and then shall the end come. Matt. 24:14. That august event, Christ's second coming, to expect which, Dr. Albert Barnes says, "became one of the marks of early Christian piety;" which, writes Dr. Hodge, "was the object of longing expectation to all the early Christians;" and which, C. H. Spurgeon declares, "is the day around which our chief hopes must centre;" and David Brown, of Scotland, styles, "The very pole-star of our hope;" — that event was lost sight of by thousands in the church, and mankind dreamed of a golden age without Christ.

* New York Independent, 1850.

CHAPTER IX.

CHRISTIANS IN AMERICA—SEVENTEENTH CENTURY.

"Behold, the Lord hath proclaimed unto the end of the world, Say ye to the daughter of Zion, Behold, thy salvation cometh; behold, his reward is with him, and his work before him."—*Isa.* 62:11.

IN presenting the prophetical views of the first Christians in America, it will not be amiss to state first that the famous discoverer of the new world was a devout Christian, a student of and writer on the sacred prophecies, and a full believer in the world's near ending. The fact is a curious one, and furnishes a suggestive introduction to this chapter.

COLUMBUS, A. D. 1504.

Christopher Columbus belonged to the last half of the fifteenth century. We know of no millenarian writers at that period, though expectations of the consummation were rife in many hearts. A hundred years before, Wycliffe had looked for the end. A volume on the Apocalypse which asserted the approaching end of the world, had been issued at Leipsic in 1481. Columbus himself declares that Cardinal Alliaco, of his time, held to the sex-millennial duration of the world, and that King Alphonso of Spain had calculated the chronology of the world. Columbus also quotes Augustine as dividing time up into seven ages. The great discoverer, who was evidently familiar with previous prophetical writers, was, says Irving, in all save a spirit of intolerance, "devotedly pious," a man of faith and prayer; and he died, it would seem, in peace and hope in the faith of Christ, May 20, 1506.

In the year 1498, Columbus prepared a paper on the prophecies, which, in 1501, was further illustrated with learned citations, by a Carthusian friar named Gaspar Gorricio, and given to the world in 1504. Humboldt, who cites the fact, says that this treatise "recalls involuntarily the great discussion of the immortal Sir Isaac Newton upon the eleventh horn of the fourth beast of Daniel." *

It is not necessary to give in detail the prophetical opinions of Columbus, except to show that he was no believer in the world's conversion. He held the doctrines of his church, and was, probably, an Anti-millenarian. He thought the ends of the earth would shortly be brought together under the sway of the Redeemer,— Mount Zion and Jerusalem be rescued from the Turks and rebuilt by the Christians; the nations know and revere the cross; the gospel, in fulfillment of our Lord's words (Matt. 24: 14), be proclaimed in all the world; and then, without further delay, the end would come. This faith made him a discoverer. "In the execution of my enterprise to the Indies," says Columbus, "human reason, mathematics, and maps of the world have served me nothing. It has accomplished simply that which the Prophet Isaiah had predicted; that before the end of the world all the prophecies should have their accomplishment." †

He is quoted again by Humboldt as saying: "St Augustine informs us that this end of the world will be in

---

* Examen Critique de l' Histoire de la Geographie du Nouveau Continent etc., 1835. I. pp. 15-19, by A. Von Humboldt.

† Quoted by Humboldt from fol. iv., of Columbus' Volume.

the seventh thousand of years after the creation. Such is also the opinion of sacred theologians, and of Cardinal Pedro de Alliaco. Your Highness* knows that from Adam to the birth of Christ one counts 5343 years and 318 days, according to the exact calculations of King Alphonso. But we have 1501 years not now entirely accomplished from the birth of our Saviour until now. The world has, therefore, already endured 6845 years. There remain, consequently, but 155 years to the time when the world may be destroyed." †

Two years later, in a letter to his sovereign, dated Jamaica, July 7, 1503, Columbus, after saying he must hasten and finish up his work of divine inspiration, namely, the opening up of the whole earth to the spread of Christianity preparatory to the coming of the Lord, added as follows: "According to my calculations there remain now to the end of the world but one hundred and fifty years!" How very striking it is that the great discoverer of the earth's western hemisphere should have been impelled to his task and have enthusiastically performed it all under a deep and solemn conviction of the fast approaching, and, we may say, the actual imminence of the Great Consummation. ‡

EARLY NEW ENGLAND PASTORS.

The well-known Increase Mather, in a work published in 1710, said : " The first and famous pastors in the New England churches did, in their public ministry, frequently insist on the doctrine of Christ's glorious kingdom on earth, which shall take place after the conversion of the Jews and when the fullness of the Gentiles shall

---

* Written to Ferdinand and Isabella.

† He probably followed the Septuagint instead of the Hebrew chronology.

‡ Humboldt's Critical Examination, etc., Vol. I. pp. 15-19. Irving's Life of Columbus, I. pp. 38, 79, 119; III. p. 201.

come in. It is a pity that this doctrine is no more inculcated by the present ministry." He adds that the too great silence of the pulpit at that time on the subject, "induced me the rather to preach, and now by the press to publish, what is emitted herewith."*

But few of these first pastors were authors of books; hence we can only judge of their views by such historic testimony as Mather and others furnished, and by the few works they published. Nevertheless we know that for a hundred years the large mass of New England Christians knew nothing of a post-millennial advent. "Millenarian doctrines," wrote Joshua Spalding, "were, beyond all dispute, favorite doctrines with the Fathers of New England." †

ELIOT, A. D. 1631.

John Eliot, the celebrated and indefatigable evangelist among the Indians, and the translator into the Indian tongue of the first Bible ever printed in America from the foundation of the world, held similar views with Huet. He was pastor at Roxbury, Mass., 1631-1689. In one place he writes of "the great kingdom of Christ, which we wait for, when all kingdoms and nations shall become his." Rev. 11:15. He does not allude to the thousand years of Rev. 20, but delighted in the hope of our Lord's return. Dr. Cotton Mather records that on his dying bed "his discourses from time to time ran upon the coming of our Lord Jesus Christ; it was the theme which he still had recourse unto, and we were sure to have something of this, whatever other subject he was upon." ‡ Christians in those days had not learned to deny *in toto* a personal second coming

---

* Faith and Fervency in Prayer. Pref., p. 18.
† Spalding's Lectures, 1796, p. 254. ‡ Magnalia, book 3, p. 257.

of their Lord, nor had they ceased to "love his appearing," and live "looking for that blessed hope."

R. MATHER AND OTHERS, A. D. 1635.

Richard Mather, pastor at Dorchester, Mass., 1635, John Higginson, born, 1616, pastor at Salem, with John Dury, a minister in Massachusetts, all held views similar to those of Shepherd, Huet, and Eliot. "The sanctifying of the Lord's name and the coming of the Lord's kingdom," writes Mather, "are the first two things in the Lord's prayer, — hence their importance." And Cotton Mather, who preached at Higginson's funeral, said that "his soul was filled with longings for the consolation of Israel, and for the time when the kingdoms of the world shall become the kingdoms of our Lord." * These three pastors say nothing about the Millennium, so far as we discover.

John Baily, pastor at Watertown, Mass., 1686, and Jonathan Mitchel, minister at Cambridge, Mass., 1635, held opinions like the pastors named. A divine kingdom was coming; it was near. So, too, did Joshua Moody, minister at Portsmouth, N. H., also at Boston, 1671. None of these wrote specially on prophecy, but all allusions to the Lord's last advent were joyful. It was the one hope. Baily said, "Let your happiness lie in the second coming of Christ;" † and Mitchel wrote, "Christ shall break out of the clouds and sit on the throne of his glory." ‡

WILLIAMS, A. D. 1635.

Roger Williams, founder of Rhode Island, 1635, and pastor of the first church in Providence, put the one

---

* Sermon, pp. 35-41.   † Man's Chief End, etc., 1689, p. 106,
‡ Sermons on Nehemiah 2: 10, 1671.

thousand years in the future, and our Lord's reign therein, "mystical," as did Cotton; but he never loses sight of a mixed age till the Lord comes in person. In his sharp controversy with John Cotton, his argument against persecution was, that the tares were never to be plucked up till the end. He constantly repeats this view, thus: "The tares are persons who ought to be tolerated till doomsday; for Christ said, Let them alone till the harvest." Again, "even hypocrites in the church must be let alone and tolerated until the harvest, or end of the world." The Lord's advent alone will destroy Antichrist. Until then there will be no extirpation of Pope, nor rest for the church. "It is the counsel of God," he says, "that Jesus Christ shall shortly appear, a most glorious judge and revenger against all his enemies, when the heavens and the earth shall flee before his most glorious presence." "The Lord will come when an evil world is ripe in sin and antichristianism, — come suddenly, and then he will melt the earth with fire and make it new, as in 2 Peter 3:13." *

In his second volume against Cotton, 1652, on pp. 54, 55, he refers to the dispute in the church concerning the millennial age, and challenges his opponent for proof that the subjection of all things to Christ would be accomplished by the ordinary proclamation of the gospel by men. With Shepherd, Cotton, Huet, etc., he disclaims possessing a clear knowledge of the future, and thought the 1260 years of the Papal domination were not ended, but hastening to their termination, then not far away.

He believed in the redemption and renovation of the earth, as the following extract shows: "The heavens and earth are growing old, and shall be changed like a

---

* Bloudy Tenent, 1644, pp. 32, 72, 73, 361.

garment. Ps. 102:26. They shall melt away, and be burned up with all the works that are therein, and the Most High Eternal Creator shall gloriously create new heavens and new earth, wherein dwelleth righteousness. 2 Peter 3:13. Till then I wait, and hope, and bear the dragon's wrath." *

NORTON, A. D. 1636.

John Norton, pastor at Ipswich, Mass., was an ardent student of the prophecies, and held advanced eschatological opinions similar to those of Thomas Shepherd. In one place I find him alluding to the "comparative speediness of Christ's coming at the resurrection, when we shall enjoy the blessedness of our persons."† As yet America's Christians had not learned to write against the doctrine of the resurrection of the body.

BULKLEY, A. D. 1636.

Peter Bulkley was minister at Concord, N. H., in 1636. In a work on the gospel, he says that at the sounding of the seventh trumpet, the glory of Christ's kingdom shall be enlarged, Jerusalem shall be a throne of glory. Isa. 4:3-6. He was looking, evidently, for some kind of a millennial reign, but he says nothing of the thousand years, and little about the advent.‡

SHEPHERD, A. D. 1640.

Rev. Thomas Shepherd was pastor at Cambridge, Mass. He rejected "an earthly kingdom here for a thousand years," but held that, at our Lord's coming in power and glory (Matthew 24:30), he will give his

---

* Bloudy Tenent, p. 32. † Orthodox Evangelist, 1657, p. 354.
‡ Gospel Covenant, 1651, p. 22.

people the kingdom named in Matthew 25:31. The Jews will first be called, and truth shine forth brightly in the world. Such passages as Hebrews 9:28, Matthew 24:30, and the 25th chapter, refer unmistakably to a personal advent and the last judgment. "I have no skill in prophecies," he wrote; but he made much of the Lord's appearing, dwelling upon the event with great delight, and saying, in his "Parable of the Ten Virgins" (1636-1640):

"Oh, be watchful! For what should they watch? For the blessed appearing and glorious coming. 1 Peter 1:10-12. They searched after and waited for his first coming, and rejoiced to see that day. So should we now for his second coming." *

Shepherd looked for a wider diffusion of Christianity, but taught that "the wheat and tares" (Matthew 13) will grow together in a mixed age, and that no separation will occur till the age ends in judgment. So also believed the first Christians in the world.

COTTON, A. D. 1642.

John Cotton was minister at Boston in 1652; and the author of numerous works. He repudiates the personal reign of Christ, puts the thousand years in the future, but held that no one will be converted to Christ during the Millennium. He interprets the first resurrection as denoting the first great reformation that occurs after the reign of Antichrist; held that his place in prophecy was under the fifth vial; and thought the Papal power would be broken and the fifth monarchy be established about the year 1655. His millennial scheme had the features of the later Whitbyan view, but he differs in

* Parable, etc., part I. pp. 95-98; part II. pp. 178, 179.

believing that even to the very end of time and during the Millennium, Satan is not deprived of his power to influence mankind. His prophetical conclusions are obscure and eccentric, but it is plain that he believed the present age would be a mixed one until the judgment day.*

HUET, A. D. 1643.

Ephraim Huet was pastor at Windsor, Conn., 1639. He was the author of "The Whole Prophecy of Daniel Explained," etc., 1643. He repudiates Chiliasm, and, with Shepherd, seems to have been an Anti-millenarian. He made much of Israel's conversion: their return will constitute a fifth monarchy, and this kingdom come "by the Lord's presence in the church militant." Singularly, he makes this fifth empire abiding,—a real, visible kingdom of converted Jews and Gentiles, who will control the earth; but it is not a spiritual reign. His views are somewhat mixed; but Dr. N. Homes, who was a staunch Millenarian, declared that both Huet and Parker, of New England, "held forth many very considerable things which are strong for our position;"† and Dr. Mather asserts truly of these, that they held the fifth divine kingdom will be visible and actual in all the world.

PARKER, A. D. 1646.

Thomas Parker was minister at Newburyport, an earnest student of divine prophecy, and author of an able and elaborate volume on Daniel, published in 1646. He argues for the consecutiveness and literality of the five universal monarchies of Dan. second and seventh; the stone, smiting the image upon the feet (Dan. 2:44), is the

---

* Pouring Out of the Seven Vials, 1642.
† Resurrection Revealed, 1653, pp. 54, 241.

Lord at his second coming, until which advent the church will be trodden under foot. He says the fourth beast of Dan. 7, extends until the coming of Christ in the clouds of heaven, which is his second coming as described in Rev. 1: 7, Matt. 24: 30, and 26: 64. Then will come the heavenly kingdom and New Jerusalem state, which will fill all the earth. He says, "The fourth beast is to extend until the last judgment by fire, and the opening of the books. 2 Thess. 2: 8; Rev. 19: 20." Parker avoided a gross chiliasm (as he thought) by putting the thousand years in the past, but ran into no novel post-millennial theories. He calculated the grand numbers, and supposed all would be ended in 1859. As we have already said, Dr. Homes cites him as favoring the doctrine of the personal reign of Christ.*

WIGGLESWORTH, A. D. 1651.

Michael Wigglesworth was minister and physician at Malden, Mass., and author of a poem entitled, "The Day of Doom," that was much read in the seventeenth century. Death, Resurrection, and the Advent are contemplated in it, and while the thousand years and new creation have no mention, he thus sings of his love for the advent:—

> "The time is short you have to serve him here,
> The day of your deliverance draweth near;
> Lift up your heads, ye upright ones in heart,
> Who in Christ's purchase have obtained a part!
> Behold, He rides upon a shining cloud,
> With angel voice and trumpets sounding loud;
> He comes to save His flock from all their foes,
> And plague the men that holiness oppose.
> So come, Lord Jesus, quickly come, we pray;
> Yea, come and hasten our redemption day!" †

---

* Work on Daniel, pp. 10, 12. † Day of Doom, 1651, p. 91.

HOLYOKE, A. D. 1658.

Edward Holyoke, of Lynn, Mass., was a layman, and the author of an interesting work on prophecy, viz., "The Doctrine of Life," 1658. Mr. Holyoke represented his town in the Massachusetts legislature. He held to a calling and conversion of Israel but not to a restoration to their former land; observing that Brightman as also many authors, "make the Jews expect things seen and temporal," while those who put the accomplishment of Zech. 14 in the future, "run into many absurdities." A. D. 606 is his date for the rise of the Papacy, which will not perish until the last advent. He opposes the post-millennial theory of the world's conversion, and says the seed of the serpent and the enemies of the church will continue to the end; in every age the vanity of this cursed world shall be manifested. He argues thus: "Such peace as many talk of under Christ's personal reign is not for this world, but for the world to come. There shall be persecution and vexation from the seed of the serpent in one place or other, more or less secret or open, while the church remaineth in this world, notwithstanding all that is alleged for the glorious personal reign of Christ here on earth."* While our author fails to comprehend a pure and proper chiliasm, at the same time his argument is sound against the post-millennial doctrine. Often, and with joyful language, he refers to "the day of Christ's bright appearing."

STOUGHTON, A. D. 1670.

Hon. William Stoughton was a Massachusetts magistrate, member of the council, chief justice of the

---

* Doctrine, etc., p. 266.

superior court, and also lieutenant governor of the state; being, says Dr. Allen, "of great learning, prudence, patriotism, and piety." Not in the regular ministry, yet, in 1668, he preached an election sermon,—one of the best,—from which we present a brief extract. He writes:

"It is not long before the Lord will finish his great works in the earth. Antichrist shall be destroyed. Israel shall be saved. Zion shall be redeemed with judgment, and her converts with righteousness. Though the Lord bear long with his elect, yet he will avenge them speedily. That he bears long hath been already fulfilled. What remains, therefore, to be accomplished, but only that now he avenge them speedily? Yet a little while, and he that shall come will come, and will not tarry. Heb. 10:37. Blessed are they that watch, and can abide the day of his coming. Shall we have our share in those times of refreshment which are so near to come?" * Could this strong Christian have been a believer in a temporal millennium?

OAKS, A. D. 1679.

Urian Oaks, President of Harvard College, 1679-1681, in some printed sermons, expressed his belief that the time of the end, Dan. 11, had come, and that evil will never be put away from the world nor Satan put down until Jesus comes. "Wait and pray," he says, "and look for and love that day." And again, "Oh! therefore, let all Christian soldiers love and long for the glorious appearance of Christ." †

Thus we see that when New England Christians could

---

* New England's True Interest Not to Lie, 1670.
† Sermon on Rom. 8: 37, 1674, p. 37.

not explain the prophetic word, they could still write of and long for our Redeemer's advent.

LEE, A. D. 1686.

Samuel Lee, minister at Bristol, R. I., 1686, wrote some noteworthy things on future events, and the last great day. Putting the thousand years of the Revelation in the future, he regarded it as the new heavens and new earth state when

———Jerusalem
"Shall be gorgeous as a gem."

Although somewhat obscure as regards his exact views concerning the personal reign, he constantly cites Justin Martyr who held it, as authority, while he wrote beautifully and eloquently of the joy of the redeemed at the resurrection day. Computing the numbers, Lee fixes 1811, '12 as the date for the happy time, but is not certain.* In his "Contemplation on Mortality," 1698, he glories in the coming of the resurrection, ending with a devout expression of love for our Lord's advent.

SEWALL, A. D. 1697.

Samuel Sewall was chief justice of the supreme court of Massachusetts, a learned, pious layman and author: a member of the Old South church, Boston. His "Description of the New Heavens as it makes to those who stand upon the New Earth," 1697, is a fanciful affair. He evidently believed in placing the Millennium in the future, as on page 31 he quotes with apparent endorsement John Cotton, who so believed. Again he observes, " Seeing the first resurrection is near at hand, it were better to wait a little and see what God will do for them (i. e. the American Indians) therein.

---

* Joy of Faith, 1687. Israel Redux, 1677.

For we are certain that if they have a part given them in the first resurrection, they will not be obnoxious to the mentioned judgment,"—that is, of fire, p. 45.

WILLARD, A. D. 1700.

Samuel Willard was President of Harvard College, minister at Boston, and author of numerous works, between 1679 and 1707. In "The Fountain Opened," 1700, he taught the national restoration of the Jews, and describes a millennial state as then to occur. "There are," he says, "better times to come. The whole creation groans for that day, and we ought to live upon the hope of it. Rom. 8:19-23. It will not be long before those days commence. Although we cannot tell the day, or month, or year, yet we are fully assured that it is hastening. Heb. 10:37. Let us, then, much ponder of the happiness of those days, and refresh our weary spirits therewithal."* It would appear as if he looked for a pre-millennial advent. But in another work he describes the advent and general judgment with no reference to the thousand years, and observes that he does not care to meddle with millennial opinions.† Very earnestly he inculcates a love for Christ's appearing. He urges: "Think of this, then, and say, 'This is the day that I love, that I wait for.'" ‡ Again, "It will not be long before that day shall come; these are the last days, and the winding up of the time that we live in." §

Continuing to quote the New England fathers, we call attention to the fact that those now to be cited during the remainder of this chapter were decided and outspoken Pre-millennialists.

---

* The Fountain, etc., pp. 10, 11, 12. † Body of Divinity, 1726, p. 554.
‡ Page 424. § Page 421.

DAVENPORT, A. D. 1637.

John Davenport, founder of and minister at New Haven, Conn., 1637-1670; was a learned man of great influence, author of seventeen different works, and an early associate of Cheever. His sermon on Matt. 24:30, we have not found; but it is quoted by Hutchinson as a pre-millennial work, and, by the Mathers and Cheevers, he is asserted to have been a sober Chiliast. In a "History of the Colony of New Haven," by E. R. Lambert, we are told that "the first settlers of New Haven were Millenarians; that is, they were believers that the second coming of Christ will precede the Millennium, and that there will be a literal resurrection of the saints, who will reign with Christ on earth a thousand years. This appears to have been a prevalent belief in New England." *

Davenport presents his chiliastic faith in a sound and sober manner, in a preface to Increase Mather's "Mystery of Israel's Salvation," 1669. With Adam Clarke, Prof. Michaelis, Dr. Coke, Matthew Henry, Dr. Gill, Prof. Bush, etc., he explained Dan. 12:4 as teaching a literal and prior reliving of the holy dead, expresses his great joy in hearing that Dr. Mather held to the personal reign, inveighs against Jewish notions of a glorious, worldly kingdom in the future, rejects the idea of a mere spiritual kingdom and reign in the heart, and holds the reign to be visible and real, and to begin at the second advent. He deals his blows against all carnal and sensuous enjoyments, as related to the thousand years' reign, and observes that these loathsome notions led learned writers to decline the literal exposition of the first resurrection. He endorses Joseph

---

* History, p. 50. Mr. Lambert might very properly have omitted his sneers at the doctrine, which follow this statement.

Mede, and styles Christ's glorious coming, "the pillar of evangelical faith."

"Yet," he says, "some explained the first resurrection in a spiritual sense, declining the literal, and understand it of the elect's effectually receiving the truth; but this hath been done in all ages, since the first publishing of the gospel, gradually, as Prov. 4:18, and, therefore, is not the meaning of this prophecy. And Dr. Thomas Goodwin proveth the bodily resurrection of the martyrs, from Rev. 20:5-7, by clear and good textual arguments, in his sermons on Eph. 1:21, 22, and on Rev. 5:9, 10. . . . . This state of things on earth, is called 'the world to come,' in Heb. 2:5. . . . Now the Lord give us understanding in all things, and bless the labors of this faithful servant of Jesus Christ for the good of many. I rest. From my study at New Haven, Sept. 18, 1667. Thine in the truth only."

From this, it may be asserted that the whole church in New Haven and vicinity were believers in the premillennial coming and personal reign of Jesus Christ.

CHEEVER, A. D. 1638.

Ezekiel Cheever, the "Patriarch of New England school-masters," "who," writes Henry Bernard, "left his mark forever on New England," was a famous teacher at New Haven, 1637-1650, and then at Ipswich, Charlestown, and Boston, till 1708,—who had governors, judges, ministers, and magistrates among his pupils, when in their teens,—was "a sober Chiliast," says Mather, who preached at his funeral. In his "Scripture Prophecies Explained," printed in 1757, after his death, Cheever, with the church of the first three centuries, sustains the personal reign of Christ in the grand millennial day, styling it, "but one day of judgment, that great and terrible day of the Lord; and there is," he says, "but one coming; that is his second, which we plead for. This is the full persuasion of my heart, that which I wait and daily pray for, saying, with the Spirit and the Bride, 'Come, Lord Jesus, come quickly.'" "The restitution of Acts 3:21-24, is not a new creation, as at the beginning, bringing a new world out of nothing, but only a restoring and refining of this present world, and bringing it into the state it was once, before the fall (Isa. 65:17, Rev. 21:1-7), all being actual and literal." And the first resurrection would be literal; "many dissenters," he asserts, holding these views.

In the style of Irenæus, whom we have previously quoted (p.61), he argues: "The promise made to Abraham, Gen. 13:15, concerning the land of Canaan, 'To thee will I give it, and to thy seed,' is to Abraham himself, as well as to his seed. God knew he should die before ever he possessed it, as appears in Acts 7:6, 'He gave him none inheritance.' Therefore Abraham himself must inherit that promised land, which he will at the resurrection. A copulative proposition is not true, except all the parts be true. If I say a man is godly, learned, and rich, except he be all three the position is not true. If one give land to a man and his children, the man has as good a right as his children, and the promise is not made good except the man have it, as well as his children. It is to no purpose to say if the man die, it falls to his children. God knew Abraham would die before he inherited the land, but he knew also that he would raise him again to possess it, at this resurrection; else why does he put him in? It had been enough to have promised it to his seed after him; but both alike are promised, and both must be fulfilled." *

* Scripture Prophecies, p. 13,

In his last will, etc., on record in the probate court in Boston, liber 16, p. 452, Cheever says he dies, "In hope of a blessed part in the first resurrection, and glorious kingdom of Christ on earth a thousand years." He evidently shaped the views of some governors, and other believers of his times.

ASPENWELL, A. D. 1641.

William Aspenwell, of New England, 1641-55, in a work entitled, "A brief description of the Fifth Monarchy, or kingdom that shortly is to come into the world," 1653; also in a second volume entitled, "A premonition of sundry sad calamities yet to come," etc., 1655, fully endorses Pre-millennialism.

HOOKE, A. D. 1644.

William Hooke, already named, was pastor, first at New Haven, and later at Taunton, Mass. Returning to England, he became chaplain to Oliver Cromwell. He wrote eight works between 1640 and 1681. At an early day, as clerical colleague, and under the tutorage of John Davenport, he became a Millenarian. In a preface to Davenport's volume, "The Saints' Anchor Hold," written by Hooke and Joseph Caryl, 1661, Hooke expresses such views. In yet another work he fully endorses Increase Mather's views on Christ's second advent. He says: "As the lightning cometh out of the east and shineth even unto the west, so shall the coming of the Son of man be; who shall come as a thief in the night, under the sixth vial, when he shall appear at the setting up of his kingdom." * Hooke curiously observes that Hallelujah is never sung in the prophetic

---

* Preface to Mather's Mystery of Israel's Salvation.

strain till the final fall of mystery Babylon at the end of time and at the personal coming of our Lord. He writes: "I subscribe to the judgment of that pious, learned, and judicious servant of God (Mr. Davenport), who hath also prefixed his epistle to this treatise. I have no more to add but my longings for the accomplishment of the great things of those last days."

Hooke loved the study of prophecy, and the dear Master's advent. In a later work, he observes that the kingdom will come at the advent, and adds: "We should love the kingdom of Christ above all other kingdoms in the world. Let the kingdom of the Lord Jesus come, whatever becomes of any or all the kingdoms under heaven." * In "Discourses on the Gospel Day," 1673, he describes the 1260 years of Papal rule as near their termination, and Satan's incarceration in the abyss, soon to come. In 1681, in another volume, he sets forth the end as coming under the seventh vial; then millennial days will come. Prayer will hasten the dawning of that happy day.

S. MATHER, A. D. 1649.

Samuel Mather, brother of Dr. Increase Mather, was minister at Rowley, and at Boston, Mass., for a year (1649), when he returned to a pastorate at Dublin, Ireland, where he died, 1671. Dr. Cotton Mather conveys the idea that he was a Pre-millennialist. He declares him to have been a thorough and earnest student of the prophetical Scriptures, and an admirer of his brother Increase's works on the divine kingdom; and also as having calculated the sacred times and numbers. "Whenever," writes Samuel Mather, "God sets up in any of the ten kingdoms which made the ten horns of

* The Privileges of the Saints, etc., 1673, p. 113.

the Papal empire, such an establishment, sovereign and independent, wherein Antichrist shall have neither power of laws nor force of arms to defend him and his corruptions, doubtless then the witnesses of our Lord are no more trodden down. Then, therefore, expire the 1260 years; and since that such a kingdom as will then arrive may well be called the Lord's, then will the seventh trumpet begin to sound, which that it is near even at the door, I may say, through grace, I doubt not." * To his brother Increase he wrote: "How much I do rejoice that it hath pleased God to stir up your spirit to search into the prophetical parts of the Scripture; of which I have often thought, and still do, that it is a great pity that they are so little minded and seen into by many, both ministers and others, who do deprive themselves of much satisfaction, which they might receive thereby." * Servants of God who are wont to despise his written prophecies, are recommended to ponder these words.

CLARKE, A. D. 1651.

John Clarke was a learned physician, who came from England to Boston in 1637, and, embracing Baptist sentiments, became the first pastor of the Baptist church at Newport, R. I., and was an associate of Roger Williams in the foundation of the commonwealth. The historian Bancroft speaks of him as "the modest and virtuous Clarke," and gives him a high Christian character.†

For preaching the gospel in the house of a member of his church, residing at Lynn, he was sentenced by the Massachusetts authorities to be fined twenty

---

* Magnalia, Book IV., chapter 2.
† Bancroft's History of the United States, vol. ii., pp. 61-65.

pounds, or to be well whipped! A friend, knowing him to be a gentleman and a scholar, without his consent, paid his fine, and the minister of Christ escaped the lash. Backus preserves Clarke's "Narrative" of the affair, in which he, as "a prisoner of the Lord," gives his "confession of faith delivered to the magistrates of Boston," 1651.* In it he refers to "the Anointed King who is gone unto his Father for his glorious kingdom, and shall ere long return again;" whom the household of faith wait for, "in hope of that glorious kingdom which shall ere long appear;" "and so wait for his coming the second time, in the form of a Lord and King, with his glorious kingdom, according to promise." These words have the true ring, and we conclude that Dr. Clarke looked for the personal reign of our Lord, in his kingdom here below.

HOLMES, A. D. 1651.

Obadiah Holmes came over from England in 1639, and became a member of Dr. Clarke's church at Newport, R. I.; and accompanying the latter to Lynn, on a religious visit to an aged member of the Newport church, and assisting in the ordinances of the gospel, he also was condemned by the superior court to be fined, or whipped; and bravely choosing the latter, he was cruelly scourged at Boston with thirty lashes of a three-corded whip.

In 1675, for the information of friends in England, Holmes wrote a confession of his faith, in which, after stating his belief in the commonly accepted evangelical doctrines, he concludes:

"33. I believe the promise of the Father concerning

---

* Backus' "History of New England, with reference to the denomination of Christians called Baptists," vol. i., pp. 182, 183 (2d edition, 1871).

the return of Israel and Judah, and the coming of the Lord to raise up the dead in Christ, and to change them that are alive, that they may reign with him a thousand years, according to the Scripture. 34. I believe the resurrection of the wicked, to receive their just judgment: Go, ye cursed, to the devil and his angels forever. 35. I believe, as eternal judgment to the wicked, so, I believe the glorious declaration of the Lord, Come, ye blessed of my Father, enter into the joy of your Lord; which joy eye hath not seen, ear hath not heard, neither can it enter into the heart of man to conceive the glory that God hath prepared for them that love and wait for his appearance; wherefore come, Lord Jesus, come quickly."

"In this faith and profession I stand, and have sealed the same with my blood, in Boston in New England." *

These testimonies and confessions of Clarke and Holmes are quite remarkable, wrung out, as they were, by persecution; and they strikingly remind us of the Baptist confession of faith presented to King Charles, in 1660.† From these confessions, we may justly conclude that the early Baptists, both in Old and New England, were, as a body, believers in the pre-millennial advent and personal reign of our Redeemer in the restored earth; and that their assertion, that for their faith, "we are not only resolved to suffer persecution to the loss of our goods, but also life itself, rather than decline from the same," was no idle boast.

WALLEY, A. D. 1663.

Thomas Walley was minister at Barnstable, Mass., 1663, and a Millenarian, although the fact does not

---

* Isaac Backus' History, vol. 1, pp. 208, 209 (second edition, 1871).
† See page 201 of this work.

appear in his only published sermon, 1669. But in the preface to Increase Mather's work, "Faith and Fervency in Prayer, and the glorious kingdom of the Lord Jesus Christ on earth, now approaching" (published in 1710), the doctor says: "Whether there will be a personal appearance of Christ, and a corporeal resurrection of saints, at the beginning of the millennium kingdom, is a more difficult point. Great divines have been for the affirmative." Then, citing Piscator, Alsted, Grossius, Brenius, Lelarierus, Mede, Burroughs, Goodwin, Worthington, and many others, he adds: "Three of the ancient pastors of the churches in New England were of this persuasion, viz., Mr. Davenport, Mr. Hooke, and Mr. Walley." * And Cotton Mather writes of him: "Thus did our pious Chiliast, Walley, it seems, come to his thoughts as Joseph Mede before him did, and as in times of more illumination learned men must and will." †
We cannot doubt the pre-millennial faith of Walley.

WHITING, A. D. 1664.

Samuel Whiting was minister at Lynn, Mass., 1664, — erudite, pious, and the author of four books. One was on the judgment day. Never having seen it, we can do no more than copy the title, thus:

"A Discourse on the Last Judgment, or short notes upon Matthew 25, from verse 31 to the end of the chapter, concerning the judgment to come, and our preparation to stand before the great Judge of quick and dead: Which are of sweetest comforts to the elect sheep, and a most dreadful amazement and terror to reprobate goats." Cambridge, 1664.‡

Dr. Cotton Mather says: "Now, though it is possible

* Mystery, etc., p. 17.   † Magnalia, i., p. 547.
‡ See Lewis' History of Lynn, 1829.

that the whole discourse (of our Lord, Matt. 25) may refer to no more than to the translation at the advent, yet, inasmuch as the generality of the interpreters have carried it unto the more general and ultimate proceedings of the last judgment, our Whiting did so too." * The radical advent character of Whiting's volume is apparent, and we judge he endorsed Mede's and Mather's opinions concerning the identity of the grand millennial reign and day of judgment. It is significant that he made it to the elect a day of "sweetest comforts."

HUTCHINSON, A. D. 1667.

Samuel Hutchinson, layman, scholar, and author of the earliest pre-millennial volume written in America, entitled, "A Declaration of a future, glorious estate of the Church to be here upon earth at Christ's personal appearance, for the restitution of all things," etc., 1667. The little volume was published in London, by a friend who signed himself, "T. T.," and whose Advent hymns, and endorsement of Hutchinson's views, abound in the same. With many other Pre-millennialists, he failed to apprehend the doctrine of the endless reign of Christ on earth, but held that our Lord would, after the personal, millennial reign, go up to, and reign in, heaven. He says of the personal reign, "Though St. Augustine fell from it, and Calvin condemned it, yet that doth not prove it an error." The thousand years he regarded as a day of judgment, as did Mede, saying: "When Christ comes to judgment, he comes accompanied only with all his saints and angels, for the restitution of all things, but not for the annihilation of all or most things, as at the ultimate day of judgment. For, as the souls of the

---

* Magnalia, ii., pp. 458, 459.

elect (Rev. 20) lived and reigned with Christ a thousand years, so the rest of the dead, that is, the wicked, rose not again till the thousand years were ended. So that it cannot be the ultimate day of judgment before the wicked rise; the beginning of the day, it may be, whilst Christ judges those that are upon the earth, being accompanied with all his saints for the judgment of them, according as the apostle speaks, 'Know ye not that the saints shall judge the world?' etc. But at the ultimate day of judgment, Christ judges the world alone. Rev. 20:11."

"And methinks it doth much derogate from the glory of Christ to deny him his personal reign upon earth. For shall we grant him his priestly office personally, and his prophetical office personally, and shall we deny him his kingly office personally? He took both his priestly and prophetical office personally, when he was here upon earth; but his kingly office personally he would not then take, because that he reserved till his second coming; and he will take it upon him in the world to come, which is this new heavens and new earth, wherein dwelleth righteousness."*

Our author was well read, and fortified his arguments by citations from the first Christians, and the reformers, Rogers, Archer, Byfield, Caryl, Brooks, Sterry, Alstead, Tillinghast, Burroughs, Homes, Goodwin, John Davenport, of New Haven, and the Catechism of King Edward VI.

I. MATHER, A. D. 1667.

Increase Mather, D. D., born at Dorchester, Mass., 1639, became minister at the North church in Boston, in 1664, continuing till 1723, and for fifteen years pres-

---

* Doctrine of Life.

ident of Harvard College, was a man much honored and of great influence, whose learning and piety are well known. During a period of fifty-three years, he wrote one hundred and ten books. Becoming a student of prophecy, and made aware that the early church, till the fourth century, taught the pre-millennial advent of Christ, "he found himself," writes his biographer, "under the necessity of becoming a sober Chiliast." The following is his lucid scriptural argument:

"When he considered that, immediately after the long tribulation under which the Jewish nation is now languishing, then the Son of man comes in the clouds of heaven with power and great glory; and that at the arrival of the kingdom under the whole heaven, given to the people of the saints of the Most High, at the expiration of the fourth monarchy, then the thrones are pitched, and the Appointer of times appears on his throne, and a fiery stream issues from it, and the judgment is set, and the body of the Romish beast is given to the burning flame; and that our Saviour is to destroy Antichrist with the brightness of his coming, and that there will be a resurrection of the dead, when the time and the times and the half time allowed for the reign of Antichrist is expired, or at the end of the four monarchies; and that when the seventh trumpet sounds, which next follows on the ceasing of the Turkish hostilities upon Europe, then comes the time of the dead, when they shall be judged, and a reward shall be given to them—and this is the time when the kingdoms of this world shall be the Lords; and that the first resurrection foretold in the Holy Oracles can be no other than (what every one owns the second is) a literal and a corporeal resurrection; he saw himself shut up to the faith of it, and compelled unto the persuasion that the second coming of our Saviour will be at the beginning of the happy state which is to be expected for the church upon the earth in the latter days." *

Writing of his experience in the study and reception of the pre-millennial view, he says:

"I was exceedingly backward to entertain such a notion, and did long oppose it, as conceiving it might be, at best, an innocent error of some who wished well to the kingdom of Christ. But blessed be the Lord God, who gave me a heart at that very time to search the Scriptures and other books which might be helpful in this case, both such as argued for, and such as argued against, the Chiliad; and to look up to Him that is in heaven, and that heareth on earth, that I might see and embrace the truth, and only the truth. And methinks I would desire no more, if I could but persuade all serious and gracious men to go that way to work in this matter. But alas! it is the great infirmity of many good men, that if anything be voiced for an error, they fall upon it in great zeal, without ever looking up to heaven, that if what they oppose be truth, they might be convinced of it, as well as, if it be otherwise, they might be strengthened in bearing witness against error; and hence the Lord never lets them see their mistakes."

We copy this from the preface of Mather's work, "The Mystery of Israel's Salvation," which appeared in 1668; a remarkable volume, in which he defends chiliastic doctrines, as held in A. D. 100-300, by a vast number of Scripture citations, and by a reference to and quotation of no less than 258 learned authors! It was his first pre-millennial work, and the preface is dated the same year that Hutchinson's work appeared. The work was greatly admired by John Caryl, of England, and was circulated and read extensively in

* Remarkables in Mather's Life, 1724, p. 63.

Europe. In it he repudiates the renewing of Jewish sacrifices in the Millennium, and vindicates the early church from the charge, sharply remarking, "A most loathsome work do they perform, both to God and man, that dig up the ceremonies out of that grave where Jesus Christ buried them, above sixteen hundred years ago." *

In a sermon on Titus 2:13, he writes: "If believers should enjoy their hoped for blessedness at the day of Christ's appearing, then they have great reason to long for the day of judgment—to long for that day of the glorious appearing of the great God and our Saviour Jesus Christ, as the saints of old did long for the first coming of Christ. Abraham, by faith, saw that day, and was glad; and many prophets and righteous men desired to see it; so believers should long for the second coming of the Lord Jesus Christ. 2 Pet. 3:12. Looking for and hasting unto the coming of the day of God: you must not only look for, not only believe that such a day will come, but you must hasten to it—that is, by earnest desires, by longing wishes. We should pray for the coming of that day. Thus Christ has taught us to pray, 'Thy kingdom come.' We must, therefore, pray for the day of judgment; for the kingdom of Christ will not come in all the glory of it before that blessed day. And when we pray, 'Thy will be done in earth as in heaven,' we pray for the day of judgment; for then, and not till then, will the will of God be done on earth as it is in heaven. Then will the saints that shall come down from heaven in the new Jerusalem, do the will of God with as much perfection on earth as now it is done in heaven: so, then, we are to pray for this coming of the Lord; and great reason

---

○ Mystery of Israel's, etc., p. 113.

believers have to do so, because of their perfect salvation, which they shall then be made partakers of. By hope we are saved. We hope for a perfect salvation in that day; therefore should we long for that day. When He shall be revealed from heaven, we shall be immortal then. Suppose we die and go to the grave before this glorious appearing of the Lord, yet he will raise us up in that day to a blessed immortality. Or suppose Christ shall come quickly, as he will,—but suppose so quickly as to be here while we are yet alive,— we shall in one moment be made immortal. All believers shall not die that shall be found alive at the appearing of Christ, but all shall be changed; therefore they have cause to long for that blessed day." *

Some ten other volumes written by Dr. Mather, dea. more or less in this question, the doctrines of the last things appearing to delight his heart. "He mightily looked up to heaven for direction and assistance in all his inquiries into the character and approaches of the holy kingdom; and by studying the prophecies, and meditating upon the paradisiacal state which then will be at the restitution of all things, he sailed so near to the land of promise, that he felt the balsamic breezes of the heavenly country upon his mind." † Mather was the first doctor of divinity in America, and the end would come, he thought, in 1866.

NOYES, A. D. 1683.

Nicholas Noyes, pastor at Haddam, Conn., and then at Salem, Mass., 1683, evidently adopted the advent views of the Mathers. In an election sermon, 1698, opinions similar to the Chiliasts', appear, but not clearly so. But decidedly placing the thousand years

* Sermons, p. 155. † Remarkables, etc., p. 64.

in the future, in a later work, 1702, he teaches that the last conflagration will not annihilate but only purify the earth, bringing the "times of restitution." Acts 3: 21. It will probably be partial at the Lord's advent, and then progressive. Christ will come at the first burst of the fire, and then, and not till then, destroy Antichrist. "But then," he writes, "whether the consummation of the conflagration will be before the end of the one thousand years, which are thus to begin with a conflagration; and what will be the difference between the inhabitants of the new heavens and new earth during the thousand years; and how the inhabitants of the new earth, enjoying the soil refined by the prodigious fires, will, according to the promise in Isa. 65, build houses and inhabit them, plant vineyards and eat the fruit of them;—these are hard to be understood." * Those who dogmatically seek to define in full the character of the millennial age, may learn something from the cautious and modest spirit of Noyes.

A year later, in 1703, Cotton Mather held a conversation with Noyes, on the millennial times, in which the latter expressed himself as hesitating what to belive about the personal reign, whereupon Mather wrote him a letter, in which he sought to draw fully over to the view that the Lord's second advent will begin the happy state, "one of the charmingest friends I have in the world." † He became a pupil in the doctor's school, and we are inclined to think that the calm, cogent, and very able argument of Dr. Mather, won the Salem pastor over to the pre-millennial doctrine.

The early divines of New England knew nothing of the later Whitbyan view of Christ's reign on earth.

* A Christian Warming Himself by the Fire, pp. 68-70.

† An essay concerning the happy state, etc., of 90 pages, 4to; unpublished, in the Antiquarian Library, Worcester, Mass.

"The sentiments we oppose," observes Spalding, "did not generally prevail, especially among the common people, till the present century;* even as late as the great earthquake, 1755, many Christians were looking, not for the modern Millennium, but for the second coming of Christ. I have the testimony of elderly Christian people, in several parts of New England, that within their remembrance this doctrine was first advanced, in the places where they lived, and have heard them name the ministers who first preached it in their churches. No doctrines can be more indisputably proved to have been the doctrines of the primitive church, than those we call Millenarian; and, beyond all dispute, the same were favorite doctrines with the Fathers of New England, with the words of one of whom, writing upon this subject, we shall conclude our observations: "They are not new, but old; they may be new to some men, but I cannot say it is their honor." †

* The eighteenth. † Spalding's Lectures, p. 254.

CHAPTER X.

CHRISTIANS IN AMERICA—EIGHTEENTH CENTURY.

"For yet a little while, and he that shall come will come, and will not tarry. Now the just shall live by faith; but if any man draw back, my soul shall have no pleasure in him."—Heb. 10 : 37, 38.

PASSING into the eighteenth century, a period marked by the rise and spread of the figurative view of the first resurrection, and by the theory of the post-millennial second coming of Christ, it is known that New England's Christian writers, to some extent, embraced and advocated the new views. President Jonathan Edwards, who flourished as a preacher and writer between 1722 and 1758, in his "History of Redemption," published, 1774; Joseph Bellamy, D. D., in "Sermons on the Millennium," 1758; Samuel Hopkins, D. D., in "A Treatise on the Millennium," 1793;—these celebrated divines, and others, taught the new Whitbyan views of a temporal millennium, and repudiated the pre-millennial advent, as cherished by the first Christians. Nevertheless, every one of them regarded the millennial kingdom as introduced, not by a soft transition, but by the most terrific outpouring of the judgments of God on the evil world-powers and antichristian organizations and peoples who desolate the earth. Rev. 11 : 15-18.

First and foremost as a champion of the chiliastic

view and the doctrine of Christ's personal reign, was Dr. Cotton Mather, who belonged in part to this century, and who, as the author of a score of works on prophecy, constantly gave prominence to the doctrine of Christ's coming. He lived and died a Chiliast. Tracing the pre-millennial believers throughout the century, we call attention to the strong, earnest testimonies of the Mathers, Prince, Gale, Spalding, and others, and are able to cite Dr. Cotton Mather as recording historically, in 1702, that such conclusions respecting Christ's personal millennial reign, "do now of late years get more ground against the oppositions of the otherwise minded, and find a kinder entertainment among them that search the Scriptures." *

Of this class we first notice,

C. MATHER, A. D. 1700.

Cotton Mather, D. D., born, 1663, minister at the North Church, Boston, was a peculiar but remarkable man, the most distinguished and learned clergyman of his day in New England, and the author of no less than three hundred and eighty-two different works, more than a score of which deal with questions of eschatology. A son of Increase Mather, he was eminent as a Chiliast, and we are indebted to him for much of our information respecting the New England pastors, given in his most celebrated work, "Magnalia."

In "The Life of Dr. Mather," written by his son, Samuel Mather, we have given us a summary of the former's prophetical views.† Of the new earth, he thus believed:

"The conflagration described by the oracles of God in strong terms, and which we are warned of by the

* Magnalia, vol. i., book iii., chap. 4.   † Life, etc., 1729, pp. 140-146.

mouth of all the prophets, this conflagration will be at the second coming of the Lord. To make the Petrine conflagration signify no more than the laying of Jerusalem and her daughter in ashes, and to make the new heavens and the new earth signify no more than the church state of the gospel,—these are shameful hallucinations. And as for the new earth, before the arrival of which no man can reasonably expect happy times for the church of God upon earth, it is the greatest absurdity to say that it will take place before the Petrine conflagration; and there is no prospect of arguing to any purpose, with such as can talk so very ridiculously." *

Concerning the Jews, Mather believed as follows:

"Such a conversion of the Israelitish nation, with a return to their ancient seats in Palestine, as many excellent persons in later years (and among the rest himself) have been persuaded of, he now thought inconsistent with the coming of the Lord and the burning of the world at the fall of Antichrist, before which fall nobody imagines that conversion. And indeed, how is it consistent with the deep sleep in which the *diluvium ignis* (fiery deluge) must, as that of water did, surprise the world? The holy people of the prophecies are found among the Gentiles, the surrogate Israel. The New Testament seems to have done with a carnal Israel; the eleventh chapter to the Romans is greatly misunderstood, where we find all Israel saved by a *filling up of the Gentiles*, which we mistranslate 'the fullness of the Gentiles.' The prophecies of the Old Testament, that seem to have an aspect on such a nation, are either already accomplished unto that nation in the return from the Chaldæan captivity; or they belong to that holy people whom a succession to

---

* Life of Mather, p. 141.

the piety of the patriarchs will render what our Bible has taught us to call them, the Israel of God. Gal. 6:16. Of what advantage to the kingdom of God can the conversion of the Jewish nation be, any more than the conversion of any other nation, except, we should suppose, to remain upon the Jewish nation after their conversion, something to distinguish them from the rest of the Christian believers? Now to suppose this, would it not be to rebuild a partition wall that our Saviour has demolished and abolished, which a Christian, one would think, would no sooner go to do, than to rebuild the fallen walls of Jericho." *

In another work, Mather describes the last days thus: "For when our Lord shall come, he will find the world almost void of true and lively faith (especially of faith in his coming); and when he shall descend with his heavenly banners and angels, what else will he find, almost, but the whole church, as it were, a dead carcass, miserably putrified with the spirit and manners and endearments of this world?" "They indulge themselves in a vain dream, not to say insane, who think, pray, and hope, contrary to the whole sacred Scripture and sound reason, that the promised happiness of the church on earth will be before the Lord Jesus shall appear in his kingdom." †

The writer has in his possession a manuscript copy of a strong pre-millennial argument from Mather, in the form of a "Letter," written to Rev. Enoch Noyes, the original being found in the library of the Antiquarian society at Worcester, Mass. There, also, is deposited what was probably intended to be his best prophetical work, now existing in manuscript, and never given to the world. The title is, "Triparadisus: the

---

* Life of Mather, p. 144. † From "Student and Preacher."

paradise of the old world; the paradise of departed spirits; the paradise of the new earth under the new heavens," etc., 4to., pp. 353. It is very learned, and in it he desired "to give the world," says Samuel Mather, "a more ample account of his persuasion." *

Dr. Mather closely watched the signs of the times, and thought the end was near. He used to say, that "for aught any man alive can say, the midnight cry may be heard before to-morrow morning." †

DUDLEY, A. D. 1703.

Joseph Dudley was first the president of Massachusetts and New Hampshire, then councilor and chief justice of New York, afterward lieutenant governor of the Isle of Wight. He was then appointed by Queen Anne to the governorship of Massachusetts, from 1702 till 1715. He was a Christian scholar and philosopher. While pursuing his official career, he began an investigation of the chiliastic doctrine, and of the end of the age. It may be supposed that Ezekiel Cheever led him into these investigations. Dr. Cotton Mather dedicated the letter written in 1703 to Nicholas Noyes, to his friend Governor Dudley, saying: "May it please your Excellency: It gave me an uncommon satisfaction, when I was informed that a person of so much erudition and sagacity, and such superior sentiments as your Excellency, has, upon the encouragement of one of the greatest literators of the age, applied his mind unto the study of those divine prophecies, which concern the kingdom of God that is to arrive, when his will is to be done on earth as it is in heaven. . . . . I have had the honor of engaging two governors, that

---

* See Life of Cotton Mather, pp. 72, 146.
† Life of Cotton Mather, p. 145.

were men of learning, to subscribe unto my sentiments." *

It was about this time that, as we have seen, the students of the Bible in New England were returning to the old paths. We have also President Increase Mather, in 1710, writing that the thousand years' reign "has ever been received as a truth in the churches of New England; nor are these churches the only ones that have thus believed." † It is evident that Gov. Dudley was a Millenarian; but who the other two governors were, who were won over to Dr. Mather's opinion, we are not informed.

Abridging much of the accumulated testimony of other witnesses to the truth in this century, we can do little more, in some instances, than name the authors whose works have been brought to our notice, and who were either fully committed to the pre-millennial faith, or held kindred doctrines touching the near advent, and restitution of all things.

BOWERS, A. D. 1709.

Bath Bowers, minister at Philadelphia, Penn., in a published sermon, 1709, proclaimed the day of judgment near at hand, and warned evil men of wrath soon to come.

FLINT, A. D. 1714.

Henry Flint, a tutor and fellow of Harvard College, in "Two Discourses on the Last Judgment," 1714, with a preface by Increase Mather, asserted an impending judgment-day "in the end of the world, when the prophecies are all fulfilled, and the wickedness of men

---

* Essay on the happy state; in Massachusetts Historical Society library, Worcester.

† Discourse Concerning Faith, etc., 1710, p. 1.

is come to the height." * Nothing hindered its coming, but the downfall of Antichrist and the calling in of Israel.

WEBB, A. D. 1714.

John Webb, pastor at Boston, 1714-1750, in "Discourses on Death, Judgment, and Heaven," 1726, applies Matt. 24:29, 30, to the end of this age; teaches a prior resurrection of the dead in Christ, and the literality of the new heavens and earth, wherein the just shall dwell. 2 Pet. 3:13.

BURNET, A. D. 1724.

William Burnet, eldest son of Bishop Burnet, was governor of New York and New Jersey, from 1720 to 1728, when he was chosen governor of Massachusetts and New Hampshire, but died, not long after, at Boston. He was a scholar, astronomer, and possessed superior talents. In 1724, only five years before his death, and while engaged in official duty at Albany, he published "An Essay on Scripture Prophecy." The work proves it possible even for Christian laymen in high positions, to pay deep attention to the sacred prophecies, as did Sir Isaac Newton. Burnet never questions the pre-millennial coming and personal reign. Proposing a scheme of the grand numbers of Daniel and John, his latest date for the final termination of all was 1790, when he supposed the Lord would come, and the Millennium begin; at its commencement, the glorious coming, and literal resurrrection of the just, would occur. He endorsed the year-day theory, and declared that the Scriptures "employ the strongest terms to recommend the study of prophecies." "Follow John's advice," he says, "in Rev. 1:3." †

---

* The Doctrine of, etc., p. 2. † An Essay on Scripture Prophecy, p. 9.

Governor Burnet affords another instance of the uselessness of time-setting, a mistake often allied to the grace of loving Christ's appearing. But laymen in high official positions may learn something from his sincere devotion to the sacred prophecies, and thus be led to take some hours from their official labors, and spend them in searching into the facts relating to that glorious period that shall give back to the earth again her Hope and Lord.

GOOKIN, A. D. 1727.

Nathaniel Gookin, minister at Hampton, N. H., in a sermon published 1727, declared the day of Christ to be at hand, referring to the great earthquake of that year as a sign. All the New England pastors so regarded it: the Lord was at hand. Very few had, at that date, dreamed of an intervening temporal millennium.

CHAUNCY, A. D. 1730.

Charles Chauncy, D. D., ministerial colleague of Thomas Foxcroft, at Boston, 1727, and for sixty years pastor of one parish; bold, learned, and author of fifty or sixty small works, was, in his private opinions, a Restorationist. In his work entitled, "Mystery Hid from Ages," etc., 1784, which, like Burnet's volume, appeared anonymously, he discourses, in the appendix, on the doctrine of the personal reign of Christ, taking strong ground in favor of a real first resurrection, and visible and eternal kingdom of our Lord, and the redeemed on earth made new. On Rev. 20, he writes: "The apostle first declares in general, that he saw thrones, and that he saw those who sat upon them, with judicial power given to them, without saying particularly who they were. He then goes on to a more particular representation of the matter. 'I saw,' he says, 'the martyrs for the sake of Christ; and I saw those who had not worshiped the beast.' These seem to me plainly distinguished from each other. The apostle saw not only the martyrs, but these also. But who are these who had not worshiped the beast? Plainly, all those whose names were written in the book of life (chapter 13:8). And these take in the whole number of those who shall *not* be cast into the lake of fire (chapter 20:15); that is, the saints universally. Besides, one of the characteristics of those whom the Apostle John saw living and reigning with Christ is, that the second death shall have no power over them (verse 6), which is a privilege common to the saints, and not peculiar to the martyrs. Further, it is said of the persons who shall live in this millennial state, that they shall be priests of God and of Christ, and shall reign with him (verse 6), which is another privilege not confined to martyrs, but extended to all the saints. Hence that song, Rev. 1:5, 6, and 5:9, 10."

Quoting Matt. 24:37-39, Luke 18:8, and 2 Thess. 1: 7-9, Dr. Chauncy adds: "It is evident from these texts, that the world will be horribly wicked at the coming of Christ, and that he will come to destroy it for its wickedness. How, then, can this Millennium immediately precede this coming of Christ, and for this end? Can it reasonably be supposed that the purest and best state of the world, and for a thousand years' continuance, should be that state of the world which should immediately precede the coming of Christ to destroy it for its abounding wickedness? To me there are insuperable objections against the figurative interpretation of this life and reign with Christ." *

---

* The Mystery, etc., London, 1784, pp. 381-384.

In a "Sermon on the Earthquake," preached at Boston, Jan. 22, 1756, from the Apocalyptic announcement, "Behold, I make all things new" (chapter 21:5), he asserts the earth's destiny to be (1) dissolution, (2) reconstruction and regeneration; and, with all his cotemporary clergymen who preached similar sermons on that memorable occasion, Dr. Chauncy regarded these convulsions of nature as tokens of the approach of that epoch when the earth would be dissolved by fire, and there should come forth out of its ashes a new heaven and a new earth, wherein dwelleth righteousness.

BYLES, A. D. 1744.

Mather Byles, D. D., who was graduated at Harvard in 1725, ordained first pastor of Hollis Street Church, Boston, in 1733, was eminent as a preacher, and also known as a writer.

In a sermon to the Artillery Company, in 1740, he said: "The day hastens when the great men, and the chief captains, and the mighty men, shall fly to hide in the dens and rocks of the mountains. Then rejoice, ye righteous, lift up your heads with joy, for your redemption draweth nigh."

In a sermon upon Phil. 3:21, are these words: "Now, perhaps, these bodies are in pain; but quickly they shall know no more pain. Now they are weary with labor; quickly they shall rest from their labor, and rise to constant exercise without weariness. Now they weep and sigh in many sorrows; quickly all tears shall be wiped from our eyes, and sorrow and sighing shall flee away." Again, on Ps. 73:26, he says: "What though the flesh be all failed, and the bones all wasted, and there be not so much as the sign of the heart remaining, yet for all that shall the text prove divinely true, and God be the strength of our heart, and our portion forever. .... *When he shall appear, we shall appear with him in glory."* These brief extracts make very evident the faith and hope of this early Boston pastor.

In 1760, an edition of Tate and Brady's Psalms was printed, which he edited, and to which he contributed a hymn, from which we take the following verses:

> When wild confusion wrecks the air,
>   And tempests rend the skies,
> Whilst blended ruin, clouds, and fire,
>   In harsh disorder rise,
>
> Safe in my Saviour's love I'll stand,
>   And strike a tuneful song;
> My harp all trembling in my hand,
>   And all inspired my tongue.
>
> I'll shout aloud: "Ye thunders, roll,
>   And shake the sullen sky!
> Your sounding voice, from pole to pole,
>   In angry murmurs try.
>
> "Thou sun, retire; refuse thy light,
>   And let thy beams decay;
> Ye lightnings, flash along the night,
>   And dart a dreadful day.
>
> "Let the earth totter on her base,
>   And clouds the heavens deform;
> Blow, all ye winds, from every place,
>   And rush the final storm.
>
> "O Jesus, haste the day when thou
>   Shalt this old earth consume;
> Build the new heavens and all below;
>   Bid a new Eden bloom.
>
> "Come quickly, blessed Lord, appear!
>   Bid thy swift chariot fly;
> Let angels tell thy coming near,
>   And snatch me to the sky.

"Around thy wheels, in the glad throng,
  I'd bear a joyous part;
All hallelujah on my tongue,
  All rapture in my heart."

The following extract from a poem entitled, "The Conflagration," relates to the effect on the earth of the flames of the last day, and is finely conceived:

"Yet shall ye flames the wasting globe refine,
And bid the skies with purer splendor shine;
The earth, which the prolific fires consume,
To beauty burns, and withers into bloom;
Improving in the fertile flame it lies,
Fades into form, and into vigor dies;
Fresh-dawning glories blush amidst the blaze,
And nature all renews her flowery face."

PRINCE, A. D. 1750.

Thomas Prince was pastor at the Old South, Boston, from 1718 to 1758, and of him Chauncy said, "He was second in learning to none but Cotton Mather in New England." Prince entered fully into Mather's millenarian views, and said of him: "And to say no more—I cannot think to wish a greater blessing in the present state of the prophetic system, than that the God of the spirits of all flesh, would, in my own dear country and every other, raise up numbers of such ministers as this, and prosper this superior example for the forming and animating them, that they might burn and shine as he, and prepare the world for the most illustrious appearance of the Great God, our Saviour Jesus Christ." * To this we add our hearty Amen.

On Matt. 24:14, he observes: "And when this whole globe shall be thus successively enlightened, then comes on the end of the present earthly scene; but it is then surprisingly to change, and it is highly likely, by the

---

* Preface to Life of Cotton Mather, p. 6.

conflagration, open into a glorious state of universal and abundant light and grace, and peace and blessedness; when the whole earth together shall be filled with saints, without a devil to tempt them, or any evil to annoy them; and Christ shall gloriously, by his Holy Spirit, angels, and raised saints, reign among them for a thousand years." *

Of the earth he writes: "He will preserve it as an everlasting theatre, though by the conflagration he will change the form, repair, refine, and leave it fit for another sort or series of inhabitants, and another scene of wondrous dispensations, over which, as the Son of God, he will reign, and so his government increase, even in this lower world, forever." †

"Prince made the prophecies a favorite study through life," says Spalding, "and was far from adopting the modern plan of the Millennium. Concerning Gog and Magog he made the following observation: 'For nearly forty years I have been more and more inclined to think that the Gog and Magog in Rev. 20, will be the wicked, raised at the end of the thousand years, whose rancored and malicious spirits, with all the devils then brought out of the dark abyss together, possessing, infatuating, and inflaming them, will be permitted to rage against the saints for a very little season, till the general judgment comes on and quells them." ‡ In this conclusion, Prince agrees with Dr. Gill, and the view explains an important point in pre-millennial doctrine. § Prince died in 1758.

SIEGVOLCK, A. D. 1753.

Paul Siegvolck, in a work issued at Germantown, Penn., 1753, supported the doctrine of the restitution as

* Six Sermons, 1785, p. 28. † Six Sermons, pp. 28, 29.
‡ Spalding's Lectures, 1796, p. 260. § See page 242, this volume.

subsequently held by Chauncy and Winchester, and fully committed himself to the old faith of the pre-millennial and glorious coming of Christ. In all save the notion that all souls will be restored, his opinions were quite sound.

IMBRIE, A. D. 1756.

David Imbrie, minister of Christ at St. Mungo, was the author of a letter on the coming of Christ, that was printed at Boston, 1756, in which the millennial opinions of Mede, Fleming, and Sir Isaac Newton, are endorsed. The end, he thought, would come in 1794.

TORREY, A. D. 1757.

William Torrey, an "aged Christian" in the state of Massachusetts, in a little work published in 1757, and fully endorsed by Rev. Thomas Prince, who wrote the preface, in a clear, vigorous, scriptural manner, presented the primitive doctrines of the Millennium and kingdom, teaching that the reign of our Redeemer will be in *person* during all the millennial season.

EDWARDS, A. D. 1761.

Morgan Edwards was minister at Philadelphia, in 1761, and at Newark, N. J., 1772. In one of Elhanan Winchester's volumes is found a valuable essay on the pre-millennial advent and personal reign of our Lord over the renewed earth, the production of Edward's pen.*

MARSH, A. D. 1762.

Edmund Marsh wrote anonymously a work on prophecy, which was published at Boston, 1762. Selecting as a leading text, the prophecy of the new earth, in Isa.

---

* Winchester's Lectures on Prophecy, Walpole, N. H., 1800, vol. ii.

65:17, 18, he maintained the doctrine that Christ will yet reign as a personal and visible king on the holy hill of Zion, in the earth made new, forever and ever.

MURRAY, A. D. 1768.

John Murray, minister at Boston in 1768, preached, from 2 Thess. 1:7-10, an eloquent and stirring discourse on "The Last Solemn Scene" of the judgment day. For its time, the discourse is unusually graphic and arousing. The scene was supposed to be not far away. He cries: "Oh, when shall the trumpet break its tedious silence, that I may fly and meet him in the air?"

GALE, A. D. 1780.

Dr. B. Gale was a resident of Killingworth, Conn., in the eighteenth century. On his monument at Killingworth is the following inscription:

"In memory of Dr. Benjamin Gale, who, after a life of usefulness in his profession, and a laborious study of the prophecies, fell asleep May 6th, A. D. 1790, Æ. 75, fully expecting to rise again under the Messiah, and to reign with him on earth. . . . I know that my Redeemer liveth, and that he shall stand at the latter day upon the earth, and mine eyes shall behold him."

John W. Barber, who published this epitaph in his Historical Collections of Connecticut, thus comments upon it: "It appears," he says, "by this inscription, that Dr. Gale was a believer in the ancient doctrine of Millenarians, a name given to those who believe that the second coming of Christ will precede the Millennium, and that there will be a literal resurrection of the saints, who will reign with Christ on earth a thousand years. This appears to have been the belief of pious persons at the time of the first settlement of New England. Even as late as the great earthquake, 1755, many Christians were looking for and expecting the second coming of Christ." * Joshua Spalding also testifies to the Millenarian belief of the early Christians of New England, and affirms that the Whitbyan view did not gain much ground till after the middle of the eighteenth century.

WINCHESTER, A. D. 1788.

Elhanan Winchester, an American divine, born, 1751, at first a Baptist at Newton, Mass., and finally at Philadelphia, adopted the views of the Restorationists. He was the able author of nine different works, between 1788 and 1795, in all of which he earnestly advocated the pre-millennial doctrine, laying much stress upon the restitution of all things to a lasting Edenic state. He is eloquent on the theme of the personal advent and endless reign of Jesus Christ, a theme that may well inspire our pens and tongues.

FISH, A. D. 1793.

Samuel Fish, minister at Windham, Conn., 1793, put forth sermons showing the certainty of Christ's personal appearance and universal reign at the head of his Zion, over all the earth; first he would reign in spirit, then a pre-millennial appearing, and a visible reign for a thousand years. His style is sober and solemn.

WATKINS, A. D. 1795.

John Watkins, layman, in an "Essay on the End of the World," published at Worcester, Mass., 1795, sustained the ancient opinion of the sex-millennial duration of the world, and gave warning of the approaching end.

* Barber's Hist. Coll., p. 531.

SPALDING, A. D. 1796.

Joshua Spalding was minister of the gospel at the Tabernacle at Salem, Mass., 1796. The Pre-Millennialism of this pious divine is well known. We make the following extracts:

"The expectation of a Millennium arises from the prophecies concerning the future kingdom of Christ—the kingdoms of this world becoming the kingdom of our Lord and of his Christ—his taking to himself his great power, and reigning before all his ancients gloriously. We are plainly told, this glorious event shall take place under the sounding of the seventh trumpet. This none disputes. All agree that the expected reign of Christ upon earth will be in the days of the voice of the seventh trumpet. The question disputed, and which we would examine, is, whether probationary time will end, and the great day of God's wrath will come at the beginning or at the ending of the seventh trumpet. It was the expectation of believers anciently, that probationary time would end, and the great day of God's wrath would come before the Millennial kingdom under the seventh trumpet: but in the last century an opinion gained currency that the Millennium would be probationary time; and therefore the coming of Christ, and overthrow of this world, of the ungodly, would not take place till some time after the Millennium. This opinion has constantly prevailed; all hands, learned and unlearned, have been employed to propogate it, and very little has been done or said to oppose it; and for about half a century it has been the most common belief, consequently people have laid aside all expectation that the day of the Lord is nigh, and old and young, ministers and people, have agreed to say, The Lord delayeth his coming. But so agrees not the voice of Revelation. The angel said at the *beginning*, not at the *close;* when the seventh angel shall *begin* to sound—then there should be time no longer—then the mystery of God should be finished—then the elders said, 'Thy wrath is come.'*

"And if our thoughts concerning the coming and kingdom of Christ be just, it is now time to watch for the midnight cry—'Behold, the Bridegroom cometh.' The sixth trumpet and also the sixth vial are now passing over us, as the events of Providence do plainly show, and are drawing towards the close; and the seventh trumpet may daily be expected to begin to sound. Who knows how soon the seventh angel, with the voice of the last trump, shall proclaim—There shall be time no longer—the mystery of God is finished? O solemn sound!"†

"That such vast multitudes are yet to be converted to Christ, as some have calculated and numbered, is what I have not been able to discover in the Scriptures. For aught I know (though to me it appears very improbable,) these calculations may be accurate, and the uncalled elect may be so many millions; still, we do not see that this proves their (the Post-millennial) scheme, for we know not why God may not call in all his elect, be they more or less, whilst the world continues in its present state, without introducing for them a state so indulgent and improper for a life of faith—a state so unlike the glorious warfare in which the worthies, through grace, have won their immortal honors and unfading crowns. Affliction worketh for us a far more exceeding and eternal weight of glory; this weight of glory they must lose without our affliction, and with it their Millennium is imaginary. Tribulation worketh patience, and patience experience. But what experience can these Millennial converts attain without tribulation? Can they know Christ in the fellowship of his sufferings? Can they be made conformable unto his death? Can they glory in his cross? Can they rejoice that they are counted worthy to suffer shame

* Lectures p. 45. † Ibid, p. 51.

for his name? Or, wherein can their lives be brought into a conformity with the lives of his people, that have followed him in his temptations, which conformity will open in their hearts such sources of sweet fellowship, to all eternity? The seed of Jacob, in all ages of the world, have been wrestlers, but these Millennial converts, at best, can be but fondlings. They are represented as a sort of Christians that I never admired; they are born without travail; their baptism is not the baptism of Christ, for it is without fire; they have not the refinement of the furnace, nor the purification of the fuller's soap; they have not the spots of God's Israel—the scars of the fight of faith; and should it be asked, 'Whence came they?' it could not be answered, 'These are they which came out of great tribulation;' therefore, they must stand without a palm or a wreath; for, no fight, no victory; no cross, no crown." *

Spalding's entire work is interesting and valuable. He notes in one place, that we read of the New Jerusalem coming down out of heaven, but nowhere do we read of its return again to heaven. We recommend his Lectures to our readers.

CUMMINGS, A. D. 1797.

Abraham Cummings, an itinerant missionary in Maine and Rhode Island, 1776–1800, in a "Dissertation on the Millennium," Boston, 1797, asserted his belief that Christ's personal advent will introduce the thousand years; and cites as authority, the first Christians, Mede, Newton, the Mathers, and Spalding.

We notice here several anonymous authors who put forth works in this century, in maintenance of our views. In 1794, a volume of 503 pages appeared at

---

* Lectures, p. 214.

New York, in which the writer essays to arrange the grand numbers in a common termination, namely, 1890, when the resurrection of the just shall occur, followed by the restitution of all things, and the eternal kingdom and reign of the Messiah. In 1798, treatises entitled, "Notes on Various Scriptures," were issued at Boston, uttering warnings of the sudden coming of Christ to judge the world of mankind, and the consummation of the age. We notice, also,

FARNHAM, A. D. 1800.

Benjamin Farnham, whose interesting little book entitled, "Dissertations on Prophecy," was published at East Windsor, Conn., 1800, advocated the literal resurrection of the martyrs and saints at our Lord's second personal appearing, to establish his millennial kingdom and renovate the whole face of the world. These positions are admirably asserted and sustained in Farnham's "Dissertations."

DOW, A. D. 1800.

Lorenzo Dow, the celebrated itinerant, born in Connecticut, 1777, and going everywhere, his name is well known to all of our readers. Mr. Dow, though eccentric, was by no means devoid of piety and talent, and was a shrewd observer of the signs of the times, and, as his works show, was quite a Bible student. He evidently interpreted the first resurrection in a literal sense, and also taught the renovation of the earth—its re-creation. On the decay of the Turkish empire, an obvious and interesting prophetical event, observed and noted by all modern writers as a remarkable sign of the times, Dow thus speaks: "The Euphrates, or Turkish empire, is drying up very fast within a few years. The

Sultans carried a half moon in their colors, to denote a government over one half of the world. The Russians have taken several provinces on the Euphrates; two provinces on the west side of the Black Sea have gone off to govern themselves; Greece, with a large territory, is gone off also. Algiers, on the coast of Barbary, is in the power of France. The Pacha of Egypt has taken Egypt, Canaan, and the plains of Babylon, etc.; hence, the Sultan has but his capital, with a small territory round, like a garden spot, left; hence, we see the waters of the Euphrates (by the vial of the sixth angel) so far dried up, that we may soon hope the three unclean spirits to appear, consolidating the whole ancient Scripture world under three heads—for Armageddon!" *

Of the "end of the world" and its precedents, he says: "How soon some of these times may be at hand, who knows? Perhaps nigher than some think. And those who are not on the watch-tower will be taken unawares, as by a thief in the night. Happy for those who shall be found watching!" † Again, on Dan. 2, "The ten toes of Nebuchadnezzar's image only remain; these times are eventful, and the signs are portentous. Let all the Israel of God be in a state of readiness for the coming of the Lord!" ‡ Let us heed his warning voice.

Many pre-millennial volumes from the pens of European authors, found publishers in America, and had a wide circulation. Dr. John Gill's "Three Sermons on the Present and Future State of the Church" were published in Boston, 1756, and also at Northampton, Mass., 1797. The work of James Purves, minister at Edinburgh, on the seals and trumpets, appeared at New York, 1788, and another volume on the Apocalypse at the same place, in 1789. Bishop Thomas Newton's

---

* Dow's Journal, p. 355.   † Ibid, pp. 343, 345.   ‡ Appendix, 2.

well-known volumes on Prophecy were issued at New York in 1787, and another edition at Northampton, 1796. The works of Joseph Priestly, LL. D., of England, were reprinted at Philadelphia in 1794. The celebrated volume of Robert Fleming, Jr., of London, was also published at Boston in 1794. The same year, the works of James Bicheno, a French minister who wrote on the signs of the times, were printed at Providence, R. I., and were again issued at West Springfield, Mass., in 1796. The works of these well-known men were spread everywhere, and being of a millenarian character, assisted to mould and form the opinions of Christians on questions of eschatology and future destiny. The old faith never died out in America.

CHAPTER XI.

PROPHETIC CONFERENCES.

THE FIRST CONFERENCE IN ENGLAND, 1826.

"We have also a more sure word of prophecy; whereunto ye do well that ye take heed, as unto a light that shineth in a dark place, until the day dawn, and the day-star arise in your hearts."—2 Peter 1:19.

THE assembling together of Christian ministers and laymen in large numbers, without regard to denomination, for the purpose of studying the sacred Scriptures, and conferring with one another concerning the prophetic word, the signs of the times, the nature of the solemn future, and the pre-millennial and near advent of our blessed Lord, was perhaps never witnessed until the present century. In 1826, the first conference of this kind was called, and held in the county of Surrey, England, at the residence of Henry Drummond, Esq., then the high sheriff of the county, subsequently a member of the British Parliament. Ministers of all denominations were invited, and twenty persons, men of every rank and church and orthodox communion in the realm, met in session for eight days. Rev. Hugh McNeile, rector of the parish, afterwards a widely known preacher, sometimes called "the star of London," presided. Joseph Wolff, the well-known converted Jew, and missionary in eastern lands, with Edward Irving, minister of the Caledonian chapel, London, were among the notable persons present.

The times of the Gentiles, the destiny of the Israelites, the doctrine of the future and last advent, and the duties of the ministry and church as related thereto, were the themes discussed. There was a great agreement, sweet charity, and a strong conviction that the end of the gospel dispensation and return of the Bridegroom "was," writes Irving, "hard at hand, yea, even at the very door." * No full report of this remarkable gathering was ever made at the time; the believers disclaimed putting the stamp of authority upon their conclusions. But with new personal convictions, these twenty men rose from their prayerful studies, to go forth and speak and work as never before; while the conference was in subsequent years repeated in Albury hall.

At this time, the comprehension of the advent of Christ had died out of many hearts, and its imminence was scarcely dreamed of. Few were watching for the Coming One; most of the pulpits were silent on the theme, and there was but little pre-millennial literature in circulation. But henceforth the Lord's advent was to take a front place on human lips, and in thoughtful hearts; a great cry went forth that was never to cease. Pulpits rang with the alarm, pens were busy, the awakening was wide and great. In 1829, 1830, 1831, 1833, and 1834, no less than six prophetical journals were established at London, Dublin, and Edinburgh, conducted by able pens and cultured minds. Between the years 1828 and 1834, some forty or fifty different volumes on prophecy were issued in Great Britain. Besides these, over thirty well-known and godly men put forth full sixty works in defense of the pre-millennial advent.† The agitation of the grand question was

---

* See Irving's account in Preliminary Discourse to Ben Ezra, vol. ii. p. 188.

† Vide Brook's Dictionary of Writers on Prophecy.

intense. Irving wrote a dozen books on prophecy, and discoursed with rare eloquence to audiences estimated at 6,000 and even 12,000 persons, in the open air, in the towns of England and Scotland. Wolff fearlessly uttered the advent cry through the wide East, and McNeile thundered the message from his pulpit in great London. Within fifteen years after the first conference at Albury, three hundred ministers of the Church of England alone were proclaiming the speedy end,* and the historian Macaulay asserted that the believers in the ancient faith, looking for the immediate appearing and kingdom, equaled in number the entire population of the Jews in Great Britain.

In mentioning the Mildmay Advent Conference of 1878, the *Messenger and Missionary Record* of the Presbyterian Church of England thus writes of what the London *Christian* calls "the remarkable and wide-spread change of Christian opinion and belief, which has taken place with regard to the close of this dispensation, during the past thirty years, and the progress of what we believe to be the truth as to our Lord's return:" †

"Since the day of these Albury conferences, premillenarian views have spread very much. They are now held by a large number in the Church of England, including most of the Evangelical party, and by many in all churches. Even those who do not accept the view of the personal reign, have had their ideas much modified and changed by the discussions that have arisen. There are, we believe, very few now who expect the world to be gradually converted, and the millennial kingdom to be peacefully ushered in. It has

* Sermon by Rev. Mourant Brock, of England.
† *The Christian*, April 24, 1879.

been shown, probably beyond question, that there will be a great final struggle between light and darkness, a grand convulsion, as it were, of the spiritual elements; in the midst of which, by some sudden manifestation of Divine power, through the presence of the Lord Jesus, the hostile forces will be smitten down, and the kingdom at once established. The Pre-millenarians have, we believe, led all earnest inquirers into prophecy as far as this,—even of those who do not hold the personal reign and the literal first resurrection. They have also drawn more attention to the serious study of prophecy, which, as may be seen from the history of the Jews, is one of the most important of all studies. Much of semi-rationalism and coldness of the professed church, arises from the neglect of this study,—fitted always to strengthen faith."

THE FIRST CONFERENCE IN AMERICA.

The first prophetic conference ever held in America, convened at Chardon street Chapel, Boston, Oct. 14, 1840, and continued two days. The sessions were crowded each day, and there were present some twenty or thirty interested ministers, with many able laymen, representing most of the orthodox denominations. A report of this conference was made, which, together with the addresses delivered, was published in an octavo volume of one hundred and seventy-five pages.* So great was the interest in the question, that in a short time, 10,000 copies of this work were issued and scattered. It contains the Call of the pastor, Rev. J. V. Himes; an Address by the chairman, Henry Dana Ward; Extracts from church creeds, and remarks by Rev. Henry Jones; a Circular to the believers; a Disser-

---

* The first Report of the General Conference of Christians Expecting the Advent of the Lord Jesus Christ. Boston, 1842.

tation on the Second Advent, by Rev. Josiah Litch; a Dissertation on the Chronology of Prophecy, by the same; a Dissertation on the Restoration of Israel, by Rev. Henry Jones; a Dissertation on Prophetic Chronology, also a Dissertation on the Judgment, prepared by Rev. William Miller (who was not present); and a very able discourse on the "History and Doctrine of the Millennium," by the chairman, H. D. Ward, then a Congregational layman, but later a well-known writer and clergyman of the Protestant Episcopal Church.

In a "Circular Address," signed by the president, Mr. Ward, and the secretaries, Rev. Henry Jones and Rev. P. R. Russell, the convention is styled, "The First General Conference on the Second Coming of our Lord Jesus Christ;" and among other excellent things, it is said:

"Our object in assembling at this time, our object in addressing you, and our object in other efforts, separate and combined, on the subject of the kingdom of heaven at hand, is to revive and restore this ancient faith, to renew the ancient landmarks, to stand in the ways and see and ask for the old paths, where is the good way in which our fathers walked. Jer. 6:16. We have no purpose to distract the churches with any new inventions, or to get to ourselves a name by starting another sect among the followers of the Lamb. We neither condemn nor rudely assail others of a faith different from our own, nor dictate in matters of conscience for our brethren, nor seek to demolish their organizations, nor build new ones of our own; but simply to express our convictions, like Christians, with the reasons for entertaining them, which have persuaded us to understand the word and promises, the prophecies and the gospel of our Lord, as the first Christians, the primitive ages of the Church, and the

FIRST CONFERENCE IN AMERICA. 351

profoundly learned and intelligent reformers have unanimously done."

Again they say: "Although in some of the less important views of this momentous subject we are not ourselves agreed, particularly in fixing the year of Christ's second advent, yet we are unanimously agreed and established in this all-absorbing point, — that the coming of the Lord to judge the world is now specially *nigh at hand*. We are also agreed and firmly persuaded that the popular theory of a thousand years or more of the spiritual and invisible reign of Christ in this present evil world, is altogether unscriptural. We are also agreed, that at the very commencement of the Millennium, the Lord will come in the glory of his Father, and all the saints with him. Again, we are agreed and harmonize with the published creed of the Episcopal, Dutch Reformed, Presbyterian, and Methodist Churches, together with the Cambridge Platform of the Congregational Church, and the Lutheran and Roman Catholic Churches, in maintaining that Christ's second and only coming now will be to judge the world at the last day." *

The influence of this united action was marked and wide; hundreds of ministers were brought to the faith of the pre-millennial and near coming, several weekly journals were established in different cities, advocating the doctrine, and in a few years there were not less than 1,500 preachers and lecturers in the United States and Canada, who were giving publicity to the theme.

The believers, as in England, were divided; some, under William Miller and others, fixing the date of the advent "about the year 1843-4;" others, represented by Henry Dana Ward, Rev. G. F. Cox, etc., saying to Mr.

---

* Proceedings, etc., pp. 13-18.

Miller, "We think you are wrong in urging the matter of the date." All dates failed, as might have been expected. "Ye know not when the time is." Mark 13: 33. But the awakened interest in prophecy, the general influence of the movement, the aroused love of our Lord's coming, did not die. In thousands of hearts, both among the various branches of the Adventists, as well as in all the churches, the hope of the speedy appearing of the Saviour still holds sway. Such are found in all denominations, and in every part of the land.

OTHER ENGLISH PROPHETICAL CONFERENCES.

A general conference of believers in the near advent was held May 5-10, 1873, in St. George's hall, London. There were no denominational lines recognized; Christians came together, drawn by a common faith, and the most distinguished clergymen, lords, noblemen, and others freely addressed full audiences on the great theme. The Church of England was largely represented by many of her most able and pious divines. The Right Honorable Earl of Shaftesbury, the foremost man of the age in philanthropic labors, occupied the chair, and on one occasion spoke as follows:

"When the thought has arisen, 'At what time will He come?' the ready answer has been, 'As a thief in the night;' and when the question has been put, 'In what manner will He come?' the reply has presented itself in the words of the angels, 'This same Jesus . . . shall so come in like manner as ye have seen him go into heaven.' With satisfaction I may say that this subject has been upon my heart for years and years; it has been much upon my inmost soul, I will not say every day, but often every hour of the day; and I may say, that in reference to the state of the times and the signs which are around us, I cannot see any remedy or solution but that suggested by the assured hope of the second coming of Christ. . . It is impossible to observe the condition of things and the aspect of society, without arriving at the conclusion that an event no less than that of the second advent itself must come to pass, before the world can be brought to a condition of piety, and purity, and peace.

"I do hope that these meetings may be the beginning of a constant, persistent course of practical preaching and faithful testimony and warning upon the subject, for hitherto we have had far too little said about it in the pulpits of our land. It is not enough to have occasional meetings and sermons in relation to this grand theme, and to read an odd book or pamphlet or tract; but it must be constantly and regularly preached by the clergy from every pulpit, and proclaimed everywhere, even at the corners of the streets. And I believe, if this great matter were so treated, you might still produce a very practical result upon all classes, and especially upon the English people, upon the refined and educated classes, as well as upon the masses of our working population. I believe there would be no one subject they would receive with greater delight — no one doctrine which would produce a greater effect upon their lives and their general conduct — than the bringing before them in their miseries, sorrows, and sufferings, the grand consolations of the second advent.

"And I know of no ground upon which we can more readily overcome our religious differences — Church and Non-conformist — than this, — to go forth and preach, day by day and night by night, the great and glorious truth of the approaching advent of our blessed Lord."

A second conference of the same character was

held at Mildmay Park, London, June 25–27, 1873, when more than a thousand persons were present. Admiral Fishbourne was in the chair, and the general sentiment of all was, that the end of this dispensation is close at hand, and our Master and King soon to come again. Other similar conferences were subsequently convened.

One of the most notable of these was held at Mildmay Park, February 26–28, 1878. The call was issued to all Christian people, in December, 1877, and signed by W. R. Freemantle, Horatius Bonar, S. A. Blackwood, J. E. Mathieson, C. Skrine, E. Auriol, E. Hoare, C. J. Goodhart, D. B. Hankin, and J. Denham Smith. The object, as stated in the circular, was "for united prayer, and for bearing testimony to the second coming of our blessed Lord as the proper hope of the Church." They said they expected a difference in details, but believed it was possible to meet and discuss the glorious theme in all brotherly love. They did so meet, and the report of the meeting was published. It contains addresses on the second coming of the Lord, by the Rev. Prebendary Auriol, Rev. Horatius Bonar, D. D., Rev. C. Skrine, Mr. S. A. Blackwood, Rev. Marcus Rainsford, Rev. H. E. Brooke, Rev. A. R. Fausset, Dr. W. P. Mackay, the Earl of Shaftesbury, Rev. Canon Hoare, Rev. C. J. Goodhart, Rev. John Wilkinson, Very Rev. Dean Freemantle, Mr. J. Denham Smith, Rev. John Richardson, Mr. A. A. Rees, Rev. J. Hudson Taylor, Rev. H. W. Webb-Peploe, Mr. T. Shouldham Henry, and Mr. H. F. Bowker.

The subjects discussed during this conference were: the second coming of Christ, personal and pre-millennial; the signs of His coming; the state of the world at the time of the second coming of Christ; the restoration and conversion of Israel; the first resurrection; the attitude of the church in expectation of His coming; with Bible readings on the second advent.*

The occasion was one of great interest, and the assembled multitudes testified by their presence, to the hold the precious doctrine had on the English heart. The speeches were plain and loving; differences were held in a Christian spirit; all agreed to the momentous importance of the doctrine; all appeared to see evidence that the advent of Christ was nigh. The noble Earl of Shaftesbury said there were many signs of its approach, and urged the clergy to go out into the streets everywhere, and tell the vast masses that the Redeemer was at hand, and might come at any moment; and if they were Christ's, the great day would bring them joy forever. It made no difference that it was unpopular — they should GO!

THE NEW YORK PROPHETIC CONFERENCE.

America witnessed a gathering of this kind, of marked importance, in November, 1878. At the "Clifton Springs Believers' Meetings for Bible Study," held June, 1878, several ministers of Jesus were moved to call a conference of Christians of all denominations, "similar," they said, "to the London Conference of February last;" to meet, and listen to carefully prepared addresses, and consider the subject of the pre-millennial advent of the Lord Jesus Christ. Rev. A. J. Gordon, of Boston; Rev. S. H. Tyng, Jr., of New York; Rev. Rufus Clark, of Albany; Prof. W. G. Morehead, of Xenia, O.; Rev. H. M. Parsons, of Buffalo; Bishop Nicholson, of the Reformed Episcopal Church, Philadelphia; and Rev. J. H. Brookes, of St. Louis, were appointed a committee, to arrange for topics, speakers, time, and place. A

---

* Our God Shall Come, 210 pp., London, 1878.

preliminary circular was sent out on June 17; a multitude of responses were returned, approving the proposed meeting; and the interest appeared to be very deep and extensive.

The committee said: "When, from any cause, some vital doctrine of God's Word has fallen into neglect, or suffered contradiction and reproach, it becomes the serious duty of those who hold it, not only strongly and constantly to reaffirm it, but to seek, by all means in their power, to bring back the Lord's people to its apprehension and acceptance. The precious doctrine of Christ's second personal appearing, has, we are constrained to believe, long lain under such neglect and misapprehension. In the word of God, we find it holding a most conspicuous place. It is there strongly and constantly emphasized as a personal and imminent event, the great object of the church's hope, the powerful motive to holy living and watchful service, the inspiring ground of confidence amid the sorrows and sins of the present evil world, and the event that is to end the reign of death, cast down Satan from his throne, and establish the kingdom of God on earth. So vital, indeed, is this truth represented to be, that the denial of it is pointed out as one of the most conspicuous signs of the apostasy of the last days."

Then, after alluding to the sad decline in our latter times from the clear, vivid, ardent faith of the early church in regard to this doctrine, the unwarranted substitution of death for the advent, the lack of love, in too many quarters, for the Lord's return, — but amid it all, of late, a powerful and wide-spread revival of this ancient faith in the coming of the Bridegroom, they add:

"In view of these facts, it has seemed desirable that those who hold to the personal, pre-millennial advent of Jesus Christ, and who are looking for that blessed hope, should meet together in conference, as our honored brethren in England have recently done, to set forth in clear terms the grounds of their hope, to give mutual encouragement in the maintenance of what they believe to be a most vital truth for the present times, and in response to our Lord's, "Behold, I come quickly,' to voice the answer by their prayers and hymns and testimony, 'Even so, come, Lord Jesus.' "

In reply to the invitation, no less than one hundred and twenty-two responses were sent in from bishops, doctors of divinity, theological professors, pastors of churches, editors of religious journals, and prominent clergymen, who endorsed the call, and expressed sympathy for the movement. When this conference convened, in the Church of the Holy Trinity, at New York city, Oct. 30, 31, and Nov. 1, 1878, the spacious edifice was, notwithstanding unfavorable weather, filled, and sometimes crowded, with audiences averaging from one to two thousand interested hearers. Dr. W. P. Mackay, from Hull, England, spoke of its unsectarian character, and said, referring to those who endorsed the call for the conference, that "one Lutheran, one Dutch Reformed, one Reformed, six Methodists, ten Congregationalists, fifteen Episcopalians, ten undenominational, twenty-seven Baptists, and forty-three Presbyterians" were there representing the churches. Besides these bishops, professors, ministers, and brethren, there were often several hundred other ministers of the various churches in the land, in attendance, scattered among the audience.

This Christian body was admitted by all to have been learned, scholarly, earnest, and pious; and to have made, in their associated action, a deep impression on the entire American community. Daily reports were given by the great press. The *Daily Tribune* published, first a newspaper, then a pamphlet, edition of the proceedings and speeches of the conference, the two editions reaching the number of 50,000 copies, which were sent to all parts of the globe. Full a dozen of the religious papers, with a few of the secular ones, were decided and outspoken in their approval of the grand doctrines announced. The opening address was made by the venerable and Rev. Dr. Stephen H. Tyng, who said:

"Union with Christ, living in Christ, following Christ, looking forward to the promised coming of Christ, and to an everlasting dwelling with Christ, have made up the character, the joy, and the hope of true believers in every age. And these constitute their significant description with equal certainty in our day. The lovers of a Saviour are looking for his appearing, longing with increasing desire to see him as he is, to be with him where he is. And thus he offers for them all the earnest supplication, for all who shall believe on him through his word, that they all may be one, that they may be with him where he is, that they may behold his glory, which he had before the foundation of the world.

"Thus in the day of his ascending triumph they beheld his glory, as a cloud received him out of their sight; and while in wonder they looked steadfastly toward heaven as he ascended, angelic messengers addressed them, 'This same Jesus, which is taken up from you into heaven, shall so come in like manner as ye have seen him go into heaven.'

"In the belief of this coming, the church of Jesus has been one in every age. In the thankful anticipation of this new manifestation of this glorious Saviour, his church on earth has always been in union, believing in his future advent, looking for his appearing, striving to seek the things which are above, that when Christ, who is our life, shall appear, we may also appear with him in glory. In this sure confidence in the reality of this personal advent of the Saviour to the earth, on which he died, in the certainty of the confidence that the time of his glorious advent draweth near, we stand and wait. Many of its preliminary facts have been accomplished. Much that was necessarily antecedent in the history and condition of man has already passed, and every passing year brings this great fact in this history of earth still nearer, and diminishes the number of earthly events which are to precede its manifestation. Knowledge and interest in connection with this great event on earth have vastly increased, and increasing multitudes are looking for the Lord's appearing, with enlarged understanding, with new convictions, with constantly brightening hopes. For some of us, necessarily, the interval of hope must be short. Our earthly period of education has come near to its conclusion, and but little more can elapse before we shall see the Lord in his glory. As a fact in our personal history, it has become almost in sight. But some of us also believe that, as a fact in the history of man, involving consequences of an immense, outspread extent, and of vast relative influence in the welfare of earth and in the eternal consequences which are to follow individual experience, this great manifestation standeth at the door; and while many sleep, the Son of man will come.

"In this solemn conviction we have assembled here, bringing together our several impressions, convictions, and studies, that we may individually contribute to the general fund of knowledge, of observation, and of conviction, in reference to this great event in the history of earth, — the coming of man's Redeemer to assume the government which he hath purchased with his death, to restore the earth to his own dominion, and to gather into one redeemed fold the flock which has strayed upon all mountains, and has been scattered, wandering through all the moves of human ignorance, waywardness, and moral and intellectual degradation. And I close with the expression of an earnest hope that infinite grace, almighty power, and everlasting love may bless the earth on which we dwell, the land which we inhabit, the nation of which we are a part, and the whole race, for which the Son of God was content to die. The Spirit of God has been ready to teach, and the faithfulness of God has covenanted, a future restoration, and opened the hope of everlasting glory."

The conference was mainly devoted to the reading of elaborate papers prepared by different ministers, and to addresses upon the subject under consideration. The following is the list of the topics there discussed:

Opening Address, by the Rev. Stephen H. Tyng, Sr., D. D.; Christ's Coming—Personal and Visible, by the Rev. Stephen H. Tyng, Jr., D. D., of the Church of the Holy Trinity, New York; Christ's Coming—Is it Premillennial, by the Rev. S. H. Kellogg, D. D., Presbyterian Seminary, Allegheny, Pa.; The First Resurrection, by the Rev. A. J. Gordon, Clarendon street Baptist church, Boston, Mass.; The Regeneration, by the Rev. C. K. Imbrie, D. D., Jersey City; The Kingdom and the Church, by Professor H. Lummis, Methodist, Monson, Mass.; The Present Age and Development of Antichrist, by the Rev. Henry M. Parsons, pastor Lafayette street Presbyterian church, Buffalo, N. Y.; The Gathering of Israel, by Bishop W. R. Nicholson, of the Reformed Episcopal Church, Philadelphia; The Judgment, or Judgments, by the Rev. J. T. Cooper, D. D., United Presbyterian Seminary, Allegheny, Pa.; The Coming of the Lord in its Relation to Christian

Doctrine, by the Rev. James H. Brookes, D. D., pastor Walnut street Presbyterian church, St. Louis, Mo.; History of the Pre-millennial Doctrine, by the Rev. Nathaniel West, D. D., Presbyterian, Cincinnati, Ohio; A Summary of the Argument in Defense of Pre-millenarianism, by the Rev. John T. Duffield, D. D., professor of mathematics in Princeton College; Hope of Christ's Coming as a Motive to Holy Living and Active Labor, by the Rev. Rufus W. Clark, D. D., Reformed Dutch church, Albany, N. Y.; The Return of Christ, and Foreign Missions, by Dr. W. P. Mackay, of Hull, England.

The essays which were read have been critically edited by Dr. Nathaniel West, of Cincinnati, whose history of pre-millennial doctrine was one of the most interesting of the papers there presented. The conference could not fail to command respect and call attention to the themes which were so eloquently discussed on that occasion. One noteworthy feature was the utter absence of all denominational distinctions and purposes. The followers of the one Lord met there in unity upon the basis of one faith and one hope of their calling, thus bearing a testimony to the substantial unity of that scattered flock, for whose oneness the Saviour again and again poured out his parting prayer.

At the closing session of the conference the following summary of faith was adopted by the large body of ministers who participated in, or were present to sympathize with, its proceedings:

"I. We affirm our belief in the supreme and absolute authority of the written word of God on all questions of doctrine and duty.

"II. The prophetic words of the Old Testament Scriptures, concerning the first coming of our Lord Jesus Christ, were literally fulfilled in his birth, life, death, resurrection, and ascension; and so the prophetic words of both the Old and the New Testaments concerning his second coming will be literally fulfilled in his visible bodily return to this earth in like manner as he went up into heaven; and this glorious Epiphany of the great God, our Saviour Jesus Christ, is the blessed hope of the believer and of the Church during this entire dispensation.

"III. This second coming of the Lord Jesus is everywhere in the Scriptures represented as imminent, and may occur at any moment; yet the precise day and hour thereof is unknown to man, and known only to God.

"IV. The Scriptures nowhere teach that the whole world will be converted to God, and that there will be a reign of universal righteousness and peace before the return of our blessed Lord, but that only at and by his coming in power and glory will the prophecies concerning the progress of evil and the development of Antichrist, the times of the Gentiles and the ingathering of Israel, the resurrection of the dead in Christ and the transfiguration of his living saints, receive their fulfillment, and the period of millennial blessedness in its inauguration.

"V. The duty of the Church during the absence of the Bridegroom is to watch and pray, to work and wait, to go into all the world and preach the Gospel to every creature, and thus hasten the coming of the day of God; and to his last promise, 'Surely I come quickly,' to respond, in joyous hope, 'Even so; come, Lord Jesus.' "

The following resolution was passed, not only unanimously by the conference, but by the vast audience voluntarily rising *en masse* to its feet — a magnificent spectacle not soon to be forgotten : "*Resolved*, That the doctrine of our Lord's pre-millennial advent, instead of paralyzing evangelistic and missionary effort, is one of the mightiest incentives to earnestness in preaching the Gospel to every creature, until He comes."

We do not refer to these things in any spirit of exultation, nor see in these any reason to expect universal acceptance of the truth of our Lord's return and reign. No such expectation is warranted by Scripture or by facts. Truth is yet a stranger in an enemy's land, and we have no reason to suppose that the great majority will ever accept the truth as it is in Christ. Every one that is of the truth heareth His voice, and He who hath given his word, gives grace to receive it. We must also expect, from the very nature of the case, the most determined opposition to the truth, and the most subtle efforts for its corruption. Satan wastes no time fighting error; he puts forth no strength to bring false doctrine into disrepute by the mistakes and inconsistencies of its defenders, nor does he waste his energies in discrediting truths which are of minor consequence. It is only against some great, grand, fundamental principle of the doctrine of Christ, that he hurls his fiery darts and pours forth his fiercest indignation. Around such great, central truths the conflicts of ages have occurred; and everything which satanic art and malice could do to pervert, destroy, and dishonor the truth as it is in Christ, has been done. The apathy of a worldly church, the ignorance of professed teachers, the mistakes of rash and imprudent men, the perversions and misjudgments of the unwise and ungracious, the errors and false doctrines which grow beside all truth like tares in the midst of wheat, the bitterness of spirit which leads so many to reject truth in consequence of the tone and temper of its defenders, and the cool contempt of the worldly-wise, who, in their hearts, know nothing of the saving power of the gospel of Christ,—

all these are instruments invoked and used by the great adversary to cast dishonor upon the truth of God, and deter people from searching the Scriptures to see for themselves if these things are so. Against such fierce and furious zealots nothing but truth can stand. Error, subjected to half the perversions and assaults that truth has borne, would be shattered in fragments, and driven like thistle-down before the whirlwind. The doctrines of men have no elements of vitality which survive alike the folly of friends and the fury of foes. After all the mistakes and absurdities which men have connected with these great truths, they still lie as foundation principles of the gospel of Christ, firm as the everlasting hills. The great facts of judgment and retribution, the glorious prospect of a reign of righteousness and peace, the gospel of the everlasting kingdom, the glorious proclamation of the reign of Him who died to save mankind, and who is henceforth expecting until his enemies be made his footstool, the grand hope of the church for which our Saviour taught us ever to pray, "Thy kingdom come, thy will be done in earth as it is in heaven,"—these are truths and facts which no malice of Satan, no fury of foes, no foolishness or fanaticism of friends, can subvert or conceal. They stand in the faith and hope of the church, and shall yet stand in the experience of the universe as the manifest triumphs of Him who is God over all, blessed evermore.

CHAPTER XII.

THE DOOM OF ANTICHRIST.

"That day shall not come except there come a falling away first, and that man of sin be revealed, the Son of Perdition. . . . And then shall that wicked be revealed whom the Lord shall consume with the spirit of his mouth, and shall destroy with the brightness of his coming."—PAUL.

IN the present chapter we exhibit the Voice of the Church on what is styled the great Pre-millennial argument. It is the one which the venerable Mr. Faber has admitted to contain " apparent evidence for the Pre-millennial advent:" and which the Rev. D. Brown, of Scotland, affirms " to have more force, than all other arguments put together," and which is "the strongest of all;" and which all Pre-millennarians, with the Hon. B. Storer, pronounce to be " the unanswerable argument;" and of which they may well declare in the decisive words of Bishop M'Illvaine, " It is wholly unanswerable."

Nearly all Protestants accord with the martyred Latimer in saying, " Antichrist is now fully known throughout all the world," and with Fleming, in testifying that, " The man of sin hath come to his full height and stature," for his power is seen every where, and his millions cover the earth. But the great question at issue is, how shall the Papal power be abolished, to make way for the Millennium? With Paul we answer, " by the Lord's coming." So said Luther and Melancthon, and giving our principles of interpretation, we proceed to exhibit the testimony of Jesus in the spirit of prophecy, and the Voice of the Church, on this momentous subject.

PRINCIPLES OF INTERPRETATION.

Luther says, "You say it *may* be interpreted thus, it *may* also be understood thus, it *may* also be answered thus, it *may* be literally interpreted thus, it *may* be mystically interpreted thus:—away with all these may be's. These, my friend Catharinus, are all refuges of lies, mere loop-holes of escape, and evidently go to confirm the truths I maintain. Speak thus : 'This is the meaning of the passage, and it cannot be understood otherwise.' You will thus keep to one simple and uniform sense of Scripture, as I always do, and always have done. This way of proceeding, is to be a divine; the former a sophist. For you know in every controverted subject we must adide by the literal sense, which is uniform throughout the whole Scriptures."*

WHAT PAUL MEANT.

Mr. Faber says, "What St. Paul then told the Thessalonians, was this: that a tyrannical and irreligious power, which he denominates the man of sin, and the lawless one, should assuredly be revealed in its own appointed time, after there had been a great apostacy from the primitive faith, but before the arrival of the day of Christ, which they erroneously deemed close at hand : that the coercing power of the Roman Empire, effectually prevented the revelation of this oppressive tyranny ; but that when the coercing law of the Roman Empire should be removed from the midst, then the man of sin, no longer restrained by the strong arm of law, but acquiring his predicted character of the lawless one, by setting himself above all law, and by having the laws and times given into his hands, should be openly revealed."†

* Luther's Pope Confounded. † Sacred Calendar, vol. i., p. 100.

With these for our principles of interpretation, and with the foregoing definition of the apostle's language, we now proceed to quote from the early church her views of the great Antichrist, and the manner by which his destruction will be accomplished, to make way for the Millennium, and reign of Christ on the earth.

FIRST CENTURY.

BARNABAS, in A. D. 70, says: "The consummate trial as has been written, and as Daniel 9: 27, says, draws near,—for the Lord has cut short the times and the days, in order that his Beloved may hasten to his inheritance. Quoting Daniel on the ten kings, and little horn, he adds: "We ought to understand. . . . . . His Son shall come and abolish the wicked one, and judge the ungodly," &c.

SECOND CENTURY.

JUSTIN MARTYR wrote: "He who is about to speak blasphemous and audacious things against the Most High, is already at the doors, whose continuance Daniel signifies to be for a time, times, and half a time. He (Christ) shall come with glory from the heavens, when also, the man of apostacy speaking great words against the Highest, will dare to do wicked things against us Christians, who, since we have known the way of worshipping God by the law, and the doctrine going forth through the apostles of Jesus, from Jerusalem, fly to the God of Israel."

IRENÆUS says: "The number of Antichrist's name shall be expressed by the word *Lateinos*. When Antichrist, reigning three years and six months, shall have laid waste all things in this world, and have sat in the Temple of Jerusalem, then shall the Lord come from heaven in the clouds, casting Antichrist and them that obey him into the lake of fire, but bringing to the just the times of the kingdom, &c.'

THIRD CENTURY.

CYPRIAN says: "We are now in the end and consummation of the world—the fatal time of Antichrist is at hand."

HIPPOLYTUS, on the image, wrote: "After these shall come the Romans, being the iron legs of the image—strong as iron: in order that the democracies which are about to rise might be pointed out, answering respectively to the ten toes of the image, in which there will be iron mingled with clay."

On Antichrist: "The seducer will seek to appear in all things like the Son of God. As Christ a lion, so he a lion; as Christ a king, so he a king; as Christ a Saviour, so he a Saviour; as Christ a Lamb, so he a Lamb, though inwardly a wolf; as Christ sent out apostles to all nations, so will he similarly send out false apostles."

ORIGEN says, on Thess. 2:8: "But there is in Daniel a prophecy about this same Antichrist, which cannot but excite the admiration of any one who will read it with common sense and candor; for there, in words truly divine and prophetic, are described the kingdoms that were to come, beginning from the time of Daniel, down to the destruction of the world; and this prophecy may be read of all men. Now see if Antichrist is not spoken of there also." He then refers to Dan., 8th chap., also in connection.

TERTULLIAN says on Thess. 2: "Who is he that letteth? Who but the Roman empire? The breaking up and dispersion of which, among the ten kings, shall bring on Antichrist: and then shall be revealed that wicked one whom the Lord Jesus shall slay with the Spirit of his mouth, and destroy with his appearance. * * * The harlot city must suffer merited destruction by the ten kings, and the Beast Antichrist, with his false prophet, make war upon the Church of God, and then the Devil, being banished for a season to the bottomless pit, the privilege of the first resurrection will be adjudged from the throne, and afterwards fire having been sent down, the sentence belonging to the universal resurrection will be pronounced from the books."

"We know that convulsions and calamities threatening the whole world, and the end of the world itself, are kept back by the intervention of the Roman empire."

FOURTH CENTURY.

LACTANTIUS says: "Antichrist * * * will persecute the righteous people; and then shall be pressure and trial such as never has been from the beginning of the world. All who believe in and receive him shall be marked by him as so many sheep, but they who reject his mark shall either fly to the mountains or be seized and put to death with exquisite torments. He shall also roll up righteous men in the books of the prophets, and so burn them. And it shall be given him to desolate the world for forty and two months. This is the period in which righteousness will be cast out and innocence detested. This is he who is called Antichrist, but who will feign himself to be Christ, and will fight against the true Christ!"

"When the capital of the world (Rome) shall fall, who will doubt that the end of human affairs and the world itself has arrived?"

CYRIL makes the fourth beast to be Rome; identifies the "little horn" and "man of sin," and writes: "This, the predicted Antichrist, will come when the times of the (Pagan) Roman empire shall be fulfilled, and the consummation of the world approach. Ten kings of the Romans shall rise together in different places, indeed, but they shall reign at the same time. Among these, the eleventh is Antichrist, who, by magical and wicked artifices, shall seize the Roman power. Satan will use this person as an instrument personally acting in him. At first, he will assume the appearance of philanthropy, but afterwards will show himself full of stern severity, especially towards the people of God, for he says, 'I beheld, and the same horn made war with the saints,' &c. Thanks be to God; for he says that for the elect's sake those days shall be shortened: Antichrist shall reign three years and a half only. I say not this from the Apocryphal writings, but from Daniel." Now, a time, is one year, &c.

GREGORY NAZIANZEN says: "Antichrist is about to appear, king of the whole Roman world, but he shall come for the desolation of the world, for he is the abomination of desolation."

AMBROSE wrote: "The abomination of desolation is the abominable advent of Antichrist, who with ill-omened sacrilege will defile the inner chambers of men's minds, and will sit literally in the temple, usurping the throne of divine power. Then will come desolation, seeing that most will fall away from true religion, and lapse into error; then will come the day of the Lord!"

FIFTH CENTURY.

CHRYSOSTOM, on 2 Thess. 2:8, says: "That hindrance is the Roman empire. When that is taken away, then Antichrist shall come."

Chrysostom—or a nearly cotemporary writer—says, on false teachers: "When thou seest the holy Scriptures regarded as an abomination by men that outwardly profess to be Christians, and them that teach God's word hated; when the people rush to hear fable-mongers and genealogies, and teachings of demons; then bethink thee of the saying. 'In the last days there shall be an apostacy from the faith.' 1 Tim 4:1."[*]

EVAGRIUS, the Historian, A. D. 420, says: "The Roman emperors are driven from their kingdoms; wars rage; all is commotion. Antichrist must be at hand."

---

[*] Horæ Apoc., vol. vi., p. 548.

JEROME, on the irruption of the northern barbarians, says: "The Roman world rushes to destruction, and we bend not our necks in humiliation;" and when Rome was taken by Alaric: "He who hindered is taken out of the way, and we consider not that Antichrist is at hand whom the Lord shall consume with the spirit of his mouth," &c. Jerome applies the tribulation of Matt. 24 : 21, to the persecutions of the Antichrist. On Daniel 8: 9, and onward: "Most of our people refer it to Antichrist, and say, that what was done under Antiochus in type, is to be fulfilled under the other—the Antichrist in reality." On Daniel 7, also Thess. 2: 'Let us say what all the ecclesiastical writers have delivered, that at the end of the world, when the kingdom of the Romans is to be destroyed, there will be ten kings who will divide the world among themselves, and an eleventh will arise, a little king, who will overcome three of the ten kings * * * who being slain, the other seven kings will submit their necks to the conqueror. And, behold, he says, in this horn were eyes like the eyes of a man. Let us not suppose him, according to the opinion of some, either to be a devil or a demon, but one of the human race, in whom all Satan shall dwell bodily; and a mouth speaking great things, for he is the Man of sin, the Son of perdition, so that he dares to sit in the temple of God, making himself to be as God."

HILARION, A. D. 402, wrote: "It now wants 101 years to the end of the sixth chiliad; about the closing of which the ten kings must arise, Babylon, now reigning, fall, Antichrist arise and be destroyed by Christ's coming, and so the saints' Sabbath Millennary begin."

THEODORET, A. D. 430. He allows but four universal kingdoms—Rome to be the fourth and last, and the little horn the Antichrist who would be a human being, made the agent of Satan, and of whom Antiochus is the type. Quoting the words of our Lord, in Matt. 24: 21, respecting the unequalled tribulation, he refers it, as Jerome, to the coming

Antichrist, and says: "It is the appointment of Almighty God that he should appear at the time of the end, and it is God's decree that now hinders his manifestation."

AUGUSTINE, on 2 Thess. 2, wrote: "No one doubts that the Apostle said these things of Antichrist, and that the day of judgment, which he here calls 'the day of the Lord,' will not come, unless he, whom he calls an apostate, that is to say from the Lord God, shall first come." He thought that the miracles done by the Antichrist, would be real miracles performed by the agency of Satan. One objection with Augustine, to the end's being near, was the non-fulfillment of Mark 16: 15, whereupon Hesychius, a contemporary Father, referred him to Paul's words in Coll. 1 : 23, uttered in A. D 64, as showing its accomplishment already.

SIXTH CENTURY.

CASSIDORUS, a Roman Senator, born 463, died 560. "John says the harlot—the city of Rome—will be utterly destroyed by those nations whose former mistress she appeared to be." Cassidorus also affirms that ten kings will have power in the earth, but that one of them, who is called Antichrist, is reserved for the end of the age, and makes war against Christ, but his iniquity will succumb under the conquering hand of the Lord.

GREGORY, OF TOURS, A. D. 590, observes: "Concerning the end of the world, I believe what I have learned from those who have gone before me. Antichrist will assume dominion, asserting himself to be the Christ."

ANDREAS. He made the Babylon of the Revelation to apply alike to Old Rome, under Nero, and New Rome, under Julian; both fulfilling, "Drunk with the blood of the saints." The Beast's eighth head is Antichrist, who is to perish not as a foreigner, but as king of the Romans. He writes: "**Out of that Beast grew one horn which is to root up three and** subdue the rest, and to become king of the Romans. And this under pretext of fostering their power, but in truth to overthrow it utterly. Therefore, if any one chooses here to understand a condensed representation of that kingdom which has ruled from the beginning until now, and which has indeed shed the blood of apostles, prophets, and martyrs, he will not err from the meaning."

GIBBON, on A. D. 500, says: "Pope, or Father, was now a name appropriated to the Roman Pontiff."

DR. GRESWELL, a thorough student of the Fathers, states their faith on the Antichrist as follows. He says that all believed and himself with them:

"That Antichrist must come, and must be destroyed by the advent of Christ. In this perfectly agree all, whether friends or foes, of the doctrine of the Millennium. The only distinction was, that the advocates of the Millennium expected their kingdom to begin and proceed after the destruction of Antichrist; the opponents of the doctrine expected the same of the kingdom of heaven.

"That Antichrist is a person, rather than a character, a bodily agent. Yet they all agree to give the name to the symbolic character of the beast in Revelation, and also to the little horn, and to the King of the north in the prophet Daniel.

"Before the appearing of Antichrist, the Roman Empire was to be broken up into ten parts, which, at his appearing, were to be reunited in him, and he should reign over them three and a half years. [NOTE.—This of course is now understood as three and a half years of symbolic days, or 1260 years.] Many understood 'he who letteth,' in 2 Thess. 2: 6, to mean the imperial power of Rome. And the end of Antichrist's power is the beginning of Christ's reign; the one will begin when the other is over, and not before."[*]

[*] Greswell's Expos. of the Parables.

Dr. GEORGE CROLY, in his exposition of the Apocalypse, presents the following testimony:

"A. D. 533. The Pope was declared head of all the churches by the Emperor Justinian.

"The circumstances of a transaction, so pregnant with the most momentous results to the Christian world, are to be found at large in the Annals of Baronius, the chief Romish Ecclesiastical historian.

"Justinian being about to commence the Vandal war, an enterprise of great difficulty, was anxious previously to settle the religious disputes of his capital. The Nestorian heresy had formed a considerable number of partizans, who conscious of the Emperor's hostility to their opinions, had appealed to the Bishop of Rome. To counteract the representations of Cyrus and Eulogius, the Nestorian deputies, the Emperor sent two distinguished prelates, Hypatius, Bishop of Ephesus, and Demetrius, Bishop of Philippi, in the character of envoys, to Rome.

"Justinian had been remarkable for taking an unkingly share in the dubious theology of the times; he felt the passions of a disputant; and to his latest days enjoyed the triumphs of a controversy with the delight of a zealot, as he sometimes signalized them by the fury of a persecutor. On this occasion, whether through anxiety to purchase the suffrage of the Roman Bishop, the Patriarch of the West, whose opinion influenced a large portion of Christendom; or to give irresistible weight to the verdict which was to be pronounced in his own favor; he decided the precedency which had been contested by the Bishops of Constantinople from the foundation of the city; and, in the fullest and most unequivocal form, declared the Bishop of Rome the **Chief of the whole Ecclesiastical body** of the empire.

"His letter was couched in these terms:

"' Justinian, pious, fortunate, renowned, triumphant, Emperor, consul, &c., to John the most holy Archbishop of our city of Rome, and patriarch.

"' Rendering honor to the Apostolic chair, and to your Holiness, as has been always and is our wish, and honoring your Blessedness as a father; we have hastened to bring to the knowledge of your Holiness all matters relating to the churches. It having been at all times our great desire to preserve the unity of your Apostolic chair, and the constitution of the holy churches of God which has obtained hitherto, and still obtains.

"' Therefore we have made no delay in *subjecting and uniting to your Holiness all the priests of the whole East.*

"' For this reason we have thought fit to bring to your notice the present matters of disturbance; though they are manifest and unquestionable, and always firmly held and declared by the whole priesthood according to the doctrine of your Apostolic chair. For we cannot suffer that anything which relates to the state of the church, however manifest and unquestionable, should be moved, without the knowledge of your Holiness, who are THE HEAD OF ALL THE HOLY CHURCHES, for in all things, as we have already declared, we are anxious to increase the honor and authority of your Apostolic chair.'

"The letter then proceeds to relate the matter in question, the heresy of the monks and the mission of the Bishops, and desires to have a rescript from Rome to Epiphanius, Archbishop of Constantinople, giving the papal sanction to the judgment already pronounced by the Emperor on the heresy. It further mentions that the Archbishop also had written to the Pope, 'he being desirous in all things to follow the Apostolic authority of his Blessedness.'

"The Emperor's letter must have been sent before the 25th of March, 533. For, in his letter of that date to Epiphanius, he speaks of its having been already despatched, and repeats his decision, that all affairs touching the church shall be referred to the Pope, 'Head of all Bishops, and the true and effective *corrector of heretics.*'

"In the same month of the following year, 534, the Pope returned an answer repeating the language of the Emperor, applauding his homage to the see, and adopting the titles of the imperial mandate. He observes that, among the virtues of Justinian, 'one shines as a star, his reverence for the Apostolic chair, to which he has subjected and united all the Churches, it being truly the Head of all; as was testified by the rules of the Fathers, the laws of Princes, and the declarations of the Emperor's piety.'

"The authenticity of the title receives unanswerable proof from the edicts in the 'Novellæ' of the Justinian code.

"The preamble of the 9th states that 'as the elder Rome was the founder of the laws, so was it not to be questioned that in her was the supremacy of the pontificate.'

"The 131st, On the ecclesiastical titles and privileges, chap. 2, states: 'We therefore decree that the most holy Pope of the elder Rome is the first of all the priesthood, and that the most blessed Archbishop of Constantinople, the new Rome, shall hold the second rank after the holy Apostolic chair of the elder Rome.'

"The supremacy of the Pope had by those mandates and edicts received the fullest sanction that could be given by the authority of the master of the Roman world. But the yoke sat uneasily on the Bishop of Constantinople; and on the death of Justinian the supremacy was utterly denied. The Greek who wore the mitre in the imperial city of the east, must have looked with national contempt on a pontiff whose city had lost the honors of the imperial residence, and whose person was in the power of the barbarians. Towards the close of the sixth century, John of Constantinople, surnamed for his pious austerities the Faster, summoned a council and resumed the ancient title of the see, 'Universal Bishop.' The Roman Bishop, Gregory the Great, indignant at the usurpation, and either hurried away by the violence of controversy, or, in that day of monstrous ignorance, unacquainted with his own distinctions, furiously denounced John, calling him an 'usurper, aiming at supremacy over the whole church,' and declaring with unconscious truth, that whoever claimed such a supremacy was Antichrist. The accession of Phocas at length decided the question. He had ascended the throne of the east by the murder of the Emperor Mauritius. The insecurity of his title rendered him anxious to obtain the sanction of the Patriarch of the west. The conditions were easily settled. The usurper received the benediction of the Bishop of Rome; and the Bishop in 606 vindicated from his rival patriarch the gorgeous title; that had been almost a century before conferred on the papal tiara by Justinian. He was thenceforth 'Head of all the Churches,' without a competitor, 'Universal Bishop' of Christendom. That Phocas repressed the claim of the Bishop of Constantinople is beyond a doubt. But the highest authorities among the civilians and annalists of Rome spurn the idea that Phocas was the founder of the supremacy of Rome; they ascend to Justinian as the only legitimate source, and rightly date the title from the memorable year 533.

"The sixth century is distinguished by other features of that extraordinary aspect which the Romish see so portentiously assumed in its ambition of boundless empire; the building of a vast number of churches in honor of the saints, and for saint worship; the creation of a multitude of festivals, adopting the forms of the abolished pagan rites; and the commencement of that sullen and benighted ignorance of Scripture and literature, which for six hundred years brought back barbarism upon the European world.

"With the title of 'Universal Bishop,' the power of the Papacy, and the Dark Ages, alike began."*

* Croly on the Apocalypse.

Pope Gregory the Great was born in 544. Died in 604. Dupin says: "He believed the Roman Empire was within a finger's breadth of its ruin; and participating in the idea that it was only to end with the world's end, he came to the conviction that the last judgment was at hand," and accordingly he sent letters throughout all Christendom, from England to Constantinople, Antioch, and Alexandria, declaring, "We know from the word of Almighty God, that the end of the world is at hand, and the reign of the saints, which shall have no end. In the approach of which consummation all nature must be expected to be disordered; seasons deranged, wars raging, and famines, and earthquakes, and pestilence. Says Dr. Elliott: "Nor in his warning cry of the judgments precursive of the world's ending being at hand, did he omit the warning of Antichrist being at hand also. He connected the one awful apprehension with the other, in his forebodings, just as had been done by most of the Fathers of the Church before him. A notable occasion had arisen to call forth the public declaration of his sentiments and his fears on this subject. The Patriarch of Constantinople, John the Faster, had just then assumed the title to himself,—though not, we may be assured in the full meaning of the words,—of Universal Bishop. Against this, Gregory—as indeed Pope Pelagius just before him—raised his most solemn protestations. In letters written and published at different times from 590 to nearly the end of the century, and addressed to the Greek emperor, the Empress, the Patriarchs of Constantinople, Antioch, and Alexandria, the Bishop of Thessalonica, and many others, he declared before Christendom that whosoever in his elation of spirit, called himself, or sought to be called universal bishop, or universal priest, that man was the likeness, the precursor, and the preparer for Antichrist, saying: 'I speak it boldly, whosoever calleth himself universal priest, or desireth so to be called in the pride of his heart, he is the forerunner of Antichrist,'—that he bore the same characteristic of boundless pride and self-exaltation; that the tendency of his assumption if consented to, was that which was the grand object of Antichrist, viz.: to withdraw all members of the church from its only true head, CHRIST JESUS, and to attach and connect them in the stead with himself;—moreover, that in so far as the priesthood might have acquiesced in it, there had been prepared an army, not of soldiers, indeed, but of priests, to assist him in carrying that design into effect, saying: 'The King of Pride is present, and what ought not to be, an army of priests is prepared for him.' It was stated, or implied in his letters that he regarded the title spoken of as the name of blasphemy connected with the ten-horned Beast in the Apocalypse; the self-exaltation manifested above all his fellow-men, as that predicted of the man of sin in St. Paul's epistle to the Thessalonians, declaring, 'By this pride of his, what else is signified, but that the time of Antichrist is even at hand,' and the consenting thereto as that departure from the faith, and that apostasy which was predicted also in the same epistle, and in that to Timothy. * * * In spite of this declaration, thus pressed as it had been on the attention of Christendom, thus dispersed, thus repeated, and even en-registered in the canon law of the Romish Church,—this very title was within 10 or 15 years afterward, officially conferred on, and assumed by Gregory's own successor in the Roman episcopate, the Greek emperor himself conferring it:—assumed by him not in its restricted meaning, as by the eastern Patriarch previously; but in its full and plain meaning of universal episcopal supremacy over the whole professing church on earth, and as a title thenceforth never to be abandoned! Surely the fact was one calculated to excite both the ponderings and the misgivings of thinking men: and to awaken enquiry whether the dreaded phantasm, the very Antichrist of prophecy, might not even then have been brought into existence, in the world, albeit under a form in some respects little expected; and, if so, with fearful evils doubtless following in his train."*

JOHN DOWLING, D. D., of New York, author of a History of the Papal Church, though admitting the anterior application of the term Pope to the Roman pontiffs—as Gibbon states—argues that previous to the year 606, in the present exclusive sense of the word as the supreme sovereign pontiff, and boasted head of the universal church, there was properly no Pope. Quoting Gregory, as does Elliott, Dr. Dowling observes: " Let the reader ponder well the sentence last quoted in this epistle of Gregory,† confessedly one of the most eminent of the Roman bishops, and who has by them been canonized as St. Gregory: in which he places the brand of Antichrist on whoever assumes this title, and then judge whether we are not justified in pronouncing the era of the Papal supremacy, when only two years after Gregory's death Pope Boniface III., sought for and obtained the title of universal bishop, as the date of the full revelation of Antichrist. We do but repeat the opinion so emphatically expressed by St. Gregory only a few years before the actual occurrence of this remarkable event in the history of Popery. Boniface, who succeeded to the Roman see in 605, was so far from having any scruples about adopting this 'blasphemous title,' that he actually applied to the emperor Phocas, a cruel and blood-thirsty tyrant, who had made his way to the throne by assassinating his predecessor; and earnestly solicited the title, with the privilege of handing it down to his successors. The profligate emperor, who had a secret grudge against the Bishop of Constantinople, granted the request of Boniface, and after strictly forbidding the former prelate to use the title, conferred it upon the latter in the year 606, and declared the Church of Rome to be head over all the churches. (Note.—These facts are related by Baronius and

* Horæ Apoc., vol. i., p. 376.   † Lib. vi., Epistle 30.

other Romish historians.) Thus was Paul's prediction accomplished, the 'man of sin' revealed, and that system of corrupt christianity and spiritual tyranny which is properly called POPERY, fully developed and established in the world. The title of universal bishop which was then obtained by Boniface, has been worn by all succeeding Popes, and the claim of supremacy which was then established, has ever since been maintained and defended by them, and still is done to the present day."*

EDWARD WINTHROP says it is generally admitted that this period of 1260 years, does not commence at a later date than the early part of the seventh century. David Lord commences it about 604. Most writers fix the full commencement about 606. Elliott suggests, as a primary beginning, A. D. 529–533, and as a secondary and complete beginning, 604–608, the difference between the two, like the difference between Daniel's 1260 and 1335, being 75 years.†

SEVENTH CENTURY.

SERENUS, Bishop of Marseilles, was the faithful Protestant of this century, protesting against image worship, and destroying the images from the churches of his diocese. An appeal was made to Rome against him. The Anglo Saxon Church in Britain protested with Serenus.‡ The dark ages begin here to set in upon the world.

EIGHTH CENTURY.

COUNCIL OF FRANKFORT, A. D. 794, under Charlemagne. This Emperor and 300 Bishops of western Christendom, protested in opposition to the Popes of Rome, against image worship and the corruptions and the idolatry of the times. The Beast had now taken the Dragon's seat, and ALCUIN,

---

* History of Romanism, p. 55.   † Letters on Proph., pp. 139, 140
‡ Horæ Apoc., vol. ii., p. 217.

preceptor and friend of Charlemagne, was a true Protestant and affirmed, that "by the Beast we understand Antichrist.' Bishop Newton says he set forth doctrines "such as a Papist would ahbor, and a Protestant would subscribe."* PAULINUS, born 726, did so also.

NINTH CENTURY.

AGOBARD, Archbishop of Lyons from A. D. 810 to 841, declared against image worship, invocation of saints, &c. CLAUDE, the Bishop of Turin, called by Waddington, "the Protestant of the ninth century," faithfully lifted his voice against the worship of saints, relics, wooden crosses, images, pilgrimages, masses, tradition, etc., which Mosheim and Gibbon affirm, in these times, "darkened God's throne;" and also against the supremacy of the Pope of Rome. Claude died A D. 840.†

TENTH CENTURY.

ARNULPH, Bishop of Orleans, at the Synod of Rheims, A. D. 991, appealed to the whole Council concerning the Pope, saying, "What think ye, reverend fathers, of this man, elevated on a lofty throne, and glittering in gold and purple? Whom do ye account him to be? Surely, if destitute of charity, and elated with the pride of science alone, he is Antichrist, 'sitting in the temple of God and showing himself that he is God'"‡ Clarke, in his Prophetic Records, says, that at this Council, GONTHIER, Bishop of Cologne, and TERGAND, Archbishop of Treves, "declared plainly and without reserve, that the Pope was Antichrist."

Genebrand and Baronius, Roman Catholic writers, call this century an iron, a leaden, and an unhappy age: "Chiefly unhappy," says Baronius, "in that for almost 150

---

* Horæ Apoc., vol. ii., p. 218. † Ibid, p. 221.
‡ Baronius Annales, A. D. 992.

years, the Popes totally degenerated from the virtue of their ancestors, being more like Apostates than Apostles." Dowling styles the period from A. D. 800 to 1073, "The world's midnight!"

ELEVENTH CENTURY.

BERENGER, Archdeacon of Angers, wrote a Comment on the Revelation, in which he declared that, "The Romish Church was a Church of malignants, and its see not the Apostolic seat, but that of Satan." Bishop Hurd supposes that Berenger originated these anti-Romish sentiments from Rev. 13: 2. These times are very dark. If the reader would fill out the picture, let him read Dowling's History of Romanism and Fox's Book of Martyrs, &c. BARONIUS says it was reported far and wide in this century that Antichrist had come.* He had truly.

TWELFTH CENTURY.

BARONIUS says that this century presented an awful picture of Popish vileness. JOHANNES ADVENTINUS, another Romish historian, said all men of this time agreed in saying that Antichrist then reigned in the Popes of Rome. ST. BERNARD, abbot of Clairvaux, born 1091, died 1153, wrote, "The Beast that is spoken of in the book of Revelation, unto which Beast is given a mouth to speak blasphemies and to make war against the saints of God, is now gotten into St. Peter's chair as a lion prepared to his prey." ARNOLD, who died 1155; PETER DE BRUYS, who was martyed 1126; HENRY, the Italian, styled "the Whitefield of his age,"† and many others, affirmed that the Papal Church was the Babylon and Whore of the Apocalypse. JOACHIM ABBAS, in his commentary, declared that the harlot city, in Revelations, which reigned over the kings of the earth, undoubtedly meant

* Horæ Apoc., vol. ii., p. 259. † Ibid, p. 268.

Rome, not the city only, but all the members of the empire. Joachim affirms that Peter says so in his first epistle, chap. 5, verse 13, the "Babylon" there referred to meaning Rome.*

THIRTEENTH CENTURY.

VITRINGA affirms that the language of pious men in general, in these centuries, was, that the Pope was Antichrist, and the Church of Rome, Babylon. PETER JOHN OLIVE says, "The Church of Rome is the Whore of Babylon, the mother of harlots, the same that St. John beheld sitting on a scarlet colored beast, full of names of blasphemy, having seven heads and ten horns." So said also HUBERT DE CASALI. So, too, MATTHEW PARIS in 1245. And PETER WALDO, the merchant of Lyons, instituted the cry, says Prof. Gaussen, of "Come out of Babylon!" And, as all know, the WALDENSES' "Treatise on Antichrist," pronounces unhesitatingly the Romish hierarchy to be the great Antichrist.†

FOURTEENTH CENTURY.

WALTER BRUTE, a Briton, in 1391, said, "The Pope is the very Antichrist and a seducer of the people. He is the chief of those fallen Christs, foretold by Christ as to come in his name, deceiving many. The Pope wageth war against infidels and Christians. Christ said that here the tares were to grow with the wheat, and the separation to be made by himself only at the time of the day of judgment; whereas the Pope would have the separation to be made by himself now; so changing times as well as laws." Of DANTE, the Italian poet, born 1265, died 1321, Bishop Jewell says: "He, by express words, called Rome the whore of Babylon." So also said FRANCIS PETRARCH, who died in 1374, and called Rome "the sanctuary of heresy and the school of error."

* Horæ Apoc., vol. iv., p. 395. † Ency. Rel. Knowledge.

FIFTEENTH CENTURY.

JOHN HUSS, and JEROME of Prague, in 1415, were burnt at the stake, on charge of affirming, among other things, "that there was no absolute necessity for a visible head of the church, and that a wicked Pope could not possibly be the vicar of Christ;" having been previously tried and condemned at the council of Constance, composed of 346 Archbishops and Bishops, 546 Abbots and Doctors, and 450 prostitutes! Says Prof. Gaussen, "When the great WICKLIFF preached the reformation in England, all eyes were turned to the Roman Pontiff with the exclamation: Behold the man of sin! When the generous HUSS and JEROME of Prague made their voices heard a hundred years before Luther, it was against the Great Whore foretold by John."* It was in this century, at the Council of Florence, held in 1436, that the Romish church avowedly and finally affirmed the great error which she had previously adopted, viz., that the Millennium was to precede the coming of the Antichrist, and she maintains the same to this day, and must, for she is infallible and must not revoke her decrees.

DR. CUMMING, in recent lectures on the Papacy, gives the names of Luther, Calvin, Beza, Rivet, Tyndal, Fox, Latimer, Jewell, Archbishop Parker, Archbishop Whitgift, Whittaker, Raynolds, Archbishop Grindal, Archbishop Abbot, Bishop Morton, Willet, Sutcliffe, Hooker, Bishop Davenant, Bishop Hall, Dr. Jackson, Edwards, the Archbishop of Canterbury, all of whom, with a host beside, agree in pronouncing the Pope the Man of Sin, and the Romish hierarchy, the Babylon of the Apocalypse. Antichrist has come; and further testimony to the fact is unnecessary. In the forcible language of the Romish official of New York city, ARCHBISHOP HUGHES " HE (THE POPE) KNOWS THAT IT IS A FUNDAMENTAL ARTICLE OF THE PROTESTANT RELIGION TO BELIEVE THAT HE IS ANTI-

---

* Gaussen on Popery.

christ."* And we venture to affirm that no Protestant can be found who will dispute it.

Having thus presented a line of witnesses down through the dark ages and reign of Antichrist to the era of the great reformation, answering in part the question sneeringly put by Rome to Protestants, i. e., "Where was your church before Luther?" we now resume more fully the strain of the early church, and proceed to show by the testimony of the great body of the reformers and elder divines that the destruction of the Papacy is to be accomplished only by the Lord's personal advent, which advent is Pre-millennial. To do this, we will consider and explain some of the terms used in 2 Thess. 2: 8, and first we call attention to the word translated "*brightness*" in this passage. This word is

EPIPHANEIA, (Greek επιφάνεια).

This word occurs in the New Testament six times, viz., in the following passages : the representative word in English we italicise. 1 Tim. 6: 14, "the *appearing* of our Lord Jesus Christ." 2 Tim. 1: 10, "the *appearing* of our Saviour Jesus Christ." Chap. 4: 1, "at his *appearing*." Verse 8, "love his *appearing*." Titus 2 : 13, "glorious *appearing* of the great God," and 2 Thess. 2: 8, "destroy with the *brightness* (i. e., the appearing) of his coming."†

H. BONAR, on the last quotation, thus writes :—"the word επιφάνεια which the apostle uses here occurs just six times in the New Testament. In one of these it refers to the first advent, which we know was literal and personal. In four it is admitted to refer to the literal and personal second coming: the fifth is the one under discussion, and it is the strongest and most unambiguous of all the six ! Not one of these others is so explicit, yet no one thinks of explaining them away. Why then fasten upon the strongest, and insist on spiritualizing it? If the strongest can be explained away so

*N Y. Cour & Enq., Nov. 22, 1851.   † English. Greek Concord

as not to denote the second coming, much more may the others, and then we shall have no passages to prove the advent at all! If the Anti-millennarian be at liberty to spiritualize the most distinct, why may not the Straussian be allowed to rationalize or mythologize the less distinct?*

That I am stating the hermeneutics of the word correctly, the following testimony from eminent lexicographers will show.

PASOR, died 1637. He defines "ἐπιφανεια appearance. In one place it is applied to the nativity of our Lord Jesus Christ, 2 Tim. 1: 10, in other places of the Scriptures for his glorious coming to judgment, as 2 Thess. 2: 8."†

STOCKIUS says: "1st. It denotes, when applied to a *genus*, any appearance whatever. 2d. When applied to a *species*, it properly denotes the appearance of some corporeal and shining matter which bursts forth with great splendor. In a metaphorical sense, it is applied to the appearance of Christ: *First*, his gracious appearance in the flesh, which is called his first coming; *Second*, his glorious appearance to judge the world, which will be gracious to the righteous and faithful, but terrible to the sinner and infidel, and which is called his second coming. 2 Thess. 2: 8; 1 Tim. 6: 14; 2 Tim. 4: 1; also 4: 8; Titus 2: 13."‡

LEIGH. Died 1671. He writes: "This word signifieth a bright, clear, glorious appearing, from which word we take our *epiphany*, specially *Adventus Numinis* (i. e. the coming of the Divinity.) It is taken for the first coming of Christ. 2 Tim. 1: 10; for his second coming as 2 Thess. 2: 8, &c."§

SUICER. Died 1705. After mentioning the use of the word—1st. The heathen use of it in reference to a manifestation of one of their gods; 2d. In reference to the first advent—he thus proceeds: 3d. This is frequently applied by

---

*Bonar's Coming and Kingdom, p. 343. †Pasor's N. T. Lex., p. 1389.
‡ Stockii Clavis, vol. ii. p. 1147.   § Critica Sacra, p 161.

the Apostle to the second coming of Christ, which will be to judgment. 2 Thess. 2: 8."*

SCULTETUS, who died in 1626, on this word—after stating that the pagan writers used to call any appearance of their gods ἐπιφάνεια—adds: "The Apostle also applies επιφανειο —appearance—to the first and last coming of Christ."†

BRETSCHNEIDER, the learned German lexicographer, says that " ἐπιφάνεια is used in the New Testament in the writings of Paul, concerning the splendid appearing and future advent in which Christ, who is now concealed from our view in the heavens, shall appear coming in the clouds (literally borne on the clouds or wafted by the clouds) to administer judgment. 2 Thess 2: 8; 1 Tim. 6: 14; 2 Tim. 4: 1-8; Titus 2: 13; and concerning his appearing in the world, which has already taken place—viz., when he was born—2 Tim. 1: 10: in other words, his first advent."

WAHL, of Germany, also defines the word as meaning an appearing, and says it is used in the New Testament in 2 Tim. 1: 10, in speaking of the advent of Jesus upon this earth; and in 2 Thess. 2: 8; 1 Tim. 6: 14; 2 Tim. 4: 1, 8; Titus 2: 13, of his future glorious return.

PICKERING says the word means appearance, and applies it to " an unexpected coming, and to the advent of Christ;" and DONNEGAN defines it as meaning " appearance or apparition, particularly that of a Divinity, or of one who comes up suddenly to offer aid, or for other purposes, &c."

LIDDELL and SCOTT define it " the appearance, manifestation—e. g., dawn of the day—specially of the appearance of deities to aid a worshipper." GREENFIELD: ' Brightness, splendor, 2 Thess. 2: 8, an appearance—i. e. the act of appearing, manifestation."‡

These authorities will suffice for this word: the second

* Thes. Eccles., vol. i. p. 1202.   † Exer. Evang., Lib. ii. ch. i.
‡ See the above named Lexicons *sub voce*.

word requiring examination is that translated "*coming*," namely,—

PAROUSIA, (Greek παρουσία.).

This word is used in the New Testament twenty-four times, the following being all the passages in which it is found, the word which represents it in English being italicised: Math. 24: 3, "sign of thy *coming*," verse 27, "the *coming* of," verse 37, "*coming* of the Son," verse 39, "the *coming* of the Son of man;" 1 Cor. 15: 23, "Christ at his *coming*," chap. 16: 17, "*coming* of Stephanus, and Fortunatus, and Achaicus;" 2 Cor. 7: 6, "*coming* of Titus," verse 7, "by his *coming*," chap. 10: 10, "his bodily *presence*;" Phil. 1: 26, "by my *coming*," chap. 2: 3, "my *presence* only;" 1 Thess. 2; 19, "at his *coming*," chap. 3: 13, "at the *coming*," chap. 4: 15, "*coming* of the Lord," chap. 5: 23, "*coming* of our Lord;" 2 Thess. 2: 1, "*coming* of our Lord," verse 8, "brightness of his *coming*," verse 9, "him whose *coming*;" James 5: 7, "*coming* of the Lord," verse 8, "*coming* of the Lord;" 2 Pet. 1: 16, "*coming* of our Lord," chap. 3: 4, "promise of his *coming*," verse 12, "the *coming* of," and 1 John 2: 18, "at his *coming*."*

The Greek word παρουσία is defined by PICKERING, "presence, arrival, to be present," by DONNEGAN, "to be present, to arrive," by GREENFIELD, "a coming, arrival, advent," by LIDDELL and SCOTT, "a being present, presence of a person or thing, especially present for the purpose of assisting, arrival." BRETSCHNEIDER refers the "coming," in 2 Thess. 2: 8, to "the advent of Christ from heaven to administer judgment." WAHL, in like manner, refers it to 'the future advent of Jesus the Messiah, to enter gloriously upon his kingdom."† We might farther quote SCAPULÆ, SCHLEUSNER, and in fact every Greek lexicographer under

* Vide Englishman's Greek Concordance.   † Vide Lexicons *sub voce*

heaven, in support of this signification. And Dr. **Duffield** justly observes that "in every instance where it occurs, (in the N. T.,) which is twenty-four times, it is used literally, and not metaphorically or anagogically."*

Claiming then this meaning for *epiphaneia* and *parousia*, we proceed to exhibit the voice of the church.

MARTIN LUTHER, his first impression in 1517. To Albert, bishop of Magdeburg and Mayence, Luther wrote on All Saint's Eve, 1517: "Prierio again attacked me, but when I found the man asserting that the authority of the Pope was superior to the councils and canons of the church, and that even the sacred Scriptures depended for their interpretation upon the mere dictum of that representative of Antichrist, I thought it unnecessary to reply farther than by simply declaring my conviction that the said Prierio's book, being a compound of blasphemies and lies, must certainly have been the work of the devil, and that if the Pope and Cardinals sanctioned such writings, which I did not then believe, though now I know it well, Rome must be the seat of Antichrist, the centre of abomination, the synagogue of Satan. Who is Antichrist if the Pope is not Antichrist? O Satan, Satan, how long wilt thou be suffered to abuse the patience of God by thy great wickedness? Unhappy, abandoned, blasphemous Rome! the wrath of God is upon thee, and thou richly deservest it, for thou art the habitation of all that is impure and disgusting! a very pantheon of impiety."†

His second impression. He wrote to Link in 1518: "My pen is ready to give birth to things much greater. I know not myself whence these thoughts come to me. I will send you what I write, that you may see if I have well conjectured in believing that the Antichrist of whom St. Paul speaks now reigns in the court of Rome."‡

---

* On Prophecy, p. 323.   † Michelet's Life of Luther, p. 80.
‡ D. Aubigne's Hist. Ref, vol. i., p. 429.

Luther's third impression, 1519, to the Elector of Saxony: "I have been turning over the Decretals of the Pope, and would whisper it in thine ears that I begin to entertain doubt whether the Pope be not the very Antichrist of Scripture."*

His fourth, to Leo, the Pope, 1520: "Rome is a sink of corruption and iniquity; for it is clearer than light itself, that the Roman church, once of all churches the most chaste and pure, has become a cavern, foul with robbers, the most obscene of brothels, the very throne of sin, of death and hell! and that its wickedness could go no further, even were Antichrist reigning there in person."†

His fifth, to Europe, 1520: "I hold the author of this Bull to be Antichrist, and Rome the kingdom of Antichrist." And then to Christian princes he says: "Ye have given your names to Christ in baptism, and can ye now abide these infernal voices of such an Antichrist?"‡

Final view. "Our Lord Jesus Christ yet liveth and reigneth, who I firmly trust will shortly come and slay with the spirit of his mouth and destroy with the brightness of his coming that Man of Sin.§ Again he says, in another place: "The Apostle expresses this Pope's destruction thus: 'Whom the Lord shall consume, &c.' The laity therefore shall not destroy the Pope and his kingdom. No, he and his wicked rabble are not deserving of so light a punishment. They shall be preserved until the coming of Christ, whose most bitter enemies they are and ever have been."‖. For the more complete testimony of Luther, the reader is referred to chapter VI. of this volume.

MELANCTHON. David N. Lord says of this reformer, "He refuted by the Scriptures the expectation of the Anabaptists of the immediate establishment of Christ's Millennial king-

---

* Ib. vol. ii. p. 13.   † Michelet's Life of Luther, p. 63,
‡ Horæ Apoc., vol. ii. p. 120.   § D'Aubigne, vol. ii. p. 166.
‖ Pope Confounded, p. 177-9.

dom. He regarded the term Antichrist as denoting both the Mohammedan empire and the Papacy, and held that they were not to be overthrown till the time of the resurrection of the dead."* Such were the views of the two great reformers, Luther and Melancthon, views doubtless shared by all their followers at that era.

THEODORE BEZA, a zealous reformer, who died in 1605, evidently took 2 Thess. 2: 8, as describing a personal advent of the Lord Jesus, as did the great reformers generally. He says, "Thus I have deemed it best to translate the name $επιφανεια$, which Paul designedly used in order to represent to our eyes that most brilliant splendor of his last coming." Again he writes, "At length by the word of the Lord that impiety will be exposed, and by the advent of Christ wholly abolished."†

ARCHBISHOP USHER.—This distinguished man observes that, "The glorious appearance of the Son of God in the latter day, shall also be the overthrow of Antichrist, whence we gather that before the last day, he shall not be utterly consumed."‡

CALVIN, in his Institutes, evidently takes the literal view of the passage making the Lord's coming the consummation of all judgment upon Antichrist, and quoting 2 Thess. 2: 8. In his commentary on Thessalonians, speaking generally of the two expressions, *consume* and *destroy*, he says: "It is uncertain whether he speaks of the final appearance of Christ, when he will be revealed from the heavens as Judge." He then remarks that this is what the words appear to mean, only the consumption is not instantaneous, but protracted, and only brought to a close "when that last day of the renewal of all things shall come." He then makes a rise of

---

* Lord's Expos. Apoc., p. 238.   † Notes on Latin Test. in loc.
‡ Body of Divinity, ch. 45.

meaning in the words *consume* and *destroy* similar to that made by Dr. Jebb.*

COUNCIL OF GAP, under Henry IV., 1603. Art. XXXI. Confession of Faith: "And since the Bishop of Rome has erected for himself a temporal monarchy in the Christian world, and usurping a sovereign authority and lordship over all churches and pastors, exalts himself to that degree of insolence as to be called God, and will be adored, &c. *** We, therefore, believe and maintain that he is truly and properly the Antichrist, the son of perdition, predicted by the holy Scriptures—that Great Whore, clothed with scarlet, sitting upon seven mountains in that great city, which had dominion over the kings of the earth; and we hope and wait that the Lord, according to his promise, and as he hath already begun, will confound him by the spirit of his mouth and destroy him by the brightness of his coming."†

S. GLASSIUS, D.D., died 1656. Referring to 2 Thess. 2: 8, this learned German writer says, "In its simplest sense, επιφάνεια, &c., is his (Christ's) coming to judgment, which is called so in this place and others as 1 Tim. 6: 14, &c."‡

KUTTNER, on 2 Thess. 2: 8: "The coming of Messiah, glorious in its splendor and majesty." Such, he affirms, is the meaning of the passage.§

SALMASIUS, died 1653. A French historian and critic of uncommon abilities and immense erudition. He dwells at considerable length upon the passage, refuting Grotius, and showing the absurdity of understanding a literal advent in the beginning of the chapter, and a spiritual one at the 8th verse, in which the apostle is bringing out the *apodosis* of his statement: "The apostle returned to the point whence he had started, and expresses the results of his reasoning which

* Inst. B. iii., ch. 20.   † Quick's Synodocon, p. 226.
‡ Philologia Sacra, p. 562.   § Hypomnemata in loc., p. 465.

14*

had so far been explanatory." He then adds: "We have received in the same manner the name of the coming of the Lord * * * it is not true that Paul in the limits of the same discourse was so wandering as to commence to speak concerning one coming of Christ, and end in speaking of another, * * * from whence ἐπιφάνεια, when applied to Christ, in my opinion, is always used to denote the *last* coming of Christ."*

SCHOETTGEN writes, "επιφανης, that manner of coming which bursts brilliantly upon the eyes of all, the majesty and exceeding splendor of which no one can deny."†

FERGUSON, died 1714. "He (Christ) shall utterly destroy him, that is, utterly abolish, enervate and make void;—and that with the brightness of his second coming, for the word rendered brightness is usually joined with his coming to judgment." So he explains the passage under consideration.‡

MATHEW HENRY says, "The apostle assures the Thessalonians that the Lord would consume and destroy him; (i. e. the Antichrist,) the consuming of him precedes his final destruction, and that is by the spirit of his mouth, by his word of command; the pure word of God accompanied by the Spirit of God, will discover this mystery of iniquity, and make the power of Antichrist to consume and waste away; and in due time it shall be totally and finally destroyed, and this will be by the brightness of Christ's coming. NOTE.—The coming of Christ to destroy the wicked will be with peculiar and eminent lustre and brightness."§

DR. WHITBY.—This bold Post-m. virtually allows the literal construction to be the most natural and proper sense to attach to the phrase "coming," in the first verse, but shuns construing the word in the same sense in verse 8th. Considering, he says, the uniform use of the phrase παρο·σια

---

* Vide Commentary. † Hebrew Commentary, p. 846.
‡ Com. on the Epistles 1656. § Henry's Com

Χριστον in the first Epistle, " it may be thought more **reasonable** to refer this passage to the same (i. e., the second personal) advent."

WESTMINSTER ASSEMBLY'S Annotators. On 2 Thess. 2, 'Destroy with the brightness of his coming,' that is, at the day of judgment, for then shall he come in flaming fire, taking vengeance, &c. Such is the early view of the English church.*

BISHOP JEWELL.—This reformer makes the "spirit of his mouth" to mean the gospel,—and then on the last clause, he thus writes: "The Lord shall come and shall make his enemies his footstool: then the sun shall be black as sackcloth, and the moon shall be like blood. Then shall Antichrist be quite overthrown * * * he will overthrow the whole power of Antichrist by his presence and by the glory of his coming."† So writes a great and good man who died in 1571.

DR. FULKE, died 1589. In his reply to the Rheimish Annotators, he thus writes: "St. Paul saith, 'The mystery of iniquity doth already work,' and shall not be utterly destroyed before the second coming of Christ. Seeing, therefore, it is impossible that one man could have continuance from the Apostle's time till the day of judgment, it is manifest that here is meant no one single man, but a continual succession."‡ This, doubtless, is the proper view of this predicted Antichrist.

DR. HAMMOND, died 1660. An Anti-m. Though he wrests the text from its proper application, yet he renders 2 Thess. 2:8, "By the breath of his own mouth, and by the appearing of his own presence."§

AUGUSTUS CALMET. Born 1672, died 1757. A man of vast erudition, and a voluminous writer On the Antichrist

* Bonar's Com. and King., p. 360
† Vide Commentary
‡ Church in Middle Ages, p. 25.
§ Works, vol. iii, p. 678.

he writes: "Our Saviour in the gospel describes the times that shall precede his coming as times of war, famine, and rebellion, and says that all this is but the beginning of sorrows. Then the just shall be given up into the hands of the wicked and put to death by them. Many good men shall be offended, and the abomination of desolation shall be seen in the Holy Place. The calamities which will then happen will be so extreme, that if they were not to be shortened no one would be saved; but for the elects' sake they will be shortened. Then shall arise false Christs and false prophets, and shall show great signs and wonders, insomuch that if it were possible, they should deceive the very elect. After all this the Son of man shall appear in all the brightness of his majesty."* Calmet was a Frenchman, and a Roman Catholic.

JOHN MILTON. On the signs of the last advent, he says: "The peculiar signs are, first, an extreme recklessness and impiety, and an almost universal apostasy. Luke 18: 18, 'When the Son of man cometh, shall he find faith in the earth?' 2 Thess. 2: 3, 'That day shall not come, except there come a falling away first.' Compare also 1 Tim. 4: 1. 'That man of sin shall be revealed, the son of perdition,' verse 8, 'And then shall that wicked be revealed, whom the Lord shall consume with the spirit of his mouth, and shall destroy with the brightness of his coming.'"† Milton evidently understood this in the literal sense.

DR. ADAM CLARKE, though a Post-millennialist, still seemingly dissatisfied with his own explanation, quotes Bishop Newton, observing of him, that "The principal part of modern commentators follow his steps." But he is forced to admit the Pre-millennial view of the passage. In his preface to 2 Thess. he allows the destruction of the Man of Sin

---

* Dictionary, fol. ed., vol. i, p. 143.
† Christian Doctrine, vol ii, chap. 33, p. 213.

to be "accomplished by a visible and extraordinary interposition of the power of Christ in the government of the world," and in Rev. chap. 17th, on verse 17, speaking of the delusions and idolatries of the Latin Church, and her defence by the ten kings, he says: " But this deplorable state of the world is not perpetual, it can only continue till every word of God is fulfilled upon his enemies; and when this time arrives, (which will be that of Christ's second advent,) then shall the Son of God slay that wicked with the spirit of his mouth, and destroy him with the brightness of his coming."*
We pause here to ask, " Is not Christ's *second* advent, his *last* advent?" Heb. 9 : 27. And where then is there room for the conversion of the world? Surely that Millennium in which the Man of Sin exists cannot be desirable.

JOHN BUNYAN. The Presbyterian Review, of Scotland, a Pre-millennial organ, observes: " The Anti-christian power is to be cut off in judgment, not merged into the church,—'the destroyers of the earth are devoted to destruction.' Rev. 11 : 18. Bunyan's Pilgrim saw at the house Beautiful. 'The sword with which the Lord will kill the Man of Sin, in the day that He shall rise up to the prey.' Zeph. 3 : 8. That 'sword' seems even now preparing, and already do we descry its distant gleam, warning us of its speedy descent, for the terms, ' I come quickly,' augur not long delay."

ROBERT FLEMING, the elder, born in Lothian, A. D. 1630, and minister at Rotterdam. He says, on 2 Thess. 2: "That this prophecy should now want an accomplishment, or Antichrist be yet to come, is a thing most repugnant to sacred truth; since it is sure that mystery of iniquity even in the times of the Apostles did begin to work, and what then for a time withheld his coming, the heathen empire of Rome, hath long since been taken out of the way, which caused some Christians in those days to wish the standing and con-

---

*Vide Clarke's Comments.

tinuance of that empire, from the terror they had of that adversary who, according to the word they knew, was to fill his room! Yea, do we not find the church's trial from Antichrist should be the most sore and lasting trial of the church under the New Testament? which after her began breathing from heathenish persecution, was to continue for many ages, wherein the word is most express and clear that the rise and fall of this enemy should be gradual and not at once; whose beginning and first appearance might be traced to the first times of the church, and his close and final ruin near the second coming of Christ, by the brightness whereof he shall be destroyed?"*

BLOOMFIELD. This learned commentator on 2 Thess. 2: 8, of the word ἐπιφάνεια therein used, honestly observes that, "It is especially suitable as here to his (Christ's) final advent to judgment."†

ROBERT FLEMING, JR., 1701. "And besides these things, seeing the twelve hundred and sixty days are the whole time of the Papal authority, which is not to be totally destroyed until the great and remarkable appearance of Christ upon the pouring out of the seventh vial; and that therefore Christ will have the honor of destroying him finally himself; therefore we may certainly conclude that it must take up some centuries of years to carry on this abomination that maketh desolate. For though the Lord will gradually consume or waste this great adversary by the spirit of his mouth, yet he will not sooner abolish him than 'by the appearing of his own presence,' as I choose to render and understand the words, 2 Thess. 2: 8."‡

BISHOP NEWTON. "But how much soever *the Man of Sin* may be exalted, and how long soever he may reign, yet at last 'the Lord shall consume *him* with the spirit of his

---

* Vide **Fulfilling** of Scripture.   † Recensio Synopt. *in loc.*
‡ Rise and Fall, &c., p. 32.

mouth and destroy him with the brightness of his coming.' This is partly taken from Isa. 11 : 4, ' and with the breath of his lips shall he slay the wicked one ;' where the Jews put an emphasis upon the words, *'the wicked one,'* as appears from the Chaldee, which renders it, '*He shall destroy the wicked Roman.*' If the two clauses, as said in the note on verse 8, relate to two different events, the meaning is, ' That the Lord Jesus shall gradually consume him with the free preaching of the gospel; and shall utterly destroy him at his second coming in the glory of the Father.' The former began to take effect at the Reformation, and the latter will be accomplished in God's appointed time. The Man of Sin is now upon the decline, and he will be totally abolished when Christ shall come in judgment."*

Dr. Jebb, died 1786. This eminent scholar first translates the words thus : " Whom the Lord Jesus will waste away with the breath of his mouth, and will utterly destroy with the bright appearance of his coming." He exhibits Dan. 7 : 26, as a parallel, and remarks that there is an advance in the sense, " the bright appearance of the Lord's coming " being a manifest rise above the " breath of his mouth;" and that " a similar progress is observable in the words *consume* and *destroy;* and, indeed, it is demanded by the laws of parallelism." Having explained the difference between the words, he adds : " It may not be improbable that the apostasy is first to be gradually counteracted by the diffusion of Christian truth, and then to be ultimately put down and annihilated by the last triumphant advent of the irresistible Messiah."†

Charles Wesley evidently would be understood in a literal sense when he thus sings :

> " Yes, we know our Lord will come—
> Smite the Antichrist of Rome ;
> All his plagues and judgments pour,
> Earth accurst with fire devour.

---

* On Prophecy, Dis. xxii. † Sacred Literature, pp. **151, 812.**

> But the curse shall soon remove;
> But the incarnate God of love,
> Sitting on his throne, shall show
> Earth renewed is heaven below."*

Dr. SCOTT.—After speaking of the wasting of Romanism by the gospel, since the Reformation, he thus comments " He will shortly destroy the whole Papal authority, and all obstinately attached to it, by the brightness of his coming, to spread the gospel through the nations; and he will finally condemn and punish with everlasting destruction all the actors in this grand delusion, when he shall come to judge the world." Scott is thus driven to refer the term, in its ultimate sense, to the day of judgment.†

Dr. WATTS.—We have not his prose writings, but by transposition of his hymns we gather the following sentiments. On the "Fall of Babylon," Rev. 15: 3; 16: 19; 17: 6; and 18: 20, 21, he says, that the stone in the angel's hand is a type of the harlot city, and as he, standing, dreadfully sinks the millstone in the flood, so terribly shall Babel sink and never rise again; her crimes speedily awakening the fury of God, she that rules the earth, drunk with the blood of martyrs, shall fulfill her plagues and drink the ready mixed cup of wrath to the dregs. Psa. 65, and Isa. 63: 4–7. On the ruin of Antichrist" he sings that God arrayed in terror, will fulfill the request of his afflicted saints in distress in Babylon, giving the promised rest in dreadful glory, and revealing his love with Almighty wrath. He will lift his banner where Antichrist has stood, and the mystic city shall be a field of blood. His patience wearied, and there being no help in his gospel, his heart studies just revenge, and bringing the day of his redeemed, he bids his fury go forth swift and fatal as the lightning, and crushes his foes with his own arm alone. Babel shall reel beneath the stroke of his devouring sword and stagger to the ground.

* Vide Hymns, vol. 2, p. 123. † Vide notes *in loc.*

"Thine honor, O victorious King,
Thine own right hand shall raise,
While we thine awful vengeance sing
And our Deliverer's praise."*

JOHN FLETCHER, of Madely, in his "Letter on the Prophecies, supposed to have been addressed to John Wesley, says, "Give me leave here, Rev. Sir, to propose to you a thing that many will look on as a great paradox, but has yet sufficient ground in Scripture to raise the expectation of every Christian who sincerely looks for the coming of the Lord—I mean the great probability, that in the midst of this grand revolution, which will destroy Rome, our Lord Jesus will suddenly come down from heaven, and go himself, conquering and to conquer." * * * "Nay, the apostle goes a great deal further; for in the same chapter, 2 Thess. 2, he assures us that the Lord will destroy the Man of Sin by the brightness of his presence. Can anything be plainer?"†

JONATHAN EDWARDS, D. D., though a Post-millennialist, says, "The destruction of Antichrist is called Christ's second coming. 2 Thess. 2: 8. And then shall that wicked be revealed whom the Lord, &c. See also Dan. 7: 13, 14, where Christ's coming to set up his kingdom on earth, and to destroy Antichrist, is called coming with the clouds of heaven." And of this coming he admits, "And this is more like Christ's last coming to judgment than any of the preceding dispensations so called—the dispensation is so much greater and more universal, and so much more like the day of judgment with respect to the whole world."‡

JOSEPH SUTCLIFFE, a noted English Methodist and Premillennialist, says: "Antichrist, whom he (Christ) will gradually consume by republishing the pure gospel, and

---

* Hymns, pp. 65, 29, 56, 59.   † Letter, 1775.
‡ Edwards on Redemption, pp. 380, 390.

totally destroy by the vengeance of his appearing. In this interpretation the primitive Fathers nearly all concur."*

WILLIAM JENKS, D. D., in the Comprehensive Commentary. On 2 Thess. 2, "The fall or ruin of the Anti-christian state is declared, verse 8. The head is called that wicked one or that lawless person . * * * * The consuming of him precedes his final destruction, and that is by the pure word of God, accompanied with the spirit of God, * * * and in due time it shall be totally and finally destroyed, and this will be by the brightness of Christ's coming. NOTE.—The coming of Christ to destroy the wicked will be with peculiar glory and eminent lustre and brightness." These last are *Henry's* words.

PROF. GAUSSEN.—"Gentlemen, I call your attention to the precious and sacred doctrine of our Fathers, * * the doctrine is, that Rome is the Babylon of which John speaks; the Pope the Man of Sin, the Son of perdition of whom Paul speaks; Popery, the little horn of which Daniel speaks."

"Nothing is so mighty as this doctrine for directly combatting Rome. Just as we lose time, if in preaching Jesus, we content ourselves with describing his virtues instead of saying: He is the Christ! so we lose much time, if in refuting the Pope, we content ourselves with showing his heresies and his crime, instead of saying: He is the Man of Sin! It is not only a weapon of controversy, but it contains for the pious mind great consolation. The Pope here preaches Christ to us: since at the end of the reign of the Man of Sin, the Scriptures always point us to that of our Redeemer, his glorious coming, our gathering together unto him, (2 Thess. 2: 1,) the blessed Millennium, and the reign of the saints."†

DR. DAVID NELSON.—Of the Antichrist he says: "His

---

* Introduction to Christianity, p. 126, 1801.
† Vide Popery an argument for the truth, &c.

career was to continue for twelve hundred and **sixty years;** for one thousand two hundred and three score **days;** for a time and times and the dividing of times; for forty and two months. Many praying people think that the judgment is now sitting, or about to sit. The last item is yet to take place. It is to come to pass hereafter. One like the Son of man; yea, one who was born one of the sons of men, will take possession of the whole earth. His kingdom will never be overturned. The greatness of the kingdom under the whole heaven shall be given to the people of the saints of the Most High." On the judgment of the Roman power, he says: "Those hours of interest and of terror (which he makes to be awful visitations of dreadful judgments,) are before us, and we do not know but they are just at hand."*

THOMAS WILLIAMS' Cottage Bible: notes, 2 Thess. 2, "That wicked (Macknight,) 'lawless one,' whom the Lord shall consume with the spirit—(Doddridge, 'breath,') of his mouth, 'which,' says Doddridge, 'shall kindle around him as a consuming flame, in which all his (Antichrist's) pomp and pride shall vanish.'" The author then refers the reader to a note on chapter 1, verse 19, as explanatory of this. It reads: "Hopkins explains this as implying, not only banishment but positive punishment, as it were, by the lightning of his eye. We think, with Macknight, that it is an allusion to the glory of the Shechinah, from which a flame came out and destroyed Nadab and Abihu, and afterwards, 250 of Korah's company."†

DR. JOHN CUMMING. On 2 Thess. 2: 8. "And then shall that wicked be revealed whom the Lord shall consume with the spirit of his mouth"—the wasting of Rome first,—"and destroy with the brightness of his ($\pi\alpha\rho ουσ ία$) personal appearance." What does this passage prove? That the great apostasy predicted by St. Paul was to reign during the

---

* Cause and Cure of Infidelity, pp. 328, 332.   † Vide Cottage Bible

whole period from Christ's first to his second advent, and that this hoary apostasy is to be consumed and utterly destroyed only by the personal advent and appearance of the Son of God."*

DR. THOMAS CHALMERS. On the Antichrist he says,— "Let us wait the coming of our Lord, who will destroy all adversaries, and will dissipate every darkening influence by the brightness of his appearance. * * * I desire to cherish a more habitual and practical faith than heretofore, in that coming which even the first Christians were called to hope for with all earnestness, even though many centuries were to elapse, ere the hope could be realized; and how much more we, who are so much nearer to this great fulfillment, than at the time they believed."†

THE OXFORD DIVINES. No. 20 of the Oxford Tracts. "With Rome, alas, a union is impossible. Their communion is infected with heresy; we are bound to flee it as a pestilence. They have established a lie in the place of God's truth; and by their claim of immutability in doctrine cannot undo the sin they have committed. They cannot repent. Popery must be destroyed. It cannot be reformed."‡

DAVID BROWN, the eminent Post-m., of Scotland, writes: "There can be no doubt, that the whole passage admits of a consistent and good explanation on the view of it above given—i. e. the Pre-millennarian view. Nor is this view confined to Pre-millennialists. Those of our elder divines who looked upon the Millennium as past already, and considered the destruction of Antichrist as the immediate precursor of the eternal state, understood this "coming of the Lord," to destroy Antichrist, of his second personal coming. There are other opponents of the Pre-millennial theory, who explain this coming to destroy the Man of Sin, of Christ's

---

* Apoc. Sketches, 1st Series. † Sab. Scrip. Readings, vol. i. p. 311
‡ Oxford Tracts, American ed. p. 136.

second coming. They make " the apostasy," " the Man of Sin," " the lawless one," here spoken of, to embrace all the evil, apostacy, and opposition to Christ, which are to exist till the consummation of all things; in which case the destruction of it will of course not be till the second advent. In neither of these views, however, can I concur."*

Dr. James Buchanan, thus solemnly writes : " We are differently situated now from the disciples in the apostolic age. They were told that the coming of the Lord would not take place until the Man of Sin was revealed. That was an event which must happen first; and it is the only event that is there mentioned as necessarily intervening betwixt the first and second coming of the Saviour. And if Antichrist has appeared, if the Man of Sin has been revealed, then there is no part of Scripture that gives any assurance that the Son of man may not very soon appear. O, to be ready! having our loins girt about, and our lights burning, as servants waiting for the coming of the Lord." †

Horatius Bonar, D. D., thus sums up the argument· " The following things are undeniable :

" It was of the literal second advent that the Apostle had written in his first epistle, making mention of it six times in the course of five brief chapters.

" It was the literal second advent that the Thessalonians were expecting. We have no evidence that they knew of any other; but whether this is the case or not, they were expecting nothing but the personal coming.

" It was some mistake as to the approach or arrival of that advent that had caused their trouble and alarm.

" It was to correct their mistake as to the *time* of this same advent that the Apostle wrote his second epistle, in which he mentions that event six times.

" It was *not* to tell them that there was no such advent as

*Brown on 2d Adv., 2d ed. p. 455.   † Warning against Popery, p. 25.

they were expecting, that he wrote, nor that the promised advent was altogether spiritual and figurative.

"It was to repeat his declarations as to the certainty of that literal advent, but also to inform them that there was a certain event between them and it.

"It was to tell them that as soon as that intervening event had come to pass, then that very advent which they had been expecting, that very advent which had been troubling them, that very advent which seemed to be waiting for the accomplishment of the one intervening event, would certainly come."*

Dr. Elliott says: "In effect, few Anti-premillennarian expositors contest the personal character of the advent in verse 1. Alike Whitby allows this, and also Scott, Brown, and others. On what principle, then, can they have justified to themselves the giving of it in verse 8, a quite different meaning; whether, as Whitby, that of Christ's coming *providentially* to destroy Jerusalem; or as Scott, Faber, and Brown, that of his coming still providentially, not personally, to inflict judgment on the apostate Roman Empire? On none most assuredly but that of escaping from the Pre-millennial inference necessarily consequent on their giving the word the same meaning. I say, necessarily consequent. For admitting the παρουσια to be Christ's second personal coming, it follows instantly and necessarily that there can intervene no Millennium of universal holiness and Gospel triumph before it."†

Dr. Duffield remarks: "The argument, therefore, we think is irresistible. It may be now summed up in a few words. The Apostle in the text is speaking of the personal coming of Jesus Christ, for he uses two words, neither of which is ever used in a figurative or metaphorical sense in the New Testament. If neither, when separately used, can

* Coming and Kingdom, p. 340. † Horæ Apoc., vol iv., p. 178.

be metaphorically understood to denote a spiritual advent, much less can both when united. If the words 'the shining forth or appearance of his presence,' do not mean the visible personal revelation or manifestation of himself, it is impossible to employ terms that can express it. Human language is utterly incapable of being interpreted on any fixed and definite principles whatever, if it be not a literal personal manifestation and coming. But this glorious personal manifestation or coming, takes place at the time, and for the express purpose, of the destruction of Popery or Antichrist, which it is conceded must take place before the Millennial day of prosperity. It follows, therefore, that JESUS CHRIST COMES IN GLORY TO JUDGE THE WORLD BEFORE THE MILLENNIUM."*

* Duffield on Proph., p. 824.

CHAPTER XIII.

THE PRESENT CENTURY.

OUR WARRANT—CHURCH CREEDS.

"But thou, O Daniel, shut up the words and seal the book, even to the time of the end; many shall run to and fro, and knowledge shall be increased."—DAN. 12: 4.

"And this Gospel of the kingdom shall be preached in all the world, for a witness unto all nations, and then shall the end come."—MATT. 24: 14.

TRUTH, said Matthew Henry, is the daughter of time. And the wonderful development of prophetic truth in the present century abundantly sustains the sentiment. Dr. Adam Clarke on the passage in Daniel's twelfth chapter thus criticizes:

"Many shall endeavor to search out the sense, and knowledge shall be increased by these means, though the meaning shall not be fully known till the events take place. Then the seal shall be broken, and the sense become plain. This seems to be the meaning of this verse, though another has been put upon it, viz.: many shall run to and fro, preaching the Gospel of Christ, and therefore religious knowledge and true wisdom shall be increased. This is true in itself; but it is not the meaning of the prophet's words.'"*

MICHÆLIS, a German scholar and critic of the last century

---

* Vide Commentary.

says of this text: "Many shall give their sedulous attention to the understanding of these things." A French translation by the A. B. S., makes it: "When many shall run all over it or through it, and to them knowledge shall be increased." A marginal note in an old English Bible, published in the sixteenth century, reads: "Many shall run to and fro to search the knowledge of these mysteries." Dr. Coke comments as follows: "Many shall run to and fro at the time of the end, when the things here spoken of begin to be fulfilled, earnestly searching into this sealed book; and knowledge shall be increased; light will then be cast on the prophecies, so that the diligent inquirer shall be able to understand them more fully than they had ever been understood before. However dark and obscure any of the prophecies may now be, the time will come when they will be clear as if written with a sunbeam."*

Matthew Henry says: "Then—i.e., at the time of the end—this hid treasure shall be opened and many shall search into it, and dig for the knowledge of it as for silver. They shall run to and fro to inquire out copies of it, shall collate them and see that they be true and authentic; they shall read it over and over, shall meditate upon it, and run it over in their minds; they shall discourse of it and talk it over among themselves, and compare notes about it, if by any means they may sift out the meaning of it, and thus knowledge shall be increased. By consulting this prophecy on this occasion, they shall be lead to search other Scriptures which shall contribute much to their advancement in useful knowledge. Those things of God which are now dark and obscure, will hereafter be made clear and easy to be understood. Scripture prophecies will be expounded by the accomplishment of them, therefore they are told us before, that when they do come to pass we may believe."†

* Coke's Commentary. † Vide Comm.

Dr. Gill comments on the passage as follows: "Towards the time of the end appointed, many shall be stirred up to inquire into these things delivered in this book, and will spare no pains or cost to get a knowledge of them, and will read and study the Scriptures, and meditate on them, compare one passage with another, or spiritual things with spiritual, in order to obtain the mind of Christ; will carefully read the writings of such who have gone before them, and who have attempted any thing of this kind, and will go far and near to converse with persons that have any understanding of such things, and by such means, with the blessing of God upon them, the knowledge of this book of prophecy will be increased, things will appear clearer and plainer the nearer the accomplishment of them, and specially when prophecy and facts can be compared."*

Dr. Duffield, on the passage, after observing that the season in which Christ will appear, is described as one of great increase of knowledge, with Gesenius for authority, he says: "The word translated run to and fro is metaphorically used to denote investigation, close, diligent, accurate observation—just as the eyes of the Lord are said to run to and fro, Zech. 4 : 10. The reference is not to missionary exertions in particular, but to the study of the Scriptures, especially the sealed book of prophecy."†

With this inspired warrant, such being the meaning of the prophet's words,—and the time of the end having undoubtedly come, how exactly is this remarkable prophecy, together with the prediction of Sir Isaac Newton, fulfilled before our eyes! The doctrine of the Pre-millennial advent and personal reign of Christ on the earth, is in various ways, at the present time, leavening the churches of God, and many eyes are earnestly turned towards that blessed hope and glorious appearing, now near, even at the doors. For the information

---

* Vide Commentary. † Duffield on Prophecy, p. 378.

of our readers, we present a brief, though necessarily an incomplete list of Pre-millennial works now circulated, together with their authors.

In the opening of this century, Edward Irving, a remarkably eloquent though somewhat misguided divine, preached the doctrine extensively in England, became the author of various works on prophecy, and translated the works of Ben Ezra, a Spanish Jew, of South America, having the title of "The coming of Messiah in Majesty and Glory."—Irving's followers are still numerous.—Charlotte Elizabeth, late of England, author of "Principalities and Powers," and other works teaching Pre-millennialism; Edward Bickersteth, author of "A Guide to the Prophecies," "Signs of the Times," etc.; John Cox, a dissenter, author of "Immanuel Enthroned," "Coming and Kingdom of Christ," "Millennarian's Answer," and other works; Joseph D'Arcy Sirr, author of "The First Resurrection Considered," "Essays on the Coming of the Kingdom of God by Philo-Basillicus;" Matthew Habershon, author of "Shadows of the Evening," and "A Guide to the Study of Chronological Prophecy;" "Abdiel's Essays;" "W. S." author of "Shadows of the New Creation;" John Hooper on "the Doctrine of the Second Advent;" G. T. Noel, author of "The Prospects of the Christian Church;" J. A. Begg, author of "The Scriptural View," and other works; Dr. Keith on "Fulfilled Prophecy," "Signs of the Times," and other works; William Rogers, author of "Jesus Comes Quickly," etc.; "The Literalist," a series of volumes, containing Sermons on the Lord's Advent, by H. M. Villiers, E. Auriol, C. J. Goodhart, W. R. Freemantle, Thomas Hill, William Dalton, etc.; Henry Woodward, author of "Sermons and Essays on the Advent;" Dr. George Croly, author of "A Treatise on the Advent," also, a work on the "Apocalypse," etc.; Henry Drummond, M. P., author of "The Fate of Christendom;" George, Duke of Manchester, author of "The Finished

Mystery;" William Wogan, Esq., author of "The Proper Lessons;" Mr. Lillingstone, whose Sermons with others appear in a volume of Bloomsbury Lectures; Francis Paget, in published "Sermons on the Second Advent;" Frederick Fysh, author of a "Divine History of the Church;" William Thorp, author of "Destiny of the British Empire;" Viscount Mandeville, who has written a "Hebrew Commentary," advocating Pre-millennial views; the eloquent Henry Melville, author of "Sermons," etc.; Dr. Joseph Wolffe, an extensive traveler, preacher, and journalist; Alexander Dallas and Joseph Tyso, authors of some note; Bishop Van Mildert, as seen in the Boyle Lectures; the late W. H. Hewitson, missionary at Maderia, as seen in his Memoirs, by Baillie; William Pym, author of "Doctrine of the New Testament on the Second Advent;" J. H. Stewart, author of the "Duty of Prayer and Watchfulness;" Mourant Brock, author of "Glorification," &c.; Ridley Herschell, author of "The Work of the Messiah;" J. W. Brooks, author of "The Elements of Prophetical Interpretation," and other valuable works; T. R. Birks, a noted author of various works on "The Four Prophetic Empires," "The Millennium," "The First Resurrection," &c.; "Extracts on Prophecy," containing the writings of W. Burgh, S. R. Maitland, S. Madden, B. A. Simon, J. W. Campbell, W. Dodsworth, J. Fry T. Erskine, Esq., J. Keeble, and others on Millennarianism: J. E. Sabin, author; also Edward Gillson; "The Investigator," devoted to the exposition of prophecy and signs of the times; John B. Sumner, lord Bishop of Chester, as seen in the Investigator; Archdeacon Browne, author of "Charge to the Clergy;" Frere, T. P. Platt, Granville, Penn., translator of "The New Covenant," Mr. Wood, Mr. Marsh, Girdlestone, Hoare, East, and and also many others of note; Hugh McNeil, an eminent preacher, and author of "Sermons on the Advent;" Dr. J. A. McCaul, author of "Plain Sermons;" Robert Murray McCheyne, author of Sermons, Dr. Thomas

Chalmers, in his 'Sabbath Scriptural Readings," "Evidences of Christianity," and other works, (see memoirs by Dr. Tyng) ; George Gilfillan, author of "Bards of the Bible;" "The London Quarterly Journal of Prophecy," edited by an association of gentlemen, and an able advocate of the Pre-millennial advent ; Andrew Bonar, author of "Redemption Draweth Nigh ;" Horatius Bonar, who has written an able work in answer to David Brown, a Post-m. of Scotland, and who is the author of "Prophetic Landmarks," "The Morning of Joy," "The Apostolicity of Chilliasm," etc. ; William Anderson, a dissenter and author of eminence ; Dr. Candlish, of the Free Church of Scotland, who, in a Pastoral Letter, written in 1845, said, "God's church, in all her various branches, has had her attention turned more earnestly to the predicted events of the latter times, and the circumstances connected with that second coming of her great Head and Lord ;" James Scott, a noted author of various Millennarian works ; William Cunninghame, Esq., author of about twenty different works on Prophecy, etc., among which are, "Vindication of the Millennial Advent," "Exposition of the Apocalypse," "Dissertations on Prophecy," and "Fullness of the Times ;" "The Presbyterian Review," the organ of the Scottish Church, now established about twenty years, is devoted to the exposition of Millennarian principles, and a year or two since stated that " the belief of the Pre-millennial advent gains wide and rapid ground among us, and the circulation of Premillennial works in Scotland, is very great ;" Dr. Ebenezer Elliott, author of the " Horæ Apocalypticæ," a work of immense erudition, having now reached its fourth edition, and received the sanction and approval of Sir Lancelott Shadwell, Sir James Stephen, the two Bishops of Winchester and Calcutta, also the Archbishop of Canterbury ; **Dr. John Cumming**, the eloquent pulpit orator, of London, now the author of over a score of valuable works on the Scriptures, all of which, with many other works are being republished in America. The foregoing list embraces Great Britain alone, and is but a meagre one indeed, for good English authorities inform us that about seven hundred clergymen of the established church alone, in the United Kingdom, teach from their pulpits the speedy advent and personal reign of the blessed Redeemer.

Other writers are, Dr. James Carlyle, of Dublin, author of "First and Second Advent," and "Latter-day Pamphlets;" Hermann Olshausen, D. D., of Germany, author of a "Commentary on the New Testament;" Dr. Capadose, of Amsterdam, who in a speech at the Free Church General Assembly, 1848, recommended that the doctrine of the personal reign be woven into the church creeds, confessions, etc.; Hengstenberg, the German commentator and author; a periodical called "The Watchman," established at Paris in 1831, and devoted to the subject of prophecy, said a few years ago, that many in that place had embraced Pre-millennialism.—The editor also makes reference to a society of pious women numbering about one hundred, and living in Paris, who receive and cherish from their ancestors an indubitable persuasion of Christ's second coming to establish his personal reign on earth."—Hans Wood, Esq., of Ireland, author of works on prophecy; Professor S. R. L. Gaussen, of Geneva, author of a work on "Inspiration," "Lectures on Popery," etc. In Wirtemburgh there is a Christian colony numbering hundreds, who look for the speedy advent of Christ; also another of like belief on the shores of the Caspian; the Molokaners, a large body of Dissenters from the Russian Greek church, residing on the shores of the Baltic— a very pious people, of whom it is said, "taking the Bible alone for their creed, the *norm* of their faith is simply the Holy Scriptures,"—are characterized by the "expectation of Christ's immediate and visible reign upon earth." In Russia the doctrine of Christ's coming and reign is preached to some extent, and received by many of the lower class. It has been extensively agitated in Germany, particularly in the south part among the Moravians. In Norway, charts and books on the advent have been circulated extensively, and the doctrine received by many. Among the Tartars in Tartary, there prevails an expectation of Christ's advent about this time. English and American publications on this doctrine have been sent to Holland, Germany, India, Ireland, Constantinople, Rome, and to nearly every missionary station on the globe. At the Turks Islands, it has been received to some extent among the Wesleyans. Mr. Fox, a Scottish missionary to the Teloogoo people, was a believer in Christ's soon coming. James McGregor Bertram, a Scottish missionary of the Baptist order at St. Helena, has sounded the cry extensively on that Island, making many converts and Pre millennialists; he has also preached it at South Africa at the missionary stations there. David N. Lord informs us that a large proportion of the missionaries who have gone from Great Britain to make known the Gospel to the heathen, and who are now laboring in Asia and Africa, are Millennarians;* and Joseph Wolffe, D. D., according to his Journals, between the years 1821 and 1845, proclaimed the Lord's speedy advent in Palestine, Egypt, on the shores of the Red Sea, Mesopotamia, the Crimea, Persia, Georgia, throughout the Ottoman Empire, in Greece, Arabia, Turkistan, Bokhara, Affghanistan, Cashmere, Hindostan, Thibet, in Holland, Scotland and Ireland, at Constantinople, Jerusalem, St. Helena, also on shipboard in the Mediterranean, and at New York city, to all denominations. He declares he has preached among Jews, Turks, Mohammedans, Parsees, Hindoos, Chaldeans, Yeseedes, Syrians, Sabeans, to Pachas Sheiks, Shahs, the kings of Organtsh and Bokhara, the Queen of Greece, etc., and of his extraordinary labors, the Investigator says· "No individual has, perhaps, given greater publicity to the doctrine of the second coming of the

* Journal, July, 1850,

Lord Jesus Christ, than has this well-known missionary to the world. Wherever he goes he proclaims the approaching advent of the Messiah in glory."*

In America the prevalence of Pre-millennialism is very considerable, and the interest on this question, in spite of much indifference and opposition, is steadily increasing. William Miller and his associates, though sadly mistaken in their attempts to ascertain the time of the Lord's return, have done much to call the attention of Christians to the nature and nearness of that glorious appearing which is the consummation of the believer's hope; and notwithstanding the errors and crudities which have often found currency among them, many individuals of standing and character might be named—editors, authors, and evangelists—who have labored earnestly and judiciously to spread far and wide the news of the Saviour's return. The "Adventists," in their various subdivisions and branches, number many thousands of adherents, including some six or eight hundred ministers. They issue half a dozen weekly and monthly periodicals, devoted more or less fully to the interpretation of prophecy and the signs of the times; besides a multitude of tracts and pamphlets of more or less importance, which are circulated in different parts of America and elsewhere.

The Congregational Journal admitted, in 1851, that "in various ways the leaven of Millenarianism is working in the community, some in nearly all denominations being its advocates."

Among the many American authors and advocates of this doctrine, whose works and faith have been known for years, some of whom have fallen asleep, may be named Dr. David Nelson, author of "The Cause and Cure of Infidelity;" Bishop Henshaw, author of "The Second Advent;" J. S. C. Abbott, the popular writer and histo-

---

* Investigator, vol. v. p. 88.

rian;* Orrin Rogers, of Philadelphia, publisher of various valuable Essays on the Kingdom of Christ; Judge Joel Jones, formerly president of Girard College, author of "Jesus and the Coming Glory;" Dr. George Duffield, author of "Dissertations on the Prophecies," and "Reply to Stuart;" James Inglis, editor of "The Witness," "Way-marks in the Wilderness," etc.; Charles Beecher, author of "Letters on Pre-millennialism;" John King Lord, author of "Sermons," inculcating this doctrine; William Ramsey, author of a work on "The Pre-millennial Advent;" Thomas Wickes, author of "An Exposition of the Apocalypse;" David N. Lord, editor for thirteen years—1848-61—of an able Quarterly, the "Theological and Literary Journal," and author of a valuable "Commentary on the Apocalypse;" Elisha Putnam, author of "The Crisis, or Last Trumpet;" Eleazer Lord, author of "The Messiah in Moses and the Prophets;" R. C. Shimeall, author of "The Age of the World and Signs of the Times," and "Our Bible Chronology;" Charles K. Imbrie, author of "The Kingdom of God;" Edward Winthrop, author of "Signs of the Times," "Letters on Prophecy," and a valuable "Premium Essay on Prophetic Symbols;" Dr. Jas. Lillie, author of " The Perpetuity of the Earth," and "Lectures on Thessalonians;" D. D. Buck, author of "Our Lord's Great Prophecy," Matt. xxiv., xxv.; H. F. Hill, author of "The World to Come, or The Saints' Inheritance;" J. C. Waller, author of "The Speedy Coming of Christ;" J. Oswald, author of "The Kingdom which shall not be Destroyed;" Alfred Bryant, author of "Views of Millenarianism;" Henry Dana Ward, author of a "History of the Millennium," "The Kingdom of God," and other works. To these publications may be added an aggregate of about a hundred thousand volumes of some twenty different books by Dr. John

* See New York Evangelist, January 12, 1843.

Cumming, of London, which have been reprinted and circulated in America; besides many of the works of Dr. H. Bonar and others;—through all of which runs like a silver thread, "that blessed hope and the glorious appearing of the great God and our Saviour Jesus Christ."

Among more recent authors may be mentioned Dr. J. A. Seiss, author of "The Last Times," "The Parable of the Virgins," and for several years the able conductor of "The Prophetic Times;" J. H. Brookes, author of "Maranatha," and other works; Dr. Willis Lord, author of "The Blessed Hope;" I. C. Wellcome, author of a "History of the Second Advent Message;" J. Litch, author of "Christ Yet to Come;" Dr. Nathaniel West, editor of "Pre-millennial Essays;" Edmond de Pressensé, of Paris, author of "Jesus Christ, His Life, Times, and Work;" H. L. Hastings, author of "The Great Controversy between God and Man;" Stephen H. Tyng, Jr., author of "He will Come;" and D. L. Moody, reports of whose sermons on "The Second Coming of Christ" have been widely scattered.

Many other preachers and authors of note may be named among the advocates of this important doctrine, such as Nathan Lord, President of Dartmouth College; Prof. A. Hopkins, of Williamstown; Prof. N. N. Whiting, translator of the New Testament; J. H. Hopkins, Bishop of Vermont; W. W. Niles, Bishop of New Hampshire; Thomas H. Vail, Bishop of Kansas; Dr. J. T. Barclay, missionary at Jerusalem; Benjamin Wilson, author of "The Emphatic Diaglott;" Dr. Richard Newton, long editor of the periodicals of the American Sunday School Union; Edwin Burnham, the well-known evangelist; Henry Jones, Elon Galusha, F. G. Brown, Henry M. Parsons, William P. Paxson, A. F. Bailey, George F. Pentecost, S. H. Tyng, A. J. Gordon, George

C. Lorimer, Thomas H. Stockton, W. I. Buddington, and a multitude of others who give the trumpet no uncertain sound.

A minister of the Protestant Episcopal Church named to the writer no less than forty-four of his brother clergymen, with twelve of the bishops of that Church, all of whom were known to be Pre-millennialists. Bishops George D. Cummins and W. R. Nicholson, of the Reformed Episcopal Church, hold the same view, which is also advocated by the organ of that body, "The Protestant Churchman."

That class of Christian believers widely known in England as "Brethren," sometimes called "Plymouth Brethren," comprehending many intelligent, able, and faithful men and women, including persons of high and low estate, are scattered through America, and are, without known exceptions, believers in the Pre-millennial advent of our Lord; and, by voice and press, have labored to diffuse the doctrine in all parts of the globe.

It is worthy of remark that those workers, in various fields of Christian labor, whom God has most signally honored, are especially interested in this subject.

Among them may be mentioned Samuel Prideaux Tregelles, whose elaborate critical edition of the Greek Testament is one of the latest and best critical authorities; Henry Alford, Dean of Canterbury, whose critical editions of the New Testament in Greek and English, with notes, have won deserved celebrity; John P. Lange, whose massive Commentary on the Bible stands unequaled by any work of this generation; E. R. Craven, the American editor of Lange's Commentary on Revelation; A. R. Fausett, one of the authors of the "Critical and Practical Commentary on the Bible;" George V. Wigram, to whose patient care and munificent liberality we are indebted for "The Englishman's Greek Concordance," "The Englishman's Hebrew Concordance," and "The Hebraist's Vade Mecum;" Henry Craik, the associate of George Müller, and author of "Hebrew Charts," and other critical publications; Charles F. Hudson, author of "A Critical Greek and English Concordance of the New Testament;" J. B. Rotherham, author of "The Emphasized New Testament;" the late Mr. Bagster, whose admirable critical and biblical publications are known throughout the globe; Henry Bewley, from whose "Dublin Tract Depository" more than four hundred millions of tracts have been scattered through all lands; the Earl of Shaftesbury, so fruitful in all gracious and philanthropic labor; George Müller, of Bristol, through whose hands thousands of orphans receive from God their daily bread; Charles H. Spurgeon, of worldwide fame among the churches of Christ; Newman Hall, whose sermons, labors, and writings have exerted wide-spread influence; J. R. Macduff and J. C. Ryle, whose devotional and expository works have been a joy to many hearts; B. W. Newton, author of scripture expositions; Horatius Bonar, Sir Edward Denny, P. P. Bliss, and Ira D. Sankey, those masters of sacred poesy and hallowed song; Dr. and Mrs. Phœbe Palmer, Lord Radstock, the Earl of Cavan, Henry Varley, H. G. Guinness, E. P. Hammond, George C. Needham, H. Morehouse, D. W. Whittle, and D. L. Moody; with a multitude of other evangelists whose names are written in heaven;—all these and many others are firm believers in and faithful witnesses to this grand, important truth, that our Saviour Christ will come in person, and reign over earth redeemed.

Such is the extent and prominence given to the doctrines we advocate, and which are fast spreading among God's faithful servants. It is true that Millenarians do not all agree with regard to the nature and character of the Millennial age; but, as an English writer has properly said, "they differ as the small clocks in a town may differ from the town clock, not by the hour, but by the minute and second." Whatever be their views of the future reign of the Messiah, all agree, to a man, in believing that Christ will come in person, not at the end, but at the commencement of the Millennium.

Regarding their views of the nearness of that day, the following, from their pens, will show. Says Elliott:

"With regard to our present position, we have been led, as the result of our investigations, to fix it at but a short time from the end of the now existing dispensation and the expected second advent of Christ. This thought, when we seriously attempt to realize it, must be felt to be a very startling as well as solemn one. And for my own part, I confess to risings of doubt, and almost scepticism, as I do so. Can it be that we are come so near to the day of the Son of man that the generation now alive shall very possibly not have passed away before its fulfillment; yea, that perhaps even our own eyes may witness, without the intervention of death, that astonishing event of the consummation? The idea falls on my mind as almost incredible. The circumstance of anticipations having been so often formed quite erroneously heretofore of the proximity of the consummation, —for example, in the apostolic age, before the destruction of Jerusalem,—then during the persecutions of Pagan Rome,— then on the breaking up of the old Roman Empire,—then at the close of the tenth century,—then at and after the Reformation, and still later, even by writers of our own day; I say the circumstance of all these numerous anticipations having been formed and zealously promulgated of the iminence of the second advent, which, notwithstanding, have by the event itself been shown to be unfounded, strongly tends to confirm us in our doubt and incredulity. Yet, to rest in scepticism simply and altogether upon such grounds, would be evidently bad philosophy For these are causes that would operate always, and that would make us be saying, even up to the very eve and moment of the advent, 'Where is the promise of his coming?'

"Our true wisdom is to test each link of the chain of evidence by which we have been led to our conclusion, and see whether it will bear the testing; to examine into the causes of previous demonstrated errors on the subject, and see whether we avoid them; finally, to consider whether the signs of the times now present be in all the sundry points that prophecy points out so peculiar as to warrant a measure of confidence in our inference such as was never warranted before."*

Such are the solemn conclusions of this ripe scholar and profound student of Prophecy, after a candid review of the whole matter, and all that himself or others had written.

Mr. Lord, too, on Christ's kingdom and speedy coming says: "There are few, probably, who have considered how largely it is treated in the ancient prophets, the gospels, the epistles, and the Apocalypse; and who would not be surprised, were they to institute the enquiry, to find that a larger space is devoted to it than to Christ's birth, crucifixion, resurrection, ascension, and reign in heaven. There are few propositions that would be received with greater incredulity by thousands whose profession it is to interpret the sacred word, than that there are no future events more clearly revealed than that Christ is within a brief period to come from heaven in person, and visibly raise the sanctified who have died, and judge and accept those who are living, destroy the civil and ecclesiastical powers who usurp his rights, and persecute his people; and renewing the nations that survive, reign over them with his glorified saints through a long round of ages; and that the Scriptures give no other view of his advent, the events that are to attend it, or the kingdom in which he and his saints are to reign."†

* Horæ Apoc., vol. iv., p. 249.   † Vide Lord's Journal.

And William Cunninghame but speaks the sentiments and hopes of the vast majority, when of that grand epoch he thus writes: "This, I conceive, is the next great event that we are now to look for. So far as I can discern, no further signs are to be expected; as it seems to me we have entered into that last period of awful expectation, during which the church is likened unto ten virgins!"*

Such a faith is no novelty. On the contrary, the doctrine of a Post-millennial advent is so novel and modern that no Christian church has ever woven it into her creeds. The following will exhibit the faith of the Church in general, as set forth in her Forms, Creeds, Articles of Faith, etc., gathered from histories of all denominations and various other sources. It is worthy of observation, that while no church of which we know has woven into her creeds the doctrine of a spiritual advent and reign of Christ as connected with Post-millennialism, many, on the other hand, hold the opposite faith of a literal resurrection of the body, personal Pre-millennial coming, and reign of Christ in a visible kingdom on earth.

"*Cerinthian Church.*—A. D. 81.—*Tenets*—1. There is one God, the maker and preserver of all things.

"2. That Jesus Christ united both the manhood and the divinity, and is thereby able to reconcile all willing souls to God.

"3. That as deity was six days creating all things, and one day being as a thousand years with God, so in six thousand years will all the wicked, with all that is cursed on the world, be destroyed forever.

"4. That the seventh thousand years shall be the rest of Millennial glory, wherein the world shall be restored to its Eden state, and the righteous shall inherit it forever."†

---

* Cunninghame's Dissertations, p. 480.
† Jeffries' Chart of the churches.

Irenæus' Creed.—" The Church, though scattered over the whole world, even to the ends of the earth, receive from the apostles, and from their disciples that belief which is in one God * * and in one Jesus Christ * * and in the Holy Ghost, who proclaimed by the prophets the dispensations of God, the advent, birth of a virgin, passion, resurrection from the dead, and bodily ascension into heaven of the beloved Jesus Christ our Lord, and his coming from heaven in the glory of the Father, to *restore all things*, and to raise up the flesh of all mankind, &c." In a following chapter he speaks of this as the one voice of the church over the whole earth, whether in Germany, Spain, Gaul, the East, Egypt, Libya, or in the middle of the world.*

The Apostles' Creed.—" I believe in God, the Father Almighty, maker of heaven and earth. And in Jesus Christ, his only Son, our Lord, who was conceived of the Holy Ghost, born of the Virgin Mary, suffered under Pontius Pilate, was crucified, dead, and buried; he descended into hell; the third day He rose again from the dead; He ascended into heaven, and sitteth on the right hand of God, the Father Almighty; from thence He shall come to judge the quick and the dead. I believe in the Holy Ghost, the holy Catholic church, the communion of saints, the forgiveness of sins, the resurrection of the body and the life everlasting." This creed is of the first centuries, and is adopted by the Roman and English churches. The Waldenses also, fully received and endorsed it.

The Nicene Creed.—A. D. 325.—" He (Christ) ascended into heaven and sitteth on the right hand of God. And he shall come again with glory to judge both the quick and the dead, whose kingdom shall have no end." This is adopted by the Roman Catholic Church, and by others.

* Irenæus, Lib. i., chap. 2.

The Athanasian Creed.—" He sitteth on the right hand of the Father, God Almighty; from whence he shall come to judge the quick and the dead. At whose coming all men shall rise again with their bodies, and shall give account for their own works. And they that have done good shall go into life everlasting, &c." Adopted by the English Episcopal Church, and others. The three Creeds last given form the basis of almost all modern creeds, on the doctrines taught in them. The wording is often the same, or similar to these. Athanasius was of the fourth century.

The Westminster Assembly, 1643.—" As Christ would have us to be certainly persuaded that there shall be a day of judgment, both to deter all men from sin, and for the greater consolation of the godly in their adversity; so will he have that day unknown to men, that they may shake off all carnal security, and be always watchful, because they know not at what hour the Lord will come, and may be ever prepared to say, ' Come, Lord Jesus, come quickly.'—Amen."

The corresponding article in the Saybrook Platform is the same. In the Directory for Public Worship, ministers are taught to pray " For the propagation of the gospel and kingdom of Christ, to all nations; for the conversion of the Jews; the fullness of the Gentiles; the fall of Antichrist, and the hastening of the second coming of our Lord."

In the Shorter Catechism is the Assembly's Exposition of the Lord's Prayer; and on the words, " Thy kingdom come," we have the following : " In the second petition we pray that Satan's kingdom may be destroyed, and that the kingdom of grace may be advanced; ourselves and others brought into it; and *that the kingdom of glory may be hastened ;*" which is explained in the corresponding clause of the Larger Catechism thus: " We pray, that Christ would *hasten the time of his second coming*, and our reigning with him forever."

This, with but little alteration, is the confession of the

Presbyterian, Congregationalist, Burgher, Anti-Burgher, Covenanter, and Associated Reformed Presbyterian Churches in the United States.

The Savoy Confession, 1658.—This confession, originally adopted by the Congregational churches in England in 1658, was also adopted by the same order in New England 1670, and agrees in substance with the Westminster, and is throughout expressed in the same language, with very little variation. The article on the day of judgment and end of the world, agrees with the 32d article of the Saybook Platform, cited below.

The Saybrook Platform, 1708.—Article xxxii: "God hath appointed a day wherein he will judge the world in righteousness by Jesus Christ, in which day all persons that died upon the earth shall appear before the tribunal of Christ, to give an account of their thoughts, words and deeds, and to receive, according to what they have done in the body, whether it be good or evil." This is the same as the Westminster Assembly's corresponding article.

Mennonites and Reformed Mennonites.—"Art. iv: He (Christ) will come again to judge the living and the dead." "Art. xviii: Of the resurrection of the dead and the last judgment. Relative to the resurrection of the dead we believe and confess, agreeably to the Scriptures, that all men who have died and fallen asleep shall be awakened, quickened and raised on the last day." The ancient Mennonites held to the personal reign of Christ on the earth.

Episcopal Church.—This church is established by law in England, the highest officer being the King or Queen. The Archbishop of Canterbury, (next the highest) with the two Bishops of Winchester and Calcutta are Pre-millennialists.
"Grant, O Lord, that as we are baptized into the death

of thy blessed Son our Saviour Jesus Christ, so by continual mortifying our corrupt affections, we may be buried with him, and that through the grave and gates of death we may pass to our joyful resurrection for his merits, who died and was buried and rose again for us," etc.—*Easter Eve. Collect.*

"Through Jesus Christ our Lord, at whose second coming in glorious majesty to judge the world, the earth and the sea shall give up their dead; and the corruptible bodies of those who sleep in him shall be changed and made like unto his own glorious body, according to the working," &c.

"Beseeching thee, that it may please thee of thy gracious goodness shortly to accomplish the number of thine elect, *and to hasten thy kingdom*, that we, with all that are departed in the true faith of thy holy name, may have our perfect consummation, both in body and soul, in thy eternal and everlasting glory, through Jesus Christ our Lord.—Amen."—*Burial Service.*

The italicised words are omitted by the Episcopal Church in the United States.

Episcopal Church in the U. S. A.—Her standards of faith are similar to those of the English Episcopal. They dwell much upon the Advent and Resurrection, teach that system of Biblical interpretation which comes nearest to the letter, and hold that at the resurrection the new body must be raised up out of the ashes of the old, the personal identity of the man being retained. The Bishops McIlvaine and Hopkins, with the late Bishops Chase and Henshaw, advocate Premillennialism.

Creed. Art. iv: "Christ did truly rise from the dead, * * he ascended into heaven, and there sitteth until he return to judge all men at the last day."

Presbyterian Churches.—This is the established church in Scotland. Her Standards and Articles of Faith are the

Westminster Assembly's Larger and Shorter Catechisms &c. In the Directory for the worship of God, under the heads " Of public prayer before sermon," and " Of prayer after sermon," ministers are taught to pray for " the fall of Antichrist and the hastening of the second coming of our Lord," and for a " watching for the coming of our Lord Jesus Christ." Both these clauses are omitted in the Directory adopted by the Presbyterian churches in the United States.

Cumberland Presbyterian.—Art. xv : " That Christ, the judge of quick and dead, will, at the last day, reward the righteous and punish the finally impenitent."

Art. xvi : " That there will be a resurrection of the bodies, both of the just and unjust."

Reformed Presbyterian.—John Knox was her founder, and her Ecclesiastical Standards, subordinate to the Bible, are the Westminster Confessions and Catechisms.

Congregational Churches.—They adopt the Assembly's Catechisms and Confessions, and on the Advent, Resurrection, and Judgment, agree substantially with the Presbyterians.

Methodist Episcopal Church.—Article iii : " Christ did truly rise again from the dead, and took again his body, with all things appertaining to the perfection of man's nature, wherewith he ascended into heaven, and there sitteth until he return to judge all men at the last day." Their creeds are called " unalterable."

The African M. E. Church holds to similar views on the Advent and Judgment.

The Wesleyan Church's articles are about the same, articles iii agreeing verbatim. Articles xviii and xix teach the general resurrection of the dead, both of the just and unjust, and the general judgment at the end of the world.

The Jewish Synagogues.—Art. xii: "We believe in the coming of King Messiah, who is to accomplish for the world and Israel, all that the prophets have foretold concerning him."

Art. xiii: "We believe in the resurrection of the dead, when it shall please the Almighty to send his Spirit to revive those who sleep in the dust, and that the Creator in his own good time will regenerate the earth, and we constantly look forward to his (the Messiah's) coming."

Baptist Churches.—Art. xvi: "God hath appointed a day in which he will judge the world in righteousness by Jesus Christ, to whom all power and judgment is given of the Father." This is her confession of faith.

Art. xvi: "Of the world to come. That the end of this world is approaching; that at the last day Christ will descend from heaven, and raise the dead from the grave to final retribution; that a solemn separation will then take place, &c." This is the declaration of faith of this church in New Hampshire, also in most other states.

Free Will Baptists.—"Doctrines and Usages. At some future period known only to God, there will be a resurrection both of the righteous and the wicked, when there will be a general judgment, etc."

Six Principle Baptists.—"Resurrection of the dead. The doctrine of the resurrection is the great pillar of the whole gospel system. The resurrection of Christ from the dead is that foundation upon which all Christianity depends, &c." They hold also to "The eternal judgment" as one essential tenet.

English Seventh Day Baptists.—Art. vii : " We believe that there will be a general resurrection of the bodies, both of the just and of the unjust.

Art. viii : We believe there will be a day of judgment for both the righteous and the wicked, etc."

Dutch Reformed Church.—Art. xxxvii : " On the judgment. Finally, we believe according to the Word of God, when the time appointed by the Lord—which is unknown to all creatures—is come, and the number of the elect complete, that our Lord Jesus Christ will come from heaven corporeally and visibly as he ascended, with great glory and majesty. * * Therefore we expect that great day with a most ardent desire, to the end that we may fully enjoy the promises of God in Christ Jesus our Lord. Even so, come Lord Jesus."

The German Reformed have similar views, and maintain that " The Bible is above all human authority, and to it alone must every appeal be made."

Evangelical Lutheran Church.—They adopt entire the Confession of the Augsburg Reformers.

Art. viii : " On the final judgment. We believe that at the end of the world, Christ will appear for judgment; that he will raise all the dead, &c."

Friends, or Quakers.—The Society of Friends believe that there will be a resurrection both of the righteous and the wicked, and that God will judge the world by that man whom he hath ordained, even Jesus Christ, the Lord.

Church of God.—Art. xxiv : " She believes in the personal coming and reign of Jesus Christ." Scriptures quoted.

Art. xxv : " She believes in the resurrection of the dead, both of the just and the unjust; that the resurrection of the just will precede the resurrection of the unjust; that the first will take place at the beginning, and the second at the end of the Millennium." Scriptures quoted.

Art. xxvi: "She believes in the creation of new heavens and a new earth." Scriptures are quoted at the end of each article.

The Christian Church.—She adopts articles corresponding with the Apostle's creed, and in the Memoirs of Elijah Shaw the writer says: "In common with other believers, the Christians everywhere believe and teach that Jesus Christ will really and visibly appear again. * * This is called his glorious appearing. It is neither figurative, nor spiritual, nor mystical, but real, literal and visible."*

Among the other churches and sects, the Evangelical Association, in Art. xxi, says: "We believe that Jesus Christ will come in the last day to judge all mankind by a righteous judgment," &c. Restorationists "believe in a future judgment." The Universalists hold to the same, and to "a final resurrection of the dead," but in a figurative sense, while the Swedenborgians and Shakers, as also Universalists, deny any future personal advent of Christ to this earth. The River Brethren, as also the United Brethren in Christ, say that in common with others, "they believe that Jesus Christ, who died on the cross for us, &c., shall come again at the last day to judge the quick and dead." The Moravians make much of the advent, and "at the grave-yard express joyful hopes of immortality and resurrection." The "Bible Christians" believe in "Jesus Christ, whom, say they, we shall meet in the air," and the Campbellites, or Disciples of Christ, affirm also their faith in " a glorious resurrection and blissful immortality," quoting Rev. 22: 20, He who testifieth these things saith, surely I come quickly, amen, even so come, Lord Jesus."

* Memoirs, p. 336.

It is worthy of note in this connection, that the early founders and eminent divines of the four most numerous and evangelical, as well as the oldest denominations in this country, viz.: the Episcopalians, the Baptists, the Presbyterians or Congregationalists, and the Methodists, were mostly Pre-millennialists. See the Confession of Faith presented to King Charles, the general Catechism of King Edward's time, the Westminster divines, and the writings of Toplady, Wesley, Fletcher, Coke and others. And with these and the general voice of the church as set forth in our volume, we now ask our readers to compare the Declaration of Principles by the Mutual General Conference of Adventists at Albany, N. Y., April 29th, 1845, who say that "among other doctrines they hold that the Scriptures teach the following important truths:—

"I. That the heavens and earth which are now, by the word of God, are kept in store, reserved unto fire against the day of judgment and perdition of ungodly men. That the day of the Lord will come as a thief in the night, in the which the heavens shall pass away with a great noise, and the elements shall melt with fervent heat, the earth also, and the works that are therein, shall be burned up. That the Lord will create new heavens and a new earth, wherein righteousness—that is, the righteous—will forever dwell, (2 Pet. 3: 7, 10, 13). And that the kingdom and the dominion under the whole heaven, shall be given to the people of the saints of the Most High, whose kingdom is an everlasting kingdom, and all dominions shall serve and obey him, (Dan. 7: 27).

"II. That there are but two advents, or appearings, of the Saviour to this earth, (Heb. 9: 28). That both are personal and visible, (Acts . : 9, 11). That the first took place in the days of Herod, (Matt. 2: 1,) when He was conceived of the Holy Ghost (Matt. 1: 18,) born of the Virgin Mary, (Matt. 1 : 25,) went about doing good, (Matt. 11: 5,) suffered on the cross, the just for the unjust, (1 Pet. 3 : 18,) died, (Luke 23 : 46,) was buried, (Luke 23 : 53,) arose again the third day, the first fruits of them that slept, (1 Cor. 15 : 4,) and ascended into the heavens, (Luke 24 : 51,) which must receive him until the times of the restitution of all things, spoken of by the mouth of all the holy prophets (Acts 3 : 21). That the second coming, or appearing, will take place when he shall descend from heaven at the sounding of the last trump, to give his people rest, (1 Thess. 4 : 15, 17; 1 Cor. 15 : 52,) being revealed from heaven in flaming fire, taking vengeance on them that know not God, and obey not the gospel, (2 Thess. 1 : 7, 8). And that he will judge the quick and the dead at his appearing and kingdom, (2 Tim. 4 : 1).

"III. That the second coming, or appearing, is indicated to be now emphatically nigh, even at the doors, (Matt. 24 : 33,) by the chronology of the prophetic periods, (Dan. 7 : 25 ; 8 : 14; 9 : 24; 12 : 7, 11, 12; Rev. 9 : 10, 15; 11 : 2, 3; 12 : 6, 14; 13 : 5,) the fulfillment of prophecy, (Dan. 2d, 7th, 8th, 9th, 11th, and 12th; Rev. 9th, 11th, 12th, 13th, 14th, and 17th,) and the signs of the times, (Matt. 24 : 29 ; Luke 21 : 25, 26). And that this truth should be preached both to saints and sinners, that the first may rejoice, knowing their redemption draweth nigh, (Luke 21: 28; 1 Thess. 4 : 18,) and the last be warned to flee from the wrath to come, (2 Cor. 5 : 11,) before the Master of the house shall rise up and shut too the door, (Luke 13 : 24, 25).

"IV. That the condition of salvation is repentance towards God, and faith in our Lord Jesus Christ, (Acts 20 : 21 · Mark 1 : 15). And that those who have repentance and faith, will live soberly, and righteously, and godly in this present world, looking for that blessed hope, and the glorious appearing of the great God and our Saviour Jesus Christ, (Tit. 2: 11, 13).

"V. That there will be a resurrection of the bodies of all the dead, (John 5 : 28, 29,) both of the just and the unjust, (Acts 24 : 15). That those who are Christ's will be raised at his coming, (1 Cor. 15 : 23). That the rest of the dead will not live again until after a thousand years, (Rev. 20: 5). And that the saints shall not all sleep, but shall be changed in the twinkling of an eye at the last trump, (1 Cor. 15: 51, 52).

"VI. That the only Millennium taught in the word of God, is the thousand years which are to intervene between the first resurrection and that of the rest of the dead, as inculcated in the 20th of Revelations, (vs. 2–7). And that the various portions of Scripture which refer to the Millennial state, are to have their fulfillment after the resurrection of all the saints who sleep in Jesus, (Isa. 11, 35: 1, 2, 5–10; 65: 17–26).

"VII. That the promise that Abraham should be the heir of the world was not to him, or to his seed through the law, but through the righteousness of faith, (Rom. 4: 13). That they are not all Israel which are of Israel, (Rom. 9 : 6.) That there is no difference under the gospel dispensation between Jew and Gentile, (Rom. 10 : 12). That the middle wall of partition that was between them is broken down, no more to be rebuilt, (Eph. 2: 14, 15). That God will render to every man according to his deeds, (Rom. 2: 6). That if we are Christ's, then are we Abraham's seed, and heirs according to the promise, (Gal. 3: 29). And that the only restoration of Israel, yet future, is the restoration of the saints to the earth, created anew, when God shall open the graves of those descendants of Abraham who died in faith, without receiving the promise, with the believing Gentiles, who have been graffed in with them into the same olive tree —and shall cause them to come up out of their graves, and bring them, with the living, who are changed, into the land of Israel, (Ezek. 37 : 12; Heb. 11 : 12, 13 ; Rom. 11 : 17; John 5 : 28, 29).

"VIII. That there is no promise of this world's conversion, (Matt. 24 : 14). That the horn of Papacy will war with the saints, and prevail against them, until the Ancient of Days shall come, and judgment be given to the saints of the Most High, and the time come that the saints possess the kingdom, (Dan. 7 : 21, 22). That the children of the kingdom, and the children of the wicked one, will continue together until the end of the world, when all things that offend shall be gathered out of the kingdom, and the righteous shall shine forth as the sun in the kingdom of their Father, (Matt. 13 : 37–43). That the Man of Sin will only be destroyed by the brightness of Christ's coming, (2 Thess. 2 : 8). And that the nations of those which are saved, and redeemed to God by the blood of Christ, out of every kindred, and tongue, and people, and nation, will be made kings and priests unto God, to reign forever on the earth, (Rev. 5 : 5, 10; 21 : 24).

"IX. That it is the duty of the ministers of the Word, to continue in the work of preaching the gospel to every creature, even unto the end, (Matt. 28 : 19, 20,)—calling upon them to repent, in view of the fact, that the kingdom of heaven is at hand, (Rev. 14 : 7,)—that their sins may be blotted out, when the times of refreshing shall come from the presence of the Lord, (Acts 3 : 19, 20).

"X. That the departed saints do not enter their inheritance, or receive their crowns, at death, (Dan. 12 : 13; Rev. 6 : 9–11; Rom. 8 : 22, 23). That they without us cannot be made perfect, (Heb. 11 : 40). That their inheritance, incorruptible and undefiled, and that fadeth not away, is reserved in heaven, ready to be revealed in the last time, (1 Pet. 1 : 4, 5). That there are laid up for them and us crowns of righteousness, which the Lord the righteous Judge shall give at the day of Christ, to all that love his appearing, (2

Tim. 4 : 8)..That they will only be satisfied when they awake in Christ's likeness, (Ps. 17 : 15). And that when the Son of man shall come in his glory, and all the holy angels with him, the King will say to those on his right hand, Come ye blessed of my Father, inherit the kingdom prepared for you from the foundation of the world, (Matt. 25 : 34). Then they will be equal to the angels, being the children of God and of the resurrection," Luke 20 : 36.

And wherein, we enquire, consists the heresy or heterodoxy of this scripturally worded confession of faith ? And in what respect does it so widely differ from the belief of the fathers, martyrs, and great reformers ? "Thus saith the Lord, stand ye in the ways, and see, and ask for the old paths, where is the good way, and walk therein, and ye shall find rest for your souls," Jer. 6 : 16. We invite special attention to the following observations from Henry Dana Ward. He says: " The earliest creeds, and all creeds of all denominations in Christendom, from the apostles to this day, recognize no other Millennium, than that of a glorious one on the renovated earth at the coming of the Lord and the resurrection of the dead—whether Greek or Roman, Apostate or Apostate Reformed, Lutheran, Episcopal, Presbyterian, Independent, Congregational, or by whatsoever name any church may be called." Again he says: "For it must be confessed by intelligent divines, that the popular doctrine of the Millennium, is a modern one totally unknown to the primitive and martyr church; so modern that it has never a place in the formula of the faith in any church—Catholic, Greek, Roman, or Protestant—but all their creeds involve the contrary."

" Consider further," he says, " that neither St. Peter, nor St. Paul, nor St. Clement, nor St. Justin, nor St. Cyprian, nor St. Cyril, nor Jerome, nor any other saint, or father, or eminent man in the primitive church, received or admitted the doctrine of the Millennium for one moment, except it

WHITBY'S INNOVATION. 437

was in the coming of the Lord Jesus with the resurrection of the dead; that neither the Greek, Latin, nor Lutheran, nor any one of the Reformed Churches, does now, or ever at any time, has acknowledged the doctrine of a Millennium in this world, by creeds, confessions, or approved standards of faith; and further, that never a man (whose writings have been enough esteemed to be preserved in the world,) came forth to preach the doctrine of "*peace and safety*" to the world, and a spiritual Millennium to the race of the first Adam, without any resurrection, until Daniel Whitby, D.D., who died A.D. 1726; and then if we do not pause with wonder, and with astonishment, and with fear, at the strong delusion that has gone over the Protestant churches; and if we do not withdraw instinctively from this "*new light*" doctrine, and enquire for the good old paths to the heavenly bliss our fathers trod, and to the true Millennium through Jesus and the resurrection, no word of exhortation from this humble source could move or persuade us. However, this I boldly say, and challenge contradiction, that Dr. Whitby's honorable name is the first and earliest that I have seen quoted in support of the doctrine, among the writers and orators of a spiritual Millennium, in this world's flesh, before the Lord's appearing, and Dr. Whitby gives credit to no other man for the discovery, but puts it roundly forth as his own opinion singly. And now one hundred years have barely gone by, since he was gathered to his fathers, and so firmly planted has this new faith become in all the churches of America, that never a religious newspaper of high standing with its own sect, can easily be found to admit an article into their columns, boldly questioning this proud Philistine, which has seized the ark of our faith, and now defies the hope of Israel. This state of things calls for mourning, as well as indignation, that in a single century, an innovation so bold in departure from the primitive faith and confessions of all churches, should have silently intrenched itself in the heart of all denominations following the reformers; which innovation those very reformers expressly condemn and brand as opposed to the Holy Scriptures."*

We impeach no article of the church's faith, exclaimed the renowned Mede, when, in the seventeenth century he boldly set his mind and hand to the recovery and support of a long buried and forgotten truth. And we, in compiling the present volume, are not aware of any trespassing on this point. If any church has woven Post-millennialism into her written creeds, we have yet to learn the fact. If it be said that all creeds teach a "general judgment" at the "last day," we answer that a general judgment by no means necessarily implies a simultaneous one, at which all men are judged at once, neither do the phrases "last day," "day of judgment," of necessity teach the judgment period to be one of but twenty-four hours duration, on the contrary, that epoch is "the great day of the Lord," with whom a thousand years is but as one day. And no creed herein presented teaches that "*at* Christ's coming *all* men shall rise again," save that of Athanasius.

A prior and Pre-millennial resurrection of the holy dead, we affirm, is taught both in the Old and New Testaments. Such, we have shown, has been the general faith of the church. And this resurrection and the Lord's advent being concomitant, the latter event must necessarily be also Pre-millennial. The true rendering of the Hebrew of Daniel 12: 2, has already been given. The translation, "And many from out of the sleepers in the dust of the earth shall awaken, these," &c., as given in the language of Winthrop, is sustained by the authority of Professors Whiting, Stuart, and Bush, of whom the latter, while denying both the resurrection of the body and also Pre-millennialism, yet stands unrivalled as an Hebraist. This makes his criticisms, with

* Hist. and Doct. of Mill., pp. 58, 59.

those of the Post-millennarian Stuart, the more invaluable. And the most learned of the Jewish Doctors concur with these, the renowned Aben Ezra interpreting for them all, when he says that the words denote that "those who awake shall be to everlasting life, and those who awake not shall be to shame and everlasting contempt." Dr. Cumming styles Gesenius "the most distinguished Lexicographer of this or any other age," and Gesenius, on the first and primary meaning of the Hebrew particle מִן (min) in Dan. 12: 2, translated "from out of," says, "It designates a part taken *from* or *out of* a whole, and corresponds to the Latin preposition *e, ex*, and the Greek εχ, εξ."* The Greek preposition εκ corresponding with this Hebrew particle our translators have rendered from the original of Rev. 5: 9th, "*out of* every kindred," &c. Thus, in the words of Bush, "the whole weight of authority compels us to this understanding of the original."

And New Testament language, referring to the resurrection of the righteous, Prof. Bush shows to have the same form of expression. Luke 20: 35, he translates, "the resurrection that is from the dead," &c. And again, Acts 4: 2, "preached through Jesus the resurrection from the dead," &c. Again, he renders Phill. 3: 11, literally, "If by any means I might attain unto the resurrection from out of the dead;" the terms teaching a resurrection "which is preëminently a privilege of some in contradistinction from others." On the last mentioned text Dr. Clarke says, the apostle meant "The resurrection of those, who, having died in the Lord, rise to glory and honor; and hence St. Paul uses a peculiar word, which occurs no where else in the New Testament, *i. e.* ἐξανάστασις (*exanastasis*) which, he says, may signify the resurrection of the blessed only."† And with these the literal interpretation of the first resurrection of Revelations 20th, is in harmonious and perfect keeping.

* Lexicon, p. 580.   † Vide Com.

And if the doctrine of the Sex-millennial duration of the world be a truth, and the Apocalyptic Millennium be the seventh chiliad, how near does it bring the golden—the blissful era! Let us cry, in the words of the pious Brainard, "The glorious times of the church are coming—are near at hand. O that his kingdom might come in the world!" and with Heber:

> "Chide the tardy seals that yet detain
> Thy Lion, Judah, from his destined reign."

"Every day," wrote Alanson Covell, "proclaims the near approach of that blessed era,"* and Mr. Brooks affirms that "in the opinion of all intelligent men, some awful and portentous crisis is at hand." In view of this solemn fact let us adopt the language of the pious Fletcher, and pray, "O that the thought, the glorious hope of Millennial blessedness may animate me to perfect holiness in the fear of God, that I may be accounted worthy to escape the terrible judgments which will make way for that happy state of things; and that I may have part in the first resurrection, if I am numbered among the dead before that happy period begins."

We have now coursed through about twenty centuries, and have found existing in the church three Millennial theories, viz: the Anti-millennarian, as held by Augustine, Andreas, Bush and others; the theory of a Post-millennial advent of Christ, as taught by Whitby and others, and its opposite, Pre-millennialism, and the personal reign, as believed by the early church, the two former of which we reject and oppose, the last mentioned we heartily receive and promulgate. What the real character of the Millennial age will be remains to be seen. It is "*night*" now, and we all "see through a glass darkly," but we shall see better and clearer when "the shadows flee away," and "the day dawns," and the "Sun"

---

* Memoirs, p. 45.

is up. But we sympathize with the Church of God in all her endeavors to interpret the Scriptures in relation to the nature of that hastening, glorious era. THE PRIEST'S LIPS SHOULD KEEP KNOWLEDGE. Meanwhile, to all those who are on the walls of Zion we say, in the earnest words of Hugh McNeil:

"My ministering brethren, watch, *preach the coming of Jesus*—I charge you, in the name of our common Master, *preach the coming of Jesus*—solemnly and affectionately in the name of God, I charge you, *preach the coming of Jesus.* 'Watch ye, therefore, (for ye know not when the master of the house cometh, at even, or at midnight, or at cock-crowing, or in the morning,) lest coming suddenly, he find the porter sleeping. Take care—'what I say unto you, I say unto all—watch.'"

CHAPTER XIV.

PRE-MILLENNIALISM.

THE STARTLING CRY—"HE COMETH."

THE Lord cometh! The heart of many an one thrills at this call. He thinks of the approaching and complete establishment of the Lord's kingdom upon earth; and he sighs, "Ah, didst thou but come!" Yes, our heart also joins in this longing of eighteen hundred years; for even so long has it been in the church, not like a flood water, which is gradually lost in the sand beneath, but like a stream, which, the nearer it draws to its destination, rolls onward with greater power. How many a prophetic omen has there been, that the grand moment of jubilee is not far distant. We already perceive signs of the publication of the gospel in all the world; that of the shaken foundations of Mohammedanism; that of the re-emergence of the Beast from the abyss; that of the decline from Christ and his word, extending through the world; and that of the powerful errors of an anti-christian spirit, acquiring domination over the cultivation of genius; of the idolization of men, and of many more similar signs.

"Never did the church witness such a constellation of signs of the near coming of Christ as now. 'The branches of the fig-trees are full of sap; and the summer is at hand.' Assuredly I am not ignorant that a portion of the Church has become gradually weary of the long tarrying, and has fallen into doubt. You also shake your head, and are of opinion, that we have long talked of 'the last time.' Well, use this language, and increase the number of the existing signs by this new one. Add that of the foolish virgins, who shortly before the midnight hour maintained 'the Lord would not come for a long time.' They ate, they drank, they wooed and were wooed, and inscribed over the festivity-decorated gate of their dwelling, 'Peace! Peace! There is no danger!' But then, however, the depths suddenly burst open, and the floods rushed forth at the command of the eternal wrath. Only Noah and those with him watched, and were preserved; upon every one else destruction came with the swiftness of a whirlwind. The Lord cometh! O, were he already here! How do we long for his revelation in these dark times!"— KRUMMACHER.

"SIGNS OF THE TIMES."

When from scattered lands afar,	Matt. 24: 6, 8
Spreads the voice of rumored war,	Luke 21: 25.
Nations in tumultuous pride,	Haggai 2: 7.
Heave like ocean's roaring tide,	Heb. 12: 26, 29.
When the solar splendors fail,	Matt. 24: 29.
When the crescent waxeth pale,	Rev. 16: 12.
And the powers that starlike reign,	Matt. 24: 39.
Sink dishonored to the plain,	Joel 11: 10, 31.
World! do thou the signal dread,	Luke 21: 26, 36.
We exalt the drooping head;	Luke 21: 37, 38.
We uplift the expectant eye,	Eph. 1: 14.
Our redemption draweth nigh.	Rom. 8: 19, 23.
When the fig-tree shoots appear,	Matt. 24: 22, 23.
Men behold their Summer near;	Luke 21: 29, 31.
When the hearts of rebels fail,	Isa 59: 18, 19.
We the coming Conqueror hail.	Rev. 19: 11, 16
Bridegroom of the weeping spouse,	Rev. 19: 7, 9.
Listen to her longing vows;	Rev. 6: 10.

Listen to her widowed moan,	Luke 18 : 3, 7, 8
Listen to Creation's groan.	Rom. 8 : 22, 23
Bid, O bid Thy trumpet sound,	1 Thess. 4 : 16
Gather thine elect around,	Matt. 24 : 31
Gird with saints Thy flaming car,	Jude 14
Summon them from climes afar,	Isa. 24 : 13–16
Call them from life's cheerless gloom,	Matt. 24 : 40, 41.
Call them from the marble tomb,	Rev. 20 : 4–6.
From the grass-grown village grave,	Luke 14 : 14.
From the deep dissolving wave,	Psalm 49 : 14, 15.
From the whirlwind and the flame,	1 Thess. 4 : 17.
Mighty Head, Thy members claim.	Col. 1 : 15.
Where are they whose proud disdain,	Luke 19 : 12, 27.
Scorned to brook Messiah's reign ?	Matt. 13 : 41, 42.
Lo, in waves of sulphurous fire,	Luke 17 ; 27, 30.
Now they taste His tardy ire;	Rev. 19 : 20, 21.
Fettered till the appointed day,	Rev. 18 : 3, 5, 9.
When the world shall pass away.	2 Peter 2 : 9.
Quelled are all thy foes, O Lord,	Rev. 19 : 15, 21.
Sheathe again the dreadful sword.	Psalm 110 : 5, 7.
Where the Cross of anguish stood,	Isa. 53 : 3, 5, 12.
Where thy life distilled in blood,	Mark 15, 27.
Where they mocked Thy dying groan,	Mark 15, 29.
King of Nations, plant Thy throne.	Isa. 24 ; 23.
Send thy law from Zion forth,	Zach. 8 : 3.
Speeding o'er the willing earth;	Dan. 2 : 35, 44
Earth, whose Sabbath glories rise,	Isa. 40 : 1, 9.
Crowned with more than Paradise;	Ps. 67 : 6.
Sacred be the impending veil!	1 Cor. 13 : 12.
Mortal sense and thought must fail,	1 John 3 : 2.
Yet the awful hour is nigh,	Luke 21 : 31.
We shall see Thee, eye to eye.	Rev. 1 : 7.
Be our souls in peace possessed,	2 Thess. 3 : 5.
While we seek our promised rest,	Heb. 4 : 9.
And from every heart and home,	2 Tim. 4 : 8.
Breathe the prayer, "O Jesus, come!"	Rev. 22 : 20.
Haste to set the captive free,	Isa. 49 : 9
All Creation groans for Thee.	Rom. 8 : 19

CHARLOTTE ELIZABETH.

THE FIRST RESURRECTION.

There is one circumstance attending the introduction of this period, that recent exegesis admits to be deducible from the text of chapter 20, which is alleged to be entirely *unique*, and which therefore, it is said, must be regarded as merely imaginary, or as belonging merely to the poetic conception and excited imagination of the writer. It is that of the *first* resurrection, Rev. 20 : 5, 6. I am aware, indeed, that this has often been asserted; and moreover, that in consequence of such a view of what the passage would teach if it were literally interpreted, a majority of commentators have deemed it necessary to give to the whole passage a sense merely *figurative*. That there are some tropical expressions in it, such as " reigning with Christ," and " being priests unto God," must, no doubt, be plain to all. But these and the like occur in the midst of simple prose, and constitute no good argument against the exegesis which deduces from the whole passage the reality of a *first* resurrection; see full references to such figurative passages in Com. on Rev. 1 : 6.

After investigating this subject, moreover, I have doubts whether the assertion is correct, that such a doctrine as that of the *first resurrection* is no where else to be found in the Scriptures. What can Paul mean, (Phil. 3 : 8–11,) when he represents himself as readily submitting to every kind of self-denial and suffering, " if by any means he might attain *unto the resurrection* of the dead ?" Of his resurrection at the end of the world, when all without exception, even the wicked as well as the good, will surely be raised, he could have no possible doubt. What sense can this passage have then, if it represents him as laboring and suffering merely in order to attain to a resurrection, and as holding this up to view, by implication, as unattainable unless he should arrive at a high degree of Christian perfection ? On the other hand; let us suppose a *first* resurrection to be appointed as a special reward of high attainments in Christian virtue, (exactly as in Rev. 20: 4–6), and all seems to be made plain and easy. Of a resurrection in a *figurative* sense, i. e. of *regeneration*, Paul cannot be speaking; for he had already attained to that on the plain of Damascus. Of the like tenor with this text, moreover, seems to be the implication in Luke 14: 14, where the Saviour promises to his disciples a sure reward for kindness to the poor and the suffering, by the declaration: "Thou shalt be recompensed at the resurrection of the just." Why the resurrection of the *just?* What special meaning can this have, unless it implies that there is a resurrection, where the just only, and not the unjust will be raised? This would agree entirely with the view in Rev. 20: 5, "But the rest of the dead *lived not again*, until the 1000 years were finished." There is the more reason to believe that such is the simple meaning of the words in Luke 14: 14, inasmuch as two recent antipodes in theology and criticism, Olshausen and De Wette, both agree in this exegesis. There are other passages, also, which are considerable in respect to number, that speak of the resurrection in respect to the *righteous*, and make no mention of that of the wicked. Some of these, at least, are susceptible of the same interpretation as that given above. In particular, what other satisfactory exegesis can we give to the $\alpha\pi\alpha\rho\chi\eta$ . . . $\epsilon\pi\epsilon\iota\tau\alpha$ . . . $\epsilon\iota\tau\alpha$ of 1 Cor. 15: 23, 24, by which the apostle marks the respective $\tau\alpha\gamma\mu\alpha$ or order of each, and represents that which is at the end ($\tau\epsilon\lambda o\varsigma$) as different from the rest.

It is well known, I may add, that among the Jews the opinion was quite common, that whenever the full development of the Messiah should take place, there would be a resurrection of the just. They appear to have deduced this opinion from Isa. 26: 19, (which no doubt describes a resurrection of some kind); from Ezek. 37; and from Dan. 12: 2. That this opinion is very old among the Jewish Rabbins is clear from the fact, that their most ancient books speak to such a purpose. In the Zohar (Genes.) we find, among many other things respecting the resurrection, the following: "The Scripture says [Isa. 26: 19], *Thy dead shall live;* they, namely, who are buried in the land of Israel. . . Therefore those bodies are raised up, viz., of the Israelites who are buried there, but not the bodies of the idolatrous nations." The reference is to the period of the Messiah. Thus in another passage of the same work: "Our Rabbins have taught us, that in the times of the Messiah, the blessed God will restore to life the just, etc," Zohar, Genes. fol. 61. See full quotations in Schoettgen, Hor. Heb. ii. p. 572, 574. So Zohar, Genes. fol. 73 : "The world cannot be freed from its guilt, until king Messiah shall come, and the blessed God shall raise up those who sleep in the dust;" (commenting on the expression, *he will swallow up death in victory*, Isa. 25 8). The same comment is made in Jalkuth Shimoni, i. fol. 188, and Shemoth Rabba, § 30. fol. 127. See Schoettg. ii. p. 167. To the same purpose speaks the Targum of Jonathan, as quoted by Wetstein on Rev. 20: 8; and Maimonides testifies that the opinion of many Rabbins is the same, as quoted by Lightfoot on John 6: 31. In fact, that the great mass of Jewish Rabbins have believed and taught the doctrine of *the resurrection of the just*, in the days of the Messiah's development, there can be no doubt on the part of him who has made any considerable investigation of this matter. The specific limitation of this to the commencement of the Millennium, seems to be peculiar to John.

No one must understand me, however, as appealing to Rabbinic authority in order to establish the doctrine of a *first* resurrection. All that I design to accomplish by such an appeal is, to show that such a doctrine was not a strange one to the Jews. We cannot say with certainty, that the book of Zohar is as ancient as the Apocalypse; but the prevailing opinion among critics seems now to be, that it belongs at least to the early ages of the Christian era, although, it has some interpolations of a much later date. If so, it seems quite probable that when John proclaimed a *first* resurrection, he would be regarded by the men of his time as free from any imputation of broaching novelties in this respect. The laws of philology oblige me to suppose, that the Saviour and Paul have both alluded to such a doctrine. That it has not been made more *prominent* in the New Testament, is no decisive objection against it. Where but in 1 Cor. 15: 24-28, have we an account of Christ's resignation of his *kingly* power? Where but in 1 Cor. 6: 2, 3, are we told that "saints shall judge the world, and judge angels?" And are these truths to be discarded, because they are no oftener brought to view and insisted on? On such ground, what must become of the authority and infallibility of scriptural teaching? Moreover it is obvious, that the *final* resurrection, *general* judgment, and the consequent distribution of rewards and punishments, are things of higher moment and deeper interest in many respects, than the resurrection of the *just only* at the commencement of the Millennium; which is a good reason for more frequently insisting upon the former. Nor should it be forgotten, that even the Old Testament contains some passages which may very naturally be applied to the Messianic or first resurrection, e. g. Isa. 26: 29.

"If there be any good foundation for what has now been said, it follows, that so far as the first resurrection and the Millennium period of prosperity to the church are concerned, they are not to be regarded as mere poetic conceptions, i. e. as the drapery only of the Apocalypse, but as *facts* which the writer designed to bring to view in a most interesting connection and relation.—*Prof. Moses Stuart.*

ADVENT EXPERIENCE.

"I have noticed in previous letters that I did not go with Mr. Howels on the subject of the Second Advent: I could not. In fact, I was a Millennarian against my will. The three particulars on which I did not believe myself to be convinced were, the vengeful dispensation against the Lord's enemies preparatory to the thousand years of blessedness; the literal nature of the first, Pre-millennial resurrection, and the personal reign. With regard to the first, I wished to believe that the gospel would be universally victorious, subduing every heart, and bringing the whole world in peaceful submission to acknowledge the Lord as King. I had once, as before stated, been startled by a reference to the sixty-third of Isaiah, and lulled to sleep again by the farfetched comments of good Matthew Henry: and I confessed I had taken up the missionary cause on the gratuitous assumption that we were to convert every body, and could not agree to a less extensive triumph. Well, I did not choose to bring this to the test of Scripture, because I did not wish to be undeceived; but just after the Irish meeting, one was held in reference to the Jews, at which I was present; and forth stepped my valued friend M'Neil, whom I had not seen for a year, and with his little Bible in his hand, preached the doctrine, to my infinite annoyance and conviction! He took up my precise objection without knowing it; he spoke of those who could not see that a part of God's *mercy* was his *judgment ;* and with that glowing ardor, tempered with deep solemnity, that always gives him so much of the prophetic characteristic, if I may so speak, he read from the 136th Psalm: 'To Him that smote Egypt in their first-born; *for his* MERCY *endureth forever:* and slew famous kings, *for his* MERCY *endureth forever.*' This was the key-note of a strain that I deeply felt resounded through the whole Scripture, though I had refused to heed it; and then he turned to the 61st of Isaiah, and read the first and part of the second verse, as quoted by our blessed Lord in the 4th of St. John, to where he shut the book, saying, 'This day is *this* Scripture fulfilled in your ears.' But did the Scripture end here? No: the first advent fulfilled so much of it; and **He who** then proclaimed 'the acceptable year of the Lord,' should at his second coming proceed with that unfinished Scripture, 'The day of vengeance of our God.' And go on thence 'To comfort all that mourn: to appoint unto them that mourn in Zion,'—and so the whole beautiful picture of Millennial gladness and glory on which Isaiah expatiates rose before me, as consequent upon that 'day of vengeance,' which Christ has not yet in person proclaimed. How angry I felt with that dauntless champion of God's whole truth, for trampling upon my darling prejudices! nevertheless he had done it; and thenceforth I opened my mind to drink in the pure, simple meaning of the literal promise.

"The first resurrection I considered to be a resurrection of the souls of the martyrs, whose spirits were to animate the happy race of believers during a thousand years. I confess some things puzzled me sorely in this interpretation: for instance, how could a soul be buried; and if not buried, how did it rise? Again, those souls were under an altar in heaven, waiting for the completion of their company by means of a new persecution on earth, and it seemed rather a heathenish doctrine to transmigrate them into other bodies; more especially as their own bodies would need them again. Besides, they were with Christ personally in heaven; and to be without Christ personally on earth, was by no means an additional privilege. I found the thing untenable, and resolved to consider it as wholly figurative; but if so, then the final judgment, described also in that chapter, might be figurative too. I would not look my own inferences in the face; so I wished to let the subject alone; but then a blessing was distinctly pronounced on such as should read or hear the words of that prophecy; and I did not like to lose a blessing.

"Thus the matter stood; I had rigidly forborne to read any book, pro or con, or to be talked to about it. One day when the subject forced itself upon me, I resolved to strengthen myself against the modern view (as I wisely supposed it,) by prayerfully reading again what I already so well knew—the 15th chapter of 1st Corinthians. I did so: and was suddenly struck by a recollection of the passage where the 'saying' is written, 'Death is swallowed up in victory.' I turned to Isa. 25, read it, and found it unequivocally a description of the church's blessedness on earth—the Millennium—at the outset of which the saying is written which 'shall come to pass,' when Christ's people rise from the dead. But will not all rise then? I went over the apostle's description once more, and found no word of the resurrection unto condemnation. The corruptible then raised would all put on incorruption; the weakness, power; the mortal, immortality; having borne the image of the earthly, they were to bear the image of the heavenly. I was quite overpowered: could I reply against God? The passage that I thought so formidable on my side failed me—'Afterwards they that are Christ's at his coming. *Then* cometh the end.' . . . . From this starting point I explored the Scriptures in reference to a literal resurrection of Christ's people, at a literal coming previous to the thousand years of Satan's binding, and the peace of the church. I saw it clearly: I received it fully: and I hold it firmly at this day. * * *

"It has often struck me what efforts the enemy has made to stifle this doctrine. . . . But shall the abuse of a sublime truth by the great enemy lead us to reject it? As well may we blot out the ninety-first Psalm, because the devil quoted it, and for a truly devilish purpose. No; he knows that the shedding forth of greater light on this important branch of Christian knowledge is one of the signs of Christ's actual coming; a token that his own time is short; therefore he endeavors to stifle it; and ere long he will bring us false Christs, to deceive, if it were possible, the very elect We have need to be found watching!"—*Charlotte Elizabeth*

THE NEW HEAVENS AND NEW EARTH.

"There is a limit to the revelations of the Bible about futurity, and it were a mental or spiritual trespass to go beyond it. The reserve which it maintains in its informations, we also ought to maintain in our inquiries—satisfied to know little on every subject, where it has communicated little, and feeling our way into regions which are at present unseen, no further than the light of Scripture will carry us.

"But while we attempt not to be 'wise above that which is written,' we *should attempt*, and that *most studiously*, to be wise *up to that which is written.* The disclosures are very few and very partial, which are given to us of that bright and beautiful economy, which is to survive the ruins of our present one. But still there are such disclosures—and on the principle of the things that are revealed belonging to us, we have a right to walk up and down, for the purpose of observation, over the whole actual extent of them. What is made known of the details of immortality, is but small in the amount, nor are we furnished with the materials of any thing like a graphical or picturesque exhibition of its abodes of blessedness. But still somewhat is made known, and which, too, may be addressed to a higher principle than curiosity, being like every other Scripture, 'profitable both for doctrine and for instruction in righteousness.'

"In the text before us, there are two leading points of information, which we should like successively to remark upon. The first is, that in the new economy, which is to be reared for the accommodation of the blessed, there will be MATERIALISM, not merely new heavens, but also a NEW EARTH. The second is, that as distinguished from the present which is an abode of rebellion, it will be an abode of righteousness.

"I. We know historically that earth, that a solid material earth, may form the dwelling of sinless creatures, in full converse and friendship with the Being who made them—that instead of a place of exile for outcasts, it may have a broad avenue of communication with the spiritual world, for the descent of ethereal beings from on high—that, like the member of an extended family, it may share in the regard and attention of the other members, and along with them be gladdened by the presence of Him who is the Father of them all. To inquire how this can be, were to attempt a wisdom beyond Scripture; but to assert that this *has been*, and therefore *may be*, is to keep most strictly and modestly within the limits of the record. For, we there read, that God framed an apparatus of materialism, which, on His own surveying, He pronounced to be all very good, and the leading features of which may still be recognized among the things and the substances that are around us—and that He created man with the bodily organs and senses which we now wear—and placed him under the very canopy that is over our heads—and spread around him a scenery, perhaps lovelier in its tints, and more smiling and serene in the whole aspect of it, but certainly made up, in the main, of the same objects that still compose the prospect of our visible contemplations—and there, working with his hands in a garden, and with trees on every side of him, and even with animals sporting at his feet, was this inhabitant of earth, in the midst of all those earthly and familiar accompaniments, in full possession of the best immunities of a citizen of heaven—sharing in the delight of angels, and while he gazed on the very beauties which we ourselves gaze upon, rejoicing in them most as the tokens of a present and presiding Deity. It were venturing on the region of conjecture to affirm, whether, if Adam had not fallen, the earth that we now tread upon would have been the everlasting abode of him and his posterity. But certain it is, that man, at the first, had for his place this world, and, at the same time, for his privilege, an unclouded fellowship with God, and, for his prospect, an immortality, which death was neither to intercept nor put an end to. He was terrestrial in respect of condition, and yet celestial in respect both of character and enjoyment. His eye looked outwardly on a landscape of earth, while his heart breathed upwardly in the love of heaven. And though he trode the solid platform of our world, and was compassed about with its horizon—still was he within the circle of God's favored creation, and took his place among the freemen and the denizens of the great spiritual commonwealth.

"This may serve to rectify an imagination, of which we think that all must be conscious—as if the grossness of materialism was only for those who had degenerated into the grossness of sin; and that, when a spiritualizing process had purged away all our corruption, then, by the stepping stones of a death and a resurrection, we should be borne away to some ethereal region, where sense, and body, and all in the shape either of audible sound, or of tangible substance, were unknown. And hence that strangeness of impression which is felt by you, should the supposition be offered, that, in the place of eternal blessedness, there will be ground to walk upon; or scenes of luxuriance to delight the corporeal senses; or the kindly intercourse of friends talking familiarly, and by articulate converse together; or, in short, any thing that has the least resemblance to a local territory, filled with various accommodations, and peopled over its whole extent by creatures formed like ourselves—having bodies such as we now wear, and faculties of perception, and thought, and mutual communication, such as we now exercise. The common imagination that we have of paradise on the other side of death, is, that of a lofty ærial region, where the inmates float in ether, or are mysteriously suspended upon nothing,—where all the warm and sensible accompaniments which give such an expression of strength, and life, and coloring, to our present habitation, are attenuated into a sort of spiritual element, that is meagre, and imperceptible, and utterly uninviting to the eye of mortals here below—where every vestige of materialism is done away, and nothing left but certain unearthly scenes that have no powers of allurement, and certain unearthly ecstasies, with which it is felt impossible to sympathize. The holders of this imagination forget all the while, that there is really no essential connection between materialism and sin,—that the world which we now inhabit had all the amplitude and solidity of its present materialism before sin entered into it —that God so far, on that account, from looking slightly upon it, after it had received the last touch of His creating hand, reviewed the earth, and the waters, and the firmament, and all the green herbage, with the living creatures, and the man whom He had raised in dominion over them, and He saw every thing that He had made, and, behold it was all VERY GOOD. They forget that on the birth of materialism, when it stood out in the freshness of those glories which the great Architect of Nature had impressed upon it, that then " the morning stars sang together, and all the sons of God shouted for joy." They forget the appeals that are made every where in the Bible to this material workmanship —and how, from the face of these visible heavens, and the garniture of this earth that we tread upon, the greatness and the goodness of God are reflected on the veiw of His worshippers.

" No, my brethren, the object of the administration we sit under, is to extirpate sin, but it is not to sweep away materialism. By the convulsions of the last day, it may be shaken, and broken down from its present arrangements; and thrown into such fitful agitations, as that the whole of its existing framework shall fall to pieces ; and with a heat so fervent as to melt its most solid elements, it may be utterly dissolved. And thus may the earth again become without form, and void, but without one particle of its substance going into annihilation. Out of the ruins of this second chaos, may another heaven and another earth be made to arise; and a new materialism, with other aspects of magnificence and beauty, emerge from the wreck of this mighty transformation; and the world be peopled as before, with the varieties of material loveliness, and space be again lighted up into a firmament of material splendor.

* * * * * *

"But the highest homage that we know of to materialism, is that which God, manifest in the flesh, has rendered to it. That He, the Divinity, should have wrapt His unfathomable essence in one of its coverings, and expatiated amongst us in the palpable form and structure of a man; and that He should have chosen such a tenement, not as a temporary abode, but should have borne it with Him to the place which He now occupies, and where He is now employed in preparing the mansions of His followers—that he should have entered within the vail, and be now seated at the right hand of the Father, with the very body which was marked by the nails upon His cross, and wherewith He ate and drank after His resurrection—that He who repelled the imagination of His disciples, as if they had seen a spirit, by bidding them handle Him and see, and subjecting to their familiar touch the flesh and the bones that encompassed Him; that He should now be throned in universal supremacy, and wielding the whole power of heaven and earth, have every knee to bow at His name, and every tongue to confess, and yet all to the glory of God the Father—that HUMANITY, that substantial and embodied HUMANITY, should thus be exalted, and a voice of adoration from every creature, be lifted up to the Lamb for ever and ever—does this look like the abolition of materialism, after the present system of it is destroyed; or does it not rather prove, that, transplanted into another system, it will be preferred to celestial honors, and prolonged in immortality throughout all ages?

"It has been our careful endeavor, in all that we have said, to keep within the limits of the record, and to offer no other remarks than those which may fitly be suggested by the circumstance, that a new earth is to be created, as well as a new heaven, for the future accommodation of the righteous. We have no desire to push the speculation beyond what is written—but it were, at the same time, well, that in all our representations of the immortal state, there was just the same force of coloring, and the same vivacity of scenic exhibition, that there is in the New Testament. The imagination of a total and diametric opposition between the region of sense and the region of spirituality, certainly tends to abate the interest with which we might otherwise look to the perspective that is on the other side of the grave; and to deaden all those sympathies that we else might have with the joys and the exercises of the blest in paradise. To rectify this, it is not necessary to enter on the particularities of heaven—a topic on which the Bible is certainly most sparing and reserved in its communications. But a great step is gained, simply by dissolving the alliance that exists in the minds of many between the two ideas of sin and materialism; or proving, that when once sin is done away, it consists with all we know of God's administration, that materialism shall be perpetuated in the full bloom and vigor of immortality. It altogether holds out a warmer and more alluring picture of the elysium that awaits us, when told, that there will be a beauty to delight the eye; and music to regale the ear; and the comfort that springs from all the charities of intercourse between man and man, holding converse as they do on earth, and gladdening each other with the benignant smiles that play on the human countenance, or the accents of kindness that fall in soft and soothing melody from the human voice. There is much of the innocent, and much of the inspiring, and much to affect and elevate the heart, in the scenes and the contemplations of materialism—and we do hail the information of our text, that after the dissolution of its present framework, it will again be varied and decked out anew in all the graces of its unfading verdure, and of its unbounded variety—that in addition to our direct and personal view of the Deity, when He comes down to tabernacle with men, we shall also have the reflection of Him in a lovely mirror of His own workmanship—and that instead of being transported to some abode of dimness and of mystery, so remote from human experience, as to be beyond all comprehension, we shall walk for ever in a land replenished with those sensible delights, and those sensible glories, which, we doubt not, will lie most profusely scattered over the 'new heavens and the new earth, wherein dwelleth righteousness.'

"But though a paradise of *sense*, it will not be a paradise of *sensuality*. Though not so unlike the present world as many apprehend it, there will be one point of total dissimilarity betwixt them. It is not the entire substitution of spirit for matter, that will distinguish the future economy from the present. But it will be the entire substitution of righteousness for sin. It is this which signalizes the Christian from the Mohammedan paradise—not that sense, and substance, and splendid imagery, and the glories of a visible creation seen with bodily eyes, are excluded from it,—but that all which is vile in principle, or voluptuous in impurity, *will be* utterly excluded from it. There will be a firm earth, as we have at present, and a heaven stretched over it, as we have at present; and it is not by the absence of these, but by the absence of sin, that the abodes of immortality will be characterized. There will both be heavens and earth, it would appear, in the next great administration—and with this specialty to mark it from the present one, that it will be a heavens and an earth, 'wherein dwelleth righteousness.'"
—*Dr. Thomas Chalmers, on* 2 *Pet.* 3: 13.

THE VINDICATION.--THE GREAT INCENTIVE.

"Do I paralyse effort when I say, 'work while it is day, for the night cometh when no man can work?' Nay, do I not thus stimulate zeal, and toil, and prayer, and love to the uttermost? Do I lull men asleep, when I say 'the coming of the Lord draweth nigh?'—or do I flatter into flesh-pleasing the great or the noble, or the beautiful of the earth, when I tell them that—

'————the tide of pomp,
That beats upon the high shore of this world,'

is ebbing fast? Do I tempt the sinner to postpone his conversion, because I speak of the 'wrath to come' as so very nigh? Or do I with less serious haste beseech men to be reconciled to God, because I add that the time of reconciliation, the acceptable year of the Lord is fast running to a close? Do I cherish idleness instead of diligence, softness of spirit instead of hardness, heedlessness about redeeming time, instead of eagerness to gather up its fragments, when I announce that 'The day goeth away, and the shadows of evening are stretched out?' Do I soothe the Bride into a deeper sleep when I say, 'Behold the Bridegroom cometh, go ye out to meet him?' Do I tempt the minister or the missionary into indolent security, when I declare that 'the Judge standeth before the door,' and that ere long the time of working, and preaching and inviting will be over? Do I persuade the soldier of the risen Jesus to ungird his weapons because I tell him that his feet are already on the battle field, and bid him listen to the loud roar afar, that forewarns of the deadly onset? Do I preach Christ crucified the less, because I preach also Christ coming to reign? or do I the less proclaim that 'here we have no continuing city,' because I can point so clearly to that which is to come, the city which hath foundations, whose builder and whose maker is God?' Or do I make saints feel the less that they are strangers here, because I set forth to them the 'new earth, wherein dwelleth righteousness?' Do I undervalue the cross because I magnify the throne? In holding up to view the crown of glory, do I deprecate the crown of thorns? Do I enfeeble my proclamation of immediate and free forgiveness to sinners, through the sin-bearer, because I enforce it with the announcement that the coming of the Lord draweth nigh? Do I foster error, or heresy, or lax walking, or any departure from the faith, when I warn men that the perilous times of the last days are setting in, when Satan will 'cast abroad the rage of his wrath,' and the unclean spirits will overflow the earth with their delusions, to deceive, if it were possible the very elect, and to gather the nations to the battle of the great day of God Almighty?

"I do not know how it may be with others, but I feel that when I can say the coming of the Lord draweth nigh, I have got a weapon in my hand of no common edge and temper. To be able to announce 'the Lord will come,' is much; but to be able to say without the reservation of an interval 'He is at hand,' is greatly more. I can go to the struggling saint against whom the battle seems to go hardly, and say, 'Faint not, the Lord is at hand, and he will bruise Satan under your feet shortly.' To the saint wearied with a vexing world, fretted with its vanities, and troubled with the thickening darkness of its midnight, I can say, 'Be of good cheer, the Lord is at hand; but a little while and that world shall cease to vex, sooner than you think the morn will break,—yea, before it is broken we shall be caught up and meet morning ere it is yet spread upon the mountains.' To the suffering saint I can say, 'Weep not, the Lord is at hand; the torn heart shall be bound up, and the bitterness of bereavement forgotten in the joy of union forever.' To the flagging saint, heavy and slothful in his walk, I can say, 'Up, for the Lord is at hand; work while it is day; look at a dying world, all unready for its Judge; cast off your selfishness and love of ease.' To the covetous saint I can say, 'The Lord is coming—it is no time for hoarding now—heap not up treasure for the last days.'

"Next our own salvation, must come the duty of sending the gospel to all. We begin at the inner circle, but woe to us if we stop there. Woe be to us if we preach not the gospel to every creature. We feel a peculiar call to this, and a peculiar urgency enforcing this call from our very system. For but little time remaineth. The night is falling. The storm is beginning to burst. We cannot tarry—we must go forth. We cannot heap up treasure for the last days. We must give liberally as long as the time allows. Those who look for a calm, long day, may sit down listlessly, but we dare not. Those who look for a mere extension of the present state of religion as all the Millennium the world is to enjoy, may excuse themselves from giving, and may heap up treasures. But we dare not, we feel that there is not a moment to be lost; and that whether there are few or many to be saved it matters not to us. We *must* fulfill our ministry, not counting even our lives dear unto us, that we may do the will of Him who sends us, and testify the gospel of the grace of God."—*Horatius Bonar*.

THE BLESSED HOPE.

"The Hope of the Body is one. The true hope of every creature is to attain its perfection. All long and strive for that which shall complete and crown their being. There is amongst all ranks of living things an instinctive or intelligent reaching forward towards that maturity which shall consummate the end for which they exist. So the hope of the church stretches onward to her perfect standing, when her Lord will present her to himself without spot, or wrinkle, or any such thing, and give to her the inheritance of the kingdom. Nothing short of that event, by which the 'one body' shall attain its predestined power and glory as the wife of the Lamb, can satisfy the desire which His promise would kindle in her heart. Death is not the perfecting of the Bride. If it is the deliverance of the spirit from sin and sorrow, it is the consummation of the curse unto the body. A disembodied spirit is not a perfect man, and cannot perform the work of a perfect man. The dead must be raised in the likeness of their Lord, before they can receive their inheritance, or serve him in the ministries of His kingdom. They rest from their labors—from *all* labors—and wait for their crown. Their hope is the redemption of the body, when Jesus shall bring them with him at his coming, and clothe them with their house which is from heaven—the body of incorruption—in which, being like him, they shall see him as he is, and be ready to be used by him in the eternal administration of his government. From beneath the altar they ever cry, 'How long, O Lord, holy and true, dost thou not judge and avenge our blood on them that dwell on the earth?' Rev. 6: 10. They look forward with joyful desire to the time when 'the kingdoms of this world shall become the kingdoms of our Lord, and of his Christ;' when 'He shall give reward unto his servants, the prophets, and to the saints, and them that fear his name;' and 'the meek shall inherit the earth.' The rest and peace in which they are now abiding, is not the glory of the kingdom when their reward shall be the fellowship of Christ's throne; and as he could not be seated at God's right hand, till first he had triumphed over death, so neither can his members reign with him so long as they lie bound under the captivity of the grave. It must be remembered, too, that the hope of the body is one, common to all, and to be obtained by all at once. Of the holy men of old, who obtained a good report through faith, the Apostle says: 'these all receive not the promise; God having provided some better thing for us, that they without us should not be made perfect.' They have not received the promise yet, nor can the dead be made perfect till the number of the elect has been completed, and all are prepared to take their places in that polity which consummates and crowns all the works of God.

"And as the hope of the sleeping saints is the resurrection of the body, so the hope of the living is, not to be unclothed in death, but to be clothed upon in the translation, when mortality shall be swallowed up of life. Enoch and Elijah were types of the faithful who shall survive unto the coming of the Lord, in whom the change from the corruptible into the incorruptible shall be accomplished without tasting of the bitterness of death. 'We shall not all sleep, but we shall all be changed, in a moment, in the twinkling of an eye, at the last trump; for the trumpet shall sound, and the dead shall be raised incorruptible, and we shall be changed.' This is the hope of our calling—the living hope unto which we are begotten by the resurrection of Jesus Christ from the dead—the hope of life, not of death. And if the faithful who sleep in Jesus, sheltered from the storms, and freed from the pollutions of this evil world, think it long till their Lord appears to raise their bodies out of the dust; how earnestly should we stretch forth the head to catch the sound of His approaching footsteps—we, to whom the battle is fierce, and the burden heavy, and the stain of sin deep in the soul! Oh, how has the Church ceased to war against death, yielding herself in passive hopelessness to its usurped dominion, and accounting its rest her chief reward, instead of pressing forward to that manifestation of the sons of God,' in the glory of the resurrection, for which even the earnest expectation of the creation waits!

"And not for our own sakes alone, nor for the sake alone of the sleeping saints should we long for the return of our Lord and Saviour; but that the earth, now groaning and travailing in pain, may be delivered from the curse. For the promise that the seed of the woman shall bruise the serpent's head, includes in its large reach of blessings the redemption of man's inheritance by the casting out of him who usurped it, and the purging away of all the evil with which his slimy presence has defiled and infected it. The earth was made for the revealing of God's glory, through the possession and enjoyment of its manifold treasures, free from all curse, by man standing in his allegiance to his Maker; and though the purpose was frustrated by the fall of the first Adam, it shall be accomplished in the second, who will cause the Father's will to be done forevermore. He has already in his own person, triumphed over the seductions of the serpent, and proved himself against all temptation, the obedient Son, worthy to take up the forfeited sceptre of man's dominion, and rule in righteousness for God; and he now waits only for the completion of the company of joint heirs that shall rule with him, to come forth to redeem and purify and bless his purchased inheritance. They are right who are looking for righteousness and peace to fill the earth, and make glad the obedient nations; but they are wrong who look for it, before the Man who is the heir shall come forth to make it his own eternal dwelling place. He was made a little lower than the angels, for the suffering of death, to pay the price of the redemption; and then crowned with glory and honor, and invested with the *right* of dominion over all the works of God's hand; 'but now we see not yet all things put under him,' and the next step shall be his *actual and visible* government of the creatures. It is an idle dream which now possesses so many that the church is to bring in the kingdom in the absence of the King. There is not one word for it in all the Scriptures. It contradicts the exhortations for continual watchfulness for Him—not for death, but for Him who is the conqueror of death,—which imply the possibility of his coming in any generation, and therefore the certainty of his coming before the long, fixed period of the Millennium, which is the time for rest, not for watching it is inconsistent with the foretold humiliation and sorrow of the church during the whole of this dispensation, in which she is to walk in his footsteps, and be perfected by the fellowship of his sufferings; it robs her of the blessed hope by which alone she can be purified, and towards which the Apostles ever struggled to lead her—the hope of being like him and seeing him as he is; and it entangles her in worldly schemes and alliances, and so eats out all faith in the heavenly citizenship. The nations *are* to be blessed, and the earth, unto the uttermost parts of it, *is* to see the salvation of God, but it shall be when the time comes that the saints possess the kingdom—Dan. 7 : 22; which is not during the Bridegroom's absence, for the church is the desolate widow called to fasting and mourning, and the word to her ever is, 'Be patient unto the coming of the Lord.' The last temptation by which Jesus was assailed when he was led up into the wilderness is now spreading its cunning seductions all around us, and we are looking to gain the kingdoms of the world, and the glory of them, before the time that the Father shall give them to his Son.

"The one great hope for the whole creation, towards which, blindly and unconsciously, if not with intelligent desire, all are reaching forward, is the 'marriage of the Lamb.' It is the hope of the Bride who shall then be one with the Lord in all his glory, and power, and fullness of blessing. It is the hope of the nations, who shall then know the blessedness of righteous rule. It is the hope of the sore-burthened earth, which longs to be delivered from the bondage of corruption into the glorious liberty of the sons of God. And it is the hope of the Lord himself, whose heart yearns over his church, purchased with his own blood, but still lying, in the desolateness of death, or amidst the defilements of this evil world, and whose word of promise is, 'Surely I come quickly.' Let our response ever be, 'Even so, come Lord Jesus.' Let our hearts be broken through our sympathy with the burdens and sorrows of all, and let us utter in His ear continually the cry that shall hasten the common deliverance."—*William W. Andrews.*

THE SOLEMN WARNING.

"Church of the living God! hast thou heard the voice that spoke from heaven, 'Surely I come quickly?' And hast thou responded to it gladly, 'Even so come, Lord Jesus?' Does the promise of his return cheer thee? And is the thought of His speedy coming a most welcome hope in these days, when men's hearts are failing them for fear? Then how is this prospect operating? Is it full of quickening, animating, stimulating power? Is it kindling up your love into greater warmth? Is it increasing the intensity of your earnestness? Is it making the separation between you and the world a more decided thing? Is it imparting a deeper solemnity to your deportment, and attaching an unutterable importance to every word and action? Is it rebuking idleness, and sloth, and vanity, and frivolity, and levity, and selfishness? Has it uprooted and destroyed in you covetousness and worldliness, those two master-sins of the evil age? And has it made you liberal and generous, enlarging your heart to give—to give with no sparing hand so long as the time remaineth? Ah! brethren in Christ, we are surely far behind! Our religion is a poor, second-rate, ineffective thing! We are dreaming when we should be working; we are pleasing and indulging the flesh when we should be serving the Lord. We are indolent and yielding when we should be energetic and indomitable. We are shrinking and fastidious when we should be resolute and hardy. We sit idly in our tents, with weapons sheathed and banners folded, when we should be in the thickest of the fight, for the world's last conflict is begun, and the armies are mustering for the battle of the great day of God Almighty.

"And you, ye men of the earth, whose portion is not among the things unseen, have you heard the voice that speaks to *you* from heaven—' Fear God, and give glory to him, for the hour of his judgment is come?' Has the warning pierced your ears and broken your mad security? How long do you count it safe to remain unreconciled? And what sort of reconciliation with God will avail you in the day when He ariseth to shake terribly the earth? And when is he to arise? Have you ascertained the time, that you sit so easy and unalarmed? The long pent-up winds are beginning to break loose; and the sudden bursts of tempest that have swept over Europe these few years past are precursors of the world's last desolating storm. At present there is a lull, but it will be brief; and behind that lull there is the more terrible tempest; and behind that tempest there is the Judge of the quick and the dead; and behind the Judge are the everlasting burnings. Has this prospect no terrors for you, and have these terrors no urgency to compel you to consider the overwhelming necessity of betaking yourselves to the provided shelter, ere another day, with all its gloomy uncertainties, shall have dawned upon you?

"The warfare has now begun in our land, which will not be ended save by the arrival of the King himself. How far the assault may prevail, or how long the tide of war may flow and reflow, we do not pretend to say. Let us prepare for the worst.

"And what, if behind and above all these, there be heard a shout and a trumpet more awful and unearthly than these— the announcement of the coming Judge in flaming fire? Are you ready? Are you hidden in the clefts of that rock to which no weapon, no storm, no fire can reach? He alone is safe who has reached the hiding-place; and that hiding-place stands with its unfolded gates ready to receive you now Will you enter? Or will you remain without? Remain without, and perish in the fiery storm! 'For every battle of the warrior is with confused noise and garments rolled in blood, but this shall be with burning and fuel of fire.' It is now, in these last days, as in the days of Noah. God's purpose of vengeance has been declared, the warning has come, and the judgment is making haste to follow. But the ark is still open, and the preacher of righteousness beckons you in. For one hundred and twenty years Noah preached, but the unheeding world heard him not. Then he entered the Ark, and, for seven days, he remained there before the deluge came, and standing at the open door of the Ark he delivered God's last message of grace, entreating men to come in. It seems as if *we* were now in the period corresponding to these seven last days—proclaiming God's last loving message to long-resisting man! For what, then, are you waiting? Are you lingering in the hope that the Millennial day will softly steal in upon the world, and that then you will be converted with all the rest? Alas for you! Do you not know that between you and that glory there lies a region as dark as midnight, and strewed with terrors such as earth has not yet witnessed? Why, then, do you wait without? There is room enough within, and will you not go in and occupy it? There is love enough, and will you not go in and taste it? There is blessedness enough, and will you not go in and enjoy it? It will cost you nothing; and you are welcome! The Father bids you welcome; and the Son bids you welcome; and the Spirit bids you welcome; and angels bid you welcome; and every saved one bids you welcome; and with so many welcomes will you still hesitate or delay—preferring death to life, shame to honor, wrath to love, the horrors of the outer darkness to the glory of that city where they need no light of the sun?"—*London Quarterly Journal of Prophecy*

LOOKING FOR HIS COMING.

"It is one of the characteristics of the Christian, that he believes that the Lord Jesus will return from heaven, and that he looks and waits for it; other men do not believe this (2 Pet. 3:4), but the Christian confidently expects it. His Saviour has been taken away from the earth, and is now in heaven; but it is a great and standing article of his faith, that the same Saviour will again come and take the believer to himself (John 14: 2, 3; 1 Thess. 4:14). This was the firm belief of the early Christians, and this expectation with them was allowed to exert a constant influence on their hearts and lives. It led them (1) to desire to be prepared for his coming; (2) to feel that earthly affairs were of little importance, as the scene here was soon to close; (3) to live above the world, and in the desire of the appearing of the Lord Jesus. This was one of the elementary doctrines of their faith, and one of the means of producing deadness to the world among them; and among the early Christians there was, perhaps, no doctrine that was more the object of firm belief, and the ground of more delightful contemplation, than that their ascended Master would return. In regard to the certainty of their belief on this point, and the effect which it had on their minds, see the following texts. [Here follow thirteen references to various passages in the New Testament.] It may be asked with great force, whether Christians in general have now any such expectations of the second appearance of the Lord Jesus, or whether they have not fallen into the dangerous error of prevailing unbelief, so that the expectation of his coming is allowed to exert almost no influence on the soul. In the passage before us, Paul says that it was one of the distinct characteristics of Christians, that they *looked for* the coming of the Saviour from heaven. They believed he would return. They anticipated important effects would follow to them from his second coming. So *we* should look."

"Let us look for the coming of the Lord. All that we hope for depends on his re-appearing. Our day of triumph and of the fullness of our joy is to be when he shall return. Then we shall be raised from the grave; then our 'vile bodies' shall be changed; then we shall be acknowledged as his friends; then we shall go to be forever with him."—*Albert Barnes, Notes on Phil.* 3:20, 21.

COMING OF THE BRIDEGROOM.

"Let us take our lamps and go forth to meet the Bridegroom. To *meet* the Bridegroom. Yes, he is coming. Let it be no scorn to any of us to avow and to act on this simple belief. Let others search and calculate, and let us reap all lawful fruit from their discovery of truth, knowing that all truth is God's. But here we take our stand; we know that that glorified form of the Son of man and the son of God lives and upholds all things by the word of his power, and is waiting to visit this earth in his person. This knowledge, this hope, we will yield for no man; persuaded that when all other knowledge fails, it shall stand; when all the rest of human hopes are disappointed, it alone shall end in perfect fulfillment.

"This coming of the Bridegroom is the most joyous day for heaven and earth, the most joyous for the church, the most joyous for every faithful soul. All nature has been earnestly expecting it; for then, first, shall the wilderness rejoice and blossom as the rose; then none shall hurt or destroy, but the redeemed of the Lord shall come with songs, and everlasting joy upon their heads, and sorrow and sighing shall flee away."

"The Lord will come in person to this earth; his risen elect will reign here with him. This is my persuasion, and not mine alone, but that of Christ's waiting people, as it was that of his primitive apostolical church, before controversy blinded the eyes of the fathers to the light of prophecy."—*Dean Alford.*

THE CHURCH'S LAST TESTIMONY.

The Church from the first has been God's witness upon earth, and when her testimony shall have been fully delivered the end will come, and the dispensation will be closed. The ripeness of the Church will be when it shall have witnessed for all the truths which are to be opposed by the heretical and the infidel. Already has the protest been uttered on behalf of those doctrines, referring both to man and the Mediator, which are nothing less than the life's blood of Christianity. If you trace heresy downward, from the apostles' days to our own, you find it fastening itself successively on the several truths of our faith, so that there is scarce a fraction which has not been assaulted, and in defense of which the Church has not shown itself a witness. What, then, remains to the rendering the Church fully ripe? We find from the Scriptures that one great feature of the last times shall be disbelief or denial of the second advent of Christ. As in other days of the dispensation, so in the concluding, there shall be abroad the covetous, the blasphemers, the traitors, the high-minded, and all those manifestations of evil which have ever called forth the protest of the Church. But, over and above these forms of wickedness, scorners shall be walking the earth, arguing, from the apparent fixedness of things, of the improbability of Christ's interference, and tauntingly asking, 'Where is the promise of his coming?' Here, it may be, will be the last and most energetic demand on the witness. The Church must oppose itself to this new and desperate infidelity. She must protest for the advent of the Lord against the denial and reviling of a profligate generation. And when the Church shall have done this, witnessed that Christ is about to re-appear, and invoke a scoffing world to prepare for his approach; then, it may be, will her perfect ripeness be reached, and then, in accordance with the parable, the fruit being brought forth, Christ shall 'immediately put in the sickle,' gather in the corn, and house his elect, ere vengeance be let loose on the impenitent and unbelieving."—*Henry Melville.*

COUNT ON CHRIST'S COMING.

"In spite of solemn prophecy, men are engaged in minding earthly things, *planning* earthly things, as the word may be rendered,—planning their own advancement in the world, planning the securing of a comfortable nest in this life, planning for their children's future, and so on,—forgetting that all these things shall be dissolved and burned up.

"Suppose a settler were busy laying out his homestead in the prairies of America. All at once a telegram reaches him: 'The prairie is on fire just beyond your horizon! The wind is carrying the flames in your direction; nothing can arrest them; they are consuming all before them!' What would the man do if he believed the message? Would he still be intent on decorating his house and completing his out-buildings?

"God has telegraphed to us from heaven to this effect, as regards the earth and all the things that are therein. The world does not believe the message. Do we believe it? The Lord is not slack concerning the promise, the promise to believers,—a threat, a terrible threat only, to the world. But Satan administers a powerful anodyne, and the world sleeps on in careless security. Yet it is only a question of time, only of a little while; all must be burned up sooner or later.

"Let us never act on anything as if we counted on the stability of the present order of things. *Let us count on the coming of Christ.* Let us train our children with this in view, lay all our plans with this in view. Let our conversation, our manner of life, be shaped by this prospect, and not by any false idea that the earth and the things that are therein are to continue. Like Noah, let us prepare for things not seen as yet; like Rahab, be ready for the coming of the Conqueror, and await, in all manner of holy conversation, the return of the Captain of our salvation." — *Lord Radstock.*

"THE SPIRIT AND THE BRIDE SAY, COME."

"The Lord said unto Moses, 'Wherefore criest thou unto me?' Now Moses had said nothing, but the voice of his heart was so loud and powerful that it ascended to the distant heavens, and was heard at the throne of God. It is a language of the same sort that the Lord heareth from the bride, and the import of it, according to his declaration, is, that he would hasten his second coming. . . . The saints long for the appearing of their Lord, because they love *him*, and not the things of the world, as the bride desires the coming of the bridegroom because her affections are transferred from all others to him.

"The coming of the bridegroom is looked forward to as the beginning of that happiness to the bride for which she has been preparing; so the appearing of the

Lord Jesus is evidently expected by the saints, in proportion to their heavenly-mindedness, as the era of their deliverance from misery, and the commencement of their perfect enjoyment. . . . Is it a wonder, then, that the saints should long for the resititution of all things? that they should be looking for and hasting to the coming of the Lord? Nay, that they should be sometimes even saying, Why is his chariot so long in coming? why stay the wheels of his chariot? . . .

"But can men in general pray for the dissolution of the world when the fibers of their hearts are so closely wound around it? Can they desire a new heaven and a new earth, wherein dwelleth righteousness, when they love the old earth so well, though there dwelleth unrighteousness?"—*Henry Martyn, on Rev.* 22:17.

THE FAITH THAT SUSTAINS.

" 'Believe on the Lord Jesus Christ and thou shalt be saved!' If there are those here who do not believe the first part of that message, there are none here who do not at least wish to believe, in some sort, the second part of it. Men do need to be saved,—saved, if not in the next, in this world,— delivered, if it might be, from some of the sin and sorrow that weigh so heavily upon every human heart and every human life. Is there no need of faith, or, if no need of faith, is there no desire for the objects of faith, among men? Have we no need of faith at this moment? The world is growing old and sick at heart. All the remedies that have been devised from time to time for the evils of society and the sorrows of humanity, have been tried to very exhaustion, and tried in vain. Idol after idol that men have set up and sacrificed to, has been rocked from its base and shivered into fragments. The gods that men have worshiped have been taken away again and again. And again and again has the cry of despair risen, 'What have we left?' Faith—faith in the future of humanity? What answer does the past give to this? In all the past ages is there one proof that in this world, constituted as it is, there shall ever be perfection of our nature? Faith in what? Faith in science? Did science ever comfort a sorrow? Did science ever heal a broken heart? Faith in civilization? Did civilization ever yet remedy the evils that are burrowing and festering into the very heart of society? Civilization! It means in the present day the gathering of men together more and more in great masses. It means the luxurious, artistic, voluptuous life of great towns. It means the wan, weary, toilsome, haggard life of those who, in those same great towns, must minister to that life of ease and wealth. It means the rich growing very rich. It means the poor growing very poor. Civilization has its dark shadow of degradation ever following on its track — the darker by contrast with its light. Civilization and science! Have they arrested war? Have they softened the heart of humanity? Civilization and art and science! Why, they are busy making mitrailleuses, and inventing the newest and most sweepingly destructive methods of murder! Where will you find, in any one of those things that men worship, a substitute for God? Where will you find, in these leaves of the tree of knowledge, 'the healing of the nations?' Yes! we should indeed be mocking you if we spoke, as some speak, of a coming millennium of science and art; we should indeed be mocking you if we spoke of the possibility of the natural condition of man being remedied without supernatural help. We believe in the perfection of humanity, but not in this life. We believe in a Millenium yet to come—not in *this* world, but in that which is yet to be revealed. We believe in an eternal peace, but it is to be at the coming of the Prince of peace. It is in this faith and this alone that we gain courage to look upon the sins and sorrows — the deadly sins, the weary sorrows — that afflict humanity. It is in the strength of this faith that we bear, each one of us, our own griefs and carry our own sorrows. It is in the strength of this faith that we can look for the last time into unclosed graves, and, though with lips that are white and quivering with agony, can raise the song of Christian triumph over death and despair, and, looking onward into the distant future, which that hour of sorrow seems to bring so very near, we can thank God again and again for the message that he has given us, and that we give you here in his name to-night: 'Blessed' — thrice blessed! — 'are they that have not seen, and yet have believed.'" — *William Connor, Bishop of Peterborough.*

THE END OF THE WORLD.

"If the body's death seems to teach the lesson that modesty is becoming to the scientific speculator, what shall we say as to the prospects of that material frame which is beyond ourselves — the general, orderly frame of the universe as we see it around us? People would suppose, from the way in which you hear men talk now, that there was not the slightest chance for any great organic change ever coming across the outward world in which we live. No doubt God works by fixed laws. No doubt the world goes on morning and evening, and summer and winter; but what reason have you to suppose that it will so go on to infinity? Have no great catastrophes befallen the world before now? Does not physical science speak itself of these catastrophes? What is there to prevent other catastrophes, produced by the operation of laws, of which, at present, we are very ignorant, coming athwart the globe on which we live, and a complete change taking place in the relations in which things, even in the outward world, stand at present, so that, in the scriptural sense of the word, there may be an end to the world, as there is certainly to be an end of earthly life? To be sure, things have gone on for a long time in the same way; but is that any proof that they are to go on in the same way forever?

"You arise morning after morning in good health and strength, and seem to say to yourselves for a time that this will last forever; but one morning something happens, you cannot explain what; the best physician in the world cannot tell you what; but something has happened that lays you on a bed of sickness, and in two days sends you off to your grave a corpse. Will the experience of the reality of the way in which everything has gone on since you were young, till you have attained maturity, save from that great mischance? Again, men for centuries had ranged over the mountains in Campagna; they thought that all would go on there,—herds and flocks feeding, and vineyards growing, as they had done for centuries; and suddenly there was a strange sound heard, and a volcano burst forth, and the greatest philosopher of the age came to look at it, and lost his life while he was looking. But neither he, nor any of the men who had speculated with him, ever expected that these great cities were to be swept to destruction, and their beautiful pastures to become for a time an arid wilderness. I do not say such instances explain or tell us distinctly that such catastrophes will befall the whole globe; but at all events, I think they ought to make us modest, seeing that the wisest know so very small a portion of the laws that regulate God's creation.

"Surely, we may not dogmatically assume that such catastrophes are beyond the range of possible or probable events. It is true, I say, things have gone on for a long time, and men say, 'Where is the promise of His coming, for all things continue as they were from the beginning of the world?' But still with Him, with whom one day is as a thousand years, and a thousand years as one day, there may be changes maturing of which no philosopher of the present or of any previous age has ever dreamed, which will bring this great catastrophe to the globe; which will answer, on the whole outward creation, to something as great as is our passage from life to death, and what is beyond it. I do not think there is anything fanciful in such an expectation. I believe that a man of that modest mind, which is the characteristic of true science, will hesitate before he pronounces with any assurance that such a change may not come over the world, as has been distinctly predicted in the Scriptures." — *A. C. Tait, Archbishop of Canterbury.*

THE NEW CREATION.

"As well in the Scriptures of the Old Testament as in those of the New, we hear the expectation most positively confessed, that with the present dispensation the earth, also, which we inhabit, shall one day have grown old, and be succeeded by a new creation. From the Old Testament there come under this head such places as Ps. 102:27; Isa. 34:4; 51:6; 65:17, 18. In the New, the plastic representation of 2 Peter 3:10–15 especially attracts our attention. If, considering the disputed authenticity of this epistle, the latter text gives rise to much more doubt than assent, it cannot pass unobserved that the Lord also makes mention of a passing away of heaven and earth as certainly impending; while also, according to John, the world passes away, and according to Paul, the whole creation, now sharing with us in the consequences of sin, sighs for an hour of deliverance and glorification. In the Jewish theology, also, of that period, yea, in heathen poets and philosophers, we meet with unequivocal traces of the same conception. And indeed, however much that is terrible may be associated with this expectation, it has nothing about it that is absurd, and it is more reasonable than the opposite one. Whatever has once been created and subjected to continual change, bears also in itself the germs of new shocks and of eventual dissolution. We have simply to read again the history of the flood, or to open a few chapters of the historic book of geology, in order to feel that what once has happened may be repeated in another manner. There is no single reason for expecting a new and perfect world from the unceasing advancement of chemistry and of industry. On the contrary, material development is made to minister infinitely more to the refinement of sensuous enjoyment than to the cause of truth and righteousness; and it becomes ever more apparent that man, in proportion as he subjects the earth to himself, also the more defiles the earth. What it *could* become for the kingdom of God, it will one day have become; but the destination of that kingdom lies higher than this visible creation, and wherefore should not the Master, when the instrument has served its purpose, replace it by another? That there are natural forces enough, present in the bowels of the earth, to be able, at a sign of Omnipotence, to accomplish the most terrible overthrow, can be doubted by none. The belief that God in his time will set free these forces, and employ them for the purifying of that which has been defiled by sin, has its solid ground in the word of prophet and apostle; and finds its support in all that, which, in accordance with that word, we expect of the life of the future. An inquiry as to the nature and effect of the fire of which the apostle speaks, lies beyond the limit we have marked out for ourselves. We need not even speak of the 'boundless universe' which shall 'fall in ruins.' Scripture does not direct our glance further than our earth, with its surrounding atmosphere. On this it points to a change, in connection with which it is, for *us* at least, impossible to think only of the destruction of Jerusalem, or of similar events. But at the same time, it leads us to expect a new heaven and a new earth, which shall be not merely the opposite, but, so to speak, the consequence, the result, of the great process of purifying and dissolution; the noblest gold, brought forth from the most terrible furnace-heat.

"It is especially to this reverse side of the picture that the eye of faith directs itself with unspeakable longing. God destroys only to create something more beautiful; and upon the ruins of the sentenced and purified world his hand raises up another, which, not only for the cleansed vision of its new inhabitants, but in a reality as yet to us unknown, shall bloom in unfading splendor. If we mistake not, the last page of the Apocalypse, especially, opens up to us the prospect of a new order of things, in which the old boundary line between heaven and earth is effaced, and this latter, now inhabited by perfectly redeemed ones, itself has become part of heaven. It is certainly a proof how even the science of faith does not always teach its student modesty, when we consider how many pages have been devoted by some, in earlier times, to all kinds of questions, e. g., as to the animal and vegetable kingdom, the light and food, etc., of the new world, with regard to which even no prophet or apostle has ventured to give us any indication. But if this folly is blameworthy, not less so is that of a modern, self-styled science, which cannot advance beyond the old doubt as to the reality of things unseen and yet future. Deeper reflection must render the opposite in the highest degree probable, namely, that as Nature has shared in the fall of man, so shall it share in his future glorifying; and teaches us to feel not only the beauty, but also the truth, of the saying of Luther, 'The earth as yet wears its working garb; then the earth also will put on its paschal and pentecostal raiment.' In this new creation we at the same time behold the theatre of the perfect blessedness, of which we have earlier spoken, and of which we in vain endeavor to shadow forth the dazzling splendor. To the question, however, what place the glorified King of the kingdom of God will occupy in this boundless circle, the answer cannot be difficult. His kingly dominion comes to an end in the sense in which we have already spoken, but everlastingly does he remain the first-born among many brethren; their guide to the living fountains of waters; their lamp, that is, the mediate cause through whom all continue to receive, out of the eternal source, their light and life; their holiness and happiness; the golden heart of the mighty paradise-rose of the blessed, to use Dante's glorious image. Where thus the God-man is seen, and in him the Father, by all who are *one* in the Holy Ghost, there we need not ask whether this new heaven and earth may truly be termed the crown of the whole work of restoration."—*J. J. Van Oosterzee, Chr. Dogmatics.*

WHERE ARE WE?

"We stand on the borders of a new era. The present dispensation is almost finished. In a few more years, if prophecy be not thoroughly misinterpreted, we shall enter upon another condition. This poor earth of ours, which has been swathed in darkness, shall put on her garments of light. She hath toiled a long while in travail and sorrow. Soon shall her groanings end. Her surface, which hath been stained with blood, is soon to be purified by love, and a religion of peace is to be established. The hour is coming when storms shall be hushed, when tempests shall be unknown, when whirlwind and hurricane shall stay their mighty force, and when 'the kingdoms of this world shall become the kingdoms of our Lord and of his Christ.' But you ask me what sort of kingdom that is to be, and whether I can show you any likeness thereof. I answer, No. 'Eye hath not seen, nor ear heard, neither have entered into the heart of man, the things which God hath prepared for them that love him,' in the next, the millennial dispensation; 'but God hath revealed them unto us by his Spirit.'

"Sometimes when we climb upwards, there are moments of contemplation when we can understand that verse, 'From whence also we look for the Saviour, the Lord Jesus Christ,' and can anticipate that thrice-blessed hour, when the King of kings shall put on his head the crown of the universe; when he shall gather up sheaves of sceptres, and put them beneath his arm; when he shall take the crowns from the heads of all monarchs, and welding them into one, shall put them on his own head, amidst the shout of ten thousand times ten thousand, who shall chant his high praises. But it is little enough that we can guess of its wonders."

"O Christians! do you know that your Lord is coming? In such an hour as ye think not, the Man who once hung quivering on Calvary will descend in glory; 'the head that once was crowned with thorns' will soon be crowned with a diadem of brilliant jewels. I do look for his pre-millennial advent, and expect he will come here again."

"Jesus, our Lord, is to be King of all the earth, and rule all nations in a glorious, personal reign. The saints, as being kings in Christ, have a right to the whole world."—*C. H. Spurgeon.*

DISTINGUISH THE TIMES.

"The ancients had a useful saying concerning the Scriptures: '*Distinguish the periods, and the Scriptures will harmonize.*' 'Distinguish the periods;' and here comes the very point — the period. The Jew had fastened his attention so on one portion of the prophecies, that he saw but one period—the glorious period of the Messiah's reign; and the Christian church has for centuries so fixed its attention on one part of the prophecies only, that it saw but one period—the coming of the Messiah to be crucified. Jewish prejudices arose from partial attention to the prophecies, and Christian prejudice has arisen from partial attention to the prophecies. It should be our privilege to distinguish the periods; and while we maintain, as Christians, the literal fulfillment of Isaiah's prophecy of the Virgin's Child, and the birth at Bethlehem, as foretold by Micah, and, therefore, that the Messiah has come, we ought to maintain, also, with the Jews, the literal interpretation of Isaiah's prophecy, that the Messiah shall reign, and believe with the Jews, that the Messiah shall come. Surely this was the real nature and genius of what the angels said to the disciples, as you may read in the first chapter of the Acts of the Apostles. The disciples, in astonishment, saw their Divine Master carried up into the air from them, and disappearing in the clouds; and while they were looking up in amazement, two angels appeared, and said: 'Ye men of Galilee, why stand ye gazing up into heaven?' What was the cause? Have you ever asked yourselves what was the cause of the amazing astonishment of the disciples? Not the mere physical miracle—they were too much accustomed to the physical miracles of their Master to be surprised at that merely, and to make us suppose that to have been the cause of their astonishment. How does what the angels said afterwards address itself to that? 'Ye men of Galilee, why stand ye gazing up into heaven? This same Jesus which is taken up . . . shall so come.' Was that calculated to abate their astonishment at the miracle which had taken place? Nay, but it was to assert another miracle. How, then, shall we interpret the incident? What was the basis and ground of their astonishment? I think it very plain and instructive. They had learned, unmistakably, that Jesus was the Messiah. They were present when they heard Peter's confession, and the remarkable approbation which was expressed of it by the Lord Jesus. They knew, then, that he was the Messiah, the one that was to come, and they expected great things for their nation; they knew that a number of the prophecies, still unfulfilled, were connected with the Messiah's name. They were looking for them; and when he was taken from them, and put to death, their expectations were dashed to the ground. When, however, they saw him again after the resurrection, their expectations revived, and they said, 'Wilt thou at this time restore again the kingdom to Israel?' Will you finish it all now? And when he had given them an answer—not, indeed, to reject their idea that the kingdom would be restored, but only to tell them the time was not for them to know—when he had done this, he was suddenly taken from among them, and they were left in amazement. What were they ready to say within their own minds and hearts: 'After all, is he not the Messiah? Is it possible that we were wrong? And if he be, how can he have gone away, leaving so much undone that was predicted of the Messiah? He has done enough to assure us that he is the Messiah. He has fulfilled some prophecies. At his word the deaf man heard; at his word the tongue of the dumb man sung; at his word the lame leaped for joy; at his word the dead came to life. He must be the Messiah; and yet he is gone! No kingdom restored to Israel! No reigning at Jerusalem!' There *was* ground for astonishment, and in that state of astonishment the angels addressed them: 'Ye men of Galilee, why stand ye gazing up into heaven?' as if he had left undone what had been promised! Do not imagine that all is to be done at one time. *Distinguish the periods.* He is gone, it is true; but he is not gone forever. That same Jesus, whom ye have seen go, 'shall so come in like manner as ye have seen him go into heaven.'

"I do not know whether I ever told you of a conversation I overheard, some years ago, between a clergyman of the Church of England and a Jew, in the vestry of a church in London. I had been preaching on Jewish prophecies, and giving to the congregation, as plainly as I could, what I have been now endeavoring to convey to your minds; and to the vestry, after the service, two Jews came, to express their gratification for what they had heard, and their willingness to hear from me more about Jesus of Nazareth, and to invite me to go the next morning to breakfast with them. They were willing to hear more. Well, I referred them to the clergyman who came in at the same moment — and he was a man of some mark in our church too. He had come into the vestry-room, holding the back of his hands towards me, and said, 'How can you preach such nonsense?' 'Well, now,' I said, 'if you will allow me, while changing my dress, I will refer you to these Jewish gentlemen to converse;' and they soon got into the thick of the argument. The Jew said to him, 'Oh, upon that interpretation, sir, I deny that a virgin ever had a son.' 'Oh! but,' said the clergyman, 'we know that it is true.' 'How do you know it?' 'It is said in the Bible.' 'Well,' said the Jew, 'what more is said in the Bible—"*He shall reign upon the throne of his father David*"—is not that in the Bible?' 'Yes.' 'Well, is not that what the gentleman has been telling us, and you don't believe it? You call it nonsense. Now, if you deny that, I deny the other.' 'Well,' said the clergyman, 'but we know that the prophecy of the birth of Christ of a virgin is true, because it is a matter of fact.' Sir, I never shall forget the Jew's face — he looked at him with such a withering sneer. 'Ay,' said he, 'YOU BELIEVE BECAUSE IT IS DONE; WE BELIEVE BECAUSE GOD HAS SAID.' "—*Hugh M'Neile, D. D.**

THE COMING OF THE LORD JESUS.

"In the days of the apostles the disciples were comforted and encouraged by the prospect of the personal return of the Lord Jesus Christ. An angel had said to them as they watched the Lord depart from the earth, 'Ye men of Galilee, why stand ye gazing up into heaven? This same Jesus, which is taken up from you into heaven, shall so come in like manner as ye have seen him go into heaven.' Acts 1:11. This, and not death, was the hope of the church; and thus it ought to have remained up to his actual return. His coming should have continued to be the hope of the church; but this, alas! for centuries has not been the case.

* Extracts from a speech delivered at the annual meeting of the Jews' Society, held in Dublin, April 8, 1856.

"In confessions of faith, the truth that the Lord Jesus will come again, may still have had a place; but practically, to by far the greater number of his disciples, it has been *a mere doctrinal statement* that has not been enjoyed, and which has had no influence upon their lives. The Lord, however, desired it should be otherwise. He intended that his church should look for him, that she should watch and wait for his return. Again and again, during his personal ministry, the Lord Jesus foretold this great event; and after his ascension the apostles referred continually to it.

"Very many passages of Scripture might be quoted in proof of this assertion, but I will only mention the following: 'When the Son of man shall *come in his glory*, and all the holy angels with him, then shall he sit upon the throne of his glory.' Matt. 25:31. 'In my Father's house are many mansions; if it were not so, I would have told you. I go to prepare a place for you. And if I go and prepare a place for you, I will *come again* and receive you unto myself; that where I am there ye may be also.' John 14:2, 3. 'As it is appointed unto men once to die, but after this the judgment; so Christ was once offered to bear the sins of many; and unto them that look for him shall he *appear the second time*, without sin unto salvation.' Heb. 9:27, 28.

" 'The Lord himself shall *descend from heaven* with a shout, with the voice of the archangel, and with the trump of God; and the dead in Christ shall rise first; then (afterward) we, which are alive and remain, shall be caught up together with them in the clouds, to meet the Lord in the air; and so shall we ever be with the Lord.' 1 Thess. 4:16, 17. These quotations suffice to prove that the second coming of the Lord Jesus means that he will return *in person*, and has no reference to the gift of the Holy Spirit on the day of Pentecost, nor to his manifesting himself in an especial manner to the believer in the way of comfort, instruction, or help of any kind; nor has it reference to our death, when we, as believers, are taken to be with him. . . .

"In connection with the return of the Lord Jesus is another event, namely, the separation between the wheat and the tares. Read, carefully, Matt. 13:24–30; also verses 37–43. In this parable, together with our Lord's own explanation of it, we see what is to be expected during this present dispensation, while Jesus tarries. Civilization, mental cultivation, and advancement in knowledge of every kind may continue to the utmost; but man, fallen man remains *a ruined creature*, except he be regenerated by the power of the Holy Spirit, through the acceptance of the gospel. Intellectually he may be improved and polished to the very highest degree; but he is a *sinner*, and, in his natural condition, remains lost, ruined, and undone. He may even possess natural religion and a form of godliness; but if he is not born again he is still at enmity with God, and as assuredly as he does not believe in the Lord Jesus Christ, 'the wrath of God abideth on him.' John 3: 36.

"Sin is not, as some suppose, *a comparatively little thing*. It is a deadly spiritual disease, as the word of God declares it to be; and no progress in education, no mental culture, can eradicate it from the heart, nor change depraved human nature. For, notwithstanding every effort at improvement, the heart *remains* 'deceitful above all things and desperately wicked.' Until the return of the Lord Jesus, therefore, the present state of things will *continue*, and, as we shall see presently from the word of God, will become worse and worse.

"This, then, plainly shows the notion entertained by many godly, excellent persons, that the world will be *converted during the present dispensation*, by the preaching of the gospel, and that the Millennium will thus finally be introduced, to be not according to the Holy Scriptures.

"The gospel, indeed, was to be preached 'for a *witness* unto all nations,' but it was not to be the means of the *conversion* of the world. Matt. 24: 14. Moreover, from Acts 15: 14 we learn the character of the present dispensation, which is, that God *takes out* from among the Gentiles 'a people for his name,' but does not *convert* all nations. This is confirmed by the parable of the wheat and the tares; for if the whole world were to be converted before the return of the Lord Jesus, there would be no truth in the explanation given of it by our Lord himself. *He* tells us that the tares (the children of the wicked one) were to grow together with the wheat (the children of the kingdom), until the end of the age, namely, up to the time of his own return. This, therefore, the word of the Lord Jesus, is in direct opposition to the common notion that the world will be converted previous to his coming again. . . .

"And now the last part of our subject remains to be considered, namely, the *practical* effect this truth should have upon our hearts. If it be really received and entered into, the child of God will say, 'What can I do for my blessed Saviour before he comes again? How can I most glorify him? His will concerning me is that I should occupy until he come. How, then, can I best use for him the talents with which I am entrusted, my physical strength, my mental powers? How can my sight, my tongue, *all* my faculties of mind and body be best devoted to his praise? How should my time, my money, all that I am, and have, be used for him? How can my whole spirit, soul, and body be best consecrated to his service?

"These are deeply important, practical questions which all believers in the Lord Jesus should ask themselves, seeing that we are not our own, but are bought with a price, even with his precious blood. Instead of indulging in inactivity and listlessness on account of the evil state of things around us, we should pray and work, and work and pray, as if it were in *our* power to stem the torrent of abounding iniquity; for who can say *how much good* one single child of God, who is thoroughly in earnest, may accomplish; and how greatly he may glorify God by walking in entire separation from all that is hateful to Him? We have especially also to guard against the temptation of slackening our efforts for the conversion of sinners, because the world will not be converted before Jesus comes. Rather should we say, 'The time that he delayeth his coming may be short; what therefore can I do to warn sinners, and to win souls for him?'

"When it pleased God in July, in 1829, to reveal to my heart the truth of the personal return of the Lord Jesus, and to show me that I had made a great mistake in looking for the conversion of the world, the effect it produced upon me was this: From my *inmost soul* I was stirred up to feel compassion for perishing sinners, and for the slumbering world around me lying in the wicked one, and considered, 'Ought I not to do what I can to win souls for the Lord Jesus while he tarries, and to rouse a slumbering church?' I determined, consequently, to go from place to place, in order to preach the gospel and arouse the church to look and to *wait* for the second coming of the Lord from heaven.

"I soon began this, but in a short time saw it plainly to be the Lord's will that I should stay for a while at Teignmouth, Devonshire, in a pastoral position, and labor in Bristol in the same way; but though I have now been a pastor for more than *fifty-one years*, my heart has always been true to these two points; and by means of 'The Scriptural Knowledge Institution for Home and Abroad,' which the Lord has permitted me to found, I have for forty-seven years been aiming at the conversion of sinners, and have sought to awaken the Church of Christ at large to look for his appearing as her great hope. . . .

"As assuredly as the practical character of the Lord's second coming is really apprehended in the power of it, the *most blessed* effects upon the life and deportment of Christians will follow. By means of it we are taught what awaits the worldly, lying in the wicked one, and what will be the end of all this world's glory, pride, and pomp. The future destiny of the children of God is also unfolded to us, even that we shall be perfectly conformed to the image of our risen Lord, both in soul and body, when we shall see him as he is.

"*Then* shall we enter upon the possession of our inheritance, which is incorruptible and undefiled, and that fadeth not away; and shall be seated with Jesus on his throne (Rev. 3: 21), to judge the world in union with Him, and to spend a happy eternity together with our Lord in glory. 'Behold, I come quickly, and my reward is with me, to give every man according as his work shall be.' Rev. 22: 12."—*George Müller*.

THE GOSPEL A WITNESS.

"Jesus shall return from his second far journey. More faithless than fond are the eyes which are at present, and for long have been, turned towards the heavens into which he has gone. Many are fearing—many more are hoping—that, as with the diver in that famous poem of Schiller's, his second plunge is his last. Let us not be deemed uncharitable if we state it as our deliberate opinion, that the theory of the Germans as to the mythic character of Christ is just the fruit, the legitimate and long-expected fruit, of the indifference of the church as to the person, personal history, and personal coming of Jesus Christ. Christ has been gradually merged in Christianity; the life has been sunk in the system, a living power changed into a dead electric apparatus which will no longer electrify.

"Christ's personal story has become a tradition; his personal coming pushed away across an imaginary period of 365,000 years, and his personal reign on earth rudely and contemptuously denied. Perish such a mythical and misty theory of the God-man, Christ Jesus! But perish also those cold and starched notions of which the doctrine of Strauss is but the consummate and detestable flower.

" 'This gospel of the kingdom,' I am told in Matthew, 'shall be preached in all the world for a witness unto all nations, and then shall the end come.' I never read these words without remembering a spectacle I, in common with thousands, saw, and which none that saw it can ever forget. It was when Her Majesty, the Queen, visited the Scottish metropolis, in 1842. Scarcely had the twilight darkened into night, than from every hill surrounding that most magnificent of cities, there seemed to rise simultaneously a crest of fire. Each mountain lifted up into his hand a torch; and from Berwick to Fife, and Fife to Sterling, the great Firth was at once illuminated. It was a witness, it was a token to the land that its sovereign was near. It was a token, too, to the approaching vessel, far out at sea, that all was ready for her reception; that loyalty had gushed out into these flaming signals. Thus, when the gospel beacons, from California to Japan, are fully lit, it will be a witness, a token to earth, that the end is approaching, and a signal to heaven for the preparation of the chariot, the harnessing of the steeds, the furbishing of the thunderbolts, the gathering together of all the elements, the witnesses, and the victims of that great day of God Almighty. Our part, meanwhile, is surely to go forward, and to light up from land to land the signals for this great and blessed advent."—*George Gilfillan.*

OUR GREAT WANT IS CHRIST.

"For six thousand years the earth has been smitten, ravaged, broken, parcelled out among the nations; the nations relatively increasing and diminishing; empires rising and falling; governments forming, flourishing, failing; but, under all circumstances, at all times, and in all places, man — sinning, sorrowing, dying! Such a world, O ye antichrists! if purposely made so, and hopelessly kept so, were a shame, a disgrace, a curse, to its Maker! And do ye still bespeak for it the innumerable and immeasurable ages? Aha! GOD knows better and will do better!"

"From the fall of Adam until now, not a year, or day, or hour, or moment, has passed, but his eye has watched our planet, and his heart has been intent on the redemption of our race. By the sufferings of his first advent he made an atonement for sin itself, and by the miracles of the second he will set us free from its consequences. At the close of his last prophetic interview with his latest surviving apostle, he declared: 'Surely I come quickly; Amen:' to which the apostle replied, in behalf of the church and the world, 'Even so, come, Lord Jesus!'

"I profess no skill or assurance, in determination of prophetic times and seasons. I simply wait on the Lord. Nevertheless, I cannot but understand that we are now nearly eighteen centuries nearer the fulfillment of the promise than when it was given. Neither can I forget that many lines of prophecy, relating to the same great event, appear to converge about the present era. And neither can I be unobservant of the fact, that the world is now open from pole to pole, — that the gospel has already performed its office, to a great extent, as a witness for Christ among all nations, — and that the condition of nature and society, everywhere, seems to invite divine intervention for the resurrection of the dead, the transformation of the living, the judgment of all, the renovation of heaven and earth, the establishment of everlasting righteousness, and the universal development and triumph of the kingdom of glory and of God.

"All we can say, is,—and this must be said with infinite reverence,—'the sooner the better:' the sooner Christ's time comes, the better for all who wait for his coming. If, amidst the conflict of empires, the revolution of kingdoms, the crumbling of republics, and the consequent amazement and alarm of all mankind, we seem to hear a repetition of the promise, 'Surely I come quickly!' —as just about to be realized,—let our hearts leap within us as we answer, 'Even so, come, Lord Jesus!'

"Here is our want, — CHRIST! 'Thou, O Christ, art *all* we want!' He, essentially and truly, whether known or unknown, is 'the desire of all nations.' Let the antichrists say what they will, the only hope of the world is in JESUS CHRIST. *I shall gain my chief object if I can only persuade you duly to remember this.*"— *T. H. Stockton, D. D., "The Book Above All."*

THE ANCIENT HOPE.

"When our Lord left his church on earth to go to the Father, he left her in a sorrowful condition. His five hundred disciples were surrounded by the whole world of his enemies, organized into antichristian religions and governments by one of the highest intelligences, animated by the most venomous malice, and educated by the experience of ages in the most effectual modes of destruction. The Lord was not ignorant of our danger; nor in his last discourses did he extenuate it, nor promise any abatement of the world's enmity and the church's tribulation. But he did promise that he himself would return to overthrow his enemies, and that he would support us till that blessed day. 'The world hateth you.' 'In the world ye shall have tribulation.' 'Ye shall weep and lament, but the world shall rejoice: and ye shall be sorrowful, but your sorrow shall be turned into joy. A woman when she is in travail hath sorrow, because her hour is come; but as soon as she is delivered of the child, she remembereth no more the anguish, for joy that a man is born into the world. And ye now therefore have sorrow, but I will see you again, and your hearts shall rejoice, and your joy no man taketh from you.' 'If I go and prepare a place for you, I will come again, and receive you unto myself; that where I am, there ye may be also.'

"Such was the blessed hope of his personal return with which he comforted his church on his personal departure. During all the period of his absence, he said we must suffer tribulation; and so it has come to pass. If we are to enjoy any period of outward peace during his absence, if his church is to be delivered from the assaults of the world, if there is to be any age of purity, when the tares shall not grow among the wheat, or if, at his coming, he shall be welcomed by the population of an earth filled with the glory of the Lord; or, indeed, even be able to find faith in the earth,—it will be to him a most unexpected surprise. Jesus did not know of this millennium. We say he did not know of it, because he did not tell us of it; and he says, 'I have called you friends, for all things which I have heard of my Father, I have made known unto you.' But in all his discourses and parables, there is not the least hint that we are to hope for any period of peace or glory before his coming. The apostles are equally ignorant of a Christless millennium. For three hundred years after our Lord's departure, the blessed hope of the church was the hope of his return.

"But when, in the progress of her predicted apostasy, the bride of Christ began to solace herself in his absence with the friendship of the kings of the earth, very naturally she averted her eyes from the eastern sky, and from that return of her Lord which would put an end to all her worldly grandeurs. When the reformers put the gospel trumpet to their mouths, and began to blow the reveille which was destined to awake the harlot of Babylon, the dreams of a Christless millennium were instantly swept away, with the rest of the popish trumpery; and the church again began to look for the coming of the Lord to destroy Antichrist. Luther hoped that it might not be much more than a hundred years from his day. In their letters, sermons, and confessions of faith, the reformers proclaimed their pre-millennial hopes."—*Robert Patterson, D. D.*

LOVING HIS APPEARING.

"Our desires pant after the end of this age, the passing away of the world at the great day of God," says Tertullian. "Holy Lord, dost thou call that 'a little while' in which I shall not see thee? Oh, this 'little' is a long little!" exclaims St. Bernard. "If I were but sure that the trumpet should sound, and the dead should rise, and the Lord appear before the period of my age, it would be the joyfullest tidings to me in the world," says Richard Baxter. And in the daily prayer which Christ himself has prescribed for all his followers, he has inserted a petition which puts every one on the anxious look-out for his return, and in which he would have his people ever beseeching him that it may not be delayed. 'Thy kingdom come,' is a prayer which shall not be answered till the King himself comes.

"Somewhere in the writings of Joanna Baillie there is a picture of a maiden whose lover had gone to the Holy Land, and was reported to be slain. With steadfast hopes that he would again return, she kindled a beacon-fire on the shore of the island where she dwelt, to guide the vessel which love imagined would restore him to her arms. And by that watch-fire she took her stand each night, looking out across the dusky Mediterranean with sad and tremulous expectation of him on whom her heart was set. It was meant only as poetry; but it may also be taken as a significant parable. That maiden is the Church. That lover is Jesus. That Holy Land is heaven. That report that he is dead is the teaching of unbelief and cold-hearted skepticism. That watch-fire is the flame of love and 'blessed hope,' fed by the midnight ministrations of waiting faithfulness. That scene beyond is the misty future. The darkness, the bleak rocks, and the rolling waters are nature's discouragements to a steadfast faith. And there, age after age, through all the night of her affliction, stands the noble maiden by her love-lit fire, bending forward to hail His coming who has pledged himself to make her his happy bride."—*Dr. J. A. Seiss.*

THE TRIUMPHANT KINGDOM OF GOD.

"That the return of the Lord will not be simply a momentarily becoming visible from heaven, but a return *to earth*, is according to the Scriptures beyond doubt.

Those dwellers on the earth, who, according to 1 Thess. 4:17, are caught up to meet him in the air, must certainly be conceived of as then returning with the heavenly host again to the earth. They form an escort to the King, who personally comes to this part of his royal domain. Simultaneously with the coming of Christ, takes place *the first resurrection*. The believers, who live to witness this appearing of Christ upon earth, are, without dying, by an instantaneous change, made meet for the new condition; and the departed who are ripe for the life of resurrection, live and reign with Christ on earth. It appears to be the meaning of the Spirit, that these chosen ones themselves, in whatever form, take part in the prolonged judgment, accomplished by the glorified King of the kingdom of God, and by means of his appearing. Paul also teaches us to look for a successive condemnation and destruction of the most powerful enemies of the kingdom of God. Thus is the power of darkness chained, in expectation that it shall yet hereafter be wholly destroyed."—*J. J. Van Oosterzee, Christian Dogmatics.*

THE FINAL CONSUMMATION.

"There is no evidence, either from Scripture or experience, that any substance has ever been annihilated. If force be motion, it may cease; but cessation of motion is not annihilation; and the common idea in our day, among men of science, is, that no force is ever lost. It is, as they say, only transformed. However this may be, it is a purely gratuitous assumption that any substance has ever passed out of existence. In all the endless and complicated changes which have been going on, from the beginning, in our earth and throughout the universe, nothing, so far as known, has ever ceased to be. Of course he who creates can destroy; the question, however, concerns the purpose, and not the power, of God; and he has never, either in his Word or in his works, revealed his purpose to destroy any thing he has once created.

"Many of the old theologians, especially among the Lutherans, understood the Bible to teach the absolute annihilation of our world. Schmid states, as the Lutheran doctrine, that the world is to be reduced to nothing. He quotes Baier, Hollaz, and Quenstedt in support of his view. Gerhard takes the same view; he admits, however, that many of the fathers, and Luther himself, were on the other side. He quotes Irenæus, Cyril, of Jerusalem, Jerome, Augustine, and Chrysostom, as in favor of mutation and against annihilation. Luther was wont to say, 'The heavens have their workday clothes on; hereafter they will have on their Sunday garments.' Most of the reformed theologians generally oppose the idea of annihilation.

"The subject of the change which is to take place at the last day is not the whole material universe, but our earth and what pertains to it. It is true the Bible says, 'Heaven and earth shall pass away,' and by heaven and earth the Scriptures often mean the universe; and it would, therefore, be consistent with the language of Scripture to hold that the whole universe is to be changed at the last day. It was natural that this interpretation should be put upon the language of the Bible, so long as our earth was regarded as the central body of the universe, and sun, moon, and stars as subordinate luminaries, intended simply for the benefit of the inhabitants of our world. The case, however, assumes a different aspect when we know that our earth, and even our solar system, is a mere speck in the immensity of God's works. It is one of the unmistakable evidences of the divine origin of the Scriptures, that they are written on such a high level that all the mutations of human science take place beneath them, without ever coming into collision with their teachings. They could be read by those who believed that the sun moves round the earth, without their convictions being shocked by their statements; and they can be read by us, who know that the earth moves round the sun, with the same satisfaction and confidence. Whether the heaven and earth which are to pass away are the whole material universe, or only our earth and its atmospheric heavens, the language of the Scripture leaves undecided. Either view is perfectly consistent with the meaning of the words employed. The choice between the two views is to be determined by other considerations. The *à priori* probability is overwhelming, in favor of the more limited interpretation. Anything so stupendous as the passing away of the whole universe, as the last act of the drama of human history, would be altogether out of keeping. The Bible concerns man. The earth was cursed for his transgression. That curse is to be removed when man's redemption is completed. The κτίσις that was made subject to vanity for man's sin, is our earth; and our earth is the κτίσις which is to be delivered from the bondage of corruption. The change to be effected is in the dwelling-place of man. According to the Apostle Peter, it is the world which once was destroyed by water, that is to be consumed. But, although the predictions of Scripture concern only our earth, it does not follow that the material universe is to last forever. As it is not from eternity, it probably will not last forever. It may be only one of the grand exhibitions of the wonderful working of God in the field of infinite space, and in the course of unending ages.

"The result of this change is said to be the introduction of a new heavens and a new earth. This is set forth not only in the use of these terms, but in calling the predicted change 'a regeneration,' 'a restoration,' a deliverance 'from the bondage of corruption' and an introduction 'into the glorious liberty of the sons of God.' The earth, according to the common opinion, that is, this renovated earth, is to be the final seat of Christ's kingdom. This is the new heavens; this is the new Jerusalem, the Mount Zion, in which are to be gathered the general assembly and church of the first-born, which are written in heaven; the spirits of just men made perfect; this is the heavenly Jerusalem, the city of the living God; the kingdom prepared for his people before the foundation of the world.

"It is, of course, in itself, no matter of interest what portion of space these new heavens and new earth are to occupy, or of what materials they are to be formed. As the resurrection bodies of believers are to be human bodies, they must have a local habitation, although it be one not made with hands, eternal in the heavens. All we know about it is, that it will be glorious, and adapted to the spiritual bodies which those in Christ are to receive when he comes the second time unto salvation."—*Charles Hodge, D. D., Systematic Theology, vol. iii. section* 3.

THE UNIVERSAL SONG.

"Sing, O ye heavens; for the Lord hath done it: shout, ye lower parts of the earth: break forth into singing, ye mountains; O forest, and every tree therein: for the Lord hath redeemed Jacob, and glorified himself in Israel."—*Isaiah* 44:23.

"This text will obtain its best fulfillment, methinks, *at the day of the Lord's appearing*,— that day around which our chief hopes must ever centre. The day will come when the gospel shall have been preached for the last time, when the chosen of God shall have been all gathered out from among men, and the dispensation shall be fulfilled. Then shall all the saints rise to glory at the call of God. The elect multitude shall be there, every one according to the redemption of the Son, every one according to the calling of the Spirit, all there; upon their faces there shall be no spot or wrinkle, and on their garments no stain nor defilement, for they are without fault before the throne of God. Then as the books are opened, and the transgressions of the ungodly are published under heaven, they shall stand without trembling, for,

>'Jesus, thy blood and righteousness
>Their beauty are, their glorious dress;
>'Midst flaming worlds, in these arrayed,
>With joy shall they lift up their heads.'

"Let us listen to the song. The angels sing, for they have deep sympathy with the redemption of man; the redeemed in glory sing, for they have been the recipients of this mighty mercy; the material heavens themselves also ring with the sweet music, and every star takes up the refrain, and, with sun and moon, praises the Most High.

"Descending from heaven, the song charms the lower earth, and the prophet calls upon creation to share in the joy; mountains and valleys, forests and trees, are charged to join the song. Why should they not? This round earth of ours has been o'ershadowed by the curse of sin; she has yet to be unswathed of all the mists which iniquity has cast upon her, 'for the creature was made subject to vanity, not willingly, but by reason of him who hath subjected the same in hope, because the creature itself also shall be delivered from the bondage of corruption into the glorious liberty of the children of God.' Therefore let creation sing."—*C. H. Spurgeon*.

PRE-MILLENNIAL CREED.

1. "I believe that the world will never be completely converted to Christianity, by any existing agency, before the end comes. In spite of all that can be done by ministers, members, and churches, the wheat and the tares will grow together until the harvest; and when the end comes, it will find the earth in much the same state that it was when the flood came in the days of Noah. Matt. 13: 24-30; 24: 37-39.

2. "I believe that the wide-spread unbelief, indifference, formalism, and wickedness, which are to be seen throughout Christendom, are only what we are taught to expect in God's word. Troublous times, departures from the faith, evil men waxing worse and worse, love waxing cold, are things distinctly predicted. So far from making me doubt the truth of Christianity, they help to confirm my faith. Melancholy and sorrowful as the sight is, if I did not see it I should think the Bible was not true. Matt. 24: 12; 2 Tim. 3: 1-4, 13.

3. "I believe that the grand purpose of the present dispensation is to gather out of the world an elect people, and not to convert all mankind. It does not surprise me at all to hear that the heathen are not all converted when missionaries preach, and that believers are but a little flock in any congregation in my own land. It is precisely the state of things I expect to find. The gospel is to be preached 'for a witness,' and then shall the end come. This is the dispensation of election, and not of universal conversion. Acts 15: 14; Matt. 24: 14.

4. "I believe that the Second Coming of our Lord Jesus Christ is the Great Event which will wind up the present dispensation, and for which we ought daily to long and pray. 'Thy kingdom come,' 'Come, Lord

Jesus,' should be our daily prayer. We look backward, if we have faith, to Christ dying on the cross, and we ought to look forward, no less, if we have hope, to Christ coming again. John 14:3; 2 Tim. 4:8; 2 Pet. 3:12.

5. "I believe that the Second Coming of our Lord Jesus Christ will be a real, literal, personal, bodily coming; that as he went away in the clouds of heaven with his body, before the eyes of man, so, in like manner, will he return. Acts 1: 11; Rev. 1: 7.

6. "I believe that, after our Lord Jesus Christ comes again, the earth will be renewed, and the curse removed; the devil shall be bound, the godly shall be rewarded, the wicked snall be punished; and that, before he comes, there shall be neither resurrection, judgment, nor Millennium; and that not till after he comes shall the earth be filled with the knowledge of the glory of the Lord. Acts 3: 21; Isa. 25: 6–9; 1 Thess. 4: 14–18; Rev. 20: 1–6.

7. "I believe that the Jews shall be ultimately gathered again, as a separate nation, restored to their own land, and converted to the faith of Christ. Jer. 30:10, 11; 31:10; Rom. 11:25, 26.

8. "I believe that the literal sense of the Old Testament prophecies has been far too much neglected by the churches, and is far too much neglected in the present day; and that, under the mistaken system of spiritualizing and accommodating Bible language, Christians have too often completely missed its meaning. Luke 24:25, 26.

9. "I believe that the Roman Catholic Church is the great predicted apostasy from the faith, and is Babylon; and the Pope, Antichrist;—although I think it highly probable that a more complete development of Antichrist will yet be exhibited to the world. 2 Thess. 2: 3–11; 1 Tim. 4:1–6;—Rev. 13:1–8.

"I believe, finally, that it is for the safety, happiness, and comfort of all true Christians, to expect as little as possible from churches or governments under the present dispensation, to hold themselves ready for tremendous conversions and changes of all things established, and to expect their good things only from Christ's second advent."—*J. C. Ryle, Bishop of Liverpool.*

ESSAY ON THE FIRST RESURRECTION---EXTRACTS.

"If now it be asked what is the practical significance of this doctrine, and what its use for Christian edification and hope, we answer, that in order to understand this we must put ourselves back into the position of the early Christians. They seem to have lived with their expectation constantly bent upon the personal reappearing of the Lord. The first resurrection was the immediate and most glorious accompaniment of this event. Therefore, to keep the command of the absent Lord, and to be always watching and waiting for his return, was to be living in the constant and joyful anticipation of receiving back their sainted dead who were sleeping in Jesus. The difference between their attitude and that which generally prevails nowadays, is this: Now, men wait for death to bring them into the presence and companionship of the departed saints. Then, they waited for the resurrection to bring their blessed dead back to them. Now, they watch for the opening inward of the gate of the grave to let them into the company of the redeemed who, in their unclothed spirit, are with Christ in Paradise. Then, they watched for the opening outward of the gate of the grave that their dead, clothed upon with immortality, might rejoin them in their transformed bodies, and, being caught up together with them to meet the Lord in the air, might be forever with the Lord. The first resurrection being thus inseparably bound up with the Parousia, all the rewards and hopes of discipleship were identified with the personal appearing of the Lord. When his word was heard, 'Behold, I come quickly, and my reward is with me,' it was the most exalted and inspiring stimulus to Christian activity and consecration. When his promise was remembered, 'Thou shalt be recompensed at the resurrection of the just,' it was a most quickening and immediate motive to zeal and steadfastness.

"It cannot be denied, we think, that the prevailing habit of our time, so different from the apostolic, of looking for the rewards of our labor so entirely at death, and for the fruition of our hope in that intermediate state to which death introduces us, has put the resurrection into a much lower place than that which it held in the beginning. Indeed, I may say that in the popular apprehension, death has very largely usurped the place that belongs to the resurrection. But death, we must remember, is an enemy. It never was, and never can be, anything but an enemy. It is cruel, repulsive, and humbling, 'Sin's great conquest and Satan's chief work, the fullness of sorrow and affliction, the triumph of corruption, the consummation of the curse.' But how has man learned to idealize this hideous enemy into a good angel! How has he accustomed himself to speak of the grim executor of the penalty of sin as though it were his bony fingers that were commissioned to bring us our reward, and unlock for us the gates of life! How he has canonized him in poetry! 'Oh how beautiful is death,' writes Richter, 'seeing we die into a world of life!' And the poet Young sings:

> 'Death is the crown of life: . . . . .
> Death gives us more than was in Eden lost;
> The King of Terrors is the Prince of Peace.'

"Indeed, I think it would be no exaggeration to say

that, in the apprehension of many Christians, death has been thrust into the place that belongs to Christ himself, and that the crown of welcome which we should ever be waiting to put upon the head of Him who at his coming will 'swallow up death in victory,' is put upon the ghastly brow of him who is daily swallowing up life in defeat. 'Oh, strange delusion of Satan,' as one has indignantly exclaimed, 'to have made the capital curse of God eclipse the capital promise of God! Satan's consummated kingdom over the body to take the place in our thoughts which Christ's consummated kingdom in the body and spirit, even the resurrection, was meant to take.'"

"And, again, as we have already intimated, the power of the first resurrection as an influential motive may be weakened by putting the Advent afar off; 'by thrusting it from the foreground to the background of the picture; by massing it up with the shadows of eternity instead of bringing it prominently forward into the clear field of time; by reducing it to a late effect instead of an early cause in the great history.' It is impossible that men should feel the power of an event which is certainly remote, as they do one that is even possibly near. Push the event of Christ's return across the period of a thousand years, and by no possibility can it continue to be an event of such startling and solemn interest as when it is known that it may be very nigh. And that which diminishes the power of the Advent, diminishes the power and influence of all the events that attend it. And so we give expression to this earnest wish, that if our gathering together in this Conference shall not impress Christians with the duty of fixing their eyes more strongly on the coming of Christ as the great hope of the Church, it shall at least lead them to divide their interest more proportionately between the two elements of that double theme of prophecy,—'The sufferings of Christ, and the glory that should follow.' Profoundly holding that we are nearer to the glory than to the sufferings, we would that that glory were rising on our larger vision, and daily kindling more and more our hope and expectation. Why should it be deemed only safe to speak of the Lord's epiphany as a far-off event, and only perilous and fanatical to think of it as nigh even at our doors? Surely it is the expectation, not the putting away of that event, that is most conducive to our preparation for it. And we know not that Matthew Henry has put it too strongly in saying that, '*Our looking at Christ's second coming as at a distance, is the cause of all those irregularities that render the thought of it terrible to us.*' At all events we wish that it were possible for the Church to keep the second advent as near to her spiritual consciousness as she keeps the first, and that as by the reminiscence of a historic faith, Jesus Christ is evidently set forth, crucified among us, so by the transfiguration of a prophetic faith, he might be constantly beheld appearing to us with his saints in glory. Surely there is enough of sorrow and woe in the present evil world to make us long for his coming; and enough in the promises and admonitions which he has left behind to make us hope for it. 'The night is far spent, the day is at hand.' At each succeeding watch we hear the ringing challenge of the great Sentinel, 'Behold, I come quickly.' As watchmen, keeping guard with him over the city of God on earth, we at least ought to be wakeful enough to give back the answer, 'Even so, come, Lord Jesus;' and faithful enough to believe that in doing so, we are sounding no meaningless watchword, and putting up no useless prayer."—*A. J. Gordon, D. D., Pre-millennial Essays, pp.* 97–99, 104–106.

TWO RESURRECTIONS.

"I cannot consent to distort its words (Rev. 20) from their plain sense and chronological place in the prophecy, on account of any considerations of difficulty, or any risk of abuses which the doctrine of the Millennium may bring with it. Those who lived next to the apostles, and the whole church for three hundred years, understood them in the plain, literal sense; and it is a strange sight in these days to see expositors who are among the first in reverence of antiquity, complacently casting aside the most cogent instance of *consensus* which primitive antiquity presents.

"As regards the text itself, no legitimate treatment of it will extort what is known as the spiritual interpretation now in fashion. If, in a passage where two resurrections are mentioned, ... the first resurrection may be understood to mean *spiritual* rising with Christ while the second means *literal* rising from the grave, then there is an end of all significance of language, and Scripture is wiped out as a definite testimony to anything. If the first resurrection is spiritual, then so is the second, which I suppose none will be hardy enough to maintain; but *if the second is literal, then so is the first*, which, in common with the whole primitive church and many of the best modern expositors, I maintain and receive as an article of faith and hope."—*Dean Alford.*

THE COMING OF THE LORD IN ITS RELATION TO CHRISTIAN DOCTRINE.

"This great truth runs like a golden cord through the entire New Testament from beginning to end, touching every doctrine, binding every duty, arousing, consoling, directing, guarding, inspiring, the believer at every step of his pilgrimage. As a motive, an incentive to an end, it has a prominence assigned to no other thought. Wherever we turn it arrests the eye; whatever the subject of inquiry, it engages the attention by its commanding presence. In the fine language of the Rev. John Ker, it is 'in the New Testament the great event that towers above every other. The heaven, that gives back Christ, gives back all that we have loved and lost, solves all doubts and ends all sorrows. His coming looks in upon the whole life of his Church, as a lofty mountain peak looks in upon every little valley and sequestered home around its base, and belongs to them all alike. Every generation lies under the shadow of it, for whatever is transcendantly great is constantly near, and in moments of high conviction it absorbs petty interests and annihilates intervals. It may surely be for us to consider whether our removal of Christ's coming further from us in feeling does not arise from a less vivid impression of its reality and surpassing moment.'"

"'By one man sin entered into the world, and death by sin; and so death passed upon all men, for that all have sinned.' Rom. 5: 12. To fallen Adam it was said: 'Cursed is the ground for thy sake; in sorrow shalt thou eat of it all the days of thy life; thorns also and thistles shall it bring forth to thee.' Gen. 3: 17, 18. From that day to this the curse has smitten the old and the young, the rich and the poor, the king and the peasant, the philosopher and the savage alike, and diffused its virulent poison through the whole system of nature. The winds with their ominous moan, the lower animals that once crouched lovingly at man's feet, the dumb earth reluctantly yielding her riches to his toil, and the waves with their resistless might, seem to have conspired against the destroyer of their peace, as if they would hurry him into the grave. But the word of God, that liveth and abideth forever, tells of a time, and that, too, while nations exist, when 'there shall be no more curse' (Rev. 22: 3); when 'the wolf also shall dwell with the lamb, and the leopard shall lie down with the kid; and the calf, and the young lion, and the fattling together; and a little child shall lead them.' Isa. 11: 6.

"It is obvious that the spread of Christianity, however widely extended; personal devotedness to the Saviour, however fervent; the suppression of moral evils, however thorough, can never arrest disease and decay and death, nor extract malaria from the soil, nor cause the fir tree to grow instead of the thorn, and the myrtle tree in place of the brier. If, however, Post-millennialists insist that the cow and the bear feeding together, the lion eating straw like an ox, the sucking child playing unharmed on the hole of the asp, the desert rejoicing and blossoming as the rose, and the thirsty land becoming springs of water, are to be understood spiritually, being nothing more than poetical metaphors to show the transforming power of the gospel, they are forced to conclude that the curse will rush onward in its desolating career through the entire period of their anticipated millennium. Storms will continue to burst in unsparing fury upon earth and sea; creation will continue to groan in her traveling throes; plague and pestilence will continue their work of destruction; sickness and pain will continue to invade every household; death will continue to lay his ruffian grasp on every quivering form; hard labor, corroding care, bitter poverty, darkened homes, blighted hopes,

"The heart-ache, and the thousand natural shocks
That flesh is heir to,'

will continue to harass, and waste, and kill, as the thousand years roll on, until a great cry would ascend to God to bring such a millennium to a speedy end.

"But He is better than men think, for 'he shall send Jesus Christ, which before was preached unto you: whom the heaven must receive until the times of restitution of all things, which God hath spoken by the mouth of all his holy prophets since the world began.' It is reserved for the Second Man in person, and on the very earth that held his cross, to remove the curse inflicted by the first man; and it is strange that one loyal to him can wish it to be otherwise. When the expectation of his personal coming dropped out of the faith and hope of the Church, after three hundred years of blessed testimony and successful service, she did little through the dark ages to bear his name to the perishing millions; and this was dishonoring to him as the Prophet and Priest of his people. But since the era of modern missions, she boasts that she can and will repair the ruins of the fall, and reign on the earth, while he has gone into a far country to receive for himself a kingdom, and to return; and this is no less dishonoring to him as the anointed King of the nations. Some, at least, thank God, do not desire her coronation until his own royal hand shall seat her beside him on the throne, for they are singing day by day, with full intelligence of its meaning,

'Bring forth the royal diadem,
And crown him Lord of all!'"

—*James H. Brookes, D.D., Pre-millennial Essays,* pp. 293, 294, 299–301.

HISTORY OF THE PRE-MILLENNIAL DOCTRINE.

"Redeemed humanity has another goal than that of common zoology, and that goal is the kingdom of the resurrection. As Dorner has beautifully said, 'Complete victor Christianity never can be, until Nature has become an organ of its service, a willing instrument of the perfect man, that is, of the righteous who are raised from the dead.' (Person of Christ, i. 412.) 'Man and the creature,' says Ellicott, 'bound together in one common feeling of longing and expectancy, are awaiting that redemption of the body which shall be the immediate precursor of the restitution of the world, and the consummation of all things in Christ.' (Destiny of the Earth, p. 18.) So Lange: 'The expectation of the future transformation of the earth into a heavenly establishment, of the conjunction of the spiritual kingdom in the other world with that in this, nay, of the reuniting of that world itself and this, is to many a mere fancy, but to every earnest Christian a great hope, an assurance of faith, a certain prediction.' (Bremen Lectures, p. 251.) Even Dr. Fairbairn avers the same belief: 'The internal links itself with the external, . . . the bodies of the saints shall be transformed, and the whole material creation shall become a fit habitation for redeemed and glorified saints.' (Hermeneutics, p. 367.) Lechler is clearly right when saying, 'To an earthly kingdom of glory, a mass of utterances refer in the letters of the apostle (Paul), if we have an open eye for them, and this is, at the same time, that eschatological point in which all his letters harmonize.' (Apostt. und Nachap. Zeit., p. 141). Tholuck was only right when saying, 'The idea that the perfected kingdom of Christ is to be transferred to heaven, is properly a modern notion. According to Paul, and the Revelation of John, the kingdom of God is to be placed upon the earth, in so far as this itself has part in the universal transformation.' (Quoted by Lee. Eschatology, p. 247.) Pre-millennialism, therefore, looks upon the old Genesis as an apocalypse of the past given to Moses, the new

Genesis as an apocalypse of the future given to John, crowned with redemption. Its eye sweeps the whole field of development from Paradise lost to Paradise restored. The relation of the dispensation of promise to that of the law is the analogue of the relation of the present dispensation to that of the Millennium; after which is the consummation and Eternal Glory, when Christ shall have surrendered the kingdom to the Father, 'that God may be all in all.' Thus does Premillennialism become a protest against the doctrine of the unbroken evolution of the kingdom of God to absolute perfection on earth, apart from the visible and miraculous intervention of Christ. And equally is it a protest against that vapid idealism which volatilizes the perfect kingdom into a spiritual abstraction, apart from the regenesis of the earth. It asserts that the literal is always the last and highest fulfillment of prophecy. It adopts the deep truth, expressed by Oetinger, that glorified 'corporcity is the end of the ways of God,' working from within outward, from the spirit to the body of the believer, and from both to the renovation of the planet. The Millennium is the transition-stage in this process of 'the regeneration,' succeeded by the everlasting state.

"The evolution and history of the doctrine run parallel with the development and progress of all revelation. It does not rest upon an isolated passage in the Apocalypse, as many suppose, but upon the whole covenant of God in Christ for the redemption of man and earth from sin and its curse, and is the central point of eschatology. Were but one verse all that announced its existence, it would still be equally valid as that other solitary verse, in all the Bible, which announces the surrender of the jurisdiction of the kingdom, by Christ, to the Father, 'that God may be all in all.' 1 Cor.

15 : 24. But six consecutive times, in six consecutive verses, John emphasizes the kingdom as the reign of a thousand years, to make it sure to our understanding. Above even this sixfold repetition, it was, in connection with the sufferings of Christ, a chief part in the burden of 'all that God hath spoken by the mouth of all his holy prophets since the world began.' Acts 3 : 21. The circumstance that some, who in ancient, as in modern times, have abused the doctrine to a carnal sense, were called 'Chiliasts,' or 'Millenarians,' no matter how perverse their doctrine might be, vacates not the fact that a true Christian Chiliasm was the orthodox faith of the primitive church in its purest days. 'Christian Chiliasm showed no favor to the fleshly Israel, nor even to its Holy City.' (Robertson, Chh. Hist., i., p. 116.) 'Christian Chiliasm,' says Dorner, 'so far from being derivable from, may in part be more justly regarded as a polemic against, Judaism, on the part of Christianity. This is, in particular, its character, where it has apparently borrowed most features from Judaism.' (Person of Christ, i. 408.) It was no device of 'later Jews' sighing for temporal deliverance from a Syrian or Roman yoke. They never admitted a 'Second Advent' in any case. They knew no Millennium save a kingdom of Solomonic and carnal splendor, under a temporal prince, with the Levitical cultus revived. Their motto was, 'Moses forever.' They believed in a resurrection of 'gross and corruptible bodies, as are here upon earth, to eat, drink, marry, and be given in marriage, and afterward to die again.' (Cudworth, Intel. Syst., ii., 606.) Of such were the Ebionite Christians, teaching a gross Apocryphal view of the thousand years, 'after the resurrection, in an earthly kingdom of Christ, according to the carnal desires and lusts of the flesh.' (August. De Hœres, ad Quod vult, etc., cap. 8. De Civit Dei,

xx. 7.) Unfortunately for the holders of the truth, their doctrine not yet wholly free from the sensuous images of that age, the name '*Chiliasts*,' derived from the thousand years, common to both, was indiscriminately applied to both. But Christian Chiliasm is not carnal. It is no 'materializing interpretation' of spiritual prophecies by which Jewish Christians were naturally 'infected,' as with some plague-spot of sensuality. It is no convenient heretical comfort, graciously permitted for a 'distressed condition' of the church. It is no Gnostic conceit, nor Patristic invention. Not Cerinthus nor Papias were its authors, but John the apostle. Not John alone, but Peter and Paul, Isaiah and Ezekiel, Daniel and Zechariah, Moses and David and Enoch, 'holy men of God, who spake as they were moved by the Holy Ghost.' 2 Pet. 1: 21. That it has an inspired Jewish origin, so far from being a prejudice against it, only entitles it to universal acceptance, for 'Salvation is of the Jews.' That it should be denied because traduced or perverted, or grossly and, in some cases, willfully misrepresented by its enemies, or that it should be held responsible for the indiscretion of its friends, is a method of estimation that files us, at once, in funeral procession to the grave of all Christian doctrine. That it is beset with difficulties and suggestive of questions none may resolve, and productive, at times, of seemingly irreconcilable contradictions, is only what is common to all the doctrines of grace, cherished by the whole church as the inspired word of God. The question, 'How can these things be?' is not of faith, but of puny reason, baffled by a mystery of glory no less than by a mystery of grace. Nicodemus would have been an Anti-Premillenarian! As the doctrine stands in the Scripture, it is the flower of the Protevangel in Eden, the glorious outcome when the veil that is spread over all nations is destroyed, and death is swallowed up in victory; the future Age, after Patriarchal, Jewish, Pagan, and Christian ages, muffled in their gray mantles, with shadowy faces, have flitted forever away. It is a symposium with Abraham, Isaac, and Jacob, the Bridegroom's wedding, the angels' delight, the overcomer's reward, the martyr's joy. It is the doctrine of the 'Day-Dawn' and 'Phosphor' of eternal glory, more sure than the vision on Tabor's height, or audible voice from heaven; part of the 'Sabbatism' that remains for the people of God; the earthly bloom of a 'kingdom that cannot be moved,' when the voice that once shook the earth shall shake once more, 'not the earth only but also heaven.'—*Nathaniel West, D. D., Pre-millennial Essays, pp.* 313-318.

DEFENSE OF PRE-MILLENARIANISM---SUMMARY.

"Our reasons for rejecting the doctrine of a millennial era of universal righteousness and peace on earth before the Advent, are summarily as follows:

"1. The doctrine is not taught by either Christ or his apostles.

"2. The uniform teaching of the New Testament respecting the condition of the church and of the world during the present dispensation, forbids the expectation of such a millennium.

"3. The Advent itself, not the millennium, is prominently presented in the New Testament as the 'blessed hope' of the church, and is uniformly presented as an event ever imminent.

"4. The Saviour's repeated command to 'watch' for his coming, because we 'know not the hour,' is inconsistent with the idea of a millennium intervening.

"5. The New Testament teaches that the manifestation of the Messianic Kingdom is to occur at, and not before, the Advent.

"6. The Apostolic church was Pre-millenarian.

"7. The church, for two centuries immediately succeeding the apostles, was Pre-millenarian.

"8. The doctrine of a millennial era before the Advent is a novelty in the history of the church, proposed but little more than one hundred and fifty years ago, and avowedly as a 'New Hypothesis.'

"We have given a summary of the argument in defense of Pre-millenarianism. Permit me, in closing, to direct attention to the summary of Christian faith and practice given by an inspired apostle: '*The grace of God that bringeth salvation hath appeared to all men, teaching us that, denying ungodliness and worldly lusts, we should live soberly, righteously, and godly, in this present world,* LOOKING FOR THAT BLESSED HOPE, AND THE GLORIOUS APPEARING OF THE GREAT GOD AND OUR SAVIOUR JESUS CHRIST.'"—*John T. Duffield, D.D., Pre-millennial Essays, pp.* 426, 427.

RETURN OF CHRIST AND FOREIGN MISSIONS.

"The church has been farming high-patches, and leaving the great mass of men untouched—settling at Jerusalem, and forgetting Samaria and the uttermost ends of the earth. There are 30,000 evangelical preachers in Great Britain alone; 50,000 and more on this continent; 80,000 men on the two hands of the body, and the rest of the body uncared for—close upon a thousand millions of people who never heard that there was a Christ. Some would persuade us that we should not go to Africa till all New York was converted. They will never get to Africa. We maintain that every man, woman, and child, in Great Britain and the United States, could hear of Christ if they desired, and it is now time for battalions of missionaries to move off to foreign lands.

"General Von Moltke, at the battle of Gravelotte, sent in regiment after regiment to certain destruction, but he turned the left flank of his enemy. We require regiments of willing brothers, faithful unto death.

"We have failed simply because we have been aiming at *universal conversion* and not at *universal evangelization*. We have been trying to convert patches, and not evangelize the whole. This is not the age of universal conversion; that is the age that is to come. Let us hearken to one of the apostles: 'Simeon hath declared how God at the first did visit the Gentiles, *to take out of them* a people for his name.' Here there is no indication whatever that the Gentiles were to be totally brought to God, and no man has need to say to his neighbor, 'Know the Lord.' So Christ taught his disciples that during his absence they were to act like fishermen with a drag net, and go over the sea and catch a net full of fishes, not the fullness of the seas.

"Instead of this, the church has been abiding by one or two favorite pools, and endeavoring to catch every fish, instead of passing along through the whole sea. The not understanding the character of the present dispensation, linked to that innate selfishness that still adheres to us all, is at the root of all this disgraceful disobedience. I trust that one great outcome from this Conference will be a deeper intelligence concerning the revealed purposes of our Lord, greater faithfulness to his parting commission, and closer sympathy with his heart of love for a perishing world. When he gave his marching orders he did not say: 'And lo, nations shall be born at once.' He did not say, 'All will be converted before you.' No such thought is ever found in the New Testament, but as witnesses to a rejected Christ, we are to go to all the world, while he says, 'Lo, I am with you alway.' He knew how much we would require his presence. He knew that the messenger would be rejected as the Messiah had been. His presence, not our success, was to be our comfort. He is a poor servant who goes merely by success. At the day of reward the word will not be, 'Well done, good and successful servant,' but, 'Well done, good and *faithful* servant.' We cannot command success. We can all aim at faithfulness. 'Be thou faithful unto death, and I will give thee a crown of life,' the Master said to those who were to be his witnesses, not to be received, but to be murdered. Faithful in the little, we shall be rewarded with the crown that he will give, for 'if we suffer with him, we shall also reign with him'—we shall be 'glorified together.' To-day is the day of the cross, and our witnessing to him to the uttermost ends of the earth. The glory, the crown, the reward, will soon be here, and, above all, he himself—the Man of Calvary—the Man that Stephen saw at the right hand, that Saul saw on his way to Damascus, will appear in royal glory, to put down all the wrong and exalt all the right; to put down all rule and authority opposed to God, and reign in righteousness over a sin-blighted world.

> "Then weep no more, 'tis all thine own,
>   His Cross and Crown divine;
> But better far than all beside,
>   Himself, the Lord, is thine.
> The Bride eyes not her garment
>   But her dear bridegroom's face;
> I will not gaze on glory,
>   But on my King of grace;
> Not on the crown he giveth,
>   But on his pierced hand.
> The Lamb is all the glory
>   Of Immanuel's land."

—*W. P. Mackay, D. D., Pre-millennial Essays, pp.* 458–461.

THE SECOND COMING OF CHRIST.

"Many thousands of the most thoughtful students of the word of God have long since been deeply convinced that the common idea that the preaching of the gospel was to continue until all nations are subdued to Christ, must be given up. We believe, on the contrary, that the end of this dispensation is most solemn judgment. I know that I may perhaps press hardly upon the thoughts of some who have been long wedded to the idea I have just expressed, and they are prepared to say, 'Sir, if I endorse that opinion, I should give up energy and missionary enterprise, and so on.' My dear brother, I do not quarrel with you in reference to the view that you hold. If the gospel is to win its way until the Millennium comes as a result, then I say I will stand with you shoulder to shoulder in the fight, and spread the glorious story of the truth unto the utmost of my power. Let no man attempt, however, to predict the day or the hour, or, if he does, it is in direct violation of the Lord's mind. But, observe, if the world be to-day as I believe it is, like a huge stranded wreck that a few more tides of time will see dashed to pieces like a potter's vessel, we should use the appliances for saving life which God has put into our hands. I see this great wreck crowded with human life from stem to stern. Let us get our fellow-men from off the wreck, men and women, fathers and mothers, brothers and sisters and children. So that, instead of want of energy, it infuses the energy of the shortness of time into every man who intelligently holds that view. Now observe what Christ himself says: 'As the days of Noah were, so shall also the coming of the Son of man be. . . . They were eating and drinking, marrying and giving in marriage, . . . and knew not until the flood came and took them all away.' He adds, 'So shall also the coming of the Son of man be.'"

"We are now come nearly to the end of the six thousand years of human history, at the close of which time, it is the deepest conviction of the most thoughtful students of the world, that we shall have the finishing of the toil and turmoil and strife of sin, and the incoming of the great ruler, the Lord Jesus Christ. Then the Sabbatical year shall be fulfilled, when righteousness shall reign throughout the world, from the river to the ends of the earth. I am aware, in entering upon this subject, of the prejudices existing in some minds, on account of certain events. Remember this, that if a man makes a caricature of a thing, however honest he may be, it does not necessarily take away from the reality of the matter itself. It does not follow that because Charles Dickens never drew a Christian character, that there are not Christian characters in the world. I want you to remember that the sign of the Lord's coming will be of the greatest moment and import to us all. First of all, he will come as a thief in the night. The thief chooses the very time when men do not anticipate his approach. When men shall say, 'Peace and safety,' then sudden destruction cometh upon them, as travail upon a woman with child. It will be a time of universal wickedness, when infidelity will be rampant. It will be a time in which the forces of human power will be set in solid array against God's Christ. This is no *ipse dixit* of mine; it is written in the book of God,—Rev. 6: 15, 16: "And the kings of the earth, and the great men, and the rich men, and the chief captains, and the mighty men, and every bondman, and every free man, hid themselves in the dens and in the rocks of the mountains; and said to the mountains and rocks, Fall on us, and hide us from the face of Him that sitteth on the throne, and from the wrath of the Lamb.' Did you ever read anything like that? The wrath of the Lamb! A contradiction in terms, you will say. No, sir; he came before as a lamb for mercy. He comes again as the Lamb of God for judgment. Listen again: 'The Lord Jesus shall be revealed from heaven . . . in flaming fire, taking vengeance on them that know not God.' Is that the Millennium? Is that the overspreading of the gospel? The world, with its boasted greatness, supposes there is to be an indefinite progress on the human side. After all the years of man's government, there is not a nation under heaven can touch the question of its people's righteousness. All that you can attend to here in your great republic, is to look after property and life, and that very imperfectly. I do not blame you. I can say that of my own country. Christian England ! No, sir. It is a lie. Cross the Channel — Christian France! No, sir! emphatically no. Christian Spain, Austria, Italy; no! Come over the Atlantic — the United States — no! distinctly no. I do not speak hastily. As God lives, the time of human rule has reached its crisis. It is breaking down, the world over."

"But I have words of blessed comfort and solemn warning. I shall not be surprised to see Jesus in person before this hair is gray. We can fix nothing about dates, but it shall be announced, — 'And at midnight there was a cry made, Behold, the bridegroom cometh!' The meeting will take place in the air. He shall descend from heaven with a shout, with the voice of the archangel and the trump of God. The clarion shout shall wake the sleeping dead in Christ — every man, woman, and child. They shall rise first, and we which are alive and remain until the coming of the Lord, shall be caught up in a moment, in the twinkling of an eye. Sirs, that is the most stupendous work that is yet in the future. This corruptible shall put on incorruption, and this mortal shall put on immortality. So sudden will it be that, as I read to you to-night, two women will be at the mill—the one shall be taken and the other left. That converted mother, sleeping perchance beside the unconverted daughter, the mother gone, and the child in vain seeking for her in the morning. Two men in the field, one, perhaps, at the hafts of the plow, and the other at the horse's head — the one taken and the other left. And mark you, after that hour is passed, there is no preacher of the gospel left, not a Christian left—they are gone to be forever with the Lord. Such is the church's hope. She waits for His Son from heaven. Mark this! The kingdom of heaven is likened unto ten virgins, emblematic of purity of character, and betrothal unto the Lord. My friend, are you betrothed unto the Lord? Then listen: 'Every man that hath this hope in him purifieth himself, even as he is pure.'"—*Henry Varley.*

CHRIST'S SECOND COMING.

"I do not want to teach anything to-day dogmatically, on my own authority, but to my mind this precious doctrine—for such I must call it—of the return of the Lord to this earth is taught in the New Testament as clearly as any other doctrine is; yet I was in the church fifteen or sixteen years before I ever heard a sermon on it. There is hardly any church that does not make a great deal of baptism, but the New Testament only speaks about baptism thirteen times, while it speaks of the return of our Lord fifty times; and yet the church has had very little to say about it. Now, I can see a reason for this: the devil does not want us to see this truth, for nothing would wake up the church so much. The moment a man takes hold of the truth that Jesus Christ is coming back again to receive his friends to himself, this world loses its hold upon him; gas-stocks and water-stocks, and stocks in banks and horse-railroads, are of very much less consequence to him then. His heart is free, and he looks for the blessed appearing of his Lord, who at his coming will take him into his blessed kingdom."

"Thank God, he is coming just as he went! We are going to see him in person; he that left this earth blessing it, for that is the way he left, is coming back to build his own church; he is coming back to receive them that have looked for him, and have waited for his return."

"The thought I want to call your attention to is this, that the disciples did not look upon Christ's coming as death at all; they kept that distinct. The coming of the Lord is one thing, and death is another. You or I may be summoned away by death before Christ comes, but we are not taught anywhere in Scripture to look for death; that is not the hope of the church. I am taught to look for the Lord, and it is something much sweeter to me to look for his return, than to look for death. Peter wanted to know what John should do. 'Jesus saith unto him, If I will that he tarry till I come, what is that to thee? Follow thou me,' and not be looking to John and to this disciple and that disciple. 'Then went this saying abroad among the brethren, that that disciple should not die; yet Jesus said not unto him, He shall not die; but, If I will that he tarry till I come, what is that to thee?'

"And there is a distinction between death and His coming. I think we have made a great mistake in saying that is the coming of the Lord. Death is one thing, and the coming of the Lord is another. Why, the year of jubilee will burst upon this world by and by, and the Lord himself shall return to this world,— and that is distinct and separate from death. There is no death when he comes; it is all life, and when all shall be changed in the twinkling of an eye. As Enoch went up to represent the first dispensation, and as Elijah went up to represent the second, so Christ went up to represent the third; and when he comes again, these vile bodies will be changed, as Enoch was changed and Elijah was translated, and we are not going to die. If we remain or tarry until Christ comes, we are not going to taste of death; death has been conquered, and by and by—I don't know when—in the fullness of time, he will return to this earth and reign, and set up his kingdom on earth. As we read in the prophecy of Daniel, that stone cut out of the mountain without hands is growing, and is going to fill the whole earth, and his kingdom is going to be over the whole of the sons of men; God has decreed it."

"You take a magnet, and you let pieces of steel be mixed up with sawdust, and every particle of steel will fly to meet the magnet. And so, when the great Magnet of heaven shall burst upon the earth, every one that he has redeemed shall fly to meet him. It is only a question of time. The hour is coming when the trump of God shall sound. 'The year of jubilee is rolling on.' Thank God, it is not far away; God has promised it, and Christ is going to return; and let us be watching, and waiting, and praying that he may come quickly."

"The church is the Lamb's wife. He has prepared a mansion for his bride, and he promises, for our joy and comfort, that he will come himself, and bring us to the place he has been all this while preparing.

"My friends, it is perfectly safe to take the word of God as we find it. If he tells us to watch, then watch! If he tells us to pray, then pray! If he tells us he will

CHRIST'S SECOND COMING—MOODY. 527

come again, wait for him! Let the church bow to the word of God, rather than trying to find out how such things can be. 'Behold, I come quickly,' said Christ. 'Even so, come, Lord Jesus,' should be the prayer of the church.

"Take the account of the words of Christ at the communion table. It seems to me the devil has covered up the most precious thing about it. 'For as often as ye eat this bread and drink this cup, ye do show the Lord's death *till he come.*' But most people seem to think that the Lord's table is the place for self-examination and repentance, and making good resolutions. Not at all; you spoil it that way; it is to show forth the Lord's death, and we are to keep it up till he comes.

"Some people say, 'I believe Christ will come on the other side of the Millennium.' Where do you get it? I cannot find it. The word of God nowhere tells me to watch and wait for the coming of the Millennium, but for the coming of the Lord. I do not find any place where God says the world is to grow better and better, and that Christ is to have a spiritual reign on earth of a thousand years. I find that the world is to grow worse and worse, and at length there is to be a separation. Two women grinding at a mill, one taken and the other left; two men in one bed, one taken and the other left. Luke 17: 34, 35. The church is to be translated out of the world. . . . We are not to wait for the great white throne judgment, but the glorified church is set on the throne with Christ, and to help to judge the world.

"Now, some of you think this is a new and strange doctrine, and that they who preach it are speckled birds. But let me tell you that most of the spiritual men in the pulpits of Great Britain are firm in this faith. Spurgeon preaches it. I have heard Newman Hall say that he knew no reason why Christ might not come before he got through with his sermon. But in certain wealthy and fashionable churches, where they have the form of godliness, but deny the power thereof, — just the state of things which Paul declares shall be in the last days, — this doctrine is not preached or believed. They do not want sinners to cry out in their meeting, 'What must I do to be saved?' They want intellectual preachers who will cultivate their taste, brilliant preachers who will rouse their imagination, but they do not want the preaching that has in it the power of the Holy Ghost. We live in the day of shams in religion. The church is cold and formal; may God wake us up! And I know of no better way to do it, than to get the church to looking for the return of our Lord.

"Some people say, 'Oh, you will discourage the young converts if you preach that doctrine.' Well, my friends, that has not been my experience. I have felt like working three times as hard ever since I came to understand that my Lord was coming back again. I look on this world as a wrecked vessel. God has given me a life-boat, and said to me, 'Moody, save all you can.' God will come in judgment and burn up this world, but the children of God do not belong to this world; they are in it, but not of it, like a ship in the water. This world is getting darker and darker; its ruin is coming nearer and nearer; if you have any friends on this wreck unsaved, you had better lose no time in getting them off.

"But some will say, 'Do you then make the grace of God a failure?' No, grace is not a failure, but man is. The antediluvian world was a failure; the Jewish world was a failure; man has been a failure everywhere, when he has had his own way and been left to himself."— *D. L. Moody, Extracts of reported Sermons.*

RELATIVE PERIOD OF THE SECOND ADVENT.

In the light of this principle of Progressive Revelation, let us now consider the most interesting and momentous question in connection with the future, the *relative period* of the return of our blessed Lord and Master.

"Before examining the revelations of the Apocalypse on this subject, we will briefly glance at the general testimony of Scripture with respect to it; first that of the Old Testament, and then that of the New.

"It is impossible that those who 'love his appearing' should be indifferent as to the *season* of their Lord's return. Even the prophets searched diligently what manner of *time* the Spirit of Christ which was in them did signify, when it testified beforehand the sufferings of Christ and the glories that should follow. With much more reason, *we*, who in his sufferings see our salvation, and in his glory our own eternal portion, *we*, who are espoused as a chaste virgin to Christ, and have his parting promise, 'I will come again and receive you unto myself,' may inquire diligently, and long to know *when* we may hope to see him as he is, and be forever with our Lord. The more we long for an event itself, the more anxious we are to ascertain the probable period of its occurrence. It argues little love to the Lord if we do not ardently desire his return; and it argues little desire for his return, if we never search the Scriptures, prayerfully seeking to learn from them when we may expect it. It is true we are to let patience have her perfect work; but our patience should be the 'patience of hope,' not the patience of careless indifference; and hope will always suggest the inquiry, 'How long?'

"'How long, O Lord our Saviour, wilt thou remain away?
Our hearts are growing weary, that thou dost absent stay.

Oh when shall come the moment, when, brighter, far, than morn,
The sunshine of thy glory, shall on thy people dawn?'"

"The teaching of Christ himself and of his apostles, led the early generations of Christians, in a very real sense, to expect the speedy return of their Lord. They took his promise, 'Behold, I come quickly,' to mean quickly according to human calculations; we have learned by experience that it meant 'quickly,' counting a thousand years as one day; and unless we have something more explicit than this by which to shape *our* expectations, we, Christians of the nineteenth century, would have little indeed to sustain our hope. A promise which has already extended over eighteen hundred years might well extend over eighteen hundred more, and the epiphany for which we wait be still ages distant.

"But Scripture contains more than general *promises* on this subject; it contains many specific, orderly, and even chronological *prophecies.* We have full and explicit inspired predictions by which to shape our expectations, and these numerous and detailed prophetic statements do not leave us like shipwrecked sailors on a dark night, on a wild and stormy sea, deprived of chart and compass, and ignorant of their bearings. If we will use them aright, they place us, rather, in the position of a weary crew, at the end of a long and dangerous voyage, exploring by the morning twilight, the chart on which their track has been marked down, noting the thousands of miles they have sailed, recognizing each highland and island they have passed on their course, and all the lights and beacons long since left behind, cheering each other as they observe that the faithful chart, whose accuracy their long experience has demonstrated, *shows but two or three way-marks ahead,*—way-marks absolutely coming into sight,—and rejoicing in hope of a speedy entrance into a peaceful port.

"But here we are met with an objection. Those who search and study the prophetic word are often rebuked by the quotation, 'Of that day and hour knoweth no man.' Now, though some students of prophecy have degenerated into prophets, and have required to be reminded of these words, yet it is a mistake to suppose that they forbid investigation, or render hopeless beforehand any well-grounded and intelligent conclusions, as to the period of our Lord's return. The day and the hour of this great event have not assuredly been revealed, but its place on the general chart of human history, has as certainly not been concealed.

"The analogy of the Old Testament would lead us to expect that dates would be given by which some approximation to a knowledge of the period of Christ's second coming, might, towards the close of the dispensation, be made. For however dark earlier generations of Israel may have been, as to the time of his *first* coming, those who lived during the five centuries immediately preceding it, had the light of distinct chronological prophecy to sustain their hopes, and guide their expectations. Though Daniel's prediction of the 'seventy weeks' was expressed in symbolic language, and perhaps not understood by the generation to whom it was first given, yet as a matter of history we know that it was correctly interpreted by later generations, that it formed a national opinion as to the probable period of the appearance of Messiah the Prince, and that it taught the faithful, like Simeon and Anna, to be waiting for the consolation of Israel. Is it not likely that the later generations of the Christian church, which is indwelt by the Spirit of truth, of whom Christ expressly said, 'He shall show you things to come,' should have as clear or clearer light, as to the period of the *second* advent?—light, *not as to its day or hour, not as to its month or year*, but as to its period, and especially as to its chronological *relation* to other future events. From the fact that the Lord Jesus, as the New Testament abundantly proves, wished his disciples in all ages to be kept constant in love, and vigilant in holiness, by means of the *continual* expectation of his return, we may be sure beforehand, that the period of that event will not be clearly revealed *in plain words*, either in the Old Testament or the New. Any revelation on the subject will be sure to be characterized by a marked and *intentional obscurity*, and to be of such a character as that only 'the wise shall understand' it."

"If there exist in Scripture an orderly chronological prophecy of future events, containing a prediction of the second coming of Christ, as one link in the chain, *its place*, in reference to all the other events, must of course be clear. And if such a prophecy contain *no* direct mention of the second advent, yet if it contain a mention of events which, from other Scriptures, we know to *synchronize* with that advent, the *relative* position of the advent will still be clear.

"Such prophecies exist; they are given for our study; and with the Holy Ghost as our guide, we may confidently expect to learn from them with certainty, the *general order* of the great incidents of the fast approaching end of the age. And not only so, but we may also expect to be able to gather from such prophecies, read in the light of the whole revelation of God, an *approximate* knowledge of the actual period of the coming of the Lord. Of this we are not, we cannot be, intended to remain in ignorance, for it is with regard to prophetic chronology that it is expressly said, 'The wise shall understand.'"—*H. Grattan Guinness.*

HOME.--THE FINAL FAREWELL.

"I believe that very soon Christ will come upon the clouds of heaven, and that, when he comes, the dead in Christ shall hear the sound of the trumpet, and shall rise to meet him in the air, and that they shall reign with him—whatever may be the nature of that reign and its details I do not pretend to specify—a thousand years, and after that shall be the general resurrection of the dead, when all shall rise and be judged, 'according to the deeds done in the body.'

"And when Christ comes, how awful and how startling the hour of the advent! The dead that have fallen asleep in Jesus shall hear, when he comes, the approach of his footsteps, and recognize the sound of his voice, and shall rise and meet him in the air. The living that are in Christ shall hear the sound of his approach too, and recognize the tones of his voice, and shall rise and meet him and the risen dead in the air, and reign with him a thousand years. Abraham, and Noah, and Job shall hear his voice, in their silent sepulchres, and join him in the air. Paul, and Peter, and John, and Luther, and Wilberforce, and Simeon of Cambridge, and Venn, and Williams, and Chalmers, shall hear his voice in their sequestered tombs, and gather around their glorious Lord. One grave shall cleave in twain, and its buried tenantry shall rise and meet the Lord, and the grave that looks equally green next to it shall not be pierced by that sound, but its dead dust shall remain unmoved. The cemeteries of stone, and the monuments of bronze shall rend, and the dead saints that are there shall come forth—for the sleeping dust shall be quickened in every sepulchre, the moment that Christ shall speak: and the stones of cathedrals, and the vaults of churches, and the green turf, and the marble mausoleum, shall alike explode, and troops of awakened dead shall come forth. Nor less startling will be the scenes that occur among the living; some families shall be together speaking of things of this world—in an instant, and without warning, one shall hear a sound significant to his heart, and rise as upon the lightning's wing, and with its splendor, too, leave you, while the rest, that know not Christ, shall remain behind. Oh! great day of separation of families—of dislocation of households—of severance of the dead—of astonishment to the world—of glory to the Lord Jesus—of happiness to the saints! But, you ask, what shall become of those who are left behind? The earth, having given up the silent dust of the saints that fell asleep in Jesus—and every living saint upon the earth having heard his voice, and responded to its call—then the fire treasured up, as I explained to you, in the very centre of the earth, shall burst forth in ten thousand crevices—' the elements shall melt as with fervent heat '—the solid rocks shall blaze as if they were oil, and the weary old earth having undergone the process of fire, shall be purified and made fit for the immediate presence of the descending Saviour and his risen saints. The earth shall be purified—its soil restored—paradise gained. The deep-toned miserere of humanity that has risen for six thousand years, shall be lost in the everlasting jubilee. There will be no tears—no sighs—no crying—no storms shall disturb its calm—there will be no decay in its verdure —no serpent's trail amid its flowers—but happiness and love, and joy, and peace, for a thousand years, in the presence of Christ and his saints.

"Some say, is not this an earthly heaven? My dear friends, earth is not essentially corrupt: there is nothing sinful in the clods of the valley—there is nothing sinful in a rose, nor in a tree, nor in a stone. I have seen spots upon the earth so beautiful, that if the clouds of winter would never overtake them, nor the sin of man blast them, I could wish to live amidst them forever. Take sin from the earth —the fever that incessantly disturbs it—the cold freezing shadow that gathers around it—and let my Lord and Saviour have his throne upon earth, its consecration and its glory, and what lovelier spot could man desire to live on? what fairer heaven could man anticipate hereafter? To me it is heaven where Christ is, whether he be throned upon earth, or reigning amid the splendors of the sky—if I am with him, I must enjoy unsullied and perpetual happiness.

"Great and solemn crisis, I cannot but again exclaim! My dear friends, if you like, reject all my views of Apocalyptic chronology, reject all my historical explanations, if you like; but do not reject this, that Christ, who died upon the cross, will come, and when ye think not, and reign, wearing his many crowns, and upon his glorious throne. Look for him, and the same Christ will come again, the husband to the widow, the bridegroom to the bride: he has promised that he will come to us, and 'we shall be forever with the Lord.'

"And when I think of the time when he does come, I can scarcely realize that glorious Sabbath which will overspread the earth! that noble song which will be heard when the saints shall sing together, Holy, holy, holy is the Lord God of Hosts! What a flood of beauty, magnificence, and glory, will roll over this now shattered orb, like the countless waves of an illuminated ocean; illuminated by Christ, the great central sun, around whom all systems revolve, and from whom all beauty comes. And, my dear friends, if there be the least probability in what I have said, is it not our duty to pause—to prepare and search if it be so? When men heard that there was a new star some where to be detected in the firmament, there were some thousands of telescopes every night directed to the skies, and countless stargazers searching if, peradventure, they might discover it. My dear friends, a star comes brighter and more beautiful than any other, 'the bright and morning star,' too long concealed by clouds which are about to be chased away; why should not our hearts look for him? why should not the be liever, who has shared in the bitterness and in the blessings of his cross, pray and pant for him, if, peradventure, he may share in the splendors of his crown ? Is not the Lord welcome to us? Crushed and bleeding humanity, amid its thousand wrongs, cries, 'Come, Lord Jesus.' The earth, weary with its groans, and the sobs of its children, cries, 'Come, Lord Jesus.' The persecuted saints in Tahiti and Madeira, in the dens, and caves, and solitary places of the earth, cry, 'Come, Lord Jesus.' And surely, many a heart that has been warmed by his love—that has been refreshed by his peace, sanctified by his grace, shall raise the same cry, 'Come, Lord Jesus;' and the sublime response will descend from heaven like a wave from the ocean of love overflowing men's hearts, 'Behold, I come quickly.'

"My dear friends, I say to many of you, Farewell; and I say that in a sense in which it is not often uttered. I say it not lightly, but solemnly. May you fare well in the first resurrection. May you fare well at the judgment day. May you fare well in time. May you fare well in eternity; and at that day when sighs and farewells shall cease, may we meet before the throne of God and of the Lamb, and so be forever with the Lord! Amen, and Amen."—*Dr. John Cumming.*

Our task is done. Such is the voice of the church, on the most thrilling and momentous question that ever engaged the human mind, or tasked its energies through the pen. On reviewing the matter, we are forced to conclude with Charlotte Elizabeth, that, "The time is past when we could regard as a matter of comparative indifference the receiving of this doctrine,—the speedy, personal, Pre-millennial appearing of the Lord Jesus Christ. We now feel it to be a matter of such vital importance, that no person rejecting it can rightly understand the Scriptures; and though he may build upon the rock, and so be personally safe, his work, if he be a minister, certainly will not prove to be either of gold or precious stones. We say *now*, because the signs are such as to leave men no excuse for closing their eyes any longer against the broad clear light of advancing day."

With us the final decision is made. While we survive and minister divine truth, we hope,—God helping us,—to "preach the coming of Jesus." The happy hour is not far hence. It is near, and hasteth greatly. And should we sleep in death—not that we would be unclothed, but clothed upon, that mortality might be swallowed up of life—instead of grieving in our last moments, like the great Robert Hall, that we had not proclaimed this doctrine, we would choose with the departing Bickersteth, to exclaim, " I have never regretted the Lord's giving me to grasp that blessed truth." And while with the eminent Post-millennialist David Brown, of Scotland, we hold that the Bride of our Lord will " BE MISERABLE" until the blessed Bridegroom's arrival, we also, firmly believing, that this generation and century will witness his glorious epiphany, and in view of speedy and everlasting redemption, would cry in her ears the solemn and dying words of the pious John King Lord : " TELL THE CHURCH TO HOLD ON TILL CHRIST COMES !"

The following Table has been prepared for the second edition of this work by Mr. Sylvester Bliss, author of a valuable work on chronology, entitled, "Analysis of Sacred Chronology ;" and the fifth column gives his estimated length of the several periods intervening between the creation and the Vulgar Era. The fourth column was drawn up by Rev. C. Bowen, of England, for the Rev E. B. Elliott, who gives it in his Horæ Apocalypticæ, as the chronology of Mr. Clinton, whence it was copied as such in the first edition. It varies, however from Mr. Clinton's 10 years in the aggregate, and in a number of places in the detail, as will be seen by a comparison of it with the first column. The remaining columns give the age of the world, as estimated by Archbishop Usher, the learned Dr. Hales, Dr. Jarvis, and Mr. Cunninghame of Scotland. The latter adopts the reading of the Septuagint instead of the Hebrew text for the chronology of the Patriarchs, and nearly coincides with that of Dr. Hales, who adopts the chronology of Josephus. Usher and Jarvis, in the periods of the Judges, are governed by the period given in 1 Kings 6 : 1, instead of the details of the periods in the history of the Judges and the statement of Paul in Acts 13 : 19–20 ; and consequently, they are obliged to reckon some of the periods in the Judges as synchronous, instead of successive, as there represented

COMPARATIVE CHRONOLOGICAL TABLE.

		Clinton.	Usher.	Jarvis.	Bowen.	Bliss.	Hales.	Cunningham.
Genesis 5 : 8	Adam	130	130	130	130	130	230	230
" 6	Seth	105	105	105	105	105	205	205
" 9	Enos	90	90	90	90	90	190	190
" 12	Cainan	70	70	70	70	70	170	170
" 15	Mahalaleel	65	65	65	65	65	165	165
" 18	Jared	162	162	162	162	162	162	162
" 21	Enoch	65	65	65	65	65	165	165
" 25	Methuselah	187	187	187	187	187	187	187
" 28	Lamech	182	182	182	182	182	182	188
" 7 : 6	Noah's age at the Flood	600	600	600	600	600	600	600
" 11 : 11	Shem	2	2	2	2	2	2	2
" 12 "	Arphaxad	35	35	35	35	35	135	135
" 14 "	Cainan	0	0	0	0	0	130	130
" 14	Selah	30	30	30	30	30	130	130
" 16	Eber	34	34	34	34	34	134	134
" 18	Peleg	30	30	30	30	30	130	130
" 20	Reu	32	32	32	32	32	132	132
" 22	Serug	30	30	30	30	30	130	130
" 24	Nahor	29	29	29	29	29	79	79
" 32	Terah's age at his death	205	205	205	205	205	205	145
Exodus 12 : 41 and Gal. 3 : 17	To the Exode	430	431	430	430	430	430	431
Joshua 5 : 6	In the wilderness	40	40	40	40	40	40	40
Josh. 14 : 7–10 and Acts 13 : 19	To the division of the land	7	6	6	6	6	6	7
Josh. 23 : 1 & 24 : 29 & Josephus	To the death of Joshua	20	2	19	19	19	20	0
Joshua 24 : 31, Judges 2 : 10, and Josephus	To the first servitude	0	30	18	11	11	10	20
Judges 3 : 8	First servitude—Mesopotamia	8	8	8	8	8	8	8
" 9–11	Othniel	40	0	40	40	40	40	40
" 12–14	Second servitude—Moab	18	80	18	18	18	18	18

CHRONOLOGY.

Judges 3:30	Ehud and Shamgar	80	0	20	80	80	80
" 4:13	Third servitude—Canaan	20	40	20	20	20	20
" 4:23 and 5:31	Deborah and Barak	40	0	40	40	40	40
" 6:1	Fourth servitude—Midian	7	40	7	7	7	7
" 8:28	Gideon	40	9	40	40	40	40
" 8:33 and 9:6–22	Abimelech	3	3	3	3	3	3
" 10:1–2	Tolah	23	23	23	23	23	23
" 3	Jair	22	22	22	22	22	22
" 6–8	Fifth servitude—Ammon	18	0	18	18	18	18
" 11:32 and 12:7	Jephthah	6	6	6	6	6	6
" 12:8–9	Ibzan	7	7	7	7	7	7
" 11	Elon	10	10	10	10	10	10
" 13–14	Abdon	8	8	8	8	8	8
" 13:1	Sixth servitude—Philistines	40	0	0	40	40	40
1 Samuel 4:18	Eli	40	0	0	0	30	40
" 7:2	Seventh servitude—Philistines	20	0	0	0	0	20
" 7:15 and Acts 13:21	Samuel	12	21	25	30	0	12
Acts 13:21	Saul	40	40	40	40	40	40
1 Kings 2:11	David	40	40	40	40	40	40
" 11:42	Solomon	40	40	40	40	40	40
" 14:21	Rehoboam	17	17	17	17	17	17
" 15:2	Abijam	3	3	3	3	3	3
" 10	Asa	41	41	41	41	41	41
2 Chron. 20:31	Jehoshaphat	24	25	25	25	26	25
" 21:5	Jehoram	7	4	8	8	8	8
2 Kings 8:26	Ahaziah	1	1	1	1	1	1
" 11:1–3	Athaliah	6	6	6	6	6	6
" 12:1	Jehoash	40	39	40	40	40	40
" 14:2	Amaziah	29	29	29	29	29	29
" 14:23 and 15:1	Interregnum	0	0	11	0	11	12
" 15:2	Azariah	52	52	52	52	52	52
2 Chron. 27:1	Jotham	15	16	16	16	16	16
" 28:1	Ahaz	15	16	16	16	16	16
2 Kings 21:1	Hezekiah	29	29	29	29	29	29
2 Chron. 33:2	Manasseh	55	55	55	55	55	55
" 34:1	Amon	2	2	2	2	2	2
" 36:2	Josiah	31	31	31	31	31	31
2 Kings 23:31	Jehoahaz	0	0	0	0	0	0
" 24:8	Jehoiakim	11	11	11	11	11	11
	Jehoiachin	0	0	0	0	0	0

CHRONOLOGY.

COMPARATIVE CHRONOLOGICAL TABLE.—(Concluded.)

	Clinton	Usher	Jarvis	Bowen	Bliss	Hales	Cunningham
To Nebuchadnezzar's death (2 Kings 25:27)	37	37	37	Zedekiah and Captivity. 81	37	37	37
Evil Merodach (Canon of Ptolemy)	Years of Ptolemy's Canon. 560	2	2	From Cyrus' decree to birth Christ 536 years. 536	2	2	Years of Ptolemy's Canon. 560
Neriglissar		4	4		4	4	
Nabonadius		17	17		17	17	
Cyrus before the conquest of Babylon		2	2		2	2	
" after "		6	7		7	7	
Cambyses		8	8		8	8	
Darius I. Hystaspes		36	36		36	36	
Xerxes		21	21		21	21	
Artaxerxes I. Longimanus		41	41		41	41	
Darius II. Nothus		19	19		19	19	
Artaxerxes Mnemon		46	46		46	46	
Ochus		21	21		21	21	
Arses		2	2		2	2	
Darius III. Codomanus		6	4		4	4	
Alexander of Macedon		7	7		7	7	
Philip Aridæus		6	7		7	7	
Alexander Ægus		26	12		12	12	
Ptolemy Lagus		37	20		20	20	
" Philadelphus		26	38		38	38	
" Euergetes I.		25	25		25	25	
" Philopater		17	17		17	17	
" Epiphanes		24	24		24	24	
" Philometer		35	35		35	35	
" Euergetes II.		28	29		29	29	
" Soter		37	36		36	36	
" Dionysius		29*	29		29	29	
Cleopatra. Died B. C. 30		21	22		22	22	
Augustus Cæsar, from Cleopatra's death to the Vulgar Era	30	29		29	29	
From Creation to the Vulgar Era	4138	4003	4019	4128	4120	5411	5478

* Including the fifteen years of the reign of Alexander, who was imposed on Egypt by Sylla of Rome.

INDEX OF NAMES.

Aben-Ezra, Abraham, 125
Adams, Thomas, 175
Agobard, 382
Alford, Dean, 470, 471, 509
Alleine, Joseph, 186
Allen, Dr., 304
Alliaco, Cardinal, 293, 295
Almeric, 125, 128
Alogians, 70
Alphonso, King, 293, 295
Alstead, John H., 222
Ambrose, Isaac, 92, 184, 370
American Encyclopædia, 106
American Prophetical Writers, 416–418
Ames, William, 220
Anderson, William, 3
Andreas, 117, 372
Andrews, W. W., 461-466
Anselm, 125
Apollinarius, 87
Apollinaris, Claudius, 87
Apollonius, 87
Aquinas, Thomas, 128
Aristides, 87
Arnold, Dr., 5
Arnulph, 382
Ascension of Isaiah, 35
Aspenwell, William, 310
Athenagoras, 87
Augustine, 97, 293, 372
Auriol, E., 354
Aztecs, The, 43

Babylonian Targum, 21
Backus, Isaac, 313
Bailee, Robert, 188
Baily, John, 297
Bale, John, 161
Barber, John W., 338
Barnabas, 51, 367
Barnes, Dr. Albert, 292, 469, 470
Baronius, 382, 383
Baxter, Richard, 182, 497
Becon, Thomas, 149
Beecher, Charles, 4, 16
Bellamy, Joseph, D. D., 324
Bengel, Dr. John Albert, 118, 133, 158, 243, 291
Ben-Israel, Menasse, 125

Benson, George, 261
Berenger, 383
Bernard, Saint, 383, 496
Beverly, Thomas, 203
Beza, Theodore, 392
Bickersteth, Edward, 1, 24, 138, 537
Blackwood, S. A., 354
Blandina, 64
Bloomfield, 398
Bonar, Horatius, 114, 354, 386, 405, 459-461
Boughton, John, 203
Bowers, Bath, 329
Bradford, John, 142
Bretschneider, 388
Brightman, T., 164, 303
Brookes, J. H., 355, 509-512
Brooks, J. W., 68, 81
Brown, David, 292, 365, 404, 537
Browne, Sir Thomas, 256
Brute, Walter, 384
Buchanan, James, 405
Bulkley, Peter, 299
Bullinger, Henry, 150
Bunyan, John, 166, 199, 397
Burgh, W., 2
Burnet, Thomas, 2, 31, 37, 72, 119, 212
Burnet, William, 330
Burroughs, Jeremiah, 194
Burton, Dr., 57, 103
Bush, Prof. George, 25, 15, 29, 47, 102, 108, 115, 307
Butler, Bishop Joseph, 277
Byles, Mather, 333

Caius, 70
Calmet, Augustus, 24, 395
Calvin, John, 3, 152, 392
Careles, John, 149
Caryl, Joseph, 310
Cassidorus, 372
Cave, Dr., 59, 75
Chabbo, Rabbi, 22
Chalmers, Dr. Thomas, 46, 404, 452-458
Channing, William, 4, 5
Charnock, Stephen, 46, 206
Chase, Bishop, 7
Chauncy, Charles, D. D., 331
Cheever, Ezekiel, 308

INDEX.

Cheever, Dr. George, 129
Chillingworth, William, 63, 100
Christian, The, London, 348
Chronological Table, 538-540
Chrysostom, 92, 370
Churches of Vienne and Lyons, 63
Chytræus, David, 146
Clarke, Dr. Adam, 3, 39, 77, 79, 225, 289, 307, 396, 408, 439
Clarke, John, 312
Clarke, Rufus, 355
Claude, 382
Clement, 50
Clement of Alexandria, 71
Cocceius, John, 221
Coke, Dr. Thomas, 271, 307, 409
Columbus, Christopher, 293, 295
Commodion, 86
Confession, Augsburg, 146
Confession, Baptist, 201
Confession, Savoy, 426
Connor, William, 474-476
Coracion, 74
Cotton, John, 300
Council of Frankfort, 381
Council of Gap, 393
Council of Nice, 87
Cowper, William, 269
Cox, G. F., 351
Cox, John, 121
Cranmer, Abp., 148
Creed, Adventists', 432-436
Creed, Apostles', 424
Creed, Athanasian, 425
Creed, Baptist, 429
Creed, Bible Christians', 431
Creed, Cerinthian Church, 423
Creed, Christian Church, 431
Creed, Church of God, 430
Creed, Congregational Church, 428
Creed, Disciples', 431
Creed, Dutch Reformed, 430
Creed, Episcopal Church, 426, 427
Creed, Evangelical Lutheran, 430
Creed, Friends', 430
Creed, Irenæus'. 424
Creed, Jewish, 429
Creed, Methodist Episcopal Church, 428
Creed, Nicene, 424
Creed, Presbyterian Church, 427, 428
Creed, Restorationists', 431
Creed, River Brethren's, 431
Creed, United Brethren's, 431
Cressener, Dr., 218
Croly, George, 374
Cumming, Dr. John, 29, 30, 112, 113, 119, 403, 533-536
Cummings, Abraham, 342
Cunninghame, William, 6, 7, 423
Cyprian, 64, 72, 368
Cyril, 369

Damasus, Pope, 115

Dante, 384
Daubuz, Charles, 236
Davenant, John, 221
Davenport, John, 307, 315
Dionysius, 84
Doddridge, Philip, 245
Donnegan, 388
Dorner, 512, 513, 515
Dowling, John, 380
Dow, Lorenzo, 343
Drummond, Henry, Esq., 346
Dudley, Joseph, 328
Duffield, Dr. George, 16, 20, 28, 51, 390, 406, 410
Duffield, Dr. John T., 517, 518
Durant, John, 185
Dury, John, 297

Edinburgh Presbyterian Review, 6
Edwards, Jonathan, 324, 401
Edwards, Morgan, 337
Edward VI., King, 148
Elias, Rabbi, 25
Eliezer, Rabbi, 21, 23
Eliot, John, 296
Elizabeth, Charlotte, 5, 443, 444, 448-451, 536
Ellicott, 513
Elliott, Dr. E. B., 15, 108, 138, 158, 378, 406, 421
Encyclopædia of Religious Knowledge, 41, 81
English Prophetical Writers, 411-414
Enoch, Book of, 34
Epiphanius, 91
Ernesti, Prof. J. A., 17
Esdras, Second Book of, 36
Eusebius, 50, 56, 88, 112
Evagrius, 370
Ezra, Fourth Book of, 35

Faber, George Stanley, 27, 64, 110, 224, 365, 366
Fairbairn, Dr., 513
Farmer, Joseph, 192
Farnham, Benjamin, 343
Felix, Minucius, 39
Ferguson, 394
Fish, Samuel, 339
Flacius, Matthias, 154
Fleming, Robert, 397
Fleming, Robert, Jr., 226, 345, 398
Fletcher, John, 264, 401, 440
Flint, Henry, 329
Freemantle, W. R., 354
Fox, H. W., 11
Foxe, John, 163
Fulke, Dr., 395

Gale, Dr. B., 338
Gale, Theophilus, 289
Gamaliel, Rabbi, 21
Gaon, Rabbi Saadias, 22, 125
Gaussen, Prof., 402

INDEX.

Gedaliah, Rabbi, 26
Gemarah, 27
Gibbon, Edward, 30, 47, 105, 114, 115, 373
Gilfillan, George, 491–493
Gill, Dr. John, 28, 121, 225, 239, 291, 307, 344, 410
Glas, John, 274
Glassius, S., 77, 393
Gonthier, 382
Goodhart, C. J., 354
Goodwin, Dr. Thomas, 6, 176, 308
Gookin, Nathaniel, 331
Gordon, A. J., 355, 505-508
Gorrico, Gaspar, 294
Greenfield, 388, 389
Gregory, David, 26
Gregory the Great, 80, 376, 378
Gregory Nazianzen, 370
Gregory of Nyssa, 86
Gregory of Tours, 372
Greswell, Dr., 57, 373
Grotius, 220
Guinness, H. Grattan, 529-532

Hagenbach, Dr., 49, 77
Hales, Dr., 7
Hall, Bishop, 1
Hall, Joseph, 203
Hall, Newman, 527
Hall, Robert, 263, 537
Hall, Thomas, 197
Hammond, Dr., 395
Hankin, D. B., 354
Heber, Reginald, 286
Henry, Matthew, 3, 208, 307, 394, 409, 508
Henshaw, Bishop, 229
Henshaw, William, 15
Hermas, 49
Hermias, 87
Higginson, John, 297
Hilarion, 371
Hilary, 93
Himes, J. V., 349
Hippolytus, 65, 368
Hitchcock, Dr. Edward, 39
Hoare, E., 354
Hodge, Dr. C., 498-501
Hody, Dr., 19
Holmes, Obadiah, 313
Holyoke, Edward, 303
Homes, Nathaniel, D. D., 277, 301
Hooke, William, 310
Hooker, 18
Hopkins, Samuel, D. D., 324
Horsley, Samuel, 255
Howe, John, 220
Huet, Ephraim, 301
Hughes, Archbishop, 385
Humboldt, A., 294
Hurd, Richard, D. D., 231
Huss, John, 385
Hussey, Joseph, 281

Hutchinson, Samuel, 316

Ignatius, 53
Imbrie, David, 337
Investigator and Expositor of Prophecy, 29
Irenæus, 60, 367
Irving, Edward, 9, 346
Irving, Washington, 294

Janeway, James, 180
Jebb, Dr., 399
Jenks, William, 402
Jeremiah, Rabbi, 23
Jerome, 4, 80, 94, 371
Jerome of Prague, 385
Jerusalem Talmud, 22
Jerusalem Targum, 21
Jewell, Bishop, 395
Jewish Rabbis, 21-27, 44, 125, 126
Joachim Abbas, 123, 383
Jochannan, Rabbi, 23
Jonathan, Rabbi, 22
Jones, Henry, 349
Josephus, 37
Juda, Leo, 149
Junckner, 138
Jurieu, Peter, 204
Justinian, 374
Justin Martyr, 57, 367

Karens, The, 42
Katturim, Rabbi Baal, 26
Ker, John, 510
Ketina, Rabbi, 27
Kimchi, Rabbi, 22
King, Edward, Esq., 257
Kitto, Dr. John, 107
Knox, John, 151
Krummacher, 442, 443
Kuttner, 393

Lactantius, 82, 369
Lambert, Francis, 284
Lancaster, Peter, 250
Lange, John P., 513
Lardner, Nathaniel, D. D., 83, 100
Latimer, Hugh, 143, 365
Lechler, 513
Lee, Samuel, 205
Leigh, 387
Liddell and Scott, 388
Lillie, John, 192
Litch, Josiah, 350
Lord, David N., 48, 422
Lord, John King, 537
Lord, Nathan, 6, 134
Lowth, William, 279
Luther, Martin, 6, 17, 134, 154, 366, 390, 499

Macaulay, 137, 348
Mackay, W. P., 357, 518-520
Maimonides, Rabbi, 21, 44, 126

INDEX.

Marsh, Edmund, 337
Martyn, Henry, 473, 474
Massillon, John B., 47, 291
Mather, Dr. Cotton, 5, 296, 308, 315, 325, 328
Mather, Increase, 295, 317, 329
Mather, Richard, 297
Mather, Samuel, 311, 325
Mathieson, J. E., 354
Maton, Robert, 174
M'Ilvaine, Bishop, 365
McNeile, Dr. Hugh, 8, 346, 441, 483-486
Mead, Matthew, 203
Mede, Joseph, 24, 28, 167, 174
Melancthon, Philip, 134, 159, 391
Melito, 66
Melville, Henry, 471, 472
Mennonites, 426
Menno, Simon, 221
Messenger and Missionary Record, 348
Methodius, 74
Michælis, Prof., 307, 408
Miller, William, 350
Milman, H. H., 1
Milner, Joseph, 78
Miltiades Modestus, 87
Milton, John, 4, 9, 178, 396
Mishna, 26
Mitchel, Jonathan, 297
Montanists, 68
Moody, D. L., 524-528
Moody, Joshua, 297
Morehead, W. G., 355
Morris, Henry, 96, 132, 136
Mosheim, John L., 75, 101, 111, 221
Müller, George, 486-491
Munscher, 69
Murray, John, 338
Mystics, 221

Napier, John, 222
Neander, J. W. A., 66, 103
Nelson, David, 402
Nepos, 74
Newcome, William, 248
Newman, John, 113
Newton, Sir Isaac, 234, 294
Newton, Bishop Thomas, 119, 248, 344, 398
New York Daily Tribune, 357
Nicholson, Bishop, 355
Noble Lesson, 130
Norton, John, 299
Noyes, Enoch, 327
Noyes, Nicholas, 321

Oaks, Urian, 304
Oetinger, 514
Olive, P. J., 384
Origen, 37, 76, 368
Osiander, Andrew, 154
Ovid, 38

Oxford Divines, 404

Pantænus, 87
Papias, 54
Pareus, David, 164
Paris, Matthew, 384
Parker, Thomas, 301
Parsons, H. M., 355
Pasor, George, 387
Patterson, Robert, 494-496
Paulikians, 126
Paulinus, 86, 382
Peel, Sir Robert, 4
Pelico, Silvo, 8
Perkins, William, 151
Perry, Joseph, 267
Petrarch, Francis, 384
Philip of Gortyra, 87
Pickering, Lexicon, 388
Pietists, 221
Pirie, Alexander, 252
Piscator, John, 143
Plato, 1, 42
Pliny the Elder, 40
Plutarch, 42
Polycarp, 54
Ponticus, 63
Pope, Alexander, 282
Presbyterian Review, 397
Prideaux, Dr. John, 204
Priestley, Joseph, LL. D., 288, 345
Prince, Thomas, 335, 337
Prophetic Expositors, 419, 420
Protestant Churchman, 148
Purves, James, 344

Quadratus, 87
Quarterly Journal of Prophecy, London, 41, 70, 107, 136, 466-468

Rabbis, Jewish, 21-27, 44, 125, 126
Radstock, Lord, 472, 473
Reader, Thomas, 233
Relatives of Our Lord, 85
Ricaut, Sir Paul, 41
Ridley, Nicholas, 145
Romaine, William, 269
Rosenmuller, 18
Rudd, Sayer, 280
Russell, Bishop, 25, 48, 102, 113, 231
Russell, P. R., 350
Rutherford, Samuel, 6, 188
Ryle, J. C., 503-505

Salmasius, 393
Sandys, Edmund, 145
Saybrook Platform, 426
Schoettgen, 394
Schultetus, 388
Scott, Dr. Thomas, 272, 400
Seiler, 45
Seiss, Dr. J. A., 496, 497
Semisch, 48, 59
Seraphion, 87

INDEX.

Sereñus, 381
Sewall, Samuel, 305
Shaftesbury, Earl of, 352
Shepherd, Thomas, 299
Sibylline Oracles, 31
Siegvolck, Paul, 336
Simai, Rabbi, 22
Skrine, C., 354
Smith, J. Denham, 354
Smith, John Pye, 3, 18
Spalding, Joshua, 7, 296, 323, 339, 340
Spanheim, 78
Spurgeon, C. H., 292, 481-483, 501, 502
Sterry, Peter, 193
Stockius, 387
Stockton, T. H., 493, 494
Storer, B., 365
Stoughton, Hon. William, 303
Stowe, Mrs. H. B., 5
Strabo, 42
Stuart, Prof. Moses, 20, 24, 114, 445-448
Suicer, 387
Sulpicius, 82, 86
Sutcliffe, Joseph, 401

Tait, Abp. A. C., 476-478
Talmud, Jerusalem, 22
Targum, Babylonian, 21
Targum, Jerusalem, 21
Taylor, Jeremy, 16, 68, 180
Taylor, Thomas, 283
Tergand, 382
Tertullian, 8, 67, 368, 496
Testament of the Twelve Patriarchs, 34
Theodoret, 371
Theological and Literary Journal, 79
Theophilus, 87
Theopompus, 27
Tholuck, 513
Tillinghast, 204
Toplady, Augustus M., 267
Torrey, William, 337
Trypho, 58
Twiss, William, 172
Tyndale, William, 140
Tyng, Dr. Stephen H., 3, 5, 358

Tyng, S. H., Jr., 355

Usher, Archbishop James, 173, 392

Van Oosterzee, J. J., 478-481, 497, 498
Varley, Henry, 521-524
Victorinus, 81
Vincent, Thomas, 195
Virgil, 41
Vitringa, 17, 384

Wahl, 388
Waldenses, 129
Waldo, Peter, 384
Walley, Thomas, 314
Ward, H. D., 85, 137, 147, 343, 349, 351
Watkins, Dr., 138
Watkins, John, 339
Watson, Thomas, 182
Watts, Dr. Isaac, 46, 250, 400
Webb, John, 330
Wells, Edmund, D. D., 236
Wesley, Charles, 262
Wesley, John, 69, 245
Westminster Assembly, 187, 395, 425
West, Dr. N., 512-517
Whiston, William, 232
Whitby, Daniel, 1, 63, 74, 75, 84, 107, 228, 252, 394
Whitefield, George, 259
Whiting, Prof. N. N., 19
Whiting, Samuel, 315
Wigglesworth, Michael, 302
Willard, Samuel, 306
Williams, Roger, 297
Williams, Thomas, 403
Winchester, Elhanan, 337, 339
Winthrop, Edward, 20, 48, 381
Wolff, Joseph, 43, 346, 415
Wood, G. H., 72
Woodhouse, Archdeacon, 229
Wycliffe, 132, 293

Young, Edward, 9

Zoroaster, 27, 28
Zuingle, 137

www.ingramcontent.com/pod-product-compliance
Lightning Source LLC
Chambersburg PA
CBHW052042290426
44111CB00011B/1587